The Trial *of* CHRISTENDOM

The Trial *of* CHRISTENDOM

Believe in God or Believe God?
There is a difference

BOOKS I – VIII

David Matthew

DISCLAIMER

Before reading "The Trial of Christendom" (Chris-ten-dom), a very important thing needs to be noted. There are 100's of scriptures used from the King James Version of the Holy Bible. Only the KJV is used to avoid any false edits or misunderstandings. The KJV is the oldest and most closely translated Bible that 'represents the original manuscripts' found of the 'Holy Word of God' for all the world today. There are Bibles that do follow close, but to be on the safe side, this book will only use the KJV.

Therefore all scriptures used in this book, "The Trial of Christendom", will have 'The Disclaimer' that any scripture used will be preceded by the original verses in the KJV. The KJV has the authority as written over any verse that is used and copied here. If a mistake or an inaccurate pro-trail of scripture is made, the KJV takes precedent first. This book takes a back seat to the true written 'Word of God'.

The difference you will find is in the **BOLDING**, Side Notes, * = + ^ Tag references made to other scriptures with *smaller fonts, and additional italicized *(clarifications)* written by the author in *(parenthesizes) ( )*. All the words written in the KJV that are *italicized* were added by the English translators. The *italicized* words in parenthesis *(italicized)* were added by me and the small font scripture tags. Always refer to the KJV as the original scripture. I, David Matthew, do not ever intend on usurping the true 'Word of God'. The Bible has warned me of this risk*.
*-Revelation 22 v 19

MISSION

The Mission of 'The Trial of Christendom' is to open the eyes of understanding to 'all walks of faith' that 'center around' the Lord Jesus Christ. What has the 'Word of God' said and not said? Who am I? Scripture will have the final say.

I, David Matthew, can hide nothing nor dare I teach a falsehood. The backing up of scriptures is the truth. I have no place to hide. I stand on 'his' written Word.

Many in Christendom (Chris-ten-dom) take what is preached from the pulpit as 'the truth'. They put their full heart-ed belief and hope of their salvation in one man/women, their pastor and/or priest by what 'they say'. What if these teachers got it wrong? What backs them up? What scriptures do they use and where is their focus of the Bible concentrated? These teachers will say, "I understand, I have read the Bible". Have they? Who would know?

I pray this book ends up in the hands of those teachers and preachers, hospitals, prisons, men and women recovering from addictions, service men and women of the armed forces, those that don't own a Bible but will read a book, and those that fear their governments, place of employment, fellow peers if they carry their Bible in public. This is also for those who were turned off by religion and what preachers have 'spouted at them' from the pulpit, the 'Red Faced Preacher'. Yes, millions hate religion because of how the minister 'preached at them' and not by what the 'Word of God' has really said or not said.

This book (for lack of a better word) is going to "God Smack" those that don't believe the 'true word of God'. These will claim they do understand and will become 'turned off' by the scriptures in this book. Many simply will not believe 'God's true Word' and will reject truth because a man (me) pointed it out.

These include 'false principalities in high places'*, religions and denominations and preachers that express to their parishioners that they had better follow what they say and teach or they are going to that very hot place. Someone unlearned in the scriptures is easily led astray. Who would know? *-Ephesians 6 v 12

Not all the scriptures written are for the world to follow but to learn from*. Many are confused and not really sure of their salvation. "How do I get saved? Show me the process and I will do it" is a major thought in Christendom. Confusion is preach from the pulpit. *-Romans 15 v 4; -II Peter 1 v 19-21

Truth be known, the King James Version (KJV) of the Holy Bible was written for everyone's learning. If you expect the Bible to be read like a novel, please reconsider your pre-supposed position. Wouldn't you want to be as close as possible to the truth?

If anything, I hope to 'poke and prod' mankind into opening their Bibles to see what was really written or what has not been written but was assumed. If you are skeptical make a study. Try to prove what is written in 'The Trial of Christendom' wrong. Use only the KJV scriptures. Ask questions, search for more truth. If it is not found in the Bible, then don't make it up.

This is the way of Religions and Denominations. These many 'differing faiths' of Christendom have their own interpretations as if they are all right and got it correct. But what does the Word of God really say or does not say? Believe in God (a god?) or believe God? There is a difference.

David Matthew

THE TRIAL OF CHRISTENDOM

Believe in God or Believe God? There is a Difference.

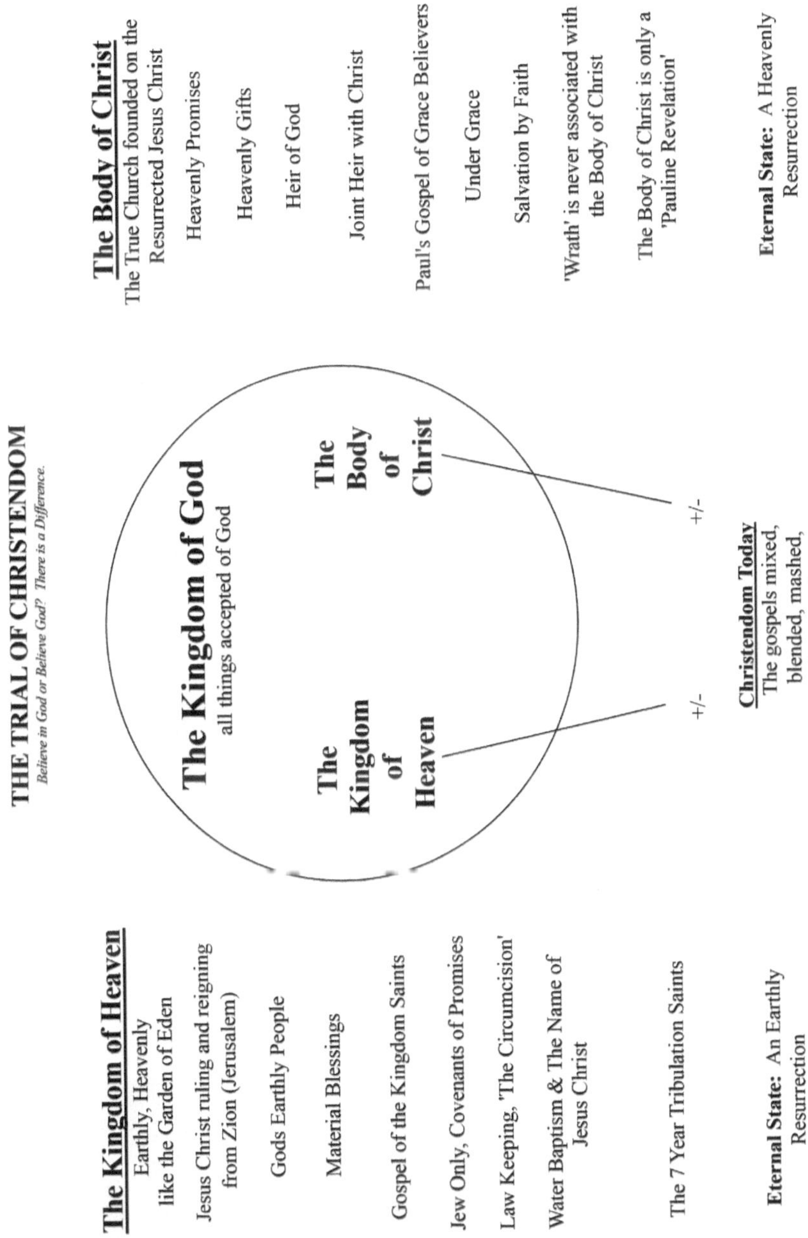
THE TRIAL OF CHRISTENDOM
Believe in God or Believe God? There is a Difference.
The Kingdom of Heaven
Earthly, Heavenly like the Garden of Eden
Jesus Christ ruling and reigning from Zion (Jerusalem)
Gods Earthly People
Material Blessings
Gospel of the Kingdom Saints
Jew Only, Covenants of Promises
Law Keeping, 'The Circumcision'
Water Baptism & The Name of Jesus Christ
The 7 Year Tribulation Saints
Eternal State: An Earthly Resurrection
The Kingdom of God
all things accepted of God
The Kingdom of Heaven
The Body of Christ
+/-
+/-
Christendom Today
The gospels mixed, blended, mashed, integrated
The Body of Christ
The True Church founded on the Resurrected Jesus Christ
Heavenly Promises
Heavenly Gifts
Heir of God
Joint Heir with Christ
Paul's Gospel of Grace Believers
Under Grace
Salvation by Faith
'Wrath' is never associated with the Body of Christ
The Body of Christ is only a 'Pauline Revelation'
Eternal State: A Heavenly Resurrection

TABLE OF CONTENTS

Book I: The Gospel of Our Salvation Declared 1

Book II: Luke: Jew or Gentile? 82

Book III: "Let Him be Accursed!" 127

Book IV: Jesus Christ Died a 'Law Keeper' 191

Book V: Dispensation: The Big Picture 265

Book VI: Israel's Interrupted Time-Line,

the Last and Latter Days 324

Book VII: The Invisible Godhead 369

Book VIII: Membership in the True Church, the Body of Christ .. 454

THE TRIAL OF CHRISTENDOM

Believe in God or Believe God? There is a Difference.

BOOK I

The Gospel of Our Salvation Declared

1- Moreover, brethren, **I** *(Apostle Paul)* **declare** unto you **the gospel** which **I preached** unto you, which also **ye have received**, and wherein **ye stand**;
2- By which also **ye are saved**, if you keep in memory what I preached unto you, unless **ye have believed** in vain.
3- For **I delivered** unto you **first** of all which **I also received**, how that **Christ died for our sins** according to the scriptures;
4- And that **he was buried**, and that **he rose again the third day** according to the scriptures:
-I Corinthians 15 v 1-4

9- That if thou shalt confess with thy mouth the Lord Jesus, and shalt **believe in thine heart that God hath raised him from the dead, thou shalt be saved.**
-Romans 10 v 9

13- In whom ye also trusted, after that ye heard the word of truth, **the gospel of your salvation**: in whom also after that ye believed, **ye were sealed with that holy Spirit of promise**.
-Ephesians 1 v 13

When you read this did you say to yourself, "I know this, of course this is 'The Gospel'"? Or did you think 'The Good News' is the Gospel and/or 'The King is Coming'? Many say that the Bible itself is the Gospel or think 'Christian music' is. Others aren't sure and most simply could care less. It gets treated as a 'generic term', a 'Christian word'. Is this the first time you have ever seen these verses in **I Corinthians 15 v 1-4?**

Nowhere in the Bible is this more easily and plainly stated. I declare **'The Gospel' by which also ye are saved!** The Apostle Paul repeats and preached the 'death, burial and resurrection Gospel' for our salvation throughout his Epistles, **Christ crucified!**

'The Gospel of the Grace of God' **began at the death** of Jesus Christ. He died for you, me and all the world. Individually he died for you! The Apostle Peter says to 'ye men of Israel', "ye killed the Prince of life"*. Whereas the Apostle Paul says, "Christ died for you"+. 'The Gospel of the Grace of God' <u>that only</u> the Apostle Paul revealed to the world <u>is not</u> 'the Gospel of the Kingdom' that was preached during 'the earthly ministry of Christ'. *-Acts 2 v 23, 36; -Acts 3 v 13-15; +-I Corinthians 15 v 1-4

Paul wrote repeatedly, being filled by the Holy Spirit, over and over 'the basis of resurrection for salvation'. This is 'Paul's Gospel of the Faith-way Grace of God'*. This is **'The Gospel of Grace'**. The Apostle Paul laid the foundation on the resurrected Lord Jesus Christ+. Not Peter, not Luke, not 'The Twelve', not even Jesus Christ himself during his earthly ministry preached 'this Gospel'. *-Galatians 3 v 21-26; +-I Corinthians 3

"Christ died for our sins". Is this what Jesus, Peter and 'The Twelve' preached? Did they go around with Jesus saying, "Christ died for our sins, and was buried, and rose again the third day"? Silly, and why would they? Jesus Christ was still alive and in their midst. 'The Kingdom of Heaven' is at hand*. *-Matthew 3 v 2; -Matthew 4 v 17; -Matthew 10 v 7

What was the message that God sent 'John the Baptist' to preach? Was John's voice heard in the wilderness saying, "Christ died for our sins, was buried and rose again the third day." Was this what Israel was hearing from John?

'John the Baptist' was 'the herald' proclaiming "the time is now, the King has come". "The Kingdom of Heaven is at hand". 'John the Baptist' preached to the Nation of Israel 'the Baptism of Repentance for the remission of sins'*. John was not preaching 'the death, burial and resurrection gospel'. *-Mark 1 v 4; -Luke 3 v 3; -Acts 13 v 24; -Acts 19 v 4

'The Twelve' disciples did not know that Jesus was going to be nailed to a cross. So how could the disciples have been preaching Paul's Gospel?:

31- Then he *(Jesus)* took unto him the twelve, and said unto them, Behold, we go up to Je-ru'sa-lem, and all things that are written by the prophets concerning the Son of man shall be accomplished.

32- For he shall be delivered unto the Gentiles, and shall be mocked, and spitefully entreated, and spitted on:

33- And they shall scourge him, and put him to death: and the third day he shall rise again.

34- **And they *(the disciples)* understood none of these things: and this saying was hid from them, neither knew they the things that were spoken.**

-Luke 18 v 31-34

How many have been told and have believed that the disciples knew Jesus Christ was going to be crucified? Scripture says they didn't know. God hid things (mysteries/secrets) until he wanted them to be known. Jesus Christ 'uttered' and spoke words concerning his coming Crucifixion, but where do the scriptures lead after saying these things? Take note, these words purposely fell on deaf ears.

17- So then faith cometh by hearing, and hearing by the word of God.

-Romans 10 v 17

29- The **secret *things* belong** unto the LORD our God: **but those *things which are* revealed *belong* unto us and to our children for ever,** that we may do all the words of this law.

-Deuteronomy 29 v 29

Until God says it, how can we believe it? Unless God opens our 'eyes and ears of understanding', the things known of God are 'spiritually discerned'*. Jesus did speak (uttered) of his coming crucifixion many times. We can read where Jesus flat out said these things to his disciples, but what that meant was 'hid from them'. *-I Corinthians 2 v 13, 14

Christendom has read these scriptures assuming, because Jesus said/ uttered them, that they were heard with understanding. He was speaking audibly, uttered out loud to his disciples these things concerning his coming crucifixion. 'The Twelve' were just 'biding the time' and patiently waiting until then?

If the disciples had understood, wouldn't they be 'high tailing it out of Israel with Jesus in tow'? Like the 'Lone Ranger' told Tonto again and again, "Tonto, don't go to town!" But what does the Word of God really say or does not say?

Paul by Holy Spirit inspiration wrote:
7- But **we speak the wisdom of God in a mystery** *(the secrets revealed)*, *even* the hidden *wisdom,* which God ordained before the world unto our glory:
8- Which none of the princes of this world knew: for had they known *it,* they would not have crucified the Lord of glory.
-I Corinthians 2 v 7, 8

Peter says the Old Testament Prophets were speaking things as was delivered to them by God since the beginning:
21- Whom the heaven must receive *(Jesus Christ)* **until** the times of restitution of all things, which God hath **spoken by the mouth of all his holy prophets since the world began**.
-Acts 3 v 21

Jesus Christ in his 'earthly ministry' spoke of things that the prophets knew and preached to Israel. Jesus Christ did not reveal the 'secrets and mysteries' that were hid by God until after 'the Resurrection'. The Lord Jesus **uttered** things but scripture says some of the understandings were hid from Israel and his disciples.

34- All these things spake Je'sus unto the multitude in parables; and without a parable spake he not unto them:
35- That it might be fulfilled **which was spoken by the prophet**, saying, I will open my mouth in parables; **I will <u>utter</u> <u>things</u> which have been kept secret from the foundation of the world**.
-Matthew 13 v 34, 35

Jesus would explain his parables in private to his disciples*. Jesus would **"<u>utter</u> <u>things</u> which have been kept secret from the foundation of the world".** Some of the things Jesus spoke (uttered) to his disciples was 'Divinely missed' or his disciples were afraid to ask. *-Matthew 13 v 3, 10, 13, 34, 35, 53; -Matthew 21 v 45; -Matthew 22 v 1; -Mark 3 v 23; -Mark 4 v 2, 11, 13, 33; -Mark 12 v 1; -Luke 8 v 10

Jesus <u>did not</u> tell his disciples that there is coming a time when the Gentiles would become 'partakers in the heavenly gifts of Christ' without them. Jesus never said to 'the Twelve' that by 'faith alone' the Gentiles could obtain a similar eternal blessing as them. He did not explain the 'mysteries and secrets' that were **"kept secret from the foundation of the world"***. These secrets and mysteries were only revealed to the Apostle Paul for us Gentiles and for the world in 'the Body of Christ+. *-Matthew 13 v 10-17; -Matthew 13 v 35; +-Romans 16 v 25

Paul writes by the Holy Spirit saying there were mysteries still hid with God that have always been secret until after 'the resurrection'. Then God made know these mysteries/secrets 'on this side of the cross'. Jesus Christ no longer was speaking in parables 'to the multitudes'. Paul writes from the ascended Jesus Christ 'by revelation from heaven'. No more secrets, no more mysteries. What was not known before the cross was made known to the Apostle Paul and for us Gentiles (the whole world) after the cross.

<u>Paul did not write concerning Christ and his earthly ministry to Israel</u> except to say:
4- But when the fulness of the time was come, God sent forth his Son, made of a woman, **made under the law,**
5- **To redeem them that were under the law,** that we might receive the adoption of sons.
-Galatians 4 v 4, 5

8- Now I say that Je'sus Christ **was a minister of the circumcision** for the truth of God, **to confirm the promises *made* unto the fathers:**
9- And that the Gen'tiles might glorify God for *his* mercy; as it is written, For this cause I will confess to thee among the Gen'tiles, and sing unto thy name.
-Romans 15 v 8, 9

Have you ever heard your pastor preach these scriptures on Sunday Morning? Better yet, were these scriptures spoken during a Christmas sermon? "God sent forth his Son, made of a woman, **made under the law, To redeem them that were under the law,** Je'sus Christ **was a minister of the circumcision** for the truth of God, **to confirm the promises *made* unto the fathers"**.

The 'mysteries and secrets' were only revealed to the Apostle Paul, not Peter, not Luke, not 'the Twelve' nor to any of the Old Testament prophets. The Apostle Paul writes by the Holy Spirit the following important and fundamental scriptures of truth below. Compare Acts 2 v 21 with Romans 16 v 25 and 26.

The Apostle Paul writes by Holy Spirit inspiration:
25- Now to **him that is of power to stablish you according to <u>my gospel</u> *(Paul)*, and the preaching of Je'sus Christ, according to the revelation of the mystery, <u>which was kept secret</u> since the world began.**
26- **But now** is made manifest, and by the scriptures of the prophets, according to the commandment of the everlasting God, made known to all nations for the obedience of faith.
-Romans 16 v 25, 26

The Apostle Peter says by Holy Spirit inspiration:
20- And he shall send Je'sus Christ, which before was preached unto you.
21- Whom the heaven must receive *(Jesus Christ)* **until** the times of restitution of all things, which God hath <u>**spoken**</u> **by the mouth of all his holy prophets <u>since the world began</u>**.
-Acts 3 v 20, 21

The overall beginning 'Mystery and Secret' that Paul revealed by the ascended Lord Jesus Christ from heaven is this following and important truth to understanding the Holy Bible. There are several 'mystery's' that Paul revealed but the start to understanding the uniqueness of Paul's Apostleship starts with this. Pay Attention!

God hid* things until the Apostle Paul. Only to the Apostle Paul did God reveal the hidden secrets and mysteries+. There is 'a new Gospel in town' and this one will save all the world by faith alone and not by doing anything in the flesh 'to merit favor with God'. How? Romans to Hebrews, and fully understanding I Corinthians 15 v 1-4. *-I Corinthians 2 v 7; -Ephesians 3 v 9; -Colossians 1 v 26; -Romans 16 v 25, 26; +-Romans 11 v 25; -Romans 16 v 25; -I Corinthians 2 v 7; -I Corinthians 15 v 51; -Ephesians 1 v 9; -Ephesians 3 v 3, 4, 9; -Ephesians 5 v 2; -Ephesians 6 v 19; -Colossians 1 v 26, 27; -Colossians 2 v 2; -Colossians 4 v 3; -I Timothy 3 v 16

This 'Gospel of Salvation' shows up all through Paul's Epistles. Blood, his shed blood, raised from the dead, Christ crucified and several more. **This is the beginning, death. Out of death comes new life.**

23- And Jesus answered them, saying, The hour is come, that the Son of man should be glorified.

24- Verily, verily, I say unto you, Except a corn of wheat fall into the ground and die, it abideth alone: but if it die, it bringeth much fruit.

-John 12 v 23, 24

1- For this cause I Paul, the prisoner of Je'sus Christ for you Gen'tiles,

2- If ye have heard of **the dispensation of the grace of God which is given me to you-ward**:

3- How that **by revelation he made known unto me the mystery** (as I wrote afore in few words,

4- Whereby, when you read, **ye may understand my knowledge in the mystery of Christ)**

5- **Whereby, in other ages was not made known unto the sons of men**, as it is **now** revealed unto his holy apostles and prophets *(Paul's ministry)* by the Spirit;

6- That **the Gentiles should be fellowheirs, and of the same body, and partakers of his promise in Christ by the gospel:**

7- **Wherefore I was made a minister**, according to the gift of the grace of God given unto me by the effectual working of his power.

8- **Unto me**, who am less than the least of all saints, **is this grace given, that I should preach among the Gen'tiles** the unsearchable riches of Christ;

9- **And to make all men see what is the fellowship of the mystery, which from the beginning of the world hath been hid in God, <u>who created all things by Je'sus Christ</u>:** *(Jesus Christ is God. -John 1 v 10; -Colossians 1 v 15-18; See the chapter The Invisible Godhead)*

10- To the intent that now unto the principalities and powers in heavenly places might be **known by 'the church'** the manifold wisdom of God,

11- According to the eternal purpose which he purposed in Christ Je'sus our Lord:

12- In whom we have boldness and access with confidence by the faith of him.

-Ephesians 3 v 1-12

Paul says 'prophets' meaning 'a preacher or a pro-claimer'. Before Paul had written the words of Jesus Christ from heaven or when Paul was absent, other men and women prophesied, spoke forth, preached the word of God that Paul had first revealed and delivered to them.

There are no prophets or preacher/teachers today revealing new things of Biblical scripture. Paul began his ministry around 40 A.D. His first epistle (Hebrews has no date of origin) was written around 54 to 58 A.D. The Gospel of Grace began with Paul and ended with Paul, Colossians 1 v 25.

'Holy Apostles' spoken of here were those with Paul, not Peter and 'the Twelve'. Barnabus, Titus, Timothy, Aquila, Priscilla and Phebe to name a few were the 'saints' that Paul could be referring to. Luke too traveled many miles with Paul. These 'saints' that Paul speaks of were not the chosen disciples by Jesus Christ during his 'earthly ministry'. <u>Peter and Paul never traveled together taking 'the gospel' to the world.</u>

24- Who now rejoice in my sufferings for you, and fill up that which is behind of the afflictions of **Christ in my flesh for his body's sake, which is the church**:
25- Whereof I am made a minister, according to **the dispensation of God** which is given to me for you, **<u>to fulfil (complete/put an end to) the word of God</u>**;
26- **Even the mystery which hath been hid from ages and from generations**, but now is made manifest to his saints *(Paul's ministry)*:
27- To whom God would make known what is the riches of the glory of **<u>this mystery among the Gen'tiles; which is Christ in you, the hope of glory:</u>**
-Colossians 1 v 24-27

Christ in you! The hope of Glory! These are Gentiles, you and me, who Paul is writing to. Peter and 'the Twelve disciples' never said such a thing that Christ also would indwell the Gentiles too. 'The Body of Christ, the Church' is all a 'Pauline Revelation'. Paul is not Peter. Peter is not Paul.

Have you read this before? In Luke 18 v 34, 'the Twelve' understood none of these things concerning what Jesus was telling them about him going to 'The Cross'. What Jesus said 'was hid' from them. Jesus told his disciples several times that he was about to be viciously beaten and then murdered. Hello!?

When Peter did speak up in protest, Jesus put him in his place*. Peter, after his rebuke, seemingly forgot what Jesus told him about his 'coming inevitable death'. It was kept secret and hid from 'the Twelve' by God. Ask yourself, why did Jesus keep secrets? *-Matthew 16 v 21-23

21- From that time forth began Je'sus to shew unto his disciples, how that he must go unto Je-ru'sa-lem, and suffer many things of the elders and chief priests and scribes, and be killed, and be raised again the third day.
22- Then Pe'ter took him, and began to rebuke him, saying, Be it far from thee, Lord: this shall not be unto thee.
23- But he *(Jesus)* turned, and said unto Pe'ter, Get thee behind me, Sa'tan: thou art an offense unto me: **for thou savourest not the things that be of God, but those that be of men**.
-Matthew 16 v 21-23

Many times Jesus told his disciples the same thing and nothing came of it*. The scriptures continue and nothing was made of such a profound statement by Jesus Christ. The disciples spoke not a word in protest or of understanding. What Jesus told them went right over their heads. Beaten! Scourged! Crucified! Murdered! Resurrect! It was by divine plan that Jesus Christ would fulfill the prophecies of Israel. His beloved disciples were not going to interfere. *-Matthew 16 v 21-23; -Matthew 17 v 22, 23; -Matthew 20 v 18, 19; -Matthew 26 v 1, 2, 45, 46, 52-56; -Mark 8 v 31-33; -Mark 9 v 31, 32; -Mark 10 v 33, 34, 45; -Luke 9 v 22

'The Word of God' said it, it is undeniable. The disciples **did not know** that Jesus was going to the cross to be crucified, though Jesus told them. **Nor did 'the Twelve' disciples know he was going to resurrect three days later** and Jesus told them that as well. **Had they known** he was going to resurrect from death, wouldn't they have been camped outside the sepulcher waiting for Jesus to appear? Or at least in 'hidden eyesight' of the tomb? None of them did. Hello!?

1- The first day of the week cometh Mary Magdalene early, when it was yet dark, unto the sepulcher, and seeth the stone taken away from the sepulcher.
2- Then she runneth, and cometh to Simon Peter, and to the other disciple *(John)*, and saith unto them, They have taken away the Lord out of the sepulcher, and we know not where they have laid him.

3- Peter therefore went forth, and that other disciple, and came to the sepulcher.

4- So they ran both together: and the other disciple did outrun Peter, and came first to the sepulcher.

5- And he stooping down, and looking in, saw the linen clothes lying; yet went not in.

6- Then cometh Simon Peter following him, and went in to the sepulcher, and seeth the linen clothes lie.

7- And the napkin, that was about his head, not lying with the linen clothes, but wrapped together in a place by itself.

8- Then went in also that other disciple *(John)*, which came first to the sepulcher, **and he saw, and believed.**

9- For as yet they knew not the scripture, that he must rise again from the dead.

-John 20 v 1-9

After Peter and John saw the burial clothes folded and Jesus not there in the sepulcher, **then they believed.** Jesus was missing and not where he had been laid, dead. A prudent grave robber wouldn't take the time to fold his burial clothes before stealing the body. Besides, there were Roman soldiers guarding the sepulcher to ensure that such a thing would not happen.

Their understanding of what Jesus had told them (uttered) now was understood. "For as yet they knew not the scripture, that he must rise again from the dead". Call man and me a liar but call the 'Word of God' a liar....? Read it, believe it for yourself. Take no person's 'supposed head knowledge' in place of the 'Word of God'.

Jesus said:

44- Let these sayings sink down into your ears: for the Son of man shall be delivered into the hands of men.

45- **But they *(the disciples)* understood not this saying, and it was hid from them, that they perceived it not:** and they feared to ask him that saying.

-Luke 9 v 44, 45

Mark writes Holy Spirit inspired:

9- Now when *Jesus* was risen early the first *day* of the week, he appeared first to Ma'ry Mag-da-le'ne, out of whom he had cast seven devils.

10- *And* she went and told them that had been with them, as they mourned and wept.

11- And they, when they had heard that he was alive, and had been seen of her, **believed not**.

12- After that he *(Jesus)* appeared in another form unto two of them, as they walked, and went into the country.

13- And they went and told it unto the residue: **neither believed they them**.

14- Afterward he *(Jesus)* appeared unto the eleven as they sat at meat, and upbraided them with their unbelief and hardness of heart, **because they believed not them which had seen him after he had risen.**

-Mark 16 v 9-14

After 'the Resurrection', Jesus appears out of thin air. Surprise! The disciples were startled by this sudden appearance:

36- And as they thus spake, Je'sus himself stood in the midst of them, and saith unto them, Peace *be* unto you.

37- But they were terrified and afrighted, and supposed that they had seen a spirit.

38- And he said unto them, Why are ye troubled? And why do thoughts arise in your hearts?

39- Behold my hands and my feet, that it is I myself: handle me, and see; for a spirit hath not flesh and bones, as ye see me have.

40- And when he had thus spoken, he shewed them *his* hands and *his* feet.

41- And while they yet believed not for joy, and wondered, he said unto them, Have ye here any meat?

42- And they gave him a piece of a broiled fish, and of an honeycomb.

43- And he took *it*, and **did eat before them.**

44- And he said unto them, These *are* the words which I spake unto you, while I was yet with you, that all things must be fulfilled*, which were written in the law of Mo'ses, and *in* the prophets, and *in* the psalms, concerning me. *-Matthew 5 v 17; -John 19 v 30; -Luke 18 v 31-33; -Luke 22 v 37; -John 19 v 28-30

45- **Then opened he their understanding, that they might understand the scriptures.**

-Luke 24 v 36-45

The chief priests and Pharisees remembered what Jesus said about him going to resurrect three days later*. They themselves did not believe in 'this resurrection' but wanted to prevent any rumors started if there happened to be a 'grave robbery' of his body. These priests and Pharisees did what they could to prevent any knowledge of 'a resurrection rumor' being made to Israel. They requested that there be Roman soldiers posted to guard the sepulcher. *-Matthew 27 v 62-66; -Matthew 28 v 11-15

62- Now the next day, that followed the day of preparation, the chief priests and Phar'i-sees came together unto Pi'late.
63- Saying, Sir, we remember that that deceiver said, while he was yet alive, After three days I will rise again.
64- Command therefore that the sepulcher be made sure until the third day, lest his disciples come by night, and steal him away, and say unto the people, He is risen from the dead: so the last error shall be worse than the first.
65- Pi'late said unto them, Ye have a watch: go your way, make it as sure as ye can.
66- So they went, and made the sepulcher sure, <u>sealing the stone</u>, and setting a watch.
-Matthew 27 v 62-66

No man can stand in the way of God:
1- In the end of the sabbath, as it began to dawn toward the first *day* of the week, came Ma'ry Mag-da-le'ne and the other Ma'ry to see the sepulcher.
2- And, behold, there was a great earthquake: for <u>the angel of the Lord</u> descended from heaven, and came and rolled back the stone from the door, and sat upon it.
3- His countenance was like lightning, and his raiment white as snow:
4- And for fear of him the keepers did shake, and became as dead *men*.
5- And the angel answered and said unto the women, Fear not ye: for I know that ye seek Je'sus, which was crucified.
6- He is not here: for he is risen, as he said. Come, see the place where the Lord lay.
7- And go quickly, and tell his disciples that he is risen from the dead; and, behold, he goeth before you into Gal'i-lee; there shall ye see him: lo, I have told you.
-Matthew 28 v 1-7

After the resurrection, Jesus was only seen by a select few for forty days*. The priests requested that the 'tomb watchers' be bribed and given money to stay quiet and speak nothing of the disappearance of Jesus Christ's crucified body. Satan (by God's design) did 'a number' on the world. Israel has believed not in the resurrected Christ. That is to say, 'the elect' believed and the rest were blinded.

*-Matthew 28 v 16, 17; -Acts 1 v 3

11- Now when they were going, behold, some of the watch came into the city, and shewed unto the chief priests all the things that were done.

12- And when they were assembled with the elders, and had taken counsel, they gave large money unto the soldiers.

13- **Saying, Say ye, His disciples came by night, and stole him** *away* **while we slept.**

14- And if this come to the governor's ears, we will persuade him, and secure you.

15- So they took the money, and did as they were taught: **and this saying is commonly reported among the Jews until this day**.

-Matthew 28 v 11-15

Jesus said:

17- Think not that I am come to destroy the law, or the prophets: I am not come to destroy, but to fulfill.

-Matthew 5 v 17

This scripture is quoted by some preachers suggesting that Israel and 'the Twelve' knew of his coming death and resurrection. Some make it seem that his crucifixion was part of 'the Law' or 'of a common knowledge'. After the resurrection, the Old Testament Messianic Prophecies concerning Christ (300+?) can now be understood that the scriptures were talking about the Lord Jesus Christ that was born in Bethlehem.

Some have led their congregations into believing that his 'dieing on the cross' was why Jesus came to Israel. They teach that Jesus Christ came in the flesh to be crucified for the sins of the world. "Everybody knows that" they have been preaching. Not according to scripture they didn't. You just read some.

Preachers like to use this next verse to show that Jesus was speaking of 'the cross' of his coming crucifixion. Sermon's 'on the blood' of Jesus Christ and how his disciples too must be willing to partake of a similar death. If 'the disciples' did not know that Jesus would be crucified, "take up the cross and follow me" has been taken out of context by so many. Why didn't this preacher read and understand the previous verses in Mathew 16 v 21-23?

24- Then said Jesus unto his disciples, If any man will come after me, let him deny himself, and take up the cross, and follow me.
-Matthew 16 v 24; -Mark 10 v 21

The burdens and persecutions that would come upon them in a world of unbeliever's was not going to be a 'cake walk'. The same is for those today that wear 'their supposed righteousness' as an a-front to the world in provoking them. Live by the sword, die by the sword. Live by the Word, Live.

Jesus Christ was that prophesied King that came to Israel. 'The Kingdom of Heaven is at hand'*. 'The Kingdom of God is within you (in their midst)'+. These were the prophecies that were being fulfilled. All of Israel was to believe in 'the Name of Jesus Christ'=. Their prophesied King and Kingdom had finally come. But 'the Nation of the Circumcision/Law' rejected their King, their Christ, their Messiah, their Kingdom. *-Matthew 3 v 2; -Matthew 4 v 17; -Matthew 10 v 7; +-Luke 17 v 21; =-Mark 16 v 17; -John 2 v 23; -John 3 v 18; -John 10 v 25; -John 20 v 31; -Acts 2 v 38; -Acts 3 v 6; -Acts 4 v 10; -Acts 8 v 12; -Acts 10 v 43; -I John 3 v 23

9- And when he *(Jesus)* had spoken these things, while they beheld, he was taken up; and a cloud received him out of their sight.
10- And while they looked steadfastly toward heaven as he went up, behold, **two men stood by them in white apparel**;
11- Which also said, Ye men of Gal'i-lee, why stand ye gazing up into heaven? This same Je'sus, which is taken up from you into heaven, shall so come in like manner as ye have seen him go into heaven.
-Acts 1 v 9-11

The exact spot and place that Jesus Christ left in Acts 1 v 11, is the same spot prophesied by Zechariah hundreds of years before Jesus Christ came in the flesh, that he would return with the 'Earthly Kingdom of Heaven':

4- And his feet <u>shall</u> stand in that day upon the mount of Ol'ives, which *is* before Je-ru'sa-lem on the east, and the mount of Ol'ives shall cleave in the midst thereof toward the east and toward the west, *and there shall be* a great valley; and half of the mountain <u>shall</u> remove toward the north, and half of it toward the south.

.....

8- **And <u>it shall be</u> in that day**, *that* living waters <u>shall</u> go out from Je-ru'sa-lem; half of them toward the former sea, and half of them toward the hinder sea: in summer and in winter shall it be.

9- And the **LORD <u>shall be</u> king over all the earth**: in that day <u>shall</u> there be one LORD, and his name one.

-Zechariah 14 v 4, 8, 9

Is the LORD king over all the earth today? Will he be? Scripture says "the LORD <u>shall be</u> king over all the earth". The Kingdom of Heaven is an 'Earthly Kingdom', perfect (Heavenly) as it was in the 'Garden of Eden'. As concerning this 'Earthly Kingdom' that was promised by God to the Jews of Israel, many don't believe in an 'Earthly Kingdom of Heaven'.

6- The wolf also <u>shall</u> dwell with the lamb, and the leopard <u>shall</u> lie down with the kid; and the calf and the young lion and the fatling together; and a little child <u>shall</u> lead them.

7- And the cow and the bear <u>shall</u> feed; their young ones <u>shall</u> lie down together: and **the lion <u>shall</u> eat straw like the ox.**

8- And the sucking child <u>shall</u> play on the hole of the asp, and the weaned child <u>shall</u> put his hand on the cockatrices' den.

9- They <u>shall not</u> hurt nor destroy in all my holy mountain *(kingdom)*: for **the earth** <u>shall be</u> full of the knowledge of the LORD, as the waters cover the sea.

10- And in that day there <u>shall be</u> a root of Jes'se, which <u>shall</u> stand for an ensign of the people; to it <u>shall</u> the Gentiles seek: and his rest <u>shall</u> be glorious.

-Isaiah 11 v 6-10

How did Isaiah know that 'a root' (Jesus Christ) would come out of Jes'se's family? He didn't. God told him. Many times in scripture people were named hundreds of years before they existed. Our Bibles are 'the Living Word of God'. Only our Bibles, and there is none other, could predict prophecy and have them be true 100%. The prophecies not fulfilled will be. Take note that in our Bible, 'time specific prophecy' concerns Israel and the Jews, not the Gentiles.

Are the carnivorous animals eating grass and straw today? Is the whole earth filled with the knowledge of the LORD? Are the wolves and lambs friends today? Can a bear and a cow live peacefully together? Can children play with poisonous snakes?

As it was in the 'Garden of Eden':
30- And to every beast of the earth, and to every fowl of the air, and to every thing that creepeth upon the earth, wherein *there is* life, **I have given every green herb for meat:** and it was so.
-Genesis 1 v 30

Peter speaks of the 'God of their fathers' after 'the resurrection':
12- And when Pe'ter saw *it*, he answered unto the people, **Ye men of Is'ra-el**, why marvel ye at this? Or why look ye so earnestly on us, as though by our own power or holiness we had made this man to walk?
13- The God of A'bra-ham, and of I'saac, and of Ja'cob, **the God of our fathers**, hath glorified his Son Je'sus; whom ye delivered up, and denied him in the presence of Pi'late, when he was determined to let *him* go.
14- But ye denied the Holy One and the Just, and desired a murderer to be granted unto you;
15- And killed the Prince of life, **whom God hath raised from the dead**; whereof we are witnesses.
16- **And his name through faith in his name hath made this man strong,** whom ye see and know: yea, the faith which is by him hath given him this perfect soundness in the presence of you all.
17- And now, brethren, I wot that through ignorance ye did *it*, as *did* also your rulers.
18- But those things, **which God before had showed by the mouth of all his prophets, that Christ should suffer, he hath so fulfilled**.
19- Repent ye therefore, and be converted, that your sins may be blotted out, **when the times of refreshing shall come** from the presence of the Lord;
20- **And he shall send Je'sus Christ**, which before was preached unto you:
21- Whom the **heaven must receive until the times of restitution of all things**, which God hath spoken by the mouth of all his holy prophets since the world began.

22- **For Moses truly said unto the fathers, A prophet** shall **the Lord your God raise up unto you of your brethren**, like unto me; him shall ye hear in all things whatsoever he shall say unto you.

23- And it shall come to pass, *that* every soul, which will not hear that prophet, shall be destroyed from among the people.

24- **Yea, and all the prophets from Sam'u-el and those that follow after, as many as have spoken, have likewise foretold of these days.**

25- **Ye are the children of the prophets, and of the covenant which God had made with our fathers, saying unto A'bra-ham, And in thy seed shall all the kindreds of the earth be blessed.**

26- **Unto you first, having raised up his Son Je'sus**, sent him to bless you, and turning away every one of you from his iniquities.

-Acts 3 v 12-26

Peter wrote (by Holy Spirit inspiration) how the Old Testament prophets searched for the meanings that they didn't understand before Jesus came in the flesh. Post resurrection, on this side of the cross, the things that Jesus had 'uttered' to his disciples now was made to be understood. The believers in the 'Name of Jesus Christ' and who he is (The Gospel of the Kingdom saints) now remembered his words.

10- Of which salvation the prophets have inquired and searched diligently, who prophesied of the grace *that should come* unto you:

11- Searching what, or what manner of time the Spirit of Christ which was in them *(those prophets)* did signify, when it testified beforehand **the sufferings of Christ and the glory that should follow**.

-I Peter 1 v 10, 11

Peter never preached 'death, burial and resurrection' for salvation (Paul's Gospel). The 'lively hope' Israel had was that Jesus was still alive and could still return to Israel with the 'Kingdom of Heaven'*. The Resurrection of Jesus Christ is stated as fact, that it did happen. It is still possible for the 'Earthly Kingdom of Heaven' to be fulfilled. Jesus is alive, not dead! *-Luke 21 v 27, 28; -Daniel 12 v 1; -Zechariah 14 v 4, 8, 9

3- Blessed *be* the God and Father of our Lord Je'sus Christ, which according to his abundant mercy **hath begotten us again unto a lively hope by the resurrection of Je'sus Christ from the dead,**
-I Peter 1 v 3

16- Because it is written, Be ye holy; for I am holy.
17- And if ye call on the Father, who without respect of persons judgeth according to every man's work, past the time of your sojourning *here* in fear:
18- Forasmuch as ye know that ye were not redeemed* with corruptible things, *as* silver and gold, from your vain conversation *received* by tradition from your fathers; (*To be redeemed physically with the promised kingdom. -Luke 21 v 27, 28; -Daniel 12 v 1*)
19- But with the precious blood of Christ, as of a lamb without blemish and without spot :
20- Who verily was **foreordained** before the foundation of the world, **but was manifest in these last times for you,**
21- Who by him do **believe in God, that raised him up from the dead,** and gave him glory; that your faith and hope might be in God.
-I Peter 1 v 16-21

Peter never said that 'Christ died for you, was buried, and rose again' as the Gospel of Salvation. But to believe that God raised Jesus from the dead and that physically he would return to set up the promised 'Kingdom of Heaven'. Redemption is something not purchased with silver and gold, but by the physical person in Jesus Christ, a man with flesh and bone, the blood of Christ*. He would return to save Israel physically and put down all their enemies. *-Luke 21 v 27, 28; -Daniel 12 v 1

In the big picture, Jesus died for the sins of the world <u>by his own submission</u>. **But this revelation of dieing for all the sins of the world, not just for the Jews, was hid from Israel until God revealed it to the Apostle Paul on this side of the cross, post resurrection.** The Jews wanted nothing to do with their LORD/JEHOVAH being a savior of the Gentiles too. Pre-crucifixion the Gentiles had "no hope and were without God"*. *-Ephesians 2 v 11-13

How many Gentiles (non-Jews) were used by God in the Old Testament? Not the Gentile nations that made war with Israel but the individuals. Who were these non-Jews? Why were there so few Gentiles in the Bible?

When the nation of Israel becomes a 'Kingdom of Priests' it would be the Jews that would bring the 'Light' to the Gentiles of the world. It was by Israel and the Jews that the world would gain the knowledge of 'their LORD God JEHOVAH'. Only the Jews of Israel knew 'the living God'. The rest of the world (Gentiles) were pagans and idol worshipers. There was no formal religion except 'cults' made by men. None of these knew 'the Living God'.

The prophet Isaiah wrote hundreds of years before Jesus:
1- Arise, shine; for thy light is come, and the glory of the LORD is risen upon thee.
2- For, behold, the darkness shall cover the earth, and gross darkness *(spiritual darkness)* the people: but the LORD shall arise upon thee, and his glory shall be seen upon thee.
3- And **the Gentiles shall come to thy light**, and kings to the brightness of thy rising.
4- Lift up thine eyes round about, and see: all they gather themselves together, they come to thee: thy sons shall come from far, and thy daughters shall be nursed at thy side.
5- **Then** thou shalt see, and flow together, and thine heart shall fear, and be enlarged; because the abundance of the sea *(mankind)* shall be converted unto thee, **the forces of the Gentiles shall come unto thee**.
-Isaiah 60 v 1-5

The history of Israel shows that they were very 'anti-Gentile'. This is not to be taken as an 'anti-Semitic' statement. God had instructed the 'Children of Israel' to have nothing to do with the people of the world. Jews 'of the Circumcision/Law' didn't have Gentile friends that they would invite to dinner. The Jews labeled the Gentiles as 'uncircumcised, heathen, unworthy and at times dogs'. Jews are not Gentiles. Gentiles are not Jews. If you are not a 'Law Keeping Jew of the Circumcision', then you are a Gentile.

The Apostle Paul makes the statement (by the Spirit of God) that he wrote the final words of our Bible*. There is debate over when John wrote the Book of Revelation. That is okay because John was not writing to us Gentiles. John was writing to 'the seven churches', an ecclesia, an assembly of Jew/Hebrews, and not 'Body of Christ Churches'. *-Colossians 1 v 24, 25

Paul had nothing to do with the audience John addresses. John never accepted Paul's Gospel of Grace. There is no indication that John, having written 'The Gospel of John, and I II III John, gave up keeping 'the law' for the writing of 'Revelation'. "Keep the commandments" John writes repeatedly. John is definitely not the Apostle of the Gentiles.

Look at the margins of your Bible. The English translators of the New Testament interpreted these assemblies, congregations, ecclesias, synagogues and gatherings as 'churches', not the original texts and manuscripts. The word 'church' has been misidentified by Christendom to include all religious gatherings and buildings.

'The Church', as Paul reveals by the ascended Lord from Heaven, is very specific. There is only one church, 'The Body of Christ'. John was not writing to 'Paul's churches' but was writing to Jews/Hebrews to encourage and prepare them for the persecutions they were presently facing and of the coming 'wrath of God'.

The 'Word of God' says by the 'pen of Paul':
24- Who now rejoice in my sufferings for you, and fill up that which is behind of the afflictions of Christ in my flesh **for his body sake, which is the church**:
25- Whereof I am made a minister, according to the dispensation of God which is given to me for you, **<u>to fulfil the word of God</u>**;
-Colossians 1 v 24, 25

Fulfill the 'Word of God'. Paul 'completed' the words of our Bible. No person is adding scripture to 'The Church, the Body of Christ'. **'To fulfill' or complete is 'to put an end to'.** It was by the Apostle Paul that wrote and 'put an end to' the words of our Bible for us in this 'Age of Grace'.

Where then does it put 'the religion' invented by the Roman Empire and those that claim they have Bibles with scripture written after Paul or books and scripture not found in the King James Version? All the Books of the KJV agree from Genesis to Revelation. These other books found in other bibles don't match up with the KJV.

The Romans themselves destroyed Jerusalem in 70 A.D. and had horribly persecuted Israel by murder and slaughter. The Roman's invented 'a religion' by a committee of men and it was by these men who decided what to believe and 'how to' believe. There is no 'Pope' or 'Cardinal' in the original manuscripts of the 'Word of God'. The Apostle Peter was a Jew 'under the law' 100% and could not have been the first Pope.

'The Trial of Christendom' speaks only for the King James Version of the Holy Bible (KJV). It is the oldest and most closely translated from the original manuscripts <u>for the world today</u>. There are other Bibles that closely follow the KJV but to be on the safe side for the writing of this Book, all scripture references will come solely from the KJV.

Every person can find a copy of the KJV. The newer translated Bibles, the KJV does not speak for them. Because by man, truth can be twisted and meanings minimized and they do. Beware of the newer translations and their <u>'fruity language'</u>!

Do you want the truth? Truth can only come from the 'Word of God'. It is by God that opens a persons heart and mind to understanding. Our Bibles trump any and all words made by a preacher, priest or any man.

Knowing that the Bible (KJV) is 'The Word of God', we can believe that Israel and the disciples did not know that Jesus Christ was going to be crucified. We know and believe then too that they did not know he was going to resurrect. These scriptures are clear and cannot be denied.

How could Peter and 'the Twelve' been preaching Paul's Gospel? Read 'The Gospel' again, I Corinthians 15 v 1-4. Paul preached 'Christ Crucified' and 'the Resurrection for Salvation' by faith*. Christ died for you, individually. The Apostle Paul did not write of the 'Earthly Ministry of Jesus Christ' but 'by Revelation from the Resurrected Lord Jesus Christ'. *-I Corinthians 1 v 23, 24; -I Corinthians 2 v 2; -Galatians 2 v 20; Galatians 5 v 24; -Galatians 6 v 14; -Acts 17 v 18, 32; -Acts 23 v 6, 8; -Acts 24 v 15, 21; -Romans 1 v 4; -Romans 6 v 5; -I Corinthians 15 v 12, 13, 21, 42; -Philippians 3 v 10, 11; -II Timothy 2 v 18

Baptism

3- Know ye not, that so **many of us as were baptized into Je'sus Christ were baptized into his death?**

4- Therefore **we are buried with him by baptism into death**: that like as Christ was raised up from the dead by the glory of the Father *(Paul's Gospel)*, even so we also should walk in newness of life.

-Romans 6 v 3, 4

13- For **by one Spirit are we all baptized** into one body, whether we be Jews or Gentiles, whether we be bond or free; and have been made to drink into one Spirit.

-I Corinthians 12 v 13

Water does not 'baptize us into Jesus' Christ's death', only the 'One Spirit' of God' can do this. **The Apostle Paul never preached Acts 2 v 38.** Water baptism was never a part of Paul's epistles nor in the 'Doctrine of Salvation' that the 'resurrected Lord Jesus Christ' sent Paul to preach.

I know for some that you are eager to jump into the Book of Acts, to show that Paul did baptize with water. Did he? This is covered in this next section.

Jesus Christ was made in the flesh under the Law. He was born of a women just like all of mankind. In the 'birthing process' there is a lot of 'water and blood'. Jesus Christ was born 'a man' (human baby). Much of Christendom have interpreted these following scriptures as 'water baptism' or they want to believe that it is, why?

Jesus the Christ was born a fleshly human: *(see the chapter: The Invisible Godhead that further clarifies the following scriptures from John)*
6- This is he that came by water and blood, even Jesus Christ; not by water only, but by water and blood. And it is the Spirit that beareth witness, because the Spirit is truth.
7- For <u>there are three that bear record in heaven</u>, **the Father, the Word, and the Ho'ly Ghost**, and these three are in one *(the Godhead)*.
8- And <u>there are three that bear witness in earth</u>, **the Spirit, and the water, and the blood** *(Jesus born of a women)*: and these three agree in one.
-I John 5 v 6-8

In Christendom, 'Water Baptism' is taught and preached that it signifies the 'death, burial and resurrection' of Jesus Christ. Going down (death), being submerged in water (burial) and then brought back up (resurrected). This interpretation could only be made **when falsely combining** Paul's God given knowledge of baptism of the 'Holy Spirit' with the Jews 'water baptism'. What?!!!

'The Baptized' by water are said to now be identified with Jesus Christ's 'death, burial and resurrection' that Paul preached? How did this happen? This is not the message that 'John the Baptist' preached. With this type of thinking, <u>the 'two Gospels' become one</u>. Most of Christendom has done this.

If 'John the Baptist' and the disciples didn't know of 'the crucifixion and resurrection', then how could they be using 'water baptism' as a metaphor of the 'crucifixion process'? It is by mans own interpretation's today, by man-made religions and denominations, that it has been taught that way. HELLO!

Peter preached 'water baptism' to 'Ye men of Israel' the same that 'John the Baptist' preached saying:
38- Then Pe'ter said unto them, Repent, and be baptized every one of you in the name of Je'sus Christ for the remission of sins, and <u>ye shall</u> receive the gift of the Ho'ly Ghost.
-Acts 2 v 38

16- John *(the Baptist)* answered, saying unto them all, I indeed baptize you with water; but one mightier than I cometh, the latchet of whose shoes I am not worthy to unloose: <u>he shall</u> baptize you with the Ho'ly Ghost and with fire:
17- Whose fan is in his hand, and he will thoroughly purge his floor, and gather the wheat into his garner; but the chaff he will burn with fire unquenchable.
-Luke 3 v 16, 17

Resist and reject the Baptism of the Holy Ghost (Holy Spirit) 'in unbelief' will result still with 'a baptism'. The unbeliever (the chaff) and the ungodly of the world too will be baptized. But this baptism is of eternal fire and damnation.
Verse 16: "he shall baptize you with the Ho'ly Ghost and with fire".
Verse 17: "but the chaff he will burn with fire unquenchable".

Baptism doesn't always mean with water. 'Baptized unto Moses', the Children of Israel didn't get wet either:
1- Moreover, brethren, I would not that ye should be ignorant, how that all our fathers were under the cloud, and all passed through the sea;
2- And were **all baptized unto Mo'ses in the cloud and in the sea**;
-I Corinthians 10 v 1, 2

By 'water baptism' the Jews would receive the Holy Spirit (Holy Ghost). God had imputed the Holy Ghost upon others in the past but these were by God's sovereign selection. The Old Testament Prophets wrote being filled with the Holy Ghost. Until 'Pentecost', the Holy Ghost wasn't given to the masses but was promised.

'The Miracle at Pentecost' did happen as was prophesied by the prophet Joel*. After Pentecost, the Jews did receive the Holy Ghost by this 'water baptism' process. **Israel and the Jews were being baptized into 'the Holy Spirit of God'.** This was for Israel at this time. They were still in anticipation of the 'Kingdom of Heaven' to come. They were being prepared to be a 'Kingdom of Priests'. It was prophesied that it was by the Jew that the world would receive knowledge of 'their LORD God JEHOVAH'. *-Joel 2 v 28, 29

For 'The Body of Christ', the 'True Church' on this side of the cross, **the Holy Spirit Baptizes us into Christ**. How? By a full faith and understanding of 'the Gospel' that Paul preached. 'We preach Christ Crucified' for 'Eternal Salvation', not the 'Earthly Ministry' of Jesus Christ to Israel for salvation.

Please don't misunderstand. The Earthly ministry of Jesus Christ to Israel is fundamental to the understanding of the 'Word of God'. What Jesus taught to Israel is accepted by 'the Body of Christ'. We fully believe the 'Earthly Ministry' and his wholesome divine words. Jesus Christ came to the nation of Israel proving who he is as was prophesied. Israel could have and should have known. Israel was not ready for their King and Messiah.

Of course we believe in 'the Earthy Ministry' and what Jesus taught. But we know in 'the Body of Christ' that Jesus came to Israel 'a Law keeper' and 'a Minister for Israel'*. The 'Fleshly Earthy Jesus Christ' was not a minister of 'the Gentiles' but a minister of 'the Circumcision'. *-Galatians 4 v 4, 5; -Romans 15 v 8, 9,

Paul <u>did not</u> preach 'water baptism' as a means for salvation to the Gentiles*. He preached 'Baptism of the Holy Spirit'. By the Holy Spirit we are Baptized into the 'Body of Christ, The Church'. *-Romans 6 v 3-10; -Ephesians 4 v 5; -Colossians 2 v 12

Luke wrote that Paul did baptize a few during the transitional period of the 'Kingdom Gospel' to the 'Gospel of Grace' in the Book of Acts. But as part of Paul's Epistles, he never wrote that water baptism is a requirement for salvation like it was for the Jews under the Law. **<u>Paul never preached Acts 2 v 38.</u>**

The few that were baptized by Paul in the Book of Acts already were baptized by the 'Holy Spirit'. These scriptures in the Book of Acts don't specifically point out that water was even used. If Paul did use water, he was qualified to do so when dealing with the 'Jews of the Circumcision/Law'.

These 'Gospel of the Kingdom saints' were promised the Holy Ghost when "they should believe on him, which should come after him *(John the Baptist)*, that is, on Christ Jesus"*. The gentiles were never promised the gift of salvation this way, only the Jews of the Circumcision' under 'the Law'. *-Acts 19 v 4

But read closely. At what point was the 'Holy Ghost' baptizing them?:
13- And on the sabbath we went out of the city by a river side, where prayer was wont to be made; and we sat down, and spake unto the women which resorted *thither.*
14- And a certain women named Lyd'i-a, a seller of purple, of the city of Thy-a-ti'ra, which worshipped God, heard us: **whose heart the Lord opened, that she attended unto the things which were spoken of Paul**.
15- And when she was baptized, and her household, she besought *us*, saying, If ye have judged me to be faithful to the Lord, come into my house, and abide *there*. And she constrained us.
-Acts 16 v 13-15

Who opened Lydia's heart? It was not Paul but the Lord after "she attended unto the things which were spoken of Paul". Then she was baptized. Was it water or the Spirit that truly baptized Lydia?

The physical act of taking them into the water is not shown. Nevertheless, Lydia was a Hebrew that worshiped God and probably was already water baptized according to 'John the Baptist' teaching. Lydia was promised the Holy Ghost under the Gospel of the Kingdom. **Did she get water baptized twice** or was it **the Holy Spirit when she/they attended unto the things which Paul spoke 'whose heart the Lord opened'?**

25- And at midnight Paul and Si'las prayed, and sang praises unto God: and the prisoners heard them.
26- And suddenly there was a great earthquake, so that the foundations of the prison were shaken: and immediately all the doors were opened, and every one's bands were loosed.
27- And the keeper of the prison awaking out of his sleep, and seeing the prison doors open, he drew out his sword, and would have killed himself, supposing that the prisoners had been fled.

28- But Paul cried with a loud voice, saying, Do thyself no harm: for we are all here.

29- Then he called for a light, and sprang in, and came trembling, and fell down before Paul and Si'las,

30- And brought them out, and said, Sirs, **what must I do** to be saved?

31- And they said, **Believe on the Lord Jesus Christ, and thou shalt be saved, and thy house.**

32- **<u>And they spake unto him the word of the Lord, and to all that were in his house.</u>**

33- **And he took them the same hour of the night, and washed *their* stripes; and was baptized, he and all his, straightway.**

-Acts 16 v 25-33

The Holy Spirit was not received in the way that Peter told 'Ye men of Israel' how to do it. **It was by faith first 'In the hearing of Paul's message' that the 'Spirit of God' baptized them.** A change in program was happening for the world in obtaining 'salvation by faith without works'. The Book of Acts is 'a Book of Transition' and not Doctrine for the 'Body of Christ'. The Book of Romans is the beginning of 'The True Church Doctrine'.

Paul encounters some Jewish disciples on his journey. These Jews had previously been baptized according to the teaching of 'John the Baptist'. They said they knew not of the 'Holy Ghost'. After Paul spoke with them, they were baptized by the 'Holy Ghost'.

1- And it came to pass, that, while A-pol'los was at Cor'inth, Paul having passed through the upper coasts came to Eph'e-sus: and finding certain disciples,

2- He said unto them, Have ye received the Ho'ly Ghost since ye believed? And they said unto him, We have not so much as heard whether there be any Ho'ly Ghost.

3- And he said unto them, Unto what then were ye baptized? And they said, Unto John's baptism.

4- Then said Paul, John verily baptized with the baptism of repentance, saying unto the people, <u>that they should believe on him which should come after him, that is, on Christ Je'sus.</u>

5- **<u>When they heard this,</u> they were baptized in the name of the Lord Jesus.**

6- And **when Paul had laid *his* hands on them, the Ho'ly Ghost *(Spiritual, not water)* came on them; and they spake with tongues, and prophesied.**
7- And all the men were about twelve.
-Acts 19 v 1-7

Did Paul use water? These were qualifying Jews that were promised the Holy Ghost by water baptism. They were not Gentiles. They had already been baptized according to the teaching of John the Baptist.

If Paul did use water, then they were water baptized <u>twice</u> with water? These twelve 'Gospel of the Kingdom' saints were promised the Holy Ghost when "they should believe on him which should come after him *(John the Baptist)*, that is, on Christ Je'sus". When they believed this, they were baptized without water, easy.

It is the same 'Gospel of the Kingdom' message. **Believe on the name of the Lord Jesus Christ.** The name is the 'Cornerstone of the Gospel of the Kingdom's' salvation. Be water Baptized and keep the full law. This too is the 'Apostles Doctrine'*. Who can follow this teaching today? *-Acts 2 v 42

Much of Christendom refuse to accept that 'Paul is thee Apostle of the Gentiles'. Many think they became 'converted Jews' when they believe in Jesus. The Apostle Paul doesn't apply to them?

By 'the spirit of this world', Christendom combines the 'ministry of the circumcision' with the 'ministry of the uncircumcision'. Christendom has 'mixed and mashed' together the 'two Gospels'. They really can't see the difference. You could show scripture after scripture and they just can't see it. They don't want to see that what they thought of as truth for years is not after the true word of God. Who is it that hardens the heart to the truth?

As Paul proclaimed by Holy Spirit inspiration:
14- I thank God that I baptized none of you, but Cris'pus and Ga'ius;
15- Lest any should say that I had baptized in mine own name.
16- And I baptized also the household of Steph'a-nas: besides, I know not whether I baptized any other.
17- **For Christ sent me not to baptize, but to preach the gospel: not with wisdom of words, lest the cross of Christ should be made of none effect.**
18- **For the preaching of the cross is to them that perish foolishness; but unto us which are saved it is the power of God.**

19- For it is written, I will destroy the wisdom of the wise, and will bring to nothing the understanding of the prudent.

20- Where *is* the wise? where *is* the scribe? where *is* the disputer of this world? hath not God made foolish the wisdom of this world.

21- For after that in the wisdom of God the world by wisdom knew not God, it pleased God by the foolishness of preaching to save them that believe.

22- For the Jews require a sign, and the Greeks seek after wisdom:

23- **But we preach Christ crucified**, unto the Jews a stumbling block, and unto the Greeks *(Gentiles)* foolishness;

24- But unto them which are called, both Jews and Greeks *(Gentiles)*, Christ the power of God, and the wisdom of God *(the preaching of Christ crucified v 23)*.

-I Corinthians 1 v 14-24

True baptism is not 'of water' but 'is of the Holy Spirit':

12- For as the body is one, and hath many members, and all the members of that one body, being many, are one body: so also *is* Christ.

13- For by **one Spirit are we all baptized into one body**, whether *we be* Jews or Gen'tiles, whether we be bond or free; and have been made all to drink into one Spirit.

….

27- **Now ye are the body of Christ**, and members in particular.

-I Corinthians 12 v 12, 13, 27

There is only One:

4- There is **one body**, and **one Spirit**, even as ye are called in **one hope** of your calling;

5- **One Lord, one faith, <u>one baptism</u>,**

6- **One God and Father** of all, who is above all, and through all, and in you all*. *(*Paul only writes to the believer.)*

-Ephesians 4 v 4-6

If Paul was Peter and Peter was Paul preaching the same thing as most of Christendom has been saying, then Paul at sometime, somewhere would have said, "Repent, and be baptized for the remission of sins and ye shall receive the Holy Ghost". In the Epistles of the 'Body of Christ Doctrine', written through Paul being Holy Spirit directed, this is not found. It is by man's 'supposed head knowledge' and not of the 'true word' of God that this is made up.

'The Apostle of the Gentiles' never followed Peter. Paul is not Peter. Peter is not Paul. Each were under a different 'dispensation'. Peter was <u>an</u> 'Apostle of the Circumcision' and Paul was <u>the</u> 'Apostle of the Uncircumcision'. Law and Grace does not mix.

7- But contrariwise, when they saw that **the gospel of the uncircumcision** was committed unto me *(Paul), as **the gospel** of the circumcision was* unto **Pe'ter**;
8- (For he that wrought effectually in Pe'ter to the apostleship of the circumcision, the same was mighty in me toward the Gen'tiles:)
9- And when James, Ce'phas *(Peter)* and John, who seemed to be pillars, perceived the grace that was given unto me, they gave to me and Bar'na-bas the right hands of fellowship; that **we *should go* unto <u>the</u> <u>heathen</u>, and they unto the circumcision.**
-Galatians 2 v 7-9

Paul never used water concerning the 'true church, the Body of Christ' as so many have falsely thought. The following scriptures have been used by those that mix the Gospels not seeing (hearing by the Word of God) the absence of water. There is no water in the following scriptures. Water is not Spirit.

Paul writes Holy Spirit inspired:
3- Know ye not, **that so many of us as were baptized into Je'sus Christ** were baptized *(by Spirit not water)* into his death?
4- Therefore we are buried with him by baptism *(Spirit not water)* into death: that like as Christ was raised up from the dead by the glory of the Father, even so we also should walk in newness of life.
5- For if we had been planted together in the likeness of his death, we shall be also *in the likeness* of *his* resurrection *(by Spirit not water)*:
6- Knowing this, that our old man is crucified with *him*, that the body of sin might be destroyed, that henceforth we should not serve sin.
7- For he that is dead is freed from sin.
8- Now if we be dead with Christ, we believe that we shall also live with him:
9- Knowing that Christ being raised from the dead dieth no more; death hath no more dominion over him.

10- For in that he died, he died unto sin once: but in that he liveth, he liveth unto God.

11- Likewise reckon ye also yourselves to be dead indeed unto sin, but alive unto God through Je'sus Christ our Lord.

12- Let not sin therefore reign in your mortal body, that ye should obey it in the lusts thereof.

13- Neither yield ye your members *as* instruments of unrighteousness unto sin: but yield yourselves unto God, as those that are alive from the dead, and your members *as* instruments of righteousness unto God.

14- For sin shall not have dominion over you: **for ye are not under the law, but under grace.**

15- What then? Shall we sin, because we are not under the law, but under grace? God forbid.

-Romans 6 v 3-15

This is where the crucifixion process (death, burial, resurrection) of Paul's 'Christ Crucified Gospel' has been used and combined with Peter and 'John the Baptist' teachings. The majority of Christendom has not understood what was written and have by their own 'blind knowledge' made 'that mixed/mashed Gospel'. Paul is not Peter. Only the 'One Spirit of God' can baptize us into 'his' death, not water.

'Christ crucified' **was not** the message that John the Baptist was preaching. John was not proclaiming salvation by the 'work of the cross' as the Apostle Paul declares. **John was baptizing the nation of Israel into the Holy Spirit. For us, without water, the Holy Spirit baptizes us into Christ, the Body of Christ, the true Church.** Not a building but 'His Glorious Spiritual Body'.

Jesus speaks to his disciples, no Gentiles here:

18- And Je'sus came and spake unto them, saying, All power is given unto me in heaven and in earth.

19- Go ye therefore, and teach all nations, **baptizing them in the name of the Father, and of the Son, and of the Ho'ly Ghost:**

20- Teaching them to observe all things whatsoever I have commanded you: and, lo, I am with you alway, *even* unto the end of the world. A-men'.

-Matthew 28 v 18-20

A Kingdom of Priest's, A Holy Royal Priesthood

'John the Baptist' message was the 'Baptism of Repentance for the Remission of Sins'. He was the chosen herald that was prophesied in the Old Testament to prepare Israel for the coming of their King and Kingdom. "The voice of him that crieth in the wilderness,..."*. *-Isaiah 40 v 3-8

To Israel and to the Jews was 'John the Baptist' message preached. There were no Gentiles being baptized by John. Only the 'Jews of the Circumcision/Law' could receive this promise of the Holy Ghost by 'water baptism'. To prepare the 'Jews of the Circumcision/Law' to be a 'Kingdom of Priest's' a 'Royal Priesthood'*. *-Exodus 19 v 6; -I Peter 2 v 5, 9

Water and cleanliness was a big part of the 'Levitical Priesthood' and the Jewish way of life. The Jews were the most clean of all the people of the world and aware of their 'Godly physical hygiene'. They practiced 'cleanliness is next to Godliness' for centuries long before the world realized it was healthy to do so. To the Jews in general, the Gentiles were dirty, uncircumcised, heathen, filthy, dogs.

There wasn't going to be a lengthy process to obtain 'Priesthood'. 'Repent and be Water Baptized' <u>and ye shall receive the Holy Ghost</u>. All of Israel were to be a 'go between', a Royal Priesthood. And they, Israel, would bring to the world the knowledge of their LORD and God.

A Kingdom of Priest's

5- Now therefore, if ye will obey my voice indeed, **<u>and keep my covenant</u>**, then **ye shall be a peculiar treasure unto me above all people**: for all the earth *is* mine:

6- And ye shall be unto me a **kingdom of priests**, and an holy nation. These *are* the words which thou shalt speak unto the children of Is'ra-el.

7- And Mo'ses came and called for the elders of the people, and laid before their faces all these words which the LORD commanded him.

8- And all the people answered together, and said, All that the LORD hath spoken **we will do**. And Mo'ses returned the words of the people unto the Lord.

-Exodus 19 v 5-8

Peter after 'the resurrection' is still in anticipation of 'the Kingdom and a Royal Priesthood':

5- Ye also, as lively stones, are built up a spiritual house, **an holy priesthood**, to offer up spiritual sacrifices, acceptable to God by Je'sus Christ.

....

9- But ye *are* a chosen generation, **a royal priesthood**, an holy nation, a peculiar people; that ye should show forth the praises of him who hath called you out of darkness into his marvelous light:

-I Peter 2 v 5, 9

John wrote in Revelation by Holy Spirit inspiration:

10- And hast made us unto our God **kings and priests: and we shall reign on the earth**.

-Revelation 5 v 10

20- Thus saith the LORD of hosts; *it shall* yet *come to pass*, that there shall come people, and the inhabitants of many cities:

21- And the inhabitants of one *city* shall go to another, saying, Let us go speedily to pray before the LORD, and to seek the LORD of hosts: I will go also.

22- Yea, many people and strong nations shall come to seek the LORD of hosts in Je-ru'sa-lem, and to pray before the LORD.

23- Thus saith the LORD of hosts; In those days *it shall come to pass*, that ten men shall take hold out of all languages of the nations, **even shall take hold of the skirt of him that is a Jew, saying, We will go with you: for we have heard *that* God is with you**.

-Zechariah 8 v 20-23

Jesus said:

17- Think not that I am come to destroy the law, or the prophets: I am not come to destroy, but to fulfill.

-Matthew 5 v 17

The Persecution of the Believers

There was a 'great persecution' against this 'newer religious sect' that believed in 'the Name of Jesus Christ'. Rome had respect for the old and ancient religion of Judaism, but this newer belief that Jesus of Nazareth is the prophesied 'King of the Jews' was admonished. Saul of Tarsus too was a major reason these Jews feared and fled for their lives. Saul of Tarsus years later becomes thee Apostle of the Gentiles, the Apostle Paul*. *-Acts 9 v 1-22; -Acts 22 v 1-16; -Acts 26 v 1-23

'The Apostles', scripture says, didn't leave Israel:
1- And Saul was consenting unto his death *(Stephens)*. And at that time there was a great persecution against the church *(assembly)* which was at Je-ru'sa-lem; and they were all scattered abroad throughout the regions of Ju-de'a and Sama'ria, **except the apostles**.
-Acts 8 v 1

19- Now they which were scattered abroad upon the persecution that arose about Stephen travelled as far as Phe-ni'ce, and Cy'prus, and An'ti-och, **preaching the word to none but unto Jews only.**
-Acts 11 v 19

What Gospel did they know? What 'word' did they know? It couldn't have been Paul's Gospel because the 'mysteries' by revelation happened years later. Paul had not written scripture as of yet. The Jews and Israel had no idea that salvation would be going to the 'world of the Gentiles' without them, 'a hidden mystery'.

They, the believers in the 'Name of Jesus Christ', were waiting and believing that the 'Earthly Kingdom of Heaven' would still happen. Their Gospel was the 'Gospel of the Kingdom'. All they had to teach from was Old Testament scripture and the words of Jesus Christ's that he spake during 'his earthly ministry'. Has Matthew, Mark, Luke or John been published yet?

Jesus speaks a warning:
9- But take heed to yourselves: for they shall deliver you to councils; and in the synagogues ye shall be beaten: and ye shall be brought before rulers and kings for my sake, for a testimony against them.
10- **And the gospel must first be published among all nations.**
-Mark 13 v 9, 10

9- Verily I *(Jesus)* say unto you, Wheresoever **this gospel** shall be preached throughout the whole world, this also that she hath done shall be spoken of for a memorial of her.
-Mark 14 v 9

15- And he *(Jesus)* said unto them, Go ye into all the world, and preach **the gospel** to every creature.
16- He that believeth and is baptized shall be saved; but he that believeth not shall be damned.
17- And these signs shall follow them that believe; **In my name** shall they cast out devils; they shall speak with new tongues;
18- They shall take up serpents; and if they drink any deadly thing, it shall not hurt them; they shall lay hands on the sick, and they shall recover.
-Mark 16 v 15-18

Jesus the Christ was staying true to the 'Law of Moses' and was fulfilling the reasons he was prophesied to accomplish by his coming to and for Israel. There is no 'Church Age' by the 'Gospel of Grace' revealed to the world yet. 'Christ Crucified' was not being taught for salvation. It was all in Israel's 'court' to believe in 'the Name of Jesus Christ'. Christ Jesus was yet in a position to fulfill the promises made to Israel's forefathers.

Was 'John the Baptist' more knowledgeable of the coming crucifixion than 'the Twelve'? 'John the Baptist' did not speak of salvation by believing in the crucifixion and resurrection without 'law keeping' (Paul's Gospel). Neither did Peter and 'the Twelve' **but stated 'the resurrection' as a fact**, that it did happen and Jesus Christ is alive and could still fulfill the prophecies by returning and setting up 'the Kingdom'. Christ would 'save them from all that hate them'. A physical 'Redemption'*. *-Luke 21 v 27, 28; -Daniel 12 v 1; -Zechariah 14 v 4, 8, 9

Jesus gives the Apostles power and a mission:
1- Then he called his twelve disciples together, **and gave them power** and authority over all devils, and to cure diseases.
2- And he sent them to preach the **kingdom of God***, and to heal the sick.
(- Paul too preached the Kingdom of God, but never the Gospel of the Kingdom).*
3- And he said unto them, take nothing for *your* journey, neither staves, nor scrip, neither bread, neither money; neither have two coats apiece.

4- And whatsoever house ye enter into, there abide, and thence depart.

5- And whosoever will not receive you, when ye go out of that city, shake of the very dust from your feet for a testimony against them.

6- And they departed, and went through the towns, **preaching the gospel**, and healing every where.

-Luke 9 v 1-6

19- Behold, **I** *(Jesus)* **give unto you power** to tread on serpents and scorpions, and over all the power of the enemy: and nothing shall by any means hurt you.

-Luke 10 v 19

35- And Je'sus went about all the cities and villages, **teaching in their synagogues,** and **preaching the gospel of the kingdom***, and healing every sickness and every disease among the people.

*-Matthew 9 v 35; -Matthew 4 v 23; -Matthew 24 v 14; -Mark 1 v 14

Is this what your church is doing? Are poisonous vipers and scorpions viewed with no fear? Are there those in your church exercising these powers given to 'the Twelve' disciples? How much does your church ignore scripture while putting fear into the congregation to follow other scriptures? Or else you can't be saved!?

Paul too preached the 'Kingdom of God' but never the 'Gospel of the Kingdom'. **You will not find the words 'Gospel of the Kingdom' in any of Paul's Epistles. Nor will you find 'the Body of Christ' anywhere outside of Paul's Epistles.**

In the Kingdom of God are all things righteous and acceptable to God. Please see 'the Kingdom of God diagram'. That which is 'claimed of God' is in the 'Kingdom of God'. These would include 'The Gospel of the Kingdom' believer which **was** Jew/Hebrew only and still under 'the Law', and 'The Body of Christ' believer that preach and teach 'Christ Crucified'. Where is most of 'Christendom' today? A mixed Gospel? Straddling the 'straight and narrow'?

Without a temple, the sacrificing for sins cannot be done. There hasn't been a temple since 70 A.D. when Titus destroyed Jerusalem. The keeping of the full law is no longer possible. Break one law and the Jew/Hebrew is guilty of 'breaking all the laws'.

Thank God for the 'Age of Grace'! I thank God that I was born and have lived at this very time. I thank God for the understanding of scripture and Paul's teaching to know that, what was written to the Jew was written to them and for my learning. What Paul writes to us in 'the Body of Christ' is 'the Gospel of Salvation'.

One of the most important scriptures:
11- Wherefore remember, that ye *being* in time past Gen'tiles in the flesh, who are called Uncircumcision by that which is called the Circumcision in the flesh made by hands;
12- **That at that time ye were without Christ *(Messiah)*, being aliens from the commonwealth of Is'ra-el, and strangers from the covenants of promise, having no hope, and without God in the world:**
13- **But now** in Christ Je'sus ye who sometimes were far off are made nigh by the blood of Christ.
-Ephesians 2 v 11-13

'The Gospel of the Kingdom' concerns the 'Heavenly/Earthly Kingdom' that is Israel's promised dominion. A perfect 'utopia' promised to Israel of no death, sickness and no fear of their enemies. The earth 'in the regeneration' after 'the tribulation' will be made again like it was in the 'Garden of Eden' for 1,000 years*, then eternity. The wild beasts would become tame and children could play with them with no fear. Then there would be new heavens and a new earth for ever and ever and ever...
*-Revelation 20 v 2-7

'The Body of Christ' already has its citizenship in heaven, in 'The Kingdom of God'. We are ambassadors on the earth, but our citizenship has already been translated into the 'Kingdom of God'*. We may not feel like we are 'citizens of heaven' while living on the earth, but by faith and the changing of our lifestyles we know. The 'Word of God' says so. Believe it! Pray. Be a worthy steward of God's word. *-Romans 8 v 16, 17; -I Corinthians 4 v 1, 2; -II Corinthians 5 v 17-21; -Ephesians 2 v 15-22; -Ephesians 3-12; -Philippians 3 v 20, 21

15- Study to shew thyself approved of God, a workman that needeth not to be ashamed, **rightly dividing the word of truth.**
-II Timothy 2 v 15; -Philippians 2 v 5 know scripture

There is no detailed description 'of Heaven' in the Bible of what this entails for 'the Body of Christ'. All we know as written is that the heaven for us shall be glorious! Words cannot describe it. All descriptions in the Bible of Heaven pertains to the 'Earthly Kingdom' that was promised to Israel.

16- The Spirit itself beareth witness with our spirit, that **we are** the children of God:
17- And if children, then heirs; **heirs of God, and joint-heirs with Christ;** if so be that we suffer with *him*, that we also may be glorified together.
18- For I reckon that **the sufferings of this present time *are* not worthy *to be compared* with the glory which shall be revealed in us**.
-Romans 8 v 16-18

These followers around that time of Jesus Christs' earthly ministry were still in anticipation of the 'Kingdom of Heaven'. They were carrying on the earthly ministry of Christ. **Jesus had given his disciples power*.** 'The Kingdom of Heaven' was in their very near future. Jesus would return and sit on his Holy hill of Zion+. *-Matthew 10 v 1; -Mark 3 v 14, 15; -Mark 6 v 7; -Luke 9 v 1; -Luke 10 v 19; -Acts 1 v 8; +-Psalm 2; -Zechariah 14 v 4, 9

Israel as a nation kept rejecting Jesus Christ, their Messiah, their King. Their final act of rejecting the King and Kingdom was 'the stoning of Stephen' if such a place could be pinpointed. Saul/Paul of Tarsus is first mentioned here in the scriptures of the 'Word of God'. God is now going to the world without the Jew and Israel. This was unheard of! Such a thing was never written in the Old Testament.

For a time, the 'Gospel of the Kingdom' and 'The Gospel of Grace' were working simultaneously. One was by 'faith plus works' the other by 'faith without works'. The Book of Acts begins all Jewish (out with the old) and ends with the Apostle Paul (Acts 28) giving up on the Jews for their unbelief (in with the new).

Prophecy Being Fulfilled Today

Prophecies are being fulfilled recently with the returning of the Jews to its ancient homeland since the mid 1800's or so. But between 70 A.D. and the mid 1800's, DESOLATION! Earthquakes, drought and malaria was rampant. Sustaining a family was never established for long and for generations. Travelers throughout history have wrote that it was a 'God forsaken land and uninhabitable'. Why didn't the 'offspring of Ishmael and Esau' take it over? It was there for thousands of years.

14- Therefore, behold, the days come, saith the LORD, that it shall no more be said, The LORD liveth, that brought up the children of Is'ra-el out of the land of E'gypt;

15- **But, The LORD liveth, that brought up the children of Is'ra-el from the land of the north, and from all the lands wither he had driven them: and I will bring them again into their land that I gave unto their fathers.**

-Jeremiah 16 v 14, 15

The Land Title Deed that was given to Abraham

18- In the same day the LORD made a covenant with A'bram, saying, Unto thy seed have I given this land, from the river of E'gypt unto the great river, the river Eu-phra'tes:

-Genesis 15 v 18

This area of land has been fought over for centuries and still no peace. The world itself has called it 'the Holy Land'. 'The Crusades' called it 'the Holy Land' but what man brought was far from Holy. Death, slaughter and desolation is the history of this land without the Jew living there. This is a fact of history.

Mo'ses speaks to the children of Israel:

6- The LORD our God spake unto us in Ho'reb saying, Ye have dwelt long enough in this mount:

7- Turn you, and take your journey, and go to the mount of the Am'or-ites, and unto all *the places* nigh thereunto, in the plain, in the hills, and in the vale, and in the south, and by the sea side, to the land of the Ca'naan-ites, and unto Leb'a-non, unto the great river, the river Eu-phra'tes.

8- Behold, I have set the land before you: go in and possess the land which the LORD sware unto your fathers, A'bra-ham, I'saac and Ja'cob, to give unto them and to their seed after them.

-Deuteronomy 1 v 6-8

There has been 'a great trespass' in this God given land to Israel. No wonder there is no peace in this area. The area has been squeezed but enough has been left to fulfill the 'end time prophecies'. Israel today has transformed 'a dead land' into one that is thriving.

The Jews have not been annihilated and pushed into the sea. What type of people would want to do this? The land is the size of New Hampshire and the world is daily in an uproar over it. Why can't they be left alone? It is not part of God's plan for Israel to be left in peace, and yet, the world can't see this.

After the Jews have returned to its God given land and have made the land productive and fruitful, 'the offspring of Ishmael' want it. They claim it as theirs saying it was always 'a good land'. Again, they had thousands of years to walk in and take that 'good land'.

False teaching has been saying that 'the Tribulation' happened in 70 A.D. when Titus, a Roman General (not a prince) destroyed Jerusalem. As bad as this was, so many things did Daniel, John, the Old Testament Prophets, Peter and even Jesus himself spake of that common sense tells me didn't happen. Daniel and John write of 'a seven year period' of 'Tribulation' that is yet to be fulfilled in 'Israel's Prophetic Time-line'. Jesus too gives a 'mid-week (seven year) in travail' description scene of the end times.

This would be 'a time of Tribulation' on the world which had never happened before nor would happen until then. Common sense tells me that 'The Wrath of God', 'The Day of the LORD', 'The Lord's Day' foretold wasn't in 70 A.D. Was 70 A.D. worse than the Holocaust? Noah's flood was pretty bad, wasn't it?

This 'Age of Grace' was hid, a mystery, a secret kept in the mind of God until it was revealed to the Apostle Paul. No one knew this was going to happen. No one knows for how long this 'Age of Grace' will last. It has been 2000 years now. Even the Apostle Paul didn't know how long. He wasn't waiting for Jesus Christ to bring in 'the Kingdom' but was looking for the 'blessed hope' of being 'caught up' and 'gathered to God'*. *-I Thessalonians 4 v 13-17; -Titus 2 v 13, 14; -I Corinthians 15 v 51-54

There is little prophecy concerning the 'Body of Christ', 'The Church'. Scripture says 'The Church' is not subject to 'the wrath' that is to come on the world and Israel. We Gentiles were never under the covenant promises made with Israel.

Would Jesus put his Body, the 'Body of Christ', the 'True Church' on the cross again? 'We are members in particular of his body'*. Paul writes that when the 'Body of Christ' is full we will be 'caught up' to meet the Lord in the air=. Then the 'son of perdition', the 'anti-Christ' would then be revealed+. The seven year tribulation would begin at some time thereafter. The Word of God has always been fulfilled. *-I Corinthians 12 v 27; +-II Thessalonians 2 v 1-6; =-I Thessalonians 4 v 17

13- Looking for that blessed hope, and the glorious appearing of **the great God and our Saviour Je'sus Christ**.
14- Who gave himself for us *(Paul's Gospel)*, that he might redeem us from all iniquity, and purify unto himself a peculiar people *(the Body of Christ)*, zealous of good works *(love not law)*.
-Titus 2 v 13, 14

Paul writes by the Holy Spirit of God:
1- Now we beseech you, brethren, **by the coming of our Lord Je'sus Christ, and by our gathering together unto him** *(caught up?)*.
2- That ye be not soon shaken in mind, or be troubled, neither by spirit, nor by word, nor by letter as from us, as that **day of Christ*** is at hand. *(*not the 2nd coming, but on that Great Resurrection Day)*
3- **Let no man deceive you by any means: for that day shall not come, except there be a falling away first, and that man of sin be revealed, the son of perdition;**
4- Who opposeth and exalteth himself above all that is called God, or that is worshipped; so that he as God **sitteth in the temple of God**, shewing himself that he is God.
-II Thessalonians 2 v 1-4

Scripture says we (The Body of Christ) will be spared from 'the wrath' that was foretold to Israel and the world to come. Law and Grace does not mix. Why put Grace now subject to Law and to Israels tribulation when the Gentiles never were under 'its covenant promises'*? *-Ephesian 2 v 11-13

9- For they themselves shew of us what manner of entering in we had unto you, and how ye turned to God from idols to serve the living and true God;

10- And to wait for his Son from heaven, whom he raised from the dead *(Paul's Gospel), even* Je'sus, **which delivered us from the wrath to come.**
-I Thessalonians 1 v 9, 10

9- **For God hath not appointed us to wrath,** but to obtain salvation by our Lord Je'sus Christ.
10- Who died for us *(Paul's Gospel),* that, whether we wake or sleep, we should live together with him.
-I Thessalonians 5 v 9, 10

14- For **if we believe** that Je'sus died and rose again *(Paul's Gospel),* even so them also which sleep in Je'sus will God bring with him.
15- For this we say unto you by the word of the Lord, that we which are alive and remain unto the coming of the Lord* shall not prevent them which are asleep *(dead). (*not the 2nd Coming of the Lord. This is the Day of Christ, the Day of Jesus Christ, the Day of the Lord Jesus Christ. No wrath of God here as it will be at his 2nd coming.)*
16- For the Lord himself shall descend from heaven with a shout, with the voice of the archangel, and with the **trump of God**: and the dead in Christ shall rise first:
17- **Then we which are alive and remain <u>shall be caught up</u> together with them in the clouds, to meet the Lord in the air: and so shall we ever be with the Lord.**
18- Wherefore comfort one another with these words.
-I Thessalonians 4 v 14-18

Psalm 2 shows a 'prophetic outline' for Israel:
1- Why do the heathen rage, and the people imagine a vain thing?
2- The kings of the earth set themselves, and the rulers take counsel together, against the LORD, and against his anointed, *saying,*
3- Let us break **their bands** asunder, and cast away **their cords** from us.
4- He that sitteth in the heavens shall laugh: the LORD shall have them in derision.
5- **Then shall he speak unto them in his wrath, and vex them in his sore displeasure.**
6- Yet have I set my king upon my holy hill in Zion.
7- I will declare the decree: the LORD hath said unto me, thou *art* my Son; **this day have I begotten thee.**

8- Ask of me, and I shall give thee the heathen *for* thine inheritance, and the uttermost parts of the earth *for* thy possession.

9- Thou shalt break them with a rod of iron; thou shalt dash them in pieces like a potter's vessel.

10- Be wise now therefore, O ye kings: be instructed, ye judges of the earth.

11- Serve the LORD with fear, and rejoice with trembling.

12- Kiss the son, lest he be angry, and ye perish *from* the way, when his wrath is kindled but a little. Blessed *are* all they that put their trust in him.
-Psalm 2

What was missed in Psalm 2? Did you see it? Prophecy went from rejection, death, ascension, tribulation, return. All the Old Testament scriptures concerning the 'Wrath of God' say this same thing. There is no mention of the 'Age of Grace' and 'The Body of Christ Church' in all of the Old Testament prophecies. It was still being hid and kept secret.

Prophecy in the Bible concerns the Nation of Israel and the Jews. At least when prophecy is put in a 'time frame'. Hello?! Prophecy concerning the 'Body of Christ' is short, if any.

'The Body of Christ' will be 'caught up' to God with 'the main harvest' on that 'Great Resurrection Day'*. Those that missed that 'Blessed Hope' never were in the 'Body of Christ'. These lost folk may be 'zealous for their faith and religion' but according to scripture they have missed 'the Gospel of Salvation'. Christendom has believed in 'a scriptural mixture, pieced and pasted together'. Confusion is preached from the pulpit. *-I Corinthians 15

Zacharias tells it like it is ...

Zacharias (John the Baptist's father) spake prophecy while being filled with the Holy Ghost:

67- And his father Zach-a-ri'as was filled with the Ho'ly Ghost, and prophesied, saying,

68- Blessed be the **Lord God of Israel**; for he hath **visited and redeemed his people,**
-Luke 1 v 67, 68

"The Lord God of Israel", not the Lord God of the world at this time. "Hath visited and redeemed his people". Who's people is God claiming to have visited and redeemed? The Jews of Israel are 'his people pre-resurrection', not Gentiles.

69- And hath raised up a horn of salvation for us in the house of his servant Da'vid.
-Luke 1 v 69

There are no Gentiles in the "House of David", only Jews/Hebrews.

70- As he spake by the mouth of his holy prophets, which have been since the world began:
-Luke 1 v 70

The Old Testament prophets gave the 'Gospel of the Kingdom' message to Israel. The prophets spoke of 'The Earthly Kingdom of Heaven' that was promised to Israel that will come.

71- That we should be **saved from our enemies**, and from the hand of all that hate us;
-Luke 1 v 71

"Saved from our enemies", not eternal salvation of the soul and Spirit. Has Israel been saved today from all that hate them? Is Israel today living peacefully and safely with no outside threats to their lives?

72- To perform the mercy *promised* to our fathers, and to remember his holy covenant:
-Luke 1 v 72

"Our fathers" were the Jews of Israel and their inheritance, not Gentiles. Holy covenants were not given to the Gentiles.

73- The oath which he sware to our father A'bra-ham,
-Luke 1 v 73

Who can claim Abraham as their father through a family bloodline? A Jew or a Gentile? **The 'Body of Christ' is connected to Abraham by faith in 'the seed' which is the 'Resurrected Jesus Christ'.**

74- That he would grant unto us, that we, being **delivered out of the hand of our enemies**, might serve him without fear,
75- In holiness and righteousness before him, all the days of our life.
-Luke 1 v 74, 75

Has Israel been "delivered out of the hands of their enemies"? Did the Holocaust happen? Is all of Israel serving the Lord God before him on the throne of David? Zacharias did not speak of the 'death, burial and resurrected for salvation' but that Israel would be 'saved from their enemies'. As long as the Nation of Israel exists, they will always be hated. Therefore, Israel will be the last Nation Standing*. *-Jeremiah 31 v 35-37; -Jeremiah 30 v 11; -Psalm 110; -Luke 21 v 32

Many times did God say 'I Will' or 'I Shall'. Because it didn't happen don't mean it won't. It is the Word of God. Believe it. It will happen. As part of God's overall divine plan, the 'Gospel of Grace' was hid and kept secret till revealed to the Apostle Paul. 'The Kingdom of Heaven' didn't happen at this time. Of course the Lord Jesus Christ knew it would be rejected by the Jews but he never revealed the 'Age of Grace' to come.

Think: What if Jesus had said, "By the way, all the prophecies and promises made to Abraham, Isaac, Jacob and David **are not** going to happen. The promised 'Kingdom of Heaven' will be delayed for 1,000's of years. But salvation will go to the Gentiles without your laws of Judaism, without your sacrificing of animals and without your devout temple worship".

The Apostle of the Gentiles reveals the truth by Holy Spirit Inspiration:
7- What then? Is'ra-el hath not obtained that which he seeketh for; but the election hath obtained it, and the rest were blinded *(spiritually)*.
8- (According as it is written, God hath given them the spirit of slumber, eyes that they should not see, and ears that they should not hear;) unto this day.
9- And Da'vid saith, Let their table *(place of position)* be made a snare, and a stumblingblock, and a recompence unto them:
10- Let their eyes be darkened, that they may not see, and bow their back always.
11- I say then, Have they stumbled that they should fall? God forbid: **but *rather* through their fall salvation is come unto the Gen'tiles, for to provoke them to jealousy.**
-Romans 11 v 7-11

17- Think not that I *(Jesus)* am come to destroy the law, or the prophets: I am not come to destroy, but to fulfill.
-Matthew 5 v 17

After the resurrection, Jesus says to the disciples:

44- And he said unto them, these *are* the words which I spake unto you, while I was yet with you, that all things must be fulfilled, which were written in the law of Mo'ses, and *in* the prophets, and *in* the Psalms, concerning me.

45- **Then opened he their understanding, that they might understand the scriptures.**

46- And he said unto them, Thus it is written, and thus it behoved Christ to suffer, and to rise from the dead the third day:

47- And that <u>repentance and remission of sins should be preached in his name</u> among all nations, beginning at Je-ru'sa-lem.

48- And ye are witnesses of these things.

49- And behold, I send the promise of my Father upon you: but tarry ye in the city of Je-ru'sa-lem, **until ye be endued with power from on high**.

50- And he led them out as far as Beth'a-ny, and he lifted up his hands, and blessed them.

51- And it came to pass, while he blessed them, he was parted from them, and carried up into heaven.

52- And they worshiped him, and returned to Je-ru'sa-lem with great joy:

53- **And were continually in the temple**, praising and blessing God. Amen'.
-Luke 24 v 44-53

All these things that Jesus was telling his disciples was in accordance with the 'Gospel of the Kingdom' message. He was speaking as if all these things that was prophesied would still happen, soon. He wasn't letting on that there would be a 2,000 year 'Church Age'. This was still being kept secret.

Israel was still in a position to receive the 'Heavenly Earthly Kingdom'. He came in the flesh to and for the Nation of Israel. Because of unbelief in the 'Name of Jesus Christ' and who he is, Israel has suffered even to this day. Haven't they? I lie not.

Scripture doesn't say 'the Great Commission' of taking the Gospel (Gospel of the Kingdom) by 'the Twelve' was fulfilled. They got as far as Samaria but scripture does not say that they took 'The Gospel of the Kingdom' beyond that. Scripture does not say that they took 'their Gospel' to the 'uttermost part of the earth' as most of 'Christendom' has been teaching and saying.

Yes, scripture does show that Peter did journey outside of the border of Israel. But scripture does not show that this journey to Antioch was for the purpose of ministering to the Gentiles. What scripture does show 'is an event of a different light' than what much of Christendom wants to believe. When Peter came to Antioch, Paul 'withstood Peter to the face' and 'blamed him for not walking uprightly according to the truth of the Gospel'*. *-Galatians 2 v 11-21

Oh, it sounds good for Christendom to think and believe that Peter and 'the Twelve' took the Gospel to the uttermost parts of the earth. And it seems to be very important for those trying to follow the 'Apostles' Doctrine'* that it was they who spread the Gospel to the world. What Gospel? But what does or doesn't the Bible say? All this has led to a 'mixing' of the truth of 'The Gospel of Grace'. *-Acts 2 v 42

6- When they therefore were come together, they asked of him *(Jesus),* saying, Lord, wilt thou **at this time restore again the kingdom to Is'ra-el**? 7- And he said unto them, It is not for you to know the times or the seasons, which the Father hath put in his own power.
8- **But ye shall receive power**, after that the Ho'ly Ghost is come upon you: and ye shall be witnesses unto me both in Je-ru'sa-lem, and in all Ju-de'a, and in Sa-ma'ri-a, and unto the uttermost part of the earth.
-Acts 1 v 6-8

After Jesus was taken up (caught up) the 'Kingdom of Heaven' was still in front of them. First, 'a Time of Tribulation' and 'the Wrath of God' and 'the Day of the Lord', then 'the Return of Christ with the Kingdom'. The Lord Jesus Christ was still in the position to fulfill the prophecies.

The physical Resurrection of Jesus Christ insured for the Nation of Israel that they would be 'saved from their enemies'. The Jews salvation came by keeping the Law, water baptizing and to believe that this Jesus Christ is that prophesied Messiah, Israel's King.

Scripture says 'the Twelve' didn't leave Israel*. So many have assumed that the Gospel (including Paul's) was taken and delivered to the world by them+. Biblical scripture would have shown this but it does not. *-Acts 8 v 1; +-Acts 11 v 19

The Jew/Hebrews require a sign. We Gentiles do not need the signs. The written Word of God is our sign, our Bible. We believe. We know for a fact that Jesus was a 'minister of the circumcision under the Law*' and that his reason for coming in the flesh was for Israel. Many of the words spoken by Jesus of course belongs in the 'Body of Christ' knowledge. If you follow the 'Earthly Ministry of Jesus Christ' for salvation you had better keep 'all the Law of Moses', right? *-Romans 15 v 8, 9; -Galatians 4 v 4, 5

'The Twelve Apostles' were not scattered, Acts 8 v 1. The disciples were not taking 'their Gospel' to the 'uttermost parts of the earth'. They still were in Jerusalem waiting for Christ to return with the Kingdom. Other Jewish believers in 'the Name of Jesus Christ' were scattered. But these Jews that 'were scattered' were preaching to fellow Jew's only, Acts 11 v 19.

The Apostle Paul writes directly to us, on this side of the cross. When reading Paul's Epistles, get used to the truth that Paul reveals so much more than Peter, Jesus (in the flesh), and the Old Testament. It is by the Apostle Paul who writes to us in 'The Body of Christ'. Paul is not Peter. Peter is not Paul.

Jews are not Gentiles, Gentiles are not Jews. The salvation for the world was made possible when God raised Jesus from the dead. Salvation for all the world is not based on 'Jesus' Earthly Ministry'*. I didn't say it, God said it through the Apostle Paul. Believe in God or believe God? *-II Corinthians 5 v 14-18

Paul writes by Holy Spirit inspiration:

14- For the love of Christ constraineth *(molds)* us, because we thus judge, that if one died for all, then were all dead:

15- And *that* he died for all, that they which live should not henceforth live unto themselves, but unto him which **died for them, and rose again** *(Paul's Gospel).*

16- Wherefore **henceforth** know we no man after the flesh: yea, **though we have known Christ after the flesh, yet now henceforth know we** *him* **no more.**

17- **Therefore if any man** *be* **in Christ,** *he is* **a new creature:** old things are passed away; behold, all things are become new.

18- And all things *are* of God, who hath reconciled us to himself by Je'sus Christ, and hath given to us the ministry of reconciliation;
-II Corinthians 5 v 14-18

Peter never said nor wrote such a thing. Paul (Holy Spirit inspired) is saying that we (Gentiles) don't know 'the Jesus that walked the earth in the flesh'. Of course we know that he did and it is profitable for our learning and for the understanding of the scriptures. The wholesome words of Jesus Christ is truth. But the 'Body of Christ' is not of 'the Twelve Apostles Doctrine' to follow*. *-Acts 2 v 42

Paul is saying that our faith and doctrine for salvation is on this side of the cross, our side, post resurrection. It is the Jesus Christ from heaven that reveals to the Apostle Paul the truth of our salvation. **It is the resurrected Christ Jesus that we know.** Yet, most church services spend the majority of the time in the 'pre-crucifixion' scriptures.

The 'Resurrected Lord Jesus Christ' is the 'Head of the Body'*, 'the Church, 'our High Priest'+. The one and only true church is the 'Spiritual Body of Christ'. This membership is by daily prayer and by the 'washing of the Word'=. All Scripture is profitable#. *-Ephesians 5 v 23; -Colossians 1 v 18; -Colossians 2 v 19; +- Hebrews 3 v 1; -Hebrews 4 v 14-15; -Hebrews 5 v 5, 10; -Hebrews 7 v 1; - Hebrews 8 v 1; =-Ephesians 5 v 25, 26; #-II Timothy 2 v 15

'The Church', 'The Body of Christ' is not a building on a street corner. We don't visit 'this church' once a week or when it is customary (Christmas, Easter, or in observance of any religious day) to do so because we have too. We want to. Our attendance is 24 Hours a day, 7 days a week, 365 days a year.

We are permanent members once we truly believe and fully understand 'The Gospel'*. We don't believe in vain. We know by scripture what we believe. This is not a free license to sin, by no means. A true believer is not also a 'part time sinner'. He/she becomes 'a new creation' in the mind and spirit+. The life in the flesh is no longer sought out. *-I Corinthians 15 v 1-4; -Romans 10 v 9; -Ephesians 1 v 13; +-II Corinthians 5 v 17; -Galatians 6 v 15

A person knows good and well when he/she has been Baptized. Not with water but by the Spirit of God. A person is convinced (faith) without a shadow of doubt that Christ Jesus, by his own submission, died for you and me individually, as well as for all the sins of the world, and that he was buried, and rose again to an eternal life never to die again. And we also have been promised the same*.

*-Philippians 3 v 21

Spiritual Tongues, 'Speaking in Tongues'

5- And when thou prayest, thou shalt not be as the hypocrites *are*: for they love to pray standing in the synagogues and in the corners of the streets, that they may be seen of men. Verily I *(Jesus)* say unto you, They have their reward.
-Matthew 6 v 5

38- And he *(Jesus)* said unto them in his doctrine, Beware of the scribes, which love to go in long clothing, and *love* salutations in the marketplaces,
39- And the chief seats in the synagogues, and the uppermost rooms at feasts:
40- Which devour widows' houses, and for a pretence make long prayers: these shall receive greater damnation.
-Mark 12 v 38-40

15- And he *(Jesus)* said unto them, Ye are they which justify yourselves before men; but God knoweth your hearts: for that which is highly esteemed among men is abomination in the sight of God.
-Luke 16 v 15

9- And he *(Jesus)* spake this parable unto certain which trusted in themselves that they were righteous, and despised others:
10- Two men went up into the temple to pray; the one a Pharisee, and other a publican.
11- The Pharisee stood and prayed thus with himself, God, I thank thee, that I am not as other men *are*, extortioners, unjust, adulterers, or even as this publican.
12- I fast twice in the week, I give tithes of all that I possess.
13- And the publican, standing afar off, would not lift up so much *his* eyes unto heaven, but smote upon his breast, saying, God be merciful to me a sinner.
14- I tell you, this man went down to his house justified *rather* than the other: for every one that exalteth himself shall be abased; and he that humbleth himself shall be exalted.
-Luke 18 v 9-14

1- **Now concerning spiritual *gifts*,** brethren, I would not have you ignorant.
2- Ye know that ye were Gentiles, carried away unto these dumb idols, even as ye were led.

3- Wherefore I give you to understand, that no man speaking by the Spirit of God calleth Je'sus accursed: and that no man can say that Jesus is the Lord, but by the Ho'ly Ghost.

4- **Now there are diversities of gifts, but the same Spirit*.**

5- **And there are differences of administrations, but the same Lord*.**

6- **And there are diversities of operations, but it is the same God* that worketh all in all.** (**The Godhead*)

7- **But the manifestation of the Spirit is given to every man to profit withal.**

8- For to one is given by the Spirit **the word of wisdom**; to another **the word of knowledge** by the same Spirit;

9- To another **faith** by the same Spirit; to another **gifts of healing** by the same Spirit;

10- To another **the working of miracles**; to another **prophecy** *(preaching)*; to another **discerning of spirits**; to another *divers* **kinds of tongues**; to another **the interpretation of tongues**.

11- **But all these worketh that one and selfsame Spirit, dividing to every man severally as he will.**

12- **For as the body is one, and hath many members, and all the members of that one body, being many, are one body: so also *is* Christ.**

13- **For <u>by one Spirit are we all</u> baptized into one body, whether *we* be Jews or Gentiles, whether *we be* bond or free; and have been all made to drink into one Spirit.**

-I Corinthians 12 v 1-13

1- And when the day of Pentecost was fully come, they were all with one accord in one place.

2- And suddenly there came a sound from heaven as of a rushing mighty wind, and it filled all the house where they were sitting.

3- And there appeared unto them cloven tongues like as of fire, and it sat upon each of them.

4- And they were all filled with the Holy Ghost, and began to speak with other tongues *(languages)* as the Spirit gave them utterance.

5- **And there were dwelling at Jerusalem Jews, devout men, out of every nation under heaven.**

6- Now when this was noised abroad, the multitude came together, and were confounded, because that every man heard them speak in his own language.

7- And they were all amazed and marvelled, saying one to another, Behold, are not all these which speak Galileans?

8- And how hear we every man in our own tongue, wherein we were born?

9- Parthians, and Medes, and Elamites, and the dwellers in Mesopotamia, and in Judea, and Cappadocia, in Pontus, and Asia,

10- Phrygia, and Pamphylia, in Egypt, and in the parts of Libya and Cyrene, and strangers of Rome, Jews and proselytes,

11- Cretes and Arabians, we do hear them speak in our tongues the wonderful works of God.

12- And they were all amazed, and were in doubt, saying one to another, What meaneth this?

13- Others mocking said, These men are full of new wine.

14- But Peter, standing up with the eleven, lifted up his voice, and said unto them, Ye men of Judea, and all ye that dwell at Jerusalem, be this known unto you, and harken to my words:

15- For these are not drunken, as ye suppose, seeing it is *but* the third hour *(9 a.m.)* of the day.

16- But this is that which was spoken by the prophet Joel*; *-Joel 2 v 28-32

17- And it shall come to past in the last days*, saith God, I will pour out of my Spirit upon all flesh: and your sons and your daughters shall prophesy, and your young men shall see visions, and your old men shall dream dreams: *(*-Last Days = the time of Christ to the Tribulation)*

18- And on my servants and on my hand maidens I will pour out in those days of my Spirit; and they shall prophesy:

-Acts 2 v 1-18

There are 'denominations that preach' that in order for a person to be saved one must 'speak in a spiritual tongue'. How many have been left behind because of this? The guilt, "Why God, how come I can't speak in tongues?" "It has been expressed to me that if I don't speak in tongues I can't be saved". "These 'professing Jews' in my church need <u>the sign</u> of me speaking in tongues!"

If this has been your experience read I Corinthians 12 v 1-13 again. If you have been told this, without a doubt, that person is of 'the mixed Gospel'. The Jews require a sign. We Gentiles in 'the Body of Christ' don't. Our sign is our 'Bible of Truth'. 'We Preach Christ Crucified and the Power of Resurrection'*. *-I Corinthians 1 v 23; -I Corinthians 2 v 2; -Galatians 3 v 1; -Galatians 6 v 14; -Romans 1 v 4; -Philippians 3 v 10

We believe our Bible from cover to cover but know that it is the Apostle Paul that God has told us to follow*. "Be ye followers of me as I follow Christ...". That is, follow Paul as he follows the 'Resurrected Lord Jesus Christ', not the 'earthly ministry'. The 'supposed Jew' needs 'the sign of the earthly ministry'. That is why they preach it. They think they are Jews, spiritual Jews? This 'earthly sign' is pushed forward into Paul's God given Gospel. *-I Corinthians 4 v 16; -I Corinthians 11 v 1; -Philippians 3 v 17; -II Thessalonians 3 v 7, 9

Israel had the 'Living Sign'. 'The Word' was made flesh. Israel's King and Messiah had come. If the Nation of Israel as a collective whole didn't believe 'the miracle machine' of Jesus Christ himself', why would the Gentiles who never saw Jesus' in action nor ever heard of him believe*? *-John 1 v 11

The Gentiles were without God, without hope and without Christ*. Jesus came in the flesh not for all the world but for 'his chosen covenanted people'. The proof to Paul that 'his Gospel of Grace' was bringing the lost to salvation was the working power of the Holy Spirit'. *-Ephesians 2 v 11-13

Paul writes Holy Spirit inspired:
1- Am I not an apostle? am I not free? have I not seen Je'sus Christ our Lord?
2- If I be not an apostle unto others, yet doubtless I am to you: for **the seal of mine apostleship are ye in the Lord**.
-I Corinthians 9 v 1, 2

Gentiles that never heard of the 'earthly ministry' (they were not Jews and were not given the 'Oracles of God'*) were 'receiving the Holy Ghost by faith' in what Paul was teaching. Paul has saved so many by the 'preaching of the cross'. Well, of course Paul didn't save them, the 'Resurrected Lord Jesus Christ' gave his Holy Spirit to those that believe what Paul has revealed. *-Romans 3 v 1, 2

Back to 'Speaking in Tongues':
In Acts 2, on that 'Famous Day of Pentecost', the 'Ye men of Israel' that Peter was preaching to were filled with the Holy Spirit/Ghost and were preaching in different tongues/languages. They were not speaking in an 'angelic unknowable tongue' though <u>it was a manifestation of the Holy Ghost</u>. These tongues/languages spoken here was not 'googly gook'. There were hearers that did understand them.

These tongues that the 'disciples were speaking in' was new to them but understood by Jews that had traveled to Israel. These were 'Jews of the Circumcision/Law' (female too remember) that had been scattered all over the then known world starting in 606 B.C. These Jews had not returned to Israel to live, but 'under the Law' <u>they had to</u> return to Jerusalem on 'Certain Feast Days' to bring their sacrifices to the Temple in Jerusalem. Many grew up speaking a language that was not Hebrew.

I Corinthians 14 gives the interpretation that Paul gives 'of tongues'. Paul does not forbid it but does question the 'value when speaking to others via this way'. Paul writes by Holy Spirit inspiration that it is 'the speech of a barbarian' if 'the hearer' does not understand*. The hearer has no interpreter. *-I Corinthians 14 v 11

Apostle Paul points out that the preaching and teaching in an 'audible, understandable language' by the Holy Spirit is a more valuable gift. Words inspired of God that is understood can be shared. Speaking in 'an unknown tongue does the unbeliever a disservice'.

1- Follow after charity *(love),* and desire spiritual *gifts*, but rather that ye may prophesy *(speak forth)*.

2- For he that speaketh in an *unknown* tongue speaketh not unto men, but unto God: **for no man understandeth *him*; howbiet in the spirit he speaketh mysteries.**

3- But he that prophesieth *(preaches)* speaketh unto men *to* edification, and exhortation, and comfort.

4- **He that speaketh in an *unknown* tongue edifieth himself; but he that prophesieth edifieth the church.**

5- I would that ye all spake with tongues *(the differing native languages*)*, but rather that ye prophesied *(preach)*: **for greater is he that prophesieth than he that speaketh with tongues**, <u>except he interpret</u>, that the church may receive edifying.

-I Corinthians 14 v 1-5

*Paul could speak in many languages. Some very well, others not as fluent but effective because of the power of the Holy Spirit/Ghost. Read I Corinthians 14 knowing this: Paul speaks of tongues or languages when it is understood by others. When Paul is speaking of languages or tongues when it is understood by others, he is not speaking of a 'Heavenly Speech' or 'Angel speech'.

Those who judge others and put themselves 'above' them that don't 'speak in a Tongue' are 'boasting'. They themselves can't explain nor interpret what they are saying. These can 'flow out the mouth' but no clarification is made.

But what did God say about Boasting?:
26- To declare, *I say*, at this time his righteousness: that he might be just, and the justifier of him which believeth in Je'sus.
27- Where *is* boasting then? It is excluded. By what law? of works? Nay: but by the law of faith.
-Romans 3 v 26, 27

You have the Holy Spirit by believing 'the Gospel' that Paul gave for all the world from the 'Resurrected Lord Jesus Christ' himself. This is the 'True Word of God'. He says it, pray, read and believe it. Do grow daily in the Spirit of the Written Word'. We are here as ambassadors for the 'Resurrected Lord Jesus Christ'. Don't hinder the Spirit. Be led by the Spirit.

The Holy Spirit is not solely manifested by 'a sign of tongues' but in other ways too as God see's fit to give. A person may say, "I have the gift of speaking in tongues'. Then tell me what you said? How did that gift edify the Body of Christ?

What are a person's daily and pervading thoughts? Does Jesus become 'top of mind'? Is Jesus thought of upon waking for the day? Is Jesus thought of when going to bed? Are you eager to read your Bible? Is prayer a staple of each day? What kind of company is being kept?

If this is you and yet you don't 'speak in tongues', you yourself are 'walking in the Spirit'. You have a spiritual gift that the 'in tongues speaker' does not have. We are all a team, members in the 'Body of Christ', each with a different function. We are all 'yoke-fellows'*. We edify each other forever. All these gifts were given by the self same Holy Spirit. There is only one! *-Philippians 4 v 3

13- For neither they themselves who are circumcised keep the law; but desire to have you circumcised *(keep the law)*, that they may glory in your flesh.
14- But God forbid that I should **glory**, save in the **cross*** of our Lord Jesus Christ, by whom the world is crucified unto me, and I unto the world.

*(*Don't glory in the earthly ministry, but in the Resurrection ministry, the cross, his shed blood of death that made salvation possible for all the world)*

15- For in Christ Jesus neither circumcision availeth anything, nor uncircumcision, but a new creature *(creation)*.

-Galatians 6 v 13-15

Some say we can fall in and out of the Grace of God, being saved one day and then lost the next. But for a membership to be revoked out of the 'Body of Christ' one must have entered fraudulently. This would not happen. There are no unbelievers in the 'Body of Christ'.

In the 'Body of Christ' we know the moment we have sinned. Who turned the light on? Before being Baptized by the Holy Spirit we would continue on thinking nothing of the sin committed. The 'believer' knows immediately and confesses to God.

But repeated 'Repentance' and 'the sinners prayer' is not required. We don't beg God for forgiveness once being a true believer in the 'Body of Christ'. We have already been forgiven. No need to beat a dead horse. But we do thank God for his mercy and forgiveness and 'his free gift of Grace'. We don't beg for it. Once you have received the gift, why are you still begging? The car is in the driveway, you can stop pleading now.

If a sinful act was real egregious, are you really in 'the Body of Christ'? We have already been forgiven by 'the finished work of the cross' by our faith. Jesus Christ died for our past, present and future sins. It is the 'Free Gift of Grace' to everyone that believes 'the Gospel'. It's what the 'Word of God' says. Believe it!

25- For I would not, brethren, that ye should be ignorant of this **mystery**, lest ye should be wise in your own conceits; that blindness *(spiritual)* in part is happened to Is'ra-el, **until** the fulness of the Gentiles *(Body of Christ)* be come in *(caught up?)*.

26- And so all Is'ra-el shall be saved: as it is written, There shall come out of Si'on *(Zion)* the deliverer, and shall turn away ungodliness from Ja'cob:

27- For this *is* my covenant unto them *(Jews of the Circumcision/Law)*, when I shall take away their sins.

28- As concerning the gospel *(Paul's), they are* enemies for your sakes: but as touching the election *(Jews of the Circumcision/Law), they are* beloved for the father's *(Abraham, Moses, David, etc.)* sakes.

29- For the gifts and calling of God *are* without repentance*. *(*God is not going to change his mind.)*

30- For as ye in times past have not believed God, yet have now obtained mercy through their unbelief *(Israels)*.

31- Even so have these *(Israel)* also now not believed, that through your mercy they may also obtain mercy.

-Romans 11 v 25-31

In other words, forsake 'the Law' and all forms of 'Denomination and Religious legalisms' and become a member in 'The Body of Christ'. Jews and every person in the world have been given this mercy, this 'pardon of grace'. Nobody deserves it in unbelief. Don't reject it. Who would reject a free gift from God? Yet billions have.

Peter at the end of his life finally see's the knowledge that God had given to Paul. This acknowledgment and endorsement of the Apostle Paul came about 68 A.D. 'Pentecost' was some 40 years before. Peter was not preaching to Gentiles.

Peter wrote by Holy Spirit inspiration:

15- And account *that* the long suffering of our Lord *is* salvation; even as our beloved brother Paul also according to **the wisdom given unto him** hath written unto you;

16- **As also it all *his* epistles**, speaking in them of these things *(salvation)*; in which are some things hard to be understood, **which they that are unlearned and unstable wrest, as *they do* also the other scriptures, unto their own destruction**.

-II Peter 3 v 15, 16

The true believer in Paul's Gospel is a permanent member of the 'Body of Christ', 'The Church':

35- Who shall separate us from the love of Christ? *Shall* tribulation, or distress, or persecution, or famine, or nakedness, or peril, or sword?

36- As it is written, For thy sake we are killed all the day long; we are counted as sheep for the slaughter *(by man)*.

37- Nay, in all these things we are more than conquerors through him that loved us.

38- For I am persuaded, that neither death, nor life, nor angels, nor principalities, nor powers, nor things present, nor things to come,
39- Nor height, nor depth, nor any other creature, **shall be able to separate us from the love of God, which <u>is in Christ Jesus our Lord</u>**.
-Romans 8 v 35-39

The key is not how much we love God and Christ but how much does he love us. When we accept the free gift by Grace (unmerited favor) of his Holy Spirit we are his forever. It's Free! Take it! Believe it! God is now just. God is the justifier to all that believe in the finished work of the cross*. *-Romans 3 v 19-31; -Romans 4 v 3-6; -Romans 5 v 1, 2, 14-21; -Romans 8 v 1, 2, 28-30; -Titus 3 v 5-7

God does not look on us as a person or a women or a man, but see's the Holy Spirit of his that was imputed to us. It is a Spiritual GPS. When we truly believe Paul's Gospel of Grace, God imputes the Spirit of Righteousness*. The 'Word of God' says so. Believe it!
*-Romans 4; -James 2 v 23

This 'Baptism of the Spirit' makes a change in the 'attitude of the heart'. It is felt by the individual but 'super natural powers' are not given to 'the Body of Christ'. These powers to drink poison and play with deadly vipers are not for us. We don't become some 'holier than thou angel' walking on the clouds.

The supernatural and the miraculous is not happening with frequency in this 'Age of Grace' like it did for Israel in the Old Testament and by Jesus Christ and his disciples. **As scripture says, "The Jews require a sign and the Gentiles wisdom". We need neither but preach and know 'Christ Crucified'*.** "The just shall live by faith"+. *-I Corinthians 1 v 23; - I Corinthians 2 v 2; -Galatians 2 v 20; -Galatians 5 v 24; +-Romans 1 v 17

Some mega church preachers claim and even attempt to show on TV. that they have 'a miracle power' that only they seem to have. Some claim to have an 'audible dialogue' with God. Is it real?

They would lay hands on someone and they would fall down showing and claiming to have been healed. Some time along the way the preacher would ask for money and from you too watching on TV. If you would give them money then you too can be healed! Just make a donation and God will bless your offering ten fold.

Healing by prayer and miracles do happen by faith. The 'Holy Spirit' imputed to us speaks through the Spirit. You better believe it! Nobody is infallible to the world of sin in which we live. Car accidents, wars, disease happen.

Our belief is that this body in the flesh has no power over 'the Holy God given Spirit' imputed within us. It will never die. **'The Holy Spirit is the Quickening Glue to the Soul', which is the mind, will and emotion.**

Quickened Scriptures: -Psalm 71 v 20; -Psalm 80 v 18; -Psalm 119 v 25, 37, 40, 50, 88, 93, 107, 149, 154, 156, 159; -John 5 v 11; -John 6 v 63; -Romans 8 v 11; -I Corinthians 15 v 36, 45; -Ephesians 2 v 1, 5; -Colossians 2 v 13; -I Timothy 6 v 13; -I Peter 3 v 18

Jesus told the 'Gospel of the Kingdom' believers:
13- And whatsoever ye shall ask in my name, that will I do, that the Father may be glorified in the son.
14- If ye shall ask any thing in my name, I will do *it*.
-John 14 v 13, 14

Who was Jesus speaking to? Is this really happening today? These 'old time religion believer's' still claim this is happening. So when they ask for anything, anything, is God doing it for them? Why not?

In the 'Kingdom of Heaven', with Jesus Christ sitting on the throne of David in Jerusalem, this will happen. This is what they are missing. There is no Kingdom on the earth today. This kingdom is not inside the body of a man.

Jesus wasn't letting on that it would not be fulfilled at this time. He came to fulfill the prophecies to Israel of 'the Gospel of the Kingdom'. It was up to the nation of Israel to accept and believe in 'the name of Jesus Christ'. A national acceptance by every Jew. Then all things requested of God would be fulfilled.

There is no 'Kingdom of Heaven' yet on this earth. At 'the end of the seven year tribulation', then anything that shall be asked for in the 'Name of Jesus Christ' will be fulfilled. Who is it at this time that would be asking?

Be honest with yourself. Do all things asked for in the 'Name of Jesus Christ' being fulfilled? Israel rejected the King and the Kingdom. The 'Age of Grace' is now. It has been called 'the Silent Years of God'.

In this 'Age of Grace' Paul writes by the 'Word of God':

6- Be careful for nothing; but in every thing by prayer and supplication with thanksgiving let your requests be known unto God.

7- And the peace of God, which passeth all understanding, shall keep your hearts and minds through Jesus Christ.

-Philippians 4 v 6, 7

Be careful for nothing. Don't sweat the small stuff. Don't ask God for foolish things. Always be thankful, even for the bad times. We don't know what is really being revealed to us during the times 'of testing'. Whatever God answers is good enough. Whether he does or doesn't fulfill is not for us to judge. Is it God's duty to fulfill all that a believer asks for? We ask and 'the peace of God' that we have through Jesus Christ is sufficient.

3- *Forasmuch as ye are* manifestly declared to be the epistle of Christ ministered by us, written not with ink, but with the Spirit of the living God; not in tables of stone, but in fleshly tables of the heart.

4- And such trust have we through Christ to God-ward:

5- Not that we are sufficient of ourselves to think any thing as of ourselves; but our sufficiency is of God;

6- Who also made us able ministers of **the new testament; not of the letter, but of the spirit: for the letter killeth, but the spirit giveth life**.

7- But if the ministration of death, written *and* engraven in stones, was glorious, so that the children of Is'ra-el could not stedfastly behold the face of Mo'ses for the glory of his countenance; **which glory was to be done away**:

8- How shall not the ministration of the spirit be rather glorious?

-II Corinthians 3 v 3-8

The Holy Spirit can bring on the believer emotion, but emotion cannot bring on the Holy Spirit. Everybody has some type of emotion that they are feeling all day long. Where did it come from?

A new believer doesn't automatically shine a bright light that 'exudes a holy spirit of emotion' on the unbelieving world. The world don't see this person's 'light' saying, "Wow! Now that guy is a Christian, he is going to heaven. It must be God given".

Emotion of the crowd can be felt and passed along. 'Sporting events' and 'music concert' crowds too can feed off of emotion. Many people take pills and drugs to be able to handle their emotions. Liqueur and alcohol have been labeled 'spirits'.

There are 'sports fans' that exuberantly show their 'faith' in their team. Before the game begins, the 'zealous sports fan' begins to 'get ready' in the mind. Even the body gets ready by wearing and showing 'their team spirit'.

At the event they let it 'all hang out'. They will cheer and rejoice or sorrow over the success and failure of their team. This feeling is kept and felt all week long or every day. Even a life time of feelings.

Like King David dancing and rejoicing before the LORD, many 'supposed Christians 'gear up' the same thoughts. "I can't wait to get to church. I will sing and dance and show God and the world how much I love Jesus".

What spirit is feeding the crowd? An emotional church service devoid of 'Paul's Gospel of Grace' may seem to be very 'spiritual'. If the truth of Gods word is not spoken, what spirit is really feeding the congregations emotions?

Who are they rejoicing for? Are they praising the 'Earthly Jesus Christ' that came for the Nation of Israel or the 'Resurrected Jesus Christ' that came for them? What is the 'Truth' that they are 'standing on'?

Paul writes by the Holy Spirit that point in which salvation was made possible:

19- And what is the exceeding **greatness of his power to us-ward who believe *(Paul's Gospel)*,** according to the working of his mighty power,

20- **Which he wrought in Christ, when he raised him from the dead *(Paul's Gospel)*,** and set him at his own right hand in the heavenly places,

21- Far above all principality, and power, and might, and dominion, and every name that is named, not only in this world, but also in that which is to come:

22- And hath put all things under his feet, **and gave him *(Christ)* to be the head over all things to the church,**

23- **Which is his body, the fullness of him that filleth all in all.**

-Ephesians 1 v 19-23

12- For we wrestle not against flesh and blood, but **against principalities,** against powers, against the rulers of the darkness of this world, **against spiritual wickedness in high places.**

-Ephesians 6 v 12

John writes (Holy Spirit inspired) of the spirit of this world:

1- Beloved, believe not every spirit *(person)*, but try the spirits whether they are of God: because many false prophets are gone out into the world.

2- Hereby know ye the Spirit of God: Every spirit *(person)* that confesseth that Je'sus Christ is come in the flesh is of God:

3- And every spirit that confesseth not that Je'sus Christ is come in the flesh is not of God: and this is that *spirit* of antichrist, whereof ye have heard that it should come; and even now already is it in the world.

4- Ye are of God, little children, and have overcome them: because greater is he that is in you, then he that is in the world.

5- They are of the world: therefore speak they of the world, and the world heareth them.

6- We are of God: he that knoweth God heareth us; he that is not of God heareth not us. Hereby know we the spirit of truth, and the spirit of error.

-I John 4 v 1-6

God knows and the believer knows 'when one has been translated' into the 'Heavenly Body of Christ'. Lives and attitudes change. Things once thought of as important are put in perspective. That which was once sought after in the flesh is now seen as vanity and of no value. We now can see that 'the gain made' was nothing more than a 'fleeting fancy'.

5- For they that are after the flesh do mind the things of the flesh; but they that are after the Spirit the things of the Spirit.

6- For to be carnally minded *is* death; but to be spiritually minded *is* life and peace.

7- Because the carnal mind *is* enmity *(an enemy)* against God: for it is not subject to the law of God, neither indeed can be.

8- So then they that are in the flesh cannot please God.

9- But ye are not in the flesh, but in the Spirit, if so be that the Spirit of God dwell in you. Now **if any man have not the Spirit of Christ, he is none of his.**

10- And if Christ *be* in you, the body is dead because of sin; but the Spirit *is* life because of righteousness

11- But if the Spirit of him that raised up Je'sus from the dead dwell in you, **he that raised up Christ from the dead shall also quicken your mortal bodies by his Spirit that dwelleth in you *(Paul's Gospel)*.**

12- Therefore, brethren, we are debtors, not to the flesh, to live after the flesh.

13- For if ye live after the flesh, ye shall die: but if ye through the Spirit do mortify the deeds of the body, ye shall live.

14- For as many as are led by the Spirit of God, they are the sons of God.

15- For ye have not received the spirit of bondage *(legalism)* again to fear, but ye have received the Spirit of adoption, whereby we cry Ab'ba, Father.

16- **The Spirit itself beareth witness with our spirit, that we are the children of God:**

17- **And if children, then heirs; heirs of God, and joint-heirs with Christ**; if so be that we suffer with *him*, that we may be also glorified together.

-Romans 8 v 5-17

Being an 'heir of God' and a 'joint-heir with Christ', our citizenship is of 'The Church, The Body of Christ', which is Heavenly. Jesus today is sitting at the right hand of the Father in Heaven. Our citizenship is in heaven and not of the earth. We are not subjects of a king, but we are joint-heirs with Christ*. *-Romans 8 v 17

20- For our conversation *(citizenship)* is in heaven; whence also we look for the Savior, the Lord Je'sus Christ:

21- **Who shall change our vile body, that it may be fashioned like unto his glorious body,** according to the working whereby he is able even to subdue all things unto himself.

-Philippians 3 v 20, 21

We are 'Sealed' with the Holy Spirit of Promise:

13- **In whom ye also *trusted*, <u>after that ye heard the word of truth, the gospel of your salvation</u> in whom also, after that ye believed, <u>ye were sealed with that holy Spirit of promise</u>,**

-Ephesians 1 v 13

17- **That Christ may dwell in your hearts by faith;** that ye, being rooted and grounded in love,

18- May be able to comprehend with all saints what *is* the breadeth, and length, and depth, and height;

19- And to know the love of Christ, which passeth knowledge, that ye might be filled with all the fullness of God.

-Ephesians 3 v 17-19

What is truth? What is the 'Gospel of Salvation'? Read Romans to Hebrews but do spend time in 'all the Word'. All the scriptures speak truth and are profitable for our learning and understanding. But it is by the 'Apostle Paul' that writes to us in this 'Age of Grace'. Could most of Paul's Epistles been written in 'Red Letter' too? They are the words of Jesus, howbeit; the Resurrected Lord Jesus Christ.

10- But God hath revealed *them* unto us by his Spirit: for the Spirit searcheth all things, yea, the deep things of God.

11- For what man knoweth the things of a man, save the spirit of man which is in him? Even so the things of God knoweth no man, but the Spirit of God.

12- Now we have received, not the spirit of the world, but the spirit which is of God; that we might know the things that are freely given to us of God.

13- Which things also we speak, not in the words which man's wisdom teacheth, but which the Ho'ly Ghost teacheth; comparing spiritual things with spiritual *(scripture with scripture)*.

14- But the natural man receiveth not the things of the Spirit of God: for they are foolishness unto him: neither can he know *them*, because they are spiritually discerned.

-I Corinthians 2 v 10-14

How do we compare Spiritual with Spiritual? By the scriptures in the 'Holy Word of God', our Bible. All scripture in the Holy Bible was given by the 'Holy Spirit of God'*. These writers were moved by the 'Holy Ghost' to write the 'Word of God'*. *-II Timothy 2 v 15; -II Timothy 3 v 16; -II Peter 1 v 21

When we compare scripture with scripture we are comparing 'truth' given to us by the 'Spirit'. The whole Bible wasn't written for us to follow but to learn from and know where to 'stand in the truth'. "Christ died for our sins", that is, know Christ from Genesis to Revelation.

11- Wherefore remember, that ye *being* in time past Gen'tiles in the flesh, who are called Uncircumcision by that which is called the Circumcision in the flesh made by hands;

12- That at that time ye were without Christ, being aliens from the commonwealth of Is'ra-el, and strangers from the covenants of promise, having no hope, and without God in the world:

13- But now in Christ Je'sus ye who sometimes were far off are made nigh by the blood of Christ.

-Ephesians 2 v 11-13

The Apostle Paul never once referred to Jesus Christ as being the 'King of the Church'. Christ is not the King of the Church but is 'The Head of the Church'. 'The Church which is his Body', Spiritually. Christ will be King and LORD of Lords without a doubt, but in 'the Body' we refer to Jesus Christ not as our King, but as the 'Divine Head of the Church', our 'High Priest', our 'Lord Jesus Christ'.

In the Body of Christ we are not working to fill 'the Kingdom' but working to fill 'the Church', 'the Spiritual Body of Christ'. We do these things out of love (charity) thereby fulfilling the Law. There is not a mandate that we must do 'righteous works'. As a believer in the 'faith-way Gospel' we become Gods' workmanship naturally*. We share 'the Gospel' in the hope of filling up 'the true Church'. When God see's that 'his Church' is full, we are out of here (caught up) whether we be dead or alive+. *-Ephesians 2 v 8-10; +-I Corinthians 15 v 51-54; -I Thessalonians 4 v 13-18; -II Thessalonians 2 v 1-3; -Titus 2 v 13, 14

What was **not said by 'The Gospel', I Corinthians 15 v 1-4**? Not 'repentance', not 'water baptism', not the 'joining of a church', 'paying tithes', 'walking the aisles', 'speaking in tongues', or any type of 'righteous works'. 'The Gospel' imposes no requirements in order to belong to the 'true church'. None of the 'Gospel of the Kingdom' requirements (legalisms) are imposed on the 'Body of Christ'.

Many 'professing Christians' think that 'The Gospel' (I Corinthians 15 v 1-4) as declared by God through the Apostle Paul is lacking and incomplete, and that things (works) need to be done and added to it. Under who's authority? These are folk that believe in a 'works religion' and are 'in a process of gaining their salvation'. These are not believing God and Paul's 'faith-way Gospel of Grace'.

It is extremely important when understanding the Apostle Paul, that Paul only writes to 'the believer' in his God given 'Gospel of Grace'. The unbeliever of course can read too, but Paul writes 'as if' the reader already believes fully and is 'a member of the Body of Christ':

1- When Paul says things like, "If you call on the name of Jesus Christ ye shall be saved" he is speaking and writing to the believer who is already in 'the Body of Christ". The unbeliever won't be saved at the point of death. What does the unbeliever believe?* *-Romans 8 v 7-9; -Romans 1 v 18-32; -I Corinthians 2 v 11-16; -II Corinthians 4 v 3, 4; -II Corinthians 13 v 3-6: and so many many more in Paul's Epistles.

2- When Paul speaks of Jesus Christ it is 'Post Crucifixion, Post Resurrection, on this side, our side of the cross. Paul is not preaching the earthly ministry of Christ*. *-Romans 10 v 2, 3, 9; -Romans 14 v 5-9; -I Corinthians 1 v 23, 17-24; -I Corinthians 2 v 2; -Galatians 1 v 11, 12; -II Corinthians 5 v 14-17: and so many more in Paul's Epistles

By not believing in the 'finished work of the cross' as the 'foundation of the Gentiles faith', teachers and preachers are making 'the Power of Resurrection' of none effect*. They unknowingly are calling God a liar by showing God that by their 'righteous works', his dieing on the cross is/was not enough. To the 'works religions', the 'work of the cross' is incomplete and unfinished. *-I Corinthians 1 v 17

Most church assemblies put little to no emphasis on 'the Resurrection'. They may have an Easter service but what significance is preached that day on 'the Power of Resurrection' if any? What purpose and significance was shown by the sermon? Jesus Christ rose from the dead...whats for lunch? Somebody say football?

Read I Corinthians 15, the whole chapter several times and say that resurrection is of no value. Read it, believe it. By adding some form of legalism men are calling God a liar and are not taking the 'Gospel of Grace' by faith. It is not our 'righteous works' that justifies us, but 'our faith in the finished work of the cross that God justifies us'.

The Apostle Paul makes it so clear we are not 'under law' but 'under grace'. Any mandate to do something is of 'a law' and not of 'Grace and Faith'. What law? The denomination, the religion, man's own ideas. Anything deemed by 'the clergy' as necessary to do in order to obtain eternal salvation is 'a law of men' and not of God.

9- But now, after that ye have known God, **or rather are known of God,** how turn ye again to the weak and beggarly elements, whereunto ye desire again to be in bondage?
10- Ye observe days, and months and times, and years *(religious traditions).*
-Galatians 4 v 9, 10

What did Jesus Christ say concerning these mega churches with many members?:

13- Enter ye in at the strait gate: for wide *is* the gate, and broad *is* the way, that leadeth to destruction, **and many there be which go in thereat**:

14- Because strait *is* the gate, and narrow *is* the way, which leadeth unto life, **and few there be that find it**.

-Matthew 7 v 13, 14; -Luke 13 v 24

Then these 'righteous works religions' would point out what James said. Read the Book of James, it is not long. One would have to be in extreme denial of truth to say that James is not 'under the law'. James made no reference to Paul or his 'Gospel of Grace'.

James writes (Holy Spirit inspired):

17- Even so faith, if it hath not works, is dead, being alone.

18- Yea, a man may say, Thou hast faith, and I have works: show me thy faith without thy works, and I will show thee my faith by my works.

19- Thou believest that there is one God; thou doest well: the devils also believe and tremble.

20- But wilt thou know, O vain man, that faith without works is dead?

21- Was not A'bra-ham our father justified by works, when he had offered I'saac his son upon the altar?

22- Seest thou how faith wrought with his works, and by works was faith made perfect?

23- And the scripture was fulfilled which saith, A'bra-ham believed God, and it was imputed unto him for righteousness: and he was called the Friend of God.

24- Ye see then how that by works a man is justified, and not by faith only.

25- Likewise also was not Ra'hab the harlot justified by works, when she had received the messengers, and had sent *them* out another way?

26- For as the body without the spirit is dead, so faith without works is dead also.

-James 2 v 17-26

We are dead to the law by 'the Body of Christ'. The 'do this and do that' for salvation is not for us. Paul writes in Romans (Holy Ghost inspired):

4- Wherefore, my brethren, **ye also are become dead to the law by the body of Christ *(the Gospel)*;** that ye should be married to another, *even to him who is raised from the dead (the Gospel),* that we should bring forth fruit unto God.

5- For when we were **in the flesh, the motions of sins, which were by the law**, did work in our members to bring forth fruit unto death.

6- But now we are delivered from the law, that being dead wherein we were held; **that we should serve in newness of spirit, and not *in* the oldness of the letter.**

-Romans 7 v 4-6

Being in the 'Body of Christ', good works come naturally and is of the heart (charity/love). There is no law mandating that we are to visit the sick and the elderly. We do these things because it is our hope that the 'truth' can be shared and taught. We are the 'ambassadors and stewards of God'*. We are God's 'workmanship'+. We work to fill the 'Body of Christ, the Church' through the truth of scripture and prayer. *-II Corinthians 5 v 20; -Ephesians 6 v 20; -I Corinthians 4 v 1, 2; -Titus 1 v 7; -I Peter 4 v 10; +-II Timothy 2 v 15; -Ephesians 2 v 10

Scripture from Ephesians 2 written by the Lord Jesus Christ from Heaven by the pen of Paul:

4- **But God,** who is rich in mercy, for his great love wherewith he loved us,

5- Even when we were dead in sins, hath quickened us together with Christ, (by grace ye are saved;)

6- And hath raised *us* up together, and made *us* sit together in heavenly *places* in Christ Je'sus:

7- That in the ages to come he might show the exceeding riches of his grace in *his* kindness toward us through Christ Je'sus.

8- **For by grace are ye saved through faith; and that not of yourselves: *it is* the gift of God:**

9- **Not of works, lest any man should boast.**

10- **For we are his workmanship, created in Christ Je'sus unto good works,** which God hath before ordained that we should walk in them.

-Ephesians 2 v 4-10

James writes his Epistle (Holy Spirit inspired) addressed to Jews not Gentiles:

1- James, a servant of God and of the Lord Jesus Christ, **to the twelve tribes which are scattered abroad**, greeting.

-James 1 v 1

James speaks of 'righteous works' of faith by keeping the Mosaic Law. Keep 'the Law' to prove your faith and thereby a man is justified. James is obviously still under 'the Law of the Circumcision'. James, Peter, John, Jesus, 'the Twelve' were all keepers of 'the Law' and all of them died under 'the Law'. They were never instructed to stop.

Have you stopped keeping 'the Law' while at the same time ignoring Paul's Gospel? Or do you do only parts of each? Under whose authority? A mixed gospel? I heard something about the 'Apostles Doctrine'. How is this achieved?

Abram was not under the 'Law of Moses'. He was given the 'Covenant of Circumcision' by God*. Under Moses, the 'Covenant of Circumcision' became part of 'the Law'. Circumcision, a Blood Covenant, began to separate and make a division between God's chosen people, the Hebrew, from the rest of the world, the Gentiles. *-Genesis 17

Back to James 2 v 17-26:

Neither was Ra'hab under 'the Law of Moses'. Abraham lived 400 years before Moses. The 'call of Abraham's faith' was 50 years before Isaac was born. Abraham had faith in what God was telling him long before Isaac was laid on the alter. God had already said that Abraham's faith was "imputed to him for righteousness"*. 'The Call of Abram'+. *-Romans 4 v 11, 22, 23, 24; +-Genesis 12 v 1-3; -Genesis 15 v 4-7; -Romans 4

The same righteousness is imputed* to us by faith in this 'Age of Grace' by believing 'The Gospel'. Like Abraham, we are not under the Jewish Law nor any man made law as a requirement, as a prerequisite or of a necessity for us to do for salvation. Such examples of 'legalisms' are found in religion's and denominations world wide. You could probably name several. Most have some form of 'the too do's' of legalism for salvation. *-Romans 4

Paul writes to us Gentiles who were never under the law and covenant promises by God to Israel:

2- Behold, I Paul say unto you, that if you be **circumcised *(keep the Law)*, Christ shall profit you nothing**.

3- For I testify again to every man that is circumcised, that he is **debtor to do the whole law.**

4- **Christ is become of no effect unto you, whosoever of you are justified by the law; ye are fallen from grace.**

-Galatians 5 v 2-4

James is not writing to Gentiles in 'The Body of Christ' in his epistle. James was still 'under the Law' and was writing to 'the Twelve Tribes scattered abroad'*. The Gentiles never had the label of 'the Twelve Tribes'. *-James 1 v 1

Note that false teaching has been saying that 'the Twelve Tribes of Israel' have been lost and are now intermingled with the world. They say the blessings and promises made to Israel have now fallen to the church. What church? You may as well throw out the whole Bible because it is all about Israel getting its promised Kingdom and being 'the Head of the nations and not the Tail'*.

*- Exodus 19 v 5, 6; -Deuteronomy 7 v 6-8; -Deuteronomy 28 v 13, 44

Israel and the Jew's will never disappear

Why do the most ungodly of men, governments, cults, the offspring of Ishmael and Esau single out the Jews to be tormented? If Israel and the Jew were to vanish, then mankind would be able to call God a liar. They are still the oldest nation and generation of people in all of world history. What has happened to all those nations that have come against Israel? Now there is a Bible and history study that without a doubt shows that God has always had 'a remnant' that will never be forsaken.

Jeremiah 31:

35- Thus saith the LORD, which giveth the sun for a light by day, *and* the ordinances of the moon and of the stars for a light by night, which divideth the sea when the waves thereof roar; The LORD of hosts *is* his name:

36- If those ordinance depart from me, saith the LORD, *then* the seed of Israel also shall cease from being a nation before me for ever.

37- Thus saith the LORD; if heaven above can be measured, and the foundations of the earth searched out beneath, I will also cast off all the seed of Israel for all that they have done, saith the LORD.
-Jeremiah 31 v 35-37

Something of extreme importance to note in the reading and understanding of our Bible is this: who is writing the book of scripture you are reading from and who is it addressed to? Jew or Gentile? When a person see's that not everything was written for them to follow but to learn from, and that there are two Gospels in the Bible, it makes sense.

James knew his audience, 'the Twelve Tribes scattered abroad', and who he was writing to. 'The Twelve Tribes' in the Book of Revelation* is spoken of by John. God knows even if man has lost track of 'the Twelve Tribes'. 1,000's (millions?) of Jews' still have not intermarried. *-Revelation 7 v 4-8

Peter asks Jesus what is in it for him? (He already had salvation by believing in 'the Name of Jesus Christ'):
27- Then answered Pe'ter and said unto him, Behold, we have forsaken all, and followed thee; what shall we have therefore?
28- And Je'sus said unto them, Verily I say unto you, That ye which have followed me *(presently)*, **in the regeneration when the Son of man shall sit in the throne of his glory *(future)*, ye also shall sit upon twelve thrones, <u>judging the twelve tribes of Israel *(future)*</u>.**
-Matthew 19 v 27, 28

Most of Biblical prophecies concern 'the Whole House of Israel'. The intermingling of the Jewish bloodline is said to be close to 50%. 49% is no longer the 'whole house'? The end then is close/closer? Jews have to be in their God given land for the fulfillment of end time prophecy. They are coming back. 'The Day of the Lord', 'The Wrath of God', 'The 'Tribulation' is coming. Current events are exposing this.

James, in his epistle writes (Holy Spirit inspired):
10- **For whosoever shall keep the whole law, and yet offend in one *point*, he is guilty of all.**
11- For he that said, Do not commit adultery, said also, Do not kill. Now if thou commit no adultery, yet if thou kill, thou art become a transgressor of the law.

12- So speak ye, and so do, as they that shall be judged by the law of liberty.
-James 2 v 10-12

Paul writes (Holy Spirit inspired) in total contradiction of James. What has happened to Christendom and what they teach? Don't take my word for it, spend time in the written word.

Paul writes Holy Spirit inspired:
10- **For as many as are of the works of the law are under the curse**: for it is written, Cursed *is* every one that continueth not in all things which are written in the book of the law to do them.
11- But that **no man is justified by the law in the sight of God**, *it is* evident: for, **The just shall live by faith.**
12- **And the law is not of faith: but, The man that doeth them shall live in them**.
-Galatians 3 v 10-12

Faith without works of a law, or a religion or a denomination **is counted for righteousness**:
1- What shall we say then that A'bra-ham our father, as pertaining to the flesh, hath found?
2- For if A'bra-ham were justified by works, he had *whereof* to glory; but not before God.
3- For what saith the scripture? A'bra-ham believed God, and it was counted unto him for righteousness.
4- **Now <u>to him that worketh</u> is the reward not reckoned of grace, <u>but of debt</u>.**
5- **But to <u>him that worketh not</u>, but believeth on him that justifieth the ungodly, <u>his faith is counted for righteousness</u>.**
6- Even as Da'vid also describeth the blessedness of the man, unto whom God imputeth **righteousness without works,**
-Romans 4 v 1-6

What a contradiction! James says one thing then Paul says the complete opposite. What are we to do? Most churches and denominations then pick and choose what they want and make a 'mixed gospel'. They say we are Jews and the Apostle Paul was preaching the same as the disciples were.

The scoffer says, "See, the Bible contradicts itself". It does if one doesn't separate 'the Two Gospels'. The 'Gospel of the Kingdom' message was preached and taught to the 'Jewish Generation of Israel'. The 'Gospel of Grace' is for all gentiles, the world. **Law and Grace does not mix**.

Most put Paul in subjection and pick and choose the scriptures that agrees with them and what they want. Is the Apostle Paul 'a selective supplement'? How many of these church leaders simply hope their parishioners don't read the Epistles from the Apostle Paul? Would they even be able to answer their questions? Most times they say that Peter and Paul were preaching the same thing and mean the same. Give a copy of this book to your pastor.

I pray this will open the eyes of understanding to Christendom worldwide. The difference between Peter and Paul's Apostleship is as clear as night and day. Same God, same Lord, same Jesus Christ but a different 'dispensation is prescribed for this Age of Grace'. We are not under any type of a law, but under Grace.

How many times did Jesus himself say to keep the commandments and 'the Law'? Where did Jesus ever say to stop keeping the commandments and 'the Law'? Who has falsely been saying that when Jesus came, 'the Law' was done away with? Where, when? Find where in scripture? Don't believe on someones 'supposed head knowledge'.

See the diagram of **The Kingdom of God**. There are two types of people in the Kingdom of God.
1- **The Kingdom of Heaven**: Earthly promises made to Israel and the Jews of the Circumcision/Law, The Gospel of the Kingdom. Jews that were under the law and died law keepers.
2- **The Body of Christ**: Heavenly promises, the Gospel of Grace, The True Church, Post Crucifixion and Resurrection. Believers saved by faith through the free gift of grace.

One of the key and most important scriptures of our Bible is:
11- Wherefore remember, that ye *being* in time past Gen'tiles in the flesh, who are called Uncircumcision by that which is called the Circumcision in the flesh made by hands;
12- **That at that time ye were without Christ *(Messiah)*, being aliens from the commonwealth of Is'ra-el, and strangers from the covenants of promise, having no hope, and without God in the world:**

13- **But now** in Christ Je'sus ye who sometimes were far off are made nigh by the blood of Christ.
-Ephesians 2 v 11-13

Memorize these verses. Take it to heart. By understanding this, the Bible becomes more easily understood and opens up. Much of the confusion and contradictions will vanish when one sees the truth in Paul's Epistles. Once the truth is perceived and imputed by the Holy Spirit, listening to a preachers message becomes easier to identify teachers that are 'Pauline' and who are not. Most are not.

It is on 'this side of the cross' that our salvation began. The sins of the whole world were paid for on the cross. The sins of the past, the sins of the present, and the sins of the future were all 'appropriated' (propitiation) for us when we believe 'The Gospel'. It's up to us individually to receive the free gift of Grace which cannot be earned nor worked for. It is a free gift to all that believe! That is good news! That is Gospel!

Paul was the last one to see Jesus Christ:
3- For I delivered unto you first of all *(the chief)* that which I also received, how that Christ died for our sins according to the scriptures;
4- And that he was buried, and that he rose again the third day according to the scriptures:
5- And that he was seen of Ce'phas *(Peter)*, then the twelve:
6- After that, he was seen of above 500 brethren at once; of whom the greater part remain unto this present, but some are fallen asleep.
7- After that, he was seen of James; then of all the apostles.
8- **And last of all he was seen of me also,** as one born out of due time.
-I Corinthians 15 v 3-8

Unlike 'Peter and the Twelve', Paul had three years or so of 'alone time' with the ascended Lord Jesus Christ:
15- But when it pleased God, who separated me from my mother's womb, and called *me* by his grace,
16- To reveal his Son in me, that I might preach him among the heathen; **immediately I conferred not with flesh and blood:**
17- **Neither went I up to Je-ru'sa-lem to them which were apostles before me;** but I went into A-ra'bi'a, and returned again unto Da-mas'cus.

18- Then after three years I went up to Je-ru'sa-lem to see Pe'ter, and abode with him fifteen days.

19- But other of the apostles saw I none, save James the Lord's brother.

20- Now the things which I write unto you, behold, before God, I lie not.

-Galatians 1 v 15-20

After Paul had his dramatic experience on the 'Road to Damascus', one would think that he would want to go to Jerusalem to visit with 'the Twelve'. You would think that Saul/Paul would want to hear from the 'horses mouth' from those that had experienced Jesus Christ in the flesh. But God had other plans. The Apostle Paul was kept from mingling with 'the chosen disciples' that knew Jesus' during 'the earthly ministry'. Law and grace does not mix and God saw to it that it didn't.

One would say to me, how is it that I can speak such things? Easily, I follow the Chief Apostle of the Gentiles, the headman, the first in line to save sinners, the one that gave 'the pattern' to follow, the one that laid the 'foundation of The Church on the Resurrected Jesus Christ', the Apostle that said 'be ye followers of me as I follow Christ, the one by whom the mysteries were revealed to, many, many more.....

16- For I am not ashamed of **the gospel of Christ**: for it is **the power of God unto salvation to everyone that believeth**; to the Jew first, and also to the Greek *(Gentile)*.

17- For therein is the righteousness of God revealed from faith to faith: as it is written, the just shall live by faith.

-Romans 1 v 16, 17

'The Gospel' and our faith and belief in it is 'our salvation'. There is only 'one Gospel' today. By 'The Gospel' we are saved. Now that is good news!

15- For though ye have ten thousand instructors in Christ, yet have ye not many fathers: for in Christ Je'sus I *(Paul)* have begotten you through the gospel.

16- Wherefore I beseech you, **be ye followers of me.**

-I Corinthians 4 v 15, 16

1- Be ye followers of me, even as I also *am* of Christ.

-I Corinthians 11 v 1

Paul is the 'called out, chosen Apostle' by the resurrected Jesus Christ to go to us Gentiles. Not Peter, James or even Jesus during his 'earthly ministry'. The Apostle Paul is the 'chosen vessel', sent by God to go to the world, the Chief! And by this 'Chief Apostle' was this 'Gospel of Salvation' revealed for all men and women.

15- But the Lord said unto him *(An-a-ni'as)*, Go thy way: for **he *(Saul/Paul)* is a chosen vessel unto me, to bear my name before the Gentiles, and Kings, and the children of Israel:**
16- For I will show him how great things he must suffer for my name's sake.
-Acts 9 v 15, 16

The Gospel that Jesus preached in the flesh:
35- And Je'sus went about all the cities and villages, teaching in their synagogues, and **preaching the gospel of the kingdom**, and healing every sickness and every disease among the people.
-Matthew 9 v 35, -Matthew 4 v 23, -Matthew 24 v 14, -Mark 1 v 14

I Corinthians 15 v 1-4 **is not** 'The Gospel of the Kingdom' that Jesus preached. This **is not** 'The Gospel of the Kingdom' that Peter preached. This **is not** 'The Gospel of the Kingdom' that 'the Twelve' disciples preached.

Only the Apostle Paul spoke and wrote of eternal salvation by Jesus dying for the sins of the whole world, including for all those saints still 'down in paradise'. Salvation has come to the whole world by 'the work of the cross'. Always remember the most important aspect of 'the work of the cross'....RESURRECTION!!

Paul says by Holy Spirit inspiration:
11- But I certify you, brethren, that the gospel which was preached of me is not after man.
12- For I neither received it of man, neither was I taught *it*, but by the revelation of Je'sus Christ.
-Galatians 1 v 11, 12

This revelation (revealing of the secrets hid/mysteries) happened after the Lord Jesus Christ 'resurrected' and returned to heaven. Scripture shows that the Apostle Paul had no dealings with Jesus during his 'earthly ministry'. So where did Paul get his authority and commission? **On this side, our side of 'the cross', post resurrection.**

Before Jesus came for his earthly ministry, Peter and Saul/Paul were on the same page. They were following the 'Mosaic Law' as all of 'the Circumcision/Law' were doing. But when Jesus came, Saul did not see Jesus as being 'that promised Messiah' of Scripture. He did not see him as the King that was to come for the Nation of Israel. Saul thought Jesus was an imposter and all those that followed him needed to be dealt with. He was in the majority and was not acting alone.

Peter on the other hand, and the disciples and many others saw Jesus for what he was. They believed that this Jesus Christ of Nazareth was the Messiah. They were 'set apart' (holy) from the rest of those still under the Law of Moses (Judaism). **They themselves still kept 'the law'.** The difference now is that they knew who Jesus really is. The 'Name of Jesus Christ' is 'the Cornerstone' of the 'Kingdom Gospel'. They were 'the elect'. They believed the prophecies.

Paul was not a chosen apostle by Jesus when he walked in the flesh. When Jesus spoke and gave his earthly ministry, the apostle Paul was not one of 'the Twelve'. Paul first became relevant several years after the Resurrection.

In Romans 2 v 16, Paul says by inspiration of the Holy Spirit:
16- **In the day when God shall judge the secrets of men by Je'sus Christ according to <u>my gospel</u>.**
-Romans 2 v 16

Peter never made such a statement. This is not being an egotist by Paul saying 'my gospel'. It wasn't the 'Gospel' that 'the Twelve' knew. It was a way for God to separate his message from the Jews of Israel to the new Gospel that was going to the Gentiles, first by Paul.

Paul is the 'chief' and first to save sinners by his Gospel:
15- This *is* a faithful saying, and worthy of all acceptation, that Christ Jesus came into the world to save sinners; of whom I am chief *(first)*.
16- Howbeit for this cause I obtained mercy, that in me first *(chief)* Je'sus Christ might show forth all long-suffering, **for a pattern to them which should <u>hereafter</u> believe on him to life everlasting.**
-Timothy 1 v 15, 16

A 'change in program', a new 'Dispensation', a new 'prescription' has been written for all of mankind. A break in the time line of the Kingdom Gospel message. Remember always that Paul wrote through the Spirit and was inspired 'of God'. God wanted Paul to use the words 'my Gospel'. Paul's Gospel was not the Gospel that Jesus preached during his earthy ministry, the 'Gospel of the Kingdom'.

To see this 'time-line break', (a parenthetical period), remove from the Bible all mention of the Apostle Paul in the book of Acts and all his Epistles from Romans to Hebrews. There it is. What was removed is 'the Church Age', the 'Age of Grace' without Judaism and the law. You will not find the 'Body of Christ', the 'Church being Caught Up', or any of the 'Revelations of the Hidden Mysteries' outside of 'Paul's Epistles'.

After the crucifixion, James, Peter, John and Jude are writing to Jews in anticipation of 'the Tribulation' to come and the 'return of Christ'. There is no word of salvation being given by them to the world by believing in 'the finished work of the cross'. Outside of Paul, there is little hint of God going to the Gentiles.

For a time, the disciples had received 'power' to carry on the ministry that Jesus had been doing. Their hopes and belief was in 'the Gospel of the Kingdom' that was promised to come to the nation of Israel. They had no idea of a 2,000 year age of Grace. Neither does the vast majority of 'supposed Christians' today. They can't comprehend that **Israel's 'prophetic time-line' was interrupted to be able to save all of mankind, us, the Gentiles**.

John writes in Revelation how he was expecting the Kingdom of Heaven to come to Israel soon:

1- The Revelation of Je'sus Christ, which God gave unto him, to show unto his servants things **which must shortly come to pass**; and he sent and signified *it* by his angel unto his servant John:

2- Who bear record of the word of God, and of the testimony of Je'sus Christ, and of all things that he saw.

3- Blessed *is* he that readeth, and **they that hear the words of this prophecy**, and keep those things which are written therein: **for the time is at hand.**

-Revelation 1 v 1-3

An important note to make concerning John and the churches (assemblies) that he writes to: Much of Christendom combine 'all churches' together, or because the interpreters called them churches that these assemblies somehow include 'the Church that Paul revealed by revelation from heaven', 'the Body of Christ'. John speaks of prophecy in Revelation 1 v 3 and in Revelation 22 v 18, 19. Israel and the Jew are shown prophecy. The Body of Christ has little to no prophecy. Who then is John writing to concerning prophecy?

There are many people that flat out deny and hate the Apostle Paul. Yes, they hate this man. Then they hate 'the Word of God'. May God have mercy on these types.

Where do they go in scripture for salvation? The 'Law' was never done away with. The Roman destruction of 70 A.D. took out 'temple sacrificing'. These would need to have a yard full of cattle to sacrifice for their sins. Where are they going to find a temple and a priest to perform the sacrifices? Repent, and be baptized and sell all your possessions and have all things common*? *-Acts 2 v 44, 45

They are indebted to do the whole law and all that is written in the Books of Exodus, Leviticus, Numbers and Deuteronomy. Peter kept 'the Law' to his dying day. There were over 600 laws in Judaism when Jesus came to Israel. Breaking one aspect of 'the Law' breaks all 'the law'. Simply picking up sticks on the Sabbath Day could get you killed. *-Acts 2 v 44-46

Paul writes by Holy Spirit inspiration:
25- For I would not, brethren, that ye should be ignorant of **this mystery**, lest ye should be wise in your own conceits; that blindness in part is happened to Is'ra-el, <u>**until**</u> **the fullness of the Gen'tiles become in** *(caught up?).*
-Romans 11 v 25

This Spiritual blindness will remain on the world of Christendom until 'the Church, the Body of Christ' is 'caught up to God'. But then it will be too late. This blindness seems to be fully accepted by the proselyte's and the 'spiritual Jew'. Paul is treated as a 'second thought' or a 'selective supplement' and only applies to them when Paul's scriptures don't contradict their teachings.

There is only one gospel for today, I Corinthians 15 v 1-4. Believe in this Gospel as it is expounded from Romans thru Hebrews. We are permanent members of 'The Body of Christ', 'an heir of God' and a 'joint-heir with Christ'*.*-Romans 8 v 1, 2, 16, 17; -Ephesians 3 v 6-12,; - II Corinthians 1 v 20-22

Paul used several names for his Gospel like 'The Gospel of Grace', 'The Gospel of Christ', 'My Gospel' and several more. **But Paul never once said 'The Gospel of the Kingdom'. Not once.** Paul preached 'Christ Crucified'! 'The Twelve disciples' never did.

The 'Gospel of the Circumcision' was by the 'Law of Moses'. 'The Gospel of the Kingdom' was for those under 'the Law'. We are not under law but under Grace. The Gospel of Grace. Christ crucified. Jesus already paid for our sins. We only have to accept the free gift by his grace. We cannot work for 'the gift' or it is not a gift.

'The Twelve' disciples speak of Jesus' death and resurrection **as fact, as an event that happened**. They don't speak of it as 'the salvation for the whole world'. They speak of their physical King that is coming back to save them. The 'precious blood of Jesus being divine.' The 'redemption' of Israel will be by saving them from their enemies, physically.

The crucifixion and dying for the sins of the whole world was not part of 'the Twelves' salvation message. Salvation is no longer exclusive to the Jew. By faith in the Gospel we obtain eternal salvation. The Word of God says so. Believe it!

After the resurrection, Peter is speaking to the Jews of Israel and uses this verse from Isaiah 110:

31- He seeing this before spake of the resurrection of Christ, that his soul was not left in hell, neither his flesh did see corruption

32- This Je'sus hath God raised up, whereof we all are witnesses.

33- Therefore being by the right hand of God exalted, and having received of the Father the promise of the Ho'ly Ghost, he hath shed forth this, which ye now see and hear.

34- For Da'vid is not ascended into the heavens: but he saith himself, The LORD said unto my Lord, Sit thou on my right hand,

35- **Until I make thy foes thy footstool.**

36- **Therefore let all the house of Is'ra-el** know assuredly, that God hath made that same Je'sus, whom ye have crucified, both Lord and Christ.

-Acts 2 v 31-36; -Psalm 110

Jesus Christ's Resurrection:
Jew Nationally = saved from their enemies.
Gentile Individually = salvation for all mankind.

For Peter and those in Israel, 'the Resurrected Jesus Christ' is still alive and could return to set up 'the Kingdom'. It was still possible. It still is. Peter pleads with the men and women of Israel to see this. Peter never preached 'Christ Crucified' as a means of salvation for the whole world. He was still in the 'Kingdom Gospel' expecting Christ to return and set up 'The Kingdom'.

1- The LORD said to my Lord, Sit thou at my right hand, <u>until</u> I make thine enemies thy footstool.
-Psalm 110 v 1

Has Israel's enemies been put down and made their footstool today? No, of course not. Israel today is not the head of the nations, nor is there a Kingdom in Israel with Jesus ruling and reigning, sitting on the throne of David. Yet Israel is in the news everyday as if they already are 'the hub of the world'. What's the big deal? What is the world afraid of?

The twisting of the truth by well intentioned men and women, churches and denominations have fallen under the anathema in Galatians. "Let him be accursed!". They combine the Gospel that Jesus preached during his earthly ministry to the Jews of Israel with that of Paul's Gospel which was preached to the Gentiles through and by the 'Ascended Jesus Christ' in Heaven. Teaching and preaching 'a mixed gospel'.

Paul took 'this Gospel' to the Jews also. Hebrews was written to them (the Jew's 'on the fence') that there was something better than 'the Law'. But in Hebrews, there is no plan of salvation or 'Body of Christ' Church language, that is 'death, burial and resurrection for salvation'. It is written to show the Jew's who Jesus really is. "The Jews require a sign, but we preach Christ Crucified"*.*-Ephesians 1; -I Corinthians 1 v 17-24; -I Corinthians 2 v 2; -see Paul's Epistles

1- For this cause I Paul, the prisoner of Je'sus Christ for you Gen'tiles,
2- If ye have heard of **the dispensation of the grace of God which is given to me to you-ward**:

3- How that by revelation he made known unto me the mystery; (as I wrote afore in few words,

4- Whereby, when ye read, ye may understand my knowledge in the mystery of Christ)

5- Which in other ages was not made known unto the sons of men, as it is now revealed unto his holy apostles and prophets by the Spirit;

6- That the Gen'tiles should be fellowheirs, and of the same body, and partakers of his promise in Christ by the gospel:

7- Wherefore I was made a minister, according to the gift of the grace of God given unto me by the effectual working of his power.

-Ephesians 3 v 1-7

If you have a newer translated Bible compare with the scriptures from the original KJV Bible used in this book. The *italicized* words were added by the translators and are not in the original manuscripts. The Bible can be understood too by skipping *these words*.

Hopefully your mind has been stimulated and you may want to show with scripture that 'The Trial of Christendom' got it wrong. The evidence of Paul's Gospel being the true message of salvation for all the world continues in this book. Compare scripture with scripture and ask yourself questions. If the answer is not found in your Bible then it doesn't exist, so don't make it. Stand on the truth of scripture. If anything, maybe you have opened your Bible.

BOOK II

Luke: Jew or Gentile?

1- What advantage then hath the Jew? Or what profit *is there* of circumcision?
2- Much every way: chiefly, because that **unto them were committed the oracles of God.**
-Romans 3 v 1, 2

Many think that Luke was a Gentile and/or want to believe that he is. The name of Luke is not a Jewish/Hebrew name. So, because of this, he must be a Gentile? Read Romans 3 v 1, 2 again. The whole Bible has been written by a Jew. From Genesis to Revelation "unto them, *(the Jew/ the circumcision)* were committed the oracles of God". Paul himself, 'the Apostle of the Gentiles', was of the 'Tribe of Benjamin'*. *-Romans 11 v 1; -Philippians 3 v 5

Romans 3 v 2 **did not say**:
-Much every way: chiefly, because that unto them were committed the oracles of God *'and that one Gentile named Luke'*.

From the time of Moses, the 'Jews of the Circumcision/Law' have always been 'anti-Gentile'. They were warned by God never to have anything to do with the people of the world, the Gentiles. Israel and the Jews were to be 'a separate and peculiar people' chosen of God. A Holy Nation and a Kingdom of Priests*. *-Exodus 19 v 5, 6; -Deuteronomy 26 v 18, 19; -Genesis 12 v 2, 3

Yet, by man's own desire to please God by their 'Religions and Denominations', many have taken an 'inclusive' view of 'the Jews directive' in the Old Testament. Gentiles are thought of as being Jews too and the Old Testament is taught that what was for the Jews and the Nation of Israel also applies to the Gentiles. In their attempt to understand the Bible, it has been taught that the Jews and Gentiles are under the same 'Dispensation'. God instructed the Jews of Israel to have nothing to do with the people of the lands, the Gentiles.

Gentiles are not Jews. Jews are not Gentiles. These preachers and teachers have become blind to scripture. By treating and believing that Jews and Gentiles are the same, this helps in their belief to understanding 'the mixed Gospel'. "It's all one and the same and there is only one Gospel", they say. "Peter and Paul were saying the same thing and there is no difference in what they preached".

In the 'Doctrine of the Grace of God' given to the Apostle Paul, there is no difference between the Jew and the Gentile. Both can achieve salvation by the 'faith-way Gospel'*. The Jew would need to forsake all the legalisms of Judaism and become a member of the Body of Christ. In essence, become a Gentile saved by Grace. There are no 'works of righteousness' in 'the Church'. No man is justified by an attempt to please God by a righteous work. Acts of love and charity come naturally. Love is the fulfilling of the Law+. *-Galatians 3 v 21-29; +-Romans 13 v 10

What is the appeal of thinking that Luke is a Gentile? Is it because Luke is not a Jewish name? Is it because he wrote the Gospel according to St. Luke and the Book of Acts? Does this legitimize that of Peter in Acts 2 v 38, that the Gentiles are to be 'water baptized' as well as the Jew? Gentiles become Jews when they get 'water baptized'?

At this 'Day of Pentecost' (Acts 2) were men and women that had traveled to Israel. Many Jewish families had been scattered previously beginning with Nebuchadnezzar and the Babylonian Empire in 606 B.C. Many had not returned to Israel with Ezra and Nehemiah but lived with their progeny and offspring, and grew up outside of Israel. They learned overtime the languages of the nations where they lived.

These 'devout Jews of the Circumcision' had not been intermarrying with Gentiles and were still 'of the Twelve Tribes of Israel'. They were 'of the circumcision' and were still under the 'Law of Moses', Judaism. These too are the 'Ye men of Israel' because they also were given the 'covenant promises'.

Peter says 'Ye men of Israel' in Acts 2 when he addressed this assembly at the 'Feast Day of Pentecost'. This we can read for ourselves and don't need a preachers interpretation of 'Ye men of Israel'. It means what it says. Peter didn't say 'Ye men of Israel and Ye Gentiles'.

From the very start of the Jewish existence, God warned Israel and the Jew not to co-mingle with the other people of the lands, the Gentiles. The 'Jews of the Circumcision under the Law' were to keep 'that Holier than thou attitude'. When the 'Earthly Kingdom of Heaven' is established with Jesus Christ sitting on the throne of David in Zion, then the Jews would be commissioned to go to the world and bring the Gentiles into a knowledge of their God, the LORD JEHOVAH. This never happened..., yet. But will. God said so. When?

The word JEHOVAH is rarely used in the Old Testament. Though it means the same as LORD by the English translators, out of respect for the Jews, 'LORD' is used in its place. The Jews throughout history have desired to not have it overused thus lessening its place of preeminence to them.

The LORD God is JEHOVAH. This is God, the same for us and all the world, but JEHOVAH is a name used by and for the Jews only. We in 'the Body of Christ' don't refer to JEHOVAH as being our God though they are one and the same. There is only one Godhead. This is further explored in the Chapter 'The Invisible Godhead'.

The LORD God of Israel is not treating the Body of Christ like he did with the Jews of the Old Testament. The acts and commands given to the Nation of Israel at times seemed harsh and of no mercy. In this age of grace, the LORD God of Israel is of patience, mercy and Grace. The LORD is not treating mankind with 'a divisional purpose' as he was in the Old Testament between the Jews and Gentiles.

Mankind operating by their own 'self will and conscience' end up violent and murderous. History is the very proof of this. The biggest mass murdering Empires were Godless. Nazi Germany, Stalin's U.S.S.R., and Mao Tse-tung of Asia. These three alone championed the murdering of over 100,000,000 people. Without the 'God of Truth' in their lives, Satan fills the vacuum. No person on their own achieve 'sainthood and righteousness'. "For all have sinned and came short of the glory of God"*. *-Romans 3 v 23

This 'Age of Grace' has been called 'The Age of the Silence of God'. God is not performing 'the supernatural' like was witnessed before the Apostle Paul. The supernatural was a more common thing to the Jews of

the Old Testament. They were not surprised to an extent that they fainted. Such acts, if performed today and mankind being natural born sinners, would make the event something to worship or even perhaps invent a new religion. "They would worship the creature rather than the creator*".
*-Romans 1 v 25

The LORD God JEHOVAH is also 'The Word'. JEHOVAH was the communicator to Israel. Scriptures say that no man has seen God and lived, but they did. No man has seen 'the Invisible Godhead' and lived. Many times JEHOVAH had appeared in many forms and was seen by men. They did not die. See the Chapter 'The Invisible Godhead'.

1- God, who at sundry times and in divers manners spake in times past unto the fathers by the prophets.
2- Hath in these last days spoken unto us by *his* Son, whom he hath appointed heir of all things by whom also he made the worlds.
-Hebrews 1 v 1, 2

John writes by Holy Ghost inspiration that 'the Word' was made flesh*. The Word, LORD God JEHOVAH was manifested to Israel in the human body of Jesus Christ. The communicator, 'The Word' is Jesus Christ. The same yesterday, today and forever. *-John 1 v 14

In this 'Age of Grace' we have the written 'Word of God'. The Apostle Paul fulfilled and finished the 'Word of God' for us*. "The Jews require a sign and the Greeks (Gentiles) wisdom". We need neither, "But we preach Christ Crucified and the Resurrection from the Dead"+. This is 'the preaching of the cross' =. We have 'the True Word' written in our Bible. Believe in God or Believe God? *-Colossians 1 v 24-28; +-I Corinthians 1 v 17-24; -I Corinthians 2 v 2; =-I Corinthians 1 v 18; -Paul's Epistles

Such directives were given by the LORD God to his chosen covenant people:
31- And I will set thy bounds from the Red Sea even unto the sea of the Philis'tines, and from the desert unto the river: for I will deliver the inhabitants of the land into your hand; and thou shalt drive them out before thee.
32- **Thou shalt make no covenant with them**, nor with their gods.
33- **They shall not dwell in thy land,** lest they make thee sin against me: for if thou serve their gods, it will surely be a snare unto thee.
-Exodus 23 v 31-33

God warns his people:

55- But if ye will not drive out the inhabitants of the land from before you; then it shall come to pass, that those which ye let remain of them *shall be* pricks in your eyes, and thorns in your sides, and shall vex you in the land wherein ye dwell.

56- Moreover it shall come to pass, *that* I shall do unto you, as I thought to do unto them.

-Numbers 33 v 55, 56

The Old Testament Anti-Gentile sentiment:

16- But of the cities of these people, which the LORD *(JEHOVAH)* thy God doth give thee *for* an inheritance, **thou shalt save alive nothing that breatheth:**

17- **But thou shalt utterly destroy them;** *namely*, the Hit'tites, and the Am'or-ites, the Ca'naan-ites, and the Per'iz-ztes, the Hi'vites, and the Jeb'u-sites; as the LORD *(JEHOVAH)* thy God hath commanded thee:

18- **That they teach you not to do after all their abominations,** which they have done unto their gods; so should ye sin against the LORD *(JEHOVAH)* your God.

-Deuteronomy 20 v 16-18

The pervading thought of the 'Circumcision/Law':

12- **Else** if ye do in any wise go back, and cleave unto the remnant of these nations, ***even* these that remain among you**, and shall make marriages with them, and go in unto them, and they to you:

13- **Know for a certainty** that the LORD *(JEHOVAH)* your God will no more drive out *any of* these nations from before you; but they shall be snares and traps unto you, and scourges in your sides, and thorns in your eyes, until ye perish from off **this good land which the LORD *(JEHOVAH)* your God hath given you.**

14- And, behold, this day I *am* going the way of all the earth *(Joshua)*: and ye know in all your hearts and in all your souls, that not one thing hath failed of all the good things which the LORD *(JEHOVAH)* your God spake concerning you; all are come to pass unto you, and not one thing hath failed thereof.

15- **Therefore it shall come to pass,** *that a*s all good things are come upon you, which the LORD *(JEHOVAH)* your God promised you; so shall the

LORD bring upon you all evil things, until he have destroyed you from off **this good land which the LORD *(JEHOVAH)* your God hath given you**. 16- When ye have transgressed the covenant of the LORD *(JEHOVAH)* your God, which he commanded you, and have gone and served other gods, and bowed yourselves to them; then shall the anger of the LORD be kindled against you, and ye shall perish quickly from off **the good land which he hath given unto you**.

-Joshua 23 v 12-16

The Jews knew their history and their plight in the world. Many today say, "Yeah, **I believe in God** or something that created life, the earth and the universe". But **do they believe God?** There is a difference. To be able to believe God we have to know what he said. How do we know what God said? He has it written for all mankind in our KJV Holy Bible.

24- For the LORD *(JEHOVAH)* thy God *is* a consuming fire, *even* a jealous God.

25- When thou shalt beget children, and children's children, and ye shall have remained long in the land, **and shall corrupt *yourselves***, and make a graven image, *or* the likeness of any *thing*, and shall do evil in the sight of the LORD *(JEHOVAH)* thy God, to provoke him to anger:

26- I call heaven and earth to witness against you this day, that ye shall soon utterly perish from off the land where unto ye go over Jor'dan to possess it; ye shall not prolong *your* days upon it, but shall utterly be destroyed,

27- **And the LORD shall scatter you among the nations, and ye shall be left few in number among the heathen, whither the LORD shall lead you.** *(Prophecy fulfilled)*

28- And their ye shall serve god's, the work of men's hands, wood and stone, which neither see, nor hear, nor eat, nor smell.

29- But if from thence thou shalt seek the LORD *(JEHOVAH)* thy God, thou shalt find *him*, if thou seek him with all thy heart and with all thy soul.

30- When thou art in tribulation, and all these things are come upon thee, *even* in **the latter days**, if thou turn to the LORD *(JEHOVAH)* thy God, and shalt be obedient unto his voice;

31- **(For the LORD *(JEHOVAH)* thy God *is* a merciful God;) he will not forsake thee, neither destroy thee, nor forget the covenant of thy fathers which he sware unto them.**

32- For ask now of the days that are past, which were before thee, since the day that God created man upon the earth, and *ask* from the one side of heaven unto the other, whether there hath been *any such thing* as this great thing *is*, or hath been heard like it?

33- Did *ever* people hear the voice of God speaking out of the midst of the fire, as thou hast heard, **and live**?

34- Or hath God assayed to go *and* take him a nation from the midst of *another* nation, by temptations *(testing)*, by signs, and by wonders, and by war, and by a mighty hand, and by a stretched out arm, and by great terrors, according to all that the LORD *(JEHOVAH)* your God did for you in E'gypt before your eyes?

35- Unto thee it was showed, that thou mightest know that the LORD *(JEHOVAH)* he *is* God; ***there is* none else beside him**.

-Deuteronomy 4 v 24-35

This is how the Jews were to deal with the Gentiles concerning their Jewish Nation:

1- When the LORD *(JEHOVAH)* thy God shall bring thee into the land whither thou goest to possess it, and hath cast out many nations before thee, the Hit'tites, and the Gir'ga-shites, and the Am'or-ites, and the Ca'naan-ites, and the Per'iz-zites, and the Hi'vites, and the Jeb'u-sites, seven nations greater and mightier than thou;

2- And when the LORD *(JEHOVAH)* thy God shall deliver them before thee; **thou shalt smite them, *and* utterly destroy them; thou shalt make no covenant with them, nor show mercy unto them**:

3- Neither shalt thou make marriages with them; thy daughter thou shalt not give unto his son, nor his daughter shalt thou take unto thy son.

4- For they will turn away thy son from following me, that they may serve other gods: so will the anger of the LORD be kindled against you, and destroy thee suddenly.

5- **But** thus shall ye deal with them; ye shall destroy their altars, and break down their images, and cut down their groves, and burn their graven images with fire.

6- **For thou *art* an holy people unto the LORD *(JEHOVAH)* thy God: the LORD thy God hath chosen thee to be a special people unto himself, above all people that *are* upon the face of the earth.**

7- The LORD did not set his love upon you, nor choose you, because ye were more in number than any people; for ye *were* the fewest of all people:

8- But because the LORD loved you, **and because he would keep the oath which he had sworn unto your fathers**, hath the LORD brought you out with a mighty hand, and **redeemed you out of the house of bondmen**, from the hand of Pha'raoh king of E'gypt.

9- Know therefore that the LORD *(JEHOVAH)* thy God, he *is* God, the faithful God, which keepeth covenant and mercy with them that love him <u>and keep his commandments</u> to a thousand generations;

10- And repayeth them that hate him to their face, to destroy them: he will not be slack to him that hateth him, he will repay him to his face.

11- **Thou shalt therefore keep the commandments, and the statutes, and the judgments, which I command thee this day, to do them.**

12- Wherefore it shall come to pass, if ye hearken to these judgments, and keep, and do them, that **the LORD *(JEHOVAH)* thy God shall keep unto thee the covenant and the mercy which he sware unto thy fathers**:

13- And he will love thee, and bless thee, and multiply thee: he will also bless the fruit of thy womb, and the fruit of thy land, thy corn, and thy wine, and thine oil, the increase of thy kine, and the flocks of thy sheep, in **the land which he sware unto thy fathers to give thee.**

14- **Thou shalt be blessed above all people:** there shall not be male or female barren among you, or among your cattle.

15- And the LORD will take away from thee all sickness, and will put none of the evil diseases of E'gypt, which thou knowest, upon thee; but will lay them upon all *them* that hate thee.

16- **And thou shalt consume all the people which the LORD *(JEHOVAH)* thy God shall deliver thee; thine eye shall have no pity upon them: neither shalt thou serve their gods; for that *will be* a snare unto thee.**

17- If thou shalt say in thine heart, These nations *are* more than I; how can I dispossess them?

18- Thou shalt not be afraid of them: *but* shalt well remember what the LORD *(JEHOVAH)* thy God did unto Pha'raoh, and unto all E'gypt;

-Deuteronomy 7 v 1-18

The Jews, chosen of the LORD God, were to be separate, peculiar and Holy:
18- **And the LORD hath avouched thee this day to be his peculiar people,** as he hath promised thee, and that *thou* shouldest **keep all his commandments;**

19- And to **make thee high above all nations** which he hath made, in praise, and in name, and in honour, and that **thou mayest be an holy people unto the LORD *(JEHOVAH)* thy God**, as he hath spoken.
-Deuteronomy 26 v 18,19

By the time Jesus Christ came, 1500 years after Moses, the history of Israel was quite the 'roller coaster' story. This attitude concerning the non-Jew didn't change over that time. The great Kingdom of Israel, David and Solomon's, are no more and the Jews are now living in Israel under the Roman Empire occupation. It would have been suicide to take the 'Jewish Directives by the LORD God JEHOVAH' now as to destroy the non-Jews. Israel was no longer in a position to do so.

The Roman Gentiles were everywhere in their God given land. Concerning adherence to their 'Law of Moses' and 'their religion of Judaism', they still carried out punishments themselves on their fellow Jew's that were breaking 'the Law'. They still performed their own 'capital punishments' and most times this was done by 'stoning to death the perceived transgressor'.

At the time of Christ's earthly ministry, the 'Religion of Judaism' and the keeping of 'the Law' was 'watered down' and not of the same doctrine that was followed early in Israel's existence. The priests and Jewish leaders were more or less following aspects of 'the Law' that would suit themselves. The same has happened to Christendom in this age of Grace.

Isaiah writes (by Holy Spirit inspiration) of the demise of 'their religion':
6- But we are all as an unclean *thing*, and all our righteousnesses are as filthy rags; and we all do fade as a leaf; and our iniquities, like the wind, have taken us away.
-Isaiah 64 v 6

11- To what purpose *is* the multitude of your sacrifices unto me? Saith the LORD: I am full of the burnt offerings of rams, and the fat of fed beasts; and I delight not in the blood of bullocks, or of lambs, or of goats.
12- When ye come to appear before me, who hath required this at your hand, to tread my courts?

13- Bring no more vain oblations; incense is an abomination unto me; the new moons and sabbaths, the calling of assemblies, I cannot away with; *it is* iniquity, even the solemn meeting.

14- Your new moons and your appointed feasts my soul hateth: they are a trouble unto me; I am weary to bear *them.*

15- And when ye spread forth your hands, I will hide mine eyes from you: yea, when ye make many prayers, I will not hear: your hands are full of blood.

-Isaiah 1 v 11-15

PROPHECY

16- And the LORD said unto Mo'ses, Behold, thou shalt sleep with thy fathers; and this people will rise up, and go a whoring *(spiritually)* after the gods of the strangers of the land, wither they *go to be* among them, and will forsake me, **and break my covenant which I have made with them**.

17- Then my anger shall be kindled against them in that day, and I will forsake them, and I will hide my face from them, and they shall be devoured, and many evils and troubles shall befall them; so that they will say in that day, Are not these evils come upon us, because our God *is* not among us?

18- And I will surely hide my face in that day for all the evils which they shall have wrought, in that they are turned unto other gods.

-Deuteronomy 31 v 16-18

PROPHECY FULFILLED

34- They did not destroy the nations, concerning whom the LORD commanded them:

35- But were mingled among the heathen, and learned their works.

36- And they served their idols: which were a snare unto them.

37- **Yea, they sacrificed their sons and their daughters unto devils,**

38- And shed innocent blood, *even* the blood of their sons and of their daughters, whom they sacrificed unto the idols of Ca'naan: and the land was polluted with blood.

39- Thus were they defiled with their own works, and went a whoring with their own inventions.

40- **Therefore was the wrath of the LORD kindled and against his people, insomuch that he abhorred his own inheritance.**

41- And he gave them into the hand of the heathen; and they that hated them ruled over them.

42- Their enemies also oppressed them, and they were brought into subjection under their hand.

43- Many times did he deliver them; but they provoked *him* with their counsel, and were brought low for their iniquity.

-Psalm 106 v 34-43

These warnings were given at the beginning of Israel's existence as well as during Israel's rein and prosperity. Don't mingle nor associate with any people who are not Jew's of 'The Circumcision', who are not under 'the Mosaic Law'. Ignore them, be not like them. Do not make marriages with them. Don't pollute the chosen generation by mixing the blood-line.

The LORD, Moses and Joshua gave stern warnings to the 'Children of Israel' that **the Gentiles would become a snare** unto them and lead to the nations downfall. The non-Jew, non-Hebrew, Gentile, Heathen, 'The Uncircumcised' were not to partake of their inheritance and the customs and service practices of Judaism. The non-Jew, the Gentile, were not given the 'Covenants of Promise'. The Gentiles can not claim Abraham as their Father nor Moses **by a family blood-line**. They (Gentiles) were never under the Commandments made by God to Israel and the Jew.

11- Wherefore remember, that ye *being* in time past Gen'tiles in the flesh, who are called Uncircumcision by that which is called the Circumcision in the flesh made by hands;

12- That at that time ye were without Christ *(Messiah)*, being aliens from the commonwealth of Is'ra-el, and strangers from the covenants of promise, having no hope, and without God in the world:

13- **But now** in Christ Je'sus ye who sometimes were far off are made nigh by the blood of Christ.

-Ephesians 2 v 11-13

The 'Blood of Christ' was at his death, not his birth. When Paul speaks of 'Blood', he is speaking the Gospel of Grace. His blood, his shed blood, his death and resurrection. This is what Paul means by the 'Blood of Christ'. New life for all of mankind began at the cross, began at his physical death, began at his resurrection, not Bethlehem as it was for the Jews.

Absolutely:

22- And almost all things are by the law purged with blood; and without the shedding of blood is no remission.

-Hebrews 9 v 22

Not all scriptural references are given here. We as believers and students of God's word can read and make note ourselves. Simply reading the Old Testament shows the separation of the Jews from the Gentiles. Very, very few Gentiles had anything to do with Israel except those nations of Gentiles that made war against Israel.

Division

The Abrahamic Covenant

1- Now the LORD had said unto A'bram, Get thee out of thy country, and from thy kindred, and from thy father's house, unto a land that I will shew thee:

2- And I will make of thee a great nation, and I will bless thee, and make thy name great; and thou shalt be a blessing:

3- And I will bless them that bless thee, and curse him that curseth thee: and in thee shall all the families be blessed.

-Genesis 12 v 1-3

Out of the sea of humanity God chose one man to bring about a nation of people that he could call his own. This began with Abram (Abraham). Abram was a Syrian and not a Jew. He is the father of 'the Jewish nation'. The first time the word 'Hebrew was used in the Bible is Genesis 14 v 13.

Maybe the following scriptures give a clue:

18- Then A'bram removed *his* tent and came and dwelt in **the plain of Mam're, which *is* in He'bron**, and built there an alter unto the LORD.

-Genesis 13 v 18

13- And there came one that had escaped, and told **A'bram the Hebrew; for he dwelt in the plain of Mam're** the Am'or-ite, brother of Esh'col, and brother of A'ner: and these *were* confederate with A'bram.

-Genesis 14 v 13

The Blood Covenant of Circumcision

9- And God said unto A'bra-ham, Thou shalt keep my covenant therefore, thou, and thy seed after thee in their generations.

10- This *is* my covenant, which ye shall keep, between me and you and thy seed after thee; Every man child among you shall be circumcised.

11- And ye shall circumcise the flesh of your foreskin; and it shall be a token of the covenant betwixt me and you.

12- And he that is eight days old shall be circumcised among you, every man child in your generations, he that is born in the house, or bought with money of any stranger, which *is* not of thy seed.

13- He that is born in thy house, and he that is bought with thy money, must needs be circumcised: and my covenant shall be in your flesh for an everlasting covenant.

14- And the uncircumcised man child whose flesh of his foreskin is not circumcised, that soul shall be cut off from his people; he hath broken my covenant.

-Genesis 17 v 9-14

The Plagues of Egypt

The first three plagues that fell on Egypt and Pharaoh's people also fell on the Hebrews in the land of Goshen. These plagues were: water was turned to blood, frogs and then an infestation of lice. The fourth plague was *flies*. The translators called the swarms *flies* and italicized the word *flies*. These swarms perhaps were the worst of flying insects and not just the typical house fly.

20- And the LORD said unto Mo'ses, Rise up early in the morning, and stand before Pha'roah, lo, he cometh forth to the water, and say unto him, Thus saith the LORD, Let my people go, that they may serve me.

21- Else, if thou wilt not let my people go, behold, I will send swarms *of flies* upon thee, and upon thy servants, and upon thy people, and into thy houses: and the houses of the E-gyp'tians shall be full of swarms *of flies*, and also the ground whereon they *are*.

22- And <u>I will sever in that day the land of Goshen</u>, in which my people dwell, that no swarms *of flies* shall be there; to the end thou mayest know that I *am* the LORD in the midst of the earth.

23- And I will put a division between my people and thy people: to morrow shall this sign be.

24- And the LORD did so; and there was a grievous swarm *of flies* into the house of Pha'roah, and *into* the servants houses, and into all the land of E'gypt: the land was corrupted by reason of the swarm *of flies.*

-Exodus 8 v 20-24

Moses warns Pharaoh that the next plague, number five, will kill all their cattle:

1- Then the LORD said unto Mo'ses, Go in unto Pha'raoh, and tell him, **Thus saith the LORD God of the Hebrews,** Let my people go, that they may serve me.

2- For if thou refuse to let *them* go, and wilt hold them still,

3- Behold, the hand of the LORD is upon thy cattle which is in the field, upon the horses, upon the asses, upon the camels, upon the oxen, and upon the sheep: *there shall be* a very grievous murrain.

4- **And the LORD shall sever between the cattle of Is'ra-el and the cattle of E'gypt: and there shall nothing die of all *that is* the children of Is'ra-el.**

5- And the LORD appointed a set time, saying, To morrow the LORD shall do this thing in the land.

6- And the LORD did that thing on the morrow, and all the cattle of E'gypt died: **but** of the cattle of the children of Is'ra-el died not one.

7- And Pha'raoh sent, and behold, there was not one of the cattle of the Is'ra-el-ites dead. And the heart of Pha'raoh was hardened, and he did not let the people go.

-Exodus 9 v 1-7

If Luke was a Gentile, would he be given 'special treatment'? At the time of Jesus Christ, the 'Jews of the Circumcision/Law' had not magically changed their attitudes toward 'the heathen'. No such scripture is found in our Bible of the Jews having a national acceptance of the 'Heathen Gentiles'. Jesus Christ himself kept his distance away from the Gentiles*.

*-Matthew 10 v 5, 6; -Matthew 7 v 6; -Matthew 15 v 22-28; -Mark 7 v 25-30

15- Study to show thyself approved unto God, a workman that needeth not to be ashamed, rightly dividing the word of truth.

-II Timothy 2 v 15

Jonah 'Walks the Plank'

Jonah's book gives good insight into the attitude of the Jew towards the non-Jew. Jonah, a good Jew, would rather have 'walked the plank' to his own death before going to a Gentile city. He understood the Law and the warnings given to Israel and the Jews from the beginning.

When God told Jonah to go to Nineveh, he rebelled. This directive was not what he was brought up and raised to believe. Now God was telling Jonah to go to a very large city of Gentiles. He understood that he was to have nothing to do with the Gentiles. Why now? Why me? God told him to go. He ran from God and tried to hide.

1- Now the word of the LORD came unto Jo'nah the son of A-mit'ta-i, saying,

2- Arise, go to Nin'e-veh, that great city, and cry against it; for their wickedness is come up before me.

3- But Jo'nah rose up to flee unto Tar'shish from the presence of the LORD, and went down to Jop'pa; and he found a ship going to Tar'shish: so he paid the fare thereof, and went down into it, to go with them unto Tar'shish from the presence of the LORD.

-Jonah 1 v 1-3

No one can hide from the 'Living God':

4- But the LORD sent out a great wind into the sea, and there was a mighty tempest in the sea, so that the ship was like to be broken.

5- Then the mariners were afraid, and cried every man unto **his god**, and cast forth the wares that *were* in the ship into the sea, to lighten *it* of them. But Jo'nah was gone down into the sides of the ship; and he lay, and was fast asleep.

6- So the shipmaster came to him, and said unto him, What meanest thou, O sleeper? Arise, call upon thy God, if so be that God will think upon us, that we perish not.

7- And they said everyone to his fellow, Come, and let us cast lots, that we may know for whose cause this evil *is* upon us. So they cast lots, and the lot fell upon Jo'nah.

-Jonah 1 v 4-7

Jonah reveals his knowledge and core beliefs:

8- Then said they unto him, Tell us, we pray thee, for whose cause this evil *is* upon us; What *is* thine occupation? And whence comest thou? What *is* thy country? And of what people *art* thou?

9- And he said unto them, I *am* an He'brew; and I fear the LORD, the God of heaven, which hath made the sea and the dry *land*.

10- Then were the men exceedingly afraid, and said unto him, Why hast thou done this? For the men knew that he fled from the presence of the LORD, because he had told them.

-Jonah 1 v 8-10

How much of the LORD God did they really know? In verse 5 they prayed to 'their gods'. Jonah told them that "his LORD was the God of Heaven, which hath made the sea and dry land". To these pagans, Jonah's God seemed to be 'all powerful'. More powerful than the gods they worshiped. Who knows what these gods were? All they knew was that Jonah's God was controlling the sea and they were in fear of drowning.

11- Then said they unto him, What shall we do unto thee, that this sea may be calm unto us? For the sea wrought, and was tempestuous.

12- And he said unto them, Take me up, and cast me forth into the sea; so shall the sea be calm unto you: for I know that for my sake this great tempest *is* upon you.

13- Nevertheless the men rowed hard to bring *it* to the land: but they could not: for the sea wrought, and was tempestuous against them.

14- Wherefore they cried unto the LORD, and said, We beseech thee, O LORD, we beseech thee, let us not perish for this man's life, and lay not upon us innocent blood: for thou, O LORD, hast done as it pleased thee.

-Jonah 1 v 11-14

It must have been quite the 'tempest' for these pagans that had once prayed to 'their gods' to turn to Jonah's God, the LORD. They tried to spare Jonah's life. They did what they could to 'lighten' the ship and to row to shore. But they were at the mercy of God, for as yet they still were afloat.

15- So they took of Jo'nah, and cast him forth into the sea: and the sea ceased from her raging.

16- **Then the men feared the LORD** exceedingly, and offered a sacrifice unto the LORD, and made vows.

-Jonah 1 v 15, 16

Because these men were Gentiles and not Jews 'under the law', what kind of a sacrifice could it have been? There was not an alter on the ship. A Jewish alter was made of 'whole stones of the earth'*. How many non-Jews would sail with such a thing (a Jewish alter) on board their ship? But for them could the sacrifice have been Jonah himself when they cast him overboard? The sea became immediately calm when Jonah hit the water.

*-Exodus 20 v 24, 25

17- Now the LORD had prepared a **great fish** to swallow up Jo'nah. **And Jo'nah was in the belly of the fish three days and three nights.**

-Jonah 1 v 17

1- Then Jo'nah prayed unto the LORD his God out of the fish's belly,
2- And said, I cried by reason of mine affliction unto the LORD, and he heard me; out of the belly of hell cried I, *and* thou heardest my voice.

-Jonah 2 v 1, 2

Jonah prays to the LORD from inside of the fishes belly. Scoffers say that to live in a fishes belly for three days is not possible. Again, they do not believe God. Jesus Christ himself endorses the story of Jonah.

Jesus Christ said during his earthly ministry:
38- Then certain of the scribes and of the Phar'I-sees answered, saying, Master, we would see a sign from thee.
39- But he *(Jesus)* answered and said unto them, An evil and adulterous generation seeketh after a sign; and there shall no sign be given to it, but the sign of the prophet Jo'nas *(Jonah)*:
40- For as Jo'nas *(Jonah)* was three days and three nights in the whale's belly; so shall the Son of man be three days and three nights in the **heart of the earth.**

41- The men of Nin'e-veh shall rise in judgment with this generation, and shall condemn it: because they repented at the preaching of Jo'nas *(Jonah)*; and, behold, a greater than Jo'nas *(Jonah)* is here.
-Matthew 12 v 38-41

Was Jonah dead? Matthew 12 v 40 says Jonah went to 'the heart of the earth'. 'The heart of the earth' is Sheol, Hades, Hell. Did Jonah die in the whales belly? Perhaps he did. Where was he going? He was swallowed whole. He was gone. He gave his visions of the hell he was in.

Jesus Christ died in the flesh but his body did not deteriorate and see corruption. Did Jonah too die in the flesh yet his body also did not deteriorate? Jonah's eternal soul and spirit did not die for those three days. He was able to pray to the LORD to spare him, "from out of the belly of hell prayed I".

Those that deny the 'Word of God' have been given a 'reprobate mind'* and are unable to understand being 'an unbeliever'. With no faith or even the smallest inkling of understanding God, this leaves them to stay in that worldly mind of death. Sin is death. Sin = Death. The 'unbeliever' themselves are in the 'fishes belly'. *-Romans 1 v 28; -II Corinthians 13 v 5; -II Timothy 3 v 8; -Titus 1 v 16

28- And even as they did not like to retain God in *their* knowledge, **God gave them over to a reprobate mind**, to do those things which are not convenient;
-Romans 1 v 28

Scripture says that God will have mercy on whom he chooses and will 'harden' the unbeliever even more against him*. Every person has been given a free will. Without ever coming and acknowledging the 'Living God of Creation' the 'spirit of unbelief' will continue to grow. *-Exodus 4 v 21; -Exodus 5 v 23; -Exodus 7 v 13; many more concerning Pharaoh

15- For he *(God)* saith to Mo'ses, I will have mercy on whom I will have mercy, and I will have compassion on whom I will have compassion.
16- So then *it is* not of him that willeth, nor of him that runneth, but of God that sheweth mercy.

17- For the scripture saith unto Pha'roah, Even for this same purpose have I raised thee up, that I might shew my power in thee, and that my name might be declared throughout all the earth.

18- **Therefore hath he mercy on whom he will *have mercy*, and whom he will he hardeneth.**

19- Thou wilt say then unto me, Why doth he yet find fault? For who hath resisted his will?

-Romans 9 v 15-19

The 'carnal mind' of **the 'unbeliever' is an enemy of God**. The unbeliever has not his 'Holy Spirit' and is unrecognizable to the 'One God who created all things'. God does not see us as men and women but he see's his own spirit within us because of our faith and belief in what God has written and done. God imputes in us the 'Spirit of Righteousness'* when we believe 'the Gospel'. What Gospel? *-Romans 4

5- For they that are after the flesh do mind the things of the flesh; but they that are after the Spirit the things of the Spirit.

6- For to be carnally minded *is* death; but to be spiritually minded *is* life and peace.

7- **Because the carnal mind *is* enmity *(an enemy)* against God:** for it is not subject to the law of God, neither indeed can be.

8- So then they that are in the flesh cannot please God.

9- But ye are not in the flesh, but in the Spirit, if so be that the Spirit of God dwell in you. Now **if any man have not the Spirit of Christ, he is none of his.**

…..

16- **The Spirit itself beareth witness with our spirit, that we are the children of God:**

17- **And if children, then heirs; heirs of God, and joint-heirs with Christ;** if so be that we suffer with *him*, that we may be also glorified together.

-Romans 8 v 5-9, 16, 17

The saying goes that there are no unbelievers in the fox hole when bombs are dropping all around them. People think that with their dying breath they can call out to God and then be saved. In order for God to hear, that person must have believed that 'he is'. Does the unbeliever diligently seek after God? Why would they? These have no faith.

This is one of the 'Absolutes' of God's Word:

6- But without faith *it is* impossible to please *him*: **for he that cometh to God must believe that he is,** and *that* he is a rewarder of them that diligently seek him.

-Hebrews 11 v 6

On the doorstep of death is hardly the place to come to God. The persons whole life was spent in unbelief and more than likely spoke out against the 'Living God of Creation'. Who heard their words of unbelief? Did they influence any person with their blasphemy?

Have they ever repented to God for forgiveness and for their sinful lives before dodging bullets? Why would the unbeliever ever repent without faith? Out of fear of being blown to smithereens they are now desperate for their very lives. Do they now **believe in** God? How can they **believe God** of whom they never knew?

In this world that we live in tragedies happen. Some very catastrophic and widespread, leaving many helpless innocent people to die. Earthquakes, typhoons and tornadoes seem to happen unmercifully. Mass shootings and the murdering of the innocent is a daily occurrence.

Throughout history 'in the name of god' many have died by these 'religious zealots'. In the name and a 'supposed duty' given from god to them, they themselves have horribly tortured, slaughtered and murdered. Today, the offspring and nations that came from Ishmael give their god the credit when they kill in his name.

In many ways the atheist have it correct. Because of 'man made religions', millions have died in the name of god. These religions of men were never in the Body of Christ, the true Church. They may claim to be in the Body, but what kind of history has this denomination blazed on mankind? No one in 'the Body of Christ' (God knows) has killed, tortured and murdered in the name of our God. The Body of Christ is not an organized religion.

The world says, "if there was a god he would not have let the tragedies happen". They say there is no God then. The unbeliever is quick to say that there is no God yet will blame God for the misfortunes in the world. They are blaming god alright, but it is their god of this world, Satan.

They say, "How can god let this happen?" After the tragedies, do they now believe in God because they blame him? How can they believe in God of whom they never knew? These may have a belief from a logical stand point that something has created life and the universe, it must be God. These may believe in 'a god' but do they believe God? His words are written in our Bible.

In the Body of Christ, we know that 'our fleshly body temple' is not permanent. We know that our soul and the God imputed Spirit will never die. We don't fear death in having no hope. Of course we do what we can to live on this earth and stay alive. We are to be 'ambassadors for Christ' while we are here*. If a tragedy kills us we would not blame God but the god of sin, Satan. Or we thank Satan for hurrying up our meeting with the God of Glory. *-II Corinthians 5 v 20; -Ephesians 6 v 20

Jonah was not such an unbeliever in doubting if there is a God. He believed the LORD GOD of Heaven. He had a moment of uncertainty and weakness. Jonah was conflicted with his upbringing in Judaism to now have the LORD God himself say for him to go to a Gentile city. He was a devout 'Jew of the Circumcision' under the Law of Moses'. Many a sermon has been given on the 'testing of a persons faith'. How does the 'professing Christian' respond to adversity?

Jonah prays to the LORD out of the belly of hell:
1- Then Jo'nah prayed unto the LORD his God out of the fish's belly,
2- And said, I cried by reason of mine affliction unto the LORD, and he heard me; out of the belly of hell cried I, and thou heardest my voice.
3- For thou hast cast me into the deep, in the midst of the seas; and the floods compassed me about: all thy billows and thy waves passed over me.
4- Then I said, I am cast out of thy sight; yet I will look again toward thy holy temple.
5- The waters compassed me about, *even* to the soul: the depth closed me round about, the weeds were wrapped about my head.
6- I went down to the bottom of the mountains; the earth with her bars *was* about me for ever: <u>yet hast thou brought up my life from **corruption**</u>, O LORD my God.
7- When my soul fainted within me I remembered the LORD: and my prayer came in unto thee, into thine holy temple.
8- They that observed lying vanities forsake their own mercy.
9- But I will sacrifice unto thee with the voice of thanksgiving; I will pay *that* that I have vowed. Salvation is of the LORD.
10- And the LORD spake unto the fish, and it vomited out Jo'nah upon the dry *land.*
-Jonah 2 v 1-10

Did God understand Jonah's rebellion? It was ingrained in the Jews since the beginning that 'the Circumcision/Law' was to have nothing to do with the Gentiles (Luke?):

1- And the word of the LORD came unto Jo'nah the second time, saying,

2- Arise, go unto Nin'e-veh, that great city, and preach unto it the preaching that I bid thee.

3- So Jo'nah arose, and went to Nin'e-veh, according to the word of the LORD. Now Nin'e-veh was an exceeding great city of three days' journey*.

4- And Jo'nah began to enter into the city a day's journey*, and he cried, and said, Yet forty days, and Nin'e-veh shall be overthrown. *(*-Nineveh was 'exceeding' in that it was 'a three days journey away by foot', not that the city was three days wide in size. Was Jonah taken on 'Eagles Wings'? -Exodus 19 v 4: -Acts 8 v 39)*

5- So the people of **Nin'e-veh believed God**, and proclaimed a fast, and put on sackcloth, from the greatest of them even to the least of them.

6- For the word came unto the king of Nin'e-veh, and he arose from his throne, and he laid his robe from him, and covered *him* with sackcloth, and sat in ashes.

7- And he caused *it* to be proclaimed and published through Nin'e-veh by the decree of the king and his nobles, saying, Let neither man nor beast, herd nor flock, taste any thing: let them not feed, nor drink water:

8- But let man and beast be covered with sackcloth, and cry mightily unto God: yea, let them turn every one from his evil way, and from the violence that *is* in their hands.

9- Who can tell *if* God will turn and repent, and turn away from his fierce anger, that we perish not?

10- And God saw their works, that they turned from their evil way; and God repented of the evil, that he had said that he would do unto them; and he did *it* not.

-Jonah 3 v 4-10

What then was Nineveh's religion? Like it is for the Body of Christ, we are not a religion nor a denomination. We believe God.

God saw something about Nineveh by which he personally wanted to get involved. They had no direction and "could not discern the right hand or the left"*. But maybe their conscience was telling them that what they were doing was against good decency and human nature. Maybe they just needed a little waking up to recognize that there is a Living God that created all things. *-Jonah 4 v 11

Jonah still doubts himself. Jonah tries to give reason to the God that knows all things. Jonah was a good Jew. He grew up his whole life believing scripture and the Mosaic Laws of Judaism. God was personally talking to Jonah. He must have been a good Jew.

1- But it displeased Jo'nah exceedingly, and he was very angry.
2- And he prayed unto the LORD, and said, I pray thee, O Lord, *was* not this my saying, when I was yet in my country? Therefore I fled before unto Tar'shish: for I knew that thou *art* a gracious God, and merciful, slow to anger, and of great kindness, and repentest thee of the evil.
3- Therefore now, O LORD, take, I beseech thee, my life from me; for *it is* better for me to die than to live.
-Jonah 4 v 1-3

Jonah was so steadfast and devout in his anti-Gentile beliefs that even after preaching to Nin'e-veh he wished to die. God points out his sovereignty. God can do what God wants to do:
4- Then said the LORD, Doest thou well to be angry?
5- So Jo'nah went out of the city, and sat on the east side of the city, and there made him a booth, and sat under it in the shadow, till he might see what would become of the city.
6- And the LORD God prepared a gourd, and made *it* come up over Jo'nah, that it might be a shadow over his head, to deliver him from his grief. So Jo'nah was exceeding glad of the gourd.
7- **But** God prepared a worm when the morning rose the next day, and it smote the gourd that it withered.
-Jonah 4 v 4-7

Jonah shows his attitude for how devout a 'Jew of the Circumcision/Law' he is:
8- And it came to pass, when the sun did rise, that God prepared a vehement east wind; and the sun beat upon the head of Jo'nah, that he fainted, and wished in himself to die, and said, *It is* better for me to die than to live.
9- And God said to Jo'nah, Doest thou well to be angry for the gourd? And he said, I do well to be angry, *even* unto death.

10- Then said the LORD, Thou hast had pity on the gourd, for the which thou hast not labored, neither madest it grow; which came up in a night, and perished in a night:

11- And should not I spare Nin'e-veh, that great city, wherein are more than sixscore thousand persons that cannot discern between their right hand and their left hand; and *also* much cattle?

-Jonah 4 v 8-11

So what was Jonah's problem? What controversy did he have? Why was he so angry and displeased?

When God told Jonah to go to Nineveh, a heathen Gentile city, Jonah became perplexed. This flew in the face of his core beliefs. God going to the Gentiles? This was unheard of!

There were few Gentiles in all of the Old Testament whom God used. These individuals could more or less be counted on one hand. These being Rahab of Jericho, Ruth the Moabitus, Naaman the Syrian, Cyrus and Darius kings of the Medes and of Persia, and these citizens of Nineveh.

Nebuchadnezzar, the king of Babylon, also was used to an extent in that he acknowledged 'the most high God', unlike the Pharaoh of Egypt. He came to fully understand that it was because of 'the Most High God' (not JEHOVAH but the same) that he was a mighty king. God used Nebuchadnezzar to be the first great Gentile empire to destroy Jerusalem and Israel.

For the most part when Gentiles were evident in the Old Testament, they were those who came and persecuted Israel and the Jews. These Gentiles were not part of God's 'covenant people'. God used Gentile nations to punish Israel for their unbelief. The Gentile city of Nineveh shows that God is sovereign. He can do as he chooses.

God's plan for the Gentiles as written, was that the Jews would bring to them 'the Light' in the knowledge of their LORD God JEHOVAH. This was to be done through the Jew/Hebrews when the 'Heavenly Kingdom' is established. Only Israel and the 'Jews of the Circumcision/Law' had knowledge of the 'Living God'*. *-Ephesians 2 v 11-13; -Romans 3 v 1, 2

Jonah was determined not to go against what he believed and knew his whole lifetime. Even so much as to stand fast in the scriptures rather than take a new directive, even a directive given by the LORD God himself. Jonah tried to flee from the face of God. He was getting a strong mixed message and would rather have died. Jonah would rather 'walk the plank' than go to a Gentile city. How many times did you count of Jonah wanting to die?

Jonah, after leaving Nineveh, sat on a hill to observe the destruction that was foretold would come. He must have thought that Nineveh wasn't going to repent and that God was not going to have mercy on them. After all, they were Gentiles.

But God saw Nineveh and knew that this city was ready for the truth of the creator God, they repented. They saw the truth behind Jonah's message. They, Nineveh, believed God's Word. They didn't just 'believe in God' but 'Believed God'. They were saved by 'faith without works of the law'. These Gentiles did not suddenly become Jews and now were keeping the 'Law of Moses'. They didn't become Proselytes.

But Jonah sat and watched. He thought he was going to get quite the spectacle. Perhaps he would witness total destruction and annihilation like that of Sodom and Gomorrah. But it didn't happen. Jonah was disappointed. This was not a city of Jews but a city of 'dirty, heathen, Gentiles'. Jonah's lifelong view was 'the LORD God of Israel' and not also 'the LORD God of the Gentiles'.

In the meantime, God prepared a gourd to grow up over him to give some shade from the sun. Jonah, perhaps thought that this was because he had done what God told him to do. The gourd was a God given reward for his 'righteous work'? But in his attitude, he was expecting Nineveh to be destroyed. So the next day God prepared a vehement wind and made it ultra hot. The gourd died, and took away Jonah's shade.

The heat of the day became so unbearable to Jonah that he wished for himself to die, again? It must have been hot. He became more upset with the gourd dying and taking away his shade then he was for Nineveh to have been destroyed which had 120,000 plus people and the cattle. He was more upset over the gourd dying than if Nineveh had been annihilated. All them Gentiles dieing was better to Jonah than the gourd dieing that took his shade away.

Nineveh was given a chance. They saw it, and took it. They believed that there was a God in control and that he had been displeased with their way of life. God spared them. Nineveh repented. Nineveh 'Believed God'.

Jesus' vast amounts of miracles, signs and wonders should have validated who he was. No man in the flesh could calm nature, walk on water, heal the lame and the sick. Jesus Christ is 'God Incarnate'. 'The

Word' (JEHOVAH/LORD) was made flesh. He came by miracles, signs and wonders proving who he is. And still, after his three year earthly ministry, the nation didn't believe in 'The Name of Jesus the Christ'.

25- And there are also many other things which Jesus did, the which, if they should be written every one, I suppose that even the world itself could not contain the books that should be written. A-men'.
-John 21 v 25

10- **He *(Jesus)* was in the world, <u>and the world was made by him</u>,** and the world knew him not.
11- He *(Jesus)* came unto his own, and his own received him not.
-John 1 v 10, 11

Who were 'his own'? Who was it that Jesus came to and for? He didn't come to fulfill the covenant promises made to the Gentiles. There were none. He came to fulfill the 'Gospel of the Kingdom' that was to and only for the Jews of 'Ye men of Israel'.

Jesus said:
17- Think not that I am come to destroy the law, or the prophets: I am not come to destroy, but to fulfil.
-Matthew 5 v 17

The second time Israel will accept Jesus. He will come at the end of 'the tribulation'. They will see his hands and his feet and they will know and believe*. The 'Word made flesh' has returned to set up his 'Kingdom of Heaven'. *-Zechariah 12 v 9, 10; -Zechariah 13 v 6-9

Most of Israel today (those not in 'the Body of Christ') still don't believe that their Messiah and King already came. They rejected God by rejecting Jesus Christ and have paid severely for it. After all those miracles made by Jesus Christ during his earthly ministry, most of Israel refused to believe. They still do.

At the end of the Tribulation they will see Christ's hands and feet and 'the evidence that it was he who was crucified'*. During the Tribulation, 'the escaping remnant of Israel' will still be in unbelief, but God will protect these Jews+. *-Zechariah 12 v 10; +-Revelation 12 v 6, 14

12- Many bulls have compassed me: strong *bulls* of Ba'shan have beset me round.

13- They gaped upon me *with* their mouths, *as* a ravening and a roaring lion.

14- I am poured out like water, and all my bones are out of joint: my heart is like wax; it is melted in the midst of my bowels.

15- My strength is dried up like a potsherd; and my tongue cleaveth to my jaws; and thou hast brought me into the dust of death.

16- For dogs have compassed me: the assembly of the wicked have enclosed me: **they pierced my hands and my feet.**

17- I may tell all my bones: they look and stare upon me.

18- They part my garments among them, and **cast lots upon my vesture.**
-Psalm 22 v 12-18

8- In that day shall the LORD defend the inhabitants of Je-ru'sa-lem; and he that is feeble among them at that day shall be as Da'vid; and the house of Da'vid *shall be* as God, as the angel of the LORD before them.

9- And it shall come to pass in that day, *that* I will seek to destroy all the nations that come against Je-ru'sa-lem.

10- And I will pour upon the house of Da'vid, and upon the inhabitants of Je-ru'sa-lem, the spirit of grace and supplications: and **they shall look upon me whom they have pierced**, and they shall mourn for him, as one mourneth for *his* only son, and shall be in bitterness for him, as one that is in bitterness for *his* firstborn.
-Zechariah 12 v 8-10

33- But when they came to Je'sus, and saw that he was dead already, they brake not his legs:

34- But one of the soldiers with a spear pierced his side, and forthwith came there out blood and water.

35- And he that saw *it* bare record, and his record is true: and he knoweth that he saith true, that ye might believe.

36- For these things were done, that the scripture should be fulfilled, **A bone of him was not broken**.

37- And again another scripture saith, **They shall look on him whom they pierced**.
-John 19 v 33-37

24- But Thom'as, one of the twelve, called Did'y-mus, was not with them when Je'sus came.

25- The other disciples therefore said unto him, We have seen the Lord. But he said unto them, Except I shall see in his hands the print of the nails, and put my finger into the print of the nails, and thrust my hand into his side, I will not believe.

26- And after eight days again his disciples were within, and Thom'as with them: *then* came Je'sus, the doors being shut, and stood in the midst, and said, Peace *be* unto you.

27- Then saith he to Thom'as, Reach hither thy finger, and behold my hands; and reach hither thy hand, and thrust *it* into my side: and be not faithless, but believing.

28- And Thom'as answered and said unto him, My Lord and my God.

29- Je'sus saith unto him, Thom'as, because thou hast seen me, thou hast believed: **blessed *are* they that have not seen, and *yet* have believed**.

-John 20 v 24-29

7- Behold, he cometh with clouds; and every eye shall see him, and they *also* which pierced him: and all kindreds of the earth shall wail because of him. Even so, A-men.

-Revelation 1 v 7

The Jewish State and Nation today is hardly what was promised to them. Israel today is a poor representative of the descriptions of 'the Kingdom of Heaven' that God promised. Israel today is the size of New Hampshire*. *-Genesis 15 v 18

The House of Cornelius – 8 Years after Pentecost

1- What advantage then hath the Jew? Or what profit *is there* of circumcision?

2- Much every way: chiefly, because that **unto them were committed the oracles of God.** -Romans 3 v 1, 2

15- Study to show thyself approved unto God, a workman that needeth not to be ashamed, rightly dividing the word of truth.

-II Timothy 2 v 15

4- For whatsoever things were written aforetime were written for our learning, that we through patience and comfort of the scriptures might have hope.
-Romans 15 v 4

20- Knowing this first, that no prophecy of the scripture is of any private interpretation.
21- For the prophecy came not in old time by the will of man: but holy men of God's spake *as they were* moved by the Holy Ghost.
-II Peter 1 v 20, 21

Another example of 'rightly dividing the word of truth' is the account of Peter going to the 'House of Cornelius'. Many use this story in Acts 10 and say, "See, Peter was taking the Gospel to the non-Jew". But this happened eight years after Pentecost. Why the delay? I thought 'the Twelve' had been evangelizing the world? That's what most of Christendom has been saying.

Like Jonah, Peter was a good 'Jew under the Law'. 'The House of Cornelius' experience show's how 'under the Law' Peter is by his very own words that he spake. The fact still remains that Jesus Christ never said to stop keeping 'the Law of Moses'. Jesus himself endorsed 'the Law' and was the perfect 'Jew of the Circumcision'. He came not to destroy 'the Law' and the prophets but to fulfill*. *-Matthew 5 v 17

The Book of Acts is a 'book of transition'. God is setting up a ministry, a dispensation/prescription for the Gentiles without the Jew. A change in the 'prophetic program' that has been all Jewish from Abraham till this time. The Jew's LORD God JEHOVAH was also going to be the same God (the Most High God) to the heathen Gentiles. This was unheard of!

1- There was a certain man in Caes-a-re'a called Cor-ne'lius, a centurion of the band called the I-tal'ian *band*,
2- A devout *man*, and one that feared God with all his house, which gave much alms to the people, and prayed to God alway.
-Acts 10 v 1, 2

Cornelius was a good man with a compassionate heart that gave money (alms) to the people. This 'cheerful giver' was seeking God, always praying scripture says. God knew that this man would be an example to the world.

Cornelius was a Gentile. He had no formal religion or doctrine he was following. 'Catholicism' appeared 100's of years later. He was a 'pagan' man that knew no better. He began to worship the man Peter as soon as Peter had come to him. Peter stopped him from doing so.

His household would receive the Holy Spirit not in the order of Acts 2 v 38, to repent, and be baptized and ye shall receive the Holy Ghost, but by faith in the words that were spoken by Peter. Without doing any 'righteous works' under 'the Law' and the 'service practices of Judaism', these Gentiles were given the 'Holy Spirit' of God. Cornelius and his household went from 'believing in God' (a god?) to 'believing God'. Their searching and seeking for the 'True Light' was revealed to them through the Apostle Peter.

3- He *(Cornelius)* saw a vision evidently about the ninth hour *(3 pm)* of the day an angel of God coming in to him, and saying unto him, Cor-ne'lius.
4- And when he looked on him, he was afraid, and said, What is it, Lord? And he said unto him, Thy prayers and thine alms are come up for a memorial before God.
-Acts 10 v 3, 4

A believer without a formal religion was seeking God, and God found him. Or is it the other way around? Good timing, after 'the seed was planted and died'*. The gentiles are now in the position to be 'saved by grace/faith' and not by 'the Law of the Jews'. *-John 12 v 24

Jesus spoke of his death, burial and resurrection:
24- Verily, verily, I say unto you, Except a corn of wheat fall into the ground and die, it abideth alone: but if it die, it bringeth forth much fruit.
-John 12 v 24

Cornelius gets instructions from the ascended Lord in Glory:
5- And now send men to Jop'pa, and call for *one* Si'mon, whose surname is Pe'ter:
6- He *(Peter)* lodgeth with one Si'mon a tanner, whose house is by the sea side: he shall tell thee what thou oughtest to do.
-Acts 10 v 5, 6

Cornelius sends trustworthy servants to seek out the Apostle Peter. If they were to find this man Peter, his belief would become more steadfast. How could it not? The name of Peter and where to find him was told to him by 'an angel of God'. This knowledge was 'divinely given' and not by any man.

7- And when the angel which spake unto Cor-ne'li-us was departed, he called two of his household servants, and a devout soldier of them that waited on him continually;
8- And when he had declared all *these* things unto them, he sent them to Jop'pa.
-Acts 10 v 7, 8

While the men sent by Cornelius were en-route seeking for Peter in Joppa, Peter too gets a vision and receives a divine instruction:
9- On the morrow, as they went on their journey, and drew nigh unto the city, Pe'ter went up upon the housetop to pray about the sixth hour *(noon)*:
10- And he became very hungry, and would have eaten: but while they made ready, he fell into a trance,
11- And saw heaven opened, and a certain vessel descending unto him, as it had been a great sheet knit at the four corners, and let down to the earth:
12- Wherein were all manner of four footed beasts of the earth, and wild beasts, and creeping things, and fowls of the air.
13- And there came a voice to him, Rise, Pe'ter; kill, and eat.
14- **But Pe'ter said, Not so, Lord; for I have never eaten any thing that is common or unclean.**
-Acts 10 v 9-14

Peter flat-out says that he only ate things which were 'lawful' to eat in the 'Mosaic Law'*. Peter was a law keeping Jew still. He was still following the 'services and practices' of 'The Law' and Judaism. So obviously, at this point, Peter was not preaching the message that Paul was going to be preaching "you are not under law but under grace". *-Leviticus 5 v 2; -Leviticus 11

15- And the voice *spake* unto him again the second time, What God hath cleansed, *that* call not thou common.
16- **This was done thrice:** and the vessel was received up again into heaven.
-Acts 10 v 15, 16

Something was happening. Jews, even the most devout followers of Judaism, that being Peter, was told directly by God 'that things that had been lawful/unlawful' was now being done away with. This 'vision of the unclean beasts' that Peter saw was told by God that it was now okay for him to eat. Three times did God give Peter this vision. God definitely wanted Peter's attention.

Peter, like Jonah, doubts himself. This vision of the 'common and unclean beasts' now being okay to eat by God himself was not what he knew his whole life 'under the law':

17- Now while **Pe'ter doubted in himself** what this vision which he had seen should mean, behold, the men which were sent from Cor-ne'li-us had made enquiry for Si'mons house, and stood before the gate,

18- And called, and asked whether Si'mon, which was surnamed Pe'ter, were lodged there.

-Acts 10 v 17, 18

Remember that it was Cornelius that had spoke with the angel of God, not these men. These men were following what their beloved master had told them to do. More or less they were on a 'blind mission' seeking for a man that goes by the name of Peter.

19- While Pe'ter thought on the vision, **the Spirit** said unto him, Behold, three men seek thee.

20- Arise therefore, and get thee down, and go with them, doubting nothing: for I have sent them.

-Acts 10 v 19, 20

Peter, as no scripture shows, was not a friend of Gentiles. Had not God sent the visions and told him to go with these strangers and to doubt nothing, Peter being a devout Jew on his own would have ignored them. Wouldn't he? Of course, none of us were there, but what has the scriptures been saying or has not been saying?

Put yourself in Peter's shoes. A group of Gentiles asking for Peter at lunch time is beyond measure! How dare they interrupt Peter's lunch. These strangers/Heathens/Gentiles where asking for Peter to take a journey with them. "Come with us Peter. Come to the home of a Roman Centurion, of whom you never met". What, are you crazy!?

Peter had not been ministering to Gentiles. Its what the Bible 'does not say' yet so many are quick to defend Peter in a 'falsehood' than to believe Paul 'in truth'. Peter was given a 'strong encouragement' by God himself that he was to go with these three men and 'to doubt nothing'. A total different directive than what Jesus had told Peter in the flesh.

5- These twelve **Je'sus** sent forth, and **commanded them**, saying, **Go not into the way of the Gen'tiles, and into** *any* **city of the Sa-mar'i-tans enter ye not:**
6- **But go rather to the lost sheep of the house of Is'ra-el.**
7- And as ye go, **preach** saying, **The kingdom of heaven is at hand**.
-Matthew 10 v 5-7

Luke continues writing by the Holy Spirit:
21- Then Pe'ter went down to the men which were sent unto him from Cor-ne'li-us; and said, I am he whom ye seek: what *is* the cause wherefore ye are come?
22- And they said, Cor-ne'li-us the centurion, a just man, and one that feareth God, and of good report among all the nation of the Jews, was warned from God by an holy angel to send for thee into his house, and to hear words of thee.
-Acts 10 v 21, 22

Peter journeys with these men back to 'the House of Cornelius':
25- And as Pe'ter was coming in, Cor-ne'li-us met him, and fell down at his feet, and worshipped *him*.
26- But Pe'ter took him up, saying, Stand up; I myself also am a man.
27- And as he talked with him, he went in, and found many that were come together.
-Acts 10 v 25-27

So obviously Cornelius was an 'idolator', a 'pagan' man. He was not under the tutelage of any formal religious doctrine. The heathen world was not given the 'Oracles of God'. But this man knew in his heart that there is a 'Living God of Heaven'. He is a rare exception to acknowledge this given his Gentile background.

A lesson for us today. God is ready to respond to anyone that seeks him*. And he will and does. I daily pray that you do. God's words are given to us in our Bible. Except for a few 'mistranslated words', the Bible (KJV) has always been 100% correct. The KJV is the closest to the foundation of truth that there is for all of mankind. *-Romans 10 v 13; -Revelation 22 v 17

Beware of the newer translated Bibles. There is an attempt to combine the 'Circumcision' ('Apostles Doctrine') with the 'Doctrine of the Gentiles' ('uncircumcision') that was only given to the Apostle Paul. Law and Grace never will mix as these newer Bibles try to do. "It's all the same, there is no difference between Peter and Paul", they say. Paul said it best, "if our Gospel be hid it is hid to them that are lost".

Man has tried to disprove this God given Word of his for 1,000's of years. The way it has been done is by men and 'their own interpretations'. The newer Bibles and by 'Religions and Denominations' can be the 'principalities of darkness in high places'*. The 'Word of God' was given to mankind to be easily understood. Who confused the masses? The god of this world has+.

*-Ephesians 6 v 12; -II Corinthians 11 v 13, 14; -Ephesians 4 v 17-19; +-II Corinthians 4 v 2-4

Cornelius was given 'a divine vision' and acted on it. He sent men to Joppa, and found that there was such a man named Peter. This message and vision had been given by God (an angel of God). He thought he was right in worshiping Peter when he saw that God was speaking the truth. So ask yourself, had this happened to you would you have done the same thing?

28- And he *(Peter)* said unto them, **Ye know how that it is an unlawful thing for a man that is a Jew to keep company, or come unto one of another nation**; but God hath showed me that I should not call any man common or unclean.

-Acts 10 v 28

Peter undoubtedly gives the knowledge of himself that he was still 'a Law keeping Jew'. He had no Gentile friends. He said, **"that it is an unlawful thing for a man that is a Jew to keep company, or come unto one of another nation"**. Peter is still keeping his distance from the common man like it always has been since Moses and the giving of 'the Law'.

'A change in dispensation' from what 'has been' is now happening. Had the words and the vision not been given by God himself, Peter would not have sought out Cornelius on his own. **'What you have been is what you are'.** Peter was instructed to go to the 'Gentile House of Cornelius' by a strong 'God given directive'.

There is no scriptural record of Peter traveling the world preaching to the non-Jews. No scripture ever says that Peter took the Gospel to the 'utter most parts of the earth'. Most of Christendom have believed in this falsehood. Scripture says that they 'were supposed to', but 'this don't mean that they did'. There was no 'Earthly Kingdom of Heaven' with Jesus Christ sitting on the throne of David to bring the Gentiles to.

Christendom has a desire and false belief that it was Peter and 'the Twelve' that took the Gospel to the world. Somehow they combined 'Paul's Gospel with their own', or parts of it. These have 'mixed the Gospels' and preach an 'elusive truth'. Peter was an Apostle of the 'Gospel of the Circumcision', Paul was the first Apostle of 'the Gospel of the Uncircumcision'*. *-Galatians 2

It is just as important to know 'what was said' and 'what was not said' by the Word of God. One of the easiest ways to recognize this is to know that Peter is not Paul and Paul is not Peter. Their Gospels are not the same.

Back to Acts 10:
34- Then Pe'ter opened *his* mouth, and said, Of a truth I perceive that God is no respecter of persons:
-Acts 10 v 34

Why would Peter say such a thing? Gentiles were not given the covenant promises made to Israel. The 'Jews of the Circumcision/Law' were to be separate and not to commune with the non-Jew. This was ingrained in Jewish beliefs since Moses and the giving of 'the Law'. Besides, Jesus Christ himself told his disciples not to go into the areas of 'the Gentiles to preach their Gospel'*.
*-Matthew 10 v 5-7

But here, Peter is shown by God that a change in 'dispensation' was happening. This experience (perhaps a bigger reason) was for Peter to see 'the grace of God' being poured out on the Gentiles so he would remember and could speak up for Paul at the 'Jerusalem Council'. Twelve years later was 'the Jerusalem Council' and still Peter wasn't evangelizing the Gentiles.

Peter speaks more evidence of him being a 'law keeper':
35- But in every nation he that feareth him, **and worketh righteousness,** is accepted with him.
-Acts 10 v 35

'Worketh Righteousness'. 'Righteous Works'. Peter was a 'Law keeping Jew'. It was the Apostle Paul that said 'you are not under law but under grace', not Peter. 'Righteous Works' to prove your faith was done away with at the cross*. *-Colossians 2 v 13, 14; -Romans 4 v 3-6, 19-25; -Romans 10 v 2-4; -Galatians 2 v 16-21; -Paul writes of many more in his Epistles

11- In whom also ye are circumcised with the circumcision made without hands, in putting off the body of the sins of the flesh by the circumcision of Christ:
12- Buried with him in baptism, wherein also ye are risen with *him* through the faith of the operation of God, who hath raised him from the dead *(Paul's Gospel)*.
13- And you, being dead in your sins and the uncircumcision of your flesh, hath he quickened together with him, **having forgiven you all trespasses;**
14- Blotting out the handwriting of ordinances that was against us, which was contrary to us, and took it out of the way, **nailing it to his cross;**
15- *And* having spoiled principalities and powers, he made a shew of them openly, triumphing over them in it.
-Colossians 2 v 11-15

But as yet, 'the elect' were still under the 'Gospel of the Kingdom Doctrine', 'the Apostles Doctrine', and were not told by Jesus/God that they were now to follow the 'Apostle of the Gentiles'. Paul had not written anything as of yet. They were still 'Jews of the Circumcision/Law' and hoping and expecting the return of Christ with the 'Kingdom of Heaven'.

Peter continues Holy Spirit inspired:
36- The word which *God* sent unto the children of Is'ra-el, preaching peace by Je'sus Christ: (he is Lord of all:)
37- That word, *I say,* ye know, which was published throughout all Ju-de'a, and begin from Gal'i-lee, after the baptism which John preached;
-Acts 10 v 36, 37

The baptism that John preached was all Jewish. Peter says in verse 36 that God sent Jesus (the Word made flesh) to the 'Children of Israel'. Gentiles were not being baptized by 'John the Baptist'. Only Jews were being 'water baptized' and it was by their 'water baptism' that they were promised the Holy Ghost. A 'righteous work' that they had faith in and believed. It was their present dispensation/prescription.

The Jews were being 'baptized with water' into the Holy Spirit. In this 'Age of Grace', we are baptized by the Holy Spirit (Holy Ghost) into Christ, the 'Body of Christ' (the True Church), without water and without 'works of righteousness'. This is all done when one wholeheartedly believes 'the faith-way Gospel' of I Corinthians 15 v 1-4. Seem simple*? Well, it is. It is 'Religions and Denominations' made by men that have added 'righteous works' to the 'faith-way doctrine of Grace'.

*-Romans 10 v 1-13; -Galatians 3

Peter continues at the Household of Cornelius:
38- How God anointed Je'sus of Naz'a-reth with the Ho'ly Ghost and with power: who went about doing good, and healing all that were oppressed of the devil; for God was with him.
39- And we were witnesses of all things which he did both **in the land of the Jews, and in Je-ru'sa-lem**; whom they slew and hanged on a tree:
-Acts 10 v 38, 39

Peter points out that Jesus stayed in the 'land of the Jews' which is Israel and Jerusalem. Some in Christendom say he ministered to the world. Here, Peter says the truth by which 'man made Religions and Denominations' have falsely been saying contrary to the 'Word of God'. "And we were witnesses of all things which he did both **in the land of the Jews, and in Je-ru'sa-lem;"** -Acts 10 v 39

May God have mercy on those that teach and preach from their own 'supposed head knowledge'. Christendom then says that Jesus did this (sent the Gospel into the world) by the 'Holy Scriptures' of our Bible. Jesus Christ was a minister for the Jews and for Israel*. His earthly ministry was for our knowledge that we may have hope+. 'Biblical Hope' is not 'a wish' but a 'sure thing'.

*-Galatians 4 v 4, 5; -Romans 15 v 8, 9; +-Romans 15 v 4

It is by the Apostle Paul, the Apostle of the Gentiles, that reveals our salvation and the mysteries of Christ*. It is the resurrected Jesus Christ that the 'Body of Christ' is identified with+. Not the Jesus Christ that gave his earthy ministry to Israel. The Gentiles had no hope and were without God before the resurrection^. *-Romans 16 v 26; -I Corinthians 2 v 7, 8; -Ephesians 1 v 9-13; -Ephesians 3 v 1-10; -Colossians 1 v 23-27; +-II Corinthians 5 v 14-18; ^-Ephesians 2 v 11-13

Peter says (Holy Ghost inspired):
40- Him God raised up the third day, and showed him openly;
-Acts 10 v 40

Peter states 'the fact of resurrection'. It really happened. Many ate and visited with the 'Resurrected Christ'. Peter was a 'first hand eye witness'. What the 'resurrection of Jesus Christ' meant for the Jew was that Christ was still alive and could bring in that 'Earthly Kingdom of Heaven' promised to the fathers of Israel. He would 'redeem' Israel and 'buy them back' like he did when he redeemed (bought back) the 'Children of Israel' out of Egypt, "...with great power, and with a mighty hand"*?
*-Exodus 32 v 11

Peter did not attribute 'salvation' to 'the resurrection' but the 'saving of the soul', the persons, the people, the Jews of Israel from their enemies. It is on this side of the cross, post resurrection that the Apostle Paul revealed by God the 'salvation of the spirit and body'. To believe in the 'Power of his Resurrection'+. "But we preach 'Christ Crucified'"*! *-I Corinthians 1 v 23; +-Romans 1 v 4; -Philippians 3 v 10

The Book of Acts starts all Jewish. The Apostles were given 'Power by God' as they waited for the 'Kingdom of Heaven'. These were carrying on the 'Earthly Ministry of Christ'. They attributed all their miracles in the 'Name of Jesus Christ'. It was through him that they had this power.

As the Book of Acts progresses it shows the 'further demise' of Israel and the Jews. They rejected the promises made to their fathers and further rejected Jesus as being the Messiah. They stoned and killed Stephen. Peter and 'the Twelve' fall off the scene. They no longer were performing miracle wonders. Halfway through the Book of Acts they vanish until James, Peter, John and Jude write their own epistles by Holy Spirit inspiration.

Much of Christendom has said that the Book of Acts is the Birth of the Church. What Church? What Acts really shows is the dying of 'Israel and the Children of the Circumcision/Law'. Rome destroyed Jerusalem in 70 A.D. The Book of Acts turns to the Apostle Paul and his missionary journeys to the Gentiles.

Luke writes an historical account of the Apostle Paul but Luke never injected his beliefs during this period. He was writing what God was telling Luke to write, not what Luke had been raised to believe. Luke writes of some of the trials and tribulations for the sake of the 'Body of Christ, the Church'.

During the historical accounts in the Book of Acts, Paul wrote some of his epistles. The Books in the Bible that follow the Book of Acts are Paul's Epistles. Romans to Philemon was written specifically to us Gentiles and all the world. Hebrews was written mostly for 'the Jew under the Law' explaining who Jesus really is and that there is now something better than 'the Law'. Hebrews is filled with 'Gems of Truth' for us also in the 'Body of Christ'. We accept all scripture as the 'Word of God'.

These newer Bibles and 'student study guides' try to make it seem that Paul, who becomes the focus of the Book of Acts half way through, was doing what 'the Twelve' were also doing. The ministry of Paul to the Gentiles is thought and taught that Peter and Paul are 'the same type of Apostles' and preaching the same message of the 'Apostles Doctrine'.

The Church! The Church! The Church!

The translators called the Jewish assemblies and Jewish congregations 'Churches'. They were still Jewish assemblies and synagogues and were not following 'the Doctrine of the Gentiles'. They were still Law keeping Jews, 'the Elect'.

It was the Apostle Paul that reveals the 'True Church' the 'Body of Christ'. Scripture does not say nor shows that 'the Twelve' forsook 'the Law' and embraced the 'Gospel of Grace'. They were not supposed to nor were they told by Jesus to stop keeping 'the Law'. "The kingdom of heaven is at hand"*. *-Matthew 3 v 2; Matthew 4 v 17; Matthew 10 v 7

'This Jerusalem Assembly' was a major thorn to Paul's ministry. This is further covered in the chapter "Let him be Accursed". Most of Christendom don't want to know this truth.

Peter continues by Holy Spirit inspiration telling them that Jesus Christ is still alive:
41- Not to all the people, but unto witnesses chosen before of God, *even* to us, who did eat and drink with him after he rose from the dead.
-Acts 10 v 41

Jesus only revealed himself in the flesh, post resurrection to the 'Jews of the Circumcision/Law'. Those that believed in 'the Name of Jesus Christ'. After 40 days he was taken up (caught up) to Heaven. These believers thought he would soon return with the Kingdom.

6- When they therefore were come together, they asked of him, saying, Lord, wilt thou at this time restore again the Kingdom to Is'ra-el?
…..
10- And while they looked steadfastly toward heaven as he went up, behold, two men stood by them in white apparel;
11- Which also said, Ye men of Gal'i-lee, why stand ye gazing up into heaven? This same Je'sus, which is taken up from you, shall so come in like manner as ye have seen him go into heaven.
-Acts 1 v 6, 10, 11; -Zechariah 14 (v 4, 9)

But the Apostle Paul is the last one to see Jesus Christ:
3- For I delivered unto you first *(chief)* of all that which I also received, how that Christ died for our sins according to the scriptures;
4- And that he was buried, and that he rose again the third day according to the scriptures:
5- And that he was seen of Ce'phas *(Peter)*, then the twelve:
6- After that, he was seen of above 500 brethren at once; of whom the greater part remain unto this present, but some are fallen asleep *(died)*.
7- After that, he was seen of James; then of all the apostles.
8- **And last of all he was seen of me also,** as one born out of due time.
-I Corinthians 15 v 3-8

Peter continues Holy Spirit inspired to the Cornelius Household:
42- And **he commanded us to preach unto the people, and to testify that it is he which was ordained of God** *to be* the judge of quick and dead.
43- To him give all the prophets witness, that **through <u>his name</u> whosoever believeth in him shall receive remission of sins.**

44- While Pe'ter yet spake these words, the Ho'ly Ghost fell on all them which heard the word.

-Acts 10 v 42-44

"And he commanded us to preach unto the people". What people? The Jews of Israel only*.

*- Acts 8 v 1; -Acts 11 v 19;

45- And **they of the circumcision which believed were astonished,** as many as came with Pe'ter, **because that on the Gen'tiles also was poured out the gift of the Ho'ly Ghost.**

-Acts 10 v 45

This surprised the 'Devout Jews of the Circumcision/Law' that traveled with Peter. These Gentiles had kept no 'Law of Moses'. These Gentiles had not made sacrifices and had gone to 'the Temple' in Jerusalem to worship. These Gentiles had not been doing 'righteous works of faith' and doing 'the services' of Judaism.

Yet, the Holy Spirit of God was manifested in them, the same as had been manifested in the Jew on that 'famous day of Pentecost'. There was a transitional change in 'dispensation' that was happening for the world concerning salvation.

46- For they heard them speak with tongues, and magnify God. Then answered Pe'ter,

47- Can any man forbid water, that these should not be baptized, which have received the Ho'ly Ghost as well as we?

48- **And he** *(Peter)* **commanded them to be baptized in the name of the Lord.** Then prayed they him to tarry certain days.

-Acts 10 v 46-48

Note the order by which the Holy Ghost came onto the Gentiles. There was not a process like that of Acts 2 v 38. The Holy Ghost came by faith, without keeping any part of the 'Mosaic Law'. These Gentiles had not been to 'the Temple' to worship, nor gave tithes, nor had done any animal sacrifices to atone for their sins. They were not Jews. God going to

Gentiles? Unheard of! In Acts 2 v 37 the people of Israel (the nation) asks Peter **what shall we do**?

36- Therefore let all the house of Is'ra-el know assuredly, that God hath made that same Je'sus, whom ye have crucified, both Lord and Christ.
37- Now when they heard *this*, they were pricked in their heart, and said unto Pe'ter and to the rest of the apostles, Men and brethren, **what shall we do**?
38- Then Peter said unto them, Repent, and be baptized **every one of you** in the name of Je'sus Christ for the remission of sins, and ye shall receive the gift of the Ho'ly Ghost.
-Acts 2 v 36-38

When Peter returned back to Jerusalem after his 'House of Cornelius' experience he was not greeted by his fellow apostles with celebration. One would think that they would be 'over joyed' of the ministry that Peter had brought to the Heathen Gentiles. They were not pleased with Peter for doing this. Why didn't Peter, after seeing the 'Holy Spirit' come on the Gentiles, continue on to the rest of the world preaching 'The Gospel of the Kingdom'?

1- And the apostles and brethren that were in Ju-de'a heard that the Gentiles had also received the word of God.
2- And when Pe'ter was come up to Je-ru'sa-lem, **they that were of the circumcision contended with him,**
3- Saying, Thou wentest in to men uncircumcised, and didst eat with them.
4- But Pe'ter rehearsed *the matter* from the beginning, and expounded *it* by order unto them, saying,
-Acts 11 v 1-4

When Peter returned to Jerusalem, the Law keeping Jews 'contended' with him. After giving his account of how the Holy Ghost came upon the Gentiles as it did on the Jews, then these fellow believers in Jerusalem were somewhat elated for the Gentiles. But 'the circumcision' continued not to reach out to the Gentiles and to the world. The 'Twelve Apostles' still were staying in Jerusalem and in Israel. When other believers (in the name of Jesus Christ) had been scattered and fled the once safe state of Israel, they still were only preaching to the Jews only*. *-Acts 11 v 19

Peter recounts the events. He explains to his fellow 'brethren of the circumcision' how the Holy Ghost fell upon the Gentiles without the 'Law and Services of Judaism':

15- And as I began to speak, the Ho'ly Ghost fell on them, as on us at the beginning.

16- Then remembered I the word of the Lord, how that he said, **John indeed baptized with water; but ye shall be baptized with the Ho'ly Ghost.**

17- For as much then as God gave them the like gift as *he did* unto us, who believed on the Lord Je'sus Christ; what was I, that I could withstand God?

18- When they had heard these things, they held their peace, and glorified God, saying, Then hath God also to the Gen'tiles granted repentance unto life.

-Acts 11 v 15-18

The next verse is one to be noted. How many have spent their whole lives in church and never heard nor read this?:

19- Now they which were scattered abroad upon the persecution that arose about Ste'phen travelled as far as Phe-ni'ce, and Cy'prus, and An'ti-och, **preaching the word to none but unto the Jews only.**

-Acts 11 v 19

What were they preaching? The Jews had not that 'new gospel'. 'The revealing of the mysteries/secrets' that have been hid since the beginning of creation were only revealed to the Apostle Paul. They could only have been preaching Old Testament scripture and possibly Matthew, Mark, Luke and John and were only focusing on Jews that had been scattered abroad. "The Kingdom of Heaven is at hand".

In this book of transition, the 'Book of Acts', Peter falls off the scene. Where did Peter's power that was given to him go? Why aren't there more accounts and record of Peter and his miracle powers being taking to the ends of the earth as most of Christendom claim that he had done.

So many have taken the liberty and preached to the world that Peter and the apostles spread 'the gospel'. These preachers and teachers following the 'Apostles Doctrine'* think and truly want to believe wholeheartedly that Peter and 'the Twelve Apostles' left Israel in taking 'their Gospel' to the uttermost parts of the earth. It is just as important to know **what was written** in the Bible and **what was not written** in the Bible. *Acts 2 v 42

The only gospel that they could have been spreading was 'the Gospel of the Kingdom'. 'The Kingdom' did not come in. The apostles miracle power was like that of Jesus Christ as he walked on the earth. What happened to it?

During the earthly ministry of Jesus Christ, he spoke of many wondrous things that would happen if they (Israel) simply were to ask him. There are scriptures that speak of things like, "whatever you shall ask in my name it shall be done unto you", etc. Is this really happening today?

Had the Kingdom come in, these things that Jesus spoke of would happen in the 'Earthly Kingdom of Heaven'. But all these things fell off the scene. Israel rejected their King and now salvation has gone to the Gentiles without the Law and without the Jew/Hebrew.

A break has happened in the 'Old Testament Prophetic Time Line'. For 2,000 years it has been the 'Age of Grace' and 'The Body of Christ'. Where in scripture did it ever say this would happen? It didn't. It was 'hid' from Israel and the Jews and was revealed to the Apostle Paul **on this side of the cross**.

The Old Testament prophecy's skip the 'Age of Grace'. Those that put the 'earthly ministry' of Jesus Christ ahead of 'the Gospel' that Paul teaches reject or are 'spiritually blind' to this. They don't want to hear it. It is God that opens the ears and eyes of understanding.

Peter writes his epistles of I Peter and II Peter still 'keeping the law' even to the end of his life. There is no 'Church language' of salvation by 'the death, burial, resurrection' in what Peter (Holy Ghost inspired) wrote. He was not preaching 'Christ Crucified'.

As Peter wrote his epistles, his language of 'keeping the Law and the Commandments' has been somewhat diminished. Has Peter changed and is now a believer more 'in a faith-way belief for salvation'? Something to note is that Peter never repeats the message he gave in Acts 2 v 38.

Finally, before being martyred, Peter endorsed the Apostle Paul:

15- And account *that* the long-suffering of our Lord *is* salvation; even as our beloved brother Paul also according to the wisdom given unto him hath written unto you;

16- As also in all *his* epistles, speaking in them of these things *(salvation)*; in which are some things hard to be understood, which they that are unlearned and unstable wrest, as *they do* also the other scriptures, unto their own destruction.

-II Peter 3 v 15, 16

What has happened to Old Testament understanding? The Law was never declared by God that it was finished. Jesus Christ never said to stop keeping the 'Law of Moses'.

So many pick and choose aspects of 'the Law' to follow but it is to no avail. The whole law has to be kept, not just bits and pieces of it. The Apostle of the Gentiles (Paul) writes by the inspiration of the Spirit that the Law was nailed to his (Jesus) cross*. Salvation for the Jew's 'under the Law' was not attributed to the 'faith in the resurrection of Jesus Christ' like it is for the world today. *-Ephesians 2 v 14-18; -Colossians 2 v 14

The 'Jews resurrection belief of Christ' is the 'saving of them from their enemies' when the 'Earthly Kingdom of Heaven' is fulfilled. The enemies of Israel would be put down and be made their footstool. Israel would be 'redeemed and bought back' by the return of Christ. They would be given a new covenant*. Jesus Christ is still alive (resurrected) and is not dead and the 'Gospel of the Kingdom' was still in a 'prophesied position' to be fulfilled. *-Jeremiah 31 v 31

Is Luke a Jew or a Gentile?
1- What advantage then hath the Jew? Or what profit *is there* of circumcision?
2- Much every way: chiefly, because that **unto them were committed the oracles of God.**
-Romans 3 v 1, 2

BOOK III

"Let Him be Accursed!"

13- For I *(Paul)* speak to you Gen'tiles, inasmuch as **I am the apostle of the Gentiles**, I magnify mine office:
14- If by any means I may provoke to emulation *them which are* my flesh, **and might save some of them**.
-Romans 11 v 13, 14

16- **In the day when God shall judge the secrets of men by Je'sus Christ according to my gospel *(Paul's)*.**
-Romans 2 v 16

25- Now to him that is of power **to stablish you according to my gospel *(Paul's)*, and the preaching of Je'sus Christ, according to the revelation of the mystery, which was kept secret since the world began.**
-Romans 16 v 25

My Gospel. Paul's Gospel that was committed to his trust. The Gospel of Christ. The Gospel of God. The glorious Gospel of the blessed God. The Gospel of his Son. The Gospel of Grace. The Gospel of your Salvation. The Gospel that was first revealed to mankind on this side of the cross, our side, post crucifixion, post resurrection through the Apostle Paul.

16- For though I preach the gospel, I have nothing to glory of: for necessity is laid upon me; yea, woe is unto me, if I preach not the gospel!

17- For if I do this thing willingly, I have a reward: but if against my will, a dispensation *of* the gospel is committed unto me.
-I Corinthians 9 v 16, 17

Why didn't the Holy Spirit instruct the Apostle Paul to write something more inclusive? Why was Paul saying "my Gospel"? Why didn't Paul say "our Gospel" that included 'the Gospel' that Jesus and 'the Twelve' knew? Most of Christendom has been teaching that there is only one Gospel and that Peter and 'the Twelve' were all on the same page preaching the same message as Paul.

19- And for me, that utterance may be given unto me, **that I may open my mouth boldly, to make known <u>the mystery of the gospel</u>,**
20- For which I am an ambassador in bonds: that therein I may speak boldly, as I ought to speak.
-Ephesians 6 v 19, 20

7- Consider what I say; and the Lord give thee understanding in all things.
8- Remember **that Jesus Christ** of the seed of David **<u>was raised from the dead according to my gospel</u>**.
9- Wherein I suffer trouble, as an evil doer, *even* unto bonds; but the word of God is not bound.
10- Therefore I endure all things for the elect's sake, that they may also obtain the salvation which is in Christ Jesus with eternal glory.
11- *It is* a faithful saying: For if we be dead with *him*, we shall also live with *him*:
12- If we suffer, we shall also reign with *him*: **if we deny *him*, he also will deny us**:
13- If we believe not, yet he abideth faithful: he cannot deny himself.
14- Of these things put *them* in remembrance, charging *them* before the Lord that they strive not about words to no profit, *but* to the subverting of the hearers.
15- **Study to shew thyself approved unto God, a workman that needeth not to be ashamed, rightly dividing the word of truth.**
-II Timothy 2 v 7-15

Peter wrote (Holy Spirit inspired) "that no prophecy *(preaching/ teaching)* of the scripture is of any private interpretation"*. All the words written in our Bible came from the 'Word of God'. Since God is perfect, he would not have made such a mistake on something so important. Why didn't the Apostle Paul ever include the 'Apostles Doctrine' ('Jews of the Circumcision/Law' and 'the Twelve') in 'the Gospel' that he took to the Gentiles? *-II Peter 1 v 19-21

Only the Apostle Paul and his ministry in 'The Body of Christ' was bringing 'the word of salvation' to the Gentile world. **Paul never preached Acts 2 v 38.** It was by 'The Gospel' given to him by the Resurrected Christ that the Gentiles were obtaining salvation and a knowledge of the 'Living God'. The Jews and 'the Twelve' had nothing to do with Paul's 'Body of Christ Church, the True Church'. Scripture shows that they were an 'impediment' to Paul's ministry as this chapter will show by the scriptures.

Paul writes by Holy Spirit inspiration that the Jesus Christ we know is not the Jesus that walked the streets of Israel. HELLO!?:

15- And *that* he died for all, that they which live should not henceforth live unto themselves, but unto him which **died for them, and rose again (Paul's Gospel).**

16- **Wherefore henceforth** know we no man after the flesh: yea, **though we have known Christ after the flesh, yet now henceforth know we *him* no more.**

-II Corinthians 5 v 15, 16

Many of the words spoken by Jesus Christ during his 'earthly ministry' does apply to the 'Pauline Gospel of Grace'. But the 'Doctrine of the Gospel of Grace' is for all of mankind. The 'Doctrine of the Circumcision/Law', 'The Gospel of the Kingdom' applies to the Jews of Israel that kept the 'Law of Moses'. These two are not the same. Law and Grace does not mix.

Jesus never told the 'Jews of the Circumcision' and 'the Twelve' to stop keeping the Law. Christendom has assumed that the Law was done away with when Jesus came in the flesh, or when he died on the cross and said, "It is finished"*. His earthly ministry and the prophecies concerning Jesus' first advent were finished, but not 'the Law'. Jesus Christ endorsed 'the Law'. The Apostle Peter was a 'Law keeping Jew' to the end of his life. *-Matthew 5 v 17; -John 19 v 30

Without the Temple in Jerusalem since 70 A.D., the 'services of atonement' by sacrificing animals for their sins no longer can be fully followed. Break one law and all the laws have been broken*. These that follow the 'Law of Moses' have transgressed. What is a good 'Law keeping Jew' to do? Peter tells them in II Peter 3 v 15, 16. Paul tells them in his Holy Spirit inspired epistles Romans to Hebrews.

*-James 2 v 10; -Galatians 3 v 10; -Galatians 5 v 2-4; -Matthew 5 v 17-19

Before this, the world of Gentiles (us) had no hope of salvation. This is shown by 'the Word of God':

11- Wherefore remember, that ye *being* in time past Gen'tiles in the flesh, who are called Uncircumcision by that which is called the Circumcision in the flesh made by hands;

12- **That at that time ye were without Christ, being aliens from the commonwealth of Is'ra-el, and strangers from the covenants of promise, having no hope, and without God in the world:**

13- But now in Christ Je'sus ye who sometimes were far off are made nigh by the blood of Christ.

-Ephesians 2 v 11-13

"Let Him Be Accursed"

It is 'the Apostle's Doctrine'* that much of Christendom is still trying to follow. Aspects of 'Law keeping' (that which they accept) while ignoring those Laws that they believe don't apply to them. Those 'Original Apostles' (the Elect) were still keeping the Law 100%. What 'professing Christian' today can do this? *-Acts 2 v 41-47

Paul writes (Holy Spirit inspired) the following to the Gentiles in Galatia and to the believer in the 'Body of Christ' today. The 'Word of God' is contrary to what most Christians assume and want to believe*. Most of Christendom can't accept nor want to acknowledge the truth that Paul writes these scriptures (Holy Spirit inspired) about them and Christendom of today. "Beware of the 'Judaizer". *-II Timothy 2 v 15

6- I *(Paul)* marvel that ye are so soon removed from him that called you into the grace of Christ unto **another gospel**:

7- **Which is not another;** but there be some that trouble you, **and would pervert the gospel of Christ.**

8- But though we, or an angel from heaven, **preach any other gospel** unto you than that which we *(Paul's ministry)* have preached unto you, **let him be accursed**.

9- As we said before, so say I now again, **If any *man* preach any other gospel unto you than ye have received, let him be accursed**.

-Galatians 1 v 6-9

What could this possibly mean? Another gospel? What does that mean? Paul writes (Holy Spirit inspired), "which is not another; but there be some that trouble you, and would pervert the gospel of Christ". So there had to be at least two Gospels being preached? Hello?

Remember who Paul is writing to. The Church of Galatia was not a Jewish synagogue. These were believers of Paul's 'Gospel of Grace'. These are Gentiles. Some may be Jews but a 'true Jew under the Law' would not be associating with the Heathen Gentiles.

These Galatians only knew one Gospel. That Gospel was brought to them by the Apostle Paul. **'The Gospel' was not brought to them by 'the Twelve' or any Jew.** The Jews were not evangelizing the world as most of Christendom has falsely been led to believe*.

*-Acts 11 v 19; -Acts 8 v 1

There was only one Gospel that the Galatians knew and it wasn't the 'Gospel of the Kingdom'. The Gentiles of the 'uncircumcision' **were never** under 'the Law of Moses'. But 'legalism' was being brought in by Jews that were infiltrating Paul's ministry. They were even following Paul from town to town. The 'Judaizers' were perverting 'The Gospel'*. *-Galatians 1 v 6-9

Christendom today has invented a 'Big Tent Concept' by their own made up 'Religions and Denominations'. "Belong to our denomination, follow our customs, traditions, service practices, take Jesus into your heart, accept Jesus as your personal savior, believe in Jesus", and on, and on. For salvation there is **'one Spirit, one faith and one baptism'***. **This is 'exclusive' and can't be added to nor diminished by 'a man's religion or a man made denomination'.** *-I Corinthians 12 v 1-13; - Ephesians 4 v 4-6

"Let him be accursed" says Galatians 1 v 8, 9. This warning is repeated. 'The Book' of God's word says this "Let him be accursed". How many Gospels could there have been at the time Paul (Holy Spirit inspired) wrote this?

Paul <u>is not</u> addressing and speaking to Jews like that of Peter on that 'Day of Pentecost', "ye men of Israel". He was writing to a church of his in Galatia (Galatians), a 'Body of Christ Church'. Paul <u>was not</u> writing to a synagogue of the Jews concerning 'their gospel'. He <u>is not</u> warning the Apostles and 'the Circumcision/Law' to beware of the Gentiles 'Gospel of Jesus Christ'. He is writing these Galatians because of the troubling news he was hearing.

'The Judaizer has Come!' 'Beware of the Judaizer!'

Paul is writing to us directly in this 'Age of Grace'. He is warning (Holy Spirit inspired) Christendom worldwide not to be 'bewitched'* and take the 'Gospel of the Kingdom' and mix in parts of 'Pauline truths'. There is a 'residue of legalism', '<u>a perversion</u>', that has been <u>made fundamental</u> to 'man made Denominations and Religions' of today. *-Galatians 3 v 1-5

Who decided what parts of 'the Jewish law and service practices' to keep and what parts to ignore? 'The Gospel' that Paul first (chief) had brought to the Galatians years before had now become 'perverted' during his absence*. The same has happened to 'Christendom' since. The world has not changed concerning 'Paul's Gospel'. If anything, Christendom and their 'Organized Religions and Denominations' keep adding new types of 'righteous works' and rules 'for a process in obtaining their salvation'. *-Galatians 1 v 6-9

At this time, the Church in Galatia were being confronted by 'the Judaizers' coming from Judea and Jerusalem. Many of these Judaizers were coming from that 'Famous Jerusalem Church' (assembly, ecclesia, synagogue) of which Peter, James and John were members. **When Paul goes to take care of this false teaching by those Judaizer's, he went to 'the top'. He went to James, Peter and John.**

These 'law keeping Jews' were claiming that the Galatians had to follow the 'Mosaic Law' and must be physically circumcised 'after the manner of Moses' in order to obtain salvation. Paul was not teaching Judaism nor preaching it. The Galatians/Gentiles were not 'Jews of the Circumcision' and following the 'Law of Moses'.

Paul writes to the Corinthians who also were being 'Judaized':

15- For though ye have ten thousand instructors in Christ, yet *have ye* not many fathers: **for in Christ Je'sus I** *(Paul)* **have begotten you through the gospel**.
16- Wherefore I beseech you, be ye followers of me.
-I Corinthians 4 v 15, 16

4- For if he that cometh preacheth **another Je'sus, whom we** *(Paul's ministry)* **have not preached**, or *if* ye receive another spirit, which ye have not received, **or another gospel**, which ye have not accepted, ye might well bear with *him*.
5- For I suppose **I was not a whit behind the chiefest apostles**.
-II Corinthians 11 v 4, 5

Paul is saying, as humbly as possible being a man, that in no way, shape or form is he behind or in subjection to any of 'the Twelve'. For us today, in the 'Age of Grace', the Apostle Paul is Chief! It was to him that the 'Revelation of the Mysteries' were revealed. One of which is that 'by faith in the finished work of the cross we are saved'. Paul is not Peter. Peter is not Paul. The gospel is hid from them that say that Peter and Paul preached the same thing.

Paul writes in I Timothy (Holy Spirit inspired):
3- As I besought thee *(Timothy)* to abide still at Eph'e-sus, when I went into Mac-e-do'ni-a, **that thou mightest charge some that they teach no other doctrine,**
4- Neither give heed to fables and endless genealogies, which minster questions, rather than edifying which is in faith: *so do*.
5- Now the end of the commandment is charity *(love)* out of a pure heart, and of a good conscience, and of faith unfeigned:
-I Timothy 1 v 3-5

Paul continues speaking of them that have <u>not stood</u> on the truth of his God given doctrine:
6- From which some having swerved have turned aside unto **vain jangling**;
7- **Desiring to be teachers of the law;** understanding neither what they say, nor whereof they affirm:
-I Timothy 1 v 6, 7; -II Peter 3 v 15, 16

Paul then speaks of the mixing of truth with the 'Law of Moses' and the civilian laws made by men:

8- But we know that the law *is* good, if a man use it lawfully;

9- Knowing this, that the law is not made for the righteous man, but for the lawless and disobedient, for unholy and profane, for murderers of fathers and murderers of mothers, for manslayers,

10- For whoremongers, for them that defile themselves with mankind, for menstealers, for liars, for purged persons, **and if there be any other thing that is contrary to sound doctrine;**

11- **According to the glorious gospel of the blessed God, <u>which was committed to my trust</u>** *(Paul).*

-I Timothy 1 v 8-11

"And if there be any other thing that is contrary to sound doctrine; <u>which was committed to my trust</u> *(Paul).* "Committed to my trust". Paul's trust. Not Peter, not Luke, not the Twelve Apostles. It was to Paul only on this side of the cross, our side that God had entrusted this new Gospel. The Apostle Paul is 'the chosen vessel' to bear God's name to the world of us Gentiles*.

*-Acts 9 v 15, 16

There are many contradictions in the Bible if this is not understood that the Gospel for the Gentiles given to the world, is different than that which was for Israel and the Jews, 'the Gospel of the Kingdom'. Paul is warning not to give in to the 'Judaizers'. "Ye are not under Law but under Grace"*. *-Romans 6 v 14

The Apostle Paul after bringing his 'Gospel of Grace' to the Corinthians are questioning themselves because of the 'Judaizers'. "Is Paul the one that we should be following"? "He is not Jesus or Peter or any of 'the Twelve'". "Paul did not walk the streets of Israel with Jesus Christ".

It was by 'the Apostle of the Gentiles' that got these 'pagan heathens' to turn to 'the Living God'. It was by 'Paul's Gospel of Grace' that turned 'a very carnal people', the Corinthians, to God' and not 'the Twelve'. "We preach Christ Crucified"*. *-I Corinthians 1 v 22-24; -I Corinthians 2 v 2; -Galatians 5 v 24; -Galatians 6 v 14

1- Do we begin again to commend ourselves? Or need we, as some *others*, epistles of commendation to you, or *letters* of commendation from you?

-II Corinthians 3 v 1

There were 'Judaizers' that were writing falsehoods and lies concerning Paul and his ministry while he was away. Paul in most of his Epistles constantly had to show his 'God given credentials' of being 'thee Apostle (Chief) of the Gentiles'. Many of Paul's opening verses in his Epistles addressed his Apostleship that was given by God and not by man*. *Acts 9 v 15; -Acts 13 v 47; -Acts 22 v 21; -Acts 26 v 17; -Acts 28 v 28; -Romans 11 v 13; -I Corinthians 1 v 1; -II Corinthians 1 v 1; -Galatians 1 v 1; -Galatians 2 v 2, 8; -Ephesians 1 v 1; -Ephesians 3 v 1, 8; -Colossians 1 v 1; -I Timothy 1 v 1; -I Timothy 2 v 7; -II Timothy 1 v 1, 11; -II Timothy 4 v 17; -Titus 1 v 1

Always remember at the time of the 'Birth of the True Church, The Body of Christ', there was no knowledge of 'The Living God' that the non-Jew knew of. 'The Most High God' to the common man (Gentiles) was not an idol that could be touched, held and displayed. If you had no knowledge of God but belonged to a 'car club' what would be your idol?

Nothing of Paul's writings while being Holy Spirit inspired contradicted itself. Paul's Epistles are in total agreement with all of 'the scriptures'. It wasn't that Paul was some sort of genius and could retain in his knowledge all of Biblical scripture. Paul was not 'carefully choosing his words' and 'sneaking behind' the 'Apostles Doctrine'. He was inspired by 'the One and only Holy Spirit of God'. He made no mistakes. God made no mistakes. His Epistles are the 'Word of God' as all of scripture is.

Before Paul had written anything or before copies were made of his Epistles, 'The Gospel' was proclaimed, preached and prophesied by men and women 'whose hearts the Lord had opened'*. Paul was first (chief) to reveal to them the Gospel of the Grace of God by the Resurrected Lord Jesus Christ. These were the Apostles in Paul's 'Body of Christ Churches' following 'The Gospel'+ and his God given 'Doctrine of Grace'. *-Acts 16 v 14; -Acts 16 v 40; +-I Corinthians 15 v 1-4

Some of the Apostles with Paul's ministry were: Barnabas, Titus, Timotheius, Apollo, Aquila, Pricella, Phebe and many more*. None of these were of 'the Twelve' during the Earthly Ministry of Christ. There is no record of Luke, John or Barnabas preaching 'The Jew's Gospel' while traveling with Paul. *-Acts 16 v 14; -Acts 18 v 2, 24-28;

2- Ye are our epistles written in our hearts, known and read of all men:

3- *Forasmuch as ye are* manifestly declared to be the epistle of Christ ministered by us, **written not with ink, but with the Spirit of the living God; not in tables of stone, but in fleshly tables of the heart.**

4- And such trust have we through Christ to God-ward:
5- Not that we are sufficient of ourselves to think anything as of ourselves; but our sufficiency is of God;
6- **Who also hath made us able ministers of the new testament; not of the letter, but of the Spirit: for the letter killeth, but the Spirit giveth life**.
-II Corinthians 3 v 2-6

"If our gospel be hid it is hid to them that are lost"

3- But if **our gospel** be hid, it is hid to them that are lost:
4- In whom the god of this world hath blinded the minds of them which believe not, lest the light of the glorious **gospel of Christ**, who is the image of God, should shine unto them.
-II Corinthians 4 v 3, 4

Here is scripture where preachers that stay in the 'pre-crucifixion' teachings like to use. They unknowingly combine 'the Gospel of the Kingdom' message with Paul's 'Gospel of Grace'. They use these scriptures from the 'pen of Paul' as a way to put their congregations in some form of 'subjection to legalism' or guilt like: paying tithes, water baptism or any type of 'righteous works' or to believe what this preacher is saying to them, that it is 'the truth' and the Word of God. Fear the preacher? Did this preacher even use the name of the Apostle Paul or did he make it seem that it was Peter who said this?

These preachers and teachers don't understand and see **the change in 'dispensation'**. So it's easier to ignore Paul. After all, Paul was not one of 'the Twelve' chosen disciples during Jesus' earthly ministry. These preachers 'cherry pick' scriptures that Paul wrote that don't contradict with them and 'their denomination/religious beliefs'. Or a man has rewritten scripture made by the newer Bibles that are not taken directly from 'The King James'.

At this very time (right now, this moment exactly, I lie not), with the KJV Bible and a rough draft of this book in front of me, a well known preacher world wide was giving his sermon on 'The Great White Throne Judgment' on T.V. He read and showed on the Big Screen two times Romans 2 v 16. But this is how he read and showed it. He stopped mid verse...?

16- *In the day when God shall judge the secrets of men by Je'sus Christ ...*

He stopped and didn't finish the verse. Two times he did this. Why did he stop? Why didn't he say, "according to my gospel" (Paul's Gospel). Why not? He, like most of Christendom preach an 'elusive truth'. He used many scriptures but only those of the Apostle Paul that agreed with his 'mixed gospel'. When he came to the real truth, he ignored and skipped it. "If our gospel be hid..."

Teachers and preachers using II Corinthians 4 v 3, 4 unknowingly are speaking this warning that is directed at themselves. What is the saying? "Wake up and smell the coffee"! They themselves can't see (smell) it. It is hidden from them. They are the ones that the god of this world has blinded. It is they whom Paul's gospel is hidden from. These are 'the principalities and spiritual wickedness in high places'*. They can't see the forest from the trees. *-Ephesians 6 v 12

They would use these verses as a way to justify what was said in Jesus' earthly ministry hoping to show that the whole Bible is all in agreement and of one and the same doctrine and the same Gospel. Using these verses (II Corinthians 4 v 3, 4) to put the fear of 'the Law' and preaching to 'do this' and 'to do that' and to follow their church beliefs and customs of their denomination. Teaching their congregations some mixed version of Law and Grace.

Paul reveals our 'Body of Christ Church Doctrine' through Jesus Christ on 'this side of the cross'. Do you put the early chapters in the Book of Acts ahead of the Book of Romans for your church doctrine? Yes, these early chapters in Acts were after 'the resurrection' but 'the Gospel of Grace' had not been revealed to the Apostle Paul yet.

This gospel that is hid is Paul's Gospel. 'The Gospel' that has been given by God to the chief Apostle for a pattern to follow'*. Not the 'Gospel of the Kingdom'. Are you a 'professing Christian', and a Bible student, and are confused when you get to the writings of Paul', that is, Romans to Hebrews?*-I Timothy 1 v 15, 16; -I Timothy 2 v 7; -I Corinthians 3 v 10, 11

How many have you stopped reading when you get to Paul? So much more is revealed that Jesus' earthly ministry to Israel and the Jew's did not. Much of Jesus Christ's ministry to the Jews does apply to us in the 'Age of Grace', but it is not the 'Doctrine for the Gentiles'. How many times did Jesus say to keep the Law and the Commandments? Too many to count?

These 'Jews of the Circumcision/Law' (Peter and 'the Twelve') were still following the 'Gospel of the Kingdom'. They are still Jews under 'the Law of Moses'. The Earthly Kingdom of Heaven was soon to come.

The Book of Romans is the beginning of 'the Church Doctrine' for us in the 'Age of Grace'. **The Book of Romans is Doctrine.** Do you follow Acts 2 v 38? How come you don't follow Acts 2 v 44, 45. Do you take the responsibility for Acts 2 v 22, 23, 36?

Peter and 'the Twelve' were not given nor preached 'The Gospel' (I Corinthians 15 v 1-4) that only Paul revealed. It is by the Apostle Paul who gives to us 'the pattern to follow'*. It is by 'The Gospel' and his Epistles that we are saved by. Don't take what was given to the Apostle Paul and add to it, like Peter's message in Acts 2 v 38. *-I Timothy 1 v 15, 16; -I Timothy 2 v 7; -I Corinthians 3 v 10, 11

Most of 'Christendom' simply justify this mixing and 'blending' of the Gospel's by saying that Peter and Paul were preaching the same thing. More than likely this teacher puts Paul in subjection to Peter. Scripture clearly shows that this is not so.

30- What shall we say then? That **the Gentiles**, which followed not after righteousness, have attained to righteousness, even **the righteousness which is of faith.**

31- But **Is'ra-el, which followed after the law of righteousness, hath not attained** to the law of righteousness.

32- Wherefore? **Because *they sought it* not by faith, but as it were by the works of the law**. For they stumbled at that stumblingstone;

33- As it is written, Behold, I lay in Si'on *(Zi'on)* a stumblingstone and rock of offense: and whosoever believeth on him shall not be ashamed.

-Romans 9 v 30-33

Now go over to Romans 10 verse 4:

4- For Christ *is* the end of the law for **righteousness to everyone that believeth**.

-Romans 10 v 4

"Righteousness to everyone that believeth"

To everyone that believes. Believe what? Not the most devout or someone that is always in the pew on Sunday morning and who was 'water baptized'. Not works, not 'righteous works', not following a Religious and Denominational Law, not tithing, not the need and pressure to belong to a church and so on. But "righteousness to everyone that believeth". Another word for believe is faith and trust. Trust in the 'finished work of the cross'. What side of the cross is most of Christendom's faith?

The Apostle Paul writes Holy Spirit inspired:
7- Consider what I say; and the Lord give thee understanding in all things.
8- Remember that Jesus Christ of the seed of David was raised from the dead according to my gospel:
-II Timothy 2 v 7, 8

As the Apostle Paul would proclaim by the Holy Spirit:
16- For I am not ashamed of the gospel of Christ: for it is the power of God unto **salvation to everyone that believeth**; to the Jew first, and also to the Greek.
17- For therein is the righteousness of God revealed from faith to faith: as it is written, **The just shall live by faith**.
-Romans 1 v 16, 17

What was said by 'The Gospel'*? Received, ye stand, saved, believed, I also received, Christ died for our sins, buried, rose again the third day. 'The Gospel' is loaded and is not something of an 'easy believism'. Every word of faith in it needs to be fully understood and by this knowledge 'we stand'. That is why we read, and continually study and enjoy the word of God+. This is not law. *-I Corinthians 15 v 1-4; +-II Timothy 2 v 15

Faith is an attitude of the heart. Not once did Paul say to 'repent and be water baptized for the remission of sins' as Peter preached to 'Ye men of Israel'. Nor did Paul ever say that to be saved you had to speak 'in Tongues'*. Salvation is a free gift of Grace to all those that believe in Paul's 'Faith-way Gospel'=. *-I Corinthians 14; =-Galatians 3 v 21-29

Who wrote the Bible scriptures? Who was it written to? Under what circumstances? What came before and what came after? Basically, the who, what, when and where, etc. A good way for understanding the Bible is to know who the message (Book) was written to. Everything in the Bible was not written to us. It is not possible to follow the 'whole Biblical scripture'.

Another rule for understanding is to know 'what was not said'. Peter is not Paul. Paul is not Peter. Beware of those with a 'supposed head knowledge' claiming to know scripture.

How many people sit in churches thinking they have salvation simply by listening to a preacher or priests sermon and attending a weekly church service? Have they read the 'Word of God' for themselves or do they rely on others and follow a man? Can such a one be influenced on a Sunday morning by principalities and false teachings? Easily if one doesn't know where to 'stand on the truth' of scripture.

Paul writes Holy Spirit inspired (not Peter, not 'the twelve'):
11- But I certify you, brethren, that **the gospel which was preached of me** is not after man.
12- For I neither received it of man, neither was I taught *it*, but **by the revelation of Je'sus Christ**.
-Galatians 1 v 11, 12

28- As concerning the gospel *(Paul's)*, *they (Jews) are* enemies for your sakes: but as touching the election, *they are* beloved for the fathers' sakes.
29- **For the gifts and calling of God *are* without repentance.** (*God's not going to change his mind.*)
30- For as ye *(Gentiles)* in times past have not believed God, yet have now obtained mercy through their *(Israel's)* unbelief:
31- Even so have these also now not believed, that through your mercy they also may obtain mercy.
32- **For God hath concluded them all in unbelief, that he might have mercy upon all.**
33- O the depth of the riches both of the wisdom and knowledge of God! How unsearchable *are* his judgments, and his ways past finding out!
34- For who hath known the mind of the Lord? Or who hath been his counselor?
35- Or who hath first given to him, and it shall be recompensed unto him again?

36- For of him, and through him, and to him, *are* all things: to whom *be* glory for ever. Amen'.

-Romans 11 v 28-36

By the Word of God, the Holy Spirit inspired the Apostle Paul to warn mankind not to fall into 'legalism' like that of the Jews. This is much of 'Christendom' today. They feel that by their 'righteous works' they are gaining and earning salvation. But by the law of any kind is no man justified. They have fallen from Grace. Christ's resurrection is of no effect to those that believe they are justified by 'righteous works' and a 'legalism for salvation'.

2- Behold, I Paul say unto you, that if you be **circumcised *(legalism's)*, Christ shall profit you nothing**.

3- For I testify again to every man that is circumcised, that he is **debtor to do the whole law.**

4- Christ is become of no effect unto you, whosoever of you are justified by the law; **ye are fallen from grace.**

-Galatians 5 v 2-4

16- Knowing that a **man is not justified by the works of the law**, but by the faith of Je'sus Christ, even we have believed in Je'sus Christ, that we might be justified by the faith of Christ, and not by the works of the law: **for by the works of the law shall no flesh be justified**.

-Galatians 2 v 16

Paul explains that the law was good (in God's eyes perfect) but had it been 'a law for salvation' it would be all a person needs. But the 'Law of Moses' could not save anyone but condemn them. Knowing that they had sinned because of 'the Law' they now could atone for their 'sins by acknowledging' them by the sacrificing of animals.

The '10 Commandments' are still a 'universal law'. Paul too endorses it but there is one by which Paul does not. He does not speak of keeping the Sabbath Day. It was for the 'Jews of the Circumcision under the Law'. In the 'Body of Christ' every day is 'in Christ'. There is no set day or time to worship like it was for the 'Jew under the Law'*. *-Acts 3 v 1

Keeping a religious law or faithfully going to church every Sunday won't save a person. Attending a yearly Bible summer school as a youth and once in awhile going to 'church' or confessing sins to a man is not the 'faith-way doctrine of Grace'. It may help, for the unlearned, if what is preached is truth by the 'faith-way Gospel of Grace'. The untaught and unlearned in the knowledge of 'Paul's Gospel exclusiveness' would not know. "Wide is the gate..."*. *-Matthew 7 v 13; -Luke 13 v 24

The need to continually prove to God ones faith shows that a full belief in the 'Gospel of Grace' was never accepted and believed. It is God that justifies us by our faith in the Gospel, not a man, not a preacher or anyone. "Not that we are sufficient of ourselves to think anything as of ourselves; but our sufficiency is of God"*. *-II Corinthians 3 v 5

Finding like minded believers in the 'Body of Christ' that put the 'Apostle of the Gentiles' first for 'the Church Doctrine' is a Blessed Day in the Lord. These good folk are out there but most of Christendom stay on the 'front end of the cross'. They don't know any better nor have understood the truth of scripture*. *-II Timothy 2 v 15

7- But if the ministration of death, written *and* engraven in stones, **was glorious**, so that the children of Is'ra-el could not steadfastly behold the face of Mo'ses for the glory of his countenance; **which *glory* was to be done away**:

-II Corinthians 3 v 7; -Exodus 34 v 29-35

Moses, as he carried down Mount Sinai the tablets of stone containing 'The Law', his face was shining so brightly that he put 'a Vail' on his face so the 'Children of Israel' could look at him. 'The Vail' was there because the 'Glory of the Law' wasn't going to be permanent. God knew this, but as far as Israel knew 'The Law' was knowledge for them, to know what was sin and how to atone for it. This was Israel's 'Dispensation'* under 'The Law'. (*Only Paul uses the word 'Dispensation')

Another 'Vail' but of the same truth is the 'Vail in the Temple' that was torn (rent) in two when Jesus was dying on the cross. This 'Vail in the Temple' was extremely thick and could not have been torn in pieces by a mans hand. This was 'Divinely' done by 'the hand of God' showing that all people, not just the priests of Israel, had access behind the vail*. *-Romans 5 v 2; -Ephesians 2 v 14-18; -Ephesians 3 v 12; -Hebrews 9 v 8

Pure 'atonement' wasn't truly accomplished for Israel and the 'Jews of the Circumcision/Law' until Christ Jesus was crucified. The blood of animals could only 'cover and hide their sins'*. 'Full Atonement' happened at the cross of Jesus Christ. The 'Blood of Christ' was unknown to Israel at the giving of 'the Law'. *-Deuteronomy 33 v 12; -Nehemiah 4 v 5; -Job 31 v 33; -Psalm 32 v 1; -Psalm 89 v 45; -Psalm 104 v 2; -Psalm 139 v 13; -Psalm 140 v 7; -Isaiah 29 v 10; -Isaiah 51 v 16; **-Isaiah 61 v 10;** -Romans 4 v 7; -I Peter 4 v 8

All sins (past, present, future) are now forgiven. The Gentiles too can now partake of the blessings of God. All sins were atoned for*. All that is needed is a full faith in 'The 'Gospel', Christ Crucified+ and the Resurrection^. *-Romans 5 v 11; +-I Corinthians 1 v 23; -I Corinthians 2 v 2; -Galatians 2 v 20; -Galatians 6 v 14; ^-Romans 1 v 4; -Romans 6 v 5; -I Corinthians 15 v 12, 13, 21, 42; -Philippians 3 v 10, 11

8- How shall not the ministration of the spirit be rather glorious?
9- For if the ministration of condemnation *(law) be* glory, much more doth the ministration of righteousness exceed in glory.
10- For even that which was made glorious had no glory in this respect, by reason of the glory that excelleth.
-II Corinthians 3 v 8-10

Symbolically, when minor league baseball teams take 'their field' to play a game, they have their respect. It's the best baseball teams on the field and they have 'the glory'. But when the Major League World Series Champions take 'their field' (the minor league teams) their glory has lost its respect "by reason of the glory that excelleth".

The ministration of the Spirit that was coming was going to far exceed (excelleth) in glory than 'the Law' that was given to the Jew and for Israel. This was unknown and kept secret until Paul reveals it through the 'Resurrected Christ'. It was revealed by revelation from Jesus Christ in Heaven, not the Jesus Christ that walked the streets of Israel.

11- For if that which is done away *was* glorious, much more that which remaineth *is* glorious.
12- Seeing then that we have such hope, we use great plainness of speech:
13- And not as Mo'ses, *which* put a vail over his face, **that the children of Is'ra-el could not steadfastly look to the end of that which is abolished**:

14- But their minds were blinded: for unto this day remaineth the same vail untaken away in the reading of the old testament; which *vail* is done away in Christ.
-II Corinthians 3 v 11-14

Although the minor league baseball team was marginalized by the appearing of the Major League Champs, the minor league team still remains in its glory in their own respect. The Law too still remains, it was never done away with. God never told the Jews to forsake the Law.

The real problem is at the source of forgiveness and atonement. The Temple is no more, the final step. Sins can no longer be atoned for and 'temporarily covered'*. At the same time in 70 A.D. when the Roman General Titus destroyed the Temple and Jerusalem, Paul's Epistles were just finished. Was this God's plan? **<u>The 'old one' can no longer be followed when along comes 'the new one'.</u>** *-Psalm 32 v 1; -Isaiah 61 v 10; -Matthew 10 v 26; -Luke 12 v 2; -Romans 4 v 7

How many church services use the Old Testament and the keeping of some aspects of 'The Full Law' for their sermons? Much of 'Christendom' have also 'this controversy' concerning what is the right day of the 'Sabbath Day'. Is it Saturday or Sunday? These churches are being hoodwinked. We are under no law and such debate is fruitless. In the 'Body of Christ' with a permanent membership, church is everyday. When we pray and open our Bibles we know where we stand and don't need a set day imposed by man when and where to worship.

It is good to find like minded believers in 'Paul's Gospel of Grace'. A church assembly in the 'Body of Christ' can be found. Bible Studies in the homes of fellow believers is where the truth can really be heard. And what a glorious day to find these like minded believers in 'the one faith'.

Daily pray to find the 'Lydia's and Apollos' of the world. We are not many like the worldwide 'Organized Religions and Denominations'. But we see the truth by the scriptures of God's Word and patiently wait for 'the blessed hope' of the appearing and gathering (caught up)* to God by Jesus Christ. *-I Thessalonians 4 v 17; -II Thessalonians 2 v 1

15- But even unto this day, when Mo'ses is read, the vail is upon their heart.
16- Nevertheless when it shall turn to the Lord, the vail shall be taken away.

17- Now the Lord is that Spirit: and where the Spirit of the Lord *is*, there *is* liberty.

18- But we all, with open face beholding as in a glass the glory of the Lord, are changed into the same image from glory to glory, *even* as by the Spirit of the Lord.

-II Corinthians 3 v 15-18

The 'Glory of the Lord'. The 'Spirit of the Lord'. The Liberty of the 'Gospel of Grace' without legalisms. Moses is read for our learning in the 'Body of Christ' but is not 'the Doctrine' by which we follow and do.

The Allegory of Law and Grace

Paul gives a vivid contrast between 'Law and Grace' in Galatians 4. The allegory that Paul makes is not necessarily that Agar and Ishmael = The Law. It is used to show the stark difference between 'Law and Grace'.

21- Tell me, ye that desire to be under the law, do ye not hear the law?

22- For it is written, that A'bra-ham had two sons, the one by a bondmaid, the other by a freewoman.

23- But he *who was* of a bondwomen *(Ishmael)* was born after the flesh; but he of the free woman *(Isaac) was* by promise.

24- Which things are **an allegory**: for these are the two covenants; the one from the Mount Si'nai, which gendereth to bondage *(legalism)*, which is A'gar.

25- For this A'gar is Mount Si'nai in A-ra'bi-a, and answereth to Je-ru'sa-lem which now is, and is in bondage *(under law)* with her children.

26- But Je-ru'sa-lem which is above is free, which is the mother of us all.

27- For it is written, Rejoice, *thou* barren that bearest not; break forth and cry, thou that travailest not: for the desolate hath many more children than she which hath an husband.

-Galatians 4 v 21-27

The descendants of Ishmael far exceed in number than the Generation of Jews by Isaac. What is it like 50 to 1? Those that follow religious 'aspects of law keeping' far out number those that follow the 'Faith-way Doctrine of Jesus Christ'.

Are not the children of the 'bondwomen' and the 'children of the free women' eternal enemies? What group of people want to annihilate Israel and want to wipe them off the face of the earth? What type of people to this day who are not descendants of Ishmael have this same attitude? What type of 'Religions and Denominations' impose 'legalisms' for salvation?

28- Now we, brethren, as I'saac was, are the children of promise.
-Galatians 4 v 28

Understand that Paul is writing to the 'Body of Christ' and not the 'Jews of the Circumcision/Law'. Abraham and Issac were never under the 'Law of Moses'. Their Dispensation was of Faith in what God said. They were not guided by 'Law Keeping'.

29- But as then he that was born after the flesh *(Ishmael)* persecuted him *that was born* after the Spirit *(Isaac)*, even so *it is* now.
-Galatians 4 v 29

Ishmael's offspring have always been an enemy of the Jews. History and current events show this. Israel is in the news everyday. The world as well has ganged up on Israel*. When was the last time the U.N. ever gave Israel a 'fair shake'? Another reason that the Bible has always been true and the 'Word of God' undeniable. **Why do we believe the Bible? The Jew.** *-Zechariah 14 v 2

There is not a truer history of a nation of people ever written. Still, through all their persecutions (Israel's), there is 'a remnant' of the 'Twelve Tribes' since Moses. These still believe in the coming of the Messiah with the 'Kingdom of Heaven'. Man may have lost track of the true bloodline of the 'Twelve Tribes', but God hasn't*. There is still to this day devout Jews who have not intermarried with Gentiles.
*-Revelation 7 v 4-8; -Revelation 21 v 12; -Matthew 19 v 28

The 'Faith-way Gospel of Grace'* is subjected by those that believe it is needful to also do 'righteous works' to prove their faith and love toward God. 'Works religions' find it unheard of to be 'justified by faith without works'. Many say that they follow the 'Doctrine that the Apostle Paul' teaches. But then these same 'supposed Christians' say that a person has to be 'water baptized' and must 'speak in tongues' and any number of 'things to do' in order to be saved. What? *-Galatians 3 v 21-29

Paul continues contrasting 'Law and Grace':
30- Nevertheless what saith the scripture? Cast out the bondwoman *(Agar)* and her son *(Ishmael)*: for the son of the bondwoman shall not be heir with the son of the freewoman.
31- So then, brethren, we are not children of the bondwoman, but of the free.
-Galatians 4 v 30, 31

Paul says to 'the Body of Christ' that we will be outnumbered because of 'the truth'. 'The Gospel' is hid to those who refuse to accept 'salvation' by the 'Pauline Gospel of Grace'. Adding to it and imposing 'legalisms' shall no man be justified*. This is not what I, a man says, but what the 'Word of God' says.
*-Galatians 2 v 16; -Galatians 3 v 11

17- **For we are not as many,** which corrupt the word of God: but as of sincerity, but as of God, in the sight of God speak we in Christ.
-II Corinthians 2 v 17

The 'Gospel of Grace' is a free gift for all mankind. It is not preached and revealed in 'hidden truths'. It is the 'Gospel of Faith' and not of any kind of 'righteous works'. Preachers and teachers themselves who are blind to the 'Apostleship of Paul' can only minister 'an elusive truth'. They have not the 'Foundation' of the Resurrected Christ' and a 'Pattern'* to follow that only the Apostle Paul has given to the world. 'The Gospel' is hid by 'the god of this world' who has blinded the lost. *-I Timothy 1 v 15, 16; -I Timothy 2 v 7; -I Corinthians 3 v 10, 11

1- Therefore seeing we have this ministry, as we have received mercy, we faint not;
2- But have renounced the hidden things of dishonesty, not walking in craftiness, nor handling the word of God deceitfully; **but by manifestation of the truth commending ourselves to every man's conscience in the sight of God.**
3- But if our gospel be hid, it is hid to them that are lost:
4- In whom the god of this world hath blinded the minds of them which believe not, lest the light of glorious gospel of Christ, who is the image of God, should shine on them.
-II Corinthians 4 v 1-4

20- O Tim'o-thy, keep that which is committed to thy trust, avoiding profane and vain babblings, and oppositions of science falsely so called:
21- Which some professing have erred concerning the faith. Grace be with thee. A-men'

-I Timothy 6 v 20, 21

Paul further encourages Timothy and us in the 'Body of Christ':
7- For God hath not given us the spirit of fear, but of power, and of love, and of a sound mind.
8- Be not thou therefore ashamed of the testimony of our Lord, nor of me *(Paul)* his prisoner*: but be thou partaker of the afflictions of the gospel according to the power of God; *(*-I Corinthians 9 v 16-18)*
9- **Who hath saved us, and called *us* with an holy calling, not according to our works, but according to his own purpose and grace, <u>which was given us in Christ Jesus before the world began*</u>,** *(*Jesus is God)*
10- <u>**But is now made manifest**</u> by the appearing *(resurrection)* of our Saviour Jesus Christ, who hath abolished death, **and hath brought life and immortality to light through the gospel:**
11- **Whereunto I am appointed a preacher, and an apostle, and teacher of the Gen'tiles.**
12- For the which cause I also suffer these things: nevertheless I am not ashamed: for I know whom I have believed, and am persuaded that he is able to keep that which I have committed unto him against that day.
13- Hold fast the form of sound words, which thou hast heard of me, in faith and love which is in Christ Je'sus.
14- That good thing which was committed unto thee keep by the Ho'ly Ghost which dwelleth in us.

-II Timothy 1 v 7-14

The Gospel of Salvation Declared for the World

1- Moreover, brethren, **I declare** unto you **the gospel** which **I preached** unto you, which also ye have **received**, and wherein **ye stand**;
2- By which also ye are **saved**, if you keep in memory what I preached unto you, unless ye have **believed** in vain.
3- For **I delivered** unto you **first** *(Paul)* of all which **I also received**, how that **Christ died for our sins** according to the scriptures;

4- And that he was **buried**, and that he **rose again the third day** according to the scriptures:
-I Corinthians 15 v 1-4

9- That if thou shalt confess with thy mouth the Lord Jesus, and shalt **believe in thine heart that God hath raised him from the dead, thou shalt be saved.**
-Romans 10 v 9

13- In whom ye also trusted, after that ye heard the word of truth, **the gospel of your salvation**: in whom also after that ye believed, **ye were sealed with that holy Spirit of promise**.
-Ephesians 1 v 13

John 3:16

John 3 v 16 is 'a staple' for most of Christendom today. You see the signs being held up at sporting events world wide. But when understanding the truth in Paul's Gospel, John 3 v 16 is incomplete. What? Combining John 3 v 16 and Paul's Gospel of Grace brings in the understanding.

Jesus is speaking to the Jews of Israel 'under the Law'. Jesus was not speaking to us Gentiles. 'The revelation of the mysteries' and the secrets that have been 'hid in God' had not been revealed to 'thee Apostle of the Gentiles' yet*. The 'Kingdom' was right there in front of them. The King and Kingdom was within them and in their midst. They had to believe that this Jesus of Nazareth is the prophesied Messiah and Christ. *-Romans 16 v 25

15- That whosoever believeth in him should not perish, but have eternal life.
16- For God so loved the world, that <u>he gave his only begotten Son</u>, that whosoever believeth in him should not perish, but have everlasting life.
-John 3 v 15, 16

Jesus speaks a mystery. 'Begotten Son' was not at his birth in Bethlehem. In Bethlehem the Son was 'Gotten to' the Nation of Israel. 'Begotten' was at his resurrection by God. Jesus was speaking before the crucifixion happened so he wasn't 'begotten' yet. As shown by scripture this revelation was still hid from Israel*. No one knew Jesus was going to be crucified and then 'begotten'. *-John 20 v 9

17- For God sent not his Son into the world to condemn the world; but that the world through him might be saved.
-John 3 v 17; -Genesis 12 v 2, 3; -Genesis 22 v 17, 18; -Genesis 26 v 4; -Genesis 28 v 14; -Acts 3 v 25; -Romans 4 v 13, 16; -Galatians 3 v 16-29

For the Jew, salvation was by 'keeping the Law' with the newly added 'Baptism of Repentance' and to believe in the 'Name of Jesus Christ'. He was the Christ, Messiah, the King that was prophesied that would come for the Nation of Israel. The 'Resurrection of Christ Jesus' meant to Israel that he was alive and in a position to bring in the 'Earthly Kingdom of Heaven' still. Old testament prophecies could still be fulfilled. "Think not*..." *-Matthew 5 v 17

18- He that believeth on him is not condemned: but he that believeth not is condemned already, because he hath not believed in **the name of the only begotten Son** of God.
-John 3 v 18; -Psalm 2 v 7; -Acts 13 v 33; -Hebrews 1 v 5; -Hebrews 5 v 5

1- Stand fast therefore in the liberty wherewith Christ hath made us free, and be not entangled again with the yoke of bondage *(legalism)*.
2- Behold, I Paul say unto you, that if ye be circumcised *(legalism)*, Christ shall profit you nothing.
3- **For I testify again to every man that is circumcised, that he is a debtor to do the whole law.**
4- **Christ is become of no effect unto you, whosoever of you are justified by the law; ye are fallen from grace.**
5- For we through the Spirit wait for the hope of righteousness by faith.
6- For in Je'sus Christ neither circumcision availeth anything, nor uncircumcision; but faith which worketh by love.
-Galatians 5 v 1-6

'The Law' was given to Israel to prepare them for the coming of their Messiah. To prepare the 'Jews of the Circumcision/Law' to be a 'Kingdom of Priests'*. It was to be by them that the world of Gentiles would receive the knowledge of 'the Light' in their LORD God JEHOVAH+. *-Exodus 19 v 6; -I Peter 2 v 5, 9; +-Zechariah 8 v 23

'The Vail' was given to Israel to keep them from seeing that 'The Law' was going to be done away with. Only God knew this. In the meantime, all of Israel was to believe the prophecy's and in the coming of the promised King and Kingdom. Israel, as a nation, rejected their King Jesus Christ. They could have and should have known*. *-John 21 v 25; -I Corinthians 2 v 8

'The Vail' remains on most of Christendom today. They can't see that the earthly ministry is now for our learning but not for us to follow to a tee*. That 'Vail' is causing the 'supposed Christian' to 'walk in an elusive faith'. To follow Paul is to follow 'his gospel', not the 'Gospel of the Law' that was only for Israel and the Jew. We believe the earthly ministry of course. *-II Corinthians 5 v 14-19

Paul writes by Holy Spirit inspiration:

1- I say then, Hath God cast away his people? God forbid. For I *(Paul)* also am an Is'ra-el-ite, of the seed of A'bra-ham, *of* the tribe of Ben'ja-min.

2- God hath not cast away his people which he foreknew. Wot ye not what the scripture saith of E-li'as *(Elijah)*. How he maketh intercession to God against Is'ra-el, saying,

3- Lord, they have killed thy prophets, and digged down thine altars; and I am left alone, and they seek my life.

4- But what saith the answer of God unto him? I have reserved to myself seven thousand men, who have not bowed the knee to *the image* of Ba'al.

5- Even so then at this present time also there is **a remnant according to the election of grace**.

6- **And if by grace, then *is it* no more of works: otherwise grace is no more grace.** But if *it be* of works, then is it no more grace: otherwise work is no more work.

7- What then? Is'ra-el hath not obtained that which he seeketh for; **but the election hath obtained It, and the rest were blinded.**

8- (According as it is written, **God hath given them the spirit of slumber, eyes that they should not see, and ears that they should not hear); unto this day**.

9- And David saith, Let their table *(place of position)* be made a snare, and a trap, and a stumblingblock, and a recompence unto them:

10- Let their eyes be darkened, that they may not see, and bow down their back alway.

11- I say then, Have they stumbled that they should fall? God forbid: **but rather through their fall salvation *is come* unto the Gentiles, for to provoke them to jealousy**.

12- Now if the fall of them *be* the riches of the world, and the diminishing of them the riches of the Gen'tiles; how much more their fulness?

13- **I speak to you Gen'tiles, inasmuch as <u>I am the apostle of the Gen'tiles, I magnify mine office</u>.**

14- **If by any means I may provoke to emulation *them which are* my flesh, and might save some of them.**

15- For if the casting away of them *be* the reconciling of the world, what *shall* the receiving *of them be*, but life from the dead?

-Romans 11 v 1-15

We Gentiles have our salvation because of the 'trial and testimony' of Israel and the Jew. Before the resurrection, the Gentiles had no hope and we were without God*. God did make a few, very few exceptions concerning Gentiles who fell into the Grace of God.

*-Ephesians 2 v 11-13

The Graffed In of The Body of Christ

16- For if the firstfruit *be* holy, the lump *is* also *holy*: and if the root *(Abraham) be* holy, so *are* the branches *(Israel)*.

17- And if some of the branches be broken off, and thou, being a wild olive tree *(Gentiles)*, wert graffed in among them, and with them partakest of the root and fatness of the olive tree;

18- Boast not against the branches. But if thou boast, thou bearest not the root, but the root thee.

19- Thou wilt say then, The branches were broken off, that I might be graffed in.

20- Well; **because of unbelief they were broken off, and thou standest by faith**. Be not high-minded, but fear:

21- For if God spared not the natural branches, *take heed* lest he also spare not thee.

22- Behold therefore the goodness and severity of God: on them which fell, severity; but toward thee, goodness, if thou continue in *his* goodness: otherwise thou also shalt be cut off.

23- And they also, if they abide not still in unbelief, shall be graffed in: for God is able to graff them in again.

24- For if thou wert cut out of the olive tree which is wild by nature, and wert graffed contrary to nature into a good olive tree: how much more shall these, which need the natural *branches*, be graffed into their own olive tree?

25- For I would not, brethren, that ye should be **ignorant of <u>this mystery</u>**, lest ye should be wise in your own conceits; that **<u>blindness</u> in part is happened to Is'ra-el, <u>until</u> the fullness of the Gentiles be come in *(caught up?)*.**

26- And so all Is'ra-el shall be saved*: as it is written, There shall come out of Si'on *(Zion)* the Deliverer, and shall turn away ungodliness from Ja'cob: *-Romans 9 v 6

27- For this *is* my covenant unto them, when I shall take away their sins.
-Romans 11 v 16-27

These scriptures of the Graffed in Gentiles say mountains of revealed truths. I hope and pray that you read these verses slowly and pray for understanding. Refer to Ezekiel 37 and 'The Dry Bones' and the promises made to Abraham. *-Genesis 12 v 1-3, -Genesis 13 v 14-17; -Genesis 15 v 5-18; -Genesis 17 v 1-8, 17-22; -Genesis 18 v 16-19; -Genesis 21 v 9-13; -Genesis 22 v 17, 18; -Genesis 25 v 20-23; -Genesis 26 v 1-5; -Genesis 28 v 13-15; -Genesis 35 v 9-13; -Genesis 45 v 4-8; -Genesis 46 v 2-4; -Genesis 50 v 24*

Has all Israel been saved? The 'Deliverer' did come but Israel rejected Jesus and crucified him by the Gentile Romans. We know some of how much the Jews have suffered since 70 A.D. They only just became a nation again in 1948. But the 'Title Deed' given by God in Genesis is a far bigger promised land given to 'The Children of Israel'*. This is still promised by God. There is a 'Great Trespass' happening today. Believe God? *-Genesis 15 v 18

18- In the same day **the LORD made a covenant with A'bram,** saying, Unto thy seed have I given this land, from the river of E'gypt unto the great river, the river Eu-phra'tes:
-Genesis 15 v 18

At his second coming, at the end of 'the Seven Year Tribulation', the 'Kingdom of Heaven' as written will be established. A 'New Covenant' will be made with Israel*. In the meantime, until 'the Body of Christ' is 'caught up' to meet the Lord in the air+, the Jew and Israel obtains salvation by 'Paul's Gospel'=. *-Jeremiah 31 v 31;+-I Thessalonians 4 v 17; -II Thessalonians 2 v 1; =-Romans 3 v 19-31; -Romans 10 v 12

Paul writes (Holy Spirit inspired) about the 'Jews under the Law' and to those of today that find it needful to do 'righteous works' in proving 'their faith' and love towards God:

1- Brethren, my heart's desire and prayer to God for **Israel** is, **that they might be saved.**

2- For I bear them record that **they have a zeal of God, but not according to knowledge.**

3- **For they being ignorant of God's righteousness, and going about to establish their own righteousness, have not submitted themselves unto the righteousness of God.**

4- **For Christ** *is* **the end of the law for righteousness to every one that believeth.**

5- For Moses describeth the righteousness which is of the law, That the man which doeth those things shall live by them.

6- But the righteousness which is of faith speaketh on this wise, Say not in thine heart, Who shall ascend into heaven? (that is, to bring Christ down *from* above:)

7- Or, Who shall descend into the deep? (that is, to bring Christ again from the dead.)

8- But what saith it? **The word is nigh thee**, even in thy mouth, and in thy heart: **that is, the word of faith, which we preach;**

9- That if thou confess with thy mouth the Lord Jesus, and shalt **believe in thine heart that God hath raised him from the dead *(Paul's Gospel)*, thou shalt be saved.**

10- For with the heart man believeth unto righteousness; and with the mouth confession is made unto salvation.

11- For the scripture saith, Whosoever believeth on him shall not be ashamed.

12- **For there is no difference between the Jew and the Greek *(Gentile)*:** for the same Lord over all is rich unto all that call upon him.

13- For whosoever shall call upon the name of the Lord shall be saved.

14- How then shall they call on him in whom they have not believed? And how shall they believe *in him of whom they have not heard? And how shall they hear without a preacher?

15- And how shall they preach except they be sent? As it is written, How beautiful are the feet of them them that preach the gospel of peace, and bring glad tidings of good things!

16- But they have not all obeyed the gospel. For Esaias *(Isaiah)* saith, Lord, who hath believed our report*? *-Isaiah 53 v 1; -John 12 v 38; -Romans 10 v 16

17- **So then faith *cometh* by hearing, and hearing by the word of God.**

18- But I say, Have they not heard? Yes verily, their sound went into all the earth, and their words unto the ends of the world.

19- But I say, Did not Israel know? **First Moses saith, I will provoke you to jealousy by *them that are* no people, *and* by a foolish nation* I will anger you.** *-Deuteronomy 32 v 21

20- But Esaias *(Isaiah)* is very bold, and saith, **All day long I have stretched forth my hands unto a disobedient and gainsaying people**.

-Romans 10 v 1-20; -Matthew 23 v 37; -Luke 13 v 34

And what is the faith of Jesus Christ that Paul speaks of? The Resurrected Christ Jesus, not the faith in the 'earthly ministry of Jesus'. Don't misunderstand, we wholeheartedly believe that Jesus Christ was here trying to save Israel. This 'earthly ministry' was for Israel and for our learning*. Christ died for all the sins of mankind, and that he was buried and rose again the third day. Salvation has came to all the world, the Gentiles, on this side of the cross, post resurrection. *-Romans 15 v 4; -II Corinthians 5 v 16

A professing Christian says, "We don't follow the Law of Moses and do animal sacrificing for our sins. We are not under law but under Grace". But what laws of their 'Organized Denomination and Religion' has replaced it? What energy of the flesh do they do? What is being taught that they 'must do' to obtain salvation? Is there 'a process' that is taught in order to gain salvation? Do this, then this and this? Now your saved?

In order to obtain salvation it is taught that a person must: be water baptized, pay tithes, speak in tongues, observe a strict adherence to church service rituals and so on and on. These are all laws (legalisms) imposed by man and not of faith. No man is justified by doing something in the flesh to please God. These, as the Word of God says, have fallen from grace*.

*-Galatians 5 v 4

1- What shall we say then that A'bra-ham our father, as pertaining to the flesh, hath found?

2- For if A'bra-ham were justified by works, he hath *whereof* to glory; but not before God.

3- For what saith the scripture? A'bra-ham believed God, and it was counted unto him for righteousness.

4- **Now to him that worketh is the reward not reckoned of grace, but of debt.**

5- **<u>But to him that worketh not, but believeth on him</u> that justifieth the ungodly, his faith is counted for righteousness.**

-Romans 4 v 1-5

The Holy Spirit is imputed (put to our account) by God in the believer by faith in 'the Gospel'*. Grace is 'the unmerited favor of God'. We don't deserve it. But God will justify us when we believe what he says+. Hadn't he always. *-I Corinthians 15 v 1-4; -Romans 4 v 11-25; -Romans 5 v 8-13; -James 2 v 23; +-Romans 3 v 20, 24, 28; -Romans 5 v 1, 9; -I Corinthians 6 v 11; -Galatians 2 v 16, 17; -Galatians 3 v 11, 24; -Galatians 5 v 4; -Titus 3 v 7

Many say they 'believe in God' and have accepted Jesus as 'their personal savior'. Is it the Jesus before the cross or the resurrected Jesus Christ? Most people would say, "well … both". But when did Jesus reveal the Gospel of Salvation to all of mankind? The 'earthly Jesus that came to and for Israel only' or the 'resurrected Jesus that came for the whole world'*? *-Romans 15 v 8; -Galatians 4 v 4; -Matthew 5 v 17

The Jerusalem Council

The 'Book of Acts account' written by Luke:

1- And certain men which came down from Ju-dae'a taught the brethren, *and said*, Except ye be circumcised after the manner of Mo'ses, ye cannot be saved.

-Acts 15 v 1

'Jews of the Circumcision/Law' were a constant harassment to Paul's 'Body of Christ Church's'. They could not accept that the 'heathen Gentiles' were obtaining salvation by their Lord God JEHOVAH too (that is, the Most High God). These Gentiles were receiving the Holy Ghost without 'their righteous works of their Law'.

By the 'faith-way Gospel'* the Gentiles were obtaining salvation. This, as scripture has said, would provoke the 'Jew's of the Circumcision' to jealousy+. Most of Christendom today too has been provoked, or has been given a heart of unbelief, yet to no avail. Most of Christendom reject or combine 'the two Gospels'. They do not put the wisdom of salvation given by the Resurrected Jesus Christ to mankind by 'his Grace' at the forefront of their faith. Saved by faith with no 'righteous works'? What? *-Galatians 3 v 21-29; +-Romans 10 v 19; -Romans 11 v 11;

2- When therefore Paul and Bar'na-bas had no small dissension and disputation with them, they determined that Paul and Bar'na-bas, and certain other of them, should go up to Je-ru'sa-lem unto the apostles and elders about this question.
-Acts 15 v 2

Paul's ministry had "<u>no small</u> dissension and disputation" with these 'Judaizers'. They strongly opposed them. There was a barrier and strong disagreement between their Gospel's. Remember, these Jews (James, Peter, John, others) still had their Temple fully functioning. There was no need for them at this time to follow Paul's new Gospel. Now that the 'new faith-way' has been revealed for almost 2,000 years, Christendom 'straddles the fence'.

After seeing that these 'Judaizers' would not stop imposing their 'Doctrine of the Circumcision/Law' on his 'Body of Christ believers', Paul saw it as a major problem that needed to be addressed. Paul confronts them on their home turf. God too was instrumental in sending Paul to the Jerusalem Church to oppose 'the Judaizers'*. *-Galatians 2 v 2

He (Paul) went to the top. He went to James, Peter and John and to the Apostles and elders of the 'Jerusalem Church' to get this problem of the 'Judaizers' dealt with. These 'Body of Christ Church's' were not following the Apostles doctrine* of James, Peter and John. James, Peter and John were still 'Law keeping Jews'. There is no scripture that ever said that they forsook the 'Law of Moses' nor did Jesus ever tell them to do so. *-Acts 2 v 42

5- But there rose up certain of the sect of the Phar'i-sees which believed *(in Jesus Christ and the Resurrection)*, saying, **That it was needful to circumcise them, and to command *them* to keep the law of Mo'ses.**
6- And the apostles and elders came together for to consider of this matter.

7- **And when there had been much disputing**, Pe'ter rose up, and said unto them, Men *and* brethren, ye know how that **a good while ago** God made choice among us, that the Gen'tiles by my mouth should hear the word of the gospel, and believe.
-Acts 15 v 5-7

"A good while ago", twelve years ago Peter went to the 'House of Cornelius'. He returned to Jerusalem. He wasn't out and about evangelizing the world as most of Christendom has been saying*. Twenty years ago was 'the Day of Pentecost' when Peter preached to 'Ye Men of Israel'. The Gospel that Peter is speaking of is not the Gospel that Paul was ministering to the world of Gentiles. *-Acts 8 v 1

8- And God, which knoweth the hearts, bare them witness, giving them the Ho'ly Ghost, even as *he did* unto us;
9- And put no difference between us and them, **purifying their hearts by faith**.
-Acts 15 v 8, 9

The 'House of Cornelius' were Gentiles and never were under the 'Jewish Law of Moses'. Now 'by faith without the works of the Law' the world was being saved, post resurrection. A change in God's program never revealed before. The 'Dispensation of Grace' after the resurrection was taking hold on the 'faith-way believers'*. *-Galatians 3 v 21-29

10- Now therefore why tempt ye God, and put a yoke upon the neck of the disciples, which neither our fathers nor we were able to bear?
11- But we believe that through the grace of the Lord Jesus Christ we shall be saved, even as they.
-Acts 15 v 10, 11

"Through the grace of the Lord Jesus Christ we shall be saved, even as they". God's grace was evident throughout the Bible, but the 'Gospel of Grace' is 'The Pauline Doctrine'. This is a bigger reason that Peter saw this grace given to the Gentiles at the 'House of Cornelius'. Peter saw 'first-hand' and was 'a witness at this Jerusalem Council' to come to the defense of the Apostle Paul.

12- Then all the multitude kept silence, and gave audience to Bar'na-bas and Paul, declaring what miracles and wonders God had wrought among the Gen'tiles by them.
-Acts 15 v 12

Luke (the writer of the Book of Acts) gives a brief account of the ministry of Paul here in Acts 15 v 12. The Apostle Paul writes more concerning his ministry in his Epistles to the Gentiles. Galatians 2 is Paul's account of this 'Jerusalem Council'.

13- And after they had held their peace, James answered, saying, Men *and* brethren, hearken unto me:
-Acts 15 v 13

After Paul and Bar'na-bas gave their testimony there must have been quite 'the heated discussion'. 'The Apostles of the Gentiles' were given space and time to speak things that the 'Jews of the Circumcision/Law' had not heard before. It took them a bit to settle down because the scripture says, "after they held their peace..."

James says (Holy Spirit inspired):
14- Sim'e-on *(Peter)* hath declared how **God at the first did visit the Gen'tiles, to take out of them a people for his name.**
15- And to this agree the words of the prophets; as it is written,
16- **After this** I will return, and will build again the tabernacle of Da'vid, which is fallen down; and I will build again the ruins thereof, and I will set it up:
-Acts 15 v 14-16; -Amos 9 v 8-15

"After this", after what? After God takes "out of them a people for his name" and then "will build again the tabernacle of Da'vid, which is fallen down". The Gentiles in the 'Body of Christ' will be 'caught up' to meet the Lord in the air and will be forever with the Lord. Then, the 'Gospel of the Kingdom' will be 'back in vogue' during the seven year tribulation. 'The King is coming'!
James and the 'Jews of the Circumcision/Law' never wrote of being "caught up to meet the Lord in the air"*. James was using Old Testament

scripture and what the prophet Amos+ said. "**After this** I will return, and will build again the tabernacle of Da'vid, which is fallen down; and I will build again the ruins thereof, and I will set it up". *-I Thessalonians 4 v 17; +-Amos 9 v 8-15

Being 'Caught Up' is a 'Pauline Revelation' and 'a mystery revealed' that was only made known to the Chief Apostle of the Gentiles. For the Jews and the Nation of Israel, Christ was returning to set up his 'Earthly Kingdom of Heaven'. He was going to save Israel from their enemies. The Resurrection of Jesus Christ was seen as a fact that would insure the return of 'the King of the Jews'. Jesus Christ, the King, the Messiah was not dead but alive. He is 'the Begotten Son'.

17- That the residue of men might seek after the Lord, and all the Gentiles, upon whom my name is called, saith the Lord, who doeth all these things. 18- Know unto God are all his works from the beginning of the world. -Acts 15 v 17-18

The Apostle Paul's account of the Jerusalem Council written in Galatians 2

1- Then fourteen years after I went up again to Je-ru'sa-lem with Bar'na-bas, and took Ti'tus with *me* also.
2- And **I went up by revelation**, and communicated unto them **that gospel which I preach among the Gen'tiles**, but privately to them which were of reputation, lest by any means I should run, or had run, in vain.
-Galatians 2 v 1, 2

"I (Paul) went up by revelation". Not only did Paul react to the 'Judaizers' disrupting the 'Body of Christ' but "by revelation" as well. A God given mission to go to 'the Jerusalem Church' and confront the leaders. These leaders were James, Peter, John and 'the Apostles and elders'.

Most of Christendom has ignored these scriptures. These are quickly passed over and thoughts of questioning and understanding by "rightly dividing the word of truth" is neglected. They can't seem to bring themselves to understand. If they don't want to they won't. It is God who opens understanding. The god of this world (Satan) don't want mankind to find the truth.

"And communicated unto them **that gospel which I preach among the Gen'tiles**". What Gospel? Wasn't James, Peter and John preaching and teaching the same Gospel as the Apostle Paul and vice versa? Why the need to explain and communicate? Were not they all on the same page preaching the same Gospel? This is what most of Christendom has been led to believe. Who led them? "Rightly dividing the word of truth"* is a revelation made by God to show this understanding and to believe it. *-II Timothy 2 v 15

3- But neither Ti'tus, who was with me, being a Greek, was compelled to be circumcised:
4- And that because of false brethren unawares brought in, who came in privily to spy out our liberty which we have in Christ Je'sus, that they might bring us into bondage:
-Galatians 2 v 3, 4

Even when 'Paul's ministry' came to Jerusalem they were being subjected to scrutiny by 'the Judaizers'. In their own privacy they were being spied on. These 'self righteous Judaizers of the Circumcision/Law' thought they knew best. Anything they could do and find of Paul and his ministry would be used against him. Paul was not keeping the 'Law of Moses' like the 'Jerusalem Church' was. To them, Paul's 'Body of Christ' believers were transgressors and sinners against their Lord God JEHOVAH.

5- **To whom we gave place by subjection, no, not for an hour; that the truth of the gospel might continue with you.**
-Galatians 2 v 5

Paul stands firm on the 'Apostleship' given to him by the 'Resurrected Jesus Christ'. Thank God for this! A key and pivotal point for the 'Body of Christ'. Most of Christendom don't see and recognize this. Paul did not back down in the face of Jesus' 'earthly chosen disciples' of James, Peter and John. Paul was not the least bit intimidated by them.
"We gave place by subjection, no, not for an hour". Paul, Barnabus and Titus never gave in nor compromised their faith in the 'finished work of the cross'. They were not 'Jews of the Circumcision/Law' like that of Peter, James and John. They were not 'under Law but under Grace'.

6- But of these who seem to be somewhat, (whatsoever they were, it maketh no matter to me: God accepteth no man's person:) **for they who seemed *to be somewhat* in conference added nothing to me**:
-Galatians 2 v 6

Paul says it like it is. **The truth!** Most of Christendom don't want to hear it in any way shape or form of 'the Twelve' being minimized. But here it is by the 'Word of God'. "These who seem to be somewhat...". James, Peter and John at one time were 'the somewhat' but no more. In the eyes of the Apostle Paul, they held no place of significance to Paul's God given 'Gospel of Grace'.

"For they who seemed to be somewhat in conference added nothing to me". James, Peter and John could not influence Paul. Paul says that they conferred (in conference) among themselves but could add nothing of truth to Paul. This is what the word of God says. Believe it. Most of Christendom don't believe this nor has understood..

7- But contrariwise, when they saw that *the gospel* of the uncircumcision was committed unto me, as *the gospel* of the circumcision *was* unto Pe'ter; 8- (For he that wrought effectually in Pe'ter to the apostleship of the circumcision, the same was mighty in me toward the Gen'tiles:)
-Galatians 2 v 7, 8

James, Peter and John began to see the 'Apostleship' given to Paul by God for 'the uncircumcision'. The same God who also had given the 'Gospel of the Circumcision' (The Gospel of the Kingdom) to them. These never did embrace Paul's 'Gospel of Grace'. Scripture never says they did. Nor were they meant to. God/Jesus never told them to forsake the 'Gospel of the Kingdom' and 'the Law'. These were 'the elect'. They had their salvation already.

9- And when James, Ce'phas *(Pe'ter)*, and John, who seemed to be pillars, perceived the grace that was given unto me, they gave to me and Bar'na-bas **the right hands of fellowship; that we *should go* unto the heathen, and they unto the circumcision.**
-Galatians 2 v 9

"And when James, Ce'phas *(Pe'ter)*, and John, **who seemed to be pillars**". To Paul they only 'seemed (past tense) to be pillars'. To the 'Gospel of the Kingdom' believer and the majority of Christendom today, these chosen disciples by Jesus are still held in high esteem 'as the pillars'. The Apostle Paul is placed in subjection to them and viewed with a diminished opinion of importance.

They shook on it. The truth that is hard to accept by so many is that only one person was 'the 'chief/captain/first', a 'chosen vessel' unto God to bear his name to the Gentiles*. It was to Paul alone that the 'Revelations of the Mysteries' that was hid till now were revealed. Not Peter, not James, not Luke or any other. Paul is the Apostle of the Gentiles, so says the Word of God. *-Acts 9 v 15; -Romans 11 v 13; -Galatians 2 v 8; -I Timothy 2 v 7; -II Timothy 1 v 11

In Galatians 2, Paul gives the account where he confronts Peter to the face and accuses him:

11- But when Pe'ter was come to An'ti-och, I *(Paul)* withstood him to the face, because he was to be blamed.

12- For before that certain came from **James**, he did eat with the Gen'tiles: **but when they were come, he withdrew and separated himself, fearing them which were of the circumcision**.

13- And the other Jews dissembled likewise with him; insomuch that Bar'na-bas also was carried away with their dissimulation.

14- But when I *(Paul)* saw that they walked not uprightly according to the **truth of the gospe**l, I said unto Pe'ter before *them* all, If thou, being a Jew, livest after the manner of Gen'tiles, and not as do the Jews, why compellest thou the Gen'tiles to live as do the Jews?

15- We *who are* Jews by nature, and not sinners of the Gen'tiles,

16- **Knowing that a man is not justified by the works of the law,** but by the faith of Je'sus Christ, even we have believed in Je'sus Christ, that we might be justified by the faith of Christ, and not by the works of the law: **for by the works of the law shall no flesh be justified**.

17- But if, while we seek to be justified by Christ, we ourselves also are found sinners, *is* therefore Christ the minister of sin? God forbid.

18- For if I build again the things which I destroyed, I make myself a transgressor.

19- **For I through the law am dead to the law, that I might live unto God.**

20- I am crucified with Christ: nevertheless I live; yet not I, but Christ liveth in me: and the life which I now live in the flesh I live by the faith of the Son of God, who loved me, and gave himself for me.
21- I do not frustrate the grace of God: **for if righteousness** *come* **by the law, then Christ is dead in vain.**
-Galatians 2 v 11-21

Peter seemed to have no problem with Paul and 'The Body of Christ Church of Gentiles' with eating and visiting with them in secret after his 'House of Cornelius experience. Peter <u>was not</u> on a 'missionary journey' taking 'his Gospel' to the Gentiles. When those of the 'Jerusalem Church' came to visit Paul, Peter withdrew from Paul and his fellow disciples and chose to simulate back with the Jews of Israel.

Again, another example that Peter was still under 'the Law' and wished not to be seen by 'the circumcision' communing with Gentiles. Peter was still keeping his distance from the common man*. Peter had not received any of the revelations from the ascended Lord Jesus that were given to Paul. *-Matthew 10 v 5, 6

So many say and think that Peter also was given these 'revelations of the mysteries'. Peter is not Paul. Paul is not Peter. Peter was an 'apostle and minister of the circumcision'. Paul was an 'apostle and minister of the uncircumcision'*. *-Galatians 2 v 7-9

Same God, same Lord Jesus but there is a transition happening to the 'Gospel of Grace'. The Book of Acts is a 'book of transition'. The Apostle Paul would be proclaiming and preaching 'the Gospel' directed by Jesus Christ himself from heaven. This was eluded to but not explained in the Old Testament that God would be going to the Gentiles without the Jew. Only the Apostle Paul reveals this truth.

2- If ye have heard of **the dispensation of the grace of God which is given me to you-ward:**
3- How that **by revelation he made known unto me** *(Paul)* **the mystery;** (as I wrote afore in few words,
4- Whereby, when ye read, ye may understand **my knowledge in the mystery of Christ)**

5- Which in **other ages was not made known unto the sons of men**, as it is now revealed unto his holy apostles *(Paul's ministry)* and prophets *(preachers/proclaimers)* by the Spirit;

6- **That the Gentiles should be fellowheirs**, and of the same body, and partakers of his promise in Christ by the Gospel:

7- **Whereof I was made a minister according to the gift of the grace of God given unto me by the effectual working of his power.**

8- Unto me, who am less than the least of all saints, **is this grace given, that I should preach among the Gentiles** the unsearchable riches of Christ;

9- And to make all *men* see what *is* **the fellowship of the mystery, which from the beginning of the world hath been hid in God**, who created all things by Jesus Christ*: *(*-Jesus is God. -John 1 v 10; -Colossians 1 v 15-18)*

-Ephesians 3 v 2-9

Only the Apostle Paul speaks of 'The Body of Christ, The Church' which is 'his body' whereby Jesus Christ is 'the Head'*. 'The Head' of the 'Body of Christ. Not the King as he would be for Israel but the 'Head of The Church'. Jesus will be King but for us Gentiles, Jesus is the 'Head of the Body' by which we are 'joint-heirs with Christ'+. *-Colossians 1 v 18-27; +-Romans 8 v 17

4- God forbid: yea, let God be true, but every man a liar; as it is written, That thou mightest be justified in thy sayings, and mightest overcome when thou art judged.

-Romans 3 v 4

By no means do we ignore any scripture like those that ignore Paul's. We take all scripture as the 'Word of God'. Understanding and "rightly dividing the word of truth"*, the 'dispensation for the Jew' at that time is not 'the dispensation for the 'Body of Christ' at this time, after 'the Resurrection'. *-II Timothy 2 v 15, 16

The whole Bible fits and is more easily understood when God opens a persons understanding of this. Some things in the Bible still are 'unknowable'. Nobody has a complete knowledge of all that is written. But what is meant to be known is found in our Bible.

Many use the excuse that the King James Version is too hard for them to understand. It's 'too English' and not written in 'today's language'. They would prefer something written that reads more like a novel.

The KJV was written for the most simple and uneducated people of the world. It was written for those who never had a formal education. Translations by man is the way in which the truth of God has been twisted and minimized. The KJV is the closest thing to the true 'Word of God' that is widely available.

The Old Testament was written in the Hebrew language*. These Jewish writers were meticulous when it came to 'the Word of God'. Their copies and manuscripts were word for word and they dare not write anything of their own. *-Romans 3 v 1, 2

The devout 'Jews of the Circumcision/Law' had a love and fear of their LORD God JEHOVAH. They had such a respect for the name of JEHOVAH that they chose not to repeatedly use it thereby diminishing the importance of the JEHOVAH name. When you see the word LORD, it is really the name JEHOVAH. JEHOVAH = LORD.

The majority of Jews did not believe in the 'Name of Jesus Christ', only that small group of 'the elect' did. Most of Israel rejected the 'Word made flesh'. They spurned the truth that JEHOVAH/LORD (The Word) was made 'in the flesh' (Jesus Christ). Israel has paid a heavy price for their unbelief. Many of Christendom today have also not believed. JEHOVAH is the Lord Jesus Christ. The Word was made flesh. See the chapter 'The Invisible Godhead'.

The transcribers knew the ultimate 'fear of God' if they were to change or rewrite anything contrary to the 'Word of God'. These newer bibles and study bibles have not understood 'that fear of God'. So many have 'wrest and twisted the truth' making biblical knowledge as something that they would want it to say and hear*. May God have mercy on these 'principalities of wickedness in high places'+.

*-II Peter 3 v 15, 16; +-Ephesians 6 v 12

18- For I testify unto every man that heareth the words of the prophecy of this book, If any man shall add unto these things, God shall add unto him the plagues that are written in this book.

19- And if any man shall take away from the words of the book of this prophecy, God shall take away his part out of the book of life, and out of the holy city, and *from* the things which are written in this book.

-Revelation 22 v 18, 19

The compilers of the New Testament around 300 A.D. kept the original manuscripts as is. There are museums that have the original texts and all agree with the KJV. The only unfortunate thing is that the Hebrew (Old Testament) and Greek (New Testament) languages have many words for the same meanings.

The English translators chose the words very carefully by well educated men. But now that 100's of years have past, some of their chosen words have lost the significance and meanings by 'their interpretations'. Our God given common sense and understanding in the 'scope in doctrine of the scriptures' helps us to see past these translations.

Our KJV Bible is not a novel. The 'Word of God' was written by his Holy Spirit*. What man is there who can skim and quickly read the 'Word of God' and retain the understanding of the 'Divine message'+? We study and read slowly, comparing spiritual with spiritual^ (scripture with scripture), and ask questions. If the answer cannot be found then it doesn't exist. Don't make the 'Word of God' fit what you think or want it to say°. *-II Peter 1 v 20, 21; +-Romans 11 v 34; -I Corinthians 2 v 16; -Isaiah 55 v 8, 9; ^-I Corinthians 2 v 10-16; °-Matthew 16 v 23; -Mark 8 v 33; -Luke 4 v 8

Example:
21- Neither shall they say, Lo here! or lo there! For, behold, the kingdom of God is within you.
-Luke 17 v 21

The original Greek word meant 'in their midst'. Look at the margins in your Bible. So many have 'spiritualized' this not understanding that Jesus was speaking. He was the King, the Messiah and where the King is, so is the Kingdom. The Kingdom was among them and in 'their midst'. The Kingdom spoken of that Israel would inherit is not an 'Earthy Kingdom' within a persons body.

For salvation in this 'Age of Grace' there is no difference between a Jew by birth and a Gentile*. All the world obtains salvation by 'one Spirit, one faith and one baptism'+. 'The Vail and Partition' has been removed=. For all the world today this is only by Paul's (Holy Spirit directed) 'no righteous works doctrine of grace'. **It is exclusive yet so easy!** *-Acts 15 v 8-11; -Romans 10 v 12; +-I Corinthians 12 v 13; -Ephesians 4 v 4-6; =-Ephesians 2 v 14

There is only one door to the sheepfold and it is at ground level. So many 'Denominations and Religions' ignore the simple truth. We don't

have to climb mountains or go through 'a rigid process of indoctrination'. It is not a wide door or a place with many entrances*.
*-Matthew 7 v 13, 14; -Luke 13 v 24

The 'Big tent concept' has the world believing that simply going to church on Sunday and believing in any of the multitudes and various forms of Denominations, the church goer will 'get there'. Because they go and attend church they are now Christians? But what does the 'Word of God' say?

16- In the day when God shall judge the secrets of men by Je'sus Christ <u>according to my gospel</u>.
-Romans 2 v 16

25- Now to him that is of power **to stablish you <u>according to my gospel</u> _(Paul's)_,** and the preaching of Je'sus Christ, **according to the revelation of the mystery, which was kept secret since the world began.**
-Romans 16 v 25

It has been said that 'Organized Religion's and Denomination's' are the many ways for mankind to go to hell. **"The road to hell is paved with good intentions"*.** There is only 'One Church, the Body of Christ'+.
*-Ephesians 6 v 12; +-Colossians 1 v 18, 24

Many say, "I follow Jesus" and their faith is in the 'pre-crucifixion' scriptures. Jesus was a 'Jew under the Law'. Peter and 'the Twelve' were all keepers of 'the Law' and died keeping 'the Law'. 'The Law' was never declared by Jesus/God to have been done away with. Following the 'earthly Jesus Christ' means following 'the Law'. Such a person has fallen from grace and is unjustified in God's eyes*. They say they follow Jesus but it is impossible to keep the 'full Law'. A man didn't say it, God's word says it. *-Galatians 5 v 3, 4

15- And _that_ he died for all, that they which live should not henceforth live unto themselves, but unto him which **died for them, and rose again _(Paul's Gospel)_.**
16- Wherefore henceforth know we no man after the flesh: yea, **though we have known Christ after the flesh, yet now henceforth know we _him_ no more.**

17- Therefore if any man *be* in Christ, *he is* a new creature: old things are passed away; behold, all things are become new.

18- And all things *are* of God, who hath reconciled us to himself by Je'sus Christ, and hath given to us the ministry of reconciliation;

-II Corinthians 5 v 15-18

Peter never said nor wrote such a thing. Paul (Holy Spirit inspired) is saying that we (Gentiles) **henceforth (from now on)** don't know 'the Jesus that walked the earth in the flesh'. We know that he did and it is profitable for our learning and for the understanding of the scriptures. Jesus earthly ministry gives us hope. But the earthly ministry of Jesus Christ was to and for the Jews and for Israel 'under the law'.

4- But when the fullness of the time was come, God sent forth his **Son,** made of a women, **made under the law,**

5- **To redeem** them that were **under the law**, that we might receive the adoption of sons.

-Galatians 4 v 4, 5

8- Now I say that **Jesus Christ was a minister of the circumcision** for the truth of God, to confirm the promises made unto the fathers:

9- And that the Gentiles might glorify God for *his* mercy; For this cause I will confess to thee among the Gentiles, and sing unto thy name.

-Romans 15 v 8, 9

Jesus said:

17- Think not that I am come to destroy the law, or the prophets: I am not come to destroy, but to fulfill.

-Matthew 5 v 17

Paul writes in the Book of Hebrews many gems of Truth for knowledge in 'The Body of Christ' (Hebrews = Jews):

1- Therefore **leaving the principles of the doctrine of Christ***, let us go on unto perfection *(spiritual maturity)*; **not laying again** the foundation of repentance from dead works, and of faith toward God. *(*-Matthew, Mark, Luke, John)*

2- Of the doctrine of baptisms, and of laying on of hands, and of resurrection of the dead, and of eternal judgment.

3- And this we will do, if God permit.

4- For *it is* impossible for those who were once enlightened, and have tasted of the heavenly gift, and were made partakers of the Ho'ly Ghost.

5- And have tasted the good word of God, and the powers of the world to come,

6- If they shall fall away, to renew them again unto repentance; seeing they crucify to themselves the Son of God afresh, and put *him* to an open shame.

-Hebrew 6 v 1-6

This is most of 'Christendom' today. So many types of 'water baptisms', who is right? Repeated repentance, confessing sins to a man and not to God? A priest is a man and in no higher place than a member 'in the Body of Christ'. He is a man and can not forgive sins, only God can.

'Legalism' of any religion or denomination is 'the falling away from grace'. These have no excuse. They have been blinded by man and 'the god of this world' to the Gospel that was given to one man by God himself, the Apostle Paul*. *-Romans 2 v 16; -Romans 16 v 25

Peter, near the end of his life, finally acknowledges the wisdom of God given to the Apostle Paul. Peter to the end of his days was a 'Law keeping Jew'. He still found the 'Gospel of Grace' hard to understand by his own words. But for Peter, he was one of the 'elect' under the 'Gospel of the Kingdom'. He was never told by Jesus and God to forsake 'the Law'.

15- And account *that* the long-suffering of our Lord *is* **salvation**; even as our beloved brother **Paul** also according to **the wisdom given unto him** hath written unto you;

16- As also in all *his* epistles, speaking in them of these things *(salvation)*; in which are some things hard to be understood, which they that are **unlearned and unstable wrest**, as *they do* also the other scriptures, **unto their own destruction**.

-II Peter 3 v 15, 16

The Deadly Opposition of 'The Truth'

Paul had a love for his fellow country men of Israel but finally in Acts 28 he gave up on the Jews. After the Jews were able to coerce the Romans to imprison Paul, he makes his final appeal to the Jewish Nation. Paul now writes his 'Prison Epistles' (Ephesians, Philippians, Colossians) and makes no mention of Old Testament scripture or any of his fellow Jews.

Paul suffered for 'The Body of Christ, our Church'. The Barjesus' of today stand against 'the Truth' of Paul's ministry claiming he wasn't worthy or he didn't have 'the scars' to validate his 'Apostleship'. They say he didn't walk with Jesus Christ in the flesh and wasn't a selected disciple as 'the Twelve' were.

Paul was constantly defending his 'Apostleship' because it came not by man but by the 'Resurrected Jesus Christ'*. He is the 'chosen vessel' by God for us Gentiles. 'The Twelve' were not+. 'The Twelve' were Apostles of the Jew and for 'the Circumcision/Law'.

*-Galatians 1 v 11, 12; -Romans 16 v 25; -Ephesians 3 v 2-12; +-Acts 9 v 15

Paul writes by Holy Spirit inspiration:

22- Are they He'brews? So *am* I. Are they Is'ra-el-ites? So *am* I. Are they the seed of A'bra-ham? So *am* I.

23- Are they ministers of Christ? (I speak as a fool) **I *am* more**; in labours more abundant, and stripes above measure, in prisons more frequent, **in deaths oft**.

24- Of the Jews five times received I forty *stripes* save one.

25- Thrice was I beaten with rods, once was I stoned, thrice I suffered shipwreck, a night and a day I have been in the deep;

26- *In* journeyings often, *in* perils of water, *in* perils of robbers, *in* perils by *mine own* country men, *in* perils by the heathen, *in* perils in the city, *in* perils in the wilderness, *in* perils in the sea, *in* perils among false brethren;

27- In weariness and painfulness, in watchings often, in hunger and thirst, and fastings often, in cold and nakedness.

28- **Beside those things that are without, that which cometh upon me daily, the care of all the churches.**

29- Who is weak, and I am not weak? Who is offended, and I burn not?

30- If I must needs glory, I will glory of the things which concern mine infirmities.

-II Corinthians 11 v 22-30

After all the physical sufferings and trials imposed on Paul by men, he viewed them as taking a back seat to his God given ministry. His number one care was not in preserving and running away to save his life, but in his ability to preach and teach the Gospel of the Grace of God. The Body of Christ Churches that he initiated were a daily care and prayer that they would stay true to his teachings. Scripture shows that not all of them did*.
*-II Timothy 1 v 15

Did Paul die and go to Heaven?

In II Corinthians 11 v 22-30, Paul writes of some of the physical sufferings he endured for the sake of 'the Gospel' and for you and me. In verse 23 he says, "in deaths oft". No man could have endured the physical trials that Paul went through had it not been for God and his life saving mercy. How many times did Paul die and/or was at 'deaths door step' and recovered?

Here is an account where Paul was left for dead. They **"drew *him* out of the city, supposing he had been dead".** How many times was Paul's body left lifeless?

19- And there came thither *certain* **Jews from An'ti-och and I-co'ni-m, who persuaded the people, and, having stoned Paul, drew *him* out of the city, supposing he had been dead.**
20- **Howbeit,** as the disciples stood round about him, **he rose up**, and came into the city: and the next day he departed with Bar'na-bas to Der'be.
21- And when they had **preached the gospel** to that city, and had taught many, they returned again to Lys'stra, and to I-co'ni-um, and An'ti-och.
-Acts 14 v 19-21

Paul miraculously recovers and stands up after being stoned to death. Once 'the stoning starts' it ends with death. The stoning of someone was not just the act of hurling and chucking stones from a distance. The act of stoning sometimes also included smashing and pulverizing the victim with large rocks.

In this account of Acts 14 that Luke wrote, did the Apostle Paul follow up on this same event in II Corinthians 12 v 1-10? Is the Apostle Paul speaking of himself here? He gives reason for not mentioning himself as being the one that went to heaven. He didn't want to glory in what he saw and was afraid to because God told him not to speak of the 'Heavenly vision' he witnessed. Knowing that the common man was eager to worship and make an idol out of most anything, Paul didn't want to be placed in a position that could possibly have usurped God himself in another persons eyes.

After being stoned and left for dead in Acts 14, was it Paul that got the glimpse of heaven? The time frame matches up but Paul says "in deaths oft" so it could have been a number of times. I can think of none other he could be writing about but you can decide for yourself.

1- It is not expedient for me to doubtless to glory. I will come to visions and revelations of the Lord.

2- I knew a man in Christ above fourteen years ago, (whether in the body, I cannot tell; or whether out of the body, I cannot tell: God knoweth;) such an one caught up to **the third heaven.**

3- And I knew such a man, (whether in the body, or out of the body, I cannot tell: God knoweth;)

4- **How he was caught up into paradise,** and heard unspeakable words, which is not lawful for a man to utter.

5- Of such an one will I glory: yet of myself **I will not glory, but in mine infirmities.**

6- For though I would desire to glory, I shall not be a fool; for I will say the truth: but *now* I forbear, lest any man should think me above that which he seeth me *to be*, or *that* he heareth of me.

7- And lest I should be exalted above measure through the abundance of the revelations, there was given to me a thorn in the flesh, the messenger of Sa'tan to buffet me, lest I should be exalted above measure.

8- **For this thing I besought the Lord thrice, that it might depart from me.**

9- And he said unto me, **My grace is sufficient for thee:** for my strength is made perfect in weakness. Most gladly therefore will **I rather glory in my infirmities,** that the power of Christ may rest upon me.

10- **Therefore I take pleasure in infirmities, in persecutions, in distresses for Christ's sake: for when I am weak, then am I strong.**

-II Corinthians 12 v 1-10

Take note of the term **'the Gospel'** in the Book of Acts. This is important. Luke used the words 'the Gospel' several times as he gave witness to the Apostle Paul's ministry. But Luke never clarified what was meant by 'the Gospel' that Paul preached. It was not the Gospel that Luke and the Twelve knew, that is, 'the Gospel of the Kingdom'. This has confused and misled most of Christendom.

Because the book of Acts repeated the words 'the Gospel' as Paul preached to the Gentiles, it has been assumed that 'the Twelve' were also preaching the same Gospel. The closest scripture that Luke used to 'the Gospel' that Paul was proclaiming was in Acts 20 v 24. Paul did preach 'the Resurrection'* but Luke in the Book of Acts didn't equate 'the Gospel of Grace' as the 'Resurrection Doctrine'. *-Acts 17 v 18, 32; -Acts 23 v 6, 8; -Acts 24 v 15, 21

It is not till Paul writes his own epistles that 'the Gospel' that Paul reveals is what he was preaching in Acts. Luke, unfortunately, never clarified that Paul preached Christ Crucified and Salvation by faith in the finished work of the cross without doing any righteous works. But maybe, God purposely left it that way for those that 'rightly divide the word of truth'.

Luke writes of Paul (Holy Spirit inspired):
24- But none of these things move me, neither count I my life dear unto myself, so that I might finish my course with joy, and **the ministry, <u>which I have received of the Lord Jesus, to testify the gospel of the grace of God</u>**.
-Acts 20 v 24

The Apostle Paul would go first to a synagogue of the Jews when he came to a city. There were Jewish synagogues spread all over the world since the time of Nebuchadnezzar and the Babylonian invasion. These 'Jews of the Circumcision' were still the 'Ye men of Israel', that kept 'the Law of Moses' and were 'under the covenant promises' made to 'their fathers'. These would make pilgrimages to Israel on the 'Jewish Feast Days' and would take their animal sacrifices to the 'Temple in Jerusalem'.

Paul would reason with the 'Jews of the Circumcision/Law' out of Old Testament scripture that 'Jesus is the Christ' and 'the prophesied messiah' that came to Israel. He preached the 'resurrection of Jesus Christ' (Christ Crucified) and that by 'this faith who believe are justified from all things which could not be justified by keeping the Law of Moses'*. This 'Gospel

of Salvation' would eventually get him thrown out of the synagogues. This happened repeatedly until Paul finally gives up on the Jews in Acts 28.
*-Acts 13 v 28-41

Paul: "lo, we turn to the Gen'tiles"

44- And the next sabbath day came almost the whole city together to hear the word of God.

45- But when the Jews saw the multitudes, they were **filled with envy** and spake against those things which were spoken by Paul, contradicting and blaspheming.

46- Then Paul and Bar'na-bas waxed bold, and said, **It was necessary that the word of God should first have been spoken to you: but seeing ye put it from you, and judge yourselves unworthy of everlasting life, lo, we turn to the Gen'tiles**.

47- **For so hath the Lord commanded us** *saying*, **I have sent thee to be a light of the Gen'tiles, that thou shouldest be for salvation unto the ends of the earth.**

48- And when the Gen'tiles heard this, they were glad, and glorified the word of the Lord: and as many as were ordained to eternal life believed.

49- **And the word of the Lord was published throughout all the region.**

50- But the Jews stirred up the devout and honorable women, and the chief men of the city, and raised persecution against Paul and Bar'na-bas, **and expelled them out of their coasts**.

51- But they shook off the dust of their feet against them, and came into I-co'ni-um.

52- And **the disciples** were filled with joy, and with the Ho'ly Ghost.
 Acts 13 v 44-52

    Verse 46- Paul would go first to his fellow beloved Jews.

    Verse 47- It was the Apostle Paul that is now commissioned by God to be a 'Light of Salvation' to the world.

    'The Twelve' were never part of 'Paul's Commission' and 'ministry'. Luke and John did for a time travel with Paul but they never had scripture written where they also were preaching Paul's Gospel. Not one.

Verse 49- **"And the word of the Lord was published throughout all the region".** It was Paul's preaching that was being published. 'The Twelve' were nowhere to be found.

Verse 50- **"the disciples"** spoken of here are not 'the Twelve' and those of 'the Circumcision' and the 'Gospel of the Kingdom Saints'. Paul too had many followers and disciples in the 'Body of Christ, the True Church'.

Paul and Barnabas in Iconium

1- And it came to pass in I-co'ni-um, that **they went both together into the synagogue of the Jews**, and so spake, that a great multitude both of the Jews and also of the Greeks believed.

2- **But** the unbelieving Jews stirred up the Gentiles, and made their minds evil affected against the brethren.

3- Long time therefore abode they speaking boldly in the Lord, which gave testimony unto the word of his grace, and granted signs and wonders to be done by their hands.

4- **But** the multitude of the city was divided: and part held with the Jews, and part held with the apostles.

5- And when there was **an assault made** both of the Gen'tiles, and also of the Jews with their rulers, to use *them* despitefully, and to stone them,

6- They were ware of *it*, and fled unto Lys'tra and Der'be, cities of Lyc-a-o'nia, and unto the region that lieth round about.

7- And there **they preached the gospel**.

-Acts 14 v 1-7

Paul would take his Gospel first to the Jews

1- Now when they had passed through Am-phip'o-lis and Ap-ol-lo'ni-a, they came to Thes-sa-lo-ni'ca, **where was a synagogue of the Jews:**

2- **And Paul, as his manner was, went in unto them,** and three sabbath days reasoned with them out of the scriptures,

3- Opening and alleging, that Christ must needs have suffered, and risen again from the dead; and that this Je'sus, whom I preach unto you, is Christ.

4- And some of them believed, and consorted with Paul and Si'las; and of the devout Greeks a great multitude, and of the chief women not a few.

5- **But** the Jews which believed not, moved with envy, took unto them certain lewd fellows of the baser sort, and gathered a company, and set all the city on an uproar, and assaulted the house of Ja'son, and sought to bring them out to the people.

6- And when they found them not, they drew Ja'son and certain brethren unto the rulers of the city, crying, **These that have turned the world upside down are come hither also**; *(Paul's ministry must have been effective, 'The World Upside Down'?)*

7- Whom Ja'son hath received: and these all do contrary to the decrees of Cae'sar, saying that there is another king, *one* Je'sus.

8- And they troubled the people and the rulers of the city, when they heard these things.

9- And when they had taken security of Ja'son, and of the other, they let them go.

-Acts 17 v 1-9

The Jew's of Berea studied the scriptures

10- And the brethren immediately sent away Paul and Si'las by night unto Be-re'a: **who coming *thither* went into the synagogue of the Jews.**

11- These were more noble than those in Thes-sa-lo-ni'ca, in that **they received the word with all readiness of mind, and searched the scriptures daily, whether those things were so.**

12- Therefore many of them believed; also of the honourable women which were Greeks, and of men, not a few.

13- **But** when the Jews of Thes-sa-lo-ni'ca had knowledge that the word of God was preached of Paul at Be-re'a, they came thither also, and stirred up the people.

14- And then immediately the brethren sent away Paul to go as it were to the sea: but Si'las and Ti-mo'the-us abode there still.

-Acts 17 v 10-14

More Jews reject the Apostle Paul and his Gospel

5- And when Si'las and Ti-mo'the-us were come from Mac-edo'ni-a, Paul was pressed in the spirit, **and testified to the Jews *that* Je'sus *was* Christ.**

6- And when **they opposed themselves, and blasphemed**, he *(Paul)* shook *his* raiment, and said unto them, Your blood *be* upon your own heads; I *am* clean: **from henceforth I will go onto the Gen'tiles**.
-Acts 18 v 5, 6

James too resists Paul's Gospel

17- And when we were come to Je-ru'sa-lem, the brethren received us gladly.

18- And the *day* following **Paul went in with us unto James; and all the elders were present**.

19- And when he had saluted them, he declared particularly what things God had wrought among the Gen'tiles by his ministry.

20- And when they heard *it*, they glorified the Lord, and said unto him, Thou seest, brother, how many thousands of Jews there are which believe; **and they are all zealous of the law**:
-Acts 21 v 17-20

"They glorified the Lord". These were 'Jews of the Circumcision' under 'the Law' and were not in agreement with 'the Gospel' that Paul was preaching. They 'glorified the Lord' in their place at 'the Lord's Table'. They were going to act and keep their attitude and 'services' being devout Jews under the 'Law of Moses'. These were vocal in their belief and 'place of position'.

"Thou seest, brother, how many thousands of Jews there are which believe; **and they are all zealous of the law**:" They were displaying 'their way' in the face of Paul. They outnumbered Paul in this multitude and regardless of what Paul may have to say, they were more in number. The same could be said for the mega churches, religions and denominations today. "Wide is the gate. And broad is the way..."*. *-Matthew 7 v 13

James continues:

21- **And they are informed of thee, that thou teachest all the Jews which are among the Gen'tiles to forsake Mo'ses, saying that they ought not to circumcise *their* children, neither to walk after the customs.**

22- What is it therefore? The multitude must needs come together: for they will hear that thou art come.

23- Do therefore this that we say to thee: We have four men which have a vow on them:
-Acts 21 v 21-23

The Apostle Paul came to Jerusalem and was at first treated with respect. Luke writes that Paul also was courteous. Paul saluted these believers in the 'Name of Jesus Christ' that were strongly accepting of the 'Gospel of the Kingdom'. These Jews were 'of the circumcision' and were "**all zealous of the law**". They were devout law keeping Jews. Who has said that these Jews of which James was present with were no longer 'under the law'?

The assemblies that gathered were aware of the Apostle Paul's teachings and that they had differed from the 'Law of Moses'. They said of Paul, **"that thou teachest all the Jews which are among the Gen'tiles to forsake Mo'ses, saying that they ought not to circumcise *their* children, neither to walk after the customs"***. *-Acts 21 v 21

For this particular day, the 'Day of Purification', the Jews imposed some legalisms on Paul under 'the Law' if he was to enter into the Jewish Temple. Along with four others, they had their heads shaved as having adhered to the 'Laws of the Circumcision'. They were 'under the gun' so to speak and would not get lost in the crowd. Identifying Paul was no problem. He was the one with all them scars on 'his bald noggin'.

24- Them take, and purify thyself with them, and be at charges with them, that they may shave *their* heads: and all may know that those things, whereof they were informed concerning thee, are nothing; but *that* thou thyself also walkest orderly, and keepest the law.
-Acts 21 v 24

The assembly of Jews were informed that Paul's doctrine was of no consequence to them. Paul would behave and he too would be observing the 'Law of the Circumcision'. Paul would show no disrespect. They need not worry that Paul was going to 'speak out' to them concerning 'his Gospel' that he preached to the Gentiles this week.

25- As touching the Gen'tiles which believe, we have written *and* concluded that they observe no such thing, save only that they keep themselves from *things* offered to idols, and from blood, and from strangled, and from fornication.

-Acts 21 v 25

They told Paul all was good. They were not imposing their Jewish Laws on the Gentiles who believed in Jesus Christ. Hadn't they? They sure tried in Acts 15 and Galatians 2. They would keep themselves from worshiping idols, from eating blood, from eating things killed in an unnatural fashion and to keep from fornication. The same things requested by James, Peter and John at 'the Jerusalem Council'. No problem. They would be allowed into the temple on 'the day of Purification'.

26- Then Paul took the men, and the next day purifying himself with them entered into the temple, to signify the accomplishment of the days of purification, until that an offering should be offered for every one of them. 27- And when the seven days were almost ended, the Jews which were of A'sia, when they saw him in the temple, stirred up all the people, and laid hands on him.

-Acts 21 v 26, 27

But at the end of the week things changed. They could not hide with their bald heads. All week long Paul's ears must have been ringing. Things were about to crescendo. This spirit of unease was not going to remain peaceful. These zealous Jews of Asia Minor had themselves a target. It was 'that one' with the scars on his bald head.

28- Crying out, Men of Is'ra-el, help: This is the man, that teacheth all *men* every where against the people, and the law, and this place: and further brought Greeks *(Gentiles)* also into the temple, and hath polluted this holy place.
29- (For they had seen before with him in the city Troph'i-mus an E-phe'sian, whom they supposed that Paul had brought into the temple.)
30- And all the city was moved, and the people ran together: and they took Paul, and drew him out of the temple: and forthwith the doors were shut.
31- **And as they went about to kill him**, tidings came unto the chief captain of the band, that all Je-ru'sa-lem was in an uproar.

32- Who immediately took soldiers and centurions, and ran down unto them: and when they saw the chief captain and the soldiers, **they left beating of Paul**.

-Acts 21 v 28-32

They were beating Paul. **<u>Where was James</u>?** What would stop them? Had not Roman soldiers been there the mob probably would have killed Paul. Many times did Paul come close to death during his 'Apostleship' at the hand of the Jews and the people of the lands. "In deaths oft..."

Paul would use the word 'Gentiles' but the Jews took it as Blasphemy

Luke gives an account with Paul himself speaking of another incident. Paul would look first for a synagogue in all the towns he traveled to. He eventually would get 'the boot' and would then take his 'Gospel of Grace' to the Gentiles.

Paul is saying to 'Jews of the Circumcision/Law' of a previous experience he had. These Jews reacted in the same manner:

17- And it came to pass, that, when I was come again to Je-ru'sa-lem, even while I prayed in the temple, I was in a trance;

18- And saw him *(Jesus)* saying unto me, Make haste, and get thee quickly out of Je-ru'sa-lem: for they will not receive thy testimony concerning me.

19- And I said, Lord, they know that I imprisoned and beat in every synagogue them that believed on thee:

20- And when the blood of thy martyr Ste'phen was shed, I also was standing by, and consenting unto his death, and kept the raiment of them that slew him.

21- **And he *(Jesus)* said unto me, Depart: for I will send thee far hence unto the Gen'tiles.**

-Acts 22 v 17-21

As Paul was relating to his audience of Jews all was well and good until he used the word 'Gentiles'. The Jews quit being cordial. That word 'Gentile' was a 'blasphemous swear word' and an insult to even speak the word in the company of Jews. Jews are not Gentiles. Gentiles are not Jews.

'Ye men of Israel' could not also have included Gentiles. This has been falsely taught to much of Christendom.

22- And they gave him audience unto this word *(Gentiles v 21)*, and *then* lifted up their voices, and said, Away with such a *fellow* from the earth: for it is not fit that he should live.
23- And as they cried out, and cast off *their* clothes, and threw dust into the air,
24- The chief captain commanded him to be brought into the castle, **and bade that he should be <u>examined by</u> <u>scourging</u>**; that he might know wherefore they cried so against him.
-Acts 22 v 22-24

They whipped and scourged Paul. Five times Paul writes that he was whipped with 39 lashes by the Jews. 40 lashes is a death sentence. How many more times was he scourged by the non-Jews? Paul's body must have been a marvel of scars.

There was no antibiotics back then. Were the whips cleaned after every time they were used on somebody? God is the antibiotic. The Apostle Paul should have been dead many times over. A normal person would not have survived. Infection took care of most scourging victims. These would later die after having survived the initial lashes.

Paul suffered for the sake of the Gospel and for the 'Body of Christ'. It is an amazing act of God that his writings were preserved and not lost nor destroyed. When Paul wrote his epistles he was 'Holy Spirit' inspired and didn't know at the time that he was actually writing 'Biblical Scripture'. He did not write with the intention 'of making a Bible'. It was the 'compilers' around 300 A.D. that gathered and organized his epistles. This had to be an 'act of God'.

The Roman imprisonment of Paul

7- And when he was come, the Jews which came down from Je-ru'sa-lem stood round about, and laid many and grievous complaints against Paul, which they could not prove.
8- While he answered for himself, Neither against the law of the Jews, neither against the temple, nor yet against Cae'sar, have I offended any thing at all.

9- **But Fes'tus, willing to do the Jews a pleasure**, answered Paul, and said, Wilt thou go up to Je-ru'sa-lem, and there be judged of these things before me?

10- Then said Paul, I stand at Cae'sars judgment seat, where I ought to be judged: to the Jews have I done no wrong, as thou very well knowest.

11- For if I be an offender, or have committed any thing worthy of death, I refuse not to die: but if there be none of these things whereof these accuse me, no man may deliver me unto them. I appeal unto Cae'sar.

12- Then Fes'tus, when he had conferred with the Council, answered, Hast thou appealed unto Cae'sar? Unto Cae'sar shalt thou go.

-Acts 25 v 7-12

The Apostle Paul had a dual citizenship. His father must have been a Jew with Roman citizenship like so many after the Babylonians had scattered them in 606 B.C. Under Roman law, a Roman citizen is awarded a trial to prove their innocence. Innocent until proven guilty. When Paul said he was a Roman they quit beating him and took him to Rome.

16- And when we came to Rome, the centurion delivered the prisoners to the captain of the guard: but Paul was suffered to dwell by himself with a soldier that kept him.

17- And it came to pass, that after three days **Paul called the chief of the Jews together**: and when they were come together, he said unto them, Men *and* brethren, though I have committed nothing against the people, or customs of our fathers, yet was I delivered prisoner from Je-ru'sa-lem into the hands of the Ro'mans.

18- Who, when they had examined me, would have let *me* go, because there was no cause of death in me.

19- But when **the Jews spake against *it***, I was constrained to appeal unto Cae'sar; not that I had ought to accuse my nation of.

20- For this cause therefore have I called for you, to see *you*, and to speak with *you*: because that **for the hope of Is'ra-el I am bound with this chain**.

21- And they said unto him, We neither received letters out of Ju'de-a concerning thee, neither any of the brethren that came showed or speak any harm of thee.

22- But we desire to hear of thee what thou thinkest: for as concerning **this sect, we know that every where it is spoken against.**

23- And when they had appointed him a day, there came many to him into *his* lodging; to whom he expounded and testified the kingdom of God*, persuading them concerning Je'sus, both out of the law of Mo'ses, and *out of* the prophets from morning till evening. *(*Paul too preached the Kingdom of God but never 'The Gospel of the Kingdom'.)*

24- And some believed the things which were spoken, and some believe not.

25- And when they agreed not among themselves, **they departed, after that Paul had spoken one word *(Gentiles v28)*,** Well spake the Ho'ly Ghost by E-sa'ias the prophet unto our fathers,

26- Saying, Go unto this people, and say, Hearing ye shall hear, and shall not understand; and seeing ye shall see, and not perceive:

27- For the heart of this people is waxed gross, and their ears are dull of hearing, and their eyes have they closed; lest they should see with *their eyes*, and hear with *their ears*, and understand with *their* heart, and should be converted, and I should heal them.

28- Be it known therefore unto you, that **the salvation of God is sent unto the Gen'tiles, and *that* they will hear it.**

29- **And when he had said these words, the Jews departed,** and had great reasoning among themselves.

30- And Paul dwelt two whole years in his own hired house, and received all that came in unto him,

31- Preaching the kingdom of God, and teaching those things which concern the Lord Je'sus Christ with all confidence, no man forbidding him.

-Acts 28 v 16-31

Are you a Barjesus?

6- And when they had gone through the isle unto Pa'phos, they found a certain sorcerer, a false prophet, a Jew, whose name *was* Bar-je'sus:

7- Which was with the deputy of the country, Ser'gi-us Pau'lus, a prudent man; who called for Bar'na-bas and Saul, and desired to hear the word of God.

-Acts 13 v 6, 7

This man of importance (Ser'gi-us Pau'lus), a deputy of the country had called (contacted) Barnabas and Saul and wanted to speak with them specifically concerning the 'Word of God':

8- But El'y-mas the sorcerer (for so is his name by interpretation) **withstood them, seeking to turn away the deputy from the faith**.
-Acts 13 v 8

Barjesus/Elymas was already available to Sergius Paulus. Why didn't the deputy get the knowledge from this Jew? Verse 7 says he was a prudent man, and so he was. He wasn't trusting in this sorcerer's knowledge concerning the word of God, even though Barjesus/Elymas was a Jew.

9- Then Saul, (who also *is called* Paul,) filled with the Ho'ly Ghost, set his eyes on him,
10- And said, O full of all subtilty and all mischief, *thou* child of the devil, *thou* enemy of all righteousness, wilt thou not cease to pervert the right ways of the Lord?
11- And now, behold, the hand of the Lord *is* upon thee, and thou shalt be blind, not seeing the sun for a season. And immediately there fell on him a mist and a darkness; and he went about seeking some to lead him by the hand.
12- Then the deputy, when he saw what was done, believed, being astonished at the doctrine of the Lord.
-Acts 13 v 9-12

Bar-jesus was made 'blind for a season'. He wasn't blind forever. This same 'spiritual blindness' has happened to Israel and the Jews. At Jesus' second coming this 'Spiritual Blindness' will be lifted. Hence, all Israel will be saved. That is, those who survived the seven year Tribulation.

25- For I would not, brethren, that ye should be ignorant of this mystery, lest ye should be wise in your own conceits; that blindness in part is happened to Is'ra-el, <u>until</u> **the fullness of the Gen'tiles be come in** *(caught up?)*.
-Romans 11 v 25

The damsel possessed with the 'spirit of divination'

16- And it came to pass, as we went to prayer, a damsel possessed with a spirit of divination met us, which brought her masters much gain by soothsaying.
-Acts 16 v 16

The power of Satan is real. He is the god of this world. There are those that embrace the spirits of darkness. Fortunetellers, soothsayers, witch doctors, voodoo priest to name a few. Satan does not have the power of salvation, only damnation.

17- The same followed Paul and us, and cried, saying, These men are the servants of **the most high God**, which show unto us the way of salvation. -Acts 16 v 17

The 'dark side' is well aware of 'the Most High God' and of Jesus Christ. To believe in this 'dark side' also acknowledges the 'Light side' though the 'man side' won't admit it. Satan keeps the 'blinders on' leaving mankind to 'stumble in the dark'. Satan can transform himself into an angel of light deceiving the world*. Mankind without God is easily deceived. A person given some kind of 'a power' from the 'dark side' doesn't go seeking the 'True Light'. *-II Corinthians 11 v 14

This damsel of the 'dark side' is speaking out uncontrollably and couldn't contain her tongue. She knew the 'True Light' had crossed paths with her shadow. What happens to a shadow when a light is manifested?

18- And this did she many days. But Paul, being grieved, turned and said to the spirit, I command thee in the name of Jesus Christ to come out of her. And he came out the same hour. -Acts 16 v 18

The damsels masters lost their money making asset. They were not at all pleased with the Apostle Paul. These 'masters of the damsel' had Paul and his Apostles beaten, whipped and thrown into the inner most prison putting their feet fast in the stocks*. *-Acts 16 v 19-24

The evil spirit that overwhelmed the vagabond Jews that were practicing 'exorcism'

13- Then certain of the vagabond Jews, exorcists, took upon them which had evil spirits the name of Lord Jesus, saying, **We adjure you by Je'sus whom Paul preacheth**.

14- And there were seven sons of one Sce'va, a Jew, and chief of the priests, which did so.

-Acts 19 v 13, 14

'Jews of the Circumcision/Law' were attempting to cast out 'evil spirits' that had possessed some men and women. Using the method that Paul had used in Acts Chapter 16, they were attempting the same way. This chief priest of the Jews and his seven sons invoked the process of exorcism after this way: "We adjure you by Jesus whom Paul preacheth".

These Jews were still under 'the Law' and had not embraced Paul's 'Faith-way Gospel of Grace, Christ Crucified'. They had no power of God behind their words. These were not following the "Jesus whom Paul preacheth" but were going to try to trick the evil spirit in this man who was possessed.

15- **And the evil spirit answered and said, <u>Je'sus I know, and Paul I know</u>; but who are ye?**

-Acts 19 v 15

That is quite the proof and endorsement of Paul's God given Apostleship! This evil spirit knew who Paul is by name.

These 'exorcist Jew vagabonds' were overwhelmed by this man possessed of the devil. They knew not the Jesus whom Paul preached. Paul preached 'Christ Crucified' and the 'Power of Resurrection'. It is the Jesus Christ on this side of the cross that is now living in us that we know, not the Jesus that walked the streets of Israel*. *-II Corinthians 5 v 16

16- And the man in whom the evil spirit was leaped on them, and overcame them, and prevailed against them, so that they fled out of that house naked and wounded.

-Acts 19 v 16

Pharaoh's magicians used the power of Satan

8- And the LORD spake unto Mo'ses and unto Aar'on, saying,

9- When Pha'raoh shall speak unto you, saying, Shew a miracle for you: then thou shalt say unto Aar'on, Take thy rod, and cast *it* before Pha'raoh, *and* it shall become a serpent.

10- And Mo'ses and Aar'on went in unto Pha'raoh, and they did so as the LORD had commanded: and Aar'on cast down his rod before Pha'raoh, and before his servants, and it became a serpent.

11- Then Pha'raoh also called the wise men and the sorcerers: **now the magicians of E'gypt, they also did in like manner with their enchantments.**

12- For they cast down every man his rod, **and they became serpents: but Aar'on's rod swallowed up their rods**.

-Exodus 7 v 8-12

When the 'Body of Christ' is 'caught up' to meet the Lord in the air, the 'Stopping Dam' will be removed. The Tribulation, The Wrath of God, The Wrath of Satan, and the Day of the Lord will be executed. The worlds population will be at its max.

The 'false godhead' will work and deceive the world. With lying wonders and magic the world will become influenced the more. The Anti-Christ is not necessarily against Christ, but will be a False-Christ.

Will Israel think that he is the Messiah of scripture and has finally come the first time? He will bring peace to Israel for 3.5 years. This is what Israel has been praying for, PEACE!

Many of 'the Twelve' suffered a horrible persecution and death at the hands of men. The martyrdom of Jesus Christ's selected disciples is really a sad story. The Nation of Israel has never recovered since the glory days of King Solomon. Because of Israel's continued unbelief they were forewarned by God that they would be chastened and scattered among the heathen*. *-Deuteronomy 30 v 3; -Jeremiah 30 v 11; -Jeremiah 31 v 10; -Ezekiel 6 v 8-10; -Ezekiel 11 v 16, 17; -Ezekiel 20 v 41, 42; -Ezekiel 28 v 25, 26; -Ezekiel 36 v 19, 20; -Zechariah 7 v 11-14

Israel never accepted their King and Messiah Jesus Christ. 'The Earthly Kingdom of Heaven' was postponed for the 'filling of the Body of Christ'. How long? The Bible don't say. It is a 'parenthetical' ( ) time in scripture

that was made relevant with the appearance of Paul's Apostleship and his ministry to the Gentiles. Jews too become Gentiles when they forsake 'the laws of Judaism' for there is no difference when it comes to the 'Gospel and Doctrine of Grace'. We are one and the same in the 'Body of Christ'*.
*-Romans 3 v 22; -Romans 10 v 12

From day one, the Apostle Paul was undermined by the Jews, by 'the Twelve', and many 'so-called Christians, 'the Barjesus'. Things and circumstances are no different today. The Apostle Paul since the beginning of his ministry has been pushed aside and ignored. The newer translations of Bibles have even changed and left out some 'Divine Scriptures of Truth'.

May God have mercy on these modern day translators, writers and publishers. Twisting out of context Paul's unique Apostleship to the Gentiles is an act of Satan. Yes, if your Bible has taken the meanings of the KJV and twisted it, your Bible is 'Satan tainted' and no good. Would you know?

Example: On TV, The Church Channel, a President from a notable 'Christian College' was reading scripture from a newer translation. He read to the world and perhaps millions this verse:
15- This *is* a faithful saying, and worthy of all acceptation, that Christ came into the world to save sinners: **of whom I am the worst *(Paul?)*.**

My KJV Bible writes:
15- This is a faithful saying, and worthy of all acceptation, that Christ came into the world to save sinners: **of whom I am chief *(Paul)*.**
-Timothy 1 v 15

Chief does not mean 'the worst'. What does a thesaurus say about the word chief? Since when has 'chief' been used in such a negative way? English 'slang' like being 'bad' means your 'real good'? And why 'this way is used' when it comes to the writings of Paul? Satan, the god of this world?

Christ came to save sinners, but on this side of the cross, Paul is the leader, the head man, the first in line, the chief. "Be ye followers of me as I follow Christ"*, the resurrected Christ. He is the 'Apostle of the Gentiles'. The Word of God says so. Saul of Tarsus may have been a bad man but throughout history there have been far worse men. *-I Corinthians 4 v 15, 16; -I Corinthians 11 v 1; -Philippians 3 v 17-21

This college president of course didn't read the next scripture, though given how out of context the previous one was I would assume his translated Bible further marginalized Paul's unique Apostleship.

The King James (KJV) reads:
16- Howbeit for this cause I obtained mercy, **that in me first *(chief)* Je'sus** Christ might shew forth all longsuffering, **for a pattern to them which should hereafter believe on him to life everlasting**.
-Timothy 1 v 16

Let's read it as this false Bible is saying:
-Howbeit for this cause I obtained mercy, **that in me first, who is the worst of all sinners,** Je'sus Christ might show forth all longsuffering, **for a pattern to them given by the worst sinner which should hereafter believe on him to life everlasting**.

Take heed ye 'Barjesus' of today:
6- And the angels which kept not their first estate, but left their own habitation, he hath reserved in everlasting chains under darkness until the judgment of the great day.
-Jude v 6

Paul writes of the constant 'spiritual warfare' ever present in this world of sinful men. Satan, the god of this world, never sleeps nor rests. Anything he can do to keep mankind from 'the truth' is his mission. The 'freewill of man' is part of God's overall plan.

12- For we wrestle not against flesh and blood, but against principalities, against powers, against the rulers of darkness of this world, against spiritual wickedness in high *places*.
13- Wherefore take unto you the whole armour of God, that ye may be able to withstand in the evil day, and having done all, to stand.
-Ephesians 6 v 12, 13

BOOK IV

Jesus Christ Died a 'Law Keeper'

5- These twelve **Je'sus** sent forth, and **commanded them**, saying, **Go not into the way of the Gen'tiles, and into** *any* **city of the Sa-mar'i-tans enter ye not:**
6- **But go rather to the lost sheep of the house of Is'ra-el.**
7- And as ye go, **preach** saying, **The kingdom of heaven is at hand**.
-Matthew 10 v 5, 6

4- But when the fullness of the time was come, God sent forth his **Son**, made of a women, **made under the law,**
5- **To redeem** them that were **under the law**, that we might receive the adoption of sons.
-Galatians 4 v 4, 5

8- Now I say that **Jesus Christ was a minister of the circumcision** for the truth of God, **to confirm the promises made unto the fathers:**
9- And that the Gentiles might glorify God for *his* mercy; For this cause I will confess to thee among the Gentiles, and sing unto thy name.
-Romans 15 v 8, 9

Jesus Christ was made in the flesh under 'the Law'. Jesus Christ came to redeem them that were under 'the Law'. Jesus Christ was a 'minister of the Circumcision'. Jesus Christ came to Israel to confirm the promises made to the fathers of Israel. The fathers of Israel are not the fathers of the Gentiles.

What did Jesus himself say?:

17- Think not that I am come to destroy the law, or the prophets: I am not come to destroy, but to fulfil.

-Matthew 5 v 17

Jesus came **"To redeem** them that were **under the law"**. Jesus Christ **was not** a minister to the whole world as he walked the streets of Israel. After 'the Resurrection' through 'the Revelations (revealing) of the hidden Secrets/Mysteries' given to Paul, the whole world of Gentiles (you and me) can now obtain salvation. This **salvation is of faith** in the 'Finished Work of the Cross' and 'the Power of his Resurrection'. 'Salvation' is not of any 'Righteous Works' or by doing 'Denominational and Religious Legalisms' of any kind.

The 'Faith-way Doctrine of Grace' was **revealed** to the Apostle Paul, not 'the Twelve', not Peter, not Luke. Jesus Christ never mentioned in his earthly ministry that the Gentiles would be able to obtain salvation and the 'Heavenly Gifts of God' without the Jew. Jesus commanded his own chosen disciples to ignore all Gentiles, you and me*. We are Gentiles. We Gentiles were never 'Jews of the Circumcision/Law'. *-Matthew 10 v 5, 6

11- Wherefore remember, that ye *being* in time past Gen'tiles in the flesh, who are called Uncircumcision by that which is called the Circumcision in the flesh made by hands;

12- **That at that time ye were without Christ *(Messiah)*, being aliens from the commonwealth of Is'ra-el, and strangers from the covenants of promise, having no hope, and without God in the world:**

13- **But now** in Christ Je'sus ye who sometimes were far off are made nigh by the blood of Christ.

-Ephesians 2 v 11-13

This knowledge of truth the majority of Christendom ignores. Most of 'Christendom' tries to place itself before the cross 'identifying themselves' with the 'earthly ministry of Jesus Christ'. The 'Jews of the Circumcision' and Jesus' disciples were still 'under and keepers' of 'the Law'. These 'supposed Christians' of today are in no such place. They are not the 'lost sheep of the House of Israel'. They are not 'Jews of the Circumcision/Law'. Read Ephesian 2 v 11-13 until it sticks. Memorize it.

The Gentiles and everyone who is not a 'Jew of the Circumcision' under the 'Law of Moses' had no hope. They, you and me, were lost. **This is the 'Word of God', the TRUTH!** Paul's Gospel revealed our salvation after 'the Resurrection'. The salvation of the Gentiles is not found in our Bible before 'the Resurrection of Christ'. Does this make a difference? Yes, why follow a Doctrine and Gospel that was never meant for you?

Most of Christendom have missed this truth. A religion or denomination not faithfully devoted to the Apostle Paul's knowledge of 'his Gospel', the truth is lost*. The parishioners devoid of Paul's Gospel have been led astray. This can be said because of what the 'Word of God' says and listening to what men have been teaching. They themselves, preachers and teachers, are blind leaders of their blind followers. *-I Corinthians 15 v 1-4

There were very few Gentiles that fell into the Grace of God in the Old Testament. Individually these could be counted on one hand and by no means could be considered a nation of people like that of the Jews of Israel. God showed mercy on whom he chose*. God is sovereign and did make exceptions but very few Gentiles were given the 'Grace of God'. *-Exodus 33 v 19; -Romans 9 v 15, 18

Jesus the Christ **did not** come in the flesh **to die** on the cross. This **was not** the purpose of 'Jesus' earthly ministry'. This was not part of 'Law keeping' that Jesus was to die on a Roman Cross for the sins of the whole world. This crucifixion of the Messiah and Christ was not part of the practices of Judaism and the Law.

Jesus Christ came to Israel to 'validate' who he was by 'signs and miracles'. God knew that Son Jesus was going to be crucified but this was hid (a mystery/secret) and was not made understandable to Israel and the disciples*. Jesus Christs' earthly ministry **was for** the purpose of confirming Old Testament prophecies of the King and the Earthly Kingdom of Heaven, not to come and die at the hands of man.
*-Luke 9 v 44, 45; -Luke 18 v 31-34

"Ye who sometimes were far off are made nigh by the blood of Christ". 'The blood' that Jesus Christ shed on 'the Cross'. His 'atoning blood' was the final sacrifice for the sins of all mankind. 'Christ Crucified' is Paul's revealed 'Gospel of Grace'. No one knew this mystery/secret of salvation until the Holy Spirit revealed it to the Apostle Paul on this side, our side of 'the Cross'. Nor did anyone know he was going to resurrect never to die again*. *-Luke 18 v 31-34; -John 20 v 1-9

He came to Israel to fulfill the prophecies of an 'Earthly Heavenly Kingdom' and he was that King, the Christ, the Messiah. Most of Israel rejected 'the Name of Jesus Christ' and who he was and what he stood for. They failed to see that this man from Nazareth is the Messiah, is the Christ, is the LORD of Lords and King of kings.

Paul (Holy Spirit inspired) writes:
7- But **we speak the wisdom of God in a mystery** *(revealed secrets)*, even the hidden wisdom, which **God ordained before the world unto our glory**:
8- Which **none of the princes of this world knew**: for **had they known** *it*, they would not have crucified the Lord of glory.
-I Corinthians 2 v 7, 8

Israel was 'spiritually blind'. They had taken their place of position 'at the LORD's Table' and turned its 'Laws' into 'a religion of filthy rags'*. Israel as a nation is spiritually blind even today. They still do not believe that Jesus Christ already came for them. They do not read and believe the New Testament. The Jews of today have no advantage over 'The Body of Christ'. Both the Jew and the Gentile will be judged by God according to Paul's Gospel+ after the resurrection. *-Isaiah 64 v 5-7; +-Romans 3 v 19-26; -Romans 10 v 12; -Romans 2 v 16; -Romans 16 v 25; -Romans 1 v 16, 17

16- **In the day when God shall judge the secrets of men by Je'sus Christ according to my gospel.**
-Romans 2 v 16

25- Now to him that is of power **to stablish you according to my gospel**, and the preaching of Je'sus Christ, **according to the revelation of the mystery, which was kept secret since the world began.**
-Romans 16 v 25

16- For I am not ashamed of the gospel of Christ: for **it is the power of God unto salvation to every one that believeth**; to the Jew first, and also to the Greek *(Gentile)*.
17- For therein is the righteousness of God revealed from faith to faith: as it is written, **The Just shall live by faith.**
-Romans 1 v 16, 17

"Salvation to every one that believeth". Salvation is not just given to the most devout Christian who goes to church every Sunday, or who was water baptized and steadily pays tithes, etc. But to EVERYONE! How? To EVERYONE THAT BELIEVETH!

Many (most) believe that Jesus came in the flesh so he could and would be crucified. "That is why he came. He came to suffer and die on the cross for our sins. Every Christian knows that", the world teaches. If this is why he came, that is to be crucified and to suffer, then what is the real significance of his resurrection? What act was bigger and more important concerning our salvation? The Crucifixion or the Resurrection?

The Old Testament prophecies spoke of 'a suffering savior' but gave no real specifics. Not until after the resurrection was it understood that it was Jesus Christ that the prophecies were speaking of*. Israel Nationally (most) are still waiting for their king to come the first time. *-John 12 v 16

Where are the preachers teaching the 'Power of Resurrection'? Most of Christendom skip the importance of 'Resurrection' and prefer to preach 'the Earthly Ministry of Jesus Christ'. It is more 'colorful'. All good and profitable of course, but the salvation for all the world happened when Jesus Christ physically died on the cross and was resurrected*. *-I Corinthians 15

In the 'Big Picture of Salvation', for all of mankind this was done. In the 'all knowing and foreknowledge of God' it was preplanned in eternity past. Nobody knew until the 'Resurrected Jesus Christ' revealed it to the Apostle Paul that resurrection is the 'Key of Salvation' for the Gentiles and for all the world.

Do these professing Christians of today realize our 'Biblical hope of salvation'? Where did salvation begin? Do these Christians know the truth behind the Resurrection? Or is 'the Resurrection' something that merely happened and is only seen as the final public presentation in the life of Jesus Christ?

Do they even know that Jesus Christ was taken up (caught up) bodily into heaven*? Do they know that this happened twice after the resurrection*? Easter service is over, what's for lunch? *-Acts 1 v 9-11; -John 20 v 14-17

Watching a preacher with a panel of four others on TV just now (these have notoriety and I remember hearing some of their names since childhood), they spoke well of scripture and even used some scriptures from the Apostle Paul. The Topic was the 'Cross of Christ'. "Look to the Cross, be sanctified by his shed blood and avoid the wrath of God". But not one time did they speak of the Resurrection and its significance concerning the Gentiles salvation. They spoke and agreed as if they knew the truth of God's word and the millions of viewers need to accept their teachings. These have been doing this their whole life time. If the 'Power of Resurrection' is not part of their ministry, it is not part of the revealed truth of salvation. Follow what the Word of God says not what men claim to know.

With this 'Show of Unbelief' by Israel, the 'Strait Gate of Salvation' was opened for all mankind. Don't forget that the Gentiles too had a hand in crucifying Jesus. The unknowing world of men try to pin all the blame on the Jew, but the Jews and Gentiles are both guilty. With God's own chosen people rejecting and viciously having him die by the hands of the Roman Gentiles, salvation has been made possible for the whole world of men and women.

Jesus is 'Just and the Justifier'* to all that believe 'The Gospel'. In the 'Big Picture', he died for the sins of the whole world. The sins of the past, present and future for all mankind. But this 'Truth of Salvation' was only revealed to the Apostle Paul several years after 'the Crucifixion' and 'the Resurrection'. * -Acts 13 v 38, 39; -Romans 3 v 20-30; -Romans 4 v 2-6; -Romans 5 v 1, 2, 8-11, 15-21; -Romans 8 v 29, 30; -I Corinthians 6 v 11; -Galatians 2 v 16, 17; -Galatians 3 v 8-29; -Galatians 5 v 2-6; -Titus 3 v 5-8; -Hebrews 10 v 38, 39

On this side of the cross, all of mankind can now receive the 'free gift of grace' for salvation. This mystery was hid and kept from Israel and the Jews. Gentiles having a chance of salvation by their LORD and God too? What? Unheard of!

Paul writes Holy Spirit inspired to the Colossians:
20- And, having made peace **through the blood of his cross, by him to reconcile all things unto himself**; by him, *I say*, whether *they be* things in earth, or things in heaven.
21- And you, that were sometime alienated and enemies in *your* mind by wicked works, yet now hath he reconciled.
22- In the body of his flesh through death, to present you holy and unblameable and unreproveable in his sight:
23- If ye continue in the faith grounded and settled, and *be* not moved away from the hope of **the gospel**, which ye have heard, *and* which was

preached to every creature which is under heaven; whereof **I Paul am made a minister**;

24- Who now rejoice in my sufferings for you, and to fill up that which is behind of the afflictions of **Christ** in my flesh for **his body's sake, which is the church**;

25- Whereof **I am made a minister**, according to **the dispensation of God** which is **given to me for you, to fulfil** *(complete)* **the word of God**;

26- Even **the mystery which hath been hid** from ages and from generations, but now is made manifest to his saints *(Paul's ministry)*:

27- To whom God would make known what *is* the riches of the glory of **this mystery among the Gentiles; which is Christ in you, the hope of glory**:

28- Whom we preach, warning every man, and teaching every man in all wisdom; that we may present every man perfect *(Spiritually mature)* in Christ Jesus:

29- Whereunto I also labour, striving according to his working, which worketh in me mightily.

-Colossians 1 v 20-29

Jesus Christ came for Israel in the Flesh

Jesus Christ **commanded** 'the Twelve Apostles' not to associate with anyone that was not a 'Jew of the Circumcision'*. This has been the same 'mod-us operand-i' for the Jewish behavior since Moses. Nothing had changed. Jesus Christ himself told his disciples not to go to anyone that was even a half Jew, the Samaritans. *-Matthew 10 v 5-7

"I thought Jesus Christ came in the flesh for the whole world"? What, Jesus is not even compromising with the Samaritans*? When Jesus did visit with the Samaritan women at the 'well of water', his disciples were not present initially. The disciples showed up awhile later "and marvelled that he talked with the women: yet no man said, What seekest thou? Or, Why talkest thou to her?"+. 'The Twelve' **were commanded** not to meet with such a one. *-Matthew 10 v 5-7; +-John 4 v 7-44

Jesus Christ was 'a minister of the circumcision'. A minister to Israel and not the whole world. He came to 'them that were under the Law'. Again I ask? To confirm what promises made to whose fathers? Have you ever heard these scriptures* during a 'Christmas or Easter service'? Have you heard these scriptures at any church service? Did you know they were in the 'Written Word of Truth'?

*-Matthew 10 v 5-7; -Galatians 4 v 4, 5; -Romans 15 v 8, 9

Everything Jesus said and did during his earthly ministry was 'under the Law' and according to 'the Law'. His disciples as well were all 'observers and doers of the Law'. The Pharisee's and Sadducees' tried to catch and trick Jesus claiming that he wasn't keeping 'the Law' or that he was breaking it.

Many of these accusations were made when Jesus performed miracles of healing on the Sabbath day. These 'religious zealots' were claiming that his miracles were 'works' and working on 'the Sabbath' was forbidden by 'the Law'. Yet they saw the miracles of healing being made, but in their hardness of heart (unbelief) couldn't see that Jesus is Son and God. They were quick to point out that he was 'working' on the Sabbath but failed to see what he was actually doing. Guilty until proven guilty? Kill him before the world see's that he is innocent!

35- And **Je'sus** went about all the cities and villages, teaching in their synagogues, **preaching the gospel of the kingdom**, and healing every sickness and every disease among the people.

-Matthew 9 v 35; -Matthew 4 v 23; -Matthew 24 v 14; -Mark 1 v 14, 15

Has all your attention been focused on 'Jesus' earthly ministry' in Matthew, Mark, Luke, John and the early chapters in the Book of Acts, the Jewish Epistles and The Old Testament? Is your doctrine and hope of salvation based off of those books? Are they the main focus of the church you attend? Are the Epistles written by Paul viewed with little acceptance as compared to the rest of the Bible?

Understood, after all, 'Jesus' earthly ministry' should be all one needs for salvation as it would 'universally seem'. Many feel safe in believing that if they follow the words of Jesus as he ministered to Israel it applies to themselves too. His words would seem to be the top and foremost of importance to all other scriptures in the Bible. After all, Jesus is Jesus. Who is there better that mankind can follow? **Answer – the Resurrected Lord Jesus Christ.**

Jesus Died a Law keeper

Who was under 'The Law'? 'The Law' of scripture are the Commandments that were given to Moses and 'the Children of Israel' around 1500 B.C.. The 10 Commandments was not 'the full Law' but a part of 'the Law' that still applies for all the world today. Only Israel as a nation and the Jew/Hebrews were under 'The Full Law'.

We Gentiles had nothing to do with the 'Covenant Promises' made to the Nation of Israel. Yet, it has been taught that when we believe in Jesus Christ we are now Jews. Did the Children of Israel in the Old Testament know who Jesus Christ is? Of course not, yet there are those that claim they did. What kind of a Bible are they reading?

Those that incorrectly divide (or not divide) the 'Word of Truth' have taken the 'Pauline revelations of God' and 'mixed and mashed' scriptures together. Even a 'round peg' can be forced into a square hole. The 'square hole' is not filled. There are empty spaces in the corners. The vessel has leaks. The Gospel of Grace has no leaks. It is easily understood, but is meaningless if not believed deeply in the heart by faith.

The 'Jerusalem Temple' was destroyed in 70 A.D. by Titus the Roman General. Without 'the Temple', the keeping of the 'full Law' is no longer possible. There is no place to sacrifice animals for the 'Jew of the Circumcision/Law' to 'atone for their sins'. Because there is no Temple, all have transgressed that are 'Law keepers'.

Today, is all of Israel following 'the Law' knowing that breaking any aspect of it is breaking all 'the Laws'? Israel Nationally is guilty. What is a Jew and the 'Jew wannabe', proselytes to do? Follow Peter? Peter kept 'the Law'. Follow Jesus' earthly ministry? He too kept 'the Law' and was the perfect example of 'Law keeping'.

The Mosaic Law was still 'in full practice' when Jesus Christ came in the flesh for the Nation of Israel. The Law was not being kept in 'its purist form' as it was originally given to Moses. The 'watered down aspects of the Law' were being observed but full adherence to the true 'Law of Moses' had been tampered with by man over time.

Working on the Sabbath day could still get a Jew stoned to death. The 'Jews of the Circumcision/Law' still were carrying out acts of capital punishment. The Jews stoned Stephen to death after Jesus Christ had died on the cross.

How many times did the Jew's want to kill Jesus themselves? These 'do gooders under the Law' were calling Jesus a blasphemer and a devil. If they could have caught him they would have killed him. But circumstances and opportunity were missed. Somehow (we know how) he was able to disappear and slip away until he knew it was time for him to be caught.

Jesus is confronted by Jewish unbelievers:
24- Then came the Jews round about him, and said unto him, How long dost thou make us to doubt? If thou be the Christ, tell us plainly.
25- Jesus answered them, I told you, and ye believed not: the works that I do in my Father's name, they bear witness of me.
26- But ye believe not, because ye are not of my sheep, as I said unto you.
27- My sheep hear my voice, and I know them, and they follow me:
28- And I give unto them eternal life; and they shall never perish, neither shall any *man* pluck them out of my hand.
29- My Father, which gave them me, is greater than all; and no *man* is able to pluck *them* out of my Fathers hand.
30- **I and *my* Father are one.**
31- **Then the Jews took up stones again to stone him.**
32- Jesus answered them, Many good works have I shewed you from my Father, for which of these works do ye stone me?
33- The Jews answered him, saying, For a good work we stone thee not; but for blasphemy; and because that thou, being a man, makest thyself God.
34- Jesus answered them, Is it not written in your law, **I said**, Ye are gods?
35- If he called them gods, unto whom the word of God came, and the scripture cannot be broken;
36- Say ye of him, whom the Father hath sanctified, and sent into the world, Thou blasphemest; because I said, I am the Son of God?
37- If I do the works of my Father, believe me not.
38- But if I do, though ye believe not me, believe the works: that ye may know, and believe, that **the Father *is* in me, and I in him**.
39- Therefore they sought again to take him: **but he escaped out of their hand**,
-John 10 v 24-39

The Lord Jesus Christ is the Word made flesh who said:
56- Your father Abraham rejoiced to see my day: and he saw *it*, and was glad.

57- Then said the Jews unto him, Thou art not yet fifty years old, and hast thou seen Abraham?

58- Jesus said unto them, Verily, verily, I say unto you, **Before Abraham was, I am**.

59- Then took they up stones to cast at him: but Jesus hid himself, and went out of the temple, going through the midst of them, and so passed by.
-John 8 v 56-59

The Moral Law (the 10 Commandments), The Levitical Law (priestly duties and how to deal with sin), and The Civil Law (how to live with fellow Jews) was 'their Law'. The 10 Commandments did make the whole world guilty by the 'knowledge of sin'. Keeping the 10 Commandments will not provide salvation, it can only condemn a person. The Law should be the natural norm. The thought of breaking it would/should never be entertained

The world of Gentiles were not keeping the 'Jewish Law of Moses'. No Gentile was making animal sacrifices to 'atone for their sins'. There were 'Proselytes' when a Gentile did become a Jew under the 'Law of the Circumcision' but these were not Jews by birth*. *-Exodus 12 v 37-51; -Nehemiah 13 v 1-3

But what did Jesus himself say concerning Proselytes?:

15- Woe unto you, scribes and Pharisees, hypocrites! For ye compass sea and land to make one proselyte, and when he is made, ye make him twofold more the child of hell than yourselves.
-Matthew 23 v 15

By the time Christ came there were over 600 plus laws, rules and regulations (legalism). 'The Law' was severe and 'a yoke of bondage'*. It was constantly pointing out sin. It was a 'Divine line' with 'no gray area'. It was 'do and observe' or 'die'. It could not save a soul but only could condemn and make man aware of their sinful natural ways. *-Galatians 5 v 1; -Acts 15 v 10; -II Corinthians 6 v 14

There are those that say, "I keep the 10 Commandments or as close as possible therefore I have salvation". Observing 'the Law' is the knowledge of sin, not salvation. Paul writes (Holy Spirit inspired):

19- Now we know that what things soever the law saith, it saith to them who are under the law: that every mouth may be stopped, and all the world may become guilty before God.

20- **Therefore by the deeds of the law there shall no flesh be justified in his sight: for by the law *is* the knowledge of sin.**

21- **But now** the righteousness of God without the law is manifested, being witnessed by the law and the prophets;

22- Even **the righteousness of God *which is* by faith of Jesus Christ** unto all and upon all them that believe: for there is no difference:

23- **For all have sinned, and come short of the glory of God;**

24- Being justified freely by his grace through the redemption that is in Christ Jesus:

25- Whom God hath set forth *to be* a propitiation *(appropriator)* through faith in his blood, to declare his righteousness for the remission of sins that are past, through the forbearance of God:

26- To declare, *I say*, at this time **his righteousness: that he might be just, and the justifier of him which believeth in Jesus**.

-Romans 3 v 19-26

Always remember that the Apostle Paul preached 'Christ Crucified' and the 'faith in the finished work of the cross'. Jesus Christ purposely died for you individually. If you were the only person alive he would have died for you. Jesus willingly submitted himself to be crucified by his own created beings so that we can have 'Eternal Salvation through Resurrection Power'.

When Paul speaks of Jesus Christ <u>it is not</u> his 'earthly ministry' but 'post resurrection'. Jesus Christ is 'just and fair'. Jesus Christ is 'the justifier' to all men that believe in 'his resurrection'. It is 'his righteousness' not man's 'righteous works'. 'God's righteousness' is a 'free gift by his Grace' given to all mankind that believe in the 'Resurrected Lord Jesus Christ'.

Mankind has its salvation on this side of the cross, post crucifixion*. He has given every person a 'free will' and a chance at eternal salvation. It is a free gift that we don't deserve. **Grace is the unmerited favor of God.** We are so lucky today with such an easy justification. This is the Grace of God. We have been given the 'Blessed Pardon'. Take it and believe! *-II Corinthians 5 v 14-17

13- **For the promise**, that he should be heir of the world, *was* not to A'bra-ham, or to his seed, through the law, but **through the righteousness of faith**.

14- **For if they which are of the law** *be* **heirs, faith is made void,** and the promise made of none effect:

15- Because the law worketh wrath: for where no law is, *there is* no transgression.

16- Therefore *it is* of faith, that it might be by grace; to the end the promise might be sure to all the seed; not to that only which is of the law, but to that also which is the faith of A'bra-ham; who is the father of us all,

17- (As it is written, I have made thee a father of many nations,) before him whom he believed, even God, who quickeneth the dead, and calleth those things which be not as though they were.

18- Who against hope believed in hope, that he might become the father of many nations, according to that which was spoken, So shall thy seed be.

19- And being not weak in faith, he considered not his own body now dead, when he was about a hundred years old, neither yet the deadness of Sa'rah's womb:

20- He staggered not at the promise of God through unbelief: but was strong in faith, giving glory to God;

21- And being fully persuaded, that what he had promised, he was able also to perform.

22- And therefore **it was imputed to him for righteousness.**

23- Now it was not written for his sake alone, that it was imputed to him;

24- **But for us also, to whom it shall be imputed, if we believe on him that raised Je'sus our Lord from the dead;**

25- **Who was delivered for our offences, and was raised again for our justification** *(Paul's Gospel).*

-Romans 4 v 13-25

Resurrection: The Power of God unto Salvation

It is one thing to believe in Jesus and take Jesus into your heart the same as 'the elect' and the Jew/Hebrews under 'the Law'. But it means far more to believe that Jesus Christ was 'raised from the dead'. **Resurrection is the power of God.**

4- And declared *to be* **the Son of God with power, according to the spirit of holiness, by the resurrection from the dead**:

5- By whom we have received grace and apostleship, for obedience to the faith among all nations, for his name:

6- Among whom are ye also the called of Jesus Christ:

-Romans 1 v 4-6

17- For Christ sent me not to baptize, but to preach the gospel: not with wisdom of words, lest the cross of Christ should be made of none effect.

18- For **the preaching of the cross** is to them that perish foolishness; but unto us which are saved it **is the power of God**.

19- For it is written, I will destroy the wisdom of the wise, and bring to nothing the understanding of the prudent.

20- Where *is* the wise? Where *is* the scribe? Where *is* the disputer of this world? Hath not God made foolish the wisdom of this world?

21- For after that in the wisdom of God the world by wisdom knew not God, it pleased God by the foolishness of preaching to save them that believe.

22- For the Jews require a sign, and the Greeks *(Gentiles)* seek after wisdom:

23- **But we preach Christ crucified,** unto the Jews a stumblingblock, and unto the Greeks *(Gentiles)* foolishness;

24- But unto them which are called, both Jew and Greeks, **Christ the power of God,** and the wisdom of God.

25- Because the foolishness of God is wiser than men; and the weakness of God is stronger than men.

26- For ye see your calling, brethren, how that not many wise men after the flesh, not many mighty, not many noble, *are called*:

27- But God hath chosen the foolish things of the world to confound the wise; and God hath chosen the weak things of the world to confound the things which are mighty;

28- And base things of the world, and things which are despised, hath God chosen, *yea*, and things which are not, to bring to nought things that are:

29- That no flesh should glory in his presence.

30- But of him are ye in Christ Jesus, who of God is made unto us wisdom, and righteousness, and sanctification, and redemption:

31- That, according as it is written, He that glorieth, let him glory in the Lord.

-I Corinthians 1 v 17-31

Saul/(Paul) was zealous of 'the Law' and was even given permission by the chief priests to search and find those who were believing in 'the Name of Jesus Christ'. Saul/(Paul) persecuted these Jew/Hebrews. But when Jesus Christ from heaven confronted Saul/(Paul) on 'the Road to Damascus' he saw the 'True Light'.

To Paul now, he viewed his material gains as a Pharisee 'under the Law' as garbage and dung*. Paul no longer was keeping 'the Law of Moses' like 'the Twelve' were still observing. Paul claimed to now know only one thing, <u>Christ and him crucified and the Power of God by the Resurrection</u>+.

*-Philippians 3 v 8; +-I Corinthians 2 v 2; -Philippians 3 v 9, 10

1- Finally, my brethren, rejoice in the Lord. To write the same things to you, to me indeed *is* not grievous, but for you *it is* safe.

2- Beware of dogs, beware of evil workers, beware of the concision.

3- For **we are the circumcision, which worship God in the spirit**, and rejoice in Christ Jesus, and have no confidence in the flesh.

4- Though I might also have confidence in the flesh. If any man thinketh that he hath whereof he might trust in the flesh, I more:

5- Circumcised the eighth day, of the stock of Israel, *of* the tribe of Benjamin, an Hebrew of the Hebrews; as touching the law, a Pharisee;

6- Concerning zeal, persecuting the church* *(not the Body of Christ)*; touching the righteousness which is in the law, blameless. *(*Church – a generic term used by the translators denoting religious gatherings)*

7- **But** what things were gain to me, those I counted loss for Christ.

8- Yea doubtless, **and I count all things *but* loss for the excellency of the knowledge of Christ Jesus my Lord: for whom I have suffered the loss of all things, and do count them *but* dung, that I may win Christ,**

9- And be found in him, **not having mine own righteousness, which is of the law,** <u>but that which is through</u> **the faith of Christ, the righteousness which is of God by faith:**

10- **That I may know him, and the power of his resurrection,** and the fellowship of his sufferings, being made conformable unto his death;

11- If by any means I might attain unto the resurrection of the dead.

12- Not as though I had already attained, either were already perfect: but I follow after, if that I may apprehend that for which also I am apprehended of Christ Jesus.

13- Brethren, I count not myself to have apprehended: **but *this* one thing *I* do, forgetting those things which are behind, and reaching forth unto those things which are before,**

14- I press toward the mark for the prize of the high calling of God in Christ Jesus.

-Philippians 3 v 1-14

The new testimony and ministry of Paul:

2- **For I determined not to know any thing among you, save Jesus Christ, and him crucified.**

3- And I was with you in weakness, and in fear, and in much trembling.

4- And my speech and my preaching *was* not with enticing words of man's wisdom, but in demonstration of the Spirit and of power:

5- **That your faith should not stand in the wisdom of men, but in the power of God.**

6- Howbeit we speak wisdom among them that are perfect *(Spiritually mature believers)*: yet not the wisdom of this world, nor of the princes of this world, that come to nought:

7- But we speak the wisdom of God in a mystery *(the revealed secrets)*, *even* the hidden *wisdom (the revealed secrets)* which God ordained before the world unto our glory:

8- Which none of the princes of this world knew: for had they known *it,* they would not have crucified the Lord of Glory.

-I Corinthians 2 v 2-8

Only the Apostle Paul received this new Gospel of Salvation to present to all of mankind:

1- **For this cause I Paul, the prisoner of Jesus Christ for you Gentiles,**

2- If ye have heard of **the dispensation of the grace of God which is given me to you-ward:**

3- How that **by revelation he made known unto me *(Paul)* the mystery;** (as I wrote afore in few words,

4- Whereby, when ye read, **ye may understand my knowledge in the mystery of Christ)**

5- Which **in other ages was not made known unto the sons of men,** as it is now revealed unto his holy apostles and prophets *(Paul's ministry)* by the Spirit;

6- That the Gentiles should be fellowheirs, and of the same body, and partakers of his promise in Christ by the gospel:
7- Whereof I was made a minister, according to the gift of the grace of God given unto me by the effectual working of his power.
8- Unto me, who am less than the least of all saints, is this grace given, **that I should preach among the Gentiles the unsearchable riches of Christ**:
9- And **to make all *men* see what *is* the fellowship of the mystery, which hath been hid in God, <u>who created all things by Jesus Christ</u>**: *(Jesus Christ is God)*
10- To the intent that now unto the principalities and powers in heavenly *places* might be known by the church the manifold wisdom of God,
11- According to the eternal purpose which he purposed in Christ Jesus our Lord:
12- In whom we have boldness and access with confidence by the faith of him.
-Ephesians 3 v 1-12

More scriptures that designate the Apostle Paul as 'Thee Apostle of the Gentiles. **This is the Word of God:**
7- For God hath not given us the spirit of fear; but of power, and of love, and of a sound mind.
8- Be not thou therefore ashamed of the testimony of our Lord, nor of me his prisoner: but be thou partaker of the afflictions of **the gospel according to the power of God;**
9- Who hath saved us, and called us with an holy calling, **not according to our works, but according to his own purpose and grace, <u>which was given us in Christ Jesus before the world began</u>**, *(Jesus Christ is God)*
10- But is now made manifest by the appearing *(resurrection)* of our Saviour Jesus Christ, who hath abolished death, and <u>hath brought life and immortality to light through the gospel:</u>
11- <u>**Whereunto I am appointed**</u> **a preacher, and an apostle, and a teacher of the Gentiles.**
-II Timothy 1 v 7-11

The Jews and Gentiles both killed Jesus, that is, his flesh and body as a man. God knew this would happen* but never revealed it to Israel. It was still up to Israel to accept the King and the Kingdom by their own choice and freewill. The Nation of Israel rejected the Christ. Now salvation has become a free gift of Grace to all that believe 'Paul's Gospel'. *-II Timothy 1 v 9

6- For when we were yet without strength, in due time **Christ died for the ungodly.**
7- For scarcely for a righteous man will one die: yet peradventure for a good man some would even dare to die.
8- But God commendeth his love toward us, in that, **while we were yet sinners, Christ died for us.**
9- Much more then, being **now justified by his blood, we shall be saved from wrath through him.**
10- For if, **when we were enemies, we were reconciled to God by the death of his Son**, much more, **being reconciled, we shall be saved by his life.**
11- And not only so, but we also joy in God through our Lord Jesus Christ, by **whom we have now received the atonement.**
-Romans 5 v 6-11

When the Apostle Paul speaks of Christ and his shed blood it has everything to do with our salvation through 'Resurrection Power'. This is the Jesus Christ we know. On this side of the cross and not before like the Jews knew him during his 'earthly ministry'. Most of Christendom believe in Jesus Christ as he was manifested in the flesh but fail to believe 'the Gospel'*. Our 'Gospel of Salvation' began at the 'Cross'. *-I Corinthians 15 v 1-4; -Romans 10 v 9; -Ephesians 1 v 13

15- **And *that* he died for all,** that they which live should not henceforth live unto themselves, but unto him which **died for them, and rose again** *(Paul's Gospel).*
16- **Wherefore henceforth** know we no man after the flesh: yea, **though we have known Christ after the flesh, yet now henceforth know we *him* no more.**
17- **Therefore if any man *be* in Christ, *he is* a new creature *(creation)*:** old things are passed away; behold, all things are become new.
18- And all things *are* of God, who hath reconciled us to himself by Je'sus Christ, and hath given to us the ministry of reconciliation;
-II Corinthians 5 v 15-18

Christendom has avoided teaching in 'absolutes'. "It's not politically correct to preach blood, suffering and Crucifixion". Some congregations have even taken out all mention of Jesus' shed blood out of their hymnals.

The 'Big Tent' concept is welcoming to all that enter a church building and who follow the teachings of their 'religion and denomination'. They are now considered Christians? Was this done by man or God? Follow 'the church rules (laws)' and ye shall be saved? Just pay tithes and be water baptized, etc?

Absolutely:
22- And almost all things are by the law purged with blood, and without the shedding of blood is no remission.
-Hebrews 9 v 22

Absolutely:
6- But without faith *it is* impossible to please *him*: for he that cometh to God must believe that he is, and *that* he is the rewarder of them that diligently seek him.
-Hebrews 11 v 6

Absolutely:
27- Where *is* boasting then? It is excluded. By what law? Of works? Nay: but by the law of faith.
28- Therefore we conclude that a man is justified by faith without the deeds of the law.
-Romans 3 v 27, 28

John writes in agreement with Paul until he writes concerning 'Law keeping'. A person must believe that Jesus Christ is the worlds advocate with the Father and he alone is the propitiation (appropriator) for mankind's sins. There is none other who can perform this. In verse 3 below, John reveals his law keeping status. He (John) kept 'the Law of Moses' to his dying day as close as possible. Remember, the Temple was destroyed in 70 A.D. so there were many years that John didn't atone for his sins. John already had his salvation.

1- My little children, these things write I unto you, that ye sin not. And if any man sin, we have an advocate with the Father, Jesus Christ the righteous:
2- And he is the propitiation *(appropriator)* for our sins: and not ours only, but also for *the sins of* the whole world.
3- And hereby **we do know that we know him, if we keep his commandments**.
-I John 2 v 1-3

44- No man can come to me, except the Father which hath sent me draw him: and I will raise him up at the last day.
-John 6 v 44

On this side of 'The Cross' under 'Grace':
10- For **as many as are of the works of the law are under the curse**: for it is written, Cursed *is* every one that continueth not in all things which are written in the book of the law to do them.
11- But that **no man is justified by the law in the sight of God**, *it is* evident: for, **The just shall live by faith**.
12- And **the law is not of faith**: but, The man that doeth them shall live in them.
13- **Christ hath redeemed us from the curse of the law**, being made a curse for us: for it is written, Cursed *is* every one that hangeth on a tree:
-Galatians 3 v 10-13

There is 'a mass assumption' (not according to scripture) that when Jesus came in 'his fleshly form' he did away with 'the Law'. This 'mass assumption' has 'Christendom' believing that his 'Twelve disciples' as well forsook 'the Law' and are now following the 'Gospel of Grace'. "Peter and Paul were preaching the same thing", they say. FALSE! Jesus said, "I am not come to destroy, but to fulfil"*.
*-Matthew 5 v 17

How and where in scripture was the 'Law of Moses' then abolished? Read the epistles of James, Peter and John. To deny that they were not under 'the Law' truly shows that "if our gospel *(Paul's Ministry)* is hid it is hid to them that are lost"*. **Only the Apostle Paul** writes by inspiration of the Holy Spirit that "we are not under law but under grace"+. Wake up Christendom before it is too late! *-II Corinthians 4 v 1-4; +-Romans 6 v 14, 15; -Galatians 3 v 10; -Galatians 5 v 18

Are you relying on your 'supposed head knowledge' of what you think the Bible says and what others have told you? **Are you believing in 'a falsehood' now knowing that there is no scripture that says Jesus quit keeping 'the Law'.** Have you thrown 'The Trial of Christendom' aside in unbelief? Before you do, be sure to justify your actions by the 'Word of God' first.

The vast majority of 'Christendom' can't see this truth or even want to see it. I speak as a man. 'Wide is the gate...'* This is not a judgment on my part but a discernment of what has been observed. 'Rightly divide the word of truth'+ doesn't just mean between the Old and New Testament. If a person rejects the 'Word of God' as written to them, they are truly lost and may God have mercy on them.

*-Matthew 7 v 13, 14; -Luke 13 v 24; +-II Timothy 2 v 15; -II Corinthians 4 v 2; -II Corinthians 6 v 7; -Ephesians 1 v 13; -Colossians 1 v 5; -I Thessalonians 2 v 13

The Trial of Christendom (this book) can fool nobody. All scriptures are taken from the KJV and shown to everybody. I pray that you read every scripture slowly and pay close attention to all punctuations.

Most people refuse and harden their heart to truth in the Bible that seems easily understood by 'The Body of Christ'. They prefer their 'supposed head knowledge' to that of scripture never questioning their teachers at the risk of personal ridicule. Many started at an early age in 'Sunday School'.

There is this need by man to want to do something and to do 'righteous works of faith'. Trying to prove to God 'their righteousness'. Trying to prove to their fellow brethren 'their faith'. These have 'negated' the work of the cross.

The true Gospel of salvation is hidden from them that are lost*. And these are good 'professing Christians'. Good people. From experience, even showing them and having them read for themselves seems futile. It is God who opens the understanding of the heart to truth. *-II Corinthians 4 v 1-4

I pray for the 'Lydia's and for the 'Apollo's of the world and those believing types like the 'Bereans of Berea'. These are examples of people that heard the truth and understood. Those of Berea searched diligently the scriptures to see if 'these things were true'*. *-Acts 17 v 10, 11

Jesus died 'under the Law'. He was the fulfillment of 'The Law'. Peter and 'the Twelve Disciples' all kept 'the Law' and died 'under the Law'. They kept 'the Law' to their dying day. There is no scripture that shows they forsook the 'Law of Moses' and accepted the Gospel that was revealed to Paul. They were not meant to nor told by God to forsake 'the Law'. Peter is not Paul. Paul is not Peter. They **were not** preaching the same thing.

The disciples and 'the elect' had salvation by keeping 'the Law' and believing in the 'Name of Jesus Christ'. They are 'the Elect'. For the 'Jew of the Circumcision' it was 'faith plus righteous works of the Law' and to 'Repent and be Baptized'.

For us in the 'Age of Grace' salvation is by the 'faith in the finished work of the cross without works of an imposed legalism'. Out of love we are 'God's workman'. Being a 'Born from above Believer' we work for God but not by the rules and custom practices of a religion. We work by 'the Faith of the Resurrected Christ'.

8- For by grace are ye saved through faith; and that not of yourselves: *it is* the gift of God:

9- Not of works, lest any man should boast.

10- For **we are his workmanship, created unto Jesus unto good works**, which God hath before ordained that we should walk in them.

-Ephesians 2 v 8-10

The Jerusalem Temple was fully operational during 'Jesus' earthly ministry'. Animal sacrificing was still being performed and was reported that over 1,000,000 sacrifices were being done per year. With the destruction of 'the Temple' in 70 A.D., the keeping and the obeisance of 'the full Law' was no longer possible. 'The whole Law' has to be kept or a person is guilty of transgressing all 'the Laws'*. So now what is a good Jew to do? The Temple in Jerusalem has not been rebuilt. *-Romans 3 v 19-21, 28; -Romans 10 v 5; -Galatians 3 v 10-13; -Galatians 5 v 3; -James 2 v 10-12; -I John 3 v 4

Jesus said in his 'earthly ministry':

18- For verily I say unto you, till heaven and earth pass, not one jot or one tittle shall in no wise pass from the law, till all be fulfilled.

19- Whosoever therefore shall break one of these least commandments, and shall teach men so, he shall be called the least in the **kingdom of heaven**: but whosoever shall do and teach *them*, the same shall be called great in the **kingdom of heaven**.

-Matthew 5 v 18, 19

Jesus is speaking to the Jews of Israel who were still 'Law keeping'. The hidden secrets/mysteries had not been given to the Apostle Paul yet. Jesus is not speaking to us here. We Gentiles were not given 'the Covenant Promises' made to Israel and 'the fathers'. Obviously, Jesus is a keeper and proponent of 'the Law'.

Had all of Israel believed in the 'name of Jesus Christ', the 'Kingdom of Heaven' would have came in as prophesied. These scriptures would have stood the test of time. But the 'Earthly Kingdom of Heaven' did not happen. Israel as a nation did not believe in the Lord Jesus Christ.

All the wonderful things spoken by Jesus of that 'utopian Kingdom life' was delayed. It didn't happen. The "B Attitudes" in Matthew 5, did they all happen and have carried on to today? Israel as a nation rejected 'their King and Kingdom'. Will it happen? It didn't at his 'first coming' but definitely will at his 'second coming'*. *-Luke 21 v 27, 28: -Daniel 12 v 1

There has been 2,000 years unaccounted for in Biblical scripture that was never prophesied to happen. But it has happened. It is today, the 'Church Age, the Age of Grace'. How long? All we know is that when the 'Body of Christ, the True Church' is full, we will be 'caught up' to God and spared from the wrath to come on the world and Israel*. *-Romans 5 v 9; -I Thessalonians 1 v 10; -I Thessalonians 4 v 17; -I Thessalonians 5 v 9

When Israel is out of its 'place of Blessing', God's time clock stops. This has fooled many Chronologists because some prophecies concerning Israel are very time specific. It throws them off when they try to piece prophecies in time when Israel is 'spiritually lost'. No other book ever written was able to foretell prophecies 100's of years in advance and have them all, 100% come true.

Hebrew time keeping in scripture: any part of a day or a year is considered the whole. One minute of a day is one day. One day of a year is one full year in scripture when spanning times. The amount of time Jesus' was in the sepulcher was less than three days (72 hours) by our time standard.

Jesus Christ was taken off the cross Friday mid afternoon and buried. This counts as one day in the tomb. Friday, Saturday, and Sunday are the three days. An Easter Service on Sunday is in agreement. Part of the day on Sunday, Jesus Christ was still in the sepulcher and rose that same day, early after midnight. The short time in the sepulcher on Sunday is counted as one day. Regardless of the actual day of 'the crucifixion', three days in the grave is according to 'the scripture'.

'The Lords Prayer' shows aspects of 'the Law':
9- After this manner therefore pray ye: Our Father which art in heaven, Hallowed be thy name.
10- **Thy kingdom come.** Thy will be done in earth, as *it is* in heaven.
11- Give us this day our daily bread.
12- **And forgive us our debts, as we forgive our debtors.**
13- And lead us not into temptation, but deliver us from evil: For thine is the kingdom, and the power, and the glory, forever. A-men'.
-Matthew 6 v 9-13

The Lord's prayer in the Book of Luke:
2- And he *(Jesus)* said unto them, When ye pray, say, Our Father which art in heaven, hollowed be thy name. **Thy kingdom come.** Thy will be done, as in heaven, so in earth.
3- Give us this day our daily bread.
4- **And forgive us our sins; for we also forgive every one that is indebted to us.** And lead us not into temptation; but deliver us from evil.
-Luke 11 v 2-4

Jesus said:
23- Therefore if thou bring thy gift to the alter, and there rememberest that thy brother hath ought against thee;
24- Leave there thy gift before the alter, and go thy way; first to be reconciled to thy brother, and then come and offer thy gift.
-Matthew 5 v 23, 24

Jesus said:
14- For if ye forgive men their trespasses, your heavenly Father will also forgive you:
15- But if ye forgive not men their trespasses, neither will your Father forgive your trespasses.
-Matthew 6 v 14, 15

Jesus said:

25- And when ye stand praying, forgive, if ye have ought against any: that your Father also which is in heaven may forgive you your trespasses.

26- But if you do not forgive, neither will your Father which is in heaven forgive your trespasses.

-Mark 11 v 25, 26

Jesus said:

3- Take heed to yourselves: If thy brother trespass against thee, rebuke him: and if he repent, forgive him.

4- And if he trespass against thee seven times in a day, and seven times in a day turn again to thee, saying, I repent; thou shalt forgive him.

-Luke 17 v 3, 4

Under 'the Law', before God would forgive, the Jew must first have forgiven. A Jew forgives those that have a debt or obligation of a liability committed to himself. Then God will forgive him*. Out of a good conscious we may forgive another but concerning God and salvation it was done already. A true believer in the 'faith-way Gospel of Grace' has already been forgiven. There is no need to repeatedly repent. *-Matthew 5 v 23, 24; -Matthew 6 v 12, 14, 15

Why was 'the Law' given?:

19- Wherefore then *serveth* the law? It was added because of transgressions, **till the seed should come to whom the promise was made**; and *it was* ordained by angels in the hand of a mediator.

20- Now a mediator is not a *mediator* of one, but God is one.

21- *Is the* law then against the promises of God? God forbid: **for if there had been a law given which could have given life, verily righteousness should have been by the law**.

22- **But** the scripture hath concluded all under sin, that **the promise by faith of Je'sus Christ might be given to them that believe**.

23- **But** before faith *(faith-way)* came, we were kept under the law, shut up unto the faith which should afterwards be revealed.

24- **Therefore** the law was our schoolmaster *to bring us* unto Christ, **that we might be justified by faith**.

25- **But** after that faith *(faith-way)* is come, we are no longer under a schoolmaster.

26- **For ye are all the children of God by faith in Christ Je'sus.**

27- For as many of you as have been **baptized into Christ have put on Christ.**

28- **There is neither Jew nor Greek,** there is neither bond nor free, there is neither male nor female: **for ye are all one in Christ Je'sus.**

29- **And if ye be Christ's, then are ye A'bra-ham's seed, and heirs according to the promise.**

-Galatians 3 v 19-29

False teachers say that 'the Law' was done away with by 'grace'. Yet these same teachers are still observing some form of legalism. These 'supposed Christians' would teach that you have to follow aspects of 'the Law', a law of their denomination, conform to the rules of 'their religion', in order to be saved. 'Repent and be water baptized, pay tithes, keep the Sabbath, etc.' Telling their parishioners that they are Jews. They mix the 'Gospel of the Kingdom' with the 'Gospel of Grace' which is not the same. Peter is not Paul. Paul is not Peter.

It has also been said by many 'supposed Christians' that they hate Paul and wish that he was not in their Bible. So take out Paul's writings then. Take out Romans to Hebrews. Where now is their 'doctrine of salvation', Acts 2 v 38?

Did they receive the Holy Ghost? Did they? Are they sharing all things common like they did in Acts 2 v 42-46? If their belief is in the early chapters of Acts, then they also (because they can't be hypocrites) accept Acts 2 v 23, 36 as speaking for them. They can't ignore what they want to, picking and choosing what is suitable.

Unfortunately this is most of Christendom. Who is right? Why do they reject the Apostle Paul? Paul's Gospel (as was given from the ascended Lord of Glory) is hid to them that are lost*. *-II Corinthians 4 v 1-4

Those that reject the Apostle Paul can't also reject Jesus, can they? Do these folk do what Jesus says? Or do they pick and choose which scriptures are suitable for them*. What kind of 'a doctrine' are they following without the Apostle Paul? *-Matthew 16 v 23; -Mark 8 v 33; -Luke 4 v 8

Those who reject the Apostle Paul, do they then observe the whole Law?:

18- If a man have a stubborn and rebellious son, which will not obey the voice of his father, or the voice of his mother, and *that*, when they have chastened him, will not hearken unto them:

19- Then shall his father and his mother lay hold on him, and bring him out unto the elders of his city, and unto the gate of his place;

20- And they shall say unto the elders of the city, This our son *is* stubborn and rebellious, he will not obey our voice; *he is* a glutton, and a drunkard.

21- And all the men of the city shall stone him with stones, that he die: so shalt thou put evil away among you; and all Is'ra-el shall hear and fear.

-Deuteronomy 21 v 18-21

Jesus the Law Keeper:

16- And, behold, one came and said unto him *(Jesus)*, Good Master, what good thing shall I do, that I may have eternal life?

17- And he said unto him, Why callest thou me good? *There is* none good but one, *that is*, God: but if thou wilt enter into life, **keep the commandments**.

18- He saith unto him, Which? Je'sus said, Thou shalt do no murder, Thou shalt not commit adultery, Thou shalt not steal, Thou shalt not bear false witness,

19- Honour thy father and thy mother: and, Thou shalt love thy neighbor as thyself.

20- The young man saith unto him, All these things have I kept from my youth up: what lack I yet?

21- **Je'sus said unto him, If thou wilt be perfect, go and sell that thou hast, and give to the poor, and thou shalt have treasure in heaven: and come and follow me.**

22- But when the young man heard that saying, he went away sorrowful: for he had great possessions.

-Matthew 19 v 16-22

These deniers of the Apostle Paul, are they then keeping 'the whole Law'? Are they doing the same as Jesus had told this man to do? Are they really following Jesus then? They did in Acts 2 v 45, 46 and had all things common. Acts 2 v 38 was only a couple scriptures before. Do they have a yard full of cattle that they can sacrifice for their sins?

Who has decided what scriptures to follow and which to ignore?:
12- For we wrestle not against flesh and blood, but against principalities, against powers, against the rulers of the darkness of this world, against spiritual wickedness in high places.
-Ephesians 6 v 12

These deciders of what to believe for salvation 'are the principalities of spiritual wickedness in high places'. Satan's work in the world is relentless. If the 'god of this world' is able to blind just one teacher or just one preacher to the truth of Paul's Gospel, what a 'false spreading influence' that is passed on, and on, from the blind, to the blind, to the... "Wide is the gate...".

'Religions and Denominational conformity' are not of faith according to the Gospel which Paul received by revelation from the ascended Lord of Glory. The Body of Christ, the True Church has not a headquarters nor a denominational name made up by men. Nothing can be done in the flesh that merits favor with God.

How many people have been murdered and killed 'in the name of god and religion'? Millions have been killed in 'the name of god'. To rephrase, millions of 'so called followers' of god have killed by the power and influence of Satan, not Christ. The torture, the murder, the persecutions by so called believers of god has been witnessed and documented throughout history.

How evil mankind can be while justifying themselves because they label themselves as being 'Christians'. Who labeled them 'Christian'? God or a man? These are Satan's followers. Murder and torture is nowhere to be found in the 'True Church, the Body of Christ'.

Do they kill because God told them too or because their interpretation of the 'Word of God' came to them by Satan, the god of this world? 'The True Church, the Body of Christ', has never partook of the evil practices of cult religions. No one can enter the 'Body, the Church' by fraud.

It was Paul's Body of Christ Churches that were called 'Christians first'*. The Jerusalem Church, of which James, Peter and John were members, was established years before Paul came on the scene. Why were they, the members of the Jerusalem Church, not called Christians? *-Acts 11 v 26

The Word of God says by Luke Holy Spirit inspired:

25- Then departed Bar'na-bas to Tar'sus, for to seek Saul *(Paul)*:

26- And when he had found him, he brought him unto An'ti-och. And it came to pass, that a whole year they assembled themselves with the church, and taught much people. **And the disciples were called Chris'tians first in An'ti-och.**

-Acts 11 v 25, 26

"And the disciples were called Chris'tians first in An'ti-och." These disciples were Paul's followers. These were not the followers of Jesus Christ's 'earthly ministry'. These were not 'Jews of the Circumcision/Law'.

Those of the 'Apostles Doctrine' were never called Christians as a Religious group. <u>Only three times was the word Christian used throughout all the Bible.</u> The first two mentions, the Apostle Paul was present*. The third time Peter is comparing Christ's suffering with their own present situation+. The Jews under 'the Law' were not under 'the Doctrine of Grace'. *-Acts 11 v 26; -Acts 26 v 28; +-I Peter 4 v 16

Paul's writes by Holy Spirit inspiration that "we are not under law but under grace"*. Yet Jesus was 'under the Law' and he 'kept the Law' and his disciples did as well. For Israel, they had to believe in the 'Name of Jesus Christ', keep 'the Law of Moses' and be 'water baptized for the remission of sins'. *-Romans 6 v 14

The Messiah did come for Israel. He was with them. They saw him and they ate with him. 'The Kingdom' was in their midst (within them). They knew him in his earthly, and fleshly form. They were the witnesses of the 'True Light'. They were 'the Elect'. They were waiting for 'The Kingdom of Heaven' yet to come.

6- When they therefore were come together, they asked of him *(Jesus)*, saying, Lord, wilt thou at this time restore again the kingdom to Is'ra-el?

7- And he said unto them, It is not for you to know the times or the seasons, which the Father hath put in his own power.

8- But ye shall receive power, after that the Holy Ghost is come upon you: and ye shall be witnesses unto me both in Je-ru'sa-lem, and in all Ju-de'a and in Sa-ma'ria, and unto the uttermost part of the earth.

9- And when he had spoken these things, while they beheld, he was taken up; and a cloud received him out of their sight.

10- And while they looked stedfastly toward heaven as he went up, behold, two men stood by them in white apparel;

11- Which also said, Ye men of Gal'i-lee, why stand ye gazing up into heaven? This same Jesus, which is taken up from you into heaven, shall come in like manner as ye have seen him go into heaven.

-Acts 1 v 6-11

As the prophet Zechariah foretold:

4- **And his feet shall stand in that day upon the mount of Ol'ives,** which *is* before Je-ru'sa-lem on the east, and the mount of Ol'ives shall cleave in the midst thereof toward the east and toward the west, *and there shall be* a great valley; and half of the mountain shall remove toward the north, and half of it toward the south.

.....

9- And the LORD shall be king over all the earth: in that day shall there be one LORD, and his name one.

-Zechariah 14 v 4, 9; -Zechariah 14

27- Then answered Pe'ter and said unto him, Behold, we have forsaken all, and have followed thee; what shall we have therefore?

28- And Je'sus said unto them, Verily I say unto you, That ye which have followed me *(presently)*, **in the regeneration when the Son of man shall sit in the throne of his glory *(future)*, ye also shall sit upon twelve thrones *(future)*, judging the twelve tribes of Is'ra-el *(future)*.**

-Matthew 19 v 27, 28

Much of Christendom think that they (the Twelve) immediately left Jerusalem and went to the whole world preaching 'the Gospel' after 'the resurrection'. What Gospel? It was prophesied that they were to 'be a Kingdom of Priest's', but there is no Kingdom with Jesus sitting on the throne of David in Zion to bring the world of Gentiles to. It was by the Jew/Hebrews that the world would receive a knowledge of their Lord God JEHOVAH. For there to be a 'Kingdom of Priest's' there has to be a kingdom.

But there is no biblical record of this happening. 'The Twelve disciples' did not take the Gospel to "the uttermost parts of the earth". There is not one scripture that shows that they did. Not one. God kept hid this 'mystery', that the Gentiles would be able to go to God directly, by faith and not by 'works of their Law'.

1- And Saul was consenting unto his death *(Stephen)*. And at that time there was a great persecution against the church *(ecclesia)* which was at Je-ru'sa-lem; and they were all scattered abroad throughout the regions of Ju-de'a and Sa-ma'ria, **except the apostles**.
-Acts 8 v 1

19- Now they which were scattered abroad upon the persecution that arose about Stephen traveled as far as Phe-ni'ce, and Cy'prus, and An'ti-och, **preaching the word to none but unto Jews only.**
-Acts 11 v 19

"And they were all scattered abroad throughout the regions of Ju-de'a and Sa-ma'ria, **except the apostles**". 'The Twelve disciples' had not left, they were still in Jerusalem. They were not commissioned to evangelize the world until they had 'their kingdom'.

The Gentiles would not need to go to a human priest or a 'go between'. The Gentiles are now able to boldly approach God in the throne room of heaven by prayer 24 hours a day. There is no set day, a Sabbath day or a church day, or a 'time of worship'. The 'Body of Christ, the True Church' is free from any rules of 'legalisms' imposed by 'Religions and Denominations'. Don't misunderstand, Church service and worship is good with fellow believers of course.

ONLY TWO GENTILES DID JESUS MEET WITH

5- And when Je'sus was entered into Ca-per'na-um, there came unto him a centurion, beseeching him,
6- And saying, Lord, my servant lieth at home sick with the palsy, grievously tormented.
7- And Je'sus saith unto him, I will come and heal him.
8- The centurion answered and said, Lord, I am not worthy that thou shouldest come under my roof: **but speak the word only, and my servant shall be healed**.

9- For I am a man under authority, having soldiers under me: and I say to this *man*, Go, and he goeth; and to another, come, and he cometh; and to my servant, Do this, and he doeth *it*.

10- When Je'sus heard *it,* he marveled, and said to them that followed, **Verily I say unto you, I have not found so great faith, no, not in Is'ra-el**.

11- And I say unto you, That **many shall come forth from the east and west, and shall sit down with A'bra-ham, and I'saac, and Ja'cob, in the kingdom of heaven**.

12- But the children of the kingdom shall be cast out into outer darkness: there shall be weeping and gnashing of teeth.

13- And Jesus said unto the centurion, Go thy way; **and as thou hast believed, so be it done unto thee**. And his servant was healed in the selfsame hour.

-Matthew 8 v 5-13

'The centurion' was not a Jew. He was a Gentile and not of 'the Circumcision/Law'. His faith and belief in who this Jesus of Nazareth is, is unmistakeable. He could see and had probably heard of the miracles being done by Jesus. His faith and belief was far more than most of Israel who should have known. "The Jews require a sign"* but even these were not good enough to convince Israel. God is sovereign and can be gracious and show mercy to whom he chooses. *-I Corinthians 1 v 22

The Second Gentile that Jesus Christ met

22- And, behold, a women of Ca'naan came out of the same coasts, and cried unto him, saying, Have mercy on me, O Lord, *thou* Son of Da'vid; my daughter is grievously vexed with a devil.

23- **But he *(Jesus)* answered her not a word.** And his disciples came and besought him, saying, **Send her away**; for she crieth after us.

24- But he answered and said, **I am not sent but unto the lost sheep of the house of Is'ra-el.**

25- Then came she and worshipped him, saying, Lord, help me.

26- But he answered and said, **It is not meet to take the children's bread, and to cast *it* to dogs**.

27- And she said, **Truth, Lord: yet the dogs eat of the crumbs which fall from their masters' table**.

28- Then Je'sus answered and said unto her, O women, great is thy faith: be it unto thee even as thou wilt. And her daughter was made whole from that very hour.
-Matthew 15 v 22-28

Why was she so disrespected by the disciples? Why did Jesus initially "answer her not a word"? They were rude to her and asked Jesus, "Send her away". What did Jesus mean when he said, "It is not meet to take the children's bread, and cast it to the dogs"?

I thought Jesus came for the whole world? This is what has been taught to much of Christendom. Jesus said, "I am not sent but unto the lost sheep of the house of Israel"*. The disciples wanted this women to leave and to quit bothering them. What? How rude! The disciples pushing people away? Jesus ignoring the 'common man'? *-Matthew 15 v 24

This Gentile women had not the promises that were made to Israel's fathers. She had not 'the place of privilege to eat at the Lords Table'. Only the 'Jews of the Circumcision/Law', the lost sheep of 'the House of Israel' had a 'formal invite'.

This women of Canaan was not one of the 'Lost Sheep of Israel'. She was simply lost by birth as we all are. She was not a recipient of the 'Covenant Promises' made to the 'Twelve Tribes of Israel'. She was viewed as a Gentile, a heathen dog. Jesus told his disciples to have nothing to do with any Gentile. They were following what Jesus had commanded them*.
*-Matthew 10 v 5, 6

Her faith and belief in who this Jesus Christ is was so steadfast unlike most of Israel. Even the smallest of blessings, a crumb, was enough for her. Jesus too made a dog reference. But this did not deter her. The smallest of crumbs that fell from Israel's place of position (table) was all she believed she needed. And it was. Her daughter was made whole (healed) that same hour.

These are the only two Gentiles in scripture that Jesus met with. Only these two. How many Gentiles did the LORD use in the Old Testament? Individually, not the nations of Gentiles that made war with Israel? Who were they?

What about the lunatic possessed by the twelve devils named 'Legion'? He was a Gaderine. Gad is one of 'the Twelve Tribes of Israel'. What about the women at the well? She was a Samaritan, a half Jew.

The Samaritan Lepers

11- And it came to pass, as he *(Jesus)* went to Je-ru'sa-lem, that he passed through the midst of Sa-ma'ri-a and Gal'i-lee.

12- And as he entered into a certain village, there met him ten men that were lepers, which stood afar off:

13- And they lifted up *their* voices, and said Je'sus, Master, have mercy on us.

14- And when he saw *them*, he said unto them, **Go shew yourselves unto the priests.** And it came to pass, that, as they went, they were cleansed.

15- **And one of them,** when he saw that he was healed, turned back, and with a loud voice glorified God,

16- And fell down on *his* face at his feet, giving him thanks: **and he was a Sa-mar'i-tan**.

17- And Jesus answering said, Were there not ten cleansed? But where *are* the nine?

18- There are not found that returned to give glory to God, save this stranger.

19- And he said unto him, Arise, go thy way: thy faith hath made thee whole.

-Luke 17 v 11-19

Verse 11 - "as he *(Jesus)* went to Je-ru'sa-lem, that <u>he passed through the midst of Sa-ma'ri-a and Gal'i-lee</u>". Jesus was passing through not planning on stopping? Jesus was not treating Samaria as the 'Lost Sheep of the House of Israel'. Jesus viewed the Samaritan's in the same light as Gentiles. "Until a seed is planted...".

Verse 14 - **"Go shew yourselves unto the priests".** Jesus was following the 'Law of Leprosy'*. *-Leviticus 13, 14

Verse 16 - "and he was a Samaritan". Scripture shows that these lepers were not of 'the lost sheep of the house of Israel'. Why did the Holy Ghost instruct Luke to point out the Lepers citizen status? What did Jesus tell the disciples concerning Samaria*? God will have mercy on those that he chooses. *-Matthew 10 v 5, 6

5- These twelve **Je'sus** sent forth, and **commanded them,** saying, **Go not into the way of the Gen'tiles, and into** *any* **city of the Sa-mar'i-tans enter ye not:**

6- **But go rather to the lost sheep of the house of Is'ra-el.**

-Matthew 10 v 5, 6

When 'rightly dividing the word of truth'* these scriptures are an eye opener. Most of Christendom has a 'supposed head knowledge' that is not based upon the scriptures. They believe in what they want to believe, not what the "Word of God' has said (or has not been said). *-II Timothy 2 v 15

Paul writes by inspiration of the Holy Ghost that is was him that 'laid the foundation' of 'the Church and the Body of Christ Doctrine'. Paul is not 'the foundation'. The Resurrected Jesus Christ is 'the foundation' of the 'True Church, the Body of Christ'*. Paul is Chief and first to present to the world the 'Doctrine of Salvation'+. All the knowledge for living the Christian life are found in his epistles, Romans to Hebrews. *-I Corinthians 3 v 6 -11; +-I Timothy 1 v 15, 16; -Paul's epistles

6- I have planted, A-pol'los watered; but God gave the increase.

7- So then neither is he that planteth any thing, neither he that watereth; but God that giveth the increase.

8- Now he that planteth and he that watereth are one: and every man shall receive his own reward according to his own labour.

9- For we are labourers together with God: ye are God's husbandry, *ye are* God's building.

10- **According to the grace of God which is given unto me, as a wise masterbuilder, I have laid the foundation, and another buildeth thereon.** But let every man take heed how he buildeth thereupon.

11- For other foundation can no man lay than that is laid, which is Jesus Christ.

-I Corinthians 3 v 6 -11

The Greek Gentiles that Wanted to Speak with Jesus

20- And there were certain Greeks among them that came up to worship at the feast:

21- The same came therefore to Phil'ip, which was of Beth-sa'I-da, and desired him, saying, Sir, we would see Je'sus.

22- Phil'ip cometh and telleth An'drew: and again An'drew and Phil'ip tell Je'sus.

23- And Je'sus answered them, saying, The hour is come, that the Son of man should be glorified.

24- Verily, verily, I say unto you, Except a corn of wheat fall into the ground and die, it abideth alone: but if it die, it bringeth forth much fruit.

-John 12 v 20-24

Jesus never spoke with these men, these Greeks, these Gentiles, but this is what he told his disciples:

Verse 24- Verily, verily, I say unto you, Except a corn of wheat fall into the ground and die, it abideth alone: but if it die, it bringeth forth much fruit. -John 12 v 24

Jesus in his own words was only "sent to the lost sheep of the House of Israel"*. Jesus said he came not to destroy the words that were prophesied of him but to fulfill them+. He didn't come in the flesh for all of mankind (but in the big picture, yes he did). To Israel only did Jesus Christ come to redeem them that are 'under the Law'=. *-Matthew 10 v 5, 6; -Matthew 15 v 24, 26; +-Romans 15 v 8, 9; =-Galatians 4 v 4, 5

He gave a picture of what would happen when he dies. He is 'the seed' that would bring forth fruit to the world, but not before his death. He first would have to be planted and die like a seed. (In nature, a seed has to die in order to grow into something alive). This truth is revealed by God to the Apostle Paul. As of yet, the disciples didn't know he was going to be crucified and resurrect*. *-John 20 v 9

So let's go back to verse 20 and read:

Verse 20- And there were certain Greeks among them that came up to worship at the feast:

-John 12 v 20

A Greek is not a Jew but a Gentile. These Greeks that came to the Jewish Feast could not claim Abraham and Moses as their fore fathers. This feast was the 'Jewish Feast of Passover'. This was a celebration of 'the Moses Exodus' when the 'angel passed over' the homes of those who had put the lamb's blood on their door posts. It was a Jewish Feast that no Gentile could claim as 'their feast'.

So why did people come to a 'Jewish Feast' when they themselves were never formally invited? More than likely they were interested in the phenomenon and rumors that they had heard surrounding this man Jesus. Like in the Exodus from Egypt, there was 'a mixed multitude' that came with Moses that were not Hebrew but they came anyways.

As it is today, there is always that curious group of onlookers who seem to be present at any event that seems to be noteworthy. This 'Feast of the Passover' had this man Jesus who was going to be present. Maybe they would see one of his miracles themselves or hear him speak words of wisdom.

Verse 21- The same came therefore to Phil'ip, which was of Beth-sa'I-da of Gal'i-lee, and desired him, saying, Sir, we would see Je'sus.
-John 12 v 21

This group of Greek Gentiles wanted to talk with Jesus themselves. Were they not comfortable with going up personally to see him or did they seek some sort of permission? Did they not feel accepted? Could this be because they were not 'Jews of the Circumcision/Law'? Did these Gentile Greeks feel that they had no right to walk right up to this man Jesus and ask him questions?

Verse 22- Phil'ip cometh and telleth An'drew: and again An'drew and Phil'ip tell Je'sus.
-John 12 v 22

Was Philip and Andrew bodyguards? Wasn't Jesus accessible to all men and women? Why this separation? Why was there a 'buffer zone' made against the people of the world (Gentiles) and Jesus?

So ask yourself, why is there a need to have a conference amongst themselves, amongst the disciples questioning whether these persons, these Greeks, these Gentiles should be able to see Jesus? Were the disciples following what Jesus had commanded them in Matthew 10 v 5, 6? They debated themselves whether they should or should not tell Jesus. But they did tell him.

Verse 23- And Je'sus answered them, saying, The hour is come, that the Son of Man should be glorified.
-John 12 v 23

What was Jesus speaking of when he said, "The hour is come, that the Son of Man should be glorified"? The full understanding of what this meant to the disciples was not made known by God to them. They did not know, as has been shown by scripture, that Jesus was going to be crucified and resurrect*. The meaning of this was still hid and a mystery to them. It was after his resurrection that they began to understand Old Testament Scripture and what Jesus had been telling them during his earthly ministry+. *-John 20 v 1-9; +-John 12 v 14-16

Verse 24- Verily, verily I say unto you, Except a corn of wheat fall into the ground and die, it abideth alone: but if it die, it bringeth forth much fruit. -John 12 v 24

Jesus <u>did not</u> have a ministry amongst the Gentiles. Jesus Christ <u>did not</u> speak with these Gentile Greeks. Don't lie to yourself nor let a preacher influence you and say that Jesus left the border of Israel. Such a journey would have been noted somewhere by Matthew, Mark, Luke and John. Nor did Jesus Christ give any indication that he would be preaching personally to the world.

Jesus said in John 12 v 24, "except a seed *(corn of wheat)* fall into the ground and die it bringeth forth much fruit". He was speaking of his death, burial and resurrection after which salvation would now be possible to go to these Greek Gentiles, the 'much fruit'. But a Gentile being saved by the Lord JEHOVAH, their God, was unheard of without keeping the Law. Nothing of the sort was ever spoken till the Apostle Paul is given the 'Gospel of Grace'.

14- And Je'sus, when he had found a young ass, sat thereon; as it is written,
15- Fear not, daughter of Si'on *(Zion)*: behold, thy King cometh sitting on an ass's colt.
16- **These things understood not his disciples at the first: <u>but when Je'sus was glorified</u>, then remembered they that these things were written of him, and *that* they had done these things unto him.**
-John 12 v 14-16; -Zechariah 9 v 9

BELIEVE IN THE 'NAME OF JESUS CHRIST'

Philip and the Eunuch
26- And the angel of the Lord spake unto Phil'ip, saying, Arise, and go toward the south unto the way that goeth down from Je-ru'sa-lem unto Ga'za, which is desert.

27- And he arose and went: and, behold, a man of E-thi-o'pi-a, an eunuch of great authority under Can'da-ce queen of the E-thi-o'pi-ans, who had the charge of all her treasure, and had come to Je-ru'sa-lem for to worship,

28- Was returning, and sitting in his chariot read E-sa'ias *(Isaiah)* the prophet*. *(*-Isaiah 53 v 7)*

29- Then the **Spirit** said unto Phil'ip, Go near, and join thyself to this chariot.

30- And Phil'ip ran thither to *him*, and heard him read the prophet E-sa'ias *(Isaiah)*, and said, Understandest thou what thou readest?

31- And he said, How can I, except some man should guide me? And he desired Phil'ip that he would come up and sit with him.

32- The place of the scripture which he read was this, He was led as a sheep to the slaughter; and like a lamb dumb before his shearer, so opened he not his mouth:

33- In his humiliation his judgment was taken away: and who shall declare his **generation**? For his life is taken from the earth.

34- And the eunuch answered Phil'ip, and said, I pray thee, of whom speaketh the prophet this? Of himself, or of some other man?

35- Then Phil'ip opened his mouth, and began at the same scripture, **and preached unto him Je'sus**.

-Acts 8 v 26-35

Philip <u>was not</u> preaching salvation by the 'finished work of the cross'. Scripture <u>does not say</u> that Philip was showing salvation by Jesus Christ dieing, being buried and resurrected. He preached Jesus. 'The Name of Jesus Christ'. "He came not to destroy the law and the prophets but to fulfill". He showed this man, the eunuch, from Old Testament scripture that this 'Jesus of Nazareth' was that 'Messiah and Christ'.

36- And as they went on *their* way, they came unto a certain water: and the eunuch said, See, *here is* water; what doth hinder me to be baptized?

37- And Phil'ip said, If thou believest with all thine heart, thou mayest. And he answered and said, **I believe that Je'sus Christ is the Son of God**.

38- And he commanded the chariot to stand still: and they went down both into the water, both Phil'ip and the eunuch; and he baptized him.

39- And when they were come up out of the water, **the Spirit** of the Lord **caught away** Phil'ip, that the eunuch saw him no more: and he went on his way rejoicing.

40- But Phil'ip was found at A-zo'tus: and passing through he preached in all the cities, till he came to Caes-a-re'a.
-Acts 8 v 36-40

'The eunuch' was 'baptized with water' the same as those in the 'Gospel of the Kingdom' doctrine. He (the eunuch) believed in 'The Name of Jesus Christ' and who he is. This is 'the Cornerstone of the Gospel of the Kingdom'. To 'believe in the Name' of the prophesied Messiah, the Christ, the Son of God.

The Ethiopian's salvation came not by Paul's 'Gospel of Grace'. Paul had not received 'the revelations' that were still hid in God. No one knew of salvation by faith in the 'finished work of the cross'. The 'Kingdom of Heaven' was still possible. Jesus Christ was still alive and was sitting at the right hand of God until he made the enemies of Israel their 'footstool'. If all of Israel would believe in the name of Jesus Christ, this was prophesied to happen. "Repent and be baptized in the name of Jesus Christ every one of you"*. *Acts 2 v 38

There is debate as to whether this eunuch was a Jew or Gentile. Many 'Jews of the Circumcision/Law' and the 'ye men of Israel' remained scattered throughout the 'then known world' after the Babylonian invasion and dispersion in 606 B.C. This Eunuch could be one of them. Regardless, Jew or Gentile, the resurrection had already happened. There is now a change in 'Dispensation' happening. It is no longer the Jew/Hebrew that held the 'privileged position at the Lord's Table'.

The Jews were to believe who he is, 'the Name of Jesus Christ'. His resurrection was a fact seen by the disciples and others that Jesus the Christ was alive and still in a position to set up the 'Kingdom of Heaven'. He would save Israel from their enemies*, not salvation by Paul's Gospel of Grace. The 'Jews of the Circumcision/Law', the 'Ye men and women of Israel' were not preaching 'The Gospel' of I Corinthians 15 v 1-4. *-Jeremiah 23 v 6, -Jeremiah 30 v 7, -Jeremiah 33 v 16, -**Isaiah 45 v 17**, -Matthew 24, -Mark 13, -Luke 1 v 67-75, -Romans 9 v 27, -Romans 11 v 26, -Revelation 21 v 24

35- Then Phil'ip opened his mouth, and began at the same scripture, **and preached unto him Jesus.**
-Acts 8 v 35

Martha's Profession of Faith

No word of salvation had been given to the world yet by believing in 'the finished work of the cross'. Jesus Christ was still alive and speaking personally with Martha. Martha's salvation was in the 'Gospel of the Kingdom Doctrine'. She was of 'the Circumcision' and was under 'the Law'.

23- Je'sus saith unto her, Thy brother *(Lazarus)* shall rise again.
24- Martha saith unto him, I know that he shall rise again in **the resurrection at the last day***. *(*-Isaiah 45 v 17)*
25- Je'sus said unto her, I am the resurrection, and the life: **he that believeth in me**, though he were dead, yet shall he live:
26- And **whosoever liveth and believeth in me shall never die**. Believest thou this?
27- She saith unto him, Yea, Lord: **I believe that thou art the Christ, the Son of God**, which should come into the world.
-John 11 v 23-27

Jesus Christ, the Son of God, did not say to Martha to believe in 'his resurrection after he was crucified'. The 'Kingdom of Heaven' was still in front of Israel. Believe in 'the Name of Jesus Christ'.

Peter's Profession of Faith

13- When Je'sus came into the coasts of Caes-a-re'a Phi-lip'pi, he asked his disciples, saying, Whom do men say that I the Son of man am?
14- And they said, Some *say that thou art* John the Bap'tist, some, E-li'as *(Elijah)*; and others, Jer-e-mi'as, or one of the prophets.
15- He saith unto them, But whom say ye that I am?
16- And Si'mon Pe'ter answered and said, **Thou art the Christ, the Son of the living God.**
17- And Je'sus answered and said unto them, Blessed art thou, Si'mon Bar-jo'na: for flesh and blood hath not revealed *it* unto thee, but my Father which is in heaven.
-Matthew 16 v 13-17

Peter did not say,"Thou art the Christ, the Son of the living God who died for me, was buried and resurrected". This is the message that much of Christendom falsely teach in combining the 'two Gospels'. The Crucifixion had not happened yet, nor did Peter know it was going to. It was still a secret/mystery being hid from them*. *-I Corinthians 2 v 7, 8; Chapter 1 of this book

Jesus the Christ speaks with 'the Twelve':
64- But there are some of you that believe not. For **Je'sus knew from the beginning** who they were that believed not, and who should betray him.
65- And he *(Jesus)* said, Therefore said I unto you, that no man can come unto me, except it were given unto him of my Father.
66- From that *time* many of his disciples went back, and walked no more with him *(Jesus)*.
67- Then said Je'sus unto the twelve, Will ye also go away?
68- Then Si'mon Pe'ter answered him, Lord, to whom shall we go? Thou hast the words of eternal life.
69- **And we believe and are sure that thou art that Christ, the Son of the living God.**
(who died and rose again for me....scripture does not say that but many preachers assume that it does...)
70- Je'sus answered them, Have not I chosen you twelve, and one of you is a devil?
71- He spake of Ju'das Is-car'iot the son of Si'mon: for he it was that should betray him, being one of the twelve.
-John 6 v 64-71

The 'True Light' was witnessed by 'the Twelve' during Jesus Christ's 'earthly ministry'. Jesus Christ came by 'signs and miracles' proving who he is. This Jesus of Nazareth is the heart of the 'Gospel of the Kingdom' to Israel. The Gospel of Grace was given to the Gentiles for all the world. Israel was still under 'the Law' and doing the things of the law.

35- And Je'sus went about all the cities and villages, teaching in their synagogues, and **preaching the gospel of the kingdom,** and healing every sickness and every disease among the people.
-Matthew 9 v 35

The Lame Man

1- Now Pe'ter and John went up together into the temple at the hour of prayer, *being* the ninth *hour.*

-Acts 3 v 1

Where did Peter and John go? The temple. When did they go? At the 'hour of prayer'.

Gentiles never had an 'official place' called 'the temple'. The 'cults and false religions' may have had a place called 'a temple' but these were not following the 'Living God'. Neither were the Gentiles ever formally invited into their 'Jewish Temple'.

Acts 3 v 1 is an example that the disciples were still under 'the law'. There are many more examples of the disciples keeping and doing the things of 'the Law'. Most of Christendom can't bring themselves to understand. There is 'only One that can open the eyes to this understanding'.

Paul, Holy Spirit inspired, warns the believer:

14- Be ye not unequally yoked together with unbelievers: for what fellowship hath righteousness with unrighteousness? And what communion hath light with darkness?

15- And what concord hath Christ with Be'li-al? Or what part hath he that believeth with an infidel?

16- And what agreement hath the temple of God with idols? For **ye are the temple of the living God**; as God hath said, I will dwell in them, and walk in *them*; and I will be their God, and they shall be my people.

17- Wherefore come out from among them, and be ye separate *(Holy)*, saith the Lord, and touch not the unclean thing; and I will receive you.

18- And will be a Father unto you, and ye shall be my sons and daughters, saith the Lord Almighty.

-II Corinthians 6 v 14-18

Jesus Christ had already ascended to heaven in Acts chapter 1. 'The elect' and those that believed in 'the Name of Jesus Christ' had not forsaken the law. They were still law abiding 'Jews of the circumcision'. Jesus never told them to stop keeping 'the Law'.

Neither did Christ Jesus tell them to believe in his 'death, burial and resurrection' for salvation without 'righteous works of the Law'. The disciples had first hand knowledge of these events: the 'earthly ministry' of miracles, signs and wonders, the resurrection and the visible ascension (taken/caught up) to heaven. They were eye witnesses. What 'this Resurrection' meant to 'the elect' was that Christ is still alive and would return with 'The Kingdom of Heaven'. Jesus Christ would save them from their enemies. The believers in the Kingdom Gospel that have died would receive an 'Earthly Resurrection'*. *-Isaiah 45 v 17, -John 11 v 24-26; -John 6 v 39, 40, 44, -I John 5 v 11-13; -Luke 21 v 27, 28

"Peter and John went up together into the temple at the hour of prayer". We in the 'Body of Christ' have not a set designated hour when it is time to pray. We can pray at any time and at any place. There is no rule or legalism (law) that says when and where we can approach God. In the 'Body of Christ', we are permanent members 24/7 and 'joint heirs with Christ'*. *-Romans 8 v 16, 17

Acts 3 continues:

2- And a certain man lame from his mothers womb was carried, whom they laid daily at the gate of the temple which is called Beautiful, to ask alms of them that entered into the temple;

3- Who seeing Pe'ter and John about to go into the temple asked an alms.

4- And Pe'ter, fastening his eyes upon him with John, said, Look on us.

5- And he gave heed unto them, expecting to receive something of them.

6- Then Pe'ter said, Silver and gold have I none: but such as I have give I thee: **In the name of Je'sus Christ of Naz'a-reth rise up and walk.**

7- And he took him by the right hand, and lifted *him* up: and immediately his feet and ankle bones received strength.

8- And he leaping up stood and walked, and entered with them into the temple, walking and leaping, and praising God:

9- And all the people saw him walking and praising God:

10- And they knew that it was he which sat for alms at the Beautiful gate of the temple: and they were filled with wonder and amazement at that which had happened unto him.

11- And the lame man which was healed held Pe'ter and John, all the people ran together unto them in the porch that is called Sol'o-mons, greatly wondering.

-Acts 3 v 2-11

Jesus Christ had given 'the Twelve disciples' power. The disciples were carrying on the ministry of 'the Gospel of the Kingdom'. Jesus Christ physically was not there but in his 'fleshly absence' these disciples were carrying on 'the ministry' till Christ returns. The Holy Spirit of God was there with them in power.

How long did they have this power? There are preachers today that claim to have the same power. Or something supernatural that God had given them personally. Satan himself can transform himself into an angel of light*. The disciples power didn't last for their whole lifetime. Israel kept rejecting their King and Kingdom. *-II Corinthians 11 v 13-15

12- And when Pe'ter saw *it*, he answered unto the people, **Ye men of Is'ra-el**, why marvel ye at this? Or why look ye so earnestly on us, as though by our own power or holiness we had made this man to walk?
13- The God of A'bra-ham, and of I'saac, and of Ja'cob, **the God of our fathers**, hath glorified his Son Je'sus; whom ye delivered up, and denied him in the presence of Pi'late, when he was determined to let *him* go.
14- But ye denied the Holy One and the Just, and desired a murderer to be granted unto you:
15- And killed the Prince of life, **whom God hath raised from the dead; whereof we are witnesses**.
16- **And his name through faith in his name hath made this man strong**, whom ye see and know: yea, the faith which is by him hath given him this perfect soundness in the presence of you all.
-Acts 3 v 12-16

Peter did not attribute anything of the Gospel of 'Christ Crucified' for 'the lame mans' healing. He never mentioned 'death, burial and resurrection' together as for the reason by which this 'lame man' was healed. It was by the 'Kingdom Gospel' and 'the Name of Jesus Christ' that healed this 'Jewish lame man'. It was by 'faith and belief of who 'Jesus of Nazareth' really is. The Name of Jesus Christ, a full heart-ed belief is the 'Cornerstone of the Gospel of the Kingdom'.

A scriptural observation:
Jesus Christ himself many times went into this temple. Scripture says the 'lame man was taken daily to the temple and put in a position to 'ask

for alms'. Jesus Christ must have passed by this man many times and did not heal him. Why? Perhaps the Lame man was left unhealed for this very purpose so Peter and John could show that, though Christ was in Heaven, he still had power on the earth and was waiting to return physically.

Paul too Preached Jesus the Christ

10- And there was a certain disciple at Da-mas'cus, named An-a-ni'as; and to him said the Lord in a vision, An-a-ni'as. And he said, Behold, I *am here*, Lord.

11- And the Lord *said* unto him, Arise, and go into the street which is called Straight, and enquire in the house of Ju'das for *one* called Saul, of Tar'sus: for, behold, he prayeth,

12- And he hath seen in a vision a man named An-a-ni'as coming in, and putting *his* hand on him, that he might receive his sight.

13- Then An-a-ni'as answered, Lord, I have heard by many of this man, how much evil he hath done to thy saints at Je-ru'sa-lem:

14- And here he hath authority from the chief priests to bind all that call on thy name.

15- **But the Lord said unto him, Go thy way: for he is a chosen vessel unto me, to bear my name before the Gen'tiles, and Kings, and the children of Is'ra-el:**

16- For I will show him how great things he must suffer for my names sake.

17- And An-a-ni'as went his way, and entered into the house; and putting his hands on him said, Brother Saul, **the Lord,** *even* **Jesus**, that appeared unto thee in the way as thou camest, hath sent me, that thou mightest receive thy sight, **and be filled with the Ho'ly Ghost.**

18- And **immediately** there fell from his eyes as it had been scales: and he received sight forthwith, and arose, **and was baptized.**

-Acts 9 v 10-18

As of yet, Saul (Paul) had not been given by God the 'Gospel of Grace'. Saul/Paul was a 'Law keeping Jew of the Circumcision' still. But the order in which salvation was received has changed. Paul received the Holy Ghost not in the order of Acts 2 v 38.

Verse 17 – "and be filled with the Holy Ghost".

Verse 18- "And immediately..." Paul was water Baptized last of all.

It wasn't "repent and be baptized in the name of Jesus Christ and ye shall receive the Holy Ghost". Saul/Paul was baptized without water by the Holy Ghost. He then later was water baptized. All the 'Jews of the Circumcision/Law' knew of no other way. They still were water baptizing.

19- And when he had received meat, he was strengthened. That was Saul certain days with the disciples which were at Da-mas'cus.
-Acts 9 v 19

Don't confuse 'these disciples at Damascus' with 'the Twelve'. Jesus' 'Twelve disciples' were still in Jerusalem*. Many Jews had fled Jerusalem to escape persecution. These Jews of the Circumcision under the Law were preaching not to the Gentiles but "preaching the word to none but unto the Jews only". *-Acts 8 v 1; -Acts 11 v 19

20- And **straightway he preached Christ in the synagogues, that he is the Son of God**.
-Acts 9 v 20

What did Saul/Paul preach? He preached Christ, that he is the Son of God. The same as Peter and 'the Twelve'. He only knew Old Testament scripture but now understood that Jesus Christ of Nazareth is the prophesied Messiah and King that was to come for the Nation of Israel. He now believed in the 'Name of Jesus Christ'. The prophecies foretold of Christ now was understood that they spoke of this man, Jesus the Christ.

21- But all that heard *him* were amazed, and said; Is not this he that destroyed them which called on this name in Je-ru'sa-lem, and came hither for that intent, that he might bring them bound unto the chief priests?
-Acts 9 v 21

Saul/Paul now had the wisdom and understanding of who the Old Testament Prophets were speaking of:
22- But Saul increased the more in strength, and confounded the Jews which dwelt at Da-mas'cus, **proving that this is very Christ**.
-Acts 9 v 22

Saul/Paul now fully understood who Jesus Christ really is. Before his 'Road to Damascus' experience, he did not believe in the 'Name of Jesus Christ'. But now he could use Old Testament scripture proving the prophecies that this man, 'Jesus of Nazareth', was that prophesied 'Messiah and Christ'.

23- And after many days were fulfilled, **the Jews took counsel to kill him**:
24- But their laying await was known of Saul. And they watched the gates day and night to kill him.
25- Then the disciples took him by night, and let *him* down by the wall in a basket.
-Acts 9 v 10-25

Paul's ministry to the Gentile world begins. When being 'humbled back down to a powerless man', the guilt and regret of what Saul had done to the believers of Jesus Christ was something hard to come to grips with. How could it not? It had to be by the 'Grace of God' that spared this man. The guilt of now knowing 'the Truth and accepting Jesus Christ' made Saul/Paul a hypocrite. The most disgusting of men. The Jews naturally became a mortal enemy of Saul/Paul.

But first though, Saul/Paul disappears into the desert for three years. Acts 15 doesn't show this but Galatians 1 does. People discounting Paul say that he wasn't one of 'the Twelve' and didn't know Jesus Christ in the flesh. <u>But better than 'the Twelve' had it</u>, he spent three years alone, 'face to face' with the ascended Jesus Christ in Heaven.

All the 'Words of God' <u>written through</u> the Apostle Paul came to him by Holy Ghost inspiration from Jesus Christ in Heaven. Romans to Hebrews all came from Heaven. The Apostle Paul did not write of Jesus' earthly ministry, but wrote of him after 'the Resurrection'. Jesus Christ was physically no longer on the earth. Everything Paul wrote came to him 'via Heaven'. Every single one of the writers of the scriptures wrote by Holy Spirit guidance that make up the King James Bible. They all did, every word, even the writers personal thoughts.

Jesus Christ selected his 'Twelve disciples' within the border of Israel. The Apostle of the Gentiles, that being Paul, was selected outside the border of Israel. Paul is 'the Chosen Vessel of God' to bear his name to the world'*. Had the Kingdom happened, the Kingdom of Jewish Priest's were to do this. **We are Saved by Grace through the Faith of the Resurrected Jesus Christ.**

KEEP the LAW, KEEP the COMMANDMENTS

The epistles that are written by James, Peter, John, Jude are still in anticipation of the 'Kingdom of Heaven'. Take out the writings of the Apostle Paul and everything in scripture left is still dealing with the same gospel, 'the Gospel of the Kingdom'. James, Peter, John and Jude are writing to their fellow 'Jews of the Circumcision/Law' to prepare them for the coming Tribulation and to not be discouraged by their present persecutions. The Kingdom of Heaven is right around the corner.

Jesus the Law Keeper:
12- Verily, verily, I say unto you, He that believeth on me, the works that I do shall he do also; and greater *works* than these shall he do; because I go unto my father.
13- And whatsoever ye shall ask in my name, that will I do, that the Father may be glorified in the son.
14- **If ye shall ask any thing in my name, I will do *it*.**
15- **If ye love me, keep my commandments.**
16- And I will pray the Father, and he shall give you another Comforter, that he may abide with you for ever;
17- *Even* the Spirit of truth; whom the world cannot receive, because it seeth him not, neither knoweth him: but ye know him; for he dwelleth with you, **and shall be in you**.
18- I will not leave you comfortless: I will come to you.
19- Yet a little while, and the world seeth me no more; but ye see me: because I live, ye shall live also.
20- At that day ye shall know that I *am* in my Father, and ye in me, and I in you.
21- **He that hath my commandments, and keep it, he it is that loveth me:** and he that loveth me shall be loved of my Father, and I will love him, and will manifest myself in him.
-John 14 v 12-21

Jesus under the law:
16- And, behold, one came and said unto him, Good Master, what good thing shall I do, that I may have eternal life?
17- And he said unto him, Why callest thou me good? *There is* none good but one, *that is*, God: but if thou wilt enter into life, **keep the commandments**.
-Matthew 19 v 16, 17

The Vine and Branch

1- I Am the true vine, and my Father is the husbandman.

2- Every branch in me that beareth not fruit he taketh away: and every *branch* that beareth fruit, he purgeth it, that it may bring forth more fruit.

3- Now ye are clean through the word which I have spoken unto you.

4- Abide in me, and I in you. As the branch cannot bear fruit of itself, except it abide in the vine; no more can ye, except ye abide in me.

5- I am the vine, *ye are* the branches. He that abideth in me, and I in him, the same bringeth forth much fruit: for without me ye can do nothing.

6- If a man abide not in me, he is cast forth as a branch, and is withered; and men gather them, and cast *them* into the fire, and they are burned.

7- If ye abide in me, and my words abide in you, ye shall ask what ye will, and it shall be done unto you.

8- Herein is my Father glorified, that ye bear much fruit; so shall ye be my disciples.

9- As the Father hath loved me, so have I loved you: continue ye in my love.

10- **If ye keep my commandments, ye shall abide in my love; even as I have kept my Father's commandments**, and abide in his love.

11- These things have I spoken unto you, that my joy might remain in you, and *that* your joy might be full.

12- This is my commandment, That ye love one another, as I have loved you.

13- Greater love hath no man than this, that a man lay down his life for his friends.

14- Ye are my friends, if ye do whatsoever I command you.

15- Henceforth I call you not servants; for the servant knoweth not what his lord doeth: but I have called you friends; for all things that I have heard of my Father I have made known unto you.

16- Ye have not chosen me, but I have chosen you, and ordained you, that ye should go and bring forth fruit, and *that* your fruit should remain: **that whatsoever ye shall ask of the Father in my name, he may give you**.

17- These things I command you, that ye love one another.

-John 15 v 1-17

The Jewish Epistles

These 'Jewish Epistles' found after the Book of Hebrews are still giving the same message as Jesus Christs' earthy ministry. The difference now is that they are waiting for the 'Return of Christ' and the 'Kingdom of Heaven'. This promised 'Earthly Heavenly Kingdom' would save them from their enemies. This is the belief they had in that word 'Resurrection' concerning Jesus the Christ, their Messiah.

The 'Jewish Epistles' are written as if the 'prophetic program' of Israel was still going to happen. There is no mention of an interruption to 'Israel's Prophecies'. 'The Kingdom of Heaven' was coming soon they thought.

The Jewish Epistles make no mention of Gentiles having salvation on their own, without the Jew. Even 'the Apostle of the Gentiles' thought he was going to be 'caught up' soon. After many years later of these events not happening and the persecution of the Jew steadily intensifying, they began to slowly realize a delay had happened.

What was the delay? The 'Age of Grace' and the filling of the 'Body of Christ, The Church'. A 'mystery and secret' kept hid from the world until it was revealed to the Apostle Paul. Israel and most of Christendom are still blind to this. They teach a mixed Gospel not able to explain this new period of time that was never included with Israel and their prophecies.

Take out Romans to Hebrews (and all mention of Paul in the Book of Acts) and you have the message of the 'Gospel of the Kingdom'. It all fits. Put back in the 'Gospel of Grace' given to Paul shows a new time line, 'a parenthetical period' added to our Bibles.

How long? We don't know but when the 'Body of Christ' is full, we will be 'caught up' and saved from going through the missing seven years of prophecy yet to be fulfilled on Israel and the world. Israel will still get its 'Kingdom of Heaven' after the 'Body of Christ, the true Church' is 'caught up to God' and the Tribulation has ran its course.

These Jewish Epistles by James, Peter, John and Jude never mention the word C-R-O-S-S. Not one time. This is all Paul claims to know after receiving the revelations of the mysteries, Christ Crucified*.

*-I Corinthians 2 v 2; -Galatians 2 v 20

The Epistle of James the 'Legalist'

1- James, a servant of God and of the Lord Jesus Christ, **to the twelve tribes which are scattered abroad**, greeting.
-James 1 v 1

Who did James address his epistle to? Many Jews had not returned to Israel after the Babylonian Invasion of 606 B.C. Many had been scattered by Saul out of Israel after 'the crucifixion'. This 'new sect' that was 'still under the Law' but had embraced the 'Name of Jesus Christ' were in the minority and came under persecution. The Gentiles were not scattered, the Jews of 'the Twelve Tribes' were.

22- But be ye **doers** of the word, and not hearers only, deceiving your own selves.
23- For if any be a hearer of the word, and not a **doer**, he is like unto a man beholding his natural face in a glass:
24- For he beholdeth himself, and goeth his way, and straightway forgetteth what manner of man he was.
25- But whoso looketh into the perfect **law of liberty**, and continueth *therein*, he being not a forgetful hearer, **but a doer of the work**, this man shall be blessed in his deed.
-James 1 v 22-25

James says to keep the whole law:
10- **For whosoever shall keep the whole law, and yet offend in one *point*, he is guilty of all.**
11- For he that said, Do not commit adultery, said also, Do not kill. Now if thou commit no adultery, yet if thou kill, thou art become a transgressor of the law.
12- So speak ye, and so do, as they that shall be judged by the **law of liberty**.
-James 2 v 10-12

James gives the message similar to the 'Four Gospels' of Matthew, Mark, Luke and John:
14- What *doth it* profit, my brethren, though a man say he hath faith, and have not works? Can faith save him?

15- If a brother or sister be naked, and destitute of daily food,

16- And one of you say unto them, Depart in peace, be *ye* warmed and filled; not withstanding ye give them not those things which are needful to the body; what *doth it* profit?

17- Even so **faith, if it hath not works, is dead, being alone**.

18- Yea, a man may say, Thou hast faith, and I have works: show me thy faith without thy works, and I will show thee my faith by my works.

19- Thou believest that there is one God; thou doest well: the devils also believe, and tremble.

20- But wilt thou know, O vain man, **that faith without works is dead?**

-James 2 v 14-20

James is led by 'the Law and Righteous Works'. The Body of Christ is led by the Spirit:

27- Pure religion and undefiled before God and the Father is this, To visit the fatherless and widows in their affliction, *and* to keep himself unspotted from the world.

-James 1 v 27

We do 'works' as God's workman* but not according to 'the Law of Moses'. Our works are of love, and charity and come naturally. We have no law or mandate that we have to do 'righteous works' proving our faith. Our faith was justified by God when we believe 'The Gospel'+. *-Ephesians 2 v 10; -II Timothy 2 v 15; +-I Corinthians 15 v 1-4; -Ephesians 1 v 13, 14; -Romans 10 v 9

5- Do ye think that the scripture saith in vain, The **spirit** that dwelleth in us lusteth to envy?

6- But he giveth more **grace**. Wherefore he saith, God resists the proud, but **giveth grace** unto the humble.

-James 4 v 5-6

James speaks of grace and spirit. The spirit is small 's' and is not leading the person like 'the Spirit'. The word 'grace' is not 'doctrine' like that of Paul. God gave 'his grace' all through the Bible but 'the 'Dispensation of the Grace of God*' was only given to one man for us, through one Chosen Vessel Apostle. *-Ephesians 3 v 1-10

James writes of Abraham's faith. But Abraham was never under the 'Law of Moses'. Abraham believed God. His faith was counted to him for righteousness. He had faith long before he offered up Isaac on an alter. Abraham was doing what God told him to do. It was not a 'righteous work under the Law'. He didn't just believe in God but fully believed God. James is obviously still a zealous 'Law Keeper'.

21- Was not A'bra-ham our father justified by works, when he had offered I'saac his son upon the altar?

22- Seest thou how faith wrought with his works, and by works was faith made perfect?

23- And the scripture was fulfilled which saith, A'bra-ham believed God, and it was imputed unto him for righteousness: and he was called the Friend of God

24- Ye see then how **that by works a man is justified, and not by faith only.**

25- Likewise also was not Ra'hab the harlot justified by works, when she had received the messengers, and had sent *them* out another way?

26- For as the body without the spirit is dead, faith without works is dead also.

-James 2 v 21-26

A Jew was to keep the 'Whole Law' or be damned:

10- **For whosoever shall keep the whole law, and yet offend in one *point*, he is guilty of all.**

11- For he that said, Do not commit adultery, said also, Do not kill. Now if thou commit no adultery, yet if thou kill, thou art become a transgressor of the law.

12- So speak ye, and so do, **as they that shall be judged by the law of liberty**.

-James 2 v 10-12

James is not Paul. Paul is definitely not James. Their message clashes and contradicts. "Rightly dividing the word of truth" is of paramount importance for understanding the 'written word of God'. Most of Christendom have missed this. James is still giving the same message to the 'Jews of the Circumcision/Law' that was preached by Jesus the Christ in the 'Four Gospels' of Matthew, Mark, Luke and John.

James preached 'the Law' and not the 'Doctrine of Grace'. He (James) is unaware that the 'revelations of the mysteries' (secrets) that have been hid have been revealed to another man, the Apostle of the Gentiles*. James was not that Apostle of the Gentiles. *-Deuteronomy 29 v 29; -Romans 16 v 25

'Faith in the resurrected Christ' **does indeed profit a man without the 'righteous works of the Law'**. James had not this new faith (faith-way) by Paul's Gospel*. James faith was by 'the Law' and doing 'righteous works'. James never wavered from the 'Gospel of the Kingdom' message fully believing in the name of Jesus Christ. *-Romans 4 v 2-6

The Epistles of I, II Peter

1- Peter, an apostle of Je'sus Christ, **to the strangers scattered** throughout Pon'tus, Ga-la'tia, Cap-pa-do'cia, A'sia, and Bi-thyn'i-a,

-I Peter 1 v 1

Peter is not writing to 'the Body of Christ'. His Epistles are not written to the Gentiles. He is writing to the "scattered Jews" that have come under persecution by their fellow Jews and the 'ungodly Gentiles' of the world. He did not receive the 'revelation of the mysteries' that were given to Paul 'after the resurrection'.

Peter does not use 'church language of salvation' based on the death, burial and the resurrection. Resurrection is referred to as 'a fact' and their hope of being saved from their enemies is still a possibility. The word 'C-R-O-S-S' is never mentioned. Nor did Peter preach Acts 2 v 38 in his epistles. Why not?

When Peter wrote his Epistles 'the Temple' was still operating. These "strangers scattered" were 'Jews of the Circumcision/Law' that believed in 'the Name of Jesus Christ' and who he is. Peter called them strangers because he must not have known them personally. But these were still the 'Ye men of Israel' and 'of the Circumcision/Law'.

Peter's Epistles have almost come full circle for today. These same Epistles by James, Peter, John and Jude once again will bring hope for the Jews in preparation for the final seven years of Tribulation that is coming. The signs are everywhere.

For the 'Jews of the Circumcision/Law' it has always been about faith. Their faith was shown by their 'righteous works' and keeping the 'whole

Law of Moses'. For the 'Body of Christ' it is 'faith in the finished work of the cross' without doing 'righteous works' of Jewish Law. When you believe the Gospel written by Paul you have salvation*. It is what the 'Word of God' says. Believe it! That is good news! That is Gospel! *-I Corinthians 15 v 1-4; -I Corinthians 12 v 13; -II Corinthians 1 v 22; -Ephesians 1 v 13; -Ephesians 4 v 30; -Romans 10 v 9

3- Blessed *be* the God and Father of our Lord Jesus Christ, which according to his abundant mercy hath **begotten us again unto a lively hope by the resurrection of Jesus Christ** from the dead,
4- To **an inheritance** incorruptible, and undefiled, and that fadeth not away, **reserved in heaven** for you,
5- Who are kept by the power of God through **faith unto salvation ready to be revealed in the last time**.
6- Wherein ye greatly rejoice, though now for a season, if need be, ye are in heaviness through manifold temptations:
7- That the trial of your faith, being more precious than of gold that perisheth, though it be tried with fire, might be found unto praise and honour and glory **at the appearing of Jesus Christ**:
-I Peter 1 v 3-7

"Salvation ready to be revealed in the <u>last time</u>". "An inheritance, reserved in heaven for you". "Honour and glory **at the appearing of Jesus Christ**'. 'The Earthly Kingdom of Heaven' is with Jesus Christ who is seated at the Father's right hand till he makes the enemies of Israel their footstool*. This is the Jewish faith and 'lively hope' in the 'Resurrected Jesus Christ'. *-Psalm 110

Peter never relates 'the resurrection' of Jesus Christ as the 'Power of God' given to the Gentiles. Peter never says it is the saving Grace and free gift for all the world. He is still focused on his fellow Jews and the soon coming 'Earthly Kingdom of Heaven'. 'The Gospel of the Kingdom' is still his Gospel to his dieing day.

13- Wherefore gird up the loins of your mind, be sober, and hope to the end for **the grace that is to be brought unto you at the revelation of Je'sus Christ;**
14- As obedient children, not fashioning yourselves according to the former lusts in your ignorance:

15- But as he which hath called you is holy, so be ye holy *(set apart)* in all manner of conversation;

16- Because it is written, Be ye holy; for I am holy *(set apart)*.

17- And if ye call on the Father, who without respect of persons judgeth according to every man's work, pass the time of your sojourning *here* in fear:

18- Forasmuch as ye know that **ye were not redeemed** with corruptible things, *as* silver and gold, from your vain conversation *received* **by tradition** from your father's;

19- **But with the precious blood of Christ,** as of a lamb without blemish and without spot:

20- Who verily was foreordained before the foundation of the world, **but was manifest in these last times for you,**

21- **Who by him do believe in God, that raised him up from the dead, and gave him glory; that your faith and hope might be in God.**

-I Peter 1 v 15-21

'Israel's hope' was further solidified by the 'physical resurrection' of Jesus Christ. 'The elect' of Israel knew by the 'Word of God' that Jesus Christ would be returning. Israel will become the 'head and not the tail' of the world*. *-Deuteronomy 28 v 13; -Deuteronomy 26 v 18, 19; -Exodus 19 v 5, 6; -Jeremiah 30 v 11

Peter writes of the 'Death, Burial and Resurrection' as a fact. He gave no basis for mankind's salvation to 'the Gospel' that Paul preaches. 'The Kingdom of Heaven' is coming, but the 'Jews of the Circumcision/Law' had no knowledge that it would be delayed for 1,000's of years. This delay was for the purpose of 'filling the Body of Christ'*. *-Romans 11 v 25

24- Who his own self bare our sins in his own body on the tree, that we, being dead to sins, should live unto righteousness: by whose stripes ye were healed.

-I Peter 2 v 24

Peter does say that he 'bared our sins' on the tree. Who is this 'our'? The 'Jews of the Circumcision/Law' that believed in 'the Name of Jesus Christ'. Don't misinterpret and include salvation for the Gentiles. Peter is still in anticipation of the Kingdom of Heaven. His Epistles did not include us Gentiles.

The same 'Climate today' is similar as to the current events when Peter wrote his Epistles:

3- For the time past of *our* life may suffice us to have wrought the will of the Gen'tiles, when we walked in lasciviousness, lusts, excess of wine, revellings, banquetings, and abominable idolatries:

4- Wherein they think it strange that ye run not with *them* to the same excess of riot, speaking evil of *you*:

5- Who shall give account to him that is ready to judge the quick and the dead.

-I Peter 4 v 3-5

Peter never promoted Paul's God's given Gospel until just before his death* around 68 A.D. It is important to not just read scripture but compare and study the scriptures. So much is said by the use of few words. This is why we study+. There is no end to the wisdom in the 'Written Word'. *-II Peter 3 v 15, 16 ; +-II Timothy 2 v 15

6- For this cause was the gospel preached also to them that are dead, that they might be judged according to men in the flesh, but live according to God in the spirit.

-I Peter 4 v 6

'The Elect' have the Holy Spirit of God. They have their salvation. They were 'baptized into the Holy Ghost'. They believed the Biblical Prophecies and in the 'Name of Jesus Christ'. They still were keepers of 'the Law' and were Holy, separated from the Gentiles and the unbelieving Jews.

Peter is expecting the Earthly Kingdom of Heaven soon:

7- But the end of all things is at hand: be ye therefore sober, and watch unto prayer.

-I Peter 4 v 7

II Peter

Peter realized that the 'Kingdom of Heaven' was not going to happen anytime soon as he thought in I Peter 4 v 7. He knew that he was soon going to die:

13- Yea, I think it meet, as long as I am in this tabernacle *(human body)*, to stir you up by putting you in remembrance;
14- Knowing that shortly I must put off this my tabernacle, even as our Lord Je'sus Christ hath shewed me.
-II Peter 1 v 13, 14; -John 21 v 18

Peter speaks (Holy Spirit inspired) of the 'Sure Words of Prophecy' that has been written in our Bible. All prophecy made by the 'Word of God' has always came true, 100%. It has been a mission by mankind to disprove the 'Word of God'. To this day they are stumped yet will never admit it.

Beware of the newer translated bibles for in these the truth of 'God's Divine Word' has been twisted and made possible by man to promote lies. 'The Solidifying Word of God' has been tampered with and been perverted when reading the Apostle Paul. Modifiers and a relentless limiting to Paul's 'chosen vessel wisdom' are the works of the god of this world that works through men. I pray that all men and women can see the difference when comparing the KJV and the newer translations.

The Truth, The Truth, The Truth

16- For we have not followed cunningly devised fables, when we made known unto you the power and coming of our Lord Je'sus Christ, but were eyewitnesses of his majesty.
17- For he received from God the Father honour and glory, when there came such a voice to him from the excellent glory, This is my beloved Son, in whom I am well pleased.
18- And this voice which came from heaven we heard, when we were with him in the holy mount.
19- We have also a more sure word of prophecy; whereunto ye do well that ye take heed, as unto a light that shineth in a dark place, until the day dawn, and the day star arise in your hearts:
20- Knowing this first, that no prophecy of the scripture is of any private interpretation.
21- For the prophecy came not in old time by the will of man: but holy men of God spake *as they were* moved by the Ho'ly Ghost.
-II Peter 1 v 16-21

Peter writes (Holy Spirit inspired):

1- But there were false prophets also among the people, even as there shall be false teachers among you, who privily shall bring in damnable heresies, even denying the Lord that bought them, and bring upon themselves swift destruction.

2- And many shall follow their pernicious ways; by reason of whom the way of truth shall be evil spoken of.

3- And through covetousness shall they with feigned words make merchandise of you: whose judgment now of a long time lingereth not, and their damnation slumbereth not.

4- For if God spared not the angels that sinned, but cast *them* down to hell, and delivered *them* into chains of darkness, to be reserved unto judgment;

5- And spared not the old world, but saved No'ah the eighth *person*, a preacher of righteousness, bringing in the flood upon the world of the ungodly;

6- And turning the cities of Sod'om and Go-mor'rha into ashes condemned *them* with an overthrow, making *them* an ensample onto those that after should live ungodly;

7- And delivered just Lot, vexed with the filthy conversation of the wicked:

8- (For that righteous man dwelling among them, in seeing and hearing, vexed *his* righteous soul from day to day with *their* unlawful deeds;)

9- **The Lord knoweth how** to deliver the godly out of temptations, and **to reserve the unjust unto the day of judgment to be punished**:

-II Peter 2 v 1-9

Peter writes by Holy Spirit inspiration these verses. See if the following scriptures could also be speaking of a certain political party in the U.S. What political party does this? What types of people could these scriptures be writing about?

10- But chiefly them that walk after the flesh in the lust of uncleanness, and despised government. Presumptuous *are they*, selfwilled, they are not afraid to speak evil of dignitaries.

11- Whereas angels, which are greater in power and might, bring not railing accusation against them before the Lord.

12- But these, as natural brute beasts, made to be taken and destroyed, speak evil of the things that they understand not; and shall utterly perish in their own corruption;

13- And shall receive the reward of unrighteousness, *as* they that count it pleasure to riot in the day time. Spots *they are* and blemishes, sporting themselves with their own deceivings while they feast with you;

14- Having eyes full of adultery, and that cannot cease from sin; beguiling unstable souls: an heart they have exercised with covetous practices; cursed children:

15- Which have forsaken the right way, and are gone astray, following the way of Ba'laam *the son* of Bo'sor, who loved the wages of unrighteousness;

16- But was rebuked for his iniquity: the dumb ass speaking with man's voice forbad the madness of the prophet.

17- These are wells without water, clouds that are carried with a tempest; to whom the mist of darkness is reserved for ever.

18- For when they speak great swelling *words* of vanity, they allure through the lusts of the flesh, *through much* wantonness, those that were clean escaped from them who live in error.

19- While they promise them liberty, they themselves are the servants of corruption: for of whom a man is overcome, of the same is he brought in bondage.

20- For if after they have escaped the pollutions of the world through the knowledge of the Lord and Savior Je'sus Christ, they are again entangled therein, and overcome, the latter end is worse with them than the beginning.

21- For it had been better for them not to have known the way of righteousness, than, after they have known *it*, to turn from the holy commandment delivered unto them.

22- But it is happened unto them according to the true proverb, The dog *is* turned to his own vomit again; and the sow that was washed to her wallowing in the mire.

-II Peter 2 v 10-22

    Peter gives warning of Christ's coming and his judgment on the world. The 'natural man' without the 'Spirit of God' cannot understand nor discern what is written in our Bible. The wisdom of men is made foolish by the 'Holy Spirit'.

Peter writes by Holy Spirit inspiration:
3- Knowing this first, that there shall come in the last days scoffers, walking after their own lusts,

4- And saying, Where is the promise of his coming? For since the fathers fell asleep *(died),* all things continue as *they were* from the beginning of creation.
5- **For this they are willingly ignorant of**, that by the word of God the heavens were of old, and the earth standing out of the water and in the water:
6- Whereby the world that then was, being overflowed with water, perished:
7- But the heavens and the earth, which are now, by the same word are kept in store, reserved unto fire against the day of judgment and perdition of ungodly men.
-II Peter 3 v 3-7

Peter gives the same end time prophecy that the prophets and Jesus himself gave. The Apostle Paul wrote little (Holy Spirit inspired) concerning end time prophecy. As well as little was written of the 'Earthly Ministry of Jesus Christ'.

10- **But the day of the Lord** will come as a thief in the night; in the which the heavens shall pass away with a great noise, and the elements shall melt with fervent heat, the earth also and the works therein shall be burned up.
11- *Seeing* then *that all* these things shall be dissolved, what manner *of persons* ought ye to be in all holy conversation and godliness,
12- Looking for and hasting unto the coming of God, wherein the heavens being on fire shall be dissolved, and the elements shall melt with fervent heat?
13- Nevertheless we, **according to his promise, look for new heavens and a new earth**, wherein dwelleth righteousness
-II Peter 3 v 10-13

Out of all these Epistles written by James, Peter, John and Jude only one reference was made of the Apostle of the Gentiles. None of these Epistles spoke of Paul's Gospel. None of them mentioned that the whole world has the 'free gift of Grace' to obtain eternal salvation. None of them spoke of 'the finished work of the cross'.

Just before Peter is martyred he finally acknowledges the wisdom that God had given to the Apostle Paul:
15- And account *that* the long-suffering of our Lord *is* salvation; even as our beloved brother **Paul** also according to **the wisdom given unto him** hath written unto you;

16- As also in all *his* epistles, speaking in them of these things *(salvation)*; in which are some things hard to be understood, which they that are **unlearned and unstable wrest**, as *they do* also the other scriptures, **unto their own destruction**.

-II Peter 3 v 15, 16

The Epistles of I, II, III John

John writes as if the 'prophetic program' laid out in scripture was in the process of still happening*. John is unaware that 'the Age of Grace' has interrupted this 'Jewish Prophetic Time Line'. The Earthly Kingdom of Heaven' has been put on hold "until the fullness of the Gentiles be come in"+. *-Psalm 2; +-Romans 11 v 25

John begins his Epistle the same way that he wrote 'the Book of John'. The 'Word was made flesh and lived among us'. The Kingdom was within them (in their midst). The disciples were eyewitness of Jesus Christ in his 'Earthly Ministry' to Israel.

1- That which was from the beginning, which we have seen with our eyes, which we have looked upon, and our hands have handled, of the Word of life;
2- (For the life was manifested, and we have seen *it*, and bear witness, and shew unto you that eternal life, which was with the Father, and was manifest unto us;)
3- That which we have seen and heard declare we unto you, that ye also may have fellowship with us: and truly our fellowship *is* with the Father, and with his Son Jesus Christ.

-I John 1 v 1-3

John shows his 'zealousness of Law keeping'. 'The Law' had not been done away with concerning the 'Jews of the Circumcision'. Though some things do agree with the Apostle Paul there is a sharp contrast in the 'Two Gospels and Doctrine' that they promoted. Can you see it?

Paul and John both acknowledge that Jesus Christ is the 'propitiation and substitute' for our sins. Jesus Christ is our Advocate with the Father. But John is still a 'Law keeping Jew', "hereby we do know that we know him, if we keep his commandments"*. Paul repeats over and over that "we are not under law but under grace"+. *-I John 2 v 3, 4; +-Romans 6 v 14; -Galatians 3 v 10; -Galatians 4 v 21;-Galatians 5 v 18; -Hebrews 7 v 11

Paul preached 'Christ Crucified' and 'faith in the finished work of the cross'. The salvation of the world (Gentiles) was made possible 'after the Resurrection'. Only the 'Jews of the Circumcision/Law' had any hope of eternal salvation before 'the Cross'*. *-Ephesians 2 v 11-13

1- My little children, these things write I unto you, that ye sin not. And if any man sin, we have an advocate with the Father, Je'sus Christ the righteous:
2- And he is the propitiation *(appropriator/substitute)* for our sins: and not for ours only, but also for *the sins* of the whole world.
3- And hereby we do know that we know him, **if we keep his commandments**.
4- He that saith, **I know him, and keepeth not his commandments**, is a liar, and the truth is not in him.
-I John 2 v 1-4

It is an eye opener to realize by the Word of God* that there has been 'Two Separate Gospels'. What was written before the cross was written to the Jew/Hebrew and for our learning and understanding+. What Paul writes after the resurrection is written for all the world. Law and Grace does not mix. *-Romans 10 v 17; +-Romans 15 v 4

John speaks of Jesus Christ's 'shed blood' as a fact but gives no basis for salvation to the Gentiles. He never included resurrection as the saving Grace for the 'Body of Christ'. John never promoted nor endorsed the 'Faith-way Gospel of Grace' that was given by God from heaven to the 'Apostle of the Gentiles'.

5- This then is the message which we have heard of him, and declare unto you, that God is light, and in him is no darkness at all.
6- If we say that we have fellowship with him, and walk in darkness, we lie, and do not the truth:
7- But if we walk in the light, as he is in the light, we have fellowship one with another, and the blood of Je'sus Christ his Son cleanseth us from all sin*. *(*-Acts 2 v 38; - I John 4 v 9, 10)*
-I John 1 v 5-7

John gives 'The Warning':

15- Love not the world, neither the things *that are* in the world. If any man love the world, the love of the Father is not in him.

16- For all that *is* in the world, the lust of the flesh, and the lust of the eyes, and the pride of life, is not of the Father, but is of the world.

17- And the world passeth away, and the lust thereof: but **he that doeth the will of God** abideth for ever.

-I John 2 v 15-17

John speaks of the 'second coming of Christ'. Only the Apostle Paul spoke of the 'Body of Christ being 'caught up' to meet the Lord in the air. For Israel, Jesus is coming! There are no words in the 'Word of God' that says the Jews too would be 'caught up'. Of course a Jew can be in the 'Body of Christ', but John here is writing to 'Jews of the Circumcision/Law'. He is writing to 'Law keeping Jews' and not to the 'Body of Christ'.

28- And now, little children, abide in him; that, when he shall appear, we may have confidence, and not be ashamed before him at his coming.

29- If ye know that he is righteous, ye know that **every one that doeth righteousness is born of him**.

-I John 2 v 28, 29

7- Little children, let no man deceive you: **he that doeth righteousness is righteous**, even as he is righteous.

…..

10- In this the children of God are manifest, and the children of the devil: **whosoever doeth not righteousness is not of God**, neither he that loveth not his brother.

…..

22- And whatsoever we ask, we receive of him, **because we keep his commandments**, and do those things that are pleasing in his sight.

23- And this is **his commandment**, That we should **believe on the name of his Son Je'sus Christ, and love one another,** as he gave us commandment.

24- And **he that keepeth his commandments dwelleth in him, and he in him**. And hereby we know that he abideth in us, by the Spirit which he hath given us.

-I John 3 v 7, 10, 22-24

John speaks of 'doing righteousness'. "He that doeth righteousness is righteous"*. Paul in contrast writes that righteousness is imputed+ (put to our account) by faith in the 'finished work of the cross'. 'The Doctrine of the Circumcision/Law' (the Gospel of the Kingdom) is not the Doctrine for us in 'the Age of Grace'. *-I John 2 v 29; -I John 3 v 7 ; -I John 3 v 10; +-Romans 4 v 22-25

The 'spirit' of antichrist:
1- Beloved, believe not every spirit *(person)*, but try the spirit whether they are of God: because many false prophets are gone out into the world.
2- Hereby know ye the Spirit of God: Every spirit *(person)* that confesseth that Je'sus Christ is come in the flesh is of God:
3- And every spirit *(person)* that confesseth not that Je'sus Christ is come in the flesh is not of God: and this is that *spirit* of anti-christ, whereof ye have heard that it should come; and even now already is in the world.
-I John 4 v 1-3

The 'Spirit of God' vs. the 'spirit of man':
4- Ye are of God, little children, and have overcome them: because greater is he that is in you, than he that is in the world.
5- They are of the world: therefore speak they of the world, and the world heareth them.
6- We are of God: he that knoweth God heareth us; he that is not of God heareth not us. Hereby know we the spirit of truth, and the spirit of error.
-I John 4 v 4-6

John writes of the Anti-Christ that dwells in the unbeliever:
22- Who is a liar but he that denieth that Jesus is the Christ? He is antichrist, that denieth the Father and the Son.
23- Whosoever denieth the Son, the same hath not the Father: *(but) he that acknowledgeth the Son hath the Father also.*
-I John 2 v 22, 23

God is love. John and Paul both agree. Many truths of God's Word are universal but do understand who is giving and receiving 'the Word'. Who is writing and who is being addressed. "Rightly divide the word of truth*". *-II Timothy 2 v 15

9- In this was manifested the love of God toward us, because that God sent his only begotten Son into the world, that we might live through him. 10- Herein is love, not that we loved God, but that he loved us, and sent his Son *to be* the propitiation *(appropriator/substitute)* for our sins.
-I John 4 v 9, 10

John encourages 'the Jews of the Circumcision' to keep the law thus proving their faith in God. This is not the 'Gospel of Grace'. We are not under Law but under Grace.

1- Whosoever believeth that Je'sus Christ is born of God: and every one that loveth him that begat loveth him also that is begotten of him.
2- By this we know that we love the children of God, **when we love God, and keep his commandments**.
3- For this is **the love of God, that we keep his commandments**: and his commandments are not grievous.
-I John 5 v 1-3

How many of the 'supposed Christians' of today that try to follow the 'Apostles Doctrine' and Acts 2 v 38 are keeping the 'Commandments and the Law'? All the Law must be followed and kept. Breaking 'one Law' makes the whole Law as having been transgressed.

John is definitely still a 'Law keeping Jew/Hebrew of the Circumcision' and never did embraced the 'Gospel of the Uncircumcision'. Nor was he expected to do so. Where does this put most of Christendom today? A mixed Gospel? Straddling the straight and narrow basing salvation on someones 'supposed head knowledge'?

Paul writes Holy Spirit (Holy Ghost) inspired:
8- Beware lest any man spoil you through philosophy and vain deceit, after the tradition of men, after the rudiments of the world, and not after Christ.
9- For in him dwelleth all the fulness of the Godhead bodily.
-Colossians 2 v 8, 9

The witness of God is greater than the witness of men. 'The Word of God', our Bible is our witness. Everything written in it came from Holy men of God as they were moved by the Spirit.

9- If we receive the witness of men, the witness of God is greater: for this is the witness of God which he hath testified of his Son.

10- He that believeth on the Son of God hath the witness in himself: he that believeth not God hath made him a liar; because he believeth not the record that God gave of his Son.

11- And this is the record, that God hath given to us eternal life, and this life is in his Son.

12- He that hath the Son hath life; and he that hath not the Son of God hath not life.

13- These things have I written unto you that believe on the Son of God; that ye may know that ye have eternal life, and that ye may **believe on the name of the Son of God**.

-I John 5 v 9-13

6- And this is love, that we walk after his commandment, That, as ye have heard from the beginning, ye should walk in it.

7- For many deceivers are entered into the world, who confess not that Je'sus Christ is come in the flesh. This is a deceiver and an antichrist.

-II John 1 v 6, 7

To keep the whole Law is not possible for us to do. Besides, keeping the Law 'shall no man be justified'*. Those that try and follow the 'Apostles Doctrine' have missed the 'Truth of the Gospel of Grace'. Thank God for the Apostle of the Gentiles. We are not under the 'Law of Moses'. *-Galatians 2 v 16; -Galatians 3 v 11

9- Whosoever transgresseth, and abideth not in the doctrine of Christ, hath not God. He that abideth in the doctrine of Christ, <u>he hath both the Father and the Son</u>.

10- If there come any unto you, and bring not this doctrine, receive him not into *your* house, neither bid him God speed.

-II John 1 v 9, 10

Obviously John is a 'Law keeping Jew of the Circumcision'. There is nothing of Paul's Gospel of Grace here. Don't be fooled like so many have that we can do all the words written in our Bible. The Bible was written for our learning and understanding. It is the Apostle Paul that we follow, not John and the Apostles Doctrine.

The Book of Jude: Be Not Deceived!

4- For there are certain men crept in unawares, who were before ordained to this condemnation, ungodly men, turning the grace of our God into lasciviousness, and denying the only Lord God, and our Lord Je'sus Christ.
5- I will therefore put you in remembrance, though ye once knew this, how that the Lord, having saved the people out of the land of E'gypt, afterward destroyed them that believed not.
6- And the angels which kept not their first estate, but left their own habitation, he hath reserved in everlasting chains under darkness unto the judgment of the Great day.
7- Even as Sod'om and Go-mor'rha, and the cities about them in like manner, giving themselves over to fornication, and going after strange flesh, are set forth for an example, suffering the vengeance of eternal fire.
8- Likewise also these *filthy* dreamers defile the flesh, despise dominion, and speak evil of dignities.
-Jude v 4-8

The wages and reward for mankind's unbelief has been forewarned. Who has believed the report? Who has believed God? Even the most devout Christians that have not accepted 'The Gospel'* that Paul teaches have not believed the 'Word of God'. These insist on following the 'Apostles Doctrine'. The Gospel of Truth has been hid from them. *-I Corinthians 15 v 1-4; -Romans 10 v 9; -Ephesians 1 v 13

The ungodly of this world:
10- But these *(the worldly)* speak evil of those things which they know not: but what they know naturally, as brute beasts, in those things they corrupt themselves.
11- Woe unto them! For they have gone in the way of Cain, and ran greedily after the error of Ba'laam for reward, and perished in the gainsaying of Co're.
12- These are spots in your feasts of charity, when they feast with you, feeding themselves without fear: clouds they are without water, carried about of winds; trees whose fruit withereth, without fruit, twice dead, plucked up by the roots.
13- Raging waves of the sea *(mankind),* foaming out their own shame; wandering stars, to whom is reserved the blackness of darkness forever.

14- And E'noch also, the seventh from Ad'am, prophesied of these, saying, Behold, the Lord cometh with ten thousands of his saints,

15- To execute judgment upon all, and to convince all that are ungodly among them of all their ungodly deeds which they have ungodly committed, and of all their hard speeches which ungodly sinners have spoken against them.

16- These are murmurers, complainers, walking after their own lusts; and their mouth speaketh great swelling words, having men's person's in admiration because of advantage.

17- But, beloved, remember ye the words which were spoken before of the apostles of our Lord Jesus Christ;

18- How that they told you there would be mockers in the last time, who should walk after their own ungodly lusts.

19- These be they who separate themselves, sensual, having not the Spirit.

-Jude v 10-19

The Book of Revelation

There are some who say that 'the Tribulation' already happened in 70 A.D. Some say 'the blessings' that were promised to Israel have been denied because the Jews of Israel rejected Jesus Christ. They say the promises made by God to Israel have now gone to the church. What church? They say the 12 Tribes of Israel have been lost and have assimilated with the rest of the world.

Did John write the book of Revelation before 70 A.D. or after? Some say yes and some say no. If the Tribulation happened before John wrote the Book of Revelation and was confirmed by the destruction of Israel in 70 A.D., then the Holy Spirit visions given to John must have been in error. Obviously the things written by John didn't happen.

If 'the Tribulation' was not in 70 A.D., then the prophecies have yet to happen. Which is it? What does our God given common sense tell us? Read the Book of Revelation. If a person can say that these things did happen in 70 A.D., then what happened to the 'Return of Christ' and his setting up of the 'Earthly Kingdom of Heaven' for a period of 1,000 years? Can a child play 'Duck, Duck, Goose' with a dozen King Cobras and the parents be at total peace and ease today?

Listen to what Jesus himself said. As bad as 70 A.D. was, the persecution of Israel by the Roman Empire did not have the 'Wrath of God' events:

15- When ye therefore shall see the abomination of desolation, spoken by Daniel the prophet, stand in the holy place, (whoso readeth, let him under stand:)

…..

21- **For then shall be great tribulation, such as was not since the beginning of the world to this time, no, nor ever shall be.**

22- And except those days be shortened, there should no flesh be saved: but for the elect's sake those days shall be shortened.

…..

29- Immediately after the tribulation of those days shall the sun be darkened, and the moon shall not give her light, and the stars shall fall from heaven, and the powers of the heavens shall be shaken:

30- And then shall appear the sign of the Son of man in heaven: and then shall all the tribes of the earth mourn, and **they shall see the Son of man coming in the clouds of heaven with power and great glory.**

31- And he shall send his angels with a great sound of a trumpet, and **they shall gather together his elect** *(the 144,000?*)* **from the four winds, from one end of heaven to the other.**

-Matthew 24 v 15, 21, 22, 29-31; *-Revelation 7

Jesus speaks in Luke 21 of both the destruction of Jerusalem that will come upon them shortly (70 A.D.) and of the 'End Time Tribulation'. False teachers and denominations prefer to use Luke's account because the 'Signs and Wrath of God' foretold follow in short succession. But did they all happen?

These types that believe the Tribulation happened in 70 A.D. have used this scripture to justify their belief:

32- Verily I (Jesus) say unto you, This generation shall not pass away, till all be fulfilled.

-Luke 21 v 32

Today's thinking says a generation is when the children beget children. When speaking of the 'Children of Israel', their generation is from Abraham until the Return of Christ. The whole Bible is written around and through this generation of people. It is an everlasting generation that will never disappear*. *-Jeremiah 31 v 35-37; -Jeremiah 30 v 11

A 'parenthetical period' ( ) has happened in the 'prophetic time line of Israel'. Psalm 2 gives a picture of this 'time line'. In all of scripture, no mention of the 'Body of Christ' and the 2,000 year 'Church Age of Grace' that is today was ever foretold and prophesied.

Jesus Christ did not reveal or speak of an interruption in the prophecies for Israel. Jesus came for the Nation of Israel and his coming for them was 'on time'*. It is after his resurrection that he gives 'the Doctrine of Grace' from heaven. This was hid and kept secret from Israel and was only revealed to one man, Paul the Apostle of the Gentiles. *-Galatians 4 v 4, 5

'The Tribulation' would have happened had the whole nation of Israel accepted Jesus Christ. But they didn't. The delay now of the final events of the tribulation have been put on hold for the filling up of the 'Body of Christ'. When God/Jesus speaks of things that will happen, though they haven't yet, they will. Believe in God or believe God?

25- And there shall be signs in the sun, and in the moon, and in the stars; and upon the earth distress of nations, with perplexity; the sea and the waves roaring;
26- Men's hearts failing them for fear, and for looking after those things which are coming on the earth: for the powers of heaven shall be shaken.
27- **And then shall they see the Son of man coming in a cloud with power and great glory.**
28- And when these things begin to come to pass, then look up, and lift up your heads; for your redemption draweth nigh.
-Luke 21 v 25-28

Almost all the Old Testament prophets spoke of the 'Wrath of God' that would happen to the world. When fulfilled at the end of the Tribulation there will be a new covenant with Israel:
31- Behold, the days come, **saith the LORD, that I will make a new covenant with the house of Israel, and with the house of Judah**:
32- Not according to the covenant that I made with their fathers in the day *that* I took them by the hand to bring them out of the land of E'gypt; which my covenant they brake, although I was an husband unto them, saith the LORD:

33- But this *shall* be **the covenant that I will make with the house of Israel; After those days**, saith the LORD, I will put my law in their inward parts, and write it in their hearts; and will be their God, and they shall be my people.

34- And they shall teach no more every man his neighbour, and every man his brother, saying, Know the LORD: for they shall all know me, from the least of them unto the greatest of them, saith the LORD: for I will forgive their iniquity, and I will remember their sin no more.

-Jeremiah 31 v 31-34

There are some religions and denominations that claim that this new covenant was fulfilled at Pentecost, when the Holy Spirit came upon them when Peter was preaching. Read Jeremiah 31 v 31-34 again. Can you justify this thought? The 'Jew wannabe's' so desperately want this to be so. It would make their belief of becoming Jews when they believe in Jesus Christ more real. Their mixed gospel would seem to fit. There are no Gentiles in the House of Israel and Judah.

The Book of Revelation written by John is all Jewish and written to them. John had not adjusted his words to now include the Gospel that Paul preached. There was not a transformation in John's attitude after writing his Epistles of John, I, II, III John.

John writes Holy Spirit inspired from the Isle of Patmos:

1- The Revelation of Je'sus Christ, which God gave unto him, to show unto his servants things **which must shortly come to pass**; and he sent and signified *it* by his angel unto his servant John:

2- Who bear record of the word of God, and of the testimony of Je'sus Christ, and of all things that he saw.

3- Blessed *is* he that readeth, and they that hear the words of this prophecy*, and keep those things which are written therein: **for the time is at hand**.

*(*Only Israel was given prophecy.)*

4- John to the seven churches which are in A'sia: Grace *be* unto you, and peace, from him which is, and which was, and which is to come; and from the seven Spirits which are before his throne;

5- And from Je'sus Christ, *who is* the faithful witness, *and* the first begotten of the dead, and the prince of the kings of the earth. Unto him that loved us, and washed us from our sins in his own blood,

6- And hath **made us kings and priests** unto God and his Father; to him *be* glory and dominion for ever and ever. Amen.
-Revelation 1 v 1-6

The English translators had interpreted the assemblies, gatherings, and congregations as being 'churches'. There is only 'One True Church' and that is 'the Body of Christ' and those that follow the Apostle of the Gentiles. John never did embrace the Revealed Gospel that was given to Paul by the ascended Lord from Heaven. Nor was he supposed to.

Contrast with the revelation given to Paul by Jesus after the resurrection:
19- Now we know that **what things soever the law saith, it saith to them who are under the law**: that every mouth may be stopped, and all the world may become guilty before God.
20- Therefore by the deeds of the law there shall no flesh be justified in his sight: for **by the law** *is* **the knowledge of sin.**
-Romans 3 v 19, 20

Before the cross:
2- But **his delight** *is* **in the law of the LORD; and in his law doth he meditate day and night**.
3- And he shall be like a tree planted by the rivers of water, that bringeth forth his fruit in his season; his leaf also shall not wither; and whatsoever he doeth shall prosper.
-Psalm 1 v 2, 3

On this side of the cross after the resurrection:
14- Blotting out the handwriting of ordinances that was against us, which was contrary to us, and took it out of the way, **nailing it to his cross**;
-Colossians 2 v 14

BOOK V

Dispensation: The Big Picture

9- Having made known unto us the **mystery** of his will, according to his good pleasure, which he purposed in himself:

10- That in **the dispensation of the fulness of time** he might gather together in one all things in Christ, both which are in heaven, and which are in earth; *even* in him:

-Ephesians 1 v 9, 10

2- If ye have heard of **the dispensation of the grace of God** which is given to me *(Paul)* to you-ward:

3- How that **by revelation** he made known unto me the **mystery**; (as I wrote afore in few words.

4- Whereby, when ye read, **ye may understand my knowledge in the mystery of Christ**)

-Ephesians 3 v 2-4

25- Whereof I *(Paul)* am made a minister, according to **the dispensation of God** which is given to me for you, **to fulfill *(complete or to put an end to)* the word of God.**

26- *Even* the mystery which hath been hid from ages and from generations, but now is made manifest to his saints *(Paul's ministry)*:

27- To whom God would make known what *is* the riches of his glory of **this mystery among the Gen'tiles; which is Christ in you, the hope of glory:**

-Colossians 1 v 25-27

16- For though I *(Paul)* preach the gospel, I have nothing to glory of: for necessity is laid upon me; yea, woe is me, if I preach not the gospel!
17- For if I do this thing willingly, I have a reward: but if against my will, **<u>a dispensation</u>** *of the gospel* **is committed unto me**.
-I Corinthians 9 v 16, 17

Rahab of Jericho, Ruth the Moabitess, Naaman the Captain of the host of the King of Syria, Cyrus the King of Persia, Darius the King of Medes, the citizens of Nineveh after Jonah preached to them, the Canaanite women and the Roman centurion in the New Testament. What do all these people have in common? That totals eight, God's number for 'completion'.

These are the only Gentiles that fell into God's grace in all of the Bible before the Apostle Paul and the 'Resurrection'. Maybe there is another but no real noteworthy person was mentioned. From Genesis to Acts, God's chosen people were Jew/Hebrews and not the Gentiles/Heathens. The Jews were commanded to have nothing to do with the people of the lands. Jesus himself during his 'earthly ministry' told his disciples the same thing*.
*-Matthew 10 v 5, 6

10- And there was a certain disciple at Da-mas'cus, named An-a-ni'as; and to him said the Lord in a vision, An-a-ni'as. And he said, Behold, I *am here* Lord.
11- And the Lord said unto him, Arise, and go into the street which is called Straight, and enquire in the house of Ju'das for one called Saul, of Tar'sus: for, behold, he prayeth,
12- And hath seen in a vision a man named An-a-ni'as coming in, and putting his hand on him, that he might receive his sight.
13- Then An-a-ni'as answered, Lord, I have heard by many of this man, how much evil he hath done to thy saints at Je-ru'sa-lem:
14- And here he hath authority from the chief priests to bind all that call on thy name.
15- But the Lord said unto him, Go thy way: **for he** *(Saul/Paul)* **is a chosen vessel unto me, to bear my name before the Gentiles, and kings, and the children of Is'ra-el.**
16- For I will shew him how great things he must suffer for my names sake.
-Acts 9 v 10-16

From Genesis to Acts 10, for 43 1/2 of the first books written in the Holy Bible, this small list of Gentiles was all that fell into God's good grace. Before the 'Resurrection' that is all. These 'select few' were chosen in the company of a Jew/Hebrew(s) and were not chosen on their own without knowledge of a Jew being present or one that had been present in their lives.

For 4,000 years only these few 'non-Jews' were chosen by God. **The Old Testament was 'Jew/Hebrew Only'.** The Gentiles had no hope and were without God*. *-Ephesians 2 v 11-13

11- Wherefore remember, that ye *being* in time past Gen'tiles in the flesh, who are called Uncircumcision by that which is called the Circumcision in the flesh made by hands;
12- That at that time ye were without Christ *(Messiah)*, being aliens from the commonwealth of Is'ra-el, and strangers from the covenants of promise, having no hope, and without God in the world:
13- **But now** in Christ Jesus ye who sometimes were far off are made nigh by the blood of Christ.
-Ephesians 2 v 11-13

How did the Gentiles become part of the heavenly gifts of God? By the blood of Jesus Christ. Not the 'divine blood' that was coursing through his body during his earthly ministry, but his shed blood, his splattered blood that poured out of his crucified body. His actual blood that was seen escaping his dead corpse of flesh.

It is this blood that Paul means when he mentions 'the blood of Christ'. Death, out of death comes new life. The preaching of the cross is to them that perish foolishness*. *-I Corinthians 1 v 18

Jesus said before he shed his blood:
24- Verily, verily, I say unto you, Except a corn of wheat fall into the ground and die, it abideth alone: but if it die it bringeth forth much fruit.
-John 12 v 24

The repeated sins by the Jews under 'the Law' were 'covered' but not completely atoned for until after the 'final sacrifice was made'. That is Jesus' shed blood of the cross. No more repeating of blood animal sacrifices.

The 'Dispensation of the Grace of God' was not given for Israel to practice. The Gentiles now could receive salvation by the shed blood of

Christ at his death. The last of the Jew's under the 'Gospel of the Kingdom' still were sacrificing for their sins. A Jew would need to forgo all the legal practices of 'the law' and become a Gentile saved by Grace, Paul's Gospel.

Only to the Apostle Paul was this revealed. The disciples (original) and those of Acts 2 and the 'Apostles Doctrine followers' were not given the 'Dispensation of the Grace of God'*. These were still under the Law. The Law was never put away as so many have falsely taught. There is no scripture that says that it was outside of Paul. *-Ephesians 3 v 2-4

'The supposed Christian' likes to use the final words of Jesus as he died on the cross:
30- When Je'sus therefore had received the vinegar, he said, **It is finished**: and he bowed his head, and gave up the ghost.
-John 19 v 30

"See", they say. "The law is finished". I say, read it again. I see no place where Jesus said, "the Law is finished". The 'mixed gospel supposed Christian' wants this to be true so they can begin their argument that the Apostles of Acts 2 were not under 'the Law' but under Grace.

But what bigger thing did these Christians miss? What would have been bigger than the Law to have been proclaimed finished? Haven't they read their Bibles?

From the 'seed of the women' in Genesis 3 to the crucified Christ was the Testament of Jesus. All the prophecies of the coming king and messiah 'was finished'. Israel killed 'the Prince of Life', their King and Savior. "He came to his own and his own received him not"*. His earthly ministry to the nation of Israel was finished, not the Law. *-John 1 v 9, 10

The Law became not possible to fulfill any longer after Titus, a Roman General, destroyed Jerusalem and the Temple in 70 A.D. The 'Law keeping Jew' is not able to keep the 'full Law' after 70 A.D. To break one law is to break all the Laws. So now what is that good Law keeping Jew to do? Their only hope is to forsake the 'Jewish thought' and become members of the 'Body of Christ'. This is the salvation for all of mankind now, Paul's Gospel.

15- And that he died for all, that they which live should not henceforth live unto themselves, but unto him which died for them, and rose again *(Paul's Gospel)*.

16- **Wherefore henceforth** know we no man after the flesh: yea, though we have known Christ after the flesh, yet now henceforth know we him no more. 17- Therefore if any man *be* **in Christ** *(the Body of Christ, the Church)*, *he* is a new creature *(creation)*: old things are passed away; behold, all things become new.

-II Corinthians 5 v 15-17

God always had a plan for the Gentiles. Through the Kingdom of Priests with Jesus Christ sitting on David's throne in Zion (Jerusalem), the Jews were the ones that were to bring the Gentiles into the knowledge of the 'Living God'. It was by the Kingdom of Priests and their Holy Nation that were to be 'the light' to the Gentiles.

It didn't happen. Israel along with Rome killed the 'King of the Jews'. But there was still hope. Jesus Christ was not dead, but alive! These Jews knew that the wrath of God was yet to happen and then the return of Christ with the 'Earthly Kingdom of Heaven'.

This is their hope in the resurrection of Christ. He would return and save Israel physically, and make their enemies their footstool, Psalm 110. Israel will be the 'head' of all nations and not the 'tail'*. It would be a physical redemption+. *-Deuteronomy 28 v 13; +-Luke 21 v 27, 28; -Daniel 12 v 1; -Zechariah 14 v 4, 8, 9

The prophetic time-line of Israel was moving right along. Psalm 2 gives a quick picture of this. But what was always missed in all the prophecies concerning Israel? This present 2,000 year Grace Age, though there were some hints.

Many of the things Paul wrote by revelation from Jesus Christ in heaven are discounted. Jesus never said them 'in the flesh'. "If Jesus never said it, I don't believe it". Paul's Epistles are treated as a 'selective supplement' to 'the mixed gospel' teachings.

So much does Paul write in his Epistles that nowhere else in the Bible is it found. Only to the Apostle Paul was he given the 'Dispensation of the Grace of God'*. Not Peter, not James, not John, and not those following the 'Apostles Doctrine'. *-Ephesians 3 v 1-12

'Dispensation' is a Biblical word and easily understood. Only the Apostle Paul uses the word 'Dispensation'. It is purely a 'Pauline word' as is 'the Body of Christ'. But in our Bible we can see the different instructions that were given to the 'chosen' of God.

Like a prescription given by a doctor for a specific illness, a person doesn't go 'willy nilly' through the medicine cabinet and take the first bottle he/she see's for an upset stomach. Taking a prescription (Dispensation) not intended to be used could/would only make the ailment worse.

This is most of Christendom. They mix and match Dispensations (prescriptions) that is not after the simple truth of the 'Gospel of Salvation' given to the Apostle Paul. Or they add 'their own prescription' following some kind of 'invented works religion' for salvation. Law and Grace does not mix. Any type of 'a rule or a regulation' promoted by 'a religion or denomination' is 'a law'. Especially when it is preached as a necessity to do in order to obtain 'eternal salvation'.

'The Dispensing' of the knowledge of God was not all given in the Book of Genesis. Our Bibles are a 'progressive revelation' of truth's. The 'Law of Moses' was not known to Adam, Eve, Cain, Abel, Abraham and Noah. These were not under the 'dispensation' of 'the Law' but 'the dispensation of faith' as we are today in this 'Age of Grace'.

There were different 'Dispensations' (prescriptions) given by God to mankind to observe and follow throughout the Old Testament. All scripture is written for our learning and for our knowledge to show us the truth in making us able 'ambassadors for Christ'*. It is not possible for a person to follow the whole Biblical Scripture and do all the 'Dispensations'. *-II Corinthians 5 v 20

9- Having made known unto us the **mystery** of his will, according to his good pleasure, which he purposed in himself:
10- That in **the <u>dispensation</u> of the fulness of time** he might gather together in one all things in Christ, both which are in heaven, and which are in earth; *even* in him:
-Ephesians 1 v 9, 10

"The dispensation of the fulness of time", that being, over time different prescriptions (dispensations) were given by God. Through these dispensations (prescriptions) "he might gather all things in Christ", not only the Jews (Earthly - Gospel of the Kingdom Saints) but all people (Heavenly - Body of Christ Saints), you and me. The final Dispensation (prescription) given to all mankind is 'The Doctrine of the Grace of God'.

I Corinthians 15 v 1-4 says it straight forward. This is where we 'stand' by which we (the believer) are 'saved'.

2- If ye have heard of **the <u>dispensation</u> of the grace of God** which is given to me *(Paul)* to you-ward:
3- How that **by revelation** he made known unto me the **mystery**; (as I wrote afore in few words.
4- Whereby, when ye read, **ye may understand my knowledge in the mystery of Christ**)
-Ephesians 3 v 2-4

"The dispensation of the grace of God". Paul alone received the revelations of the mysteries, the revealed hidden secrets that were hid by God from the beginning. Paul was shown by God the things that have been secret from eternity past. Only to the Apostle of the Gentiles was this manifested to, not Peter, not John, not James, not Luke nor did Jesus Christ himself in the flesh speak of this dispensation.

25- Whereof I *(Paul)* am made a minister, according to **the <u>dispensation</u> of God** which is given to me for you, **to fulfill the word of God**.
26- *Even* the mystery which hath been hid from ages and from generations, but now is made manifest to his saints:
27- To whom God would make known what is the riches of his glory of **this mystery among the Gen'tiles; which is Christ in you, the hope of glory:**
-Colossians 1 v 25-27

"The dispensation of God to fulfill the word of God". The Apostle Paul completed the words of our Bible. 'To fulfill' is 'to put an end to' or 'complete'. Nobody is adding any more scripture to the truth of God. **When Paul was given the new Gospel of Grace, it started with Paul and ended with Paul.**

16- For though I (Paul) preach the gospel, I have nothing to glory of: for necessity is laid upon me; yea, woe is me, if I preach not the gospel!
17- For if I do this thing willingly, I have a reward: but if against my will, **<u>a dispensation</u>** *of the gospel* **is committed unto me**.
-I Corinthians 9 v 16, 17

Paul is the epitome of God's Grace. If Paul can be saved, we all can be no matter what kind of lifestyle we previously led. Grace is the 'unmerited favor' of God.

Given the Grace of God and not being struck down dead on the 'Road to Damascus', "necessity was laid upon Paul to preach the Gospel". "Woe is me, if I preach not the gospel"! Paul says he has a reward for doing so, "a dispensation is committed unto me". Paul was prescribed the Gospel of Salvation to take to all the world.

That word 'Dispensation' was not used in the Old Testament but the way of God (prescription and dispensation) was made known. That which was made known to do and follow was for that time and for their present situation. God is eternal and everlasting but 'his Dispensations' were revealed as he 'prescribed' them. Until the Law was given, it was by faith in what God had said to observe and do. Take the 'prescribed medicine' and all would be well.

29- The secret *things belong* unto the LORD our God: but those *things which* are revealed *belong* unto us and to our children for ever, that *we* may do all the words of this law.
-Deuteronomy 29 v 29

The earthly ministry of Jesus Christ was not known to Adam and Eve. The Law of Moses had not been given for Adam and Eve to follow. There were no 'Jews so called' with that name. Crucifixion by a Roman Cross was unknown. To Adam and Eve, "What's a Roman?"

Only to the Apostle Paul was it revealed 'the way of salvation' for all mankind. This Gospel of Salvation included all of man, not just the Jew/ Hebrews. This salvation was made known to the Apostle Paul, the Apostle of the Gentiles, **after** Jesus' earthly ministry, **after** the Lord Jesus Christ was crucified and had resurrected and ascended back to heaven. Man has been 'pardoned' and given eternal salvation by 'Faith in the Gospel of his (Jesus Christ's) Resurrection'.

The Two Basic School's of Thought

The majority (90%?) of professing Christians believe that the Holy Bible gives the same message and that it applies for all people. Gentiles become Jew's and what was written to them applies to us today as well.

"There is only 'one Gospel' and Peter and Paul were preaching the same thing", they say.

"Peter and Paul were teaching and preaching in the same 'dispensation'" they try to show. With this, most of Christendom remains unsure of their 'eternal belief'. It doesn't quite make complete sense. These follow the 'elusive truth', the 'mixed Gospel'.

The other school of thought not as widely held is that Paul is 'thee Apostle of the Gentiles'. This truth is repeated over and over in Paul's epistles yet 'Christendom' doesn't take it to heart. "Peter too must have been an apostle of the Gentiles". "He must have been", is the majority of 'false thought'.

Only the Apostle Paul received the 'hidden mysteries and secrets' that God had hid from the beginning of time. And only to Paul was it revealed. Not to Peter, James, John, nor did Jesus Christ reveal them in the flesh.

The first and overall scoop of the hidden mysteries revealed is the following truth. **God hid things until it was only revealed to the apostle of the Gentiles.** Only to one man were these shown to. And God knew this from eternity past.

Remember, the Jews never did have a 'national acceptance' of all the people of the world. Just the opposite. It is Paul's Gospel of Grace that "hath broken down the middle wall of partition between us"*, between the Jew and the Gentile. The Gospel of the Grace of God is accepting of all people, regardless of race or any perceived differences. *-Ephesians 2 v 14-18

13- In whom ye also *trusted*, **after that ye heard the word of truth**, the gospel of your salvation in whom also, after that ye believed, **ye were sealed with that holy Spirit of promise,**
14- Which is the earnest of our inheritance until the redemption of the purchased possession, unto the praise of his glory.
-Ephesians 1 v 13, 14

And what is the word of truth? The Gospel of our salvation:
1- Moreover, brethren, **I declare** unto you **the gospel** which **I preached** unto you, which also ye have **received**, and wherein **ye stand;**
2- By which also ye are **saved**, if you keep in memory what I preached unto you, unless ye have **believed** in vain.

3- For **I delivered** unto you **first** of all which **I also received**, how that **Christ died for our sins** according to the scriptures;
4- And that he was **buried**, and that he **rose again the third day** according to the scriptures:
-I Corinthians 15 v 1-4

9- That if thou shalt confess with thy mouth the Lord Jesus, and shalt **believe in thine heart that God hath raised him from the dead, thou shalt be saved.**
-Romans 10 v 9

13- In whom ye also *trusted*, after that ye heard the word of truth, **the gospel of your salvation**: in whom also after that ye believed, **ye were sealed with that holy Spirit of promise.**
-Ephesians 1 v 13

John 3 v 16 doesn't quite say it all. I Corinthians 15 v 1- 4 completes it. 'The Begotten Son' happened when God raised Jesus from the dead. Jesus wasn't 'Begotten' at his birth in Bethlehem'. Here he was 'Gotten to Israel'.

Jesus was speaking 'a mystery' in John 3 v 16. Israel did not know he was going to be crucified, buried and then resurrect. Jesus Christ was not 'Begotten' while he was speaking. He was speaking of the future. He knew he was going to be crucified. He told his disciples this over and over but God hid the understanding. Chapter One covers this more in detail.

14- And as Mo'ses lifted up the serpent in the wilderness, even so must the Son of man be lifted up:
15- That whosoever believeth in him should not perish, but have eternal life.
16- For God so loved the world, that he gave his only begotten Son, that whosoever believeth in him should not perish, but have everlasting life.
-John 3 v 14-16

Psalm 2 gives a quick 'prophetic prophecy' of the future of Israel:
1- Why do the heathen rage, and the people *(Israel)* imagine a vain thing?
2- The kings of the earth set themselves, and the rulers take council together, against the LORD, and against his anointed *saying,*
3- Let us break their bands asunder, and cast away their cords from us.

4- He that sitteth in the heavens shall laugh: the LORD shall have them in derision.

-Psalm 2 v 1-4

The following has yet to happen. Jesus has been 'begotten' but has yet to pour out his wrath and vexation. This will be a time more destructive than in any age before.

5- Then shall he speak to them in his wrath, and vex them in his sore displeasure.

6- **Yet have I set my king upon my holy hill of Zi'on.**

7- **I will declare the decree:** the LORD hath said unto me, Thou art my Son; **this day have I begotten thee.**

-Psalm 2 v 5-7

During the time of Christ's 'earthly ministry', the 'Jews of the Circumcision' were still under the 'Law of Moses'. The non-Jew, the Gentiles/Heathen, never were given the promises made to 'The Children of Israel'. Before the 'Resurrection' the world of Gentiles had no hope and were without God. They, you and me, were lost*. God is sovereign and there were exceptions but very few Gentiles fell into the 'Grace of God' in the Old Testament. God will have mercy on whom he chooses+. *-Ephesians 2 v 11-13; +-Exodus 33 v 19

Keep not 'the law' and a Jew could be taken outside the city and stoned to death. And they did. During the ministry of Christ to Israel, the keeping of 'the Law' and its punishments were still being observed. Jesus Christ never said for the 'Jews of the Circumcision' to stop keeping 'the Law'. False 'principalities in high places'* have preached this lie. Find in scripture where Jesus Christ said to stop keeping 'the law' during his 'earthly ministry'. If your following Jesus then keep 'the law' for he never said to stop. *-Ephesians 6 v 12

A mass deception to Christendom has assumed and falsely been taught that between the last book of the Old Testament, Malachi to Matthew, 'the Law' was done away with. "The book of Matthew begins the Age of Grace", they teach. Somehow, somewhere it has been taught that during these '400 years of Silence' the 'Law of Moses' was made null and void. By whom?

What has happened to the truth of scripture? Don't they read? They believe in God but don't believe God. Like Cain, in his heart, he believed that what he brought to the sacrifice was going to have to be good enough. Cain thought that what was good enough for him was going to have to be good enough for God. An everlasting and eternal mistake.

How many times did Jesus Christ himself say to keep the commandments? Was Jesus Christ the only one under 'the Law' then? Was Jesus Christ under a 'pseudo Law of Moses'? Was Jesus Christ following a 'special type' of 'the Law'. Gentiles have now magically became Jews and are also the 'Ye men of Israel'? The Word of God said no such things.

'The True Church, 'the Body of Christ', is under no such laws but believe the 'Faith-way Gospel of Grace' in the 'Resurrection of Jesus Christ'*. Righteousness is imputed+ (put to our account) to every one that believes without any 'righteous works' of 'imposed denominational legalisms'. **Not one time did the Apostle Paul say to 'Repent and be Baptized' with water for salvation.**

*-I Corinthians 15 v 1-4; -Galatians 3 v 22-29 and all through Paul's Epistles; +-Romans 4 v 11, 22-24; -Romans 5 v 13; -James 2 v 23

9- For we are labourers together with God: ye are God's husbandry, *ye are* God's building.

10- According to **the Grace of God which is given unto me *(Paul)*, as a wise masterbuilder, I have laid the foundation, and another buildeth thereon.** But let every man take heed how he buildeth thereupon.

11- **For other <u>foundation</u> can no man lay than that is laid, <u>which is Je'sus Christ</u>.**

-I Corinthians 3 v 9-11

Always concerning Paul, that when he speaks of Jesus Christ it is the resurrected Jesus Christ. The Apostle Paul did not preach 'the earthly ministry'. This is so vitally important to understand. The Gospel and Jesus Christ are based on the foundation of his blood, his death, his resurrection.

1- **Paul, an apostle of Je'sus Christ by the commandment of God our Saviour, and Lord Je'sus Christ, *which is* our hope;**

2- Unto Tim'o-thy, *my* own son in the faith: Grace, mercy, and peace, from God our Father and Je'sus Christ our Lord.

3- As I besought thee to abide still at Eph'e-sus, when I went into Mac-e-do'ni-a, **that thou mightest charge some that they teach no other doctrine**,
4- Neither give heed to fables and endless genealogies, which minister questions, rather than godly edifying which is in faith: so do.
5- Now **the end of the commandment is charity** *(love)* out of a pure heart, and *of* good conscience, and *of* faith unfeigned:
6- From which **some having swerved have turned aside unto vain jangling**;
7- Desiring to be teachers of the law; understanding neither what they say, nor whereof they affirm.
8- But we know that the law *is* good, if a man use it lawfully;
9- Knowing this, **that the law is not made for a righteous man**, but for the lawless and disobedient, for the ungodly and for sinners, for unholy and profane, for murderers of fathers and murders of mothers, for manslayers,
10- For whoremongers, for them that defile themselves with mankind, for menstealers, for liars, for perjured persons, **and if there be any other thing that is contrary to sound doctrine**;
11- **According to the glorious gospel of the blessed God, which was committed to my trust.**
12- And I thank Christ Je'sus our Lord, who hath enabled me, for that he counted me faithful, putting me into the ministry.
13- Who was before a blasphemer, and a persecutor, and injurious: <u>but I obtained mercy, because I did *it* ignorantly in unbelief</u>.
14- And the grace of our Lord was exceeding abundant with faith and love which is in Christ Jesus.
15- This *is* a faithful saying, and worthy of all acceptation, that **Christ Je'sus came into the world to save sinners; of whom I am chief** *(first)*.
16- Howbeit **for this cause I obtained mercy, <u>that in me first *(Paul)*</u> Je'sus Christ might shew forth all longsuffering, for a pattern to them which should hereafter believe on him to life everlasting.**
-I Timothy 1 v 1-16

Dispensation(s) given in The Garden of Eden

'Dispensation' is 'purely a Pauline word'. So is the 'Body of Christ' and also being 'caught up' to meet the Lord in the air. Only the Apostle Paul uses these words being inspired of the Holy Ghost. You will not find them outside of Paul's Epistles.

Here are some directions/instructions/prescriptions/dispensations that God gave in the Old Testament. To take his word by 'faith' one has to believe what he says. Not all 'the prescriptions' were to be taken one after the other. If we were to do all the directions and prescriptions we would 'O.D.'. And that's what has happened in Christendom. Preachers and teachers pick and choose 'their own poison' that they understand and can teach to the unlearned. This is a main purpose for writing this book.

28- And God blessed them, and God said unto them, **Be fruitful** and **multiply,** and **replenish** the **earth**, and **subdue it**: and have **dominion** over the fish of the sea, and over the fowl of the air, and over every living thing that moveth **upon the earth**.

29- And God said, Behold, I have given you every **herb bearing seed**, which is upon the face of all the earth, and **every tree** in which is the **fruit** of a tree yielding seed; to you it shall be **for meat** *(food)*.

30- And to every beast of the earth, and to every fowl of the air, and to every thing that creepeth upon the earth, wherein there is life, **I have given every green herb for meat** *(food)***:** and it was so.

-Genesis 1 v 28-30

16- And the LORD God commanded the man, saying, Of **every tree** of the garden thou mayest freely eat:

17- **But** of the **tree** of the **knowledge of good and evil**, thou shalt **not eat** of it: for in the day that thou eatest thereof **thou** shalt surely **die**.

-Genesis 2 v 16, 17

Any word of repentance and baptism given to Adam? In the Commandments and Laws given to Moses, was Adam following them? 'The Cross and Resurrection' that would come thousands of years later was Adam and Moses knowledgeable? Did Adam know of the Romans' and their crucifixion practices of death by nailing a person to a cross?

Some say that Adam, Abraham, Moses and others in the Old Testament knew that Jesus Christ of Nazareth was going to be crucified on a Roman Cross. These try to show that the whole Biblical scripture was always saying and teaching the same thing, a similar 'Dispensation'? They say that there is only one Gospel and Peter and Paul were on the same page.

Paul (Holy Spirit inspired):

7- But **we speak the wisdom of God in a mystery** *(revealed secrets)*, *even* the hidden *wisdom*, which **God ordained before the world unto our glory**:

8- Which **none of the princes of this world knew**: for **had they known** *it*, **they would not have crucified the Lord of glory.**

-I Corinthians 2 v 7, 8

God revealed things on 'his own time-line'. The Bible (the Word of God) is a 'progressive revelation'. Until God speaks it, then the Word is sure. The 'earthly ministry' of Jesus Christ and a 'Roman cross' was not revealed in detail to the Old Testament prophets. No one knew the 'knowledge and details of 'what is' and 'who is to be' the 'suffering savior'*. *-I Peter 1 v 10, 11

17- So then **faith** *cometh* by **hearing**, and hearing by **the word of God**.

-Romans 10 v 17

Moses speaks prophecy by Holy Spirit inspiration. Moses does not mention the Prophet by name (which is Jesus the Christ), nor does he give any details of a Roman cross crucifixion and 'the Resurrection'. A mystery/secret still being withheld from Israel. **The Word of God is a progressive revelation, a progressive revealing.**

15- The LORD thy God will raise up unto thee a Prophet from the **midst of thee**, of thy brethren, like unto me; unto him shall ye hearken;

16- According to all that thou desiredst of the LORD thy God in Ho'reb in the day of **the assembly** *(church?)*, saying, Let me not hear again the voice of the LORD my God, neither let me see this great fire anymore, that I die not.

17- And the LORD said unto me *(Moses)*, They have well *spoken that* which they have spoken.

18- **I will raise them up a Prophet from among their brethren, like unto thee, and will put my words in his mouth; and he shall speak unto them all that I shall command him.**

19- And it shall come to pass, *that* whosoever will not hearken unto my words which he shall speak in my name, I will require it of him.

-Deuteronomy 18 v 15-19

A person can't believe what God says until God speaks it. Today we have our own personal Bible and many have mixed it all together thinking it is all one and the same message, not correctly dividing the word of truth*. Compare again **Acts 3 v 21** and **Romans 16 v 25**. Study these two scriptures. If you think they are saying the same thing then pray. Pray to God to show you the understanding and he will. *-II Timothy 2 v 15

Peter said to the Jews' of Israel:
20- And he shall send Jesus Christ, which before was preached unto you:
21- Whom the heaven must receive *(Jesus Christ)* **until the times of restitution** of all things, **which God hath spoken by the mouth of all his holy prophets <u>since the world began</u>**.
-Acts 3 v 20, 21

Compare with Paul, 'the Apostle of the Gentiles':
25- Now to him that is of power to establish you according to my gospel, and the preaching of Je'sus Christ, **according to the revelation of the mystery, which <u>was kept secret since the world began</u>,**
26- **<u>But now is made manifest,</u>** and by the scriptures of the prophets, according to the commandment of the everlasting God, made known to all nations for the obedience of faith:
-Romans 16 v 25, 26

Have you heard the 'professing Christian' say "I follow and do what the Bible says'? "I try to keep the 10 Commandments as best as I can, thereby I should be OK". Then by their own mouth they would be observing and doing the following:

23- And Moses spake to the children of Israel, that they should bring forth him that had cursed out of the camp, and stone him with stones. And the children of Israel did as the LORD commanded Moses.
-Leviticus 24 v 23

32- And while the children of Is'ra-el were in the wilderness, they found a man that gathered sticks upon the Sabbath day.
33- And they that found him gathering sticks brought him unto Moses and Aaron, and unto all the congregation.

34- And they put him in a ward, because it was not declared what should be done to him.

35- And the LORD said unto Moses, The man shall surely be put to death: all the congregation shall stone him with stones without the camp.

36- And all the congregation brought him without the camp, and stoned him with stones, and he died; as the LORD commanded Moses.

-Numbers 15 v 32-35

12- And the Lord spake unto Moses, saying,

13- Speak thou also unto the children of Israel, saying, Verily my sabbaths ye shall keep: for it *is* a sign between me and you throughout your generations; that *ye* may know that I *am* the Lord that doth sanctify you.

14- Ye shall keep the sabbath therefore; for it *is* holy unto you: everyone that defileth it shall surely be put to death: for whosoever doeth *any* work therein, that soul shall be cut off from among his people.

15- **Six days may work be done; but in the seventh *is* the Sabbath of rest, holy to the LORD: whosoever doeth any work in the sabbath day, he shall surely be put to death.**

-Exodus 31 v 12-15

Here is a scriptural example of a man that believed in Jesus Christ but didn't follow the words of Jesus Christ (as far as was revealed by scripture). This is the same as those that say they follow the words of Christ as he ministered to Israel. But do they really or only picking and choosing what they personally want? Believe in God or believe God?

20- The young man saith unto him, All these things have I kept from my youth up: what lack I yet?

21- **Jesus said unto him, If thou be perfect, go *and* sell that thou hast, and give to the poor, and thou shalt have treasure in heaven: and come *and* follow me.**

22- But when the young man heard that saying, he went away sorrowful: for he had great possessions.

-Matthew 19 v 20-22

Many stand firm on Acts 2 v 38 as 'doctrine for their salvation'. Then Acts 2 v 44 and 45 also speaks for them. How much of Acts 2 has fully been taken to heart? How much of Acts 2 is ignored by the 'professing Christian' of today? Many claim to be here as Peter was preaching to Israel. If they are in a similar place then they believe Acts 2 v 23, 36 as well. What an admittance! This is not 'Pauline Doctrine' at all.

44- And all that believed were together, and had all things common:
45- And sold their possessions and goods, and parted them to all *men*, as every man had need.
-Acts 2 v 44, 45

22- Ye men of Is'ra-el, hear these words; Je'sus of Naz'a-reth, a man approved of God among you by miracles and wonders and signs, which God did by him in the midst of you, as ye yourselves also know:
23- Him, being delivered by the determinate counsel and foreknowledge of God, ye have taken, and by wicked hands have crucified and slain:
…..
36- Therefore let all the house of Is'ra-el know assuredly, that God hath made that same Je'sus, whom ye have crucified, both Lord and Christ.
-Acts 2 v 22, 23, 36

Acts 2 v 38 is only two scriptures away. We Gentiles in 'the Body of Christ' were never given the 'Earthly Promises' made to Israel and the Patriarchs. Our salvation was made possible after the crucifixion and the resurrection. To embrace being a Jew here is to say that I killed the Lord of Glory. Absolutely not!

We do, however, crucify Jesus Christ and put him to an open shame when we pollute 'the Gospel of Grace'*. When we add 'righteous works' as a necessity for our salvation then we have made the blood of Christ of none effect+. **By adding any 'works of the flesh', or a law of the denomination, we are saying to God that his dieing on the cross was not good enough.** *-Hebrews 6 v 1-6; +-Romans 4 v 13, 14; I Corinthians 1 v 17-25

1- Therefore leaving the principles of the doctrine of Christ*, let us go on unto perfection; not laying again the foundation of repentance from dead works, and of faith toward God. *(*the principles of the doctrine of Christ = the Gospel's of Matthew, Mark, Luke, John)*

2- Of the doctrine of baptisms, and of laying on of hands, and of resurrection of the dead, and of eternal judgment.

3- And this we will do, **if** God permit.

4- For *it is* **impossible** for those who were once enlightened, and have tasted of the heavenly gift, and were made partakers of the Ho'ly Ghost.

5- And have tasted the good word of God, and the powers of the world to come.

6- **If they shall fall away, to renew them again unto repentance; seeing they crucify to themselves the Son of God afresh, and put *him* to an open shame.**

-Hebrews 6 v 1-6

Peter says you killed Jesus, you killed the Prince of life:

13- The God of A'bra-ham, and of I'saac, and of Ja'cob, the God of our fathers, hath glorified his Son Je'sus; whom ye delivered up, and denied him in the presence of Pi'late, when he was determined to let *him* go.

14- But ye denied the Holy One and the Just, and desired a murderer to be granted unto you;

15- And killed the Prince of life, whom God hath raised from the dead; whereof we are witnesses.

-Acts 3 v 13-15

Paul says Christ died for us:

6- For when we were yet without strength, in due time Christ died for the ungodly.

7- For scarcely for a righteous man will one die: yet peradventure for a good man some would even dare to die.

8- But God commendeth his love toward us, in that, while we were yet sinners, Christ died for us.

9- Much more then, being now justified by his blood, we shall be saved from wrath through him.

10- For if, when we were enemies, we were reconciled to God by the death of his Son, much more, being reconciled, we shall be saved by his life.

11- And not only so, but we also joy in God through our Lord Je'sus Christ, by whom we have now received the atonement.

-Romans 5 v 6-11

33- Who shall lay any thing to the charge of God's elect? *It is* God that justifieth.

34- Who is he that condemneth? It is Christ that died, yea rather, that is risen again *(Paul's Gospel)*, who is even at the right hand of God, who also maketh intercession* for us.

*-Romans 8 v 33, 34; -Romans 8 v 26, 27, 34; -Hebrews 7 v 25

14- For the love of Christ constraineth *(molds)* us; because we thus judge, that if one died for all, then we are all dead:

15- And *that* he died for all, that they which live should not henceforth live unto themselves, but unto him which died for them, and rose again.

16- <u>Wherefore henceforth</u> know we no man after the flesh: yea, though we have known Christ after the flesh, **yet now henceforth know we *him* no more**.

17- Therefore if any man *be* in Christ *(the Body of Christ, the Church)*, he *is* a new creature *(creation)*: old things are passed away; behold, all things are become new.

18- And all things *are* of God, who hath reconciled us to himself by Je'sus Christ, and hath given to us the ministry of reconciliation;

19- To wit, that God was in Christ, reconciling the world unto himself, not imputing their trespasses unto them; and hath committed unto us the word of reconciliation.

20- Now then we are ambassadors for Christ, as though God did beseech *you* by us: we pray *you* in Christ's stead, be ye reconciled to God.

21- For he hath made him *to be* sin for us, who knew no sin; that we might be made the righteousness of God in him.

-II Corinthians 5 v 14-21

9- For God hath not appointed us to wrath, but to obtain salvation by our Lord Je'sus Christ,

10- **Who died for us**, that, whether we wake or sleep, we should live together with him.

-I Thessalonians 5 v 9, 10

The 'supposed Christian' of today has no fear of the following in this 'Age of Grace':

1- But a certain man named An-a-ni'as, with Sap-phi'ra his wife, sold a possession,

2- And kept back part of the price, his wife also being privy to *it*, and brought a certain part, and laid *it* at the apostles' feet.

3- But Pe'ter said, An-a-ni'as, why hath Sa'tan filled thine heart to lie to the Holy Ghost, and to keep back *part* of the price of the land?

4- Whiles it remained, was it not thine own? And after it was sold, was it not in thine own power? Why hast thou conceived this thing in thine heart? Thou hast not lied unto men, but unto God.

5- And An-a-ni'as hearing these words fell down, and gave up the ghost: and great fear came on all them that heard these things.

6- And the young men arose, wound him up, and carried *him* out, and buried *him*.

7- And it was about the space of three hours after, when his wife, not knowing what was done, came in.

8- And Pe'ter answered unto her, tell me whether ye sold the land for so much? And she said, Yea, for so much.

9- Then Pe'ter said unto her, How is it that ye have agreed together to tempt the Spirit of the Lord? Behold, the feet of them which have buried thy husband are at the door, and shall carry thee out.

10- Then fell she down straightway at his feet, and yielded up the ghost: and the young men came in, and found her dead, and, carrying *her* forth, buried *her* by her husband.

11- And great fear came upon all the church *(assembly)*, and upon as many as heard these things.

-Acts 5 v 1-11

This law keeping mentality of the 'Jews of the Circumcision/Law' was still in their minds all the way through the time of Christ. To take such a profound action under 'the Law' as stoning someone that had broke the 'Law of Moses' was still a punishment that was and could be observed. 'The Law' was still applicable for the Jew/Hebrews. Rome allowed the Jews to carry out punishments concerning the 'Jew's religion'.

Jesus never said to stop keeping the Law nor did he narrow its scope. Keep the commandments. Keep the Sabbath. Keep the full law. To break one law is the same as breaking all the laws*. *-James 2 v 10; -Romans 3 v 19, 20; -Matthew 5 v 17-19

Jesus was crucified on a cross. The cross was a Roman invention. As scripture says he would be lifted up*. It was according to prophecy of the Bible. The Romans didn't know that this was so. They didn't know that they were actually fulfilling Biblical prophecy. How could they? The 'Oracles of God' were not given to the Romans nor to any Gentile+. *-II Samuel 22 v 47-49; -Psalm 27 v 6; -Psalm 30 v 1; -Psalm 83 v 2; -John 3 v 14; -John 12 v 34; +-Romans 3 v 1, 2

11- Verily, verily, I say unto thee, We speak that we do know, and testify that we have seen; and ye receive not our witness.

12- If I have told you earthly things, and ye believe not, how shall ye believe, if I tell you of heavenly things?

13- And no man hath ascended up to heaven, but he that came down from heaven, even the Son of man which is in heaven.

14- And as Mo'ses lifted up the serpent in the wilderness, even so must the Son of man be lifted up:

15- That whosoever believeth in him should not perish, but have everlasting life.

16- For God so loved the world that he gave his only begotten Son, that whosoever believeth in him should not perish, but have everlasting life.

17- For God sent not his son into the world to condemn the world; but that the world through him might be saved.

18- He that believeth on him is not condemned: but he that believeth not is condemned already, because he hath not believed in the name of the only begotten Son of God.

19- And this is the condemnation, that light is come into the world, and men loved darkness rather than light, because their deeds were evil.

20- For every one that doeth evil hateth the light, neither cometh to the light, lest his deeds should be reproved.

21- But he that doeth truth cometh to the light, that his deeds may be made manifest, that they are wrought in God.

-John 3 v 11-21

1- Keep not thou silence, O God: hold not thy peace, and be not still, O God.

2- For, lo, thine enemies make a tumult: and they that hate **thee have lifted up** the head.

3- They have taken crafty counsel against thy people, and consulted against thy hidden ones.

4- They have said, Come, and let us cut them off from *being* a nation; that the name of Is'ra-el may be no more in remembrance.
5- For they have consulted together with one consent: they are confederate against thee:
-Psalm 83 v 1-5

The Jews, if they had it their way, perhaps would've taken Jesus out of the city and stoned him with stones as they had been doing all through their history. They tried several times to catch Jesus but could not get their hands on him. Jesus allowed himself to be caught. He died for us. He didn't run till he was finally nabbed.

The Romans had respect for ancient religions. Though they knew not the 'Living God', they had religions of idols that sprang from the 'Tower of Babel'. To the Romans, an ancient religion was an ancient religion. 'Judaism' was such a religion. But 'the newer belief' that Jesus Christ came in the flesh to be 'King of the Jews' was not accepted. "There is no King but Caesar*". *-John 19 v 15

This small group, 'the elect', came under intense persecution. Those that believed in 'the Name of Jesus Christ' as being the prophesied Messiah of scripture were seen as an enemy of the Jews (the non-believers in who Jesus Christ is) and the Romans. The Pharisee's that believed in the 'Name of Jesus Christ' were few in number. 'The whole house of Israel' was to fully believe in Jesus Christ, then the 'Earthly Kingdom of Heaven would be fulfilled as was prophesied.

But even after the ministry of Jesus Christ there were only a small number of Jews that understood and believed. After all the signs and miracles performed by this man, of which only God (a god?) could do, they still could not believe. Israel as a nation was spiritually blinded* as they still are today. This is according to scripture and not according to me or any man. *-Romans 11 v 25

14- For the love of Christ constraineth *(molds)* us; because we thus judge, that if one died for all then we are all dead:
15- And *that* he died for all, that they which live should not henceforth live unto themselves, but unto him which died for them, and rose again *(Paul's Gospel).*

16- Wherefore henceforth know we no man after the flesh: yea, though we have known Christ after the flesh, yet now henceforth know we *him* no more.

17- Therefore if any man *be* in Christ, *he* is a new creature *(creation)*: old things are passed away; behold, all things become new.

-II Corinthians 5 v 14-17

This 'spiritual blindness' would also apply to those claiming to be Jews because they attempt to follow the 'Apostles Doctrine'. Calling themselves Jews, obviously they don't understand the Doctrine of Grace that was given by Jesus Christ from Heaven. They can't distinguish the difference between Peter and Paul. These believe and say that they both (Peter and Paul) were preaching and under the same 'Dispensation'.

Paul writes by the Holy Spirit:

1- Brethren, my heart's desire and prayer to God for Is'ra-el is, that they might be saved.

2- For I bear them record that they have a zeal of God, but not according to knowledge.

3- For they being ignorant of God's righteousness, and going about to establish their own righteousness, have not submitted themselves unto the righteousness of God.

4- For Christ *is* the end of the law for righteousness to every one that believeth.

5- For Mo'ses describeth the righteousness which is of the law, That the man which doeth those things shall live by them.

6- But the righteousness which is of faith speaketh on this wise, Say not in thine heart, Who shall ascend into heaven? (that is, to bring Christ down *from above*:)

7- Or, Who shall descend into the deep? (that is, to bring up Christ again from the dead.)

8- But what saith it? The word is nigh thee, *even* in thy mouth, and in thy heart: that is, **the word of faith, which we preach;**

9- **That if thou shalt confess with thy mouth the Lord Jesus, and shalt believe in thine heart that God hath raised him from the dead *(Paul's Gospel)*, thou shalt be saved.**

10- For with the heart man believeth unto righteousness; and with the mouth confession is made unto salvation.

11- For the scripture saith, Whosoever believeth on him shall not be ashamed.
12- For there is no difference between the Jew and the Greek: for the same Lord over all is rich unto all that call upon him.
13- For whosoever shall call upon the name of the Lord shall be saved.
-Romans 10 v 1-13

When the understanding by the Holy Ghost reveals this to us (the believer) that Peter and Paul were not under the same 'Dispensation', the whole Bible becomes clearer and understandable. We cannot possibly follow all the words and 'Dispensations' given in the Bible. The Bible was written to us for our understanding and knowledge, but all of scripture was not written for us to follow. The Gentiles never were given the promises made to Israel and the patriarchs.

The new Dispensation added to 'the Law' was the 'Baptism of Repentance'. More so now because they, along with Rome, killed the Lord of Glory. The Kingdom was still possible. The 'Baptism of Repentance' was 'the prescription/dispensation' for Israel to be a 'Kingdom of Priests' and to perform that which was promised to the Nation of Israel. All of the Jews were to 'Repent and be Baptized'. Jesus the Christ would return and sit on his Holy Hill in Zion (Jerusalem).

Some 6-8 years after Pentecost was the stoning of Stephen. While Stephen was dying he saw Jesus standing*, not sitting+, ready to bring in the Kingdom? But Israel continued to reject Jesus as they still do today. God put Israel on hold, gave them 'spiritual blindness'= and interrupted the 'prophetic time line' for the Jews. God now is going to the Gentiles without the Jew. *-Acts 7 v 55; +-Psalm 110, =-Romans 11 v 25

Saul of Tarsus (Paul) is first introduced at the 'stoning of Stephen'. Sometime after, the Lord Jesus Christ confronts Saul on his way to persecute more 'Jews of the Circumcision/Law' that were following the earthly ministry of Christ. Paul is struck down on the 'Road to Damascus'. He returns back to the world of the living with a New Gospel three years after. Not the same Gospel as 'the Twelve' and Jesus in the flesh knew, but a new Gospel of salvation for the whole world of Gentiles/Heathen.

It should be noted that when Paul returns from the desert of Sinai three years later* he had not written anything yet. His first Epistle was I Thessalonians written about 54 to 58 A.D. Hebrews still has an unknown date of origin. From 40 A.D. to 54 A.D. or so, no new testament scriptures had been written. All that the world had to go by was the Old Testament scriptures. *-Galatians 1 v 17, 18

Paul's ministry had it's disciples and apostles too. Don't mix in the disciples that were with Jesus Christ and his earthly ministry. Peter and Paul never traveled together taking the gospel to the world.

Before Paul had written anything, he taught his followers what the Resurrected Christ was teaching him. 'Paul is Chief', the 'Chosen Vessel Apostle of the Resurrected Jesus Christ'. His 'able ministers' were spreading his Gospel of the Grace of God to the world.

Before Paul had written scripture, he fully encourages and indorses the ministry of his disciples:

2- Ye are our epistle written in our hearts, known and read of all men:

3- *Forasmuch as ye are* manifestly declared to be the epistle of Christ ministered by us, written not with ink, but with the Spirit of the living God; not in tables of stone, but in fleshly tables of the heart.

4- And such trust have we through Christ to God-ward.

5- Not that we are sufficient of ourselves to think any thing as of ourselves; **but our sufficiency *is* of God**.

6- **Who also hath made us able ministers of the new testament; not of the letter but of the spirit: for the letter killeth, but the spirit giveth life.**

-II Corinthians 3 v 2-6

The 'elect' may have been more accepting of Paul but these were not following the new Gospel that Paul revealed from the Lord in Heaven. The 'Judaizers from Jerusalem' tried interfering with the 'Body of Christ' claiming that they had to be circumcised and keep the Law of Moses or they could not be saved*. *-Acts 15 v 1

Peter, near the very end of his life finally endorses the Apostle of the Gentiles, but still did not accept Paul's Holy Spirit inspired Doctrine of Grace. He found that what Paul had been preaching was still hard to be understood being a devout Jew under 'the Law'*. But for Peter, his dispensation was in the 'Gospel of the Kingdom'. Peter had his salvation. He believed in the 'Name of Jesus Christ'. *-II Peter 3 v 15, 16

Peter still thought the 'Earthly Kingdom of Heaven' was going to happen, but was now realizing that he was probably going to die first*. Peter gave a good fight and pleaded with Israel to see and recognize who

Jesus Christ really is. But Israel continues even to this day in rejecting that the Messiah had already came for their nation. *-II Peter 1 v 13-15

Even today, the 'Faith-way Gospel of Grace'* is pushed aside in favor of a 'works religion'. "We have to do something to show God our faith" says most of Christendom. No man is justified in God's sight that believe this way. So says the 'Word of God'. Believe it and read the revealed word of truth. Man nor I has said this but God himself. *-Galatians 3 v 21-29

16- Knowing that a man is not justified by the works of the law, but by the faith of Je'sus Christ, even we have believed in Je'sus Christ, that we might be justified by the faith of Christ, and not by the works of the law: for by the works of the law shall no flesh be justified

17- But if, while we seek to be justified by Christ, we ourselves also are found sinners, *is* Christ therefore the minister of sin? God forbid.

18- For if I *(Paul)* build again the things I destroyed, I make myself a transgressor.

19- For I through the law am dead to the law, that I might live unto God.

20- I am crucified with Christ: nevertheless I live; yet not I, but Christ liveth in me: and the life which I now live in the flesh I live by the faith of the Son of God, who loved me, and gave himself for me.

21- I do not frustrate the grace of God: for if righteousness *come* by the law, then Christ is dead in vain.

-Galatians 2 v 16-21

10- For as many as are of the works of the law are under the curse: for it is written, Cursed *is* every one that continueth not in all things which are written in the book of the law to do them.

11- But that no man is justified by the law in the sight of God, *it is* evident: for, The just shall live by faith

12- And the law is not of faith: but, The man that doeth them shall live in them.

13- Christ hath redeemed us from the curse of the law, being made a curse for us: for it is written, Cursed *is* every one that hangeth on a tree.

14- That the blessing of A'bra-ham might come on the Gen'tiles through Jesus Christ; that we might receive the promise of the Spirit through faith.

-Galatians 3 v 10-14

Contrast with James 'the Legalist'. James never stopped keeping the law nor was he instructed to. The Temple was destroyed in 70 A.D.. 'The Law' can no longer be fully followed. Was this God's plan? Paul's epistles were now finished. So what is the option?

For Israel and all the world 'there is only one'. All of mankind are equal, we all have sinned. Under Paul's Gospel of Grace, there is no difference now between the Jew and Gentile. Today's difference is man-made and not of the true word of God. It is now 'Paul's Gospel of Grace', the only option.

14- What *doth it* profit, my brethren, though a man say he hath faith, and have not works? can faith save him?
-James 2 v 14

Absolutely, sure can. James obviously was not following the 'Apostle of the Gentiles'.

15- If a brother or a sister be naked, and destitute of daily food,
16- And one of you say unto them, Depart in peace, be *ye* warmed and filled; notwithstanding ye give them not those things which are needful to the body; what *doth it* profit?
17- Even so faith, if it hath not works, is dead, being alone.
-James 2 v 15-17

Not according to the revelation given to the Apostle Paul. Law and Grace don't mix. Of course we help those in need.

18- Yea, a man may say, Thou hast faith, and I have works: shew me thy faith without thy works, and I will shew thee my faith by my works.
19- Thou believest that there is one God; thou doest well: the devils also believe, and tremble.
20- But wilt thou know, O vain man, that faith without works is dead?
-James 2 v 18-20

Definitely not Paul's teachings. James is not writing to 'the Body of Christ'.

21- Was not A'bra-ham our father justified by works, when he had offered I'saac his son upon the altar?
-James 2 v 21

Abraham was already counted as righteous and faithful 50 years before Isaac was put on the altar.

22- Seest thou how faith wrought with his works, and by works was faith made perfect?
23- And the scripture was fulfilled which saith, A'bra-ham believed God, and it was imputed unto him for righteousness: and he was called the Friend of God.
24- Ye see then how that by works a man is justified, and not by faith only.
-James 2 v 22-24

A complete contradiction to the Gospel of Grace.

25- Likewise also was not Ra'hab the harlot justified by works, when she received the messengers, and had sent *them* out another way?
26- For as the body without the spirit is dead, so faith without works is dead also.
-James 2 v 25-26

James is a long way from the 'Gospel of Grace'. The disciples that followed Jesus' earthly ministry were never given the Gospel that Paul would be preaching, 'death, burial and resurrection'. James is writing to 'the Twelve Tribes' scattered abroad. James is not writing to Paul's 'Body of Christ' believers. There is no account of James being accepting of any Gentile nor any scripture showing that James is now preaching 'Paul's Gospel'.

Satan has done many falsehoods to keep mankind from finding 'the Truth'. Yet, in our Bibles, the truth is there. It is amazing that Satan has influenced the world by keeping them from the truth of salvation by Paul's God given Gospel. The truth has all been in our Bible, yet for centuries, the word of God is unable to be read with understanding. The word of God was written for everyone to understand. Who is confusing the people*?
*-Ephesians 6 v 12

1- Therefore seeing we have this ministry, as we have received mercy, we faint not;
2- But have renounced the hidden things of dishonesty, not walking in craftiness, nor handling the word of God deceitfully; but by manifestation

of the truth commending ourselves to every man's conscience in the sight of God.

3- But if our gospel be hid, it is hid to them that are lost:

4- In whom the god of this world hath blinded the minds of them which believe not, lest the light of the glorious gospel of Christ, who is the image of God, should shine unto them.

-II Corinthians 4 v 1-4

Many that believe in this 'mixed Gospel', I love and live among. Maybe God will make an exception because they really have had life changing testimonies. They have not bowed 'the knee to Baal'. They daily pray and live 'spiritual lives'. These type of people are the best friends anyone could have. They don't lie, steal, cheat, murder or do anything contrary to good human nature. Yet, somehow they refuse to see that 'Paul is thee Apostle of the Gentiles', the Chief! They prefer to preach Peter and the earthly ministry of Jesus Christ.

The Bible, as written for us to understand, shows that through the revealing (revelations) of the mysteries/secrets that every person will be judged by Jesus Christ according to Paul's Gospel. Not Peter's, John's or the Gospel of the Kingdom that Jesus came to fulfill. By 'Paul's Gospel' alone can a man be saved.

16- In the day when God shall judge the secrets of men by Je'sus Christ **according to my gospel**.

-Romans 2 v 16

25- Now to him that is of power to stablish you **according to my gospel**, and the preaching of Je'sus Christ, according to the revelation of the mystery, which was kept secret since the world began.

-Romans 16 v 25

Do these 'professing Christians' of today that claim to be following what the Bible says do these things? Have they stopped or are they picking and choosing specific scriptures to follow while ignoring others? A type of 'pseudo law' that all believers now do and follow? Read the Book of Leviticus. Is it possible to follow all that is written today?

Then they say, we are 'not under law but under grace'. Who said that? Was it Jesus or Peter? You mean the Law, the full law isn't being kept? Why not? Jesus never said to stop keeping the law.

The Dispensation/Prescription(s) for Cain and Abel

3- And **in the process of time** it came to pass, that Cain brought of the fruit of the ground an offering unto the LORD.
-Genesis 4 v 3

"And **in the process of time**"... There must have been a time of instruction by God on how to prepare a sacrifice for Cain and Abel's sins. They were making a sacrifice to God. Why would they simply go and sacrifice their best offerings unless God had instructed them on how to do it. "And **in the process of time**".

Abel believed the LORD:
4- And Abel, he also brought of the firstlings of his flock and of the fat thereof. And the LORD had respect unto Abel and to his offering:
-Genesis 4 v 4

Cain did not believe the LORD:
5- But unto Cain and to his offering he had not respect. And Cain was very wroth, and his countenance fell.
6- And the LORD said unto Cain, Why art thou wroth? And why is thy countenance fallen?
7- If thou doest well, shalt thou not be accepted? And if thou doest not well, sin lieth at the door. And unto thee *shall* be his desire, and thou shalt rule over him.
-Genesis 4 v 5-7

Through "the process of time" Cain knew what was expected of him concerning a 'blood sacrifice'. The LORD tells Cain that there is a 'proper sacrifice' at his door (tent). This animal was not going to put up a fight. "And unto thee shall be his desire, and thou shalt rule over him".

Cain could have made the proper sacrifice and was even given a second chance. But Cain was rebellious and did not believe God. In Cain's own heart, he believed that what he brought to be his sacrifice would be good enough. If it wasn't good enough for God, then, oh well. Maybe he did bring his best sacrifice that was good enough for him, but it was not the 'dispensation' that God expected.

God would accept Cain and Able by their faith because they brought a 'blood sacrifice'. They were to follow and believe what God had said to them in the time (process) of instruction. There was no formal religion nor the 'Law of Moses' that Cain and Abel were following. They had no knowledge of the 'crucifixion'. They had no knowledge of Jesus the Christ.

The knowledge they did have was to believe God and do what was instructed of them. It was by faith in the words of God. If they were to follow the dispensation given, God would accept their 'blood sacrifice' and bless them.

4- By faith A'bel offered unto God a more excellent sacrifice than Cain, by which he obtained witness that he was righteous, God testifying of his gifts: and by it he being dead yet speaketh.
-Hebrews 11 v 4

11- For this is the message that ye heard from the beginning, that we should love one another.
12- Not as Cain, *who* was of that wicked one, and slew his brother. And wherefore slew he him? Because his own works were evil, and his brother's righteous.
13- Marvel not, my brethren, if the world hate you.
-I John 3 v 11-13

Without God a man is vain in his thoughts and is nothing more than a brute beast, so says the Holy Word of God:
10- But these *(men)* speak evil of those things which they know not: but what they know naturally, as brute beasts, in those things they corrupt themselves.
11- Woe unto them! for they have gone in the way of Cain, and ran greedily after the error of Ba'laam for reward, and perished in the gainsaying of Co're.
12- These are spots in your feasts of charity, when they feast with you, feeding themselves without fear: clouds *they are* without water, carried about of winds; trees whose fruit withereth, without fruit, twice dead, plucked up by the roots;

13- Raging waves of the sea *(mankind)*, foaming out their own shame; wandering stars, to whom is reserved the blackness of darkness for ever.
-Jude v 10-13

Unbelief is the Ultimate and Unpardonable Sin

Jesus Christ says:

31- Wherefore I say unto you, All manner of sin and blasphemy shall be forgiven unto men: but the blasphemy *against* the *Ho'ly* Ghost shall not be forgiven unto men.

32- And whosoever speaketh a word against the Son of man *(Jesus Christ)*, it shall be forgiven him: but whosoever speaketh against the Ho'ly Ghost, it shall not be forgiven him, neither in this world, neither in the *world* to come.
-Matthew 12 v 31, 32

An unenlightened person of the Grace of God has no belief. They are lost. They have no faith. The Holy Ghost of God was never imputed to the 'unbeliever'. They can speak blasphemy because they have a reprobate mind and no faith. They don't believe God and what he says. They will be rewarded for their unbelief at the Great White Throne.

Before dying, this 'unbeliever' will still have a chance at salvation. But the moment they die their souls, being separated from the body, will forever be in hell. At the time appointed, at the Great White Throne, they will be cast into the lake of fire for ever, and ever, and ever*. There will be no remedy once a person dies in unbelief. *-Revelation 20 v 12-15

But, the person who has believed and "speaketh against the Ho'ly Ghost, it shall not be forgiven him, neither in this world, neither in the *world* to come"*. There are no unbelievers in the 'Body of Christ'. We still are of the 'old Adam' and are not sinless but recognize sin as it happens and confess. Once a true believer there is no need to repeatedly repent. We have already been forgiven and have obtained that 'blessed pardon by faith'. *-Matthew 12 v 31, 32

6- But without faith *it is* impossible to please *him*: for he that cometh to God must believe that he is, <u>and *that* he is a rewarder of them that diligently seek him</u>.
-Hebrews 11 v 6

7- Wherefore (as the Ho'ly Ghost saith, To day if ye will hear his voice,

8- Harden not your hearts, as in the provocation, in the day of temptation in the wilderness:

9- When your fathers tempted (tested) me, proved me, and saw my works forty years.

10- Wherefore I was grieved with that generation, and said, They do always err in *their* heart; and they have not known my ways.

11- So I sware in my wrath, They shall not enter into my rest.)

12- **Take heed, brethren, lest there be <u>an evil heart of unbelief</u>, in departing from the living God.**

-Hebrews 3 v 7-12

Dispensation/Prescription(s) given to Noah

5- And God saw that the wickedness of man *was* great in the earth, and *that* every imagination of the thoughts of his heart *was* only evil continually.

6- And it repented the LORD that he had made man on the earth, and it grieved him at his heart.

7- And the LORD said, I will destroy man whom I have created from the face of the earth; both man and beast, and the creeping thing, and the fowls of the air; for it repenteth me that I have made them.

8- **But** No'ah found grace in the eyes of the LORD.

…..

11- The earth also was corrupt before God, and the earth was filled with violence *(murder)*.

12- And God looked upon the earth, and, behold, it was corrupt; for all flesh had corrupted his way upon the earth.

13- And God said unto No'ah, The end of all flesh is come before me; for the earth is filled with violence through them; and, behold, I will destroy them with the earth.

14- **Make thee an ark** of gopher wood; rooms shalt though make in the ark, and shall **pitch** it within and without with **pitch**.

-Genesis 6 v 5-8, 11-14

17- And, behold, I, even I, do bring a flood of waters upon the earth, to destroy all flesh, wherein *is* the breath of life, from under heaven; and every thing that *is* in the earth shall die.

18- **But with thee will I establish my covenant;** and thou shalt come into the ark, thou, and thy sons, and thy wife, and thy sons' wives with thee.
…..
22- Thus did No'ah; according to all that God commanded him, so did he.
-Genesis 6 v 17, 18, 22

A new dispensation/prescription when Noah's family emerged from the ark:
1- And God blessed No'ah and his sons, and said unto them, Be fruitful, and multiply, and replenish the earth.
2- And the fear of you and the dread of you shall be upon every beast of the earth, and upon every fowl of the air, upon all that moveth *upon* the earth, and upon all the fishes of the sea; into your hand are they delivered.
3- **Every moving thing that liveth shall be meat for you;** even as the green herb have I given you all things.
4- **But** flesh with the life thereof, *which is* the blood thereof, shall ye not eat.
-Genesis 9 v 1-4

God introduces Capital Punishment:
5- And surely your blood of your lives will I require; at the hand of every beast will I require it, and at the hand of man; at the hand of every man's brother will I require the life of man.
6- Whoso sheddeth man's blood, by man shall his blood be shed: for in the image of God made he man.
7- And you, be ye fruitful, and multiply; bring forth abundantly in the earth, and multiply therein.

…..

18- And the sons of No'ah, that went forth of the ark, were Shem, and Ham, and Ja'pheth: and Ham *is* the father of Ca'naan.
19- **These *are* the three sons of No'ah: and of them was the whole earth overspread.**
-Genesis 9 v 1-7, 18, 19

Noah believed God. This 'dispensation' was of faith. Noah was not following 'the law' or any type of religion. He knew of the 'God of Creation' and spoke with him. He believed God.

Dispensation/Prescription(s) given to Abraham

1- Now the LORD had said unto A'bram, Get thee out of thy country, and from thy kindred, and from thy father's house, unto a land that I will shew thee.
2- And I will make of thee a great nation, and I will bless thee, and make thy name great; and thou shalt be a blessing:
3- And I will bless them that bless thee, and curse him that curseth thee: and in thee shall all the families of the earth be blessed.
-Genesis 12 v 1-3

    A'bram was a Syrian. His family knew not the 'living God'*. They were idolaters and pagans as all the world was at this time. God saw something in A'bram that made him different. God chose A'bram to be the Father of the Jewish Nation. Along the way, through Sarah's and Abraham's impatience for an heir, he also became the Father of all the descendants of Ishmael and Esau. Ishmael was 'of the flesh' and 'not by promise'. *-Joshua 24 v 2

2- And Josh'u-a said unto all the people, Thus saith the LORD God of Is'ra-el, Your fathers dwelt on the other side of the flood* in old time, *even* Te'rah, the father of A'bra-ham, and the father of Na'chor: **and they served other gods.** (*-Euphrates River floods it banks yearly*)
3- And I took your father A'bra-ham from the other side of the flood, and led him throughout all the land of Ca'naan, and multiplied his seed and gave him I'saac.
-Joshua 24 v 2, 3

The Covenant (Dispensation/Prescription) of Circumcision

10- This *is* my covenant, which ye shall keep, between me and you and thy seed after thee; Every man child among you shall be circumcised.
11- And ye shall circumcise the flesh of your foreskin; and it shall be a token of the covenant betwixt me and you.
12- And he that is eight days old shall be circumcised among you, every man child in your generations, he that is born in the house, or bought with money of any stranger, which *is* not of thy seed.

13- He that is born in thy house, and he that is bought with thy money, must needs be circumcised: and my covenant shall be in your flesh for an everlasting covenant.

14- And the uncircumcised man child whose flesh of his foreskin is not circumcised, that soul shall be cut off from his people; he hath broken my covenant.

-Genesis 17 v 10-14

Dispensation/Prescriptions(s) given to Moses

There were several instructions (Dispensations) given by God for Moses to follow. Moses had the strength and the faith to believe the mighty work that God was going to accomplish through him. Moses was going to bring out of Egypt a great nation.

The most notable 'Dispensation' was 'the Law' given by God to the Children of Israel. This prescription (Dispensation) was going to prepare them for the 'Earthly Kingdom of Heaven' of which all of Israel were to be a Kingdom of Priests. It was by Israel's priests that the knowledge of their LORD God JEHOVAH would be made known to the world.

5- Now therefore, if ye will obey my voice indeed, and keep my covenant, then ye shall be a peculiar treasure unto me above all people: for all the earth *is* mine.

6- And ye shall be unto me **a kingdom of priests, and an holy nation**. These *are* the words which thou shalt speak unto the children of Is'ra-el.

-Exodus 19 v 5, 6

Why was the law given?:

19- Wherefore then *serveth* the law? It was added because of transgressions, till the seed should come to whom the promise was made; *and it was* ordained by angels in the hand of a mediator.

20- Now a mediator is not a *mediator* of one, but God is one.

21- *Is* the law then against the promises of God? God forbid: for if there had been a law given which could have given life, verily righteousness should have been by the law.

-Galatians 3 v 19-21

Dispensation/Prescription(s) given to Joshua

6- Be strong and of a good courage: for unto this people shalt thou divide for an inheritance the land, which I sware unto their fathers to give them.
7- Only be thou strong and very courageous, that thou mayest observe to do according to all the law, which Mo'ses my servant commanded thee: turn not from it *to* the right hand or *to* the left, that thou mayest prosper whithersoever thou goest.
8- This book of the law shall not depart out of thy mouth; but thou shalt meditate therein day and night, that thou mayest observe to do according to all that is written therein: for then thou shalt make thy way prosperous, and then thou shalt have good success.
-Joshua 1 v 6-8

1- And it came to pass, when all the kings of the Am'or-ites, which *were* on the side of Jor'dan westward, and all the kings of the Ca'naan-ites, which *were* by the sea, heard that the LORD had dried up the waters of Jor'dan from before the children of Is'ra-el, until we were passed over, that their heart melted, neither was there spirit in them any more, because of the children of Is'ra-el.
2- At that time the LORD said unto Josh'u-a, Make thee sharp knives, and circumcise again the children of Is'ra-el the second time.
3- And Josh'u-a made him sharp knives, and circumcised the children of Is'ra-el at the hill of the foreskins.
4- And this *is* the cause why Josh'u-a did circumcise: All the people that came out of E'gypt, *that were* males, *even* all the men of war, died in the wilderness by the way, after they came out of E'gypt.
5- Now all the people that came out were circumcised: but all the people *that were* born in the wilderness by the way as thy came forth out of E'gypt, *them* they had not circumcised.
6- For the children of Is'ra-el walked forty years in the wilderness, till all the people *that were* men of war, which came out of E'gypt, were consumed, because they obeyed not the voice of the LORD: unto whom the LORD sware that he would not shew them the land, which the LORD sware unto their fathers that he would give us, a land that floweth with milk and honey.
7- And their children, *whom* he raised up in their stead, them Josh'u-a circumcised: for they were uncircumcised, because they had not circumcised them by the way.

8- And it came to pass, when they had done circumcising all the people, that they abode in their places in the camp, till they were whole.

9- And the LORD said unto Josh'u-a, This day have I rolled away the reproach of E'gypt from off you. Wherefore the name of the place is called Gil'gal unto this day.

-Joshua 5 v 1-9

As Israels history unfolded, through all the good times and bad, the Dispensation that they were to follow was 'the full law and to love their God with all their hearts and minds'. Some did and some didn't. Those that did, were blessed of God. Those that didn't, lost their souls.

Dispensation/Prescription - Water Baptism

(Note: remember that Paul was the only one to use the word 'Dispensation and is only found in his Epistles.)

2- As it is written in the prophets, Behold I send my messenger before thy face, which shall prepare thy way before thee.

3- The voice of one crying in the wilderness, Prepare ye the way of the Lord, make his paths straight.

4- John did baptize in the wilderness, and **preached the baptism of repentance** for the remission of sins.

5- And there went out unto him all the land of Judea, and they of Je-ru'sa-lem, and were all baptized of him in the river Jor'dan, confessing their sins.

….

8- I indeed have baptized you with water: **but he *(Jesus)* shall baptize you with the Holy Ghost**.

-Mark 1 v 2-5, 8

Who was under the Law? The Jews of Israel and only to them were given the 'Mosaic Law'. With the giving of the moral law (the 10 Commandments) all the world can now see their 'conscience acts of freewill' as being good or bad. There is now 'a standard' for the world. Not according to the ways of man but of God. But without 'an enforcement' who would know? "No one saw me drive through the stop sign. I didn't break the law. I have been given no ticket".

A persons conscience can be 'seared' and changed by the acts of man and the world. The 'freewill' of man can be influenced by the god of this world. Without the 'Moral Commandments' of God, what becomes the end of man? Sin and death. World history has shown this over and over.

The wickedness of mankind is beyond description. The things that have been done by man to another man is horrific and utterly 'non-human'. You yourself can think of many examples. The murder and torture by the 'supposed Christians' throughout history acting in the name of God is not of God but of Satan.

5- And God saw that the wickedness of man *was* great in the earth, and *that* every imagination of **the thoughts of his heart *was* only evil continually.**
-Genesis 6 v 5

11- The LORD knoweth the thoughts of man, that they *are* vanity.
-Psalm 94 v 11

11- The earth also was corrupt before God, and the earth was filled with **violence**.
12- And God looked upon the **earth**, and, behold, it was **corrupt**; for all flesh had corrupted his way upon the earth.
-Genesis 6 v 11, 12

Noah's flood and the destroying of the planet and all that lived followed this 'consciousness of freewill'. Mankind must have been real bad for God to punish them this way. Only eight believed in the 'Living God'. Only eight survived this catastrophe. This is the way of mankind when left up to their own 'freewill' moralities and conscience. Sin and Death. Sin = Death.

Paul writes by the Holy Spirit:
24- Who now rejoice in my sufferings for you, and fill up that which is behind of the afflictions of Christ in my flesh **for his body sake, which is the church**:
25- Whereof I *(Paul)* am made a minister, according to the **dispensation of God** which is given to me for you, **to fulfil the word of God;**
-Colossians 1 v 24, 25

If anything could be learned I pray that these verses are taken to heart. These 'words of God' say so much. **"For his body sake, which is the church"**. 'The Church' is the spiritual 'Body of Christ', not a building or a gathering of 'supposed Christians'. The Holy Spirit baptizes us into Christ without water and without any type of 'religious denominational legalisms'.

"I (Paul) am made a minister". No man or a convent or a college of study made the Apostle Paul a minister. It was the resurrected Jesus Christ in Heaven that did.

"According to the dispensation of God which is given to me for you". Who was given the prescription (Dispensation)? Why was it given? "For you", meaning us Gentiles.

"To fulfil the word of God". 'To fulfill' or 'to complete the word of God'. Before the English translators, the Greeks had the meaning of 'to put an end to'. It was by the Dispensation given to the Apostle Paul for us Gentiles that finished our knowledge for salvation.

Our written Bible of the Word of God is done, finished. No man is adding anymore scripture of truth to the 'Body of Christ'. All that is needed for salvation is found between Genesis 1 v 1 to Revelation 22 v 21. Specifically for the world and the Gentiles, Romans thru Hebrews. Most don't view Paul's Epistles with understanding.

The Crusades, the death, the torture, the persecutions of man by the religion created by 'the Roman Empire' is not a 'Body of Christ Church' as it was 'Dispensed' to the Apostle Paul. Though they claim to be in the 'Body of Christ', history has shown me otherwise. Nobody in the 'True Church, The Body of Christ' has persecuted or killed anyone. Once a believer and in 'the Body of Christ', the past transgressions of a man is no longer remembered by God*. *-Hebrews 8 v 12; -Hebrews 10 v 17; -Romans 4; -Ephesians 1 v 7; -Ephesians 4 v 32; -Colossians 1 v 14; -Colossians 2 v 13

1- If ye then be risen with Christ, seek those things which are above, where Christ sitteth on the right hand of God.

2- Set your affection on things above, not on things on the earth.

3- For ye are dead, and your life is hid with Christ in God.

4- When Christ, *who is* our life, shall appear, then shall ye also appear with him in glory.

-Colossians 3 v 1-4

17- Therefore if any man be in Christ *(the True Church)*, he is a new creature *(creation):* old things are passed away; behold, all things are become new.
18- And all things are of God, who hath reconciled us to himself by Je'sus Christ, and hath given to us the ministry of reconciliation;
19- To wit, that God was in Christ, reconciling the world unto himself, not imputing their tresspasses unto them; and hath committed unto us the word of reconciliation.
-II Corinthians 5 v 17-19

If a murderer claiming to have been 'saved' but then continues in the sinful ways of men, this person is obviously a hypocrite. I dare not judge any person but the discerning of the Word of God has been clear. Becoming a true believer does not excuse the crimes that are punishable by the laws of men.

Being jailed or even executed by 'capital punishments' is 'the law of the land'. It would take a full and wholehearted belief in Paul's Gospel of Salvation that would save the murderer. Only God would know. If Saul of Tarsis can be saved, we all can be. Saul is the 'Epitome of God's Grace'. Discard the 'Old Man Adam'* and become a new creation. *-Romans 6 v 6; -II Corinthians 5 v 17; -Ephesians 4 v 22; -Colossians 3 v 9

This is the deception of the world. All Christians are heaped and lumped into one entity. A person going to any building 'called a church' is considered now to be a Christian? Denominations and religion's are all viewed as being the same and there are many ways and forms to obtain salvation. Go to church then your now a Christian?

The world takes a wide view of salvation but **the written Word of God is narrow**. These mega churches with large congregations may seem that they got it right. Because of the wealth and assets that these mega churches have obtained, even TV air time, they hold a lot of sway in the Word of God. These are 'principalities in high places'. Are these large churches the ones to follow? New religions are invented constantly. Who is right? What does the 'Holy Ghost inspired Apostle of the Gentiles (Paul) say?

There is only One Way

12- For as the body is one, and hath many members, and all the members of that one body, being many, are one body: so also *is* Christ.

13- For by one Spirit are we all baptized into one body, whether *we be* Jews or Gen'tiles, whether *we be* bond or free; and have been made to drink into one Spirit.

-I Corinthians 12 v 12, 13

4- *There is* one body, and one Spirit, even as ye are called in one hope of your calling;

5- One Lord, one faith, one baptism,

6- One God and Father of all, who *is* above all, and through all, and in you all *(believers)*.

-Ephesians 4 v 4-6

    The first ones to be called 'Christians' in the Bible were a 'Body of Christ Church' that was established by the Apostle Paul. These were Gentiles and not Jews. There may have been Jews there too, but in the Body of Christ there is no difference.

    The Jerusalem Church (an ecclesia, a congregation, an assembly) were not called Christians first. What? The Jerusalem Church of which Peter, James and John were members was older than these newer gatherings following the Gospel that was given to Paul. The Bible (the Word of God) didn't designate the Jerusalem Church as Christians?

    Millions follow the Apostles Doctrine* and label themselves as 'Christians'. <u>The 'Body of Christ, the Church' are not following the Apostles Doctrine.</u> The revelations of the mysteries were only given to the Apostle Paul. Many refuse to see this. Prove to yourself then. Make a Bible study. Find in scripture (the Word of God) that shows that Peter and the Disciples were also shown the 'Mysteries and Secrets' that have always been hid until it was revealed to them. *-Acts 2 v 42

    This is another falsehood that has blinded mankind. The culprit most likely is the understanding that most of Christendom stopped their knowledge somewhere in Acts Chapter 2. They ignore the Epistles of Paul and only see and focus on his God given scriptures that agree with the Apostles Doctrine. Read Galatians Chapters 1 and 2. It could not be more clear yet the god of this world seems to be able to blind Christendom to these truths, even after reading these chapters.

    The unique Apostleship given to Paul by the resurrected Jesus Christ from heaven to all of mankind is lost on most of Christendom. This is not judgment but a discernment by the truth of the 'written Words of God'. Study and read what is and is not in our Bibles. The easiest way to see this is to know the difference between the 2 Gospels (the Gospel of the Kingdom and the Gospel of Grace). They are not the same Gospels. Study and understand 'both sides of the cross'.

The 'supposed Christians' that follow Peter, James and John were not called Christians at all by the Word of God. The world calls everyone a Christian or calls themselves Christians because they went to a church or want to be accepted in such a place of men and women. Or a person says, "I believe in God" I am now a Christian.

Only three times was the word 'Christian' used in the Bible. Not one time was the word 'Christian' used in the Old Testament. Who is calling themselves Christians?

Luke writes **the First mention of the word 'Christian'.** He writes concerning Paul and his disciples:

25- Then departed Bar'na-bas to Tar'sus, for to seek Saul *(Paul).*

26- And when he had found him, he brought him unto An'ti-och. And it came to pass, that a whole year they assembled themselves with the church, and taught much people. <u>And the disciples were called Chris'tians first in An'ti-och.</u>

-Acts 11 v 25, 26

The Second mention of the word 'Christian'. Paul is stating his case in front of King Agrippa reasoning that the Jews had nothing against him by which they could accuse him. Paul gets sent to Rome where he writes his prison epistles, Ephesians, Philippians and Colossians.

24- And as he thus spake for himself, Fes'tus said with a loud voice, Paul, thou art beside thyself; much learning doth make thee mad.

25- But he said, I am not mad, most noble Fes'tus; but speak forth the words of truth and soberness.

26- For the king knoweth of these things, before whom also I speak freely: for I am persuaded that none of these things are hidden from him; for this thing was not done in a corner.

27- King A-grip'pa, believest thou the prophets? I know that thou believest.

28- Then A-grip'pa said unto Paul, Almost thou persuadest me to be a Christian.

29- And Paul said, I would to God, that not only thou, but also all that hear me this day, were both almost, and altogether such as I am, except these bonds.
-Acts 26 v 24-29

The Third time the word Christian is used. Peter is writing to the Jews who were scattered abroad, strangers*. Peter never addressed a Body of Christ Church under the 'Banner of Paul's Gospel'. He is writing these Jews encouraging them to stay strong in the face of the persecutions and the 'wrath of God' that was thought to soon be coming. Peter is comparing the suffering of Jesus Christ with what they are now facing. *-I Peter 1 v 1

12- Beloved, think it not strange concerning the fiery trial which is to try you, as though some strange thing happened unto you:

13- But rejoice, inasmuch <u>as ye are partakers of Christ's sufferings</u>; that, when his glory shall be revealed, ye may be glad also with exceeding joy.

14- If ye be reproached for the name of Christ, happy *are ye*; for the spirit of glory and of God resteth upon you: on their part he is evil spoken of, but on your part he is glorified.

15- But let none of you suffer as a murderer, or *as* a thief, or *as* an evil doer, or as a busy body in other men's matters.

16- Yet <u>if *any man suffer*</u> as a Christian *(like Christ suffered)*, let him not be ashamed; but let him glorify God on this behalf.

17- For the time *is come* that judgement must begin at the house of God: and if *it* first *begin* at us, what shall the end *be* of them that obey not the Gospel of God*. *(*-Do I need to say it? What Gospel was Peter promoting?)*

18- And if the righteous scarcely be saved, where shall the ungodly and sinner appear*? *(*-Revelation 20 v 11)*

19- Wherefore <u>let them that suffer according to the will of God</u> commit the keeping of their souls *to him* in well doing, as unto a faithful Creator.
-I Peter 4 v 12-19

Do practicing Jews of today call themselves Christians? Or is it a misinterpretation for Christians to call themselves Jews? I have been in a church service and the pastor called the congregation Jews. Absolutely not. I am a Gentile saved by Grace.

No disrespect meant to the Jews. It is because of the Jew/Hebrew that we have hope but there are sects of religions that claim this. They have not understood the difference in Dispensations in the 'Kingdom Doctrine' to that of the 'Gospel of Grace'. They preach a mixed/mashed gospel in hopes of making the Bible understandable. They have not separated the Word of Truth but have mixed it together. This is most of Christendom.

Beware of the 'professing Christian' that has been in a church or denomination for years that have 'this supposed head knowledge' where they insist that they know the truth. Don't be intimidated by pastors, preachers and Bible teachers. These become adamant to what they know (think they know) when confronted with real genuine readable scripture. When they show their scriptures supporting 'their faith' we can see and understand now. What scriptures are they using and to whom were the scriptures written for? Jew or Gentile?

Listening to 'these' does help us solidify the truth of the 'written Word' when they reveal (unknowingly by themselves) their lack of knowledge as written. Just because they have a congregation and followers by no means is 'justification' as to what they are saying is 'truth'. " Wide is the gate...*"
*-Matthew 7 v 13

Follow the scripture first and foremost. It (the Word of God) pre-empts any spoken word from the 'pulpit'. You could show them scripture to their face. Even have them read for themselves, yet they refuse to see and make all kinds of reasons for their 'supposed knowledge'. "It always has been one Gospel, one dispensation and one message to the world", they say.

Understand the means by which mankind will be judged. It will not be by any man or priest:
16- In the day when God shall judge the secrets of men by Je'sus Christ according to <u>my gospel</u>.
-Romans 2 v 16

They have lived and believed 'this way' perhaps their whole lives and no one, not even scripture (truth) will change their minds. Many have said "I follow what my Church says". "I will follow Jesus before I follow any man". Is this the 'resurrected Jesus Christ' or the 'earthly Jesus Christ'? Paul only writes of the 'Resurrected Lord Jesus Christ'.

I pray to find the 'Apollo's and Lydia's' who readily accept the truth and are able to embrace Paul's knowledge given to him on 'this side of the cross'. It is God that opens the heart to understanding. A man can read but understanding comes by the Holy Spirit of God.

Does your church spend most of its time 'outside' the writings of the Apostle Paul? That is, does your church rarely use Paul's Epistles and spends its time devoted to Jesus' earthly ministry, the Old Testament and the 'Jewish Epistles'? If so, 'Dispensational' teaching and understanding is 'hid'. The Gospel is hid to them that are lost*. Nobody wants to hear that what they have believed in is not according to the scriptures. *-II Corinthians 4 v 3, 4

A denomination won't save you. A works religion won't save you. A preacher won't save you. Confessing to a Catholic priest won't save you. Attending a weekly church service won't save you. Sitting in the pew every Sunday morning won't save you. But what will save you? The Gospel! Paul's God given Gospel of Grace revealed from heaven by the resurrected Jesus Christ*.*-I Corinthians 15 v 1-4; -Romans 10 v 8, 9; -Ephesians 1 v 13 and all through Paul's Epistles

Paul repeats the death, burial, and resurrection Gospel of Grace throughout his epistles. He is the only one to reveal that salvation has came to us Gentiles on 'this side of the cross'. Not Peter, not Luke nor even Jesus Christ in the flesh taught salvation by 'Paul's Gospel'.

For 'the elect' and 'Jews of the circumcision' under the 'Law of Moses', resurrection was seen as a fact, an event that happened. Jesus Christ was not dead but alive and could still return and set up 'the Kingdom'. He is sitting at the Father's right hand until the enemies of Israel have been 'put down'.

For the Jew it was by keeping 'the Law' and to believe in the 'Name of Jesus Christ'. His name denoting that it is he, Jesus Christ, that was prophesied to come for the nation of Israel, the King, the Messiah, the Christ. 'The elect' were also given 'the dispensation of water baptism'. When 'John the Baptist' came to Israel, repentance and water baptism for the remission of sins was added for these Jews and not Gentiles. (Remember 'Dispensation' is only a 'Pauline' word).

Some even say when they are shown scripture, 'that's not what it says and means, I don't believe it'. Or 'it means the same thing...' Where is their Bible? Or do they have a 'supposed head knowledge' that is better and greater than the 'written Word of God'? Call me and man a liar but don't call God a liar. Read the scriptures. What does the Word of God say? Not what man wants it to say.

Don't be contentious and argumentative. Simply rely on the Holy Words of God written for us. Show the scriptures and let them read them. It is God that opens the heart to understanding. It is God that accepts and not a religion or a denomination. A wise Christian will be like Apollos and understand because only God can show understanding and open the heart.

All of Paul's teachings are based on the 'Resurrected Jesus Christ', not his earthly ministry:

6- I *(Paul)* have planted, A-pol'los watered; but God gave the increase.

7- So then neither is he that planteth any thing, neither he that watereth; but God that giveth the increase.

8- Now he that planteth and he that watereth are one: and every man shall receive his own reward according to his own labor *(not for salvation but for reward)*.

9- For we are labourers together with God: ye are God's husbandry, *ye are* God's building.

10- According to the grace of God which is given unto me, as a wise masterbuilder, I have laid the foundation, and another buildeth thereupon. But let every man take heed how he buildeth thereupon.

11- For other foundation can no man lay than that is laid, which is Je'sus Christ.

-I Corinthians 3 v 6-11

Peter said to them:

20- And he shall send Jesus Christ, which before was preached unto you:

21- Whom the heaven must receive until the times of restitution of all things, which God hath spoken **by the mouth of all his holy prophets since the world began**.

-Acts 3 v 20, 21

Compare with Paul, 'the Apostle of the Gentiles':

25- Now to him that is of power to establish you according to my gospel, and the preaching of Je'sus Christ, **according to the revelation of the mystery, which was kept secret since the world began,**

26- **But now** is made manifest, and by the scriptures of the prophets, according to the commandment of the everlasting God, made known to all nations for the obedience of faith:

-Romans 16 v 25, 26

Peter said, "by the mouth of his holy prophets since the world began". Paul said, "according to the revelation of the mystery, which was kept secret since the world began". Only to the Apostle Paul were revealed the 'mysteries' that were hid and kept secret. Not Peter, not Luke, not Abraham, not Moses, not the prophets but to Paul alone were the 'mysteries/secrets of Christ' revealed. Even 'the Twelve' did not know these 'revelations of the mysteries'.

29- The **secret *things*** belong unto the LORD our God: but those *things* which are revealed *belong* unto us and our children for ever, that we may do all the words of this **law**.
-Deuteronomy 29 v 29

Has there ever been a time in history where mankind has not suffered by the hands of others? Has any person who has ever lived escaped mans own devices and peacefully died at an old age with the society around them too? Has man by himself ever achieved a perfect 'utopian' society, directed solely by 'their conscience' and 'self willed morality' and not that of God?

There is no understandable hint in the Bible prior to Paul of an 'Age of Grace' or 'the Body of Christ as being the Church'. The 'prophetic time line' in the Old Testament said that there would be a 'Suffering Savior and Messiah'. Many of these scriptures are found in the Book of Psalm. He would return and bring in 'wrath and the tribulation' unlike the world has ever seen nor ever will see again. Then the return of Jesus Christ who would sit on the 'Throne of David' in Zion.

During the period of time after the Crucifixion and before the Tribulation is the 'calling out' of the 'Body of Christ'. This is what the Bible calls **'the last days'**. None of Israel's Biblical Prophecies ever included the Church Age and this Age of Grace. It was hid and kept secret apart from Israel's prophecies.

A new segment in our Bible never before eluded to, in any detail whatsoever, as it was revealed to the Apostle Paul (not Peter). 'The Body of Christ Church' was never spelled-out nor explained during Jesus' earthly ministry nor in the Old Testament. The Lord God of Israel is also going to the Gentiles without the Jew? What? Unheard of!

This is key. Understanding this 'parenthetical period' that is not a part of the 'Jewish time-line'. It is not Jewish but Gentile in nature. The whole

Bible was written by Jew's*. Paul was a Jew but he was designated by God to be 'The Apostle of the Gentiles'. *-Romans 3 v 1, 2

13- For I speak to you Gen'tiles, inasmuch as **I am the apostle of the Gen'tiles, <u>I magnify mine office</u>**.
14- If by any means I may provoke to emulation *them which are* my flesh *(Jews)*, and might save some of them.
-Romans 11 v 13, 14

Hebrews was written to the Jew/Hebrew mostly but much of it does contain gems of spiritual truths for the 'Body of Christ'. This is where so many have messed up the scriptures. They combine Peter and Paul. Paul was a chosen vessel by God himself to go to us Gentiles. Had the Kingdom been realized, the Jew would have their commission to bring to the world the knowledge of their God, JEHOVAH. It didn't happen... yet.

John in Revelation gives a Seven year time period (Daniel's 70th week), when it will happen. In a sense, today we are at the same place. As they wrote in their Jewish epistles by James, Peter, John, Jude and in Revelation, they were expecting the seven-year tribulation to happen shortly after Jesus ascended to heaven. Even Paul thought he would be 'caught up to meet the Lord in the air' before the tribulation was to happen.

Paul writes (Holy Spirit inspired always remember) that the 'Body of Christ' would be 'caught up' in a blink of an eye to meet the Lord in the air*. These are those that had embraced Paul's Gospel of Grace by faith and not of anything under any 'Denominational or Religious' law. *-I Corinthians 15 v 51-54; -I Thessalonians 1 v 10; -I Thessalonians 4 v 13-18; -Titus 2 v 13, 14; -II Thessalonians 2 v 1

There is nowhere in Biblical Scripture for the 'Jews of the Circumcision/ Law' to be 'caught up' to meet the Lord in the air. Only the Apostle Paul reveals this mystery. For the Jews and Israel, Jesus Christ is coming to the earth to set up the 'Kingdom of Heaven'. So many have discounted the words of God concerning this being 'caught up' and do not teach it or believe it. In essence, they have called God a liar. What is the number one cardinal sin? Unbelief!

What happened? The tribulation did not come in. This is the break in the prophetic time line the Old Testament never alluded to nor mentioned that God would go to the Gentiles and 'take out of them a people for his name'*. At least this was never directly said. Paul writes that the 'Body of Christ' <u>will not</u> go through the tribulation and will be spared the wrath and vexation that will come during those 7 years.

*-Acts 15 v 13-16; -Romans 11 v 25

1- For this cause I Paul, the prisoner of Je'sus Christ for you Gen'tiles,

2- If ye have heard of the dispensation of grace of God which is given me to you-ward:

3- How that by revelation he made known unto me the mystery; (as I wrote afore in few words,

4- Whereby, when ye read, ye may understand my knowledge in the mystery of Christ)

5- Which in other ages was not made known unto the sons of men, as it is now revealed unto his holy apostles and prophets *(Paul's ministry)* by the Spirit;

6- That the Gen'tiles should be fellowheirs, and of the same body, and partakers of his promise in Christ by the gospel:

7- Wherefore I was made a minister, according to the gift of the grace of God given unto me by the effectual working of his power.

8- Unto me, who am less than the least of all saints, is this grace given, that I *(Paul)* should preach among the Gen'tiles the unsearchable riches of Christ;

9- And to make all *men* see what *is* the fellowship of the mystery, which from the beginning of the world hath been **hid in God, who created all things by Je'sus Christ**: *(Jesus is God, see the Invisible Godhead chapter)*

10- To the intent that now unto the principalities and powers in heavenly *places* might be known by the church the manifold wisdom of God.

11- According to the eternal purpose which he purposed in Christ Je'sus our Lord:

12- In whom we have boldness and access with competence by the faith of him.

-Ephesians 3 v 1-12

23- If ye continue in the faith *(faith-way)* grounded and settled, and *be* not moved away from the hope of the gospel, which ye have heard, *and* which was preached to every creature which is under heaven; **wherefore I Paul am made a minister;**

24- Who now rejoice in my sufferings for you, and fill up that which is behind of the affliction of **Christ in my flesh for his body's sake, which is the church**:

25- **Whereof I am made a minister, according to the dispensation of God** which is given to me for you, **to fulfill** *(complete/finish)* **the word of God**;

26- **Even the mystery which hath been hid from ages and from generations**, but now is made manifest to his saints *(Paul's Ministry)*.

27- To whom God would make known what *is* the riches of **the glory of this mystery among the Gen'tiles; which is Christ in you, the hope of glory**:

28- Whom we preach, warning every man, and teaching every man in all wisdom; that we may present every man perfect in Christ Je'sus:

29- Where unto I also labor, striving according to his working, which worketh in me mightily.

-Colossians 1 v 23-29

18- And immediately there fell from his eyes as it had been scales: and he received site forthwith, and arose, and was baptized.

19- And when he had received meat, he was strengthened. Then was Saul certain days with the disciples which were at Damascus. *(Note: These disciples were not the twelve, because it acts 8 v 1 they were still in Jerusalem.)*

20- <u>And straightway he preached Christ in the synagogues, that he is the Son of God.</u>

21- But all that heard *him* were amazed, and said; Is not this he that destroyed them which called on this name in Je-ru'sa-lem, and came hither for that intent, that he might bring them bound unto the chief priest?

22- But Saul increased the more in strength, and confounded the Jews which dwelt at Damascus, proving that this is very Christ.

23- And after many days were fulfilled, the Jews took counsel to kill him:

24- But their laying await was known of Saul. And they watched the gates day and night to kill him.

25- Then the disciples took him by night, and let *him* down by the wall in a basket.

-Acts 9 v 18-25

Saul was preaching the 'Kingdom Gospel'. He was preaching Christ, the name of Jesus the Christ, the Messiah, the Son of God. He was not preaching salvation by his 'death and burial and resurrection' yet. He was also water baptized. At this time Saul had not received the mysteries and the 'Gospel of Grace'. He was preaching 'the name of Jesus Christ' and who he was.

Most of the Jews, the Pharisees and Sadducees didn't believe in the 'Name of Jesus the Christ'. They were following, as well as most of Israel was, the message that Saul had been crusading to Israel. But now they were looking at Saul as a hypocrite. He was preaching the very thing that he was against.

After Paul's Damascus experience you would think he would immediately go to Jerusalem to be with 'The Twelve' to get first hand information on what they knew of Jesus themselves. For they lived with Jesus for three years. One would think this is the logical place for Paul to go, but Paul did not. God purposely kept Paul from interacting with 'the Jews under the law'.

God had a special plan and task for the Apostle Paul. Law and Grace does not mix. He was given by 'progressive revelation', the Doctrine of Grace. Paul started his God given Apostleship around 40 A.D. His first letter came out around 54 A.D. There is no sure date of when the Book of Hebrews was written.

The time frame when Saul was let down in the basket to the time he came to Jerusalem is a three-year span. In Acts, written by Luke, there was no gap given. Luke writes as if Paul immediately went back to Jerusalem. Paul writes in Galatians 1 of the same event. He gives the account that it was three years later that he comes back to Jerusalem. During these three years, Paul spent face time 'one-on-one' with the resurrected Jesus Christ himself. Paul was the last to see the Lord Jesus Christ*. *-I Corinthians 15 v 8

11- But I I certify you, brethren, that **the gospel** which was preached of me is not after man.

12- For I neither received it of man, neither was I taught it, but **by the revelation of Je'sus Christ.**

13- For ye have heard of my conversation in time past in the Jews' religion, how that beyond measure I persecuted the church of God, and wasted it:

14- And profited in the Jews' religion above many my equals in mine own nation, being more exceedingly zealous of the traditions of my father's.

15- But when it pleased God, who separated me from my mother's womb, and called *me* by his grace,

16- To reveal his Son in me, **that I might preach him among the heathen; immediately I conferred not with flesh and blood:**

17- Neither went I up to Je-ru'sa-lem to them which were apostles before me; but I went into A-ra'bia, and returned again unto Da-mas'cus.
18- Then after three years I went up to Je-ru'sa-lem to see Pe'ter, and abode with him fifteen days.
19- But other of the apostles saw I none, save James the Lord's brother.
20- Now the things which I write unto you, behold, before God, I lie not.
-Galatians 1 v 11-20

15- So, as much as in me is, I am ready to preach the gospel to you that are at Rome also.
16- For I am not ashamed of the gospel of Christ: for it is the power of God unto salvation to everyone that believeth; to the Jew first, and also to the Greek *(Gentile).*
17- For therein is the righteousness of God revealed from faith to faith: as it is written, The just shall live by faith.
-Romans 1 v 15-17

15- Nevertheless, brethren, I have written the more boldly unto you in some sort, as putting you in mind, because of the grace that is given to me of God.
16- That I should be the minister of Je'sus Christ to the Gen'tiles, ministering the gospel of God, that the offering up of the Gen'tiles might be acceptable, being sanctified by the Ho'ly Ghost.
-Romans 15 v 15,16

25- Now to him that is of power to establish you according to my gospel, and the preaching of Je'sus Christ, according to the revelation of the mystery, which was kept secret since the world began,
-Romans 16 v 25

15- For though ye have ten thousand instructors in Christ, yet *have ye* not many fathers: for in Christ Je'sus I have begotten you through the gospel.
16- Wherefore I beseech you, be ye followers of me.
-I Corinthians 4 v 15, 16

1- Be ye followers of me, even as I also *am* of Christ.
-I Corinthians 11 v 1

Paul did not walk with Jesus during his earthly ministry. Paul was not a chosen disciple before the crucifixion. So where did Paul receive his knowledge of Jesus Christ? Paul didn't reveal his 'revelation of the mysteries' till many years after the resurrection.

Before Paul had his 'Road to Damascus experience', as 'Saul of Tarsus' he was hunting down and persecuting those that had embraced Jesus as being the Messiah, Christ and King of Israel. He was an enemy of 'the elect' and an enemy of the Lord Jesus.

When Paul revealed the 'hidden secrets/mysteries' they were done progressively. They were not all revealed at one time. They were 'Dispensation-ally' revealed.

Note that during the time of Christ's earthly ministry the printed word had not been made. We have the luxury of reading our Bible 'as if in a real time' that they were written. The Old Testament was all that could be used for scriptural knowledge. Matthew, Mark, Luke and John referred to as 'The Four Gospel's of Jesus Christ' had not been written yet, or were in the process? The Book of Acts, a 'transitional book', written by Luke was not published either.

Paul would start his ministry to the Jew/Hebrews first. But the Jews hated the Apostle Paul and his doctrine of Grace. The Apostle Paul was kicked out of every synagogue eventually. Grace and Law does not mix. Not only was the 'pagan world' an enemy of Paul but 'the Jews of the Circumcision/Law' would follow Paul and disrupt his 'Body of Christ Churches'.

Yes, the 'Gospel of the Kingdom' believers (the elect) were a major thorn in the Apostle Paul's ministry. Nothing has changed. "Paul is just that guy that we take incredible scripture of spiritual truths when it agrees with our religion and our denomination".

Writers of the Bible (Holy Spirit Inspired) may not have known each other, may not have read other texts, may have been hundreds of years apart but not one thing written has ever been disproved by man as being 'amiss, false or a fable'. Historical findings made constantly prove over and over that the 'Word of God' has always been right, 100%. The detailed genealogies kept for thousands of years have always been 100% correct. What generation can claim that?

The only Book ever written where prophecies have came true. No other history of people on the planet earth has such a book. Does any other religion have a book of prophecies that were fulfilled?

Paul writes in II Timothy:

16- All scripture *is* given by inspiration of God, and *is* profitable for **doctrine**, for **reproof**, for **correction**, for **instruction** in righteousness:

17- That the man of God may be perfect *(spiritually mature)*, thoroughly furnished unto all good works.

-II Timothy 3 v 16, 17

Good works, not 'righteous works' of the flesh. As members in the 'Body of Christ' we do those things out of love, fulfilling the law. There is no rule that we have to do this and that (legalism) for us to obtain salvation. 'The just shall live by faith'.

There are 'traditions', 'works', and 'church customs' that denominations feel that must be done and followed to be 'saved'. Such as joining their church, water baptism, paying tithes, repentance, 'speaking in tongues', and so on. Was Christmas and Easter a holiday to follow because the Bible said too?

Don't lie to yourself nor let any denomination or preacher tell you that when Christ came it was understood that he did away with 'the Law' and the Jewish customs. That during Jesus' earthly ministry the Jewish system was abolished. Or part of it was and they are following what the Bible says, a 'pseudo law'. It is just as important to know what the Bible says as well as what it does not say.

The 'earthly ministry of Christ written in Matthew, Mark, Luke and John is still part of the Old Testament. It is still 'the Kingdom Message', 'The Gospel of the Kingdom'. 'The King of the Jews' had come and all that was prophesied could be fulfilled. Believe in the Name of Jesus Christ.

The Epistles written by James, Peter, John and Jude is still 'the Kingdom Message' and 'the Gospel of the Kingdom' Doctrine. The difference is that they are now in anticipation of the return of Jesus Christ. The 'prophetic time line' of Old Testament prophecies is moving right along and in accordance with Biblical scripture. The next order of business was the Tribulation then Christ and the Earthly Kingdom.

Oh, the push back at this by those that 'peace meal' the word of God to make it fit 'their own desires'. In their attempt to understand, they discount the understanding of 'the Dispensations'. This way they can stay in Matthew, Mark, Luke, John and the beginning of Acts and build 'a doctrine', picking and choosing scriptures that will fit what 'they want' out of the rest of the Bible.

Often times 'the piece-mealers of the Gospels' use Old Testament scriptures of 'the Law' to put the parishioners in some type of subjection. These 'church members' had better follow what is spoken from behind the pulpit or they will go to a very warm place. Do what the priest and preacher says not what the 'Word of God' has said?

12- For we wrestle not against flesh and blood, but against principalities, against powers, against the rulers of the darkness of this world, against spiritual wickedness in high *places.*
-Ephesians 6 v 12

These are found every Sunday and on TV in 'so called' churches. Much of Christendom thinks they are following the 'Word of God', as it is doled out by their pastors and their preachers. Their faith rests on what these preachers and teachers are saying. What if they are wrong? They are only men and women. Read and understand for yourself 'the truth in the Dispensations' given that have been given by God to Man.

Peter writes near the end of his life:
15- And account *that* the long-suffering of our Lord is salvation; even as our beloved brother Paul also according to the wisdom given unto him hath written *(Hebrews)* unto you;
16- As also in all *his* epistles, speaking of these things; in which are some things hard to be understood, which they that are unlearned and unstable wrest, as *they do* also the other scriptures *(Romans to Hebrews),* unto their own destruction.
-II Peter 3 v 15, 16

Peter, a law keeping Jew, finally at the end of his life acknowledges the wisdom that was given to the 'Apostle of the Gentiles', the Apostle Paul. Only to Paul did Jesus Christ reveal the 'mysteries that have been kept secret since the world began'*. These were revealed to Paul 'on this side of the cross' after Christ's resurrection and ascension to heaven. Jesus Christ did not reveal the secrets/mysteries to his disciples during his earthly ministry. *-Romans 16 v 25

Peter is not Paul. Paul is not Peter. Many being 'unlearned and unstable' have said they wrote and agreed on the same thing. In essence, they are believing (want to believe) that Peter and Paul were in the same 'dispensation'. It's the difference between night and day. These ignore the truth of scripture. Or quite simply, because of the hardness of their heart' and their 'know it all attitude' they have been blinded by the god of this world and are unable to see the truth.

The vast majority of Christendom is in denial of this. They don't want to hear it. Perhaps the church and your denomination are of this 'supposed head knowledge'. The preachers and teachers will fight you 'tooth and nail' when shown the 'Words of Truth'. These are not in 'the Body of Christ, the True Church' though they claim to be while ignoring and refuting these scriptures shown to them.

These 'principalities in high places' can talk a good game and will attempt to make you question your own faith. They will want to make you feel inferior and guilty for questioning 'their supposed head knowledge'. This man/women, teacher, preacher cannot give you the 'free gift of Grace'.

14- Be ye not unequally yoked together with unbelievers: for what fellowship hath righteousness with unrighteousness? and what communion hath light with darkness.
-II Corinthians 6 v 14

Peter found Paul's message hard to understand*. Why? Peter was a 'law keeping Jew' and was never told by Jesus Christ to stop keeping 'the law', nor was he expected to. The 'Gospel of the Kingdom' was still paramount in his mind. Peter was still in Jerusalem waiting for Jesus to re-appear with the Kingdom of Heaven. *-II Peter 3 v 15, 16

Before the crucifixion, Peter asks Jesus:
27- Then answered Peter and said unto him, Behold, we have forsaken all, and followed thee; what shall we have therefore?
28- And Jesus said unto them, Verily I say unto you, That ye which have followed me *(presently)*, in the **regeneration** *(future)* when the Son of man shall sit in the throne of his glory *(future)*, ye also shall sit upon twelve thrones *(future)*, judging the twelve tribes of Is'ra-el *(future)*.
-Matthew 19 v 27, 28

Note the word 'regeneration'. What is going to be regenerated? Planet earth after the tribulation "when the Son of man shall sit in the throne of his glory'. A 1,000 year time frame given in the Book of Revelation*. Heaven on earth. The Kingdom of Heaven. The Gospel of the Kingdom. *-Revelation 20

Has Peter and 'the Twelve' sat on thrones? Are 'the Twelve' judging 'the Tribes of Israel' today? Has the 'Regeneration' happened and the 'Son of man' (Jesus the Christ) is sitting on his throne of glory? False teachers say that because the Jews rejected Jesus Christ the blessings promised to Israel has fallen to 'the church'.

What church? There is only 'one true church' and it is not a religion or denomination. 'The Body of Christ' is 'the Church', a spiritual body of which Jesus Christ is the head. It is not a physical building on a street corner. Going to a church service at a specific location is not 'the Body of Christ'. Though 'The Body of Christ' does congregate in 'church buildings'.

The blessings and promises made to Israel is still going to happen. God said so. Believe God not what someone has told you. Israel is out of its place of blessing today. Israel stumbled at that stumbling stone which is Christ*. The prophetic time line of Israel's prophecies have been set aside but not forgotten. *-Romans 9 v 32

The 'Age of Grace' and the filling of the 'Body of Christ' is now, today. You won't find this in the 'Jewish parts of the Bible'. It is all a 'Pauline revelation' that was never made known to any man except the Apostle Paul.

The 'Wrath of God' and 'the Day of the Lord' has yet to happen (the latter days). The prophets in the Old Testament spoke of this 'time of Tribulation'. 70 A.D. may have been horrific and bad but does not compare with 'the Holocaust' or 'Noah's flood'. Daniel and John give a 7 year period for this. A specific time frame that has yet to happen. Jesus Christ speaks of this time as being worse than all times, past, present and future.

What Dispensation are you taking daily?

BOOK VI

Israel's Interrupted Time-Line, the Last and Latter Days

6- For unto us a child is born, unto us a son is given: *and the government **shall be** upon his shoulder: and his name **shall be** called Wonderful, Counselor, The mighty God, The Everlasting Father, The Prince of Peace. 7- Of the increase of *his* government *there* **shall be** no end, upon the throne of Da'vid, and upon his kingdom, to order it, and to establish it with judgement and with justice **from henceforth** even for ever. The zeal of the LORD of hosts will perform this.

-Isaiah 9 v 6, 7

*All that follows in v6 and v7 has yet to happen. We can call the LORD all these names of course, but Jesus today does not have the 'Kingdom of Heaven's government' on his shoulder. Jesus Christ is not ruling and reigning from Zion. He will one day because scripture says "the Government **shall be**..." After the Kingdom is established, "**from henceforth**..." it will then be forever.

In these next scriptures, Jesus quotes Isaiah but stops at 'the Break in the Prophetic Time Line'. Jesus knew of course what he was doing, not giving it away, but keeping it secret. Jesus stops reading at the place where he knew it was not going to happen, ... yet.

16- And he *(Jesus)* came to Naz'a-reth, where he had been brought up: and, as **his custom was, he went into the synagogue on the sabbath day***, and stood up for to read. *(*Jesus Christ the law keeper. -Matthew 5 v 17)*

17- And there was delivered unto him the book of the prophet E-sa'ias *(Isaiah)*. And when he had opened the book, he found the place where it was written,

18- The Spirit of the Lord *is* upon me, because he hath anointed me to preach the gospel to the poor; he hath sent me to heal the brokenhearted, to preach deliverance to the captives, and recovering of sight to the blind, to set at liberty them that are bruised,

19- To preach the acceptable year of the Lord*. *(*-v21; -Galatians 4 v 4)*

20- And he closed the book and gave *it* again to the minister, and sat down. **And the eyes of all them that were in the synagogue were fastened on him.**

21- And he began to say unto them, **This day is this scripture fulfilled in your ears.**

-Luke 4 v 16-21; -Isaiah 61 v 1; Isaiah 61 v 2 and the following scriptures has yet to happen

Why were their eyes fastened on Jesus? What did they know that Jesus had not read? They knew these scriptures that Isaiah wrote. Jesus stop reading and sat down. Why?

Jesus was quoting Isaiah 61 but he stopped. He stopped at the prophecies of the coming kingdom. **Jesus never gave away the secret that he would be turning his focus towards the Gentiles without the Jew.** When the Jews are out of their place of blessing, God's time-clock for Israel stops.

Isaiah 61 v 1-6:

1- The Spirit of the LORD God *is* upon me; because the LORD hath anointed me to preach good tidings unto the meek; he hath sent me to bind up the brokenhearted, to proclaim liberty to the captives, and the opening of the prison to *them that are* bound.

2- To proclaim the acceptable year of the LORD*, and the day of vengence of our God; to comfort all that mourn; *(*the following has yet to happen.)*

3- To appoint them that mourn in Zion, to give unto them beauty for ashes, the oil of joy for mourning, the garment of praise for the spirit of heavyness; that they might be called trees of righteousness, the planting of the LORD, that he might be glorified.

4- And they shall build the old wastes, they shall raise up the former desolations, and they shall repair the waste cities, the desolations of many generations.

5- And strangers shall stand and feed your flocks, and the sons of the alien *shall be* your plowman and your vinedressers.

6- **But ye shall be named the Priests of the LORD*:** *men* shall call you **the ministers of our God**: ye shall eat the riches of the Gen'tiles, and in their glory shall ye boast yourselves. *(*-Exodus 19 v 6)*
-Isaiah 61 v 1-6

As of yet, there is no word of the 'Gospel of Grace' and the Lord bringing salvation to the Gentiles without the Jew. All that can be understood is that by the Jew the rest of the world would get the knowledge of Israel's LORD God JEHOVAH. Israel was to be a kingdom of priests*. *-Exodus 19 v 6; -I Peter 2 v 5, 9

But in order for a successful priesthood to be accomplished, Jesus must be ruling and reigning the 'Earthly Kingdom of Heaven' from David's throne in Zion. This hasn't happened, ... yet. There is no kingdom to bring the Gentiles to (into).

Early in the Book of Acts, the disciples asks Jesus:

6- When they therefore were come together, they asked of him, saying, Lord, wilt thou at this time restore again the kingdom to Is'ra-el?

7- And he said unto them, It is not for you to know the times or the seasons, which the Father hath put in his own power.

8- But ye shall receive power, after that the Ho'ly Ghost is come upon you: and ye shall be witnesses unto me both in Je-ru'sa-lem, and in all Ju-dae'a, and in Sa-ma'ri-a, and unto the uttermost part of the earth*. *(*-these disciples never left Israel (Acts 8 v 1) in preaching 'their Gospel'.)*
-Acts 1 v 6-8

Jesus told them these things just before he was 'taken up' to heaven. The disciples did receive power and performed many miracles continuing on 'the earthly ministry of Christ'. At this time the Earthly Kingdom could still be fulfilled. Jesus is not dead but alive. They thought that it wouldn't be much longer and Jesus would be returning with the Kingdom of Heaven.

But what happened to the miracle power that was given to them? There is no scriptural record of them taking 'their gospel' to the ends of the earth. The kingdom did not happen. Israel is out of its place of blessing. It still is according to scripture*. *-Romans 11 v 25

Up to Acts 10, the Bible has been all Israel and the Jew mostly, with a few exceptions. The Gentiles that were noted were always in the presence of a Jew/Hebrew or one that the Gentile had been involved with. There is nothing of Gentiles receiving a knowledge of the Living God on their own. The Book of Acts starts all Jewish 100%. Halfway through the Book of Acts, Peter and the rest vanish from scripture. They reappear when they write their own epistles. The Book of Acts ends with the Apostle Paul officially giving up on the Jews.

Jesus Christ knew that the Earthly Kingdom of Heaven was going to be delayed. What was the reason to put on hold the prophecies and promises made to Israel? Israel rejected as a Nation the Name of Jesus Christ. They (Israel) murdered along with the Roman Empire the Messiah, the Christ, Israel's prophesied King.

The 'earthly ministry' and the prophecies were 'fulfilled and finished'*. Jesus now turns his attention to all of mankind through 'thee Apostle of the Gentiles', Romans to Hebrews. Israel's blessings will have to wait. They proved themselves unworthy of the Kingdom of Heaven. *-John 19 v 30

But the Kingdom was promised to Abraham, Issac and Jacob (Israel). When 'the times of the Gentiles'* has run its course (been almost 2,000 years now), God will return for his covenanted people. After the crucifixion Israel is no longer the 'blessed nation of God'. But God promised he would never forget them nor forsake them+. There is always a 'remnant'=. *-Luke 21 v 24; +- Leviticus 26 v 44; -Jeremiah 31 v 35-36; -Jeremiah 33 v 25, 26; -Nehemiah 9 v 31; -Hebrews 13 v 5; =-II Kings 19 v 30, 31; -Ezra 9 v 8; -Isaiah 1 v 9; -Isaiah 10 v 20-22; -Isaiah 11 v 11, 16; -Isaiah 37 v 31, 32; -Jeremiah 31 v 7; -Jeremiah 44 v 28; -Ezekiel 5 v 10; -Ezekiel 11 v 13-17; -Ezekiel 14 v 22; -Joel 2 v 32; -Micah 2 v 12; -Micah 5 v 3-8; -Micah 7 v 8; -Zephaniah 2 v 7-9; -Zephaniah 3 v 13; -Zechariah 8 v 12; -Romans 9 v 27; -Romans 11 v 5, 6

Scripture does not show that 'these Jews still under the law' were now accepting of all types of people, the Gentiles. There was never a 'national acceptance or inclusion' were a Gentile could now simply walk into a synagogue. What scripture does show is what much of Christendom does not want to hear.

1- And Saul was consenting unto his death *(Stephen)*. And at that time there was a great persecution against the church which was at Je-ru'sa-lem; and they were all scattered abroad throughout the regions of Ju-da-e and Sa-ma'ri-a, **except the Apostles**.
-Acts 8 v 1

The stoning of Stephen happened 6 to 8 years after Jesus was 'taken up'. His disciples were still in Jerusalem. They were not out evangelizing the world as much of Christendom has falsely taught. These truths are hard for the 'supposed Christian' to accept.

19- Now they which were scattered abroad upon the persecution that arose about Stephen travelled as far as Phe-ni'ce, and Cy'prus, and An'ti-och **preaching the word to none but unto the Jews only**.
-Acts 11 v 19; -Galatians 2 v 9 shook on it

Those of 'the Circumcision/Law' that had left Israel were not evangelizing the Gentiles. Acts 11 was written approximately 10-12 years after Jesus was 'taken up'. There is no scriptural record of the Jews and the 'original disciples' as having preached to the non-Jew.

What about Peter going to the House of Cornelius? This was approximately 8 years after Pentecost. Why the delay? After Peter saw the power of the Holy Spirit being received by Gentiles, who never were under 'the Law', he returned back to Israel. Peter was 'contended with' by his fellow Jews for going to the Gentiles in the first place*. *-Acts 11 v 1-18

Why didn't Peter continue on to the rest of the world when he left the House of Cornelius? He saw that the Gentiles too were being accepted by God. Peter 'was not to be' the apostle of the Gentiles. This 'office' was given to the Apostle Paul*. *-Romans 11 v 13

1- The Spirit of the LORD God *is* upon me; because the LORD hath anointed me to preach good tidings unto the meek; he hath sent me to bind the brokenhearted, to proclaim liberty to the captives, and the opening of the prison to *them that are* bound;
2- To proclaim the acceptable year of the LORD, *and the day of vengeance of our God; to comfort all that mourn;
-Isaiah 61 v 1, 2

*"The day of vengeance of our God". This has yet to happen. The rest of the scripture has. God will soon be turning his focus of salvation towards the Gentiles without the Jew after his resurrection of which Israel (the non-saints) knew nothing of.

Resurrection significance to Israel is that Jesus would return with the Kingdom of Heaven and put down all their enemies forever. For the Gentiles, the belief that Jesus rose from the dead is everything. Gentiles and the world being in the favor of God over his covenant people? Unheard of in scripture before Paul.

From Genesis to Christ's earthly ministry the Bible has been all Jewish. Only the Jew had a knowledge of the 'Living God'. "I was told and led to believe that we become Jews when we believe the Apostle's Doctrine", says some of Christendom. Those of 'the Apostle's Doctrine' were under the Law.

The Apostle Peter quotes Joel Holy Spirit inspired. Peter is unaware that there is going to be an interruption in the scriptures he quotes. Jesus never told his disciples of the soon coming 'Age of Grace' and the Wrath of God being delayed for the 'filling of the Body of Christ'. The Prophetic Time-line of Israel is still being fulfilled early in the Book of Acts. Peter and all the true believers in Israel had only the 'prophesied vision' of the future as God gave them*. Paul's Gospel has yet to be revealed. *-Acts 3 v 21

14- But Pe'ter, standing up with the eleven, lifted up his voice, and said unto them, Ye men of Ju-de'a, and all *ye* that dwell at Je-ru'sa-lem, be this known unto you, and hearken to my words.

15- For these are not drunken, as ye suppose, seeing it is *but* the third hour of the day *(9 a.m.)*.

16- But this is that which was spoken by the prophet Jo'el.

17- And it shall come to pass in the last days, saith God, I will pour out of my Spirit upon all flesh: and your sons and your daughters shall prophesy, and your young men shall see visions, and your old men shall dream dreams:

18- And on my servants and on my handmaidens I will pour out in those days of my Spirit; and they shall prophesy:

19- *And I will shew wonders in heaven above, and signs in the earth beneath; blood, and fire, and vapour of smoke:

20- The sun shall be turned into darkness, and the moon into blood, **before that great and terrible day of the Lord come**:

21- And it shall come to pass, *that* whosever shall call on the name of the Lord shall be saved.

-Acts 2 v 14-21; -Joel 2 v 28-32

*This has yet to happen. Peter did not know that the fulfillment of Joel's words were not going to happen all at once, together. Jesus never told 'the Twelve' that the 'Earthly Kingdom of Heaven' was going to be postponed for thousands of years.

What would be the reasons for delaying the promised Kingdom to Israel? Israel collectively, as 'the whole', rejected their King and Messiah, the Lord Jesus Christ. God knew this would happen. Jesus himself told his disciples flat out that he was going to be beaten, scourged, mocked, crucified and murdered. Had not the meanings of what Jesus told them been hidden, the disciples I am sure would have interceded and caused some kind of a protest.

Peter did speak up 'that one time', but what was Jesus' reply*? After the rebuke, that was it. The many times that Jesus spoke those things of his coming crucifixion was 'divinely missed'. The disciples never fully understood. Had they perceived the meaning, they would have fled Israel with Jesus 'in tow'. Wouldn't they? *-Matthew 16 v 23, -Mark 8 v 33, -Luke 4 v 8

The Prophet Joel wrote by Holy Spirit inspiration:

28- And it shall come to pass afterward, *that* I will pour out of my spirit upon all flesh; and your sons and your daughters shall prophesy, your old men shall dream dreams, your young men shall see visions:

29- And also upon the servants and upon the handmaids in those days will I pour of my spirit.

30- *And I will shew wonders in the heavens and in the earth, blood, fire, and pillars of smoke.

31- The sun shall be turned into darkness, and the moon into blood, **before the great and the terrible day of the Lord come.**

32- And it shall come to pass, *that* whosoever shall call on the name of the Lord shall be delivered: for in mount Zi'on and in Je-ru'sa-lem shall be deliverance, as the Lord hath said, and in **the remnant** whom the Lord shall call.

-Joel 2 v 28-32

*These are all visions and prophecies spoken and written by the prophets concerning the 'Latter Days', the Wrath of God, and the Day of the Lord. All terrible and frightening the second coming of Jesus Christ. He will not be coming with love and mercy but death and destruction. He will fulfill Psalm 110. Jesus Christ will make all the enemies of Israel their footstool. Israel will be the Head of all the remaining nations and kingdoms+. +-Deuteronomy 28 v 13, -Jeremiah 30 v 11

27- Then answered Pe'ter and said unto them, Behold, we have forsaken all, and followed thee; what shall we have therefore? *(Peter is not speaking of salvation, he had that, but is speaking of reward.)*

28- And Je'sus said unto them, Verily I say unto you, That ye which have followed me *(presently)*, in the regeneration *(future)* when the Son of man <u>shall</u> sit in the throne of his glory *(future)*, ye also <u>shall</u> sit upon twelve thrones *(future)*, judging the twelve tribes of Is'ra-el *(future)*.

-Matthew 19 v 27, 28

Planet earth will be regenerated and made new again like the 'Garden of Eden' for one thousand years, and then a new heaven and a new earth for all eternity*. When the Tribulation ends with the 2nd coming of Christ, there will be survivors. Even after the intense bombing raids on Japan (these raids killed more Japanese than the two atom bombs did) and the bombs dropped on Hiroshima and Nagasaki, there were people that lived. Incredible, there always seems to be someone that lives. *-Revelation 20

No different after the Tribulation. There will be survivors that can "take hold of the skirt of him that is a Jew, saying, "We will go with you: for we have heard *that* God *is* with you"*. During 'the regeneration', the filth of sin and wickedness will be cleaned up and discarded. There will be nothing left with 'a sin nature' on the earth. It will be 'heaven on earth'. Planet earth will be 'regenerated and made new'. <u>The Kingdom of Heaven is an 'earthly kingdom'</u> that was promised to Israel by God. *-Zechariah 8 v 23

20- Thus saith the LORD of hosts; *It shall yet come to pass,* that there shall come people and the inhabitants of many cities;

21- And the inhabitants of one *city* shall go to another, saying, Let us go speedily to pray before the LORD, and to seek the LORD of hosts: I will go also.

22- Yea, many people and strong nations shall come to seek the LORD of hosts in Je-ru'sa-lem, and to pray before the LORD.

23- Thus saith the LORD of hosts; **In those days** *it shall come to pass*, that **ten men shall take hold out of all languages of the nations** *(speaking in tongues?)*, even take hold of the skirt of him that is a Jew, saying, We will go with you: for we have heard *that* God *is* with you.

-Zechariah 8 v 20-23

Daniel writes the following scriptures by Holy Spirit inspiration:

11- And from the time *that* the daily sacrifice shall be taken away, and the abomination that maketh desolate set up*, *there shall be* a thousand two hundred and ninety days *(three and a half years)*. *(*-Matthew 24 v 15)*

12- Blessed *is* he that waiteth, and cometh to the thousand three hundred and five and thirty days.

13- But go thou thy way till the end *be*: for thou shalt rest, and stand in thy lot at the end of days.

-Daniel 12 v 11-13

There are 45 days added after the completion of the tribulation (1335 - 1290 = 45). Are these the days needed to 'regenerate the earth' and to separate the 'Goats from the Sheep'? Is this the time when the Gospel of the Kingdom Saints inherit their kingdom and be resurrected+ from the dead by their order and lot*? *-Daniel 12 v 13; +-Isaiah 45 v 17; -John 6 v 39, 40, 44, 54; -John 11 v 24-26; -I John 5 v 11-13; -Luke 21 v 27, 28

There will be survivors but not all will be saints. There will be sinners and non-believers that will survive 'the Tribulation', but no 'unbeliever' will make it into the Kingdom of Heaven. The earth will completely be regenerated, even the population.

13- But he that shall endure unto the end shall be saved.

-Matthew 24 v 13

Living to the end of the 'wrath of God' and 'the Tribulation' is not how the sinner will receive 'his salvation'. The 'believer' physically will be saved and can now walk into the Kingdom of Heaven. The 'unbeliever' may live through the horrible Tribulation but there will be no 'unbelievers' in the Kingdom of Heaven. The 'goats' will be separated from the 'sheep'.

Jesus/God speaks of **those that will be taken:**

40- As therefore the tares are gathered and burned in the fire; <u>so shall it be in the end of this world.</u>

41- The Son of man shall send forth **his angels**, and they **shall gather out of his kingdom** all things that offend, and them which do iniquity;

42- And shall cast them into a furnace of fire: there shall be wailing and gnashing of teeth.

43- **Then** shall the righteous shine forth as the sun in the kingdom of their father. Who hath ears to hear, let him hear.

-Matthew 13 v 40-43

Jesus said:

36- But of that day and hour knoweth no *man*, no, not the angels of heaven, but my Father only.

37- But as the days of No'e *(Noah) were*, so shall also the coming of the Son of man be.

38- For as in the days that were before the flood they were eating and drinking, marrying and giving in marriage, until the day that No'e entered into the ark,

39- And knew not until the flood came, **and took them all away;** so shall also the coming of the Son of man be.

40- Then shall two be in the field; the **one shall be taken**, and the other left.

41- Two *women shall be* grinding at the mill; the **one shall be taken**, and the other left.

-Matthew 24 v 36-41

Jesus said:

34- I tell you, in that night there shall be two *men* in one bed, the **one shall be taken**, and the other shall be left.

35- Two *women* shall be grinding together; the **one shall be taken**, and the other left.

36- Two *men* shall be in the field; the **one shall be taken**, and the other left.

-Luke 17 v 34-36

49- Behold, this was the iniquity of thy sister Sod'om, pride, fullness of bread, and abundance of idleness was in her and in her daughter's, neither did she strengthen the hand of the poor and needy.

50- And they were haughty, and committed abomination before me: **therefore I took them away** as I saw *good*.

-Ezekiel 16 v 49, 50

Read Matthew 24 v 36. The wording is that 'the flood' took them away. These that were taken, died. There are going to be those left alive on the earth who will be able to walk into the Earthly Heavenly Kingdom. The non-believer will be taken out of the land of the living. There will be no unbelievers left on the planet earth.

Those that are 'taken' are not being 'caught up' to God. Only the Apostle Paul speaks of the 'Body of Christ' being 'caught up' to meet the Lord in the air. The Jews and Israel never were given this revelation. For them, Jesus Christ is coming to the earth. The Jews are God's 'earthly people', the Body of Christ is God's 'heavenly people'. The promises to Israel have been 'earthly', the promises made to 'the true church' are 'heavenly'.

31- When the Son of man shall come in his glory, and all the holy angels with him, then shall he sit upon the throne of his glory.

32- And before him shall be gathered all nations: and he shall separate them one from another, as a shepherd divideth *his* sheep from the goats:

33- And he shall set the sheep on his right hand, but the goats on the left.

34- Then shall the King say unto them on his right hand, Come, ye blessed of my Father, inherit the kingdom prepared for you from the foundation of the world:

35- For I was an hungred, and ye gave me meat: I was thirsty, and ye gave me drink: I was a stranger, and ye took me in:

36- Naked, and ye clothed me: I was sick, and ye visited me: I was in prison, and ye came unto me.

37- Then shall the righteous answer him, saying, Lord, when saw we thee an hungred, and fed *thee*? or thirsty, and gave *thee* drink?

38- When saw we thee a stranger, and took *thee* in? or naked, and clothed *thee*?

39- Or when saw we thee sick, or in prison, and came unto thee?

40- And the King shall answer and say unto them, Verily I say unto you, Inasmuch as ye have done it unto one of the least of these my brethren*, ye have done *it* unto me. *(*-Jesus is identifying 'my brethren' that were hungry,* *thirsty, stranger, naked, sick, in prison at this time. The 144,000 preaching the 'Gospel of the Kingdom'?)*

41- Then shall he say also unto them on the left hand, Depart from me, ye cursed, into everlasting fire, prepared for the devil and his angels:

42- For I was an hungred, and ye gave me no meat: I was thirsty, and ye gave me no drink:

43- I was a stranger, and ye took me not in: naked, and ye clothed me not: sick, and in prison, and ye visited me not.

44- Then shall they also answer him, saying, Lord, when saw we thee an hungred, or athirst, or a stranger, or naked, or sick, or in prison, and did not minister unto thee?

45- Then shall he answer them, saying, Verily I say unto you, Inasmuch as ye did *it* not to one of the least of these, ye did *it* not to me.

46- And these shall go away into everlasting punishment: but the righteous into life eternal.

-Matthew 25 v 31-46; -Luke 14 v 13, 14; -Acts 24 v 15

After the tribulation, after the 1,000 year reign of the Kingdom of Heaven, there will be a final insurrection against Jesus Christ. But God will waste no time in dealing with this final rebellion:

1- And I saw an angel come down from heaven, having the key of the bottomless pit and a great chain in his hand.

2- And he laid hold on the dragon, that old serpent, which is the Dev'il, and Sa'tan, and bound him a thousand years.

3- And cast him into the bottomless pit, and shut him up, and set a seal upon him, that he should deceive the nations no more, **till the thousand years should be fulfilled**: and after that he must be loosed a little season.

4- And I saw thrones, and they sat upon them, and judgment was given unto them: and I *saw* the souls of them that were beheaded for the witness of Je'sus, and for the word of God, and which had not worshipped the beast, neither his image, neither had received *his* mark upon their foreheads, or in their hands; and they lived and reigned with Christ a thousand years.

5- But the rest of the dead lived not again **until the thousand years were finished**. This is the first resurrection *(v4)*.

-Revelation 20 v 1-5

Those that have died without the Spirit of the Living God imputed to them will also receive eternal life+. The Soul (mind, will and emotion) are 'of Gods image'* and are eternal. This is the invisible image of God. It will never die whether in the body or out of the body. But this resurrected state is of eternal damnation. There is no hope or prayers that will effect the unbelievers salvation once a person has died in unbelief. The ultimate unpardonable sin = unbelief. *-Genesis 1 v 26, 27; +-Luke 14 v 14, -Acts 24 v 15

6- Blessed and holy *is* he that hath part in the first resurrection: on such **the second death** hath no power, but **they shall be priests of God and Christ**, and **shall reign with him a thousand years.**
7- **And when the thousand years are expired, Sa'tan shall be loosed out of his prison.**
8- And shall go out to deceive the nations which are in the four quarters of the earth, Gog and Ma'gog, to gather them together to battle: the number of whom *is* as the sand of the sea.
9- And they went up on the breadeth of the earth, and compassed the camp of the saints about, and the beloved city: **and fire came down from God out of heaven, and devoured them.**
-Revelation 20 v 6-9

During the 1,000 year Kingdom of Heaven Earthly Reign there will be no sickness nor death. 'Heaven on earth'. Those that received this promise will live full fruitful lives. There will be no more pain in child bearing. There will be a population explosion. How could there not be. A perfect world, 'heaven'.

God is going to test this new generation of Jews. Like those that died in the wilderness following Moses, 'unbelief' will again show its Satan inspired deception. These will be tried.

Israel for the most part rejected the earthly ministry of Jesus Christ and don't believe and read the new Testament. Do they have the New Testament scriptures written by John concerning these 'latter days'? If they did, they would know what is coming. In the all knowing and foreknowledge of God, many "as the sand of the sea*" will be cast into the lake of fire. These obviously had not read the 'New Testament warnings'. *-Revelation 20 v 8

10- And the devil that deceived them was cast into the lake of fire and brimstone, where the beast and the false prophet *are,* and shall be tormented day and night for ever and ever.

11- And I saw a great white throne, and him that sat on it, from whose face the earth and the heaven fled away; and there was found no place for them.

12- And I saw the dead, small and great, stand before God; and the books were opened: and another book was opened, which is *the book* of life: and the dead were judged out of those things which were written in the books, according to their works.

13- And the sea gave up the dead which were in it; and death and hell delivered up the dead which were in them: and they were judged every man according to his works.

14- **And death and hell were cast into the lake of fire. This is the second death.**

15- And whosoever was not found written in the book of life was cast into the lake of fire.

-Revelation 20 v 10-15, -Luke 14 v 14, -Acts 24 v 15

During the tribulation, the 'Kingdom Gospel' will be the hope and salvation again for the world. The King is coming! The Kingdom of Heaven is at hand! The Jewish Epistles of James, Peter, John, Jude and Revelation will be able to give comfort and promise again.

But Israel and those that don't believe in Jesus Christ don't read the New Testament. Most will be clueless to the signs and warnings given. The Body of Christ will not be here. Law and Grace does not mix.

The Anti-Christ will give Israel what they have always wanted, PEACE! At least for 3.5 years. Unfortunately, what Israel has wanted (having denied Jesus their Christ/King/Messiah) will come for them as the Anti-Christ. What they describe and want is the Anti-Christ, not the Lord Jesus Christ. These have renounced Jesus/God their Messiah and still do.

Jesus said:

14- And this **gospel of the kingdom** shall be preached in all the world for a witness unto all nations; and then shall the end come.

15- When ye therefore shall see the abomination of desolation, spoken of by Dan'iel the prophet, stand in the holy place, (whoso readeth, let him understand:)

16- Then let them which be in Ju-de'a flee into the mountains:

17- Let him which is on the housetop not come down to take anything out of his house:

18- Neither let him which is in the field return back to take his clothes.

19- And woe unto them that are with child, and to them that give suck in those days!

20- But pray ye that your flight be not in winter, <u>neither on the sabbath day</u>: *(*Jews again will be under 'the Law'?)*

21- For then shall be great tribulation, such as was not since the beginning of the world to this time, no, nor ever shall be.

22- Except those days should be shortened *(end on time),* there should no flesh be saved: but for the elect's sake those days shall be shortened.
-Matthew 24 v 14-22

29- Immediately after the tribulation of those days shall the sun be darkened, and the moon shall not give her light, and the stars shall fall from heaven, and the powers of the heavens shall be shaken:

30- And then shall appear the sign of the Son of man in heaven: and then shall all the tribes of the earth mourn, and they shall see the Son of man coming in the clouds of heaven with power and great glory.

31- And he shall send his angels with a great sound of a trumpet, and they shall gather together his elect *(the 144,000*?)* from the four winds, from one end of heaven to the other. (*-Revelation 7 v 1-8)
-Matthew 24 v 29-31

10- Then said he *(Jesus)* unto them, Nation shall rise against nation, and kingdom against kingdom:

11- And great earthquakes shall be in divers places, and famines, and pestilences; and fearful sights and great signs shall there be from heaven.
-Luke 21 v 10, 11

20- And when ye shall see Je-ru'sa-lem compassed with armies, then know that the desolation thereof is nigh.

21- Then let them which are in Ju-de'a flee to the mountains; and let them which are in the midst of it depart out; and let not them that are in the countries enter thereinto.

22- For these be **the days of vengence, that all things which are written may be fulfilled**.

23- But woe unto them that are with child and to them that give suck in those days! for there shall be great distress in the land, and wrath upon this people.

24- And **they shall fall** by the edge of the sword, and **shall be led away captive into all nations**; and **Je-ru'sa-lem shall be trodden down of the Gen'tiles** *(70 A.D.)*, <u>**until the times of the Gen'tiles be fulfilled**</u>.

-Luke 21 v 20-24

Make note concerning 'the times of the Gentiles' vs. the 'fullness of the Gentiles'. Simultaneously, two things are happening in bringing about the end of this world. The 'times of the Gentiles' is the filling up of 'the cup of iniquity'. As man progresses to the end times, so will their sins and wickedness. They will wax worse and worse. The earths population will be at it's max.

The 'fullness of the Gentiles' concerns 'the true church' and the 'Body of Christ'. While the earth progresses in its' path of unbelief, the 'Body of Christ' will also be growing. When God see's that the time has come and the church is full, we are out of here. The Tribulation will start sometime after. Law and Grace does not mix.

Here in the Gospel of Luke, Jesus combines the destruction by the Roman Empire in 70 A.D. and the end-time tribulation. Jesus Christ was still keeping things secret. Use the God given common sense to see the things of scripture that has happened and scripture that has yet to be fulfilled. Some in Christendom believe that the Tribulation happened and was fulfilled in 70 A.D.

25- And there shall be signs in the sun, and in the moon, and in the stars; and upon the earth distress of nations, with perplexity; the sea and the waves roaring *(mankind in derision)*;

26- Men's hearts failing them for fear, and for looking after those things which are coming on the earth: for **the powers of heaven shall be shaken**.

27- And then shall they see the Son of man coming in a cloud with power and great glory.

28- And when these things begin to come to pass, then look up, and lift up your heads; for **your redemption draweth nigh**.

-Luke 21 v 25-28

31- So likewise ye, when ye see these things come to pass, know ye that the kingdom of God is nigh at hand.

32- Verily, I say unto you, This generation *(the children of Israel)* shall not pass away, till all be fulfilled.

33- Heaven and earth shall pass away: but my words shall not pass away.

34- And take heed to yourselves, lest at any time your hearts be overcharged with surfeiting, and drunkenness, and cares of this life, and so that day come upon you unawares.

35- <u>For as a snare shall it come on all them that dwell on the face of the whole earth.</u>

36- Watch ye therefore, and pray always, that ye may be accounted worthy to escape all things that shall come to pass, and to stand before the Son of man.

-Luke 21 v 31-36

The Kingdom of Heaven was soon coming... the Elect thought

1- The Revelation of Je'sus Christ, which God gave unto him, **to show unto his servants things which must shortly come to pass**; and he sent and signified *it* by his angel unto his servant John:

2- Who bare record of the word of God, and of the testimony of Je'sus Christ, and of all things that he saw.

-Revelation 1 v 1, 2

7- Be patient therefore, brethren, unto the coming of the Lord. Behold, the husbandman waiteth for the precious fruit of the earth, and hath long patience for it, until he receive the early and latter rain.

8- Be ye also patient; establish your hearts: **the coming of the Lord draweth nigh**.

-James 5 v 7, 8

7- But **the end of all things is at hand**: be ye therefore sober, and watch unto prayer.

-I Peter 4 v 7

18- Little children, **it is the last time**: and as ye have heard that antichrist shall come, even now are there many antichrist; whereby **we know that it is the last time**.

-I John 2 v 18

This same thought is in much of Christendom

Believe in God or Believe God?:

2- That ye may be mindful of the words which were spoken before by the holy prophets, and of the commandment of us the apostles of the Lord and Savior:

3- Knowing this first, that there shall come in the last days scoffers, walking after their own lusts,

4- And saying, Where is the promise of his coming? For since the fathers fell asleep *(died)*, all things continue as *they were* from the beginning of the creation.

5- **For this they willingly are ignorant of**, that by the word of God the heavens were of old, and the earth standing out of the water and in the water:

6- Whereby the world that then was, being overflowed with water, perished:

7- But the heavens and the earth, which are now, by the same word are **kept in store, reserved unto fire against the day of judgment and perdition of ungodly men**.

-II Peter 3 v 2-7

11- In the six hundredth year of No-ah's life, in the second month, the seventeenth day of the month, **the same day were all the fountains of the great deep broken up***, and the windows of heaven were opened.

-Genesis 7 v 11; -Genesis 8 v 2

*Fountains of the great deep also would include volcanoes. Not only did it rain for 40 days and nights but a world wide eruption of volcanic destruction. There are artifacts and fossils found in the strangest places.

On the top of mountains discoveries of fish bones have been made from the sea world wide. Man wants to say that the ice glaciers carved the earth bringing these bones with them. Glaciers move down by gravity not up.

Under the Ark of Noah as they floated in safety, the world below was being 'mixed up' by earthquakes and volcanic eruptions. There is found a layer of volcanic ash worldwide at the same depths from this time. A fact that unbelieving geologist conveniently ignore.

These same geologists claim that the Grand Canyon was formed by glaciers. The rivers by now should have made the canyon deeper they claim and still hold to it. It is no deeper than when it was first discovered.

Geologist show charts of 'their studies' claiming that the deeper you dig in the earth the older fossils are found buried farther down. But the truth be known, fossils are all mixed together from the oldest to the newest. Dinosaur bones have been found on the surface of the earth.

Evolutionist want to say that 'a nothing' progressed to 'a something' over millions of years of time. There is no fossil evidence of a creature changing through 'a progression' into what it is today. Fossils found represent the original created being as God made them in 'the beginning'.

'Global Warmers' can't lie their way out of this one:
22- While the earth remaineth, seedtime and harvest, and cold and heat, and summer and winter, and day and night shall not cease.
-Genesis 8 v 22

The day of the Lord

the wrath of God

the Lord's day

the day of God

the slain of the LORD

that day, those days

the coming of the LORD

the day of his wrath

the day of the LORD of hosts

a destruction from the Almighty

the wrath of the LORD of hosts

the day of his fierce anger

the day of the LORD's vengeance

the day of the LORD's anger

the wrath of the LORD
the terrible day of the LORD come
the day of the LORD's sacrifice
the great and dreadful day of the LORD

8- Be sober, be vigilant; because your adversary the devil, as a roaring lion, walketh about, seeking whom he may devour:

-I Peter 5 v 8

With a lion you know your in trouble:

13- For such *are* false apostles, deceitful workers, transforming themselves into the apostles of Christ.

14- And no marvel; for Sa'tan himself is transformed into an angel of light.

-II Corinthians 11 v 13, 14

1- The LORD said unto my Lord, Sit thou at my right hand, **until** I make thine enemies thy footstool.

2- The LORD shall send the rod of thy strength out of Zi'on: rule thou in the midst of thine enemies.

3- Thy people *shall be* willing in the day of thy power, in the beauties of holiness from the womb of the morning: thou hast the dew of thy youth.

4- The LORD hath sworn, and will not repent, Thou *art* a priest for ever after the order of Mel-chiz'e-dek.

5- The Lord at thy right hand shall strike through kings **in the day of his wrath**.

6- He shall judge among the heathen, he shall fill *the places* with the dead bodies; he shall wound the heads over many countries.

7- He shall drink of the brook in the way: therefore shall he lift up his head.

-Psalm 110

8- But, beloved, be not ignorant of this one thing, that one day *is* with the Lord as a thousand years, and a thousand years as one day.

9- The Lord is not slack concerning his promise, as some men count slackness; but is <u>longsuffering to us-word, not willing that any should perish</u>, but that all should come to repentance.

10- But **the day of the Lord** will come as a thief in the night; in which the heavens shall pass away with a great noise, and the elements shall melt with fervent heat, the earth also and the works that are therein shall be burned up.
11- *Seeing* then *that* all these things shall be dissolved, what manner *of persons* ought ye to be in *all* holy conversation and godliness,
12- Looking for and hastening unto **the coming of the day of God**, wherein the heavens being on fire shall be dissolved, and the elements shall melt with fervent heat?
13- Nevertheless **we, according to his promise, look for new heavens and a new earth**, wherein dwelleth righteousness.
-II Peter 3 v 8-13

30- Therefore prophesy thou against them all these words, and say unto them, **The LORD shall roar from on high**, and utter his voice from his holy habitation; he shall mightily roar upon his habitation; he shall give a shout, and they that tread *the grapes*, against all the inhabitants of the earth.
31- A noise shall come *even* to the ends of the earth; for the LORD hath a controversy with the nations, he will plead with all flesh; he will give them *that are* wicked to the sword, saith the LORD.
32- Thus saith the LORD of hosts, Behold, evil shall go forth from nation to nation, and a great whirlwind *(WMD's?)* shall be raised up from the coast of the earth.
33- And **the slain of the LORD shall be at that day from *one* end of the earth even unto the *other* end of the earth**: they shall not be lamented, neither gathered, nor buried; they shall be dung upon the ground.
34- Howl, ye shepherds, and cry; and wallow yourselves *in the ashes*, ye principle of the flock: for the days of your slaughter and of your dispersions are accomplished; and ye shall fall like a pleasant vessel.
35- And the shepherds shall have no way to flee, nor the principal of the flock to escape.
36- A voice of the cry of the shepherds, and an howling of the principal of the flock, *shall be heard*: for the LORD hath spoiled their pasture.
37- And the peaceable habitations are cut down because of **the fierce anger of the LORD**.
38- He hath forsaken his covert, as the lion: for their land is desolate because of the fierceness of the oppressor, and because of his fierce anger.
-Jeremiah 25 v 30-38

All of the Old Testament scriptures concerning the Jews dealt with the 'top line of prophecy'. The 'Body of Christ' and the Gentiles were never included with their 'Heavenly Earthly Kingdom'. Israel's prophecies never foretold of a 2,000 year 'Grace Age'. But it has happened.

37- O Je-ru'sa-lem, Je-ru'sa-lem, *thou* that killest the prophets, and stonest them which are sent unto thee, how often would I have gathered thy children together, even as a hen gathereth her chickens under *her* wings, and ye would not!
38- Behold, your house is left unto you desolate.
39- For I say unto you, Ye shall not see me henceforth, till ye shall say, Blessed *is* he that cometh in the name of the Lord.
-Matthew 23 v 37-39

Paul writes briefly of the 'Last Days'. When he says 'they and them' he is not speaking of the Body of Christ, but those that missed being 'caught up to God':
3- For when they shall say Peace and safety; then sudden destruction cometh upon them, as travail upon a woman with child; and they shall not escape.
4- But ye, brethren, are not in darkness, that **that day** should overtake you as a thief.
-I Thessalonians 5 v 3, 4

James writes in anticipation of the Lord coming:
3- Your gold and silver is cankered; and the rust of them shall be a witness against you, and shall eat your flesh as it were fire. Ye have heaped treasure together for **the last days**.
4- Behold, the hire of the labourers who have reaped down your fields, which is of you kept back by fraud, crieth: and the cries of them which have reaped are entered into the ears of the Lord of Sab'a'oth.
5- Ye have lived in pleasure in the earth, and been wanton; ye have nourished your hearts, as in a day of slaughter.
6- Ye have condemned *and* killed the just; *and* he doeth not resist you.
7- Be patient therefore, brethren, unto **the coming of the Lord**. Behold, the husbandman waiteth for the precious fruit of the earth, and hath long patience for it, until he receive the early and latter rain.

8- Be ye also patient; stablish your hearts: **for the coming of the Lord draweth nigh.**

-James 5 v 3-8

Peter encourages his brethren to stay strong during the tribulation ('tried with fire'):

7- That the trial of your faith, being much more precious than of gold that perisheth, though it be tried with fire, might be found unto praise and honour and glory at **the appearing of Je'sus Christ**.

-I Peter 1 v 7

1- The word that came to Jer-e-mi'ah from the LORD, saying,

2- Thus speaketh <u>the LORD God of Is'ra-el</u>, saying, Write thee all the words that I have spoken unto thee in a book.

3- For, lo, the days come, saith the LORD, that I will bring again the captivity of my people Is'ra-el and Ju'dah, saith the LORD: and I will cause them to return to the land that I gave to their fathers, and they shall possess it.

4- And these *are* the words that the LORD spake concerning Is'ra-el and concerning Ju'dah.

5- For thus saith the LORD; We have heard a voice of trembling, of fear, and not of peace.

6- Ask ye now, and see whether a man doth travail with child? wherefore do I see every man with his hands on his loins, as a woman in travail, and all faces are turned into paleness?

7- Alas! **For that day *is* great, so that none is like it: it *is* even the time of Ja'cob's trouble**; but he shall be saved out of it.

-Jeremiah 30 v 1-7

Not all of Israel will be saved:

8- **And it shall come to pass, *that* in all the land, saith the LORD, two parts therein shall be cut off *and* die; but the third shall be left therein.**

9- And **I will bring the third part through the fire**, and will refine them as silver is refined, and will try them as gold is tried: they shall call on my name, and I will hear them: I will say, it *is* my people: and they shall say, the LORD *is* my God.

-Zechariah 13 v 8, 9

End time prophecy has become more understandable by the mid 1800's. But before then, end time prophecy was not a perceived reality. What's a smart phone? It was hard to be understood. Technology has now made the 'Last and Latter Day' prophecies more real and believable.

Daniel writes Holy Spirit inspired:

1- And at that time shall Mi'chael stand up, the great prince which standeth for the children of <u>thy people</u>: and there shall be a time of trouble, such as never was since there was a nation *even* to that same time: and at that time <u>thy people</u> shall be delivered, every one that shall be found written in the book. *(Thy people? What happened to 'my people'?)*

2- And many of them that sleep in the dust of the earth shall awake, some to everlasting life, and some to shame *and* everlasting contempt.

3- And they that be wise shall shine as the brightness of the firmament; and they that turn many to righteousness as the stars for ever and ever.

4- But thou, O Dan'iel, shut up the words, and seal the book, even to the time of the end: many shall run to and fro, and knowledge* shall be increased. *(*Scriptural knowledge as well.)*

5- Then I Dan'iel looked, and, behold, there stood other two, the one on this side of the bank of the river, and the other on that side of the bank of the river.

6- And *one* said to the man clothed in linen, which *was* upon the waters of the river, How long *shall it be* to the end of these wonders?

7- And I heard the man clothed in linen, which *was* upon the waters of the river, when he held up his right hand and his left hand unto heaven, and sware by him that liveth for ever that *it shall be* for a time, times, and a half *(3.5 years)*; and when he shall have accomplished to scatter the power of the holy people, all these *things* shall be finished.

8- And I heard, but I understood not: then said I, O my Lord, what *shall be* the end of these *things?*

9- And he said, Go thy way, Dan'iel: for the words *are* closed up and sealed till the time of the end.

10- Many shall be purified, and made white, and tried; but the wicked shall do wickedly: and none of the wicked shall understand; but the wise shall understand.

11- And from the time that the daily sacrifice shall be taken away, and the abomination that maketh desolate set up, there shall be a thousand two hundred and ninety days *(3.5 years)*.

12- Blessed *is* he that waiteth, and cometh to the thousand three hundred and five and thirty days.
13- But go thou thy way till the end *be*: **for thou shalt rest, and stand in thy lot at the end of days**.
-Daniel 12

The 7 year tribulation can be studied in three parts. The beginning events, the middle when the anti-christ turns on Israel, the end. It is referred to by 3.5 years and 3.5 years, or other time measurements like the number of days. Prophecy for Israel is often times in a 'time-frame'. When the anti-christ appears, rest assured, there is 7 years left.

Anti-christ does not mean that this man is against Christ only. He will be a false-christ. People will worship this man. He will bring to Israel what they always have been praying for, PEACE. At least for 3.5 years.

Jesus said:
15- When ye therefore shall see the abomination of desolation, spoken of by Dan'iel the prophet, stand in the holy place, (whoso readeth, let him understand:)
16- Then let them which be in Ju-de'a flee into the mountains:
17- Let him which is on the housetop not come down to take any thing out of his house:
18- Neither let him which is in the field return back to take his clothes.
19- And woe unto them that are with child, and to them that give suck in those days!
20- But pray ye that your flight be not in the winter, neither on the **sabbath day**:
21- **For then shall be great tribulation, such as was not since the beginning of the world to this time, no, nor ever shall be.**
-Matthew 24 v 15-21

Take a special note and understand that the prophets at times were speaking of 'the coming destruction' of Jerusalem in 606 B.C. by Nebuchadnezzar, 'the overthrow' by the Medes and Persians, 'the destruction' by Rome in 70 A.D., 'the last days' and 'the latter days' and more. They wrote what God wanted them to write. So when you read prophecy, what time frame is it concerning? Like Daniel, he would write of the very near future then jump ahead to 'the end times'. **There was no understanding of a 2,000 year Grace Age and the Body of Christ.**

1- And Je'sus went out, and <u>departed from the temple*</u>: and his disciples came to *him* for to shew him the buildings of the temple. *(*The Lord Jesus Christ died in the flesh a 'law keeper'.)*
2- And Je'sus said unto them, See ye not all these things? verily I say unto you, There shall not be left here one stone upon another, that shall not be thrown down *(70 A.D.).*
3- And as he sat upon the mount of Ol'ives, the disciples came unto him privately, saying, Tell us, when shall these things be? and what *shall be* <u>the sign of thy coming*</u>, <u>and of the end of the world?</u> *(*Thy coming? They knew he would be leaving and then returning with the Kingdom. These believers understood a time of tribulation was coming.)*
4- And Je'sus answered and said unto them, Take heed that no man deceive you.
5- For many shall come in my name, saying, I am Christ; and shall deceive many.
6- And ye shall hear of wars and rumors of wars: see that ye be not troubled: for all *these things* must come to pass, but the end is not yet.
7- For nation shall rise against nation, and kingdom against kingdom*: and there shall be famines, and pestilences, and earthquakes, in divers places. *(*70 A.D. had only one nation and kingdom that destroyed Jerusalem, not many.)*
8- All these things **are** the beginning of sorrows.
-Matthew 24 v 1-8

1- The fool hath said in his heart, *There is** no God. Corrupt are they, and have done abominable iniquity: *there is* none that doeth good. *(*-read without 'There is')*
2- God looked down from heaven upon the children of men, to see if there were *any* that did understand, that did seek God.
3- Every one of them is gone back: they are altogether become filthy; *there is* none that doeth good, no, not one.
4- Have the workers of iniquity no knowledge? who eat up my people *as* they eat bread: they have not called upon God.
5- There were they in great fear, *where* no fear was: for God hath scattered the bones of him that encampeth *against* thee: thou hast put *them* to shame, because God hath despised them.

6- Oh that the salvation of Is'ra-el *were come* out of Zion! When God bringeth back the captivity of his people, Ja'cob shall rejoice, *and* Is'ra-el shall be glad.
–Psalm 53 v 1-6

8- The beast that thou sawest was, and is not; and shall ascend out of the bottomless pit, and go into perdition: and they that dwell on the earth shall wonder, whose **names were not written in the book of life from the foundation of the world**, when they behold the beast that was, and is not, and yet is.
-Revelation 17 v 8

19- And I saw the beast, and the kings of the earth, and their armies, gathered together to make war against him that sat on the horse, and against his army.
20- And the beast was taken, and with him the false prophet that wrought miracles before him, with which he deceived them that had received the mark of the beast, and them that worshiped his image. These both were cast alive into a lake of fire burning with brimstone.
-Revelation 19 v 19, 20

1- And I saw an angel come down from heaven, having the key of the bottomless pit and a great chain in his hand.
2- **And he laid hold on the dragon, that old serpent, which is the Dev'il, and Sa'tan, and bound him a thousand years,**
3 - And cast him into the bottomless pit, and shut him up, and set a seal upon him, that he should deceive the nations no more, till **the thousand years should be fulfilled: and after that he must be loosed a little season.**
4- And I saw thrones, and they sat upon them, and judgment was given unto them: and I *saw* the souls of them that were beheaded for the witness of Je'sus, and for the word of God, and which had not worshiped the beast, neither his image, neither had received *his* mark upon their foreheads, or in their hands; **and they lived and reigned with Christ a thousand years.**
5- **But the rest of the dead lived not again until the thousand years were finished.** This *is* the first resurrection *(verse 4).*
6- Blessed and holy *is* he that hath part in the first resurrection: on such **the second death** hath no power, but **they shall be priests of God and of Christ,** and they shall reign with him a thousand years.

7- And when the thousand years are expired, Sa'tan shall be loosed out of his prison,

8- And shall go out to deceive the nations which are in the four quarters of the earth, Gog and Ma'gog, to gather them together to battle: the number of whom is as the sand of the sea.

9- And they went up on the breadth of the earth, and compassed the camp of the saints about, and the beloved city: and fire came down from God out of heaven, and devoured them.

10- And the devil that deceived them was cast into the lake of fire and brimstone, where the beast and the false prophet *are*, **and shall be tormented day and night for ever and ever.**

-Revelation 20 v 1-10

6- And the angels which kept not their first estate, but left their own habitation, he hath reserved in everlasting chains under darkness **until the judgement of the great day.**

-Jude v 6

1- The word that came to Jer-e-mi'ah from the LORD, saying,

2- Thus speaketh the LORD God of Is'ra-el, saying, Write thee all the words that I have spoken unto thee in a book.

3- For, lo, the days come, saith the LORD, that I will bring again the captivity of my people Is'ra-el and Ju'dah, saith the LORD: and I will cause them to return to the land that I gave to their fathers, and they shall possess it *(1948?)*.

4- And these *are* the words that the LORD spake concerning Is'ra-el and concerning Ju'dah.

5- For thus saith the LORD; We have heard a voice of trembling, of fear, and not of peace.

6- Ask ye now, and see whether a man doth travail with child? Wherefore do I see every man with his hands on his loins, as a woman in travail, and all faces are turned into paleness?

7- Alas! For that day is great, so that none is like it: it *is* even the time of Ja'cob's trouble; but he shall be saved out of it.

-Jeremiah 30 v 1-7

1- But there were false prophets also among the people, even as there shall be false teachers among you, who privily shall bring in damnable heresies, even denying the Lord that bought them, and bring upon themselves swift destruction.

2- And many shall follow their pernicious ways; by reason of whom the way of truth shall be evil spoken of.

3- And through covetousness shall they with feigned words make merchandise of you: whose judgment now of a long time lingereth not, and their damnation slumbereth not.

4- For if God spared not the angels that sinned, but cast *them* down to hell, and delivered *them* into chains of darkness, to be reserved unto judgment;

5- And spared not the old world, but saved No'ah the eighth *person*, a preacher of righteousness, bringing in the flood upon the world of the ungodly;

6- And turning the cities of Sod'om and Go-mor'rha into ashes condemned *them* with an overthrow, making *them* an ensample onto those that after should live ungodly;

7- And delivered just Lot, vexed with the filthy conversation of the wicked:

8- (For that righteous man dwelling among them, in seeing and hearing, vexed *his* righteous soul from day to day with *their* unlawful deeds;)

9- The Lord knoweth how to deliver the godly out of temptations, and to reserve the unjust unto the day of judgment to be punished:

-II Peter 2 v 1-9

Did this happen between Genesis 1 v 1 and v 2?:

7- And there was war in heaven: Mi'chael and his angels fought against the dragon; and the dragon fought and his angels,

8- And prevailed not; neither was their place found any more in heaven.

9- And the great dragon was cast out, that old serpent, called the Dev'il, and Sa'tan, which deceiveth the whole world: he was cast out into the earth, and his angels were cast out with him.

-Revelation 12 v 7-9

3- Then shall the Lord go forth, and fight against those nations, as when he fought in the day of battle.

4- And his feet shall stand in that day upon the mount of Ol'ives, which *is* before Je-ru'sa-lem on the east, and the mount of Ol'ives shall cleave in the midst thereof toward the east and toward the west, *and there shall be* a very great valley; and half of the mountain shall remove toward the north, and half of it toward the south.

.....

9- And the **LORD shall be king over all the earth**: in that day shall there be **one LORD**, and his name **one**.
-Zechariah 14 v 3, 4, 9

8- **In that day** shall the LORD defend the inhabitants of Je-ru'sa-lem; and he that is feeble among them and **that day** shall be as Da'vid; and the house of Da'vid *shall be* as God, as the angel of the LORD before them.

9- And it shall come to pass, *that* I will seek to destroy all the nations that come against Je-ru'sa-lem.

10- And I will pour upon the house of Da'vid, and upon the inhabitants of Je-ru'sa-lem the spirit of grace and of supplications: <u>and they shall look upon me whom they have pierced</u>, and they shall mourn for him, as one mourneth for *his* only *son*, and shall be in bitterness for him, as one that is in bitterness for *his* firstborn.

11- In that day shall there be a great mourning in Je-ru'sa-lem, as the mourning of Ha'dad-rim'mon in the valley of Me-gid'don.

12- And the land shall mourn, every family apart; the family of the house of Da'vid apart, and their wives apart; the family of the house of Na'than apart, and their wives apart;

13- The family of the house of Le'vi apart, and their wives apart; the family of Shim'e-i apart, and their wives apart;

14- All the families that remain, every family apart, and their wives apart.
-Zechariah 12 v 10-14

1- The Revelation of Je'sus Christ, which God gave unto him, to show unto his servants **things which must shortly come to pass**; and he sent and signified *it* by his angel unto his servant John:

2- Who bear record of the word of God, and of the testimony of Je'sus Christ, and of all things that he saw.

3- Blessed *is* he that readeth, and they that hear the words of **this prophecy**, and keep those things which are written therein: **for the time is at hand**.

4- John to the seven churches which are in A'sia: Grace *be* unto you, and peace, from him which is, and which was, and which is to come; and from the seven Spirits which are before his throne;

5- And from **Je'sus Christ**, *who is* the faithful witness, *and* **the first begotten of the dead**, and the prince of the kings of the earth. Unto him that loved us, and washed us from our sins in his own blood*, (*The Lord Jesus Christ is the final blood sacrifice.)*

6- And hath **made us kings and priests** unto God and his Father; to him *be* glory and dominion for ever and ever. Amen.
-Revelation 1 v 1-6

14- And E'noch also, the seventh from Ad'am, prophesied of these, saying, Behold, the Lord cometh with ten thousand of his saints,

15- To execute judgment upon all, and to convince all that are ungodly among them of all their ungodly deeds which they have ungodly committed, and of all their hard *speeches* which ungodly sinners have spoken against him.
-Jude v 14, 15

All prophecies in the Bible centered around the Jews and Israel. There is no mention of the 'Body of Christ' in the Old Testament. There is no detailed hint of God going to the Gentiles without the Jew. It was the Jew that was 'to bring in' the Gentiles. It was by them that they would bring the knowledge of their LORD God JEHOVAH to the world.

Saved by faith only, and not by faith plus righteous works, unheard of? The Jews 'under the Law' were instructed by God to have nothing to do with the Gentiles until the 'Earthly Kingdom of Heaven' is fulfilled. To this day it has not been fulfilled. There is no Kingdom in Israel with Jesus Christ ruling and reigning from the throne of David in Zion.

The Old Testament writes of the promises to Israel of an Earthly Heavenly Kingdom. Yet, after all 33 books of the Old Testament, that one verse in Luke 17 v 21, "... the kingdom of God is within you", has some in Christendom believing that those prophecies and promises specifically made only to the Jews of Israel has somehow spiritually manifested itself in the heart of the believer.

This Kingdom where the wolf shall lay down with the Lamb is now within the believer? Israel will be the head of the nations with Jesus ruling and reigning on David's throne from Mt. Zion is now inside a persons body? The plowman will overtake the reaper?

Silly. The Earthly Heavenly Kingdom was in their midst (within them). Jesus physically was there. So much of Christendom take the words by the English translators not seeing the Big Picture. Where Jesus Christ is, there is the Kingdom. It is not a Kingdom without a king. Jesus Christ is/was that prophesied King and Messiah.

For the record, not once did the Apostle of the Gentiles say the words 'Gospel of the Kingdom'. Paul was not preaching this Kingdom Gospel. Paul preached the Kingdom of God, but not the Jew's gospel*. Because of the fall of the Jew we are given grace by faith in the finished work of the cross. We have been translated into the Kingdom of God, which today is in heaven. Where Jesus Christ is there is the Kingdom. *See the Kingdom of God Diagram

Jesus Christ may indwell the believer but the promised kingdom of scripture is 'earthly' and was promised to Israel. Only the Jews were given the 'covenant promises'. The Gentiles were lost and without hope and God until after the resurrection*. There were exceptions of course, God is sovereign and always had a plan for the Gentile world. But the natural man led by their own conscience never sought out the God of all Creation. Except perhaps Cornelius the Roman Centurion though he probably observed and seen the Jews practice Judaism.

*-Ephesians 2 v 11-13

Right off the top of our Bibles (so to speak), take out all mention of the Apostle Paul in the Book of Acts and remove the Books of Romans through Hebrews. There is the break in the time-line. Paul, the chosen Apostle by God, reveals the Grace Age Church and the Body of Christ. This was never mentioned anywhere outside of Paul that this was going to happen. Gentiles going to God without the Jew was never in Israels prophecies. It was by the Jew that they would bring in the Gentiles after the Kingdom has come to earth for them.

With these sections (Books) figuratively removed from our Bible it is all the 'Gospel of the Kingdom' message. The Jewish epistles after the Book of Hebrews is written with the expectation that Jesus was returning back for Israel with the Kingdom. Jesus Christ had resurrected, was still alive, and would save Israel from their enemies and all that hate them.

What happened? Why wasn't the Kingdom established? Most of Christendom don't see that the 'Body of Christ' and what is called 'the

Age of Grace' has interrupted Israel's prophecies. They can't see what was written concerning 'the promise of an Earthly Kingdom of Heaven', and some have surmised that the Kingdom is inside the believer now. The Kingdom is the kingdom, is the kingdom, is the kingdom...

Some in Christendom teach that when a person believes in Jesus Christ they have become a Jew. What kind of Jew? Israel is as secular and 'worldly' as the rest of mankind. They are not in a position today ahead of anybody. There is 'no respect of person's' when it comes to God and salvation*. They are sinners like the rest of the world. *-II Chronicles 19 v 7; -Acts 10 v 34; -Romans 2 v 11; -Colossians 3 v 25

Jews too can be in the Body of Christ, of course. Anybody that believes the words (Holy Ghost inspired) that were revealed by revelation to Paul can be a member of the Body of Christ. The Jew becomes a Gentile saved by Grace, not the Gentile becomes a Jew by believing in Jesus Christ. No such words are in the Bible.

There is no difference between the Jew and Gentile concerning the Body of Christ. There is only one way to get there. Romans to Hebrews.

22- Even the righteousness of God *which* is by faith of Jesus Christ unto all and upon all them that believe: <u>for there is no difference</u>:
23- For all have sinned, and come short of the glory of God;
24- Being justified freely by his grace through the redemption that is in Christ Jesus:
-Romans 3 v 22-24

12- For <u>there is no difference between the Jew and the Greek</u>: for the same lord over all is rich unto all that call upon him.
13- Forwhosever shall call upon the name of the Lord shall be saved.
-Romans 10 v 12, 13

13- But now in Christ Jesus ye who sometimes were far off are made nigh by the blood of Christ.
14- **For he is our peace, who hath made both one, and hath broken down the middle wall of partition *between* us.**
15- Having abolished in his flesh the enmity, *even* the law of commandments *contained* in ordinances; for to make in himself of twain one new man, so making peace;

16- And that he might reconcile both unto God in one body by the cross, having slain the enmity thereby:

17- And came and preached peace to you which were afar off, and to them that are nigh.

-Ephesians 2 v 13-17

It was revealed to Paul only that 'faith in the Lord Jesus Christ's <u>resurrection</u> is salvation'. Faith in the 'finished work of the cross'. We preach Christ crucified*. 'The elect' never did. *I Corinthians 1 v 23

Nowhere in the Apostles Doctrine does it say that believing in the 'death, burial and resurrection of Jesus Christ' was salvation. Take all scriptures written by the Jews concerning the resurrection. Pray and look closely. Was the resurrection of Jesus equated to eternal salvation of the soul and spirit or a saving of them physically from their enemies?

The Gospel of the Kingdom Saints believed in their own resurrection in 'the last days' when they will inherit their Kingdom. Under the Kingdom Gospel they have been promised eternal life. They will receive an 'earthly resurrection'*. *-Isaiah 45 v 17; -John 6 v 39, 40, 44, 54; -John 11 v 24, 25; -I John 5 v 11-13; -Luke 21 v 27, 28; -Daniel 12 v 1

At the heart of the Gospel of Grace is to believe in Jesus Christ's resurrection. That he purposely died for you and me individually and rose again to eternal life. We have been promised the same by faithfully believing and following the Apostle of the Gentiles*.

*-Philippians 3 v 21

27- And he shall confirm the covenant with many for one week *(seven years)*: and in the **midst of the week** he shall cause the **sacrifice and the oblation to cease**, and for the overspreading of abominations he shall make it desolate, even unto the consummation, and that determined shall be poured upon the desolate.

-Daniel 9 v 27

3- Let no man deceive you by any means: for *that day shall not come*, except there come a falling away first, and that man of sin be revealed, the son of perdition;

4- Who opposeth and exalteth himself above all that is called God, or that is worshiped; so that he as God sitteth in the temple of God, showing himself that he is God.

-II Thessalonians 2 v 3, 4

11- The lofty looks of man shall be humbled, and the haughtiness of men shall be bowed down, and the LORD alone shall be exalted in that day.

12- For **the day of the LORD of hosts** *shall be* upon every *one that is* proud and lofty, and upon every *one that is* lifted up; and he shall be brought low:

.....

17- And the loftiness of man shall be bowed down, and the haughtiness of men shall be made low: and the LORD alone shall be exalted **in that day**.

18- And the idols he shall utterly abolish.

19- And they shall go into holes of the rocks, and into the caves of the earth, for fear of the LORD, and for the glory of his majesty, **when he ariseth to shake terribly the earth**.

20- **In that day** a man shall cast his idols of silver, and his idols of gold, which they made *each one* for himself to worship, to the moles and to the bats:

21- To go into the clefts of the rocks, and into the tops of the ragged rocks, for fear of the LORD, and for the glory of his majesty, **when he ariseth to shake terribly the earth**.

22- Cease ye from man, whose breath *is* in his nostrils: for wherein is he to be accounted of?

-Isaiah 2 v 11, 12, 17-22

4- The noise of a multitude in the mountains, like as of a great people; a tumultuous noise of the kingdoms of nations gathered together: **the LORD of hosts mustereth the host of the battle**.

5- They come from a far country, from the end of heaven, *even* the LORD, and the weapons of his indignation, to destroy the whole land.

6- Howl ye; for **the day of the LORD** is at hand; it shall come as **a destruction from the Almighty**.

7- Therefore shall all hands be faint, and every man's heart shall melt:

8- And they shall be afraid: pangs and sorrows shall take hold of them; they shall be in pain as a women that travaileth: they shall be amazed one at another; their faces *shall be as* flames.

9- Behold, **the day of the LORD cometh, cruel both with wrath and fierce anger, to lay the land desolate: and he shall destroy the sinners thereof out of it.**

10- For the stars of heaven and the constellations thereof shall not give their light: the sun shall be darkened in his going forth, and the moon shall not cause her light to shine

11- And **I will punish the world** for *their* evil, and the wicked for their iniquity; and I will cause the arrogancy of the proud to cease, and I will lay low the haughtiness of the terrible.

12- I will make a man more precious than fine gold; even a man than the golden wedge of O'phir.

13- Therefore I will shake the heavens, and the earth shall remove out of her place, in **the wrath of the LORD of hosts**, and in **the day of his fierce anger**.

14- And it shall be as the chased roe, and as a sheep that no man taketh up: they shall every man turn to his own people, and flee every one into his own land.

15- Every one that is found shall be thrust through; and every one that is joined *unto them* shall fall by the sword.

16- Their children also shall be dashed to pieces before their eyes; their houses shall be spoiled, and their wives ravished.
-Isaiah 13 v 4-16

1- Come near, ye nations, to hear; and hearken, ye people: let the earth hear, and all that is therein; the world, and all things that come forth of it.

2- For **the indignation of the LORD** *is* upon all nations, and *his* fury upon all their armies: he hath utterly destroyed them, he hath delivered them to the slaughter.

3- Their slain also shall be cast out, and their stink shall come up out of their carcases, and the mountains shall be melted with their blood.

4- And all the host of heaven shall be dissolved, and the heavens shall be rolled together as a scroll: and their host shall fall down, as the leaf falleth off from the vine, as a falling *fig* from the fig tree.

5- For my sword shall be bathed in heaven: behold, it shall come down upon I-du-me'a, and upon the people of my curse, to judgement.

6- The sword of the LORD is filled with blood, it is made fat with fatness, *and* with the blood of lambs and goats, with the fat of the kidneys of rams:

for **the LORD hath a sacrifice** in Boz'rah, **and a great slaughter** in the land of I-du-me-a.

7- And the unicorns *(wild ox)* shall come down with them, and the bullocks with the bulls; and their land shall be soaked with blood, and their dust made fat with fatness.

8- For *it is* **the day of the LORD's vengeance**, and the year of recompences for the controversy of Zi'on.

9- And the streams thereof shall be turned into pitch, and the dust thereof into brimstone, and the land thereof shall become burning pitch.

10- It shall not be quenched night or day; the smoke thereof shall go up for ever: from generation to generation it shall lie waste; none shall pass through it for ever and ever.

-Isaiah 34 v 1-10

10- For this *is* **the day of the LORD of hosts, a day of vengeance**, that he may avenge him of his adversaries: and the sword shall devour, and it shall be satiate and made drunk with their blood: for the LORD God of hosts hath a sacrifice in the north country by the river Eu-phra'tes.
-Jeremiah 46 v 10

22- Thou hast called as in a solemn day my terrors round about, so that in **the day of the LORD's anger** none escaped nor remained: those that I have swaddled and brought up hath mine enemy consumed.
-Lamentations 2 v 22

19- They shall cast their silver in the streets, and their gold shall be removed: their silver and their gold shall not be able to deliver them in the day of **the wrath of the LORD**: they shall not satisfy their souls, neither fill their bowels: because it is the stumblingblock of their iniquity.
-Ezekiel 7 v 19

Could the following scriptures also be speaking of the preachers and teachers that preach the 'elusive truth, the mixed/mashed gospel'?:

3- Thus saith the LORD God; Woe unto the foolish prophets, that follow their own spirit, and have seen nothing!

4- O Is'ra-el, thy prophets are like the foxes in the deserts.

5- Ye have not gone up into the gaps, neither made up the hedge for the house of Is'ra-el, to stand in the battle in **the day of the LORD**.

6- They have seen vanity and lying divination, saying, The LORD saith: and the LORD hath not sent them: and they have made *others* to hope that they would confirm the word.

7- Have ye not seen a vain vision, and have ye not spoken a lying divination, whereas ye say, The LORD saith *it*; albeit I have not spoken?

8- Therefore thus saith the LORD God; Because ye have spoken vanity, and seen lies, therefore, behold, I *am* against you, saith the LORD God.

9- And mine hand shall be upon the prophets that see vanity, and that divine lies: they shall not be in the assembly of my people, neither shall they be written in the writing of the house of Is'ra-el, neither shall they enter into the land of Is'ra-el; and ye shall know that I *am* the LORD God.

10- Because, even because they have seduced my people, saying, Peace; and *there was* no peace; and one built up a wall, and, lo, others daubed it with untempered *morter.*

11- Say unto them which daub *it* with untempered *morter*, that it shall fall: there shall be an overflowing shower, and ye, O great hailstones, shall fall; and a stormy wind shall rend *it.*

12- Lo, when the wall is fallen, shall it not be said unto you, Where *is* the daubing wherewith ye have daubed *it*?

13- Therefore, thus saith the LORD God; I will even rend *it* with a stormy wind in my fury; and there shall be an overflowing shower in mine anger, and great hailstones in *my* fury to consume *it.*

14- So will I break down the wall that ye have daubed with untempered *morter*, and bring it down to the ground, so that the foundation thereof shall be discovered, and it shall fall, and ye shall be consumed in the midst thereof: and ye shall know that I *am* the LORD.

15- Thus will I accomplish my wrath upon the wall, and upon them that have daubed it with untempered *morter*, and will say unto you, The wall *is* no *more*, neither they that daubed it;

16- To *wit*, the prophets of Is'ra-el which prophesy concerning Je-ru'sa-lem, and which see visions of peace for her, and there *is* no peace, saith the LORD God.

-Ezekiel 13 v 3-16

15- Alas for the day! for **the day of the LORD** *is* at hand, and as a destruction from the Almighty shall it come.

-Joel 1 v 15

1- Blow ye the trumpet in Zi'on, and sound an alarm in my holy mountain *(kingdom)*: let all the inhabitants of the land tremble: for **the day of the LORD** cometh, for *it is* nigh at hand;

.....

11- And the LORD shall utter his voice before his army: for his camp *is* very great: for *he is* strong that executeth his word: for **the day of the LORD *is* great and very terrible**; and who can abide it?

.....

31- The sun shall be turned into darkness, and the moon into blood, before the great and **the terrible day of the LORD come**.
-Joel 2 v 1, 11, 31

14- Multitudes, multitudes in the valley of decision: for **the day of the LORD** *is* near in the valley of decision.
-Joel 3 v 14

37- O Je-ru'sa-lem, Je-ru'sa-lem, *thou* that killest the prophets, and stonest them which are sent unto thee, how often would I have gathered thy children together, even as a hen gathereth her chickens under *her* wings and you would not!
38- Behold, your house is left unto you desolate.
39- **For I say unto you, Ye shall not see me henceforth, till ye shall say, Blessed *is* he that cometh in the name of the Lord.**
-Matthew 23 v 37-39, -Luke 13 v 34

18- Woe unto you that desire **the day of the LORD!** to what end *is* it for you? **the day of the LORD *is* darkness, and not light.**

.....

20- *Shall* not **the day of the LORD** *be* darkness, and not light? even very dark, and no brightness in it.
-Amos 5 v 18, 20

15- For **the day of the LORD** is near upon all the heathen: as thou hast done, it shall be done unto thee: thy reward shall return upon thine own head.
-Obadiah v 15

7- Hold thy peace at the presence of the LORD God: for **the day of the LORD** *is* at hand: for the LORD hath prepared a sacrifice, he hath bid his guests.

8- And it shall come to pass in **the day of the LORD's sacrifice**, that I will punish the princes, and the king's children, and all such as are clothed with strange apparel *(spiritual diversities)*.

.....

10- And it shall come to pass **in that day**, saith the LORD, *that there shall be* the noise of a cry from the fish gate, and a howling from the second, and a great crashing from the hills.

.....

14- **The great day of the LORD** *is* near, *it is* near, and hasteth greatly, *even* the voice of **the day of the LORD**: the mighty man shall cry there bitterly.

15- That day is a day of wrath, a day of trouble and distress, a day of wasteness and desolation, a day of darkness and gloominess, a day of clouds and thick darkness,

.....

18- Neither their silver nor their gold shall be able to deliver them in **the day of the LORD's wrath**; but the whole land shall be devoured by the fire of his jealousy: for he shall make even a speedy riddance of all them that dwell in the land.

-Zephaniah 1 v 7, 8, 10, 14, 15, 18

1- Behold, **the day of the LORD cometh**, and thy spoil shall be divided in the midst of thee.

.....

3- Then shall the LORD go forth, and fight against those nations, as when he fought in the day of battle.

-Zechariah 14 v 1, 3

5- Behold, I will send you E-li'jah the prophet before the coming of **the great and dreadfull day of the LORD.**

-Malachi 4 v 5

19- And I will shew wonders in heaven above, and signs in the earth beneath; blood, and fire, and vapour of smoke:

20- The sun shall be turned into darkness, and the moon into blood, before that great and notable **day of the LORD** come.

-Acts 2 v 19, 20

10- But **the day of the LORD** will come as a thief in the night; in the which the heavens shall pass away with a great noise, and the elements shall melt with fervent heat, the earth also and the works therein shall be burned up.
-II Peter 3 v 10

10- I was in the Spirit on **the LORD's day** *(a tribulation vision)*, and heard behind me a great voice, as of a trumpet,
-Revelation 1 v 10

The Day of Jesus Christ
The Day of Christ
The Day of our Lord Jesus Christ
The Day of the Lord Jesus
Rejoice in the Day of Christ
the coming of our Lord Je'sus Christ
the coming of the Lord

The True Church, the Body of Christ, is never associated in scripture with the 'wrath and vexation' foretold that will happen to the 'world'. Would Jesus Christ go back on the cross? 'The Church' which 'is his body'*, has never been a part of Israel's promises, laws, practices or customs. *-Colossians 1 v 24

"For in that he died, he died unto sin once...*" Why would God throw 'his Body' under the bus and make 'the True Church' now responsible for the wrath that is coming on Israel and "the world"? As if it was also our fault? That is not scripture. *-Romans 6 v 10

Law and Grace does not and never will mix. Else, the Word of God has been in vain. The Body of Christ, according to scripture, is to be spared from such a thought and action. Believe in God or believe God?

6- Even as the testimony of Christ was confirmed in you:
7- So that ye come behind in no gift; waiting for **the coming of our Lord Jesus Christ**:
8- Who shall also confirm you unto the end, *that ye may be* blameless in **the day of our Lord Jesus Christ.**
.....

18- For the preaching of the cross* is to them that perish foolishness; but unto us which are saved it is the power of God. *(*The 'preaching of the cross' is not the 'preaching of the earthly ministry'.)*
-I Corinthians 1 v 6-8, 18

5- To deliver such an one unto Sa'tan for the destruction of the flesh, that the spirit may be saved in **the day of the Lord Jesus**.
-I Corinthians 5 v 5

The Body of Christ is not associated with the 'spiritual whoredoms' of Israel:
14- And God hath both raised up the Lord, and will also raise up us by his own power.
15- Know ye not that <u>your bodies are the members of Christ</u>? **shall I then take the members of Christ, and make *them* the members of an harlot? God forbid.**
-I Corinthians 6 v 14, 15

13- For we write none other things unto you, than what ye read or acknowledge, and I trust ye shall acknowledge even to the end;
14- As also ye have acknowledged us in part, that we are your rejoicing, even as ye also *are* ours in **the day of the Lord Je'sus**.
-II Corinthians 1 v 13, 14

5- For your fellowship in the gospel from the first day until now;
6- Being confident of this very thing, that he which hath begun a good work in you will perform *it* until **the day of Je'sus Christ**.
.....
9- And this I pray, that your love may abound yet more and more in knowledge and *in* all judgement;
10- That ye may approve things that are excellent; that ye may be sincere and without offence till **the day of Christ**;
-Philippians 1 v 5, 6, 9, 10

13- For it is God which worketh in you both to will and to do of *his* good pleasure.
14- Do all things without murmurings and disputings:

15- That ye may be blameless and harmless, the sons of God, without rebuke, in the midst of a crooked and perverse nation, among whom ye shine as lights in the world:

16- Holding forth the word of life; that I may **rejoice in the day of Christ**, that I have not run in vain, neither laboured in vain.

-Philippians 2 v 13-16

1- Now we beseech you, brethren, by **the coming of our Lord Je'sus Christ**, <u>and *by* our gathering together unto him,</u>

2- That ye be not soon shaken in mind, or be troubled, neither by spirit, nor by word, nor by letter as from us, as that **the day of Christ** is at hand.

.....

13- But we are bound to give thanks alway to God for you, brethren beloved of the Lord, because <u>God hath from the beginning chosen you</u> to salvation through sanctification of the Spirit and belief of the truth:

14- Whereunto <u>he called you by our Gospel</u>, to the obtaining of the glory of our Lord Jesus Christ.

-II Thessalonians 2 v 1, 2, 13, 14

22- For we know that the whole creation groaneth and travaileth in pain together until now.

23- And not only *they*, but ourselves also, which have the firstfruits of the Spirit, even we ourselves groan within ourselves, waiting for the adoption, *to wit*, <u>the redemption of our body</u>.

-Romans 8 v 22, 23

51- Behold, **I shew you a mystery** *(a never before revealed secret);* We shall not all sleep *(die)*, but we shall all be changed,

52- In a moment, in the twinkling of an eye, at the last trump: for the trumpet shall sound, and the dead shall be raised incorruptible, and **we shall be changed**.

53- For this corruptible must put on incorruption, and this mortal *must* put on immortality.

54- So when this corruptible shall have put on incorruption, and this mortal shall have put on immortality, then shall be brought to pass the saying that is written, Death is swallowed up in victory*. *(*These saints in the Body of Christ will escape death altogether.)*

-I Corinthians 15 v 51-54

3- For ye are dead, and **your life is hid with Christ in God**.

4- **When Christ**, *who is* our life, **shall appear**, then shall **ye also appear with him in glory**.

-Colossians 3 v 3, 4

10- And to wait for his Son from heaven, whom he raised from the dead, *even* Je'sus which delivered us from the wrath to come.

-I Thessalonians 1 v 10

13- To the end he may stablish your hearts unblameable in holiness before God, even our father, at **the coming of our Lord Je'sus Christ with all his saints.**

-I Thessalonians 3 v 13

13- But I would not have you to be ignorant, brethren, concerning them which are asleep *(dead),* that ye sorrow not, even as others which have no hope.

14- For if we believe that Je'sus died and rose again *(Paul's Gospel)*, even so them also which sleep in Je'sus will God bring with him.

15- For this we say unto you by the word of the Lord, that we which are alive *and* remain unto **the coming of the Lord** shall not prevent them which are asleep.

16- For the Lord himself shall descend from heaven with a shout, with the voice of the archangel, and with the trump of God: and the dead in Christ shall rise first:

17- **Then we which are alive *and* remain shall be caught up together with them in the clouds, to meet the Lord in the air: so shall we ever be with the Lord.**

18- Wherefore comfort one another with these words.

-I Thessalonians 4 v 13-18

9- For **God hath not appointed us to wrath**, but to obtain salvation by our Lord Je'sus Christ.

-I Thessalonians 5 v 9

Paul realizes that 'being caught up to God' wasn't going to happen in his lifetime:

6- For I am now ready to be offered, and the time of my departure is at hand.

7- I have fought a good fight, I have finished *my* course, I have kept the faith:

8- Henceforth there is laid up for me a crown of righteousness, which the Lord, the righteous judge, shall give me at that day: and not to me only, but **unto all them also that love his appearing**.

-II Timothy 4 v 6-8

BOOK VII

The Invisible Godhead

9- And to make all *men* see what is the fellowship of **the mystery, which from the beginning of the world hath been hid in <u>God, who created all things by Je'sus Christ</u>**.

-Ephesians 3 v 9

1- God, who at sundry times and **in divers manners spake in time past unto the fathers by the prophets,**
2- **Hath in these last days spoken unto us by <u>*his*</u>* Son**, whom he *(God)* hath appointed heir *(Son)* of all things, **by whom also he *(Son)* made the worlds**. (**note: 'his' was added by the English translators. Read without that word 'his'.)*
3- Who being the brightness of *his* glory, and the express image of his person, and **upholding all things by the word of his *(Son)* power**, when he had **by himself purged our sins, sat down on the right hand of the Majesty on high:**
4- Being made so much better than the angels, as he hath by inheritance obtained a more excellent name than they.

-Hebrews 1 v 1-4

These next scriptures from John seem to have controversy in Christendom. Some claim that they were never in the original manuscripts. These 'believers' say they stand and firmly trust the Bible 100%, yet there are several scriptures they conveniently reject. These scriptures usually center around the 'Eternal Invisible Godhead'. <u>This chapter will prove these next scriptures true, over and over.</u>

6- This is he that came by water and blood, *even* Jesus Christ; not by water only, but by water and blood. And it is the Spirit that beareth witness, because the Spirit is truth.

7- For <u>there are three that bear record in heaven</u>, **the Father, the Word, and the Ho'ly Ghost**, and these <u>three are one</u> *(the Godhead)*. *(God is one but there are three that bear record in heaven.)*

8- And <u>there are three that bear witness in earth</u>, **the Spirit, and the water, and the blood**: and <u>these three agree in one</u>. *(Jesus born of a women v 6)*.
-I John 5 v 6-8

The claim is made that before the 16th Century, in v7 from "the Father" to v8 "in earth", this was not written in the original manuscripts. So lets read it that way:

6- This is he that came by water and blood, *even* Jesus Christ; not by water only, but by water and blood. And it is the Spirit that beareth witness, because the Spirit is truth.

7- For there are three that bear record in heaven,

8- **the Spirit, and the water, and the blood**: and these three agree in one.
-I John 5 v 6-8

I John 5 v 7, 8 don't make sense now. v7 – who are the three that bear record in heaven? Because in v8, water and blood is 'earthly'. Only the 'Spirit' is heavenly. Uh-Oh!

Maybe the KJV should have been italicized:

6- This is he that came by water and blood, *even* Jesus Christ; not by water only, but by water and blood. And it is the Spirit that beareth witness, because the Spirit is truth.

7- For there are three that bear record in heaven, ***the Father, the Word, and the Ho'ly Ghost***, *and these* <u>*three are one*</u> *(the Godhead)*.

8- *And there are three that bear witness in earth*, **the Spirit, and the water, and the blood**: and these three agree in one. *(Jesus born of a women v 6)*.
-I John 5 v 6-8

v6 During 'the birthing process' there is water and blood, which are of the earth, 'earthly'. The Spirit is of God, 'heavenly'. It is the Spirit that beareth witness with 'the earthy', Jesus Christ the Word made flesh.

v7 Water and blood are earthly, but the Spirit is Heavenly, right.? Who are the three that bear record in Heaven? What three Heavenly witnesses are missing? See v7.

1- **In the beginning was the Word**, and the Word was with God, and **the Word was God**.
2- The same was in the beginning with God.
3- **All things were made by him; and without him was not anything made.**
-John 1 v 1-3

1- **In the beginning God created the heaven and the earth.**
-Genesis 1 v 1

18- And Je'sus came and spake unto them, saying, All power is given unto me in heaven and in earth.
19- Go ye therefore, and teach all nations, <u>**baptizing them in the name of the Father, and of the Son, and of**</u> **the Ho'ly Ghost**.
-Matthew 28 v 18, 19

8- **I am Al'pha and O-me'ga,** the beginning and the ending, **saith the Lord**, which is, and which was, and which is to come, **the Almighty**.
-Revelation 1 v 8

What more needs to be said? God, at different times ('Sundry times') and in many ways ('Divers Manners'), spoke and was made a visible form for man to see and hear all through the Old Testament. But doesn't scripture say that no man has seen God and lived?

If no one can see God and live, then what are all these appearances by God to men mean? Many saw God yet did not die. Does scripture tell lies?

18- **No man hath seen God at any time;** the only begotten Son, which is in the bosom of the Father, he hath declared *him*.
-John 1 v 18

12- **No man hath seen God at any time.** If we love one another, God dwelleth in us, and his love is perfected in us.
-I John 4 v 12

20- And he said, Thou canst not see my face: **for there shall no man see me, and live.**
21- And the LORD said, Behold, *there is* a place by me, and thou shalt stand upon a rock:
22- And it shall come to pass, while my glory passeth by, that I will put thee in a clift of the rock, and will cover thee with my hand while I pass by:
23- And I will take away mine hand, and thou shalt see my back parts: **but my face shall not be seen**.
-Exodus 33 v 20-23

God spoke by various ways (Divers Manners) to some of the fathers of Israel and by the prophets for the 'Children of Israel'. Sometimes God spoke to the 'Children of Israel' as a nation by these 'divers manners' directly to them. 'The Children of Israel', at times, heard audibly 'the voice of God'.

"Hath in these last days spoken to us by Son*". 'These last days' are from the time of Jesus Christ to the Tribulation. 'The Latter Days' are the final seven years yet to be fulfilled in Israel's Biblical 'Time-Line' Prophecy and eternity. We are in 'the last days' today. And in 'these last days' Jesus Christ ministered to Israel proving who he is. *-Hebrews 1 v 2; -Matthew 5 v 17

Who is Son? If Son made the worlds* is not Son, God? Who is the one and only that can purge men of their sins? God? Son? A priest? The Angel who redeemed me? When man's sins were purged, where did Son go? The Son sat down on the right hand (figuratively) of the Majesty on high*. Are there more than one God? *-Hebrews 1 v 1-4

14- And **the Word was made flesh**, and dwelt among us, (and we beheld his glory, the glory as of the only begotten of the Father,) full of grace and truth.
15- John *(the baptist)* bare witness of him, and cried, saying, This was he of whom I spake, He that cometh after me is preferred before me: **for he was before me.**
-John 1 v 14, 15

'John the Baptist' was 6 months older than his cousin Jesus but says, **"for he *(Jesus)* was before me"***. John claims (by Holy Spirit inspiration) that Jesus is **'the Word', that by Son, "All things were made by him; and without him was not anything made".** *-John 1 v 1-3, -Hebrews 1 v 1-4, -John 1 v 15

John the Baptist, seeing the man Jesus (his first cousin in the flesh), announced and proclaimed to Israel that this is "the Word made flesh*". "The Kingdom of Heaven is within you *(in your midst)*"+. The Word (God) created all things=. *-John 1 v 14; +-Luke 17 v 21; =-John 1 v 1-3

The Word was made flesh. Jesus is the Word. Jesus created all things. Only God could do this. Yet, scripture says that no man has seen God and lived. **No man has seen 'the Invisible Godhead'* (the Father, the Word the Holy Ghost) all at one time and lived.** But they did see God many times before 'the Word was made flesh'. How? *-Colossians 1 v 15-20

The LORD, the LORD God JEHOVAH, the Word, the communicator between God and man was who was made visible to men. 'The Word' at times took on many different appearances, even sometimes as a man. 'The Word' was made flesh. 'The Word' from eternity past is Jesus the Christ. Not known by that name till his 'earthly birth in Bethlehem' but the same. Jesus was made a human (by whom?) for the suffering of death in the flesh.

That is why those that understand the Godhead as originally written for us in the KJV (the Father, the Word, the Holy Spirit) say, "God the Father, God the Son, and God the Holy Spirit". Take it to the obvious it also could be said, God/Father, God/Son, God/Holy Spirit or even say God = Father, God = Son, God = Holy Spirit/Ghost. Is the word <u>"the"</u> the reason the 'God in a box Christian' reject saying, 'God <u>the</u> Son'?

We understand that Son = Jesus the Christ. Is he not God? Is he not Son? Is he not Jesus Christ? Is he not Son and God? Then he is God the Son. No?

Many refuse because the words "God the Son" was not 'spelled out' in scripture. But "the Son of God" is. These can't seem to connect (don't want to see) the 'eternal Godhead'. These can see by a man's thinking, 'a God in a Box'. But thinking 'outside the box' is beyond their biblical risk taking.

If I was to surmise, these are the same 'supposed Christians' that can't separate the 'ministry of Peter from that of Paul', Law vs. Grace, Circumcision vs. Uncircumcision, the Apostles Doctrine vs. the Body of Christ, the Earthly Ministry of Jesus vs. the Resurrected Ministry, the Gospel of the Kingdom vs. the Gospel of the Grace of God...

These 'supposed Christians' put the 'Earthly Ministry of Christ' ahead of Romans to Hebrews. These claim the scriptures of Acts 2 v 42 as if it applies to them for today's teaching. The 'New Testament Church' people neglect the truth behind the True Church, the Body of Christ, though they claim to be in it.

'The New Testament Church' is a made up name by man and is never mentioned in the Bible. These folk accept this 'made up name' but reject using the name of 'God <u>the</u> Son'. Which has more truth? I believe that God = Son, and Son = God.

Jesus said, **"Before A'bra-ham was, I am":**

51- Verily, verily, I say unto you, If a man keep my *(Jesus)* saying, he shall never see death.

52- Then said the Jews unto him, Now we know that thou hast a devil. A'bra-ham is dead, and the prophets; and thou sayest, If a man keep my saying, he shall never taste of death.

53- Art thou greater than our father A'bra-ham, which is dead? and the prophets are dead: whom makest thou thyself?

54- Je'sus answered, If I honor myself, my honour is nothing: **it is my Father that honoreth me;** of whom ye say, that he is your God:

55- Yet ye have not known him; but I know him: and if I should say, I know him not, I shall be a liar like unto you: but I know him, and keep his saying.

56- **Your father A'bra-ham rejoiced to see my day: and he saw it, and was glad.**

57- Then said the Jews unto him, Thou art not yet fifty years old, and hast thou seen A'bra-ham?

58- **Jesus said unto them, Verily, verily, I say unto you, <u>Before A'bra-ham was, I am.</u>**

59- Then took they up stones to cast at him: but Je'sus hid himself, and went out of the temple, going through the midst of them, and so passed by.

-John 8 v 51-59

Jesus, 'the Word made flesh', says that **"it is my Father that honoreth me"***. In John 8, the Jews speaking and seeing Jesus claim to know the Father, God, JEHOVAH the LORD. But this man Jesus must be an imposter. "Who does he think he is? Miracles and the power to heal the sick? That doesn't mean a thing". *-John 8 v 54

Israel was 'spiritually blinded' by their 'know it all place of position' at the LORD's table'*. Many in Christendom act and believe the same way. Only to Israel was it given 'the Oracles of God' and only the Jew knew of the 'Living God'+. But having this dedication and 'their self importance' of keeping 'the traditions and service practices' of their religion=, they lost focused of the true word that Mo'ses spoke to them. *-Romans 11 v 9; -Psalm 69 v 22, 23; +-Romans 3 v 1, 2; =-Mark 7 v 6-9

Mo'ses said Holy Spirit inspired:
15- **The LORD thy God <u>will</u>** raise up unto thee a Prophet from the midst of thee, of thy brethren, like unto me, unto him ye shall hearken:
16- According to all that thou desiredst of **the LORD thy God** in Ho'reb in the day of the assembly *(church?)*, saying, Let me not hear again the voice of **the LORD my God**, neither let me see this great fire any more, that I die not.
17- And **the LORD said** unto me, They have well *spoken that* which they have spoken.
18- <u>**I will**</u> raise them up a Prophet from among their brethren, like unto thee, and will put my words in his mouth; and he shall speak unto them all that I shall command him.
-Deuteronomy 18 v 15-18

How can this man Jesus, being 'a Jew of the Circumcision' under 'the Law of Moses', get away with working on the Sabbath day*? Jesus was not working under 'their Law' but healing and proving to Israel who he really is. He is Israel's Christ, their Messiah, their King, their Saviour with the Earthly Kingdom of Heaven if all of the Children of Israel were to accept him. They should have known and been prepared for 'their Kingdom'. *-Exodus 31 v 12-15

It was a 'spiritual blindness' beyond measure. They saw the many miracles that Jesus was doing that only God could do, yet did not believe that <u>'Jesus is Son and God'</u>. Israel did not see that it was God doing the miracles. All one and the same. Do you see?

Jesus said:
37- If I do not the works of my Father, believe me not.
38- But if I do, though ye believe not me, believe the works: that ye may know, and believe, that **the Father *is* in me, and I in him**.
-John 10 v 37, 38

'John the Baptist' was 'the herald' specifically chosen by God to announce to Israel to 'be ready' for 'their King and Earthly Heavenly Kingdom':

6- There was **a man sent from God**, whose name *was* **John**.

7- The same *(John)* came for a witness, **to bear witness of the Light**, that all *men* through him might believe.

8- He *(John)* was not that Light, but *was sent* to bear witness of that Light.

9- *That* was the true Light, which lighteth every man that cometh into the world.

10- He *(the Light, Jesus)* was in the world, **and <u>the world was made by him *(Je'sus)*</u>, and the world knew him not.**

11- **He came unto <u>his own</u>, and <u>his own</u> received him not.**

12- But as many as received him, to them gave he power to become the sons of God, *even* **to them that believe on his name:**

13- Which were born *(**to them that believe on his name v12**)*, not of blood, nor of the will of the flesh, nor of the will of man, but of God.

14- And <u>**the Word was made flesh**</u>, and dwelt among us, (and we beheld his glory, the glory as of **the only begotten of the Father**), full of grace and truth.

-John 1 v 6-14

1- That which was **from the beginning**, which we have heard, which we have seen with our eyes, which we have looked upon, and our hands have handled, of **the Word of life**;

2- (For the life was manifested, and we have seen *it*, and bear witnesses, and show unto you that **eternal life, which was with the Father**, and was manifested unto us;)

3- That which we have seen and heard declare we unto you, that ye also may have fellowship with us: and truly **our fellowship *is* with <u>the Father, and with <u>his Son Jesus Christ</u></u>**.

-I John 1 v 1-3

15- Who *(Jesus)* is the image of the invisible God, the firstborn of every creature:

16- For by him were all things created, that are in heaven, and that are in earth, visible and invisible, whether *they be* thrones, or dominions, or principalities, or powers: all things were created by him and for him:

17- And he is before all things, and by him all things consist.

18- **And he is the head of the body, the church: <u>who is the beginning, the firstborn from the dead*</u>;** that in all *things* he might have preeminence. *(*The resurrected Jesus Christ became the head of the Body, the Church, who is the firstborn from the dead.)*
19- For it pleased *the Father* that in him should all fullness dwell;
20- And, having made peace through the blood of his cross *(Paul's Gospel)*, by him to reconcile all things unto himself; by him, *I say,* whether *they be* things in earth, or things in heaven.
-Colossians 1 v 15-20

John writes by Holy Spirit inspiration that the 'true Light is Jesus'. He, the Light, Jesus, made the worlds. Does this not make Jesus, God? "He *(the Light, Jesus)* was in the world, **and <u>the world was made by him *(Je'sus)*</u>, and the world knew him not*"**. The Word was made flesh. The Word is Jesus. Jesus is the Light. *-John 1 v 10, 11

To Israel, the LORD God JEHOVAH is One, "I am he":
4- Who hath wrought and done *it,* **<u>calling</u> the generations from the beginning? I the LORD, the first, and with the last; I *am* he.**
-Isaiah 41 v 4

Who called the generations from the beginning? **I the LORD, the first, and with the last; I *am* he.** The Word <u>called</u> (calling/spoke by reason being 'The Communicator') the generations from the beginning.

In the Beginning

The first scripture in our Bible says that God created every thing:
1- In the beginning **God created** the heaven and the earth.
-Genesis 1 v 1

2- And the earth was without form, and void; and darkness was upon the face of the deep. And the **Spirit of God** moved upon the face of the waters.
-Genesis 1 v 2

The second verse of our Bible introduces the **Spirit of God**. The Spirit of God was acting independently and "moved upon the face of the waters".

Why doesn't scripture say, "God moved upon the face of the waters"? One would say, "God is the Spirit". Why then was 'a plurality made of God' in the first two scriptures of our Bibles? Maybe it's important to note. <u>This individuality shows itself all through the Bible</u>. Have you seen it?

In chapter 1 of Genesis we have **God** and the **Spirit of God.** In Genesis 2 v 4, 5 the **LORD God**:

4- These *are* the generations of the heavens and of the earth when they were created, in the day that **<u>the LORD God</u> made the earth and the heavens**. 5- And every plant of the field before it was in the earth, and every herb of the field before it grew: for <u>the Lord God</u> had not caused it to rain upon the earth, and *there was* no a man to till the ground.
-Genesis 2 v 4, 5

In Genesis 2 we are introduced to the LORD God. Scripture says, **"the LORD God made the earth and the heavens"**. Genesis 1 v 1 says that God created everything. "For <u>there are three that bear record in heaven</u>, **the Father, the Word, and the Ho'ly Ghost**, and these <u>three are one</u> *(the Godhead)**". **Scripture does not say 'this one is three' but says 'these three are one'.** *-I John 5 v 7

The plural pronouns of God when man was created a living being:
26- And God said, **Let <u>us</u> make man in <u>our</u> image**, after <u>our</u> likeness: and let them have dominion over the fish of the sea, and over the fowl of the air, and over the cattle, and over all the earth, and over every creeping thing that creepeth upon the earth.
27- So God created man in his *own** image, in the image of God created he him; male and female created he them.
(*'own' was added by the translators.)
-Genesis 1 v 26, 27

God did not say, <u>I will</u> make man in <u>my image</u> and <u>my likeness</u>. <u>God said, us and our</u>. **This image is not our bodies of flesh but 'his invisible image of the mind, will and emotion', the Soul.** He was speaking as the Godhead, God the Father. But in actuality, who really in the Godhead did the speaking?

4- Who hath wrought and done *it*, **calling the generations from the beginning? I the LORD, the first, and with the last; I *am* he.**
-Isaiah 41 v 4

In scripture you can find where the Father, the Word and the Spirit at 'sundry times' and in' diver's manners' acted independently (though always one and the same) with 'a mind, a will and a (an) emotion'. All invisible to every person but very real. This is the 'invisible image of God', the Soul.

Because of science and medical technology we can surmise the locations of the brain where these may be. But cutting into the brain does not reveal the soul, it is invisible. This 'image of God' is forever alive, either in the body or out of the body. The body may die, but the soul is eternal. The image of God will never die because 'it is of God'. **The Holy Spirit of God is the 'quickening glue' of the soul.**

We can't see 'the mind, will and emotion', they are invisible but very real. It is what guides the living. This is the 'Soul of Man'. Man has been given 'a will, a free will' to choose either life or death.

A person confronted with a challenge can decide by his or her own 'free will' whether to act or not, 'fight or flight'. A dog has a mind, <u>instinct</u> and emotion. An animal by instinct will act to preserve it's life. We can make free choices, whether good or bad, even to the point of death. An animal would throw all 'caution to the wind' for a morsel of food when starvation is eminent.

The Godhead Bodily

8- Beware lest any man spoil you through philosophy and vain deceit, after the tradition of men, after the rudiments of the world, and not after Christ. 9- For in him *(Jesus Christ)* dwelleth all the <u>fullness</u> of <u>the Godhead</u> bodily.
-Colossians 2 v 8, 9

Jesus in the flesh was filled with 'all the <u>fullness of the Godhead</u>' for he is God. The Father, the Word and the Holy Ghost/Spirit was the man Jesus the Christ. To look on the man Jesus, he wasn't bursting out of his skin with the fullness of the God of creation. **Scripture does not say that Jesus was filled with the 'fullness of God', but 'the fullness of the Godhead**

bodily'. What possibly could contain God knowing he is everywhere in the universe? Jesus looked like a simple man, but was God.

As Jesus Christ walked the streets of Israel, the Godhead was still everywhere on the earth and in the heavens. No matter where we go, God is there. If God is there, then so also is the Word and the Spirit.

The 'world of men' thinking themselves wise through education, the reading of their own Bibles, reasoning and philosophy, and 'worldly' vain deceit, follow 'a man's logic' and 'a man's spirit'. These reject the written 'Word of God' and accept scripture by their own reasoning so that it fits with their thinking. Believe in God or believe God?

"We will make the scriptures make sense!" This putting of 'God in a Box' is the 'vision of men' that they can understand. Faith is taking God at his word, not a man's word. Christendom has 'over thought' themselves. These try to make the 'one God' as something that can be understood in 'the natural man way'.

11- For what man knoweth the things of a man, save the spirit of man which is in him? Even so the things of God knoweth no man, but the Spirit of God.

12- Now we have not received, not the spirit of the world, but the spirit which is of God; that we might know the things that are freely given to us of God.

13- Which things also we speak, not in the words which man's wisdom teacheth, but which **the Ho'ly Ghost teacheth; comparing spiritual things with spiritual** *(scripture with scripture)*.

14- **But the natural man receiveth not the things of the Spirit of God**: for they are foolishness unto him: neither can he know *them*, **because they are spiritually discerned**.

15- But he that is spiritual judgeth all things, yet he himself is judged of no man.

16- For who hath known the mind of the Lord, that he may instruct him? But we have the mind of Christ*. (**the written Word, our Bibles and prayer.*)

-I Corinthians 2 v 11-16

Before Jesus Christ was made a physical body of flesh in the appearance as a human person, God spoke to whom he chose. God also made many visible appearances to whom he chose to show himself to. But scripture also says that no man has ever seen God at any time and lived. How can this be? Does scripture tell lies? Does the 'Word of God' contradict itself? It will if 'God is put in a box'. God forbid.

Who raised Jesus from death?

Scripture says Jesus physically died. A fact of scripture. If, like many have taught, 'God is One' and Jesus is this 'One', then according to the masses that 'put God in a box', God is dead. If God and Jesus are dead (scripture says Jesus died), who or what could have resurrected him? There is no 'Deity' left because the 'Holy Spirit' too is thrown in 'the same box'. According to the strict belief that "Hear O Israel, the LORD our God is one LORD", how do they answer? Who raised Jesus from the dead?

I hope the mountain of scriptural evidence shown in this chapter may open the eyes of some. Only God can do this, but how many scriptures does it take showing the example of the 'Godhead'? One? Twenty? One Hundred? A person will not believe if they don't want too. Believe in God or believe God?

22- Ye men of Is'ra-el, hear these words; Je'sus of Naz'a-reth, a man approved of God among you by miracles and wonders and signs, which God did by him in the midst of you, as ye yourselves also known:
23- Him, being delivered by the determinate counsel and foreknowledge of God, ye have taken, and by wicked hands have crucified and slain:
24- **Whom God hath raised up**, having loose the pains of death: because it was not possible that he should be holden of it.
-Acts 2 v 22-24

31- He seeing this before spake of the resurrection of Christ, that his soul was not left in hell, neither his flesh did see corruption
32- **This Je'sus hath God raised up**, whereof we all are witnesses.
33- **Therefore being by the right hand of God exalted, and having received of the Father the promise of the Ho'ly Ghost,** he hath shed forth this, which ye now see and hear.
34- For Da'vid is not ascended into the heavens: but he saith himself, **The LORD** *(the Father)* **said unto my Lord** *(the Word)***, Sit thou on my right hand*,** (*-*Psalm 110; spoken before the Word was made flesh revealing a Father and Son, or that there is only one LORD and that which follows is Lord.)*

35- Until I make thy foes thy footstool.

36- Therefore let all the house of Is'ra-el know assuredly, that God hath made that same Je'sus, whom ye have crucified, both Lord and Christ.

-Acts 2 v 31-36

33- **God hath fulfilled** the same unto us their children, **in that he** *(God)* **hath raised up Je'sus again**; as it is also written in the second psalm, **Thou art my Son, this day have I begotten thee**.

34- And as concerning that he *(God)* raised him from the dead, *now* no more to return to corruption, he said on this wise, I *(God)* will give you the sure mercies of Da'vid.

-Acts 13 v 33, 34

14- Knowing that **he** *(God)* **which raised up the Lord Jesus** <u>shall raise up us also by Jesus</u>, and shall present *us* with you.

-II Corinthians 4 v 14

1- Paul, an apostle, (not of men, neither by man, but by Jesus Christ, and **God the Father, who raised him** *(Jesus)* **from the dead**;)

-Galatians 1 v 1

20- **Which he** *(God)* **wrought in Christ, when he raised him from the dead, and set** *him* **at his own right hand in the heavenly places,**

-Ephesians 1 v 20

14- **And God hath both raised up the Lord, and will also raise up us by his own power.**

-I Corinthians 6 v 14

3- Concerning his Son Jesus Christ our Lord, which was made of the seed of David according to the flesh;

4- And **declared** *to be* **the Son of God** with power, according to the spirit of holiness, **by the resurrection from the dead** *(Paul's Gospel)*:

-Romans 1 v 3, 4

When and how will 'righteousness be imputed to us'?

22- And therefore it was imputed to him for righteousness.

23- Now it was not written for his sake alone, that it was imputed to him;

24- **But for us also, to whom <u>it shall be imputed, if we believe on him</u> <u>(God) that raised up Jesus our Lord from the dead (Paul's Gospel)</u>;**
25- Who was delivered for our offenses, **and was raised again for our justification**.
-Romans 4 v 22-25

15- Yea, and we are found false witnesses of God; because **we have testified of God that he raised up Christ: whom he raised not up, if so be that the dead rise not.**
16- For if the dead rise not, then is not Christ raised:
17- And **if Christ be not raised, your faith *is* vain;** ye are yet in your sins.
18- Then they also which are fallen asleep in Christ are perished.
19- **If in this life only we have hope in Christ***, we are of all men most miserable. (**saying that if salvation is only for those living contemporary and during the Earthly Ministry, where is there hope for the rest? But now v 20...*)
20- **But now is Christ risen from the dead,** *and* become the first fruits of them that slept.
21- For since by a man *came* death, by man *came* also the resurrection of the dead.
22- For as in Ad'am all die, even so in Christ shall all be made alive.
23- But every man in his own order: Christ the firstfruits; afterword they that are Christ's at his coming*. (**this is not the 2nd coming of Christ but 'The Day of Jesus Christ' on the 'Great Resurrection Day'. v 24- is speaking of what people?*)
24- Then *cometh* the end, when he shall have delivered up the kingdom to God, even the Father; when he shall have put down all rule and all authority and power.
25- For he must reign, till he hath put all enemies under his feet.
26- The last enemy *that* shall be destroyed *is* death
-I Corinthians 15 v 15-26

Scripture never said that Jesus raised himself from the dead. Then who did? Jesus was buried a dead, dead man. But the 'Invisible Godhead' is eternal.

24- **Whom God hath raised up,** having loosed the pains of death: because it was not possible that he should be holden of it.

…..

30- Therefore being a prophet, and knowing that God had sworn an oath to him, that of the fruit of his loins, according to the flesh, <u>he would raise up Christ to sit on his throne</u>;

31- He seeing this before spake of the resurrection of Christ, that his soul was not left in hell, neither his flesh did see corruption.

32- **This Jesus hath God raised up,** whereof we all are witnesses.

33- **Therefore** being by the right hand of God exalted, and having received of the Father the promise of the Holy Ghost, he hath shed for this, which you now see and hear.

34- For David is not ascended into the heavens: but he saith himself, the LORD *(the Father)* said unto my Lord (the Word), Sit thou on my right hand,

35- **Until** I make thy foes thy footstool*. *(*this has yet to happen.)*

36- Therefore let all the house of Is'ra-el know assuredly, that God hath made that same Jesus, whom ye have crucified, both Lord and Christ.

-Ats 2 v 24, 30-36

13- The **God** of A'bra-ham, and of I'saac, and of Ja'cob, the God of your fathers, **hath glorified his Son Jesus**; whom ye delivered up, and denied him in the presence of Pi'late, when he was determined to let *him* go.

14- But ye denied the Holy One and the Just, and desired a murderer to be granted unto you;

15- And killed the Prince of life, **whom God hath raised from the dead;** whereof we are witnesses.

16- And **his name through faith in his name hath made this man strong**, whom you see and know: yea, the faith which is by him hath given him this perfect soundness in the presence of you all.

.....

26- **Unto you first *(Ye men of Israel)* God, having raised up his Son Jesus,** sent him to bless you, in turning away every one of you from his iniquities.

-Acts 3 v 13-16, 26

10- Be it known unto you all, and to all the people of Is'ra-el, that by the name of Je'sus Christ of Naz'a-reth, whom ye crucified, **whom God raised from the dead,** *even* by him doth this man stand here before you whole.

-Acts 4 v 10

30- **The God of our fathers raised up Je'sus,** whom ye slew and hanged on a tree.

31- Him hath God exalted with his right hand *to be* a Prince and a Savior, for to give repentance to Is'ra-el, and forgiveness of sins.

-Acts 5 v 30, 31

40- **Him** *(Jesus)* **God raised up the third day,** and shewed him openly;

41- Not to all the people, but **unto witnesses chosen before of God**, *even* to us, **who did eat and drink with him after he rose from the dead**.

-Acts 10 v 40, 41

29- And when they had fulfilled all that was written of him*, they took *him* down from the tree, and laid *him* in a sepulcher. (*-John 19 v 30)

30- **But God raised him from the dead:**

31- And **he was seen many days** of them which came up with him from Gal'i-lee to Je-ru'sa-lem, **who are his witnesses unto the people**.

32- And we declare unto you glad tidings, how that the promises which were made unto the fathers,

33- God hath fulfilled the same unto us their children, **in that he** *(God)* **hath raised up Je'sus again;** as it is also written in the second psalm, **Thou art my Son, this day have I begotten* thee**.

**The only 'Begotten Son' was at Jesus' resurrection, not his birth in Bethlehem. John 3 v 16 speaks a mystery. Christ had not been crucified yet nor did they know he was going to be. For Israel, 'the resurrection belief' is that Jesus is not dead but alive. His resurrection solidified to the 'Ye men of Israel' that Jesus could still bring in the 'Earthly Heavenly Kingdom'.*

John the Baptist never preached that the Gentiles and those not under 'the Law' would be able to obtain salvation by believing in the 'Resurrected Jesus Christ'. 'The Gospel' that Paul delivered to the world began with him and ends with him. Only the Apostle Paul taught salvation on the basis of resurrection, not the 'earthly ministry'. We believe the 'earthly ministry' of course but can differentiate between 'law and grace'.

34- And as concerning that **he** *(God)* **raised him up from the dead,** *now* no more to return to corruption, he said on this wise, I will give you the sure mercies of Da'vid.

35- Wherefore he saith also in another *psalm*, Thou shalt not suffer thine Ho'ly One to see corruption.

36- For Da'vid, after he had served his own generation *(the children of Israel, past, present, future)* by the will of God, fell on sleep, and was laid unto his father's, and saw corruption:

37- **But he *(Jesus)*, whom God raised again,** saw no corruption.

-Acts 13 v 29-37

11- **But if <u>the Spirit</u> of him that raised up Je'sus from the dead dwell in you, he that raised up Christ from the dead shall also quicken your mortal bodies by his Spirit that dwelleth in you.**

.....

34- Who *is* he that condemneth? *It is* **Christ that died, yea rather, that is risen again, who is even at the right hand of God, who also maketh intercession for us.**

-Romans 8 v 11, 34

5- Je'sus answered, Verily, verily, I say unto thee, Except a man be born of water *(earthly)* and *of* the Spirit *(heavenly)*, he cannot enter into the kingdom of God*. *(*only a man or a women can enter once born of the Spirit.)*

6- That which is born of the flesh is flesh; and that which is born of the Spirit is spirit.

7- Marvel not that I said unto thee, Ye must be born again. (*only the Holy Ghost/Spirit can do this, not water, 'the 'earthly'.)

8- The wind bloweth where it listeth, and thou hearest the sound thereof, but canst not tell whence it cometh, and whither it goeth: so is every one that *is* born of the Spirit.

.....

31- He that cometh from above is above all: he that is of the earth is earthly, and speaketh of the earth: he that cometh from heaven is above all.

32- And what he hath seen and heard, that he testifieth; and no man receiveth his testimony.

33- He that hath received his testimony hath set to his seal that God is true.

34- For **he whom God hath sent** speaketh the words of God: for God giveth not the Spirit by measure *unto him*.

35- **The Father loveth the Son, and hath given all things into his hand.**

36- He that believeth on the Son hath everlasting life: and he that believeth not the Son shall not see life; but the wrath of God abideth on him.
-John 3 v 5-8, 31-36

6- For unto us a child is born, unto us a son is given: *and the government <u>shall be</u> upon his shoulder: and his name <u>shall be</u> called Wonderful, Counsellor, The mighty God, The everlasting Father, The Prince of Peace. *(*has yet to happen, Jesus Christ is not ruling from the throne of David, ... yet.)*
7- Of the increase of *his* government and peace *there shall be* no end, upon the throne of Da'vid, and upon his kingdom, to order it, and to establish it with judgment and with justice from henceforth even for ever. The zeal of the LORD of hosts will perform this.
-Isaiah 9 v 6, 7

The Godhead Evidenced in the Same Place

16- And <u>**Je'sus**</u>, when he was baptized, went up straightway out of the water: and, lo, the heavens were opened unto him, and **he saw the <u>Spirit of God</u> descending like a dove**, and lighting upon him:
17- And lo **a <u>voice from heaven</u>, saying, This is my beloved Son, in whom I am well pleased**.
-Matthew 3 v 16, 17

10- And straightway coming up out of the water, **he <u>*(Jesus)*</u>** saw the heavens opened, and **the <u>Spirit</u> like a dove descending upon him**:
11- And there came **a <u>voice from heaven</u>,** *saying*, **Thou art my beloved Son, in whom I am well pleased**.
12- And immediately **the Spirit driveth him** into the wilderness.
-Mark 1 v 10-12

32- And John bare record, saying, **I saw the <u>Spirit</u> descending from heaven like a dove**, and it abode upon him.
33- And I knew him not: but <u>he that sent me to baptize with water, the same said unto me</u>, **Upon whom thou shalt see the Spirit descending, and remaining on him, the same is he which baptizeth with the Ho'ly Ghost.**
34- And I saw, and bare record that this is the <u>Son of God</u>.
-John 1 v 32-34

The Stoning of Stephen:
8- And Stephen, full of faith and power, did great wonders and miracles among the people.
9- Then there rose certain of the synagogue, which is called *the synagogue* of the Lib'er-tines, and the Cy-re'ni-ans, and Alex-an'dri-ans, and of them of Ci-li'cia, and of A'sia, disputing with Ste'phen.
10- **And they were not able to resist the wisdom and the spirit by which he spake.**

.....

15- And all that sat in the council, looking steadfastly on him, **saw his face as it had been the face of an angel**.
-Acts 6 v 8-10, 15

55- But he *(Stephen),* being **full of the <u>Ho'ly Ghost</u>,** looked up stedfastly into heaven, **and saw the glory of <u>God</u>, and <u>Jesus standing</u> on the right hand of <u>God</u>.**
56- And said, Behold, **I see** the heavens opened, and **the <u>Son of man standing</u> on the right hand of <u>God</u>.**
-Acts 7 v 55, 56

Jesus was standing? Why was he not sitting? These Jews did not want to hear this statement at all. If Stephen saw Jesus standing and not sitting, then the only explanation is that Jesus Christ is about to return with the Kingdom of Heaven. They had not heard of Jesus standing in heaven but that he was sitting 'until he made the enemies of Israel their footstool'. "Let God arise"*... Jesus would return with the wrath of God foretold by the prophets of the Old Testament. *-Psalm 68 v 1-3

These Jews knew the following scriptures:
1- The LORD said to my Lord, <u>Sit</u> thou at my right hand, <u>until</u> I make thine enemies thy footstool.
2- The LORD shall send the rod of thy strength out of Zi'on: rule thou in the midst of thine enemies.

.....

5- The Lord at thy right hand shall strike through kings in **the day of his wrath** *(the latter day's).*

6- He shall judge among the heathen, he shall fill *the places* with the dead bodies; he shall wound the heads over many countries.
-Psalm 110 v 1, 2, 5, 6

NOTE: "The LORD said to my Lord..." David wrote this. Is David calling out 2 Lord's of his? One of them is the LORD, Israel's LORD God JEHOVAH. Who is 'Lord' then?

To Israel, at this time, there is no understanding that the 'Word', LORD God JEHOVAH would be made flesh. Some of the Old Testament saints and prophets spoke and wrote of a 'suffering savior'. But until Jesus came in the flesh, there was no direct interpretation of 'this Jesus' being 'their future king'.

This revelation of the 'messianic prophecies' (over 300 of them) was in 'a veiled language' and was something that God purposely did not spell out to the Nation of Israel. They were to believe in what God told them. To this day, after the proof of the earthly ministry of Jesus Christ, most humans still will never believe. Even God's own chosen people rejected Jesus their Christ and Messiah.

David was a prophet of Israel. He is speaking 'prophetically'. He was writing being filled by the 'Holy Spirit of God'. He is not making it up. David could see (understand?) 'the Godhead' but could not explain it. He never met Jesus Christ, but he did know the LORD. Who then is the LORD calling Lord.

In this case, because they knew not of the 'earthly ministry of the Word', ... God the Father, the Godhead (Father, Word, Holy Spirit) is LORD speaking to 'the Word'. The Word was made a little lower than the angels for the suffering of death. Jesus was still God totally in the flesh, but his body is 'earthly'. He was slightly lower in the Godhead. He was a man. His flesh could die.

5- Let this mind* be in you, which was also in Christ Je'sus. *(*Know scripture. Christ died for our sins. Know Jesus Christ from Genesis to Revelation.)*
6- Who, being in the form of God, thought it not robbery to be equal with God.
7- But made himself of no reputation, and took upon him the form of a servant, and was made in the likeness of men:

8- And being found and fashion as a man, he humbled himself, and became obedient unto death, even the death of the cross.

9- Wherefore God also hath highly exalted him, and given him a name which is above every name:

10- That at the name of Je'sus every knee should bow, of *things* in heaven, and *things* in earth, and *things* under the earth;

11- And that every tongue should confess that **Je'sus Christ is Lord, to the Glory of God the Father.**

-Philippians 2 v 5-11

5- For unto the angels hath he not put in subjection the world to come, whereof we speak.

6- But one in a certain place testified, saying, What is man, that thou art mindful of him? or the son of man, that thou visitest him?

7- **Thou madest him a little lower than the angels;** thou crownest him with glory and honour, and didst set him over the works of thy hands:

8- Thou hast put all things in subjection under his feet. For in that he put in subjection under him, he left nothing that is not put under him. But now we see not yet things put under him.

9- **But we see Je'sus, who was made a little lower than the angels for the suffering of death, crowned with glory and honour; that he by the grace of God should taste death for every man.**

.....

14- Forasmuch then as the children are partakers of flesh and blood, he himself likewise took part of the same; that **through death he might destroy him that had the power of death, that is, the devil.**

15- And deliver them who through fear of death were all their lifetime subject to bondage.

16- For verily he took not on *him the nature of* angels; but he took on *him* the seed of A'bra-ham.

17- Wherefore in all things it behoved him to be made like unto *his* brethren, that he might be a **merciful and faithful <u>high priest</u>** in things *pertaining* to God, **to make reconciliation for the sins of the people.**

18- For in that he himself hath suffered being tempted, he is able to succor them that are tempted.

-Hebrews 2 v 5-9, 14-18

33- Therefore **being by the righthand of God exalted**, and **having received of the Father the promise of the Ho'ly Ghost**, he hath shed forth this, which ye now see and hear.

34- For Da'vid is not ascended into the heavens: but he saith himself, The LORD said unto my Lord, Sit thou on my right hand,

35- Until I make thy foes thy footstool.

36- **Therefore let all the house of Is'ra-el know assuredly, that God hath made that same Je'sus, whom ye have crucified, both Lord and Christ.**

-Acts 2 v 33-36

Jesus would stand when he is prepared to bring in the 'Earthly Heavenly Kingdom'. He was standing. Stephen, being filled with the Holy Spirit saw Jesus standing at the right hand of God. The Jews did not want to hear this. They murdered Stephen.

This is the place where Jesus (if such a place can be pinpointed), who is now seen standing, turned to the rest of the world (Gentiles) without the Jew. 'Israel's Prophetic Time-line' has been interrupted. Because of this break, the 'Age of Grace' is now. The whole world has a chance at 'the free gift of grace'. How?

This 2,000 years of 'the Church Age' was never foretold, but it has happened. 'The Dispensation to the Faith-way for Salvation' begins, without the Jew and their Law. When Israel is out of its 'place of blessing', God's time-clock stops. When Jesus came for his 'triumphal entry', where is the first place he went? What did he find? Did Jesus find Israel ready for him?

Here is the first place where the Apostle Paul (Saul) is mentioned in Biblical scripture. Saul was a witness of the 'Stoning of Stephen'. The 'stoners' laid their clothes at the feet of Saul. Saul, more than likely, was an instigator of this murder because of the reputation that preceded him.

57- Then they cried out with a loud voice, and stopped their ears, and ran upon him with one accord,

58- And cast *him (Stephen)* out of the city, and stoned *him*: and **the witnesses laid down their clothes at a young man's feet, whose name was Saul.**

59- And they stoned Ste'phen, calling upon *God,* and saying, Lord Jesus, receive my spirit.

60- And he kneeled down, and cried with a loud voice, Lord, lay not this sin to their charge. And when he had said this, he fell asleep.
-Acts 7 v 57-60

The Mount of Transfiguration:
28- Verily I say unto you, there be some standing here, which shall not taste of death, **till they see the Son of man coming in his kingdom**.
-Matthew 16 v 28

Matthew 17 six days later:
1- And after six days **Je'sus** taketh Pe'ter, James, and John his brother, and bringeth them all into an high mountain apart,
2- And **was transfigured before them: and his face did shine as the sun, and his raiment was white as light**.
3- And, behold, there appeared unto them Mo'ses and E-li'as *(Elijah)* talking with him.
4- Then answered Pe'ter, and said unto Je'sus, Lord, it is good for us to be here: if thou wilt, let us make here three tabernacles; one for thee, and one for Mo'ses, and one for E-li'as.
5- While he yet spake, behold, a bright cloud overshadowed them: **and behold a voice out of the cloud, which said, This is my beloved Son, in whom I am well pleased; hear ye him**.
6- And when the disciples heard *it*, they fell on their face, and were sore afraid.
7- And Je'sus came and touched them, and said, Arise, and be not afraid.
8- And when they had lifted up their eyes, they saw no man, save Je'sus only.
-Matthew 17 v 1-8

Luke 2:
25- And, behold, there was a man in Je-ru'sa-lem, whose name *was* Sim'e-on; and the same man *was* just and devout, **waiting for the consolation of Is'ra-el**: and **the Ho'ly Ghost was upon him.**
26- And **it was revealed unto him by the Ho'ly Ghost, that he should not see death, before he had seen <u>the Lord's Christ</u>**.
27- And **<u>he came by the Spirit</u> into the temple**: and when the parents brought in **the child <u>Je'sus, to do for him after the custom of the law,</u>**
28- **Then took he *(Jesus)* him up in his arms, and <u>blessed God</u>**, and said,

29- **Lord**, now lettest thou thy servant depart in peace, according to thy word:

30- **For mine eyes have seen thy salvation,**

31- Which thou hast prepared before the face of all people;

32- **A light to lighten the Gen'tiles, and <u>the glory of thy people Is'ra-el</u>.**

-Luke 2 v 25-32

1- **That which was from the beginning**, which we have **heard**, which we had **seen** with our eyes, which we have **looked upon**, and **our hands have handled, the Word of life *(Jesus Christ, Son);***

2- (For the life was manifested, and we have seen *it*, and bear witness, and shew unto you that eternal life, which was with the Father *(the Godhead)*, and was manifested unto us;)

3- That which we have seen and heard declare we unto you, that ye also may have fellowship with us: and truly **our fellowship *is* with the Father, and with his Son Je'sus Christ.**

-I John 1 v 1-3

8- I am Al'pha and O-me'ga, the beginning and the ending, saith the Lord, which is, and which was, and which is to come, the Almighty.

9- I John, who also am your brother, and companion in tribulation, and in the kingdom and patience of Je'sus Christ, was in the isle that is called Pat'mos, for the word of God, and for the testimony of Je'sus Christ.

10- I was in the Spirit on **the Lord's day***, and heard behind me a great voice, as of a trumpet, *(*the 'Lords day', a vision given to John of the 'Latter Day's'.)*

11- Saying, I am Al'pha and O-me'ga, the first and the last: and, What thou seest, write in a book, and send *it* unto the seven churches *(Jewish assemblies)* which are in A'sia; unto Eph'e-sus, and unto Smyr'na, and unto Per'ga-mos, and unto Thy-a-ti'ra, and unto Sar'dis, and unto Phil-a-del'phi-a, and unto La-od-i-ce'a.

12- And I turned to see the voice that spake with me. And being turned, I saw seven golden candlesticks;

13- And in the midst of the seven candlesticks *one* like unto the Son of man, clothed with a garment down to the foot, and girt about the paps with a golden girdle.

14- His head and *his* hairs *were* white like wool, as white as snow; and his eyes *were* as a flame of fire;

15- And his feet like unto fine brass, as if they burned in a furnace; and his voice as the sound of many waters.

16- And he had in his right hand seven stars: and out of his mouth went a sharp twoedged sword *(his words)*: and his countenance *was* as the sun shineth in his strength.

-Revelation 1 v 8-16

Daniel writes, Holy Spirit inspired, some 650 years before 70 A.D.:

9- I beheld till the thrones were cast down, and the Ancient of days *(the Father)* did sit, whose garment *was* white as snow, and the hair of his head like the pure wool: his throne *was like* the fiery flame, *and* his wheels *as* burning fire.

…..

13- I saw in the night visions, and, behold, **one like the Son of man came with the clouds of heaven, and came to the Ancient of days *(the Father)*,** and they brought him near before him.

14- And there was given him dominion, and glory, and a kingdom, that all people, nations, and languages, should serve him: his dominion *is* an everlasting dominion, which shall not pass away, and his kingdom *that* which shall not be destroyed.

-Daniel 7 v 9, 13, 14

16- For God *(the Father)* so loved the world, that he gave his only begotten **Son**, that whosoever believeth in him should not perish, but have everlasting life.

17- For **God sent** not his **Son** into the world to condemn the world; but that the world through him *(Son)* might be saved.

18- He that believeth on him *(Son)* is not condemned: but he that believeth not is condemned already, **because he hath not believed in <u>the name of the only begotten Son of God</u>**.

19- And this is the condemnation, that light is come into the world, and men loved darkness rather than light, because their deeds were evil.

20- For every one that doeth evil hateth the light, neither cometh to the light, lest his deeds should be reproved.

21- But he that doeth truth cometh to the light, that his deeds may be made manifest, that they are wrought in God.

-John 3 v 16-21

NOTE: before Moses and the giving of 'the Law', LORD = God Almighty = the Most High God. Then JEHOVAH = LORD = God Almighty = the Most High God. LORD is JEHOVAH. The translators in every place of scripture where the word LORD is used in all Capital letters, substitute in the name JEHOVAH. It is the same. LORD = JEHOVAH.

25- And Ad'am knew his wife again; and she bare a son, and called his name Seth: For God, *said she*, hath appointed me another seed instead of A'bel, whom Cain slew.
26- And to Seth, to him also there was born a son; and he called his name E'nos: **then began men to call upon the name of the LORD**.
-Genesis 4 v 25, 26

2- And **God spake** unto Mo'ses and said unto him, **I** *am* **the LORD**.
3- **And I appeared** unto A'bra-ham, unto I'saac, and unto Ja'cob, **by** *the name* **God Almighty, but by my name JE-HO'VAH was I not known to them**.
4- And **I have also established my covenant with them, to give them the land of Ca'naan**, the land of their pilgrimage, wherein they were strangers.
-Exodus 6 v 2-4

3- Hear therefore, O Is'ra-el, and observe and do *it;* that it may be well with thee, and that ye may increase mightily, as **the LORD God of thy fathers** hath promised thee, in the land that floweth with milk and honey.
4- Hear, O Israel: **The LORD our God** is one LORD:
5- And thou shalt love **the LORD thy God** with all thine heart, and with all thy soul, and with all thy might.
-Deuteronomy 6 v 3-5

Revisit Isaiah 41 v 4 as an example:
4- Who hath wrought and done *it*, **calling the generations from the beginning? I the LORD** *(JEHOVAH)*, **the first, and with the last; I** *am* **he.**
-Isaiah 41 v 4

Who created all things?
12- Giving thanks unto the Father, which hath made us meet to be partakers of the inheritance of the saints in light:
13- Who hath delivered us from darkness, and hath translated *us* into the kingdom of his dear Son:

14- In whom we have redemption through his blood, *even* the forgiveness of sins:

15- Who is the image of the invisible God, the firstborn of every creature:

16- **For by him** *(Son/Jesus)* **were all things created**, that are in heaven, and that are in earth, visible and invisible, whether *they be* thrones, or dominions, or principalities, or powers: **all things were created by him** *(Son/Jesus)* **and for him**:

-Colossians 1 v 12-16

Who is before all things? Does this not make Jesus, God?:

17- **And he** *(Son/Jesus)* **is before all things, and by him all things consist.**
18- And **he is the head of the body, the church: who is the beginning, the firstborn from the dead**; that in all *things* he might have the preeminence.
19- For it pleased *the Father* that <u>in him should all fulness dwell</u>.
20- And, having made peace through the blood of his cross, by him to reconcile all things unto himself, *I say*, whether *they be* things in earth, or things in heaven.

-Colossians 1 v 17-20

The Father ordained that 'the fullness of the Godhead' would dwell in Jesus Christ the man. 'The Invisible Godhead' is not seen by man. The Son, JEHOVAH, the Word was the communicator between God the Father (the Godhead), to the world of men. <u>The Word is the communicator.</u> Scripture says that no man has seen God, the Invisible Godhead, the Father and lived.

The Invisible Godhead is the Father, the Word, and the Spirit. This is 'the fullness of God'. This is the one true God. Our God. No one else can claim to know him but by prayer and the studying of our Holy Bibles. We have his sign for 'the Body of Christ', Paul's Epistles. The 'supposed Christians' of today rely heavily on the 'earthly sign' of Jesus' first advent. Jesus Christ came in the flesh for Israel and the Jew and for us, our learning*. *-Ephesians 2 v 11-13; -Romans 15 v 6, 7; -Galatians 4 v 4, 5

God is one but there are three that bear record in heaven:

7- For <u>there are three that bear record in heaven</u>, **the Father, the Word, and the Ho'ly Ghost**, and these <u>three are one</u> *(the Godhead)*.

-I John 5 v 7

The Holy Spirit/Holy Ghost

The Holy Spirit, the Holy Ghost, is as much God as Jesus Christ is. The Spirit at times acted independently of the Father and Son and is an equal in the Godhead. They are all one and the same. "These three are one*, these three agree in one+".

*-I John 5 v 7; +-I John 5 v 8

Of course God is able to do as he wishes. God is sovereign, beyond all the comprehension of men. The Godhead could not possibly be bound and restricted. God is always everywhere.

Instead of appearing as 'an angel of the LORD' or in 'a flame of fire', at times the 'Spirit of God' indwelt and directed the individual. Samson was given incredible strength when the 'Spirit of God' came upon him. But the Spirit was not a permanent indwelling fixture of superhuman strength. Samson strength came and went as God saw fit and when Samson prayed and obeyed. "Do not go to the Barber Shop!"

This 'indwelling Holy Spirit' was not given to all that believed in the LORD God JEHOVAH in the Old Testament. The Holy Spirit would come and go. It wasn't the 'Comforter' (though it is the same Holy Ghost/Spirit) that was promised by Jesus Christ after he resurrected and ascended*. **The same Spirit of God is acting in a 'different Dispensation' towards mankind <u>after the resurrection</u>.**

*-John 16 v 7

'The Elect' and those of Israel were promised the gift of the Holy Ghost/Holy Spirit, the Comforter, by:

1- faith in the 'Name of Jesus Christ' and that it is he that came to be their Messiah.

2- keeping 'the Law'

3- being 'water baptized'.

These believing Jews were being 'water baptized into the Holy Spirit'. 'The Holy Ghost' indwelling 'the believer' was not a reward because they 'kept the Law' only. Jesus called the indwelling and permanent 'Holy Ghost/Spirit the Comforter'.

The Church, 'which is his body spiritually', are baptized by the Holy Ghost into Christ. In God, in Christ, that is our position in 'the Body of

Christ, the True Church. Not by water is this done. By faith in Paul's Gospel is this done by the Holy Spirit.

Examples of Diverse Manners

Adam and the Women:

8- And they heard **the voice of the <u>LORD God</u> walking** in the garden in the cool of the day: and Ad'am and his wife hid themselves from **the presence of the <u>LORD God</u>** amongst the trees of the garden.

9- And **the <u>LORD God</u>** called unto Ad'am, and said unto him, Where *art* thou?

10- And he said, I heard thy voice in the garden, and I was afraid, because I *was* naked; and I hid myself.

11- And he said, Who told thee that thou *wast* naked? Hast thou eaten of the tree, whereof I commanded thee that thou shouldest not eat?

-Genesis 3 v 8-11

Verse 8- **"the voice of the LORD God walking"**, **"the presence of the LORD God"**.

Before the 'food chain of life and death' fell upon all the living, Adam and the Women (she wasn't called Eve until after they ate of 'the Tree of the Knowledge of Good and Evil'), had a special relationship with God. They **"heard the voice of the LORD God walking"**. Can a voice walk? In what form was the voice of the LORD God walking in?

"The presence of the LORD God". The LORD God had a presence that Adam and the Women were well aware of. Did they actually see a visible presence of the LORD God? Something invisible is 'not seen'.

The LORD spoke to Cain:

6- And **the LORD said** unto Cain, Why art thou wroth? And why is thy countenance fallen?

7- If thou doest well, shalt thou not be accepted? And if thou doest not well, sin lieth at the door. And unto thee *shall be* his desire, and thou shalt rule over him.

-Genesis 4 v 6, 7

The LORD gave Cain a second chance. The LORD gave to Cain the 'proper sacrifice'. Cain had been taught through instruction by God in 'the process of time'* the 'correct way of what God expected of him. God left a submissive proper sacrifice at Cain's tent door. All Cain had to do was believe and accept. Cain was rebellious with no faith. The condemnation of mankind = unbelief. *-Genesis 4 v 3

8- And Cain talked with A'bel his brother: and it came to pass, when they were in the field, that Cain rose up against A'bel his brother and slew him.
9- And **the LORD said** unto Cain, Where is A'bel thy brother? And he said, I know not: *Am* I my brothers keeper?
10- And he said, What hast thou done? The voice of thy brother's blood crieth unto me from the ground.
11- And now *art* thou cursed from the earth, which hath opened her mouth to receive thy brother's blood from thy hand.
12- When thou tillest the ground, it shall not henceforth yield unto thee her strength; a fugitive and a vagabond shalt thou be in the earth.
-Genesis 4 v 8-12

Enoch walked with God. Did he walk with the voice only or was it a visible presence?:
22- And **E'noch walked with God** after he begat Me-thu'se-lah three hundred years, and begat sons and daughters:
23- And all the days of E'noch were three hundred sixty and five years:
24- **And E'noch walked with God: and he *was* not; for God took him.**
-Genesis 5 v 22-24

God speaks with Noah:
8- But No'ah found grace in the eyes of **the LORD.**

…..

13- And **God said** unto No'ah, The end of all flesh is come before me; for the earth is filled with violence through them; and, behold, I will destroy them with the earth.
14- Make thee an ark of gopher wood; rooms shalt thou make in the ark, and shalt <u>pitch it within and without with pitch.</u>

…..

18- But with thee will I establish my covenant; and thou shalt come into the ark, thou, and thy sons, and thy wife and thy sons' wives with thee.
-Genesis 6 v 8, 13, 14, 18

1- And **the LORD said** unto No'ah, Come thou and all thy house into the ark, for thee have I seen righteous* before me in this generation. *(*Noah's righteousness is by faith in what God said for Noah to do. Same as Abraham and for us. Noah's righteousness was not by 'the Law' but 'righteousness to every one that believeth'.)*
.....
16- And they that went in, went in male and female of all flesh, **as God had commanded** him: and **the LORD shut him in**.
-Genesis 7 v 1, 16

8- And God spake unto No'ah, and to his sons with him, saying,
9- And I, behold, **I establish my covenant with you, and with your seed after you:**
10- And with every living creature that *is* with you, of the fowl, of the cattle, and of every beast of the earth with you; from all that go out of the ark, to every beast of the earth.
11- And **I will** establish my covenant with you; neither shall all flesh be cut off any more by the waters of a flood; neither shall there any more be a flood to destroy the earth.
12- And **God said**, This *is* the token of the covenant which I make between me and you and every living creature that *is* with you, for perpetual generations.
13- I do set my bow in the cloud, and it shall be for a token of a covenant between me and the earth.
-Genesis 9 v 8-13

Here is scripture for the 'global warmers' and those that take 'man's science and knowledge' as usurping the power and Word of God. Believe in God or believe God?:
22- **While the earth remaineth, seedtime and harvest, and cold and heat, and summer and winter, and day and night shall not cease.**
-Genesis 8 v 22

16- For I am not ashamed of **the gospel of Christ**: for it is the power of God unto **salvation to every one that believeth**; to the Jew first, and also to the Greek *(Gentiles)*.

17- For therein is the righteousness of God revealed from faith to faith: as it is written, The just shall live by faith.

18- For the wrath of God is revealed from heaven against all ungodliness and unrighteousness of men, who hold the truth in unrighteousness;

19- Because that which may be known of God is manifest in them; **for God hath showed it unto them.**

20- For **the invisible things** of him from the **creation** of the world are **clearly seen**, being **understood by the things that are made**, *even* **his eternal power and <u>Godhead</u>**; so that **they are without excuse**:

21- Because that, when they knew God, they glorified *him* not as God, neither were thankful; but **became vain in their imaginations**, and their foolish heart was darkened.

22- **Professing themselves to be wise, they became fools,**

23- And changed the glory of the uncorruptible God into an image made like to corruptible man, and to birds, and four-footed beasts, and creeping things.

24- Wherefore **God also gave them up** to uncleanness through the lusts of their own hearts, to dishonor their own bodies between themselves:

25- **Who changed the truth of God into a lie, and worshipped and served the creature more than the Creator**, who is blessed for ever. A'men.

26- For this cause **God gave them <u>all up</u>** unto vile affections: for even their women did change the natural use into that which is against nature:

27- And likewise also the men, leaving the natural use of the woman, burned in their lust one toward another; men with men working that which is unseemly, and receiving in themselves that recompense of their error which was meet.

28- And even as they did not like to retain God in *their* knowledge, **God <u>gave them over</u> to a reprobate mind**, to do those things which are not convenient;

29- Being filled with all unrighteousness, fornication, wickedness, covetousness, maliciousness; full of envy, murder, debate, deceit, malignity; whisperers,

30- Backbiters, haters of God, despiteful, proud, boasters, inventors of evil things, disobedient to parents,

31- Without understanding, covenant breakers, without natural affection, implacable, unmerciful:

30- Who knowing the judgment of God, that they which commit such things are worthy of death, not only do the same, but have pleasure in them that do them.

-Romans 1 v 16-30

'The invisible things' that are far beyond the thinking of a man is subjected to unfounded scrutiny by unbelievers. Nature itself should prove to the world that there is a God. Yet, what did 'the spirit of men' come up with as an explanation? <u>Evolution</u>, where '<u>a nothing</u>' <u>becomes</u> '<u>a double nothing</u>', and over billions of years '<u>nothing became eventually something</u>'? 'The spirit of the natural man' can now explain the existence of life and mankind? Evolution?

Who taught the spiders there craftsmanship of web building? Is there a 'Spidey U School of Web Building'? Who instructed the birds on how to make a nest? Do the birds go to 'Fowl University'? Who can explain all the mysteries of the human body? Who set 'the invisible balance in nature'?

Take the brightest and most brilliant of men and have them create 'one simple cell living organism from scratch', no cloning. 'The simple confounds the wise'. No man, or any number of men can create even the most basic of life forms. Not so simple the gift of life.

God speaks with Abram. These scriptures are a staple for all Biblical knowledge. Understanding 'the Call of Abraham' and the Covenant promise made by God to him is of paramount foundational knowledge of the Holy Bible. The whole Bible from Genesis to Revelation was all written by the 'offspring' of Abraham.

The Abrahamic Covenant:

1- God 'sovereignly selected his chosen people'

2- God promised a nation and a kingdom. To survive as a cohesive 'great nation' there will have to be laws and rules to survive, a government

3- God gives these 'families' a place to establish their nation, an area of land, 'The Title Deed*'. *-Genesis 15 v 18

1- Now **the LORD had said** unto A'bram, Get thee out of thy country, and from thy kindred, and from thy father's house, unto a land that I will shew thee:
2- And I will make of thee a great nation, and I will bless thee, and make thy name great; and thou shalt be a blessing:
3- And I will bless them that bless thee, and curse him that curseth thee: and **in thee shall all families of the earth be blessed**.
-Genesis 12 v 1-3

7- And **the LORD appeared unto A'bram**, and said, Unto thy seed will I give this land: and there builded he an alter unto **the LORD, who appeared unto him**.
-Genesis 12 v 7

"the LORD appeared unto A'bram". Abram saw God. Is not the LORD, God? Yet no man has seen God and lived?

Melchizedek

Before the Law was delivered to Moses, **Jesus appeared in the person of Melchizedek**. Who else could it have been? Abraham was not seeing 'the LORD God of Israel' but 'the priest of the most High God'. All one and the same, but Abram, an Hebrew and not a child of Israel (he will be the father of the Jews, but as of yet, Abram is a Syrian) knew the LORD as God ALMIGHTY*, the most high God.
*-Genesis 17 v 1; -Genesis 28 v 3; -Genesis 35 v 11; -Genesis 43 v 14; -Genesis 48 v 3; -Genesis 49 v 25; -Exodus 6 v 3; -Numbers 24 v 4, 16; -Job 5 v 17; -Job 6 v 4; -Job 8 v 3, 5; -Job 11 v 7; -Job 13 v 3; -Job 15 v 25; -Job 22 v 17, 26; -Job 23 v 16; -Job 27 v 2, 10, 11, 13; -Job 31 v 2; -Job 33 v 4; -Job 34 v 10, 12; -Job 35 v 13; -Job 40 v 2; -Ezekiel 10 v 5

Melchizedek presents himself as 'the priest of the most high God':
18- And Mel-chiz'e-dek king of Sa'lem brought forth bread and wine: and **he *was* the priest of the most high God**.
19- And he blessed him, and said, **Blessed *be* A'bram of the most high God**, possessor of heaven and earth.
20- And **blessed be the most high God**, which hath delivered thine enemies into thy hand. And he gave him tithes of all.
-Genesis 14 v 18-20

Hebrews 7:

1- For this **Mel-chis'e-dec, king of Salem, priest of the most high God**, who met A'bra-ham returning from the slaughter of the Kings, and blessed him;

2- To whom also A'bra-ham gave a tenth part of all; first being by interpretation King of righteousness, and after that also king of Salem, which is, king of peace;

3- **Without father, without mother, without descent, having neither beginning of days, nor end of life; but made like unto the Son of God; abideth a priest continually.**

-Hebrews 7 v 1-3

Melchisedec was "without father, mother, descent, nor beginning, nor end, but made like unto the Son of God, abiding as a priest forever". You could say, "Melchisedec is God having such credentials". But scripture says no man has seen God and lived. Who is it then that Abraham communed with? Who really is this Melchisedec?

Hebrews 4:

12- For the word of God *is* quick, and powerful, and sharper than any twoedged sword, piercing even to the dividing asunder of soul and spirit, and of the joints and marrow, and *is* a discerner of the thoughts and intents of the heart.

13- Neither is there any creature that is not manifest in his sight: but all things *are* naked and opened unto the eyes of him with whom we have to do.

14- Seeing then that we have **a great high priest, that is passed into the heavens, Jesus the Son of God**, let us hold fast *our* profession.

15- **For we have not an high priest which cannot be** touched with the feeling of our infirmities; but was in all points tempted like as *we are, yet* without sin.

16- **Let us therefore come boldly unto the throne of grace,** that we may obtain mercy, and find grace to help in time of need.

-Hebrews 4 v 12-16

Hebrews 5:

1- For every high priest taken from among men is ordained for men in things *pertaining* to God, that he may offer both gifts and sacrifices for sins:

2- Who can have compassion on the ignorant, and on them that are out of the way; for that he himself also is compassed with infirmity.

3- And by reason hereof he ought, as for the people, so also for himself, to offer for sins.

4- And **no man taketh this honour unto himself, but he that is called of God**, as *was* Aar'on.

5- So also Christ glorified not himself to be made an high priest; but he that said unto him, **Thou art my Son, to day have I begotten thee**.

6- As he saith also in another *place*, **Thou *art* a priest for ever after the order of Mel-chiz'e-dec.**

7- <u>Who in the days of his flesh *(Melchizedec/Jesus?)*</u>, when he had offered up prayers and supplications with strong crying and tears unto him that was able to save him from death, and was heard in that he feared;

8- Though he were a **Son**, yet learned he obedience by the things which he suffered;

9- And being made perfect, **he became the author of eternal salvation unto all them that obey him;**

10- **Called of God an high priest <u>after the order of</u> Mel-chiz'e-dec.**

11- Of whom we have many things to say, and hard to be uttered, seeing ye are dull of hearing.

12- For when for the time ye ought to be teachers, ye have need that one teach you again which *be* the first principles of the oracles of God; and are become such as have need of milk, and not of strong meat,

13- For every one that useth milk *is* unskilled in the word of righteousness: for he is a babe.

14- But strong meat belongeth to them that are of full age, *even* those who by reason of use have their senses exercised to discern both good and evil.
-Hebrews 5 v 1-14

Hebrews 6:

10- For God *is* not unrighteous to forget your work and labor of love, which ye have shewed toward his name, and that ye have ministered to the saints, and do minister.

11- And we desire that every one of you do show the same diligence to the full assurance of hope unto the end.

12- That ye be not slothful, but followers of them who through faith and patience inherit the promises.

13- For when God made promise to A'bra-ham, because he could swear by no greater, he swear by himself.

14- Saying, Surely blessing I will bless thee, and multiplying I will multiply thee.

15- And so, after he had patiently endured, he obtained the promise.

16- For men verily swear by the greater: and an oath for confirmation *is* to them an end of all strife.

17- Wherein God, willing more abundantly to shew unto the heirs of promise the immutability of his counsel*, confirmed *it* by on oath. (*counsel, a plurality)

18- That by two immutable things, in which *it was* impossible for God to lie, we might have a strong consolation, who have fled for refuge to lay hold upon the hope set before us:

19- Which *hope* we have as an anchor of the soul, both sure and stedfast, and which entereth into that within the veil;

20- **Whither the forerunner is for us entered,** *even* **Jesus, made an high priest for ever after the order of Mel-chis'e-dec.**

-Hebrews 6 v 10-20

Hebrews 8:

1- Now of the things which we have spoken *this is* the sum: **We have such an high priest, who is set on the right hand of the throne of the Majesty in the heavens;**

2- **A minister of the sanctuary, and of the true tabernacle, which the Lord pitched, and not man.**

-Hebrews 8 v 1, 2

Examples of Visible Appearances by God

NOTE: Any partial scriptures used in this chapter will have as always 'the final say and disclaimer' from the King James Version of the Holy Bible. The scriptures used 'in partiality' in this chapter is to show how that in one chapter of the Holy Bible, the Godhead (the Father, the Word, the Holy Spirit/Ghost) are 'not restricted and put in a box'. Meaning, without reading the whole chapter these separate names for God were used and identified in their own respective individual-actualities as God has written.

Genesis 16: angel of the LORD = I will multiply = God

    verse 7- angel of the LORD

    verse 8- and he said

    verse 9- angel of the LORD

    verse 10- And the angel of the LORD said unto her *(Ha'gar)*, **I will** multiply thy seed exceedingly, that it shall not be numbered for multitude.

    verse 11- angel of the LORD

Only God, the LORD, the Word could say, "**I will** multiply thy seed exceedingly, that it shall not be numbered for multitude". The angel of the LORD visibly appeared many times in the Old Testament. They did not die that saw God.

Genesis 17: The LORD = I *am* the Almighty God.

    verse 1- **the LORD appeared to A'bram**, and said unto him, **I *am* the Almighty God**

    verse 3- and God talked with him

    verse 9- and God said unto A'bra-ham

    verse 15- and God said unto A'bra-ham

    verse 19- and God said,

    verse 22- and God went up from A'bra-ham

The LORD said, "I *am* the Almighty God". Who is the Almighty God? The LORD = the Almighty God = God.

The LORD visibly appeared to Abraham many times. Abraham did not die. A man cannot possibly behold and see the Godhead at one time (the Father, Word, Holy Spirit) and live. But the LORD JEHOVAH (who is God) was manifested in a visible form that men could see. The LORD God JEHOVAH is the one LORD, the one God that Israel knew. The Word, LORD, JEHOVAH, SON was made flesh in the person of Jesus Christ.

Genesis 18: The LORD appeared = the LORD said = the LORD left communing with Abraham

    verse 1- the LORD appeared unto him *(A'bra-ham)*

    verse 13- the LORD said unto A'bra-ham

    verse 33- And the LORD went his way, as soon as he had left communing with A'bra-ham

The LORD appeared to Abraham. God appeared to Abraham. The LORD said to Abraham. God said to Abraham. The LORD left communing with Abraham. God left communing with Abraham. God appeared and spoke through the Word, the LORD God JEHOVAH. The Word, this communicator, the LORD was made flesh in the body of Jesus Christ.

Genesis 20: Dream visions = a 'Divers manner'
verse 3- But God came to A'bra-ham in a dream by night

A 'divers manner' that only God could do. God came to Abraham in a dream. God, the LORD God JEHOVAH appeared to others via this way, a 'divers manner'.

Genesis 21: LORD = God = angel of God
verse 1- And the LORD visited Sa'rah
verse 12- God said unto A'bra-ham
verse 17- the angel of God called to Ha'gar out of heaven
verse 19- God opened her eyes

In one chapter we have the LORD, God, and the angel of God. There are not three God's but one. They are all one and the same. God the Father, the Godhead was communicating to men through the Son, who is the one LORD, the Word, at times the angel of the LORD.

Genesis 22: angel of the LORD = LORD = God
verse 11- angel of the LORD called to A'bra-ham out of heaven
verse 12- for now I know thou fearest God
verse 14- And A' bra-ham called the name of that place Je-ho'vah-ji'reh: and it is said to this day, In the mount of the LORD it shall be seen.
verse 15- And the angel of the LORD called unto A'bra-ham the second time,
verse 16- By myself have I sworn, saith the LORD,

Genesis 26: LORD = God
verse 2- the LORD appeared unto him *(I'ssac)*,
verse 24- the LORD appeared unto him *(I'ssac)* the same night, and said, I am the God of A'bra-ham thy father: fear not,

Genesis 28: 'Jacob's Ladder' Dream, LORD = LORD God

verse 12- And he dreamed, and behold a ladder set up on the earth, and the top of it reached to heaven: and behold <u>the angels of God</u> ascending and descending on it.

verse 13- **the LORD stood above it,** and said, **I am the LORD God** of A'bra-ham thy father, and the God of I'saac

Genesis 31: angel of God = God = God of Bethel

verse 11- And the angel of God spake unto me in a dream, *saying,* Jacob: and I said, Here *am* I.

verse 13- I *am* the God of Beth'-el* *(*Beth-el = house of God, ancient and seat of worship)*

verse 24- And God came to La'ban the Syr'i-an in a dream by night

Genesis 32: **Jacob says he saw God face to face.** If no man has seen God and lived then who was Jacob wrestling with?

1- And Ja'cob went on his way, and the angels of God met him.

2- And when Ja'cob saw them, he said, This *is* God's host: and he called the name of that place Ma-ha-na'im.

…..

24- And Ja'cob was left alone, and **there wrestled a man with him** until the breaking of the day.

25- And when he saw that he prevailed not against him, he touched the hollow of his thigh; and the hollow of Ja'cob's thigh was out of joint, as he wrestled with him.

26- And he said, Let me go, for the day breaketh. And he said, I will not let thee go, except thou bless me.

27- And he said unto him, What is thy name? And he said, Ja'cob.

28- And he said, **Thy name shall be called no more Ja'cob, but Is'ra-el:** for as a prince hast thou power with God and with men, and hast prevailed.

29- And Ja'cob asked *him,* and said, Tell *me,* I pray thee, thy name. And he said, Wherefore *is* it *that* thou dost ask after my name? And he blessed him there.

30- And Ja'cob called the name of the place Pe-ni'el: for <u>**I have seen God face to face, and my life is preserved**</u>.

-Genesis 32 v 1, 2, 24-30

Genesis 35: God = I *am* God almighty. Who of the Godhead was Jacob able to see? No man has seen God and lived scripture says.

>   verse 9- And God appeared unto Ja'cob again
>   verse 10- And God said unto him
>   verse 11- And God said unto him, I *am* God almighty
>   verse 13- And God went up from him in the place where he talked with him.

Genesis 46: 'Divers manners'

>   verse 2- And God spake unto Is'ra-el in the visions of the night
>   verse 3- I *am* God, the God of thy father

Genesis 48: God = the Angel which redeemed me. There is only one redeemer. Angel is capitalized.

>   verse 15- And he *(Israel/Jacob)* blessed Joseph, and said, God, before whom my fathers A'bra-ham and I'saac did walk, the God which fed me all my life long unto this day.
>   verse 16- <u>the Angel which redeemed me</u>

Exodus 3: angel of the LORD = LORD = God = I AM THAT I AM = the LORD God

2- And the **angel of the LORD** appeared unto him *(Moses)* in **a flame of fire** out of the midst of a bush: and he looked, and, behold, the bush burned with fire, and the bush *was* not consumed.

3- And Mo'ses said, I will now turn aside, and see this great sight, why the bush is not burnt.

4- And **when the LORD saw** that he turned aside to see, **God called** unto him out of the midst of the bush, and said, Mo'ses, Mo'ses. And he said, Here *am* I.

5- And he *(God)* said, Draw not nigh hither: put off thy shoes from off thy feet, for the place whereon thou standest *is* holy ground.

6- Moreover he said, **I *am* the God of thy father, the God of A'bra-ham, the God of I'saac, and the God of Ja'cob.** And Mo'ses hid his face; for he was afraid to look upon God.

7- And **the LORD said**, I have surely seen the affliction of **my people** which *are* in E'gypt, and have heard their cry by reason of their taskmasters; for I know their sorrows;

8- And **I am come down to deliver them** out of the hand of the E-gyp'tians, and to bring them up out of that land unto a good land and a large, unto a land flowing with milk and honey; unto the place of the Ca'naan-ites, and the Hit'tites, and the Am'or-ites, and the Per'iz-zites, and the Hi'vites, and the Jeb'u-sites.

9- Now therefore, behold, the cry of the children of Is'ra-el is come unto me: and I have also seen the oppression wherewith the E-gyp'tians oppress them.

10- Come now therefore, and I will send thee unto Pha'raoh, that thou mayest bring forth **my people the children of Is'ra-el** out of E'gypt.

11- And Mo'ses said unto God, Who *am* I, that I should go unto Pha'raoh, and that I should bring forth the children of Is'ra-el out of E'gypt?

12- And he said, Certainly I will be with thee; and this *shall be* a token unto thee, that I have sent thee: When thou hast brought forth the people out of E'gypt, ye shall serve God upon this mountain.

13- And Mo'ses said unto God, Behold, *when* I come unto the children of Is'ra-el, and say unto them, The God of your fathers hath sent me unto you; and they shall say to me, What is his name? What shall I say unto them?

14- And **God said** unto Mo'ses, **I AM THAT I AM**: and he said, Thus shalt thou say unto the children of Is'ra-el, **I AM** hath sent me unto you.

15- And God said moreover unto Mo'ses, Thus shalt thou say unto the children of Is'ra-el, **The LORD God of your fathers, the God of A'bra-ham, the God of I'saac, and the God of Ja'cob, hath sent me unto you: this *is* my name for ever, and this *is* my memorial unto all generations.**

16- Go, and gather the elders of Is'ra-el together, and say unto them, **The LORD God of your fathers**, the God of A'bra-ham, of I'saac, and of Ja'cob, **appeared unto me**, saying, I have surely visited you, and *seen* that which is done to you in E'gypt.

-Exodus 3 v 2-16

I AM = the angel of the LORD = LORD = God = the LORD God of your (Israel's) fathers. All of God (the Father, the Godhead) was not in the flaming bush, but 'the communicator', the Word, Son, the LORD, the angel of God was manifested in the flame. These are not 'god's of many but 'one God' appearing in different ways, divers manners.

Exodus 4: LORD = LORD God

    verse 1- for they will say, The LORD hath not appeared unto thee.

    verse 2- And the LORD said unto him, What *is* that in thine hand? And he said, A rod.

    verse 3- And he said, Cast it on the ground, and it became a serpent

    verse 4- And the LORD said unto Mo'ses, take it by the tail, and it became a rod in his hand.

    verse 5- That they may believe that the LORD God of their fathers, hath appeared unto thee.

    verse 27- And the LORD said to Aar'on

Exodus 6: God = I am the LORD = God Almighty = JEHOVAH

    verse 2- And God spake unto Mo'ses, and said unto him, I *am* the LORD:

    verse 3- And I appeared unto A'bra-ham, unto I'saac, and unto Ja'cob, by *the name of* God Almighty, but by my name JE-HO'VAH was I not known to them.

The LORD God of the Hebrews Only

Exodus 7: The LORD God of the Hebrews, not the LORD God of all men.

    verse 16- The LORD God of the Hebrews hath sent me *(Mo'ses)* unto thee *(Pha'raoh)*

Exodus 9: LORD = The LORD God of the Hebrews

    verse 1- the LORD said unto Mo'ses, thus saith the LORD God of the Hebrews

Exodus 10: The LORD God of the Hebrews

    verse 3- Thus saith the LORD God of the He'brews

Diverse Manners continued:

Exodus 13: 'Divers Manners' of the LORD = cloud by day and fire by night

21- And the LORD went before them by day in a pillar of a cloud, to lead them the way; and by night in a pillar of fire, to give them a light; to go by day and night:

22- He took not away the pillar of the cloud by day, nor the pillar of fire by night, *from* before the people.

-Exodus 13 v 21, 22

Exodus 14: 'Divers Manners' of the angel of God = cloud and fire

19- And **the angel of God**, which went before the camp of Is'ra-el, removed and went behind them; and the pillar of the cloud went from before their face, and stood behind them.

20- And it came between the camp of the E-gyp'tians and the camp of Is'ra-el; and it was a cloud and darkness *to them*, but it gave light by night *to these*: so that the one came not near the other all night.

-Exodus 14 v 19, 20

Exodus 19: 'Divers Manners' of thunders, lightnings, trumpet. God = the LORD descends in fire = the LORD

16- And it came to pass on the third day in the morning that there were thunders and lightenings, and a thick cloud upon the mount, and the voice of the trumpet exceeding loud; so that all the people that *was* in the camp trembled.

17- And Mo'ses brought forth the people out of the camp **to meet with God**; and they stood at the nether part of the mount.

18- And mount Si'nai was altogether on a smoke, because **the LORD descended upon it in fire**: and the smoke thereof ascended as the smoke of a furnace, and the whole mount quaked greatly.

19- And when the voice of the trumpet sounded long, and waxed louder and louder, Mo'ses spake, and God answered him by a voice.

20- And **the LORD came down upon the mount Si'nai**, on the top of the mount. and the Lord called Moses *up* to the top of the mount; and Mo'ses went up.

21- And the LORD said unto Mo'ses, Go down, charged the people, lest they break through unto the LORD to gaze, and many of them perish.

-Exodus 19 v 16-21

Exodus 20: 'Divers Manners' of thunderings, lightnings, noise of a trumpet, mountain smoking, thick darkness. God = the LORD

18- And all the people saw the thunderings, and the lightnings, and the noise of the trumpet, and the mountain smoking: and when the people saw *it*, they removed, and stood afar off.

19- And they said unto Mo'ses, Speak thou with us, and we will hear: but let not God speak with us, lest we die.

20- And Mo'ses said unto the people, Fear not: for God is come to prove you, and that his fear may be before your faces, that ye sin not.

21- And the people stood afar off, and Mo'ses drew near unto **the thick darkness where God** *was*.

22- And **the LORD said unto Mo'ses**, Thus thou shalt say unto the children of Is'ra-el, **Ye have seen that I have talked with you from heaven**.

23- Ye shall not make with me gods of silver, neither shall ye make unto you gods of gold.

24- <u>An altar of earth</u> thou shalt make unto me, and shalt sacrifice thereon thy burnt offerings, and thy peace offerings, thy sheep, and thine oxen: in all places where I record my name I will come unto thee, and I will bless thee.

25- And if thou wilt make me an altar of stone, thou shalt not build it of hewn stone: for if thou lift up thy tool upon it, thou hast polluted it.

-Exodus 20 v 18-25

Exodus 23: Angel is capitalized. Who is this Angel?

God said, "for my name is in him, obey his voice and do all that <u>I</u> speak".

20- Behold, I send an **Angel** before thee, to keep thee in the way, and to bring thee into the place which I have prepared.

21- Beware of him, and obey his voice, provoke him not; for he will not pardon your transgressions: **for my name** *is* **in him**.

22- But if thou shalt indeed obey **his voice**, and do all **that I speak**; then **I will be** an enemy unto thine enemies, and an adversary unto thine adversaries.

23- For **mine Angel** shall go before thee, and bring thee in unto the Am'or-ites, and the Hit'tites, and the Per'iz-zites, and the Ca'naan-ites, the Hi'vites, and the Jeb'u-sites: **and I will** cut them off.

-Exodus 23 v 20-23

Exodus 24: 'Divers Manners' of a cloud being the glory of the LORD and a devouring fire. God of Israel = God = glory of the LORD = called to Moses out of the cloud = like a devouring fire

> verse 9- Then went up Mo'ses, and Aaron, Nadab, and Abihu, and seventy of the elders of Is'ra-el:

> verse 10- And <u>they saw the God of Is'ra-el</u>

> verse 11- <u>the nobles of the children of Is'ra-el saw God</u>

> verse 16- <u>the glory of the LORD</u> abode upon mount Sinai, and the cloud covered it six days: and on the seventh day **he called unto Moses out of the midst of the cloud.**

> verse 17- And the sight of **the glory of the LORD** was like devouring fire on top of the mount in the eyes of the children of Is'ra-el.

Exodus 33: 'Divers Manners' = LORD = cloudy pillar = my glory.

> verse 9- And it came to pass, as Moses entered into the tabernacle, **the cloudy pillar** descended, and stood *at* the door of the tabernacle, and *the LORD* **talked with Moses.**

> verse 11- And **the LORD spake unto Moses <u>face to face</u>,** as a man speaketh unto his friend

> verse 20- And he said, Thou canst not see my face: **for there shall no man see me, and live.**

> verse 21- And the LORD said, Behold, *there is* a place by me, and thou shalt stand upon a rock:

> verse 22- And it shall come to pass, while **my glory passeth by**, that I will put thee in a clift of the rock, and will cover thee with my hand while I pass by:

> verse 23- And I will take away mine hand, and thou shalt see my back parts: **but my face shall not be seen.**

Exodus 40: 'Divers Manners' = The glory of the LORD = Cloud by day = fire by night.

34- Then a cloud covered the tent of the congregation, and **the glory of the LORD** filled the tabernacle.

35- And Mo'ses was not able to enter into the tent of the congregation, because the cloud abode thereon, and **the glory of the LORD** filled the tabernacle.

36- And when the cloud was taken up from over the tabernacle, the children of Is'ra-el went onward in all their journeys.

37- But if the cloud were not taken up, then they journeyed not till the day that it was taken up.

38- For the cloud of the LORD was upon the tabernacle by day and fire was on it by night, in the sight of all the house of Is'ra-el, throughout all their journeys.

-Exodus 40 v 34-38

Leviticus 9: 'Divers Manners' = glory of the LORD = the LORD

23- And Mo'ses and Aar'on went into the tabernacle of the congregation, and came out, and blessed the people: and the glory of the LORD appeared unto all the people.

24- And there came a fire out from before the LORD, and consumed upon the alter the burnt offering of the fat: *which* when all people saw, they shouted and fell on their faces.

-Leviticus 9 v 23, 24

Numbers 9: 'Divers Manners' = cloud covering the tent of the testimony, cloud by day, fire by night

15- And on the day that the tabernacle was reared up the cloud covered the tabernacle, *namely* the tent of the testimony: and at even there was upon the tabernacle as it were the appearance of fire, until the morning.

16- So it was alway: the cloud covered it by day, and the appearance of fire by night.

17- And when the cloud was taken up from the tabernacle, then after that the children of Is'ra-el journeyed: and in the place where the cloud abode, there the children of Is'ra-el pitched their tents.

-Numbers 9 v 15-17

Numbers 11: 'Divers Manners' = the Lord = the fire of the LORD = a cloud spake = the LORD smote the people

1- And *when* the people complained, it displeased the LORD: and the LORD heard *it;* and his anger was kindled; and the fire of the LORD burnt among them, and consumed *them that were* in the uttermost parts of the camp.

2- And the people cried unto Mo'ses; and when Mo'ses prayed unto the LORD, the fire was quenched.

…..

25- And the LORD came down in a cloud, and spake unto him, and took of the spirit that *was* upon him, and gave *it* unto the seventy elders:, and *it* came to pass, *that,* when the spirit rested upon them, they prophesied and did not cease.

…..

31- And there went forth a wind from the LORD, and brought quails from the sea, and let *them* fall by the camp, as it were a day's journey on this side, and as it were a day's journey on the other side, round about the camp, and as it were two cubits *high* upon the face of the earth.

32- And the people stood up all that day, and all *that* night, and all the next day, and they gathered the quails: he that gathered least gathered ten homers: and they spread *them* all abroad for themselves round about the camp.

33- And while the flesh *was* yet between their teeth, ere it was chewed, the wrath of the LORD was kindled against the people, and the LORD smote the people with a very great plague.

34- And he called the name of that place Kib'roth-hat-ta'a-vah: because there they buried the people that lusted.

35- *And* the people journeyed from Kib'roth-hat-ta'a-vah unto Ha-ze'roth; and abode at Ha-ze'roth.

-Numbers 11 v 1, 2, 25, 31-35

Numbers 12: 'Divers Manners' = The LORD = pillar of cloud = he said = spoke of the visions and dreams the LORD would use in selecting the prophets.

5- And the LORD came down in the pillar of the cloud, and stood *in* the door of the tabernacle, and called Aar'on and Mir'i-am: and they both came forth.

6- And he said, Hear now my words: If there be a prophet among you, *I* the LORD will make myself known unto him in a vision, *and* will speak unto him in a dream.

7- My servant Mo'ses *is* not so, who *is* faithful in all mine house.

8- With him will I speak mouth to mouth, **even apparently**, and not in dark speeches; and **the similitude of the LORD shall he behold**: wherefore then were ye not afraid to speak against my servant Mo'ses?

9- And the anger of the LORD was kindled against them; and he departed.

10- And the cloud departed from off the tabernacle; and, behold, Mir'i-am *became* leprous, *white* as snow: and Aar'on looked upon Mir'i-am, and, behold, *she was* leprous.
-Numbers 12 v 5-10

Numbers 14: 'Divers Manners' = The glory of the LORD = the LORD
10- But all the congregation bade stone them with stones. And the glory of the LORD appeared in the tabernacle of the congregation before all the children of Is'ra-el.
11- And the LORD said unto Mo'ses, How long will this people provoke me? and how long will it be ere they believe me, for all the signs which I have shewed among them?
12- I will smite them with the pestilence, and disinherit them, and will make of thee a greater nation and mightier than they.
-Numbers 14 v 10-12

Numbers 16: 'Divers Manners' = The glory of the LORD appeared unto all the congregation = the LORD spake
19- And Ko'rah gathered all the congregation against them unto the door of the tabernacle of the congregation: and the glory of the LORD appeared unto all the congregation.
20- And the LORD spake unto Mo'ses and unto Aar'on, saying,
21- Separate yourselves from among this congregation, that I may consume them in a moment.
-Numbers 16 v 19-21

Numbers 22: 'Diverse Manners' = God = angel of the LORD = the LORD
22- And God's anger was kindled because he went: and the angel of the LORD stood in the way for an adversary against him. Now he was riding upon his ass, and his two servants *were* with him.
23- And the ass saw the angel of the LORD standing in the way, and his sword drawn in his hand: and the ass turned aside out of the way, and went into the field: and Ba'laam smote the ass, to turn her into the way.
24- But the angel of the LORD stood in the path of the vineyards, a wall *being* on this side, and a wall on that side.
25- And when the ass saw the angel of the LORD, she thrust herself unto the wall, and crushed Ba'laam's foot against the wall: and he smote her again.

26- And the angel of the LORD went further, and stood in a narrow place, where *was* no way to turn either to the right hand or to the left.

27- And when the ass saw the angel of the LORD, she fell down under Ba'laam: and Ba'laam's anger was kindled, and he smote the ass with a staff.

28- And the LORD opened the mouth of the ass, and she said unto Ba'laam, What have I done unto thee, that thou hast smitten me these three times?

29- And Ba'laam said unto the ass, Because thou hast mocked me: I would there were a sword in mine hand, for now would I kill thee.

30- And that ass said unto Ba'laam, *Am* not I thine ass, upon which thou hast ridden ever since *I was* thine unto this day? was I ever wont to do so unto thee? And he said, Nay.

31- Then the LORD opened the eyes of Ba'laam, and he saw the angel of the LORD standing in the way, and his sword drawn in his hand: and he bowed down his head, and fell flat on his face.

32- And the angel of the LORD said unto him, Wherefore hast thou smitten thine ass these three times? behold, I went out to withstand thee, because *thy* way is perverse before me:

33- And the ass saw me, and turned from me these three times: unless she had turned from me, surely now also I had slain thee, and saved her alive.

34- And Ba'laam said unto the angel of the LORD, I have sinned; for I knew not that thou stoodest in the way against me: now therefore, if it displease thee, I will get me back again.

35- And the angel of the LORD said unto Ba'laam, Go with the men: but only the word that I shall speak unto thee, that thou shalt speak. So Ba'laam went with the princes of Ba'lak.

-Numbers 22 v 22-35

Numbers 23: 'Diverse Manners' = God = the LORD

4- And **God met** Ba'laam: and he said unto him, I have prepared seven altars, and I have offered upon *every* alter a bullock and a ram.

5- And **the LORD put a word** in Ba'laam's mouth, and said, Return unto Ba'lak, and thus thou shalt speak.

-Numbers 23 v 4, 5

Deuteronomy: the LORD spake with Moses many times. At times the LORD spoke to the children of Israel.

1 v 6- the LORD our God spake unto us in Ho'reb, saying,

4 v 12- And the LORD spake unto you out of the midst of the fire:

5 v 4- The LORD talked with you face to face in the mount out of the midst of the fire,

Deuteronomy 5: LORD = our God = voice of the living God

22- These words the LORD spake unto all your assembly *(church?)* in the mount out of the midst of the fire, of the cloud, and of the thick darkness, with a great voice: and he added no more. And he wrote them in two tables of stone, and delivered them unto me.

23- And it came to pass, when ye heard the voice out of the midst of the darkness, (for the mountain did burn with fire,) that ye came near unto me, *even* all the heads of your tribes, and your elders;

24- And ye said, Behold, the LORD our God hath shewed us his glory and his greatness, and we have heard his voice out of the midst of the fire: **we have seen this day that God doth talk with man, and he liveth**.

25- Now therefore why should we die? For this great fire will consume us: if we hear the voice of the LORD our God any more, then we shall die.

26- **For who *is there of* all flesh, that hath heard the voice of the living God speaking out of the midst of the fire, as we *have*, and lived?**

-Deuteronomy 5 v 22-26

Deuteronomy 6: the LORD = our God = one LORD

4- Hear O Is'ra-el the LORD our God *is* one LORD:

-Deuteronomy 6 v 4

Deuteronomy 9: The LORD delivered the two tables of stone = written with the finger of God = spake out of the midst of the fire

10- And **the LORD delivered unto me two tables of stone written with the finger of God**; and on them *was written* according to all the words, which **the LORD spake with you in the mount out of the midst of the fire**; in the day of assembly *(church?)*.

-Deuteronomy 9 v 10

Deuteronomy 31: the LORD = pillar of a cloud

15- And **the LORD appeared in the tabernacle in a pillar of a cloud**: and the pillar of the cloud stood over the door of the tabernacle.

16- And the Lord said unto Mo'ses, Behold, thou shalt sleep with thy fathers; and **this people will** rise up, and go a whoring *(spiritually)* after the gods of the strangers of the land, whither they go *to be* among them, and will forsake me, and break my covenant which I have made with them.

-Deuteronomy 31 v 15, 16

Deuteronomy 34: The LORD showed all 'the promised land' given to Israel. If Mo'ses never moved from the top of Pisgah, how did the LORD do this?

1- And Mo'ses went up from the plains of Mo'ab unto the mountain of Ne'bo, to the top of Pis'gah, that *is* over against Jer'i-cho. And the LORD shewed him all the land of Gil'e-ad, unto Dan,

2- And all Naph'ta-li, and the land of E'phra-im, and Ma-nas'seh, and all the land of Ju'dah, unto the utmost sea,

3- And the south, and the plain of the valley of Jer'i-cho, the city of palm trees, unto Zo'ar.

4- And the LORD said unto him, This *is* the land which I sware unto A'bra-ham, unto I'saac, and unto Ja'cob, saying, I will give it unto thy seed: **I have caused thee to see *it* with thine eyes, but thou shalt not go over thither.**

5- So Mo'ses the servant of the LORD died there in the land of Mo'ab, according to the word of the LORD.

-Deuteronomy 34 v 1-5

Deuteronomy 34: The LORD knew Mo'ses face to face. If the LORD is God, then why did not Moses die? Scripture says that 'No man has seen God and lived'. Who of the Godhead has been seen by man and did not die?

10- And there arose not a prophet since in Is'ra-el like unto **Mo'ses, whom the LORD knew face to face.**

-Deuteronomy 34 v 10

The LORD God JEHOVAH was seen by man and they did not die. 'The communicator' of the Godhead is the LORD. The LORD = the Word. The Word, the LORD, JEHOVAH God was made flesh in the body of Jesus Christ. The LORD God JEHOVAH = the Lord Jesus Christ = God = Son

Jesus Christ himself refers to 'The Father' and his relationship with the Godhead. When the Word became flesh, the man Jesus (though God himself) prayed not to himself but to God the Father, the Godhead. All three are one. The Father, the Word and the Holy Ghost. All three are 'heavenly witnesses'.

The LORD God JEHOVAH being a man suffered like men do. Jesus felt physical pain, he got tired, he got hungry, he got thirsty. Jesus Christ is the 'righteous advocate' and our High Priest, our representative, our propitiation (the 'appropriator' of all our sins), having the same human, earthy, day to day challenges. Jesus is just, and the justifier* to **all that believe** on 'his resurrection' as 'the Gospel of Salvation'. *-Romans 1 v 17; -Romans 3 v 24, 26, 28, 30; -Romans 4 v 2, 5, 25; -Romans 5 v 1, 9, 16; -Romans 8 v 30, 33; -I Corinthians 6 v 11; -Galatians 2 v 16; -Galatians 3 v 8, 11; -Titus 3 v 7; -Hebrews 10 v 38

Beware! Paul writes Holy Spirit inspired. Scripture does not say 'the fulness of God' dwells in Jesus but says 'the fulness of the Godhead' = the Father, the Word and the Holy Spirit:
8- Beware lest any man spoil you with philosophy and vain deceit, after the tradition of men, after the rudiments of the world, and not after **Christ**.
9- **For in him *(Son)* dwelleth all the fulness of the Godhead bodily.**
-Colossians 2 v 8, 9

17- And he *(Son)* is before all things, and by him *(Son)* all things consist.
18- And he *(the resurrected Jesus)* is the head of the body, the church: who is the beginning, the firstborn from the dead; that in all *things* he may have the preeminence.
19- **For it pleased the Father that in him *(Son)* should all fulness dwell.**
-Colossians 1 v 17-19

19- Because that which may be known of God is manifest in them; for God hath showed *it* unto them.
20- For the invisible things of him from the creation of the world are clearly seen, being understood by the things that are made, *even* his eternal power and **Godhead**; so that **they are without excuse**:
21- Because that, when they knew God, they glorified *him* not as God, neither were thankful; but became vain in their imaginations, and their foolish heart was darkened.
-Romans 1 v 19-21

The Jews left off believing or never did believe that Jesus is the Son of God, the Word made flesh. Most of Christendom believe in the 'earthly ministry' of Jesus Christ to Israel, not understanding that the LORD is the Word, is God, and it is Jesus Christ that represents the Godhead, The Father, the Word and the Holy Ghost.

Read the following scriptures from John. This is what God wrote through John, not what John wrote through God. Whether he understood or not, it is God's word not John's words. It is God that opens the eyes of understanding of what John was Holy Spirit inspired to write.

30- I *(Jesus)* can of mine own self do nothing: as I hear, I judge; and my judgment is just; because **I seek not mine own will, but the will of the Father which hath sent me**.

31- **If I bear witness of myself, my witness is not true.**

32- There is another that beareth witness of me*; and I know what the witness which he witnesseth of me is true. *(*The Godhead, the Father)*

33- Ye sent unto John, and he bare witness unto the truth.

34- But I received not testimony from man: but these things I say, that ye might be saved.

35- He was a burning and a shining light: and ye were willing for a season to rejoice in his light.

36- But I *(Jesus)* have greater witness than *that* of John *(the Baptist)*: for **the works which the Father hath given me to finish**, the same works that I do, bear witness of me, that **the Father hath sent me**.

37- **And the Father himself, which hath sent me, hath borne witness of me. Ye have neither heard his voice at any time, nor seen his shape.**

…..

43- **I *(Jesus)* am come in my Father's name**, and ye receive me not: if another shall come in his own name, him ye will receive.

44- How can ye believe, which receive honour one of another, and seek not the honor that cometh from God only?

45- Do not think that I will accuse you to the Father: there is *one* that accuses you, *even* Moses, in whom ye trust.

46- **For had ye believed Mo'ses, ye would have believed me: for he wrote of me.**

47- **But if ye believe not his writings, how shall ye believe my words?**

-John 5 v 30-37, 43-47

John 14: Jesus Christ speaks not one word of the 'Earthly Heavenly Kingdom' being delayed. There is no mention of the 'Church, the Body of Christ'. Israel still at this time has the opportunity to accept their messiah and kingdom. Jesus is speaking as if the 'prophetic time-line for Israel' would keep right on going, uninterrupted.

1- Let not your heart be troubled: **ye believe in God, believe also in me (Jesus)**.

2- In my father's house are many mansions: if *it were* not *so*, I would have told you. I go to prepare a place for you.

3- And if I go and prepare a place for you, I will come again, and receive you unto myself; that where I am, *there* ye may be also.

4- And whither I go ye know, and the way ye know.

5- Thom'as saith unto him, Lord, we know not whither thou goest; and how can we know the way?

6- Jesus saith unto him, I am the way, the truth, and the life: **no man cometh unto the Father, but by me**.

7- **If ye had known me, ye should have known my Father also: and from henceforth ye know him, and have seen him.**

8- Phil'ip saith unto him, Lord, shew us the Father, and it sufficeth us.

9- Je'sus saith unto him, Have I been so long time with you, and yet hast thou not known me, Phil'ip? **He that hath seen me hath seen the father;** and how sayest thou *then*, Shew us the Father?

10- Believest thou not that **I am in the Father, and the Father in me?** The words that I speak unto you **I speak not of myself: but the Father that dwelleth in me, he doeth the works.**

11- Believe me that **I *am* in the Father, and the Father in me: or else believe me for the very works sake.**

12- Verily, verily, I say unto you, He that believeth on me, the works that I do shall he do also; and greater *works* than these shall he do; **because I go unto my Father.**

13- And whatsoever ye shall ask in my name, that will I do, that **the Father may be glorified in the Son.**

14- If ye shall ask any thing in my name, I will do *it*.

15- If ye love me, keep <u>my commandments</u>.

NOTE: v15- Jesus is speaking, 'my commandments', given by God, given by the LORD, given by Jesus? Jesus, the Son, was in the Old Testament. LORD = Jesus Christ = God = Son

16- And I will pray the Father, and he shall give you another Comforter, that he may abide with you for ever;

17- *Even* the Spirit of truth; whom the world cannot receive, because it seeth him not, neither knoweth him: but ye know him; for **he dwelleth with you** *(Jesus is with them)* **and <u>shall be</u> in you** *(after the ascension via the Holy Spirit).*

18- I will not leave you comfortless: I will come to you.

v18- "I will come to you", how? By the Holy Ghost, the Comforter. All are one and equal in the Godhead, The Father, the Word and the Holy Ghost. In this case, God isn't going to visit in his earthly visible form but by the Holy Spirit.

19- Yet a little while, and the world seeth me no more; but ye see me: because I live, ye shall live also.

20- <u>At that day</u> **ye shall know that I** *am* **in my Father, and ye in me, and I in you.**

21- **He that hath <u>my *(Jesus)* commandments</u>**, and keepeth them, he it is that loveth me: and he that loveth me shall be loved of **my Father**, and I will love him, and will manifest myself to him.

22- Ju'das saith unto him, not Is-car'i-ot, Lord, how is it that thou wilt manifest thyself unto us, and not unto the world?

23- Je'sus answered and said unto him, If a man love me, he will keep my words: and **my Father will love him, and we will come unto him, and make our abode with him.**

24- He that loveth me not keepeth not my sayings: and the word which ye hear is not mine, but <u>the Father's which sent me</u>.

25- These things have I spoken unto you, being *yet* present with you.

26- But **the Comforter,** *which is* **the Holy Ghost*, whom the Father* will send in my name*,** he shall teach you all things, and bring all things to your remembrance, whatsoever I have said unto you. *(*The Godhead)*

27- Peace I leave with you, my peace I give unto you: not as the world giveth, give I unto you. Let not your heart be troubled, neither let it be afraid.

28- Ye have heard how I said unto you, I go away, and come *again* unto you. If ye loved me, ye would rejoice, because I said, **I** *(Jesus)* **go unto the Father**: for **my Father is greater than I***. *(*Jesus speaking as a man and has not been resurrected/glorified/begotten yet. A little lower than the angels for the suffering of death, "the LORD said to my Lord"...)*

29- And now I have told you before it come to pass, that, when it is come to pass, ye might believe.

30- Hereafter I will not talk much with you: for the prince of this world cometh, and hath nothing in me.

31- But that the world may know that **I love the Father**; and as **the Father gave me commandment, even so I do**. Arise, let us go hence.

-John 14

John 15:

1- **I Am** the true vine, and **my Father** is the husbandman.

.....

9- As **the Father hath loved me, so have I loved you**: continue ye in my love.

10- If ye keep my commandments*, ye shall abide in my love; even as I have kept my Father's commandments, and abide in his love. *(*my commandments, Jesus = my Fathers commandments = LORD = I Am = Jesus Christ)*

.....

15- Henceforth I call you not servants; for the servant knoweth not what his lord doeth: but I have called you friends; for all **things that I have heard of my Father I have made known unto you**.

.....

21- But all these things will they do unto you for my name's sake, because **they know not him that sent me**.

.....

23- **He that hateth me hateth my Father also.**

24- If I had not done among them the works which none other man did, they had not had sin: but now have they both seen and hated both me and my Father.

25- But *this cometh to pass*, that the word might be fulfilled that is written in their law, **They hated me without a cause**.

26- **But when the Comforter* is come, whom I* will send unto you from the Father*, *even* the Spirit* of truth, which proceeded from the Father*, he shall testify of me*:** *(*The Godhead)*

27- And ye also shall bear witness, because ye have been with me from the beginning.

-John 15 v 1, 9, 10, 15, 21-27

John 16:

3- And these things will they do unto you, because **they have not known the Father, nor me**.

…..

5- But now **I go my way to him that sent me**; and none of you asketh me, Whither goest thou?

…..

7- Nevertheless I tell you the truth; It is expedient for you that I go away: for if I go not away, **the Comforter** will not come unto you; but if I depart, **I will send <u>him</u> unto you**.

…..

10- Of righteousness, because **I go to my Father**, and ye see me no more;

…..

13- Howbeit when **he, the Spirit of truth**, is come, **he will guide you** into all truth: for **he shall not speak of himself**; but **whatsoever he shall hear, *that* shall he speak**: and **he will shew you** things to come.

…..

15- **All things that the Father hath are mine**: therefore said I, that he shall take of mine, and shall shew *it* unto you.

…..

23- And in that day ye shall ask me nothing. Verily, verily, I say unto you, **Whatsoever ye shall ask the Father in my name**, he will give *it* you.

-John 16 v 3, 5, 7, 10, 13, 15, 23

Jesus is speaking during his 'earthly ministry'. Paul and 'the Gospel of the Grace of God' is still a hidden mystery and a secret. There were no Gentiles under the 'Kingdom Gospel'. When Jesus is sitting on his Holy Hill in Zion, as the King of Kings, and Lord of Lords, all things asked of him will be fulfilled. It has been promised to be 'an Earthly Heavenly Kingdom'.

Are all things that are asked of God given to those who ask? Answers to prayers do happen in the Age of Grace, but all things asked for? When the Earthly Kingdom of Heaven is fulfilled, then all things asked for will be received.

Be honest with yourself. There is no Kingdom on the Earth with Jesus Christ ruling and reigning from Jerusalem. Go ahead, drink poison, play with scorpions and vipers. Why not? Many say, "I follow Jesus", but how can you if you don't obey his directions and keep 'the Law of Moses'?

24- Hitherto have **ye asked nothing in my name: ask, and ye shall receive**, that your joy may be full.

25- These things have I spoken unto you in proverbs: but the time cometh, when I shall no more speak unto you in proverbs, but **I shall shew you plainly of the Father.**

26- **At that day ye shall ask in my name**: and I say not unto you, that **I will pray the Father for you:**

27- For **the Father himself loveth you**, because **ye have loved me**, and have believed that **I came out from God.**

28- **I came forth from the Father**, and am come into the world: again, **I leave the world, and go to the Father**.

…..

32- Behold, the hour cometh, yea, is now come, that ye shall be scattered, every man to his own, and shall leave me alone: and yet **I am not alone, because the Father is with me**.

33- These things I have spoken unto you, that in me ye might have peace. In the world ye shall have tribulation: but be of good cheer, I have overcame the world.

-John 16 v 24-28, 32, 33

Joshua

13- And it came to pass, when Josh'u-a was by Jer'i-cho, that he lifted up his eyes and looked, and, behold, there stood a man over against him with his sword drawn in his hand: and Josh'u-a went unto him, and said unto him, *Art* thou for us, or for our adversaries?

14- And he said, Nay; but *as* **captain of the host of the LORD am I now come. And Josh'u-a fell on his face to the earth, and did worship**, and said unto him, What saith my lord unto his servant?

15- And **the captain of the LORD's host** said unto Josh'u-a, Loose thy shoe from off thy foot; for the place whereon thou standest *is* holy. And Josh'u-a did so.
-Joshua 5 v 13-15

Joshua visibly see's 'the captain of the host of the LORD'. Who did Joshua really see? Joshua fell down and worshiped 'the captain of the LORD's host'. Joshua never would have worshiped anything unless it was the LORD God JEHOVAH himself. Joshua recognized who the captain really is. Can you?

Joshua 10: The LORD God of Israel fought for Israel.

11- And it came to pass, as they fled from before Is'ra-el, *and* were in the going down to Beth-ho'ron, that **the LORD cast down great stones from heaven upon them unto A-ze'kah, and they died:** *they were* **more which died with hailstones than** *they* **whom the children of Is'ra-el slew with the sword**.

12- Then spake Josh'u-a to the LORD in the day when the LORD delivered up the Am'or-ites before the children of Is'ra-el, and he said in the sight of Is'ra-el, Sun, stand thou still upon Gib'e-on; and thou, Moon, in the valley of Aj'a-lon.

13- And the sun stood still, and the moon stayed, until the people had avenged themselves upon their enemies. *Is* not this written in the book of Ja'sher? So the sun stood still in the midst of heaven, and hasted not to go down about a whole day.

14- And there was no day like that before it or after it, that the LORD hearkened unto the voice of a man: for **the LORD fought for Is'ra-el**.

42- And all these kings and their land did Josh'u-a take at one time, because **the LORD God of Is'ra-el fought for Is'ra-el**.
-Joshua 10 v 11-14, 42

"The LORD God of Is'ra-el fought for Is'ra-el". If the LORD God JEHOVAH = the Word = Jesus Christ, then before the Word became flesh, Jesus Christ fought for Israel. Not as 'the messiah' that came to minister and be their king, but as the LORD God JEHOVAH. The same LORD and God. He fought for Israel. He killed enemies of Israel. God was ruthless concerning his directives and will. There was no gray area.

Christians today (most?) have this peaceful loving concept of Jesus Christ, as they should. We are in the 'Age of Grace'. Thank God for the free gift! But seeing the truth, that the LORD God JEHOVAH was at times a warring killing machine in the Old Testament, they don't want to hear it. Many today have 'a rosy picture' of God. They don't want to hear about blood, death and crucifixion which is the 'foundation of Paul's Gospel'*.
*-I Corinthians 3 v 9-11

They desire the things that mankind wants to believe in, and think by 'the spirit of men' that the LORD God has always been a peaceful, always a loving God of mercy. This is not what the word of God has shown to us. We fear God out of respect. "The fear of God is the beginning of wisdom*". All men (not the Body of Christ because we already were judged 'faithful' when we believe Paul's Gospel) will one day stand in front of him without excuse. *-Psalm 111 v 10; -Proverbs 1 v 7; -Proverbs 9 v 10

What did Jesus tell Peter of 'a man's desire' to that of the will of God*? A man's desire comes from Satan, the spirit of this world. What God wants and expects, the natural man, 'the Old Adam' is clueless and lost. *-Matthew 16 v 23; -Mark 8 v 33

31- And he began to teach them, that the Son of man must suffer many things, and be rejected of the elders, and *of* the chief priests, and scribes, and be killed, and after three days rise again.
32- And he spake that saying openly. And Pe'ter took him, and began to rebuke him.
33- But when he had turned about and looked on his disciples, he rebuked Pe'ter, saying, Get thee behind me, Sa'tan: for thou savourest not the things that be of God, but the things that be of men.
-Mark 8 v 31-33

Judges 2: angel of the LORD = LORD = I will = I sware = I will not
1- And the **angel of the LORD** came up from Gil'gal to Bo'chim, and said, I made you to go up out of E'gypt, and have brought you unto the land which **I sware** unto your fathers; and I said, **I will** never break my covenant with you.
2- And ye shall make no league with the inhabitants of this land; ye shall throw down their alters: but **ye have not obeyed my voice**: why have ye done this?

3- Wherefore I also said, **I will not** drive them out from before you; but they shall be as *thorns* in your sides, and their gods shall be a snare unto you. 4- And it came to pass, when **the angel of the LORD spake these words unto all the children of Is'ra-el**, that the people lifted up their voice, and wept. -Judges 2 v 1-4

Judges 3: the Spirit of the LORD = LORD

>   verse 10- the Spirit of the LORD came upon Oth'ni-el son of Ke'naz, Ca'leb's brother
>
>   verse 12- the LORD strengthened Eg'lon the King of Mo'ab against Is'ra-el
>
>   verse 15- when the children of Is'ra-el cried unto the LORD, the LORD raised them up a deliverer, E'hud

Judges 6: angel of the LORD = angel of God = angel of the LORD God = Spirit of the LORD = God

>   verse 11- there came an angel of the LORD, and sat under an oak
>
>   verse 12- the angel of the LORD appeared unto him *(Gid'e-on)*
>
>   verse 20- the angel of God said unto him,
>
>   verse 21- the angel of the LORD put forth the end of the staff, the angel of the LORD departed
>
>   verse 22- **I have seen an angel of the LORD God!, I have seen an angel of the LORD face to face**
>
>   verse 23- the LORD said unto him, Peace be unto thee; fear not: thou shalt not die.
>
>   verse 34- the Spirit of the LORD came upon Gid'e-on
>
>   verse 37-39: 'divers manners' = fleece of wool and the dew
>
>   verse 40- and God did so that night

Judges 11: the Spirit of the LORD acting independently yet is always equal in the Godhead:

>   verse 29- the Spirit of the LORD came upon Jeph'thah

Judges 13: The angel of the LORD appeared as a man. The angel looked like a man. Who really is it?

1- And the children of Is'ra-el did evil again in the sight of the LORD; and the LORD delivered them into the hand of the Phi-lis'tines forty years.

2- And there was a certain man of Zo'rah, of the family of the Dan'ites, whose name *was* Ma-no-ah; and his wife *was* barren, and bare not.

3- And **the angel of the LORD appeared unto the woman**, and said unto her, Behold now, thou *art* barren, and bearest not: but thou shalt conceive, and bear a son.

4- Now therefore beware, I pray thee, and drink not wine nor strong drink, and eat not any unclean *thing*:

5- For, lo, thou shalt conceive, and bear a son; and no razor shall come on his head: for the child shall be a Naz'a-rite unto God from the womb: and he shall begin to deliver Is'ra-el out of the hand of the Phi-lis'tines.

6- Then the woman came and told her husband, saying, **A man of God came unto me, and his countenance *was* like the countenance of an angel of God, very terrible:** but I asked him not whence he *was*, neither told he me his name:

7- But he said unto me, Behold, thou shalt conceive, and bear a son; and now drink no wine nor strong drink, neither eat any unclean *thing*: for **the child <u>shall be</u> a Naz'a-rite to God** from the womb to the day of his death.

8- Then Ma-no'ah intreated the LORD, and said, O my Lord, let the man of God which thou didst send come again unto us, and teach us what we shall do unto the child that shall be born.

9- **And God hearkened to the voice of Ma-no'ah; and the angel of God came again unto the woman** as she sat in the field: but Ma-no'ah her husband *was* not with her.

10- And the woman made haste, and ran, and shewed her husband, and said unto him, Behold, the man hath appeared unto me, that came unto me the *other* day.

11- And Ma-no'ah arose, and went after his wife, **and came to the man**, and said unto him, ***Art* thou the man that spakest unto the woman? And he said, I *am*.**

12- And Ma-no'ah said, Now let thy words come to pass. How shall we order the child, and *how* shall we do unto him?

13- And **the angel of the LORD said unto Ma-no'ah**, Of all that I said unto the woman let her beware.

14- She may not eat of any *thing* that cometh of the vine, neither let her drink wine or strong drink, nor eat any unclean *thing*: all that I commanded her let her observe.

15- And Ma-no'ah said unto the angel of the LORD, I pray thee, let us detain thee, until we shall have made ready a kid *(goat)* for thee.

16- And the angel of the LORD said unto Ma-no'ah, Though thou detain me, I will not eat of thy bread: and **if thou wilt offer a burnt offering, thou must offer it unto the LORD. For Ma-no'ah knew not that he** *was* **an angel of the LORD**.

17- And Ma-no'ah said unto the angel of the LORD, What *is* thy name, that when thy sayings come to pass we may do thee honour?

18- And the angel of the LORD said unto him, Why askest thou thus after my name, seeing it *is* secret?

19- So Ma-no'ah took a kid with a meat offering, and offered *it* upon a rock unto the LORD: and *the angel* did wondrously; and Man-o'ah and his wife looked on.

20- For it came to pass, when the flame went up toward heaven from off the altar, that **the angel of the LORD ascended in the flame of the altar**. And Ma-no'ah and his wife looked on *it*, and fell on their faces to the ground.

21- But the angel of the LORD did no more appear to Ma-no'ah and to his wife. **Then Ma-no'ah knew that he** *was* **an angel of the LORD.**

22- **And Ma-no'ah said unto his wife, We shall surely die, because we have seen God.**

23- But his wife said unto him, If the LORD were pleased to kill us, he would not have received a burnt offering and a meat offering at our hands, neither would he have shewed us all these *things*, nor would as at this time have told us *such things* as these.

24- And the woman bare a son, and called his name Sam'son: and the child grew, and the LORD blessed him.

25- And **the Spirit of the LORD began to move him at times** in the camp of Dan between Zo-ah and Esh'ta-ol.

-Judges 13

Judges 14: the Spirit of the LORD and its independence yet is always an equal in the Godhead:

    verse 6- the Spirit of the LORD came mightily upon him *(Samson)*

    verse 19- the Spirit of the LORD came upon him *(Samson)*, and slew
        thirty men

Judges 15: the Spirit of the LORD did not 'clave an hollow place in the jaw for water', God did. The Father, the Word, and the Spirit are all one in God, the Godhead:

verse 14- and the Spirit of the Lord came mightily upon him, and the cords that *were* upon his arms became as flax that was burnt with fire, and his bands loosed from off his hands

verse 19- But God clave an hollow place that was in the jaw, and there came water thereout;

I Samuel 3:

verse 4- the LORD called Sam'u-el: and he answered, Here *am* I.

verse 6- the LORD called yet again, Sam'u-el

verse 7- **Now Sam'u-el did not yet know the LORD, neither was the word of the LORD yet revealed unto him.**

verse 8- the LORD called Sam'u-el again the third time

verse 10- And **the LORD came, and stood**, and called as at other times, Sam'u-el, Sam'u-el. Then Sam'u-el answered, Speak; for thy servant heareth.

verse 11- the LORD said to Sam'u-el,

verse 21- And the LORD appeared again in Shi'loh: **for the LORD revealed himself to Sam'u-el in Shi'loh by the word of the LORD.**

I Sam'u-el 8:

22- And the LORD said to Sam'u-el, Hearken unto their voice, and make them a king. And Sam'u-el said unto the men of Is'ra-el, Go ye every man unto his city.

-I Samuel 8 v 22

The Gifts and Power of the Holy Spirit

Exodus 35: the LORD called = the spirit of God in all manner of workmanship:

30- And Mo'ses said unto the children of Is'ra-el, See, **the LORD hath called** by name Be-zal'e-el the son of U'ri, the son of Hur, of the tribe of Ju'dah.

31- And **hath filled him with the spirit of God**, in wisdom, in understanding, and in knowledge, and in all manner of workmanship;

32- And to devise curious works, to work in gold, and in silver, and in brass.

33- And in the cutting of stones, to set *them*, and in carving of wood, to make any manner of cunning work.

34- And **he hath put in his heart that he may teach**, *both* he, and A-ho'li-ab, the son of A-his'a-mach, of the tribe of Dan.

35- Them **hath he filled with wisdom of heart**, to work all manner of work, of the engraver, and of the cunning workman, and of the embroiderer, in blue, and in purple, in scarlet, and in fine linen, and of the weaver, *even* **of them that do any work**, and of those that devise cunning work.

-Exodus 35 v 30-35

Exodus 36: the LORD directed the work = gave wisdom and knowledge for the building of the tabernacle:

1- Then wrought Be-zal'e-el and A-ho'li-ab, and every **wise hearted man, in whom the LORD put wisdom and understanding to know how to work all manner of work** for the service of the sanctuary, according to all that the LORD had commanded.

2- And Mo'ses called Be-zal'e-el and A-ho'li-ab, and every **wise hearted man, in whose heart the LORD had put wisdom**, *even* every one whose heart stirred him up to come unto the work to do it:

-Exodus 36 v 1, 2

I Samuel 10:

6- And the Spirit of the LORD will come upon thee *(Saul)*, and thou shalt prophesy with them, and shalt be turned into another man.

.....

9- And it was *so*, that when he had turned his back to go from Sam'u-el, **God gave him another heart**: and all those signs came to pass that day.

10- And when they came thither to the hill, behold, a company of prophets met him; and **the Spirit of God came upon him, and he prophesied among them.**

-I Samuel 10 v 6, 9, 10

I Samuel 11:

4- Then came the messengers to Gib'e-ah of Saul, and told the tidings in the ears of the people: and all the people lifted up their voices, and wept.

5- And, behold, Saul came after the herd out of the field; and Saul said, what *aileth* the people that they weep? And they told him the tidings of the men of Ja'besh.

6- And **the Spirit of God came upon Saul** when he heard those tidings, and **his anger was kindled greatly**.

7- And he took a yoke of oxen, and hewed them in pieces, and sent *them* throughout all the coasts of Is'ra-el by the hands of messengers, saying, Whosoever cometh not forth after Saul and after Samuel, so shall it be done unto his oxen. And **the fear of the LORD fell on the people**, and they came out with one consent.

-I Samuel 11 v 4-7

I Samuel 16:

10- Again, Jes'se made seven of his sons to pass before Sam'u-el. And Sam'u-el said unto Jes'se, The LORD hath not chosen these.

11- And Sam'u-el said unto Jes'se, Are here all *thy* children? And he said, There remaineth yet the youngest, and behold, he keepeth the sheep. And Sam'u-el said unto Jes'se, Send and fetch him: for we will not sit down till he come hither.

12- And he sent, and brought him in. Now he *was* ruddy, *and* withal of a beautiful countenance, and goodly to look to. And **the LORD said, Arise, anoint him**: for this *is* he.

13- Then Sam'u-el took the horn of oil, and anointed him in the midst of his brethren: and **<u>the Spirit of the LORD came upon Da'vid from that day forward</u>**. So Sam'u-el rose up, and went to Ra'mah.

14- **But the Spirit of the LORD departed from Saul**, and **an evil spirit from the LORD troubled him.**

.....

23- And it came to pass, when **the *evil* spirit from God was upon Saul,** that Da'vid took an harp, and played with his hand: so Saul was refreshed, and was well, and **the evil spirit departed from him**.

-I Samuel 16 v 10-14, 23

I Samuel 19:

18- So Da'vid fled, and escaped, and came to Sam'u-el to Ra'mah, and told him all that Saul had done to him. And he and Sam'u-el went and dwelt in Na'ioth.

19- And it was told Saul, saying, behold, Da'vid *is* at Na'ioth in Ra'mah.

20- And Saul sent messengers to take Da'vid: and when they saw the company of the prophets prophesy, and Sam'u-el standing *as* appointed over them, **the Spirit of God was upon the messengers of Saul, and they also prophesied**.

21- And when it was told Saul, **he sent other messengers, and they prophesied likewise. And Saul sent messengers again the third time, and they prophesied also**.

22- Then went he also to Ra'mah, and came to a great well that is in Se'chu: and he asked and said, Where *are* Sam'u-el and Da'vid? And *one* said, Behold, *they be* at Na'ioth in Ra'mah.

23- And he went thither to Na'ioth in Ra'mah: and **the Spirit of God was upon him also**, and he went on, **and prophesied**, until he came to Na'ioth in Ra'mah.

24- And he stripped off his clothes also, and prophesied before Sam'u-el in like manner,and lay down naked* all that day and all that night. Wherefore they say, *Is* Saul also among the prophets? (*-*not completely. To shed ones outer apparel, in this case 'Royal Apparel', is thought of as being naked. Like walking around in your underwear.)*

-I Samuel 19 v 18-24

II Samuel 23:

1- Now these *be* the last words of Da'vid. David the son of Jes'se said, and the man *who was* raised up on high, the anointed of the God of Ja'cob, and the sweet psalmist of Is'ra-el, said,

2- **The Spirit of the Lord spake by me, and his word *was* in my tongue**.

-II Samuel 23 v 1, 2

II Chronicles 15:

1- And **the Spirit of God** came upon Az-a-ri'ah the son of O'bed:

2- And he went out to meet A'sa, and said unto him, Hear ye me, A'sa, and all Ju'dah and Ben'ja-min; the LORD *is* with you, while ye be with him; and if you seek him, he will be found of you; but if you forsake him, he will forsake you.

3- Now for a long season Is'ra-el *hath been* without the true God, and without a teaching priest, and without law.

4- But when they in their trouble did turn unto **the LORD God of Israel**, and sought him, he was found of them.

5- And in those times *there was* no peace to him that went out, nor to him that came in, but great vexations *were* upon all the inhabitants of the countries.

6- And nation was destroyed of nation, and city of city: for God did vex them with all adversity.

7- Be ye strong therefore, and let not your hands be weak: for your work shall be rewarded.

8- And when A'sa heard these words, and the prophecy of O'bed the prophet, he took courage, and put away the abominable idols out of all the land of Ju'dah and Ben'ja-min, and out of the cities which he had taken from mount E'phra-im, and renewed the altar of the LORD, that *was* before the porch of the LORD.

-II Chronicles 15 v 1-8

II Chronicles 20:

13- And **all Ju'dah stood before the LORD**, with their little ones, their wives, and their children.

14- **Then upon Ja-ha'zi-el** the son of Zech-a-ri'ah, the son of Be-na'iah, the son of Je-i'el, the son of Mat-ta-ni'ah, a Le'vite of the sons of A'saph, **came the Spirit of the LORD** in the midst of the congregation;

15- And he said, **Hearken ye, all Ju'dah, and ye inhabitants of Je-ru'sa-lem**, and thou King Je-hosh'a-phat, Thus saith the LORD unto you, Be not afraid nor dismayed by reason of this great multitude; for the battle *is* not your's, but God's.

16- To morrow go ye down against them: behold, they come up by the cliff of Ziz; and ye shall find them at the end of the brook, before the wilderness of Jer'u-el.

17- Ye shall not *need* to fight in this *battle*: set yourselves, **stand ye *still***, and see the salvation of the LORD with you, O Ju'dah and Je-ru'sa-lem: fear not, nor be dismayed; tomorrow go out against them: for the LORD *will be* with you.

18- And Je-hosh'a-phat bowed his head with *his* face to the ground: and all Ju'dah and the inhabitants of Je-ru'sa-lem fell before the LORD, worshipping the LORD.

19- And the Le'vites, of the children of the Ko'hath-ites, and of the children of the Kor'hites, stood up to praise **the LORD God of Israel** with a loud voice on high.

-II Chronicles 20 v 13-19

II Chronicles 24:

17- Now after the death of Je-hoi'a-da came the princes of Ju'dah, and made obeisance to the king. Then the king hearkened unto them.

18- And <u>they left the house of</u> **the LORD God of their fathers**, and served groves and idols: and wrath came upon Ju'dah and Je-ru'sa-lem for this their trespass.

19- Yet he sent prophets to them, to bring them again unto the LORD; and they testified against them: but they would not give ear.

20- And **the Spirit of God came upon Zech-a-ri'ah** the son of Je-hoi'a-da the priest, which stood above the people, and said unto them, Thus saith God, Why transgress ye the commandments of the LORD, that ye cannot prosper? Because ye have forsaken the Lord, he hath also forsaken you.

-II Chronicles 24 v 17-20

Isaiah 48:

12- Hearken unto me, O Ja'cob and Is'ra-el, my called; **I *am* he; I *am* the first, I also *am* the last**.

13- Mine hand also hath laid the foundation of the earth, and my right hand hath spanned the heavens: *when* I call unto them, they stand up together.

14- All ye, assemble yourselves, and hear; which among them hath declared these *things*? The LORD hath loved him: he will do his pleasure on Bab'y-lon, and his harm *shall be on* the Chal-de'ans.

15- I, *even* I, have spoken; yea, I have called him: I have brought him, and he shall make his way prosperous.

16- Come ye near unto me, hear ye this; I have not spoken in secret **from the beginning; from the time that it was, there *am* I: and now the LORD God, and his Spirit,** hath sent me.

17- **Thus saith the LORD, thy Redeemer, the Holy One of Is'ra-el; I am the LORD thy God** which teacheth thee to profit, which leadeth thee by the way *that* thou shouldest go.

18- O that thou hadst hearkened to my commandments! then had thy peace been as a river, and thy righteousness as the waves of the sea:

19- Thy seed also had been as the sand, and the offspring of thy bowels like the gravel thereof; his name should not have been cut off nor destroyed from before me.

-Isaiah 48 v 12-19

Isaiah 61:

1- The Spirit of the LORD God *is* upon me; because the LORD hath anointed me to preach good tidings unto the meek; he hath sent me to bind up the brokenhearted, to proclaim liberty to the captives, and the opening of the prison to *them that* are bound.

2- To proclaim the acceptable year of the LORD, * and the day of vengeance of our God; to comfort all that mourn;

*This has not happened, 'the day of vengeance of our God'. Between this is the 'Age of Grace'. Israel and the 'Circumcision/Law' never had this knowledge of 'the mysteries and the secrets' that only the Apostle of the Gentiles revealed by the 'resurrected Jesus Christ'.

3- To appoint unto them that mourn in Zi'on, to give unto them beauty for ashes, the oil of joy for mourning, the garment of praise for the spirit of heaviness; that they might be called trees of righteousness, the planting of the LORD, that he might be glorified.

4- And they shall build the old wastes, they shall raise up the former desolations, and they shall repair the waste cities, the desolations of many generations.

5- And strangers shall stand and feed your flocks, and the sons of the alien *shall be* your plowman and your vinedressers.

6- But **ye shall be named the <u>Priests of the LORD</u>**: *men* shall call you the **<u>Ministers of our God</u>**: ye shall eat the riches of the Gentiles, and in their glory shall ye boast yourselves.

7- **For your shame *ye shall have* double; and *for* confusion they shall rejoice in their portion:** therefore in their land they shall possess the double: everlasting joy shall be unto them.

8- For I the LORD love judgment, I hate robbery for burnt offering; and I will direct their work in truth, and **I will make an everlasting covenant with them***. *-Jeremiah 31 v 31

9- And their seed shall be known among the Gen'tiles, and their offspring among the people: all that see them shall acknowledge them, **that they *are* the seed *which* the LORD hath blessed**.

10- I will greatly rejoice in the LORD, my soul shall be joyful in my God; <u>for he hath clothed me with the garments of salvation, he hath covered</u>

<u>me with the robe of righteousness</u>, as a bridegroom decketh *himself* with ornaments, and as a bride adorneth *herself* with her jewels.

11- For as the earth bringeth forth her bud, and as the garden causeth the things that are sown in it to spring forth; so the LORD God will cause righteousness and praise to spring forth before all the nations.

-Isaiah 61

Isaiah 63:

7- I will mention the loving kindness is of the LORD, *and* the praises of the LORD, according to all that the LORD hath bestowed on us, and the great goodness toward <u>the house of Is'ra-el</u>, which he hath bestowed on them according to his mercies, and according to the multitude of his lovingkindnesses.

8- **For he said, Surely they** *are* **my people**, children *that* will not lie: so he was their Savior.

9- In all their affliction he was afflicted, and **the angel of his presence saved them**: in his love and in his pity **he redeemed them**; and he bare them, and carried them all the days of old.

10- **But they rebelled, and vexed his holy Spirit:** therefore he was turned to be **their enemy,** *and* **he fought against them**.

11- Then he remembered the days of old, Mo'ses, *and* his people, *saying*, Where *is* he that brought them up out of the sea with the shepherd of his flock? Where is he that put his holy Spirit within him?

12- That led *them* by the right hand of Mo'ses with his glorious arm, dividing the water before them, to make himself an everlasting name?

13- That led them through the deep, as an horse in the wilderness, *that* they should not stumble?

14- As a beast goeth down into the valley, **the Spirit of the LORD caused him to rest**; so didst thou lead thy people, to make thyself a glorious name.

15- Look down from heaven, and behold from the habitation of thy holiness and of thy glory: where *is* thy zeal and thy strength, the sounding of thy bowels and of thy mercies toward me? Are they restrained?

16- Doubtless thou *art* our father, though A'bra-ham be ignorant of us, and Is'ra-el acknowledge us not: **thou, O LORD,** *art* **our father, our redeemer; thy name** *is* **from everlasting**.

17- O LORD, why hast thou made us to err from thy ways, *and* hardened our heart from thy fear? Return for thy servant's sake, the tribes of thine inheritance.

18- The people of thy holiness have possessed *it* but a little while: our adversaries have trodden down thy sanctuary.

19- We are *thine*: thou never barest rule over them; **they were not called by thy name**.

-Isaiah 63 v 7-19

Ezekiel 11:

1- Moreover **the spirit lifted me up**, and brought me unto the <u>east gate of the LORD's house, which looketh eastward</u>: and behold at the door of the gate five and twenty men; among whom I saw Ja-az-a-ni'ah the son of A'zur, and Pel-a-ti'ah the son of Be-na'iah, princes of the people.

2- Then said he unto me, Son of man, these *are* the men that devise mischief, and give wicked counsel in this city:

3- Which say, *It is* not near; let us build houses: this *city is* the cauldron, and we *be* the flesh.

4- Therefore prophesy against them, prophesy, O son of man.

5- And **the Spirit of the LORD fell upon me**, and said unto me, Speak; Thus saith the LORD; Thus have ye said, O house of Is'ra-el: for I know the things that come into your mind, *every one* of them.

…..

24- Afterwords **the spirit took me up, and brought me in a vision by the Spirit of God into Chal-de'a, to them of the captivity**. So the vision that I had seen went up from me.

25- Then I spake unto them of the captivity all the things that the LORD had shewed me.

-Ezekiel 11 v 1-5, 24, 25

The Spirit Count (S not s)

 33 - Old Testament

 11 - Matthew, Mark, Luke

 10 - John

 11 - Acts

 81 - Romans to Hebrews – the Apostle Paul

 26 - James to Revelation

Isaiah writes, by the Holy Spirit, approximately 750 years before Christ's first advent. If you didn't know when it was written, these scriptures could have came from the New Testament. Israel could have and should have known. After the resurrection, it is obvious who the Old Testament prophets were writing about. To us that is, but most of Israel nationally and the world is still blind to who Jesus Christ really is. The condemnation of the world, unbelief.

Isaiah 53:

1- Who hath believed our report? And to whom is the arm of the LORD revealed?

2- For he shall grow up before him as a tender plant, and as a root out of a dry ground: he hath no form nor comeliness; and when we shall see him, *there is* no beauty that we should desire him.

3- He is despised and rejected of men; a man of sorrows, and acquainted with grief: and we hid as it were *our* faces from him; he was despised, and we esteemed him not.

4- Surely he hath borne our griefs, and carried our sorrows: yet we did esteem him stricken, smitten of God, and afflicted.

5- But he *was* wounded for our transgressions, *he was* bruised for our iniquities: the chastisement of our peace *was* upon him; and with his stripes we are healed.

6- All we like sheep have gone astray; we have turned everyone to his own way; and the LORD hath laid on him the iniquity of us all.

7- He was oppressed, and he was afflicted, yet he opened not his mouth: he is brought as a lamb to the slaughter, and as a sheep before her shearers is dumb, so he openeth not his mouth.

8- He was taken from prison and from judgment: and who shall declare his generation? For he was cut off out of the land of the living: for the transgression of my people was he stricken.

9- And he made his grave with the wicked, and with the rich in his death; because he had done no violence, neither *was any* deceit in his mouth.

10- Yet it pleased the LORD* to bruise him; he hath put *him* to grief: when thou shalt make his soul an offering for sin, he shall see *his* seed, he shall prolong *his* days, and the pleasure of the LORD shall prosper in his hand. *(*-to Israel, 'The LORD our God is one LORD'. The concept of the Word made Flesh was unknown. A suffering Saviour?)*

11- He shall see of the travail of his soul, *and* shall be satisfied: but his knowledge shall my righteous servant justify many; for he shall bear their iniquities.

12- Therefore will I divide him *a portion* with the great, and he shall divide the spoil with the strong; because he hath poured out his soul unto death: and he was numbered with the transgressors; and he bare the sin of many, and made intercession for the transgressors.

-Isaiah 53

Psalm 22: Written approximately 1,000 years before Christ. These scriptures are of David speaking of himself, then words of Jesus that <u>he will</u> speak in the future from the cross, then back and forth. A Spiritual vision. A Roman cross crucifixion of Jesus Christ was unknown. There were no Romans when David was king.

1- My God, my God, why hast thou forsaken me? *Why art thou* so far from helping me, *and from* the words of my roaring?

2- O my God, I cry in the daytime, but thou hearest not; and in the night season, and am not silent.

3- But thou *art* holy, *O thou* that inhabitest the praises of Is'ra-el.

4- Our fathers trusted in thee: they trusted, and thou didst deliver them.

5- They cried unto thee, and were delivered: they trusted in thee, and were not confounded.

6- But I *am* a worm, and no man; a reproach of men, and despised of the people.

7- All they that see me laugh me to scorn: they shoot out the lip, they shake their head, *saying,*

8- He trusted on the LORD *that* he would deliver him: let him deliver him, seeing he delighted in him.

9- But thou *art* he that took me out of the womb: thou didst make me hope *when I was* upon my mother's breasts.

10- I was cast upon thee from the womb: thou *art* my God from a mother's belly.

11- Be not far from me; for trouble *is* near; for *there is* none to help.

12- Many bulls have compassed me: strong *bulls* of Ba'shan and have beset me round.

13- They gaped upon me *with* their mouths, *as* a ravening and a roaring lion.

14- I am poured out like water, and all my bones are out of joint: my heart is like wax; it is melted in the midst of my bowels.

15- My strength is dried up like a potsherd; and my tongue cleaveth to my jaws; and thou hast brought me into the dust of death.

16- For dogs have compassed me: the assembly of the wicked have inclosed me: **they pierced my hands and my feet**.

17- I may tell all my bones: they look *and* stare upon me.

18- **They part my garments among them, and cast lots upon my vesture.**

19- But be not thou far from me, O LORD: O my strength, haste thee to help me.

20- Deliver my soul from the sword; my darling from the power of the dog.

21- Save me from the lion's mouth: for thou hast heard me from the horns of the unicorn's *(wild ox)*.

22- I will declare thy name unto my brethren: in the midst of the congregation will I praise thee.

23- Ye that fear the LORD, praise him; all ye the seed of Ja'cob, glorify him; and fear him, all ye the seed of Is'ra-el.

24- For he hath not despised nor abhorred the affliction of the afflicted; neither hath he hid his face from him; but when he cried unto him, he heard.

25- My praise *shall be* of thee in the great congregation: I will pay my vows before them that fear him.

26- The meek shall eat and be satisfied: they shall praise the LORD that seek him: your heart shall live for ever.

27- All the ends of the world shall remember and turn unto the LORD: and all the kindreds of the nations shall worship before thee.

28- For the kingdom *is* the LORD's: and he *is* the governor among the nations.

29- All *they that be* fat on the earth shall eat and worship: all they that go down to the dust shall bow before him: and none can keep alive his own soul.

30- A seed shall serve him; it shall be accounted to the LORD for a **generation***.

31- <u>**They**</u> **shall come,** <u>**and shall**</u> **declare his righteousness** <u>**unto a people**</u> <u>**that shall**</u> **be born, that** <u>**he had**</u> **done** *this**. *(*The Body of Christ? A seed of faith? Faith in the Earthly or resurrected Jesus Christ?)*

-Psalm 22

45- Now from the sixth hour *(noon)* there was darkness over all the land unto the ninth hour *(3 pm.)*.

46- And about the ninth hour **Je'sus cried** with a loud voice, saying, E'li, E'li, la'ma sa-bach'tha-ni? That is to say, **My God, my God,** why hast thou forsaken me?

-Matthew 27 v 45, 46

33- And when the sixth hour *(noon)* was come, there was darkness over the whole land until the ninth hour *(3 pm)*.

34- And at the ninth hour **Je'sus cried** with a loud voice, saying, E-lo'i, E-lo'i, la'ma sa-bach'tha-ni?, which is, being interpreted, **My God, my God,** why hast thou forsaken me?

-Mark 15 v 33, 34

44- And it was about the sixth hour *(noon)*, and there was a darkness over all the earth until the ninth hour *(3 pm)*.

45- And the sun was darkened, and the veil of the temple was rent in the midst.

46- And when **Je'sus had cried** with a loud voice, he said, **Father,** into thy hands I commend my spirit: and having said thus, he gave up the ghost.
-Luke 23 v 44-46

28- After this, **Je'sus** knowing that all things were now accomplished, that **the scripture might be fulfilled**, saith, I thirst.

29- Now there was set a vessel full of vinegar: and they filled a sponge with vinegar, and put *it* upon hyssop, and put *it* to his mouth.

30- When **Je'sus** therefore had received the vinegar, he said, <u>It is finished*</u>: and he bowed his head, and gave up the ghost. *(*-the law was never declared finished but the prophecies and earthly ministry of Jesus Christ were now finished.)*
-John 19 v 28-30

Why the small variations of scripture? The writers of scripture (all of them are the offspring of Abraham) wrote as the Holy Spirit directed them*. They wrote what God wanted to be written, not what a man may desire. The newer translated bibles are the ways that God's words are changed and marginalized. *-Romans 3 v 1, 2

1- And when the day of Pen'te-cost was fully come, they were all with one accord in one place.

2- And suddenly there came a sound from heaven as of a rushing mighty wind, and it filled all the house where they were sitting.

3- And there appeared unto them cloven tongues like as of fire, and it sat upon each of them.

4- And they were all filled with the Ho'ly Ghost, and began to speak with other tongues, as the Spirit gave them utterance.

…..

12- And they were all amazed, and were in dought, saying one to another, What meaneth this?

13- Others mocking said, These men are full of new wine.

14- But Pe'ter, standing up with the eleven, lifted up his voice, and said unto them, Ye men of Ju-dae'a, and all ye that dwell at Je-ru'sa-lem, be this known unto you, and hearken to my words.

15- For these are not drunken, as ye suppose, seeing it is *but* the third hour of the day *(9 am)*.

16- But this is that which was spoken by the prophet Jo'el*. *-Joel 2 v 28-32

17- And it shall come to pass in **the last days**, saith God, I will pour out of my Spirit upon all flesh: and your sons and your daughters shall prophesy *(speak forth)*, and your young men shall see visions, and your old men shall dream dreams.

18- And on my servant's and on my handmaidens I will pour out in those days of my Spirit; and they shall prophesy *(speak forth)*.

-Acts 2 v 1-4, 12-18

Jesus said:

19- But when they deliver you up, take no thought how or what ye shall speak: for it shall be given you in that same hour what ye shall speak.

20- For it is not ye that speak, but the Spirit of your Father which speaketh in you.

-Matthew 10 v 19, 20

25- And Je'sus knew their thoughts, and said unto them, Every kingdom divided against itself is brought to desolation; and every city or house divided against itself shall not stand:

26- And if Sa'tan cast out Sa'tan, he is divided against himself; how shall then his kingdom stand?

27- And if I by Be-el'ze-bub cast out devils, by whom do your children cast *them* out? Therefore they shall be your judges.

28- But if I cast out devils by the Spirit of God, then the kingdom of God is come unto you.

-Matthew 12 v 25-28

9- And it came to pass in those days, that Je'sus came from Naz'a-reth of Gal'i-lee, and was baptized of John in Jor'dan.

10- And straightway coming up out of the water, he saw the heavens opened, and the Spirit like a dove descending upon him.

11- And there came a voice from heaven, *saying*, Thou art my beloved Son, in whom I am well pleased.

12- **And immediately the Spirit driveth him into the wilderness.**

-Mark 1 v 9-12

1- And **Je'sus being full of the Ho'ly Ghost** returned from Jor'dan, **and was led by the Spirit into the wilderness**.

-Luke 4 v 1

14- And **Je'sus returned in the power of the Spirit** into Gal'i-lee: and there went out a fame of him through all the region round about.

-Luke 4 v 14

17- *Even* the Spirit of truth; whom the world cannot receive, because it seeth him not, neither knoweth him: but ye know him; for he dwelleth with you, **and shall be** in you.

-John 14 v 17

26- But when **the Comforter** is come, whom **I will send unto you from the Father**, *even* the Spirit of truth, which proceedeth from the Father *(the Godhead)*, he shall testify of me:

27- And ye also shall bear witness, because ye have been with me from the beginning.

-John 15 v 26, 27

29- **Then the Spirit said unto Phil'ip,** Go near, and join thyself to this chariot.

…..

39- And when they were come up out of the water, **the Spirit of the Lord caught away Phil'ip,** that the eunuch saw him no more: and he went on his way rejoicing.

-Acts 8 v 29, 39

19- While **Pe'ter** thought on the vision, **the Spirit said unto him,** Behold, three men seek thee.

-Acts 10 v 19

12- And **the Spirit bade me go with them, nothing doubting.** Moreover these six brethren accompanied me, and we entered the man's house.

-Acts 11 v 12

11- But if **the Spirit of him that raised up Jesus from the dead *(Paul's Gospel)*** dwell in you, he that raised up Christ from the dead shall also quicken your mortal bodies by the Spirit that dwelleth in you.

…..

16- The Spirit itself beareth witness with our spirit, that we are the children of God.

…..

23- And not only *they*, but ourselves also, which have the firstfruits of the Spirit, even we ourselves groan within ourselves, waiting for the adoption, *to wit*, the redemption of our body.

…..

26- Likewise the Spirit also helpeth our infirmities: for we know not what we should pray for as we ought: but the Spirit itself maketh intercession for us with groanings which cannot be uttered.

27- And he that searcheth the hearts knoweth what *is* the mind of the Spirit, because he maketh intercession for the saints according *to the will of* God.

-Romans 8 v 11, 16, 23, 26, 27

4- Now there are diversities of gifts, but the same Spirit.

…..

7- But the manifestations of the Spirit is given to every man to profit withal.

8- For to one is given by the Spirit the word of wisdom; to another the word of knowledge by the same Spirit.

9- To another faith by the same Spirit; to another the gifts of healing by the same Spirit.

10- To another the working of miracles; to another prophecy *(preaching)*; to another discerning of spirits; to another *divers* kinds of tongues; to another the interpretation of tongues:

11- But all these worketh that one and selfsame Spirit, dividing to each man severally as he will.

-I Corinthians 12 v 4, 7-11

21- Now he which stablisheth us with you in Christ, and hath annointed us, *is* God.

22- **Who hath also sealed us**, and given the earnest of the Spirit in our hearts.

-II Corinthians 1 v 21, 22

3- *Forasmuch as ye are* manifestly declared to be the epistle of Christ ministered by us, written not with ink, but with the Spirit of the living God; not in tables of stone, but in fleshly tables of the heart.

-II Corinthians 3 v 3

5- Now he that wrought us for the selfsame thing is God, who also hath given unto us the earnest of the Spirit.

-II Corinthians 5 v 5

12- That we should be to the praise of his glory, who first trusted in Christ.

13- In whom ye also *trusted*, **after that ye heard the word of truth, the gospel of your salvation** in whom also, **after that ye believed, ye were sealed** with that holy Spirit of promise.

14- Which is the earnest of our inheritance until the redemption of the purchased possession, unto the praise of his glory.

-Ephesians 1 v 12-14

18- For through him we both have access by one Spirit unto the Father.

19- Now therefore ye are no more strangers and foreigners, but fellowcitizens with the saints, and of the household of God;

20- And are built upon the foundation of the apostles and prophets, Je'sus Christ himself being the chief corner *stone*.

21- In whom all the building fitly framed together groweth unto an holy temple in the Lord:

22- In whom ye also are builded together for an habitation of God through the Spirit.

-Ephesians 2 v 18-22

4- *There is* one body, and one Spirit, even as ye are called in one hope of your calling.

5- One Lord, one faith, one baptism,

6- One God and Father of all, who *is* above all, and through all, and in you all *(only the believer)*.

7- But unto every one of us is given grace acccording to the measure of the gift of Christ.

.....

30- And grieve not the holy Spirit of God, whereby *ye are sealed* unto the day of redemption.

-Ephesians 4 v 4-7, 30

17- And take **the helmet of salvation, and the sword of the Spirit, which is the word of God**:

18- Praying always with all prayer and supplication in the Spirit, and watching thereunto with all perseverance and supplication for the saints;

19- And for me, that utterance may be given unto me, **that I may open my mouth boldly, to make known the mystery of the gospel**.

20- For which I am an ambassador in bonds: that therein I may speak boldly, as I ought to speak.

-Epheslans 6 v 17-20

8- He therefore that despiseth, despiseth not man, but God, who hath also given unto us his holy Spirit.

-I Thessalonians 4 v 8

13- But we are bound to give thanks alway to God for you, brethren beloved of the Lord, because **God hath from the beginning chosen you to salvation through sanctification of the Spirit and belief of the truth**:

14- **Whereunto he called you by our gospel, to the obtaining of the glory of our Lord Je'sus Christ.**

15- Therefore, brethren, stand fast, and hold the traditions *(faith and love, not law)* which ye have been taught, whether by word, or our epistle.

-II Thessalonians 2 v 13-15

22- Seeing ye have purified your souls in obeying the truth through the Spirit unto feigned love of the brethren, *see that ye* love one another with a pure heart fervently.

-I Peter 1 v 22

18- For Christ also hath once suffered for sins, the just for the unjust, that he might bring us to God, being put to death in the flesh, but quickened by the Spirit.

-I Peter 3 v 18

22- And whatsoever we ask, we receive of him, because we keep his commandments, and do those things that are pleasing in his sight.

23- And this is his commandment, That we should believe on the name of his Son Jesus Christ, and love one another, as he gave us commandment.

24- And he that keepeth his commandments dwelleth in him, and he in him. And hereby we know that he abideth in us, by the Spirit which he hath given us.

-I John 3 v 22-24

10- I was in the Spirit on the Lord's day *(latter days, tribulation)*, and heard behind me a great voice, as of a trumpet,

11- Saying, I am Al'pha and O-me'ga, the first and the last: and, What thou seest, write in a book, and send *it* unto the seven churches which are in A'sia; unto Eph'e-sus, and unto Per'ga-mos, and unto Thy-a-ti'ra, and unto Sar'dis, and unto Phil-a-del'phia, and unto La-od-i-ce'a.

-Revelation 1 v 10, 11

7- He that hath an ear, let him hear what the Spirit saith unto the churches; To him that overcometh will I give to eat of the tree of life, which is in the midst of the paradise of God.

.....

11- He that hath an ear, let him hear what the Spirit saith unto the churches; He that overcometh shall not be hurt of the second death.

.....

17- He that hath an ear, let him hear what the Spirit saith unto the churches; To him that overcometh will I give to eat of the hidden manna, and will give him a white stone, and in the stone a new name written, which no man knoweth saving he that receiveth *it*.

.....

29- He that hath an ear, let him hear what the Spirit saith unto the churches.
-Revelation 2 v 7, 11, 17, 29

6- He that hath an ear, let him hear what the Spirit saith unto the churches.

.....

13- He that hath an ear, let him hear what the Spirit saith unto the churches.

.....

22- He that hath an ear to hear, let him hear what the Spirit saith unto the churches.
-Revelation 3 v 6, 13, 22

17- And the Spirit and the bride say, Come. And let him that heareth say, Come. And let him that is athirst come. <u>And whosoever will</u>, let him take the water of life freely.
-Revelation 22 v 17

BOOK VIII

Membership in the True Church, the Body of Christ

4- For if he that cometh preacheth another Je'sus, whom we have not preached, or *if* ye receive another spirit, which ye have not received, or another gospel, which ye have not accepted, ye might well bear with *him*. 5- For I *(Paul)* suppose I was not a whit behind <u>the very chiefest apostles</u>. -II Corinthians 11 v 4, 5

v4- "... if he that cometh preacheth another Je'sus..." Paul only claims to know one thing, "Christ and him crucified*..." Paul made little reference to the 'earthly ministry' but more important to note, he did not preach it, ever. He preached the Gospel that began with the death of the Lord Jesus Christ, not his life in the flesh. *-I Corinthians 2 v 2

How many churches and denominations favor the earthly ministry for salvation? I ask, then where is it? Where is the plan of salvation <u>for all the world</u> in the 'earthly ministry'? There is no temple by which to keep the commandments and adherence to the full law. A person cannot fully follow Jesus. Hello?

v5- "...the very chiefest apostles". When Paul was confirmed by God as being the 'chief apostle' of the Gentiles, what was to be understood? Who are the 'chiefest apostles' spoken of here? Who were the 'most important apostles' before Paul?

In scripture, the word 'chief' (chief, chiefest, chiefly, etc...) was written at least 293 times. 293 times all of them meant 'the top', the 'first', the 'leader' and the 'one to follow'. But when it comes to the Apostle Paul, man has in a very important scripture twisted the truth of God's written word and translated the word 'chief' into 'worst'.

15- This is a faithful saying and worthy of all acceptation, that Christ Jesus came into the world to save sinners; of whom I am chief *(the worst?)*.
-I Timothy 1 v 15

There is a popular translated bible (I suppose more than one) that has taken the word 'chief' and substituted the word 'worst' for I Timothy 1 v 15. After all the examples of 'chief' as being 'preeminent' all through the Bible, when it comes to 'thee Apostle of the Gentiles', the made up denominations and religions by man diminish the 'Apostle Paul'. Why the continued subjugation of God's 'Chosen Vessel Apostle'*? The spirit of this world? I pray you can see this. *-Acts 9 v 15, 16

Why, when it comes to Paul? Much of Christendom can't accept the truth that they can't see. "...for if our gospel be hid, it is hid to them that are lost*". The wickedness of principalities in high places has been at work for centuries concerning our 'Chief Apostle'. The god of this world has even influenced what most professing Christians see as sacred and holy, the bibles of the world.
*-II Corinthians 4 v 3

The next verse in I Timothy reads:
16- Howbeit for this cause I obtained mercy, <u>that in me first</u> *(chief/worst?)* Jesus Christ might shew forth all longsuffering, for a pattern to them which should hereafter believe on him to life everlasting.
-I Timothy 1 v 16

Who was shown the 'pattern to follow first'? For all of mankind now it is Paul, not Jesus in the flesh, not Peter, not James, not John, not Luke. Believe in God or believe God?

May God have mercy on those that support such a Bible. Follow Paul because he is first in line after the 'resurrected Lord Jesus Christ'. You cannot pass the Apostle Paul by using and believing in some other doctrine for salvation. This is much of Christendom. Man invented religions and denominations. What is the spirit of men? Where did it come from?

2- For I *(Paul)* determined not to know any thing among you, save Je'sus Christ, and him crucified.

-I Corinthians 2 v 2

23- But we *(Paul's Ministry)* preach Christ crucified, unto the Jews a stumbling block, and unto the Greeks foolishness;
24- But unto them which are called, both Jews and Greeks, Christ the power of God, and the wisdom of God.

-I Corinthians 1 v 23

v23- "...unto the Jews a stumbling block..." There are those that firmly believe that the earthly ministry must be preached for salvation. **Christendom has stumbled at the cross.** To begin at the cross is not where the majority of 'professing Christians' think. Most denominations and man made religions need the sign of the earthly ministry. But we teach it for our learning and for the 'eternal hope' of salvation*, but <u>the earthly ministry was for Israel+</u>. Don't misunderstand, the earthly ministry is fundamental to know. *-Acts 28; -Romans 5 v 2; +-Ephesians 2 v 11-13; -II Corinthians 5 v 16

17- For Christ sent me *(Paul)* not to baptize, but to preach the gospel: not with wisdom of words, lest the cross of Christ should be made of none effect.
18- For the preaching of the cross is to them that perish foolishness; but unto us which are saved it is the power of God.

-I Corinthians 1 v 17, 18

v17- "For Christ sent me *(Paul)* not to baptize",... "lest the cross of Christ should be made of none effect". The Apostle of the Gentiles did not preach and teach Acts 2 v 38. And if you do, what does the Word of God say? "lest the cross of Christ should be made of none effect". The true Gospel of salvation was nullified by the work of the flesh. So says the word of God.

v18- "For the preaching of the cross is to them that perish foolishness..." The 'preaching of the cross' is not the preaching of the earthly ministry. Religions and denominations have blurred the line of truth*. *-I Corinthians 15 v 1-4

25- Now to him that is of power to stablish you according to my gospel *(Paul's)*, and the preaching of Je'sus Christ, according to the revelation of the mystery, which was kept secret since the world began.
-Romans 16 v 25

'The Body of Christ' is not established according to Matthew, Mark, Luke, John or Acts 2 v 42, but by Paul's Gospel. Our high priest is not after the order of Aaron and the Law, but of Melchisedec who is, was, and always will be the Lord Jesus Christ.

Paul writes in Hebrews:
9- And being made perfect, he became the author of eternal salvation unto all them that obey him;
10- Called of God an high priest after the order of Mel-chis'e-dec.
11- Of whom we have many things to say, and hard to be uttered, seeing ye are dull of hearing.
12- For when for the time ye ought to be teachers, ye have need that one teach you again which *be* the <u>first principles*</u> of the oracles of God; and are <u>become such as have need of milk</u>, and not of strong meat. *(The Gospel's of Matthew, Mark, Luke, John, 'milk')*
13- For every one that useth milk *is* unskilled in the word of righteousness: for he is a babe.
14- But strong meat belongeth to them that are of full age, *even* those who by reason of use have their senses exercised to discern both good and evil.
-Hebrews 5 v 9-14

Chapter 6 begins. Remember that Paul wrote originally (Holy Spirit inspired) with no title breaks. It was all one continuous message. The English translators inserted the title breaks, not Paul.

1- Therefore leaving <u>the principles</u> of the doctrine of Christ*, let us go on unto perfection; <u>not laying again the foundation of repentance from dead works, and of faith toward God</u>. *-Hebrews 5 v 12; (The Gospel's of Matthew, Mark, Luke, John, 'milk')*
2- **Of the doctrine of baptisms***, and of laying on of hands, and of resurrection of the dead, and of eternal judgment. *(*Water Baptism for the remission of sins and not by faith/Grace alone.)*
3- And this we will do, **if** God permit.

4- For *it is* **impossible** for those who were once enlightened, and have tasted of the heavenly gift, and were made partakers of the Ho'ly Ghost.

5- And have tasted the good word of God, and the powers of the world to come.

6- **If they shall fall away, <u>to renew them again unto repentance*</u>; seeing they crucify to themselves the Son of God afresh, and put *him* to an open shame.** *(*-repeated repentance shows God that the Gospel of Grace was never accepted. You were already forgiven when you believe Paul's Gospel. The 'sinners prayer' is not necessary.)*

-Hebrews 6 v 1-6

There are those who say that 'the old patriarchs' knew that Jesus Christ was going to die for them, be buried and God would raise him up to eternal life. Don't believe it! The Bible (KJV) never said they had this understanding. There is no mention of the 'Body of Christ' in the Old Testament.

The first (the Gospel of the Kingdom) was only for Israel and the Jews. The second Gospel, the Gospel of the Grace of God is for all of mankind, Jew and Gentile. And only to Paul was he given the 'Dispensation of the Grace of God'*, not Peter, Luke, John nor did Jesus in the flesh reveal 'the Gospel of Grace'. *-Ephesians 3 v 2-12

24- But for us also, to whom it shall be imputed, if we believe on him that raised up Je'sus our Lord from the dead *(Paul's Gospel)*;

25- Who was delivered for our offences, and was raised again for our justification.

-Romans 4 v 24, 25

v24- "...it shall be imputed, if we believe on him that raised up Je'sus our Lord from the dead *(Paul's Gospel),*" Paul's Gospel of salvation begins at the cross, not the streets of Israel, not in the Book of Genesis.

12- That we should be to the praise of his glory, who first trusted in Christ.

13- In whom ye also *trusted,* **<u>after that ye heard</u> the word of truth, the gospel of your salvation** in whom also, **<u>after that ye believed</u>, <u>ye were sealed</u>** with that holy Spirit of promise.

14- Which is the earnest *(down payment by faith alone)* of our inheritance until the redemption of the purchased possession, unto the praise of his glory.

-Ephesians 1 v 12-14

The Gospel of Salvation Declared

1- Moreover, brethren, **I** *(Apostle Paul)* **declare** unto you **the gospel** which **I preached** unto you, which also ye have **received**, and wherein **ye stand**;
2- By which also ye are **saved**, if you keep in memory what I preached unto you, unless ye have **believed** in vain.
3- For **I delivered** unto you **first** of all which **I also received**, how that **Christ died for our sins** according to the scriptures;
4- And that he was **buried**, and that he **rose again the third day** according to the scriptures:
-I Corinthians 15 v 1-4

9- That if thou shalt confess with thy mouth the Lord Jesus, and shalt **believe in thine heart that God hath raised him from the dead, thou shalt be saved.**
-Romans 10 v 9

13- In whom ye also trusted, after that ye heard the word of truth, **the gospel of your salvation**: in whom also after that ye believed, **ye were sealed with that holy Spirit of promise.**
-Ephesians 1 v 13

23- If ye continue in the faith grounded and settled, and *be* not moved away from the hope of the gospel, which ye have heard, *and* which was preached to every creature* which is under heaven; whereof I Paul am made a minister; *(*only one creature denies God - man)*
24- Who now rejoice in my sufferings for you, and fill up that which is behind of the afflictions of Christ in my flesh for **his body's sake, which is the church.**
25- **Whereof I am made a minister, according to the dispensation of God which is given to me for you, to fulfill** *(complete/put an end to)* **the word of God;**
26- *Even* the mystery which hath been hid from ages and from generations, **but now is made manifest to his saints:**
27- To whom God would make known what *is* the riches of the glory of **this mystery among the Gen'tiles; which is Christ in you, the hope of glory:**

28- Whom we preach, warning every man, and teaching every man in all wisdom; that we may present every man perfect in Christ Je'sus:
29- Whereunto I also labour, striving according to his working, which worketh in me mightily.
-Colossians 1 v 23-29

11- Wherefore remember, that ye *being* in time past Gen'tiles in the flesh, who are called Uncircumcision by that which is called the Circumcision in the flesh made by hands;
12- That at that time ye were without Christ *(Messiah)*, being aliens from the commonwealth of Is'ra-el, and **strangers from the covenants of promise, having no hope, and without God in the world**:
13- <u>But now</u> in Christ Je'sus ye who sometimes were far off are made nigh by the blood of Christ*.
*(*The Blood of Christ = his shed blood = dying for all of us on the cross = his death and resurrection.)*
-Ephesians 2 v 11-13

14- For the love of Christ constraineth *(molds)* us; because we thus judge, that if one died for all, then we are all dead;
15- And *that* he died for all, that they which live should not henceforth live unto themselves, but unto him which died for them, and rose again *(Paul's Gospel)*.
16- **Wherefore henceforth** know we no man after the flesh: yea, though we have known Christ after the flesh, yet now henceforth know we *him* no more.
17- Therefore if any man *be* <u>in Christ</u>*, *he is* a new creature: old things are passed away; behold, all things are become new. *(*in Christ = the Body of Christ, the True Church.)*
-II Corinthians 5 v 14-17

The 'Body of Christ' is purely 'Pauline'. The 'Body of Christ' has nothing to do with the 'assemblies of Jews' in the early chapters of the Book of Acts including those 'of the Apostles Doctrine'*. Paul is still an unknown with his God given 'Gospel of Grace. *-Acts 2 v 42

In the early chapters of Acts, these Jewish believers were still 'under and keeping the Law', 100%. They were not preaching salvation by 'faith alone in the resurrected Jesus Christ'. These Jews, those of the 'Apostles Doctrine', are not following Paul and are not the 'Body of Christ'.

The 'Apostles Doctrine believers' have their salvation under the 'Gospel of the Kingdom'. They believe that Jesus Christ came in the flesh to be Israel's King and Messiah. They were 'water baptizing' for the 'remission of sins' and were still keeping 'the Law'. Jesus never said for them to stop 'keeping the Law'. A falsehood taught in many gatherings.

The Body of Christ

Romans

1- I beseech you therefore, brethren, by the mercies of God, that ye present your bodies a living sacrifice, holy, acceptable unto God, *which is* your reasonable service.

2- And be not conformed to this world: but be ye transformed by the renewing of your mind, that ye may prove what *is* that good, and acceptable, and perfect, will of God.

3- For I say, through the grace given unto me, to every man that is among you, not to think *of himself* more highly than he ought to think; but to think soberly, according as God hath dealt to every man the measure of faith.

4- For as we have many members in one body, and all members have not the same office:

5- **So we, *being* many, are one body in Christ,** and every one members one of another.

6- Having then gifts differing according to the grace that is given to us, whether prophecy *(preaching)*, *let us prophesy* according to the proportion of faith;

7- Or ministry, *let us wait* on *our* ministering: or he that teacheth, on teaching;

8- Or he that exhorteth, on exhortation: he that giveth, *let him do it* with simplicity; he that ruleth, with diligence; he that sheweth mercy, with cheerfulness.

9- *Let* love be without dissimulation. Abhor that which is evil; cleave to that which is good.

10- *Be* kindly affectioned one to another with brotherly love; in honoring preferring one another;

11- Not slothful in business; fervent in spirit; serving the Lord;

12- Rejoicing in hope; patient in tribulation; continuing instant in prayer;

13- Distributing to the necessity of saints; given to hospitality.

14- Bless them which persecute you: bless, and curse not.

15- Rejoice with them that do rejoice, and weep with them that weep.

16- *Be* of the same mind one toward another. Mind not high things, but condescend to men of low estate. Be not wise in your own conceits.

17- Recompense to no man evil for evil. Provide things honest in the sight of all men.

18- **If it be possible, as much as lieth in you, live peaceably with all men*.**

19- Dearly beloved, avenge not yourselves, but *rather* give place unto wrath: for it is written, Vengeance *is* mine, I will repay, saith the Lord.

20- Therefore if thine enemy hunger, feed him; if he thirst, give him drink: for in so doing thou shalt heap coals of fire on his head.

21- Be not overcome of evil, but overcome evil with good.

-Romans 12

*I have heard said on several occasions that those that claim to be Christians avoid all trouble and confrontation. They don't want to 'stir the pot' and be seen as being disruptive. "I am not a trouble maker". I have even heard that though 'the believer' was owed a large sum of money, because of his 'faith', he didn't take 'the debtor' to court. "The Bible says to forgive thy neighbor".

Who really is 'the believers' neighbor? The 'guy next door' or the person that reads and shares scripture with you? Is your real neighbor a man or a women of 'the world' that seeks not after 'his Word' or the fellow believer that has laughed and cried with you? Or someone who would defraud another and do you harm or someone that could care less about the repercussions of the friendship though they live next door? Who is the 'believers' true neighbor?

We are not 'under the law'. Concerning our salvation, we have already been forgiven by God when we believe Paul's Gospel. That's what the word of God says*. Forgiving another for the trespass against you my give you peace of mind and prove to yourself that your the better man or women, but forgiving another has nothing to do with our 'eternal salvation'. *-II Corinthians 1 v 22-24, -Ephesians 1 v 13, -Ephesians 4 v 30

Paul writes to us Holy Spirit Inspired:

13- Forbearing one another, and forgiving one another, if any man have a quarrel against any: even as Christ forgave you, so also *do* ye.

-Colossians 3 v 13

Under the law, in order for God to forgive, the Jew must have forgiven the other first. "Forgive us our debts as we..." We are not 'under the law' but under grace, thank God.

'The Lords Prayer' shows aspects of 'the Law':
9- After this manner therefore pray ye: Our Father which art in heaven, Hallowed be thy name.
10- **Thy kingdom come.** Thy will be done in earth, as *it is* in heaven.
11- Give us this day our daily bread.
12- **And forgive us our debts, as we forgive our debtors.**
13- And lead us not into temptation, but deliver us from evil: For thine is the kingdom, and the power, and the glory, forever. A-men'.
-Matthew 6 v 9-13

The Lord's prayer in the Book of Luke:
2- And he *(Jesus)* said unto them, When ye pray, say, Our Father which art in heaven, hollowed be thy name. **Thy kingdom come.** Thy will be done, as in heaven, so in earth.
3- Give us this day our daily bread.
4- **And forgive us our sins; for we also forgive every one that is indebted to us.** And lead us not into temptation; but deliver us from evil.
-Luke 11 v 2-4

Jesus said:
23- Therefore if thou bring thy gift to the alter, and there rememberest that thy brother hath ought against thee;
24- Leave there thy gift before the alter, and go thy way; first to be reconciled to thy brother, and then come and offer thy gift.
-Matthew 5 v 23, 24

Jesus said:
14- For if ye forgive men their trespasses, your heavenly Father will also forgive you:
15- But if ye forgive not men their trespasses, neither will your Father forgive your trespasses.
-Matthew 6 v 14, 15

Jesus said:

25- And when ye stand praying, forgive, if ye have ought against any: that your Father also which is in heaven may forgive you your trespasses.

26- But if you do not forgive, neither will your Father which is in heaven forgive your trespasses.

-Mark 11 v 25, 26

Jesus said:

3- Take heed to yourselves: If thy brother trespass against thee, rebuke him: and if he repent, forgive him.

4- And if he trespass against thee seven times in a day, and seven times in a day turn again to thee, saying, I repent; thou shalt forgive him.

-Luke 17 v 3, 4

Paul writes Holy Spirit inspired:

31- Let all bitterness, and wrath, and anger, and clamour, and evil speaking, be put away from you, with all malice:

32- And be ye kind one to another, tenderhearted, forgiving one another, even as God for Christ's sake hath forgiven you.

-Ephesians 4 v 31, 32

Paul writes Holy Spirit Inspired:

11- In whom also ye are circumcised with the circumcision made without hands, in putting off the body of the sins of the flesh by the circumcision of Christ:

12- Buried with him in baptism, wherein also ye are risen with him through the faith of the operation of God, who hath raised him from the dead.

13- And you, being dead in your sins and the uncircumcision of your flesh, hath he quickened together with him, having forgiven you all trespasses;

14- Blotting out the handwritting of ordinances that was against us, which was contrary to us, and took it out of the way, nailing it to his cross.

-Colossians 2 v 11-14

Our rulers, governors and laws of the world we follow. We 'tote the line'. We are not above 'the law'. We are still subject to the 'laws of men'. But the final judge will not be man but 'Jesus Christ' the 'Just and Justifier' of all mankind.

1- Let every soul be subject unto the higher powers. For there is no power but of God: **the powers that be <u>are ordained</u> of God**.

2- Whosoever therefore resisteth the power, resisteth the ordinance of God: and they that resist shall receive to themselves damnation.

3- For rulers are not a terror to good works, but to the evil. Wilt thou then not be afraid of the power? do that which is good, and thou shalt have praise of the same:

4- For he is the minister of God to thee for good. But if thou do that which is evil, be afraid; for he beareth not the sword in vain: for he is the minister of God, a revenger to *execute* wrath upon him that doeth evil.

5- Wherefore *ye* must needs be subject, not only for wrath, but also for conscience sake.

6- For for this cause pay ye tribute also: for they are God's ministers, attending continually upon this very thing.

7- **Render therefore to all their dues:** tribute to whom tribute is *due*; custom to whom custom; fear to whom fear, honour to whom honour.

8- Owe no man any thing *(defraud not)*, but to love one another: for he that loveth another hath fulfilled the law.

9- For this, Thou shalt not commit adultery, Thou shalt not kill, Thou shalt not steal, Thou shalt not bear false witness, Thou shalt not covet; and if there be any other commandment, it is briefly comprehended in this saying, namely, Thou shalt love thy neighbour *(a fellow believer)* as thyself.

10- Love worketh no ill to his neighbour: therefore love *is* the fulfilling of the law.

11- And that, knowing the time, that now *it is* high time to awake out of sleep: for now *is* our salvation nearer than when we believed.

12- The night is far spent, the day is at hand: let us therefore cast off the works of darkness, and let us put on the armour of light.

13- Let us walk honestly, as in the day; not in rioting and drunkenness, not in chambering and wantonness, not in strife and envying.

14- But put ye on the Lord Jesus Christ, and make not provision for the flesh, to *fulfil* the lusts *thereof.*

-Romans 13

1- Him that is weak in the faith receive ye, *but* not to doubtful disputations.

2- For one believeth that he may eat all things: another, who is weak eateth herbs.

3- Let not him that eateth despise him that eateth not; and let not him which eateth not judge him that eateth: for God hath received him.

4- Who art thou that judgest another man's servant? to his own master he standeth or falleth. Yea, he shall be holden up: for God is able to make him stand.

5- One man esteemeth one day above another: another esteemeth every day *alike**. Let every man be fully persuaded in his own mind. *(*A day of worship: Sunday Church or every day?)*

6- He that regardeth the day, regardeth *it* unto the Lord; and he that regardeth not the day, to the Lord he doth not regard *it*. He that eateth, eateth to the Lord, for he giveth God thanks; and he that eateth not, to the Lord he eateth not, and giveth God thanks.

7- For none of us liveth to himself, and no man dieth to himself.

8- For whether we live, we live unto the Lord; and whether we die, we die unto the Lord: whether we live therefore, or die, we are the Lord's.

9- For to this end Christ both died, and rose, and revived *(Paul's Gospel)*, that he might be Lord both of the dead and living.

10- But why dost thou judge thy brother? or why dost thou set at nought thy brother? for we shall all stand before the judgement seat of *Christ**. *(*Beama Seat for reward - see further explanation below)*

11- For it is written, *As* I live, saith the Lord, every knee shall bow to me, and every tongue shall confess to God. *(We in the Body of Christ already have,)*

12- So then every one of us shall give account of himself to God.

13- Let us not therefore judge one another any more: but judge this rather, that no man put a stumblingblock or an occasion to fall in *his* brother's way.

14- I know, and am persuaded by the Lord Je'sus, that *there is* nothing unclean of itself: but to him that esteemeth any thing to be unclean, to him *it is* unclean.

15- But if thy brother be grieved with *thy* meat*, now walkest thou not charitably. Destroy not him with thy meat, for whom Christ died.

16- Let not then your good be evil spoken of:

17- For the kingdom of God is not meat and drink; but righteousness, and peace, and joy in the Ho'ly Ghost.

18- For he that in these things serveth Christ *is* acceptable to God, and approved of men.

19- Let us therefore follow after the things which make for peace, and things wherewith one may edify another.

20- For meat* destroy not the work of God. All things indeed *are* pure; but *it is* evil for that man who eateth with offence.

21- *It is* good neither to eat flesh, nor to drink wine, nor *any thing* whereby thy brother stumbleth, or is offended, or is made weak.

22- Hast thou faith? have *it* to thyself before God. Happy *is* he that condemneth not himself in that thing which he alloweth.

23- And he that doubteth is damned if he eat, because *he eateth* not of faith: for whatsoever *is* not of faith is sin.

-Romans 14

*Eating food unknowingly that was dedicated to idols is harmless to the believer. But knowingly eating food after it was revealed that it had be dedicated to idols in the presence of others is. Walk the walk, practice what you preach. Someone new in the faith would be unsure when they see 'believers' acting like they are still 'of the world'. The believer may be strong in his faith but the 'new believer' may be weakened by the example you are setting. What kind of company do you keep?

1- We then that are strong ought to bear the infirmities of the weak, and not to please ourselves.

2- Let every one of us please *his* neighbour *(a fellow believer)* for *his* good to edification.

3- For even Christ pleased not himself; but, as it is written, The reproaches of them that reproached thee fell on me.

4- **For whatsoever things were written aforetime* were written for our learning, that we through patience and comfort of the scriptures might have hope.** *(*Written before Paul and/or not 'Pauline scripture': -Colossians 1 v 24-28)*

5- Now the God of patience and consolation grant you to be likeminded one toward another according to Christ Je'sus.

6- That ye may with one mind *and* one mouth glorify God, even the Father of our Lord Je'sus Christ.

7- Wherefore receive ye one another, as Christ also received us to the glory of God.

-Romans 15 v 1-7

The Gospel of Grace Doctrine began with Paul and ended with Paul:

17- Now I beseech you, brethren, mark them which cause divisions and offences **contrary to the doctrine which ye have learned**; and avoid them.

18- For they that are such serve not our Lord Je'sus Christ, but their own belly; and by good words and fair speeches deceive the hearts of the simple.

19- For your obedience is come abroad unto all *men*. I am glad therefore on your behalf: but yet I would have you wise unto that which is good, and simple concerning evil.

20- And the God of peace shall bruise Sa'tan under your feet shortly. The grace of our Lord Je'sus Christ *be* with you. A-men'.

.....

25- Now to him that is of power to stablish you according to **my gospel**, and the preaching of Je'sus Christ, according to the revelation of the mystery, which was kept secret since the world began,

26- But now is made manifest, and by the scriptures of the prophets, according to the commandment of the everlasting God, made known to all nations for the obedience of faith:

27- To God only wise, *be* glory through Je'sus Christ for ever. A-men'.

-Romans 16 v 17-20, 25-27

<u>I Corinthians</u>

10- We are fools for Christ's sake, but ye *are* wise in Christ; we *are* weak, but ye *are* strong; ye *are* honourable, but we *are* despised.

11- Even unto this present hour we both hunger, and thirst, and are naked, and are buffeted, and have no certain dwellingplace.

12- And labour, working with our own hands: being reviled, we bless; being persecuted, we suffer it:

13- Being defamed, we intreat: we are made as the filth of the world, *and are* the offscouring of all things unto this day.

14- I write not these things to shame you, but as my beloved sons I warn *you*.

15- For though ye have ten thousand instructors in Christ, yet *have ye* not many fathers: for **in Christ Je'sus I** *(Paul)* **have begotten you through the gospel**.

16- **Wherefore I beseech you, be ye followers of me.**

-I Corinthians 4 v 10-16

31- Whether therefore ye eat, or drink, or whatsoever ye do, do all to the glory of God.

32- Give none offence, neither to the Jews, nor to the Gentiles, nor to the church of God.

33- Even as I please all *men* in all *things*, not seeking mine own profit, but the *profit* of many that they may be saved.

-I Corinthians 10 v 31-33

1- Now concerning spiritual *gifts*, brethren, I would not have you ignorant.

2- Ye know that ye were Gentiles, carried away unto these dumb idols, even as ye were led.

3- Wherefore I give you to understand, that no man speaking by the Spirit of God calleth Je'sus accursed: and *that* no man can say that Je'sus is the Lord, but by the Ho'ly Ghost.

4- Now there are diversities of gifts, but the same Spirit*.

5- And there are differences of administrations, but the same Lord*.

6- And there are diversities of operations, but it is the same God* which worketh all in all. *(* the Godhead)*

7- But the manifestation of the Spirit is given to every man to profit withal.

8- For to one is given by the Spirit the word of wisdom; to another the word of knowledge by the same Spirit;

9- To another faith by the same Spirit; to another the gifts of healing by the same Spirit;

10- To another the working of miracles; to another prophecy *(preaching/teaching)*; to another discerning of spirits; to another *diverse* kinds of tongues *(languages)*; to another the interpretation of tongues *(languages)*:

11- But all these worketh that one and the selfsame Spirit, dividing to every man severally as he will.

12- For as the body is one, and hath many members, and all the members of that one body, being many, are one body: so also *is* Christ.

13- **For by one Spirit are we all baptized into one body,** whether *we be* Jews or Gentiles, whether *we be* bond or free; and have been all made to drink into one Spirit.

14- For the body is not one member, but many.

15- If the foot shall say, Because I am not the hand, I am not of the body; is it therefore not of the body?

16- And if the ear shall say, Because I am not the eye, I am not of the body; is it therefore not of the body?

17- If the whole body *were* an eye, where *were* the hearing? If the whole *were* hearing, where *were* the smelling?

18- <u>But now</u> hath God set the members every one of them in the body, as it hath pleased him.

19- And if they were all one member, where *were* the body?

20- But now *are they* many members, yet but one body.

21- And the eye cannot say to the hand, I have no need of thee: nor again the head to the feet, I have no need of you.

22- Nay, much more those members of the body, which seem to be more feeble, are necessary:

23- And those *members* of the body, which we think to be less honourable, upon these we bestow more abundant honour; and our uncomely *parts* have more abundant comeliness.

24- For our comely *parts* have no need: but God hath tempered the body together, having given more abundant honour to that *part* which lacked:

25- That there should be no schism in the body: but *that* the members should have the same care one for another.

26- And whether one member suffer, all the members suffer with it; or one member be honoured, all the members rejoice with it.

27- Now ye are the body of Christ, and members in particular.

28- And God hath set some in the church, first apostles, secondarily prophets, thirdly teachers, after that miracles, then gifts of healings, helps, governments, diversities of tongues.

29- *Are* all apostles? *are* all prophets? *are* all teachers? *are* all workers of miracles?

30- Have all the gifts of healing? <u>do all speak with tongues?</u> do all interpret?

31- But covet earnestly the best gifts: and yet shew I unto you a more excellent way.

-I Corinthians 12

Charity is Love

1- Though I speak with the tongues of men and of angels, and have not charity, I am become *as* sounding brass, or a tinkling cymbal.

2- And though I have *the gift of* prophecy, and understand all mysteries, and all knowledge; and though I have all faith, so that I could remove mountains, and have not charity, I am nothing.

3- And though I bestow all my goods to feed *the poor*, and though I give my body to be burned, and have not charity, it profiteth me nothing.

4- Charity suffereth long, *and* is kind; charity envieth not; charity vaunteth not itself, is not puffed up,

5- Doth not behave itself unseemly, seeketh not her own, is not easily provoked, thinketh no evil;

6- Rejoiceth not in iniquity, but rejoiceth in the truth;

7- Beareth all things, believeth all things, hopeth all things, endureth all things.

8- Charity never faileth: but whether *there be* prophecies, they shall fail; whether *there be* tongues, they shall cease; whether *there be* knowledge, it shall vanish away.

9- For we know in part, and we prophesy in part.

10- But when that which is perfect is come, then that which is in part shall be done away.

11- When I was a child, I spake as a child, I understood as a child, I thought as a child: but when I became a man, I put away childish things.

12- For now we see through a glass, darkly; but then face to face: now I know in part; but then shall I know even as also I am known.

13- And now abideth faith, hope, charity, these three; but the greatest of these *is* charity *(love)*.

-I Corinthians 13

1- Follow after charity, and desire spiritual *gifts*, but rather that ye may prophesy.

2- For he that speaketh in an *unknown* tongue speaketh not unto men, but unto God: for no man understandeth *him*; howbeit in the spirit he speaketh mysteries.

3- But he that prophesieth *(preach/teach)* speaketh unto men *to* edification, and exhortation, and comfort.

4- He that speaketh in an *unknown* tongue edifieth himself; but he that prophesieth edifieth the church.

5- I would that ye all spake with tongues, but rather that ye prophesied: for greater *is* he that prophesieth than he that speaketh with tongues, except he interpret, that the church may receive edifying.

.....

12- Even so ye, forasmuch as ye are zealous of spiritual *gifts*, seek that ye may excel to the edifying of the church.

13- Wherefore let him that speaketh in an *unknown* tongue pray that he may interpret.

14- For if I pray in an *unknown* tongue, my spirit prayeth, but my understanding is unfruitful.

15- What is it then? I will pray with the spirit, and I will pray with the understanding also: I will sing with the spirit, and I will sing with the understanding also.

16- Else when thou shalt bless with the spirit, how shall he that occupieth the room of the unlearned say A-men' at the giving of thanks, seeing he understandeth not what thou sayest.

17- For thou verily givest thanks well, but the other is not edified.

18- I thank my God, I speak with tongues *(languages)* more than ye all:
*(*Paul had the gift of many languages. He is the Chief Missionary, Chosen Vessel of God to bear 'his name' to the Gentiles.)*

19- Yet in the church I had rather speak five words with my understanding, that *by my voice* I might teach others also, than ten thousand words in an *unknown* tongue.

.....

22- Wherefore tongues are for a sign, not to them that believe, but to them that believe not: but prophesying *(preaching/teaching)* serveth not for them that believe not, but for them which believe.

23- If therefore the whole church be come together into one place, and all speak with tongues, and there come in *those that are* unlearned, or unbelievers, will they not say that ye are mad?

24- But if all prophesy, and there come in one that believeth not, or *one* unlearned, he is convinced of all, he is judged of all:

25- And thus are the secrets of his heart made manifest; and so falling down on *his* face he will worship God, and report that God is in you of a truth.

26- How is it then, brethren? when ye come together, every one of you hath a psalm, hath a doctrine, hath a tongue, hath a revelation, hath an interpretation. **Let all things be done unto edifying.**

27- If any man speak in an *unknown* tongue *(different language), let it be* by two, or at most *by* three, and that by course; and let one interpret.

28- But if there be no interpreter, let him keep silence in the church; and let him speak to himself, and to God.

29- Let the prophets speak two or three, and let the other judge.

30- If *any thing* be revealed to another that sitteth by, let the first hold his peace *(the unknown tongues)*.

31- For ye may all prophesy one by one, that all may learn, and all may be comforted.

32- And the spirits of the prophets are subject to the prophets.

33- For God is not *the author* of confusion, but of peace, as in all churches of the saints.

34- Let your women keep silence in the churches: for it is not permitted unto them to speak; but *they are commanded* to be under obedience, as also saith the law*.

-I Corinthians 14 v 1-5, 12-19, 22-34

*When Paul speaks of women this way, understand that Paul writes his epistles of the 'Grace of God', he is 'first', the Chief, to bring in this 'new doctrine of salvation'. Paul's Gospel was brought first by him and his ministry. The world knew not the living God, it was Paul that brought in the knowledge.

There were cults and false religious practices that had priestesses that worked in their 'temples' during the day who would then go and be partakers of 'houses and businesses of ill repute'. Paul at all costs wanted to avoid any confusion and the fleshly temptations of women, especially so early in the establishing of his early church's.

Paul was not anticipating a 2,000 year Grace Age. But today, there are women of course worthy to preach and teach the 'Dispensation of the Grace of God'. A female too can lead a person to the knowledge of 'the Gospel of Salvation'. But think on how and why Paul saw the potential of misguiding the new believer at this time. Scantly clad females preaching and teaching from the pulpit? What were the moral values of the Roman Empire at this time?

There are several women in Paul's ministry that he spoke highly of. Some of these names are found in Romans 16. One of special note is Phebe. After the last scripture in Romans 16, see if there are words concerning Phebe. These words are in my KJV: "Written to the Ro'mans from Co-rinth'us, and sent by Phe'be servant of the church at Cen'chre-a".

Phebe was entrusted with the Book of Romans to be delivered to them. She was given a high responsibility and she delivered. The Book of Romans has since stood the test of time.

35- And if they will learn any thing, let them ask their husbands at home: for it is a shame for women to speak in the church *(early assemblies)*.

36- What? came the word of God out from you? or came it unto you only?

37- If any man think himself to be a prophet, or spiritual, let him acknowledge that the things that I write unto you are the commandments of the Lord.

38- But if any man be ignorant, let him be ignorant.

39- Wherefore, brethren, covet to prophesy, and forbid not to speak with tongues.

40- Let all things be done decently and in order.

-I Corinthians 14 v 35-40

II Corinthians

14- Now thanks *be* unto God, which always causeth us to triumph in Christ, and maketh manifest the saviour of his knowledge by us in every place.

15- For we are unto God a sweet savour of Christ, in them that are saved, and in them that perish:

16- To the one *we are* the savour of death unto death; and to the other the savour of life unto life. And who *is* sufficient for these things?

17- **For we are not as many, which corrupt the word of God: but as of sincerity, but as of God, in the sight of God speak we in Christ.**

-II Corinthians 2 v 14-17

Paul encourages his apostles to stay true to what he has been teaching from the resurrected Lord Jesus Christ. Though Paul had not written anything yet for these disciples to follow, their faith and belief in Christ will guide them. Because of their foundation based on the resurrected Christ, they were walking, living epistles. What they spoke was Holy Spirit directed and guided.

1- Do we begin again to commend ourselves? or need we, as some *others*, epistles of commendation to you, or *letters* of commendation from you?

2- Ye are our epistle written in our hearts, known and read of all men:

3- *Forasmuch as ye are* manifestly declared to be the epistle of Christ ministered by us, written not with ink, but with the Spirit of the living God; not in tables of stone, but in fleshly tables of the heart.

4- And such trust have we through Christ to God-ward:

5- Not that we are sufficient of ourselves to think any thing as of ourselves; **but our sufficiency *is* of God**.

6- **Who also hath made us able ministers of the new testament; not of the letter, but of the spirit: for the letter killeth, but the spirit giveth life.**

-II Corinthians 3 v 1-6

10- Always bearing about in the body the dying of the Lord Je'sus, that the life also of Je'sus might be made manifest in our body.

11- For we which live are alway delivered unto death for Je'sus' sake, that the life also of Je'sus might be made manifest in our mortal flesh.

12- So then death worketh in us, but life in you.

13- We having the same spirit of faith, according as it is written, I believed, and therefore have I spoken; we also believe, and therefore speak;

14- **Knowing that he which raised up the Lord Je'sus shall raise up us also by Je'sus, and shall present us with you.**

15- For all things *are* for your sakes, that the abundant grace might through the thanksgiving of many redound to the glory of God.

16- For which cause we faint not; but though our outward man perish, yet **the inward *man* is renewed day by day**.

17- For our light affliction, which is but for a moment, worketh for us a far more exceeding *and* eternal weight of glory.

18- Which we look not at the things which are seen, but at the things which are not seen: for the things which are seen *are* temporal; but the things which are not seen *are* eternal.

-II Corinthians 4 v 10-18

1- We then, *as* workers together *with him*, beseech *you* also that ye receive not the grace of God in vain.

2- (For he saith, I have heard thee in a time accepted, and in the day of salvation have I succoured thee: behold, now *is* the accepted time; behold, now *is* the day of salvation.)

3- Giving no offence in any thing, that the ministry be not blamed:

4- But in all *things* approving ourselves as the ministers of God, in much patience, in afflictions, in necessities, in distresses,

5- In stripes, in imprisonments, in tumults, in labours, in watchings, in fastings;

6- By pureness, by knowledge, by longsuffering, by kindness, by the Ho'ly Ghost, by love unfeigned,

7- By the word of truth, by the power of God, by the armour of righteousness on the right hand and on the left,

8- By honour and dishonour, by evil report and good report: as deceivers, and *yet* true;

9- As unknown, and *yet* well known; as dying, and, behold, we live; as chastened, and not killed;

10- As sorrowful, yet alway rejoicing; as poor, yet making many rich; as having nothing, and *yet* possessing all things.

.....

14- Be ye not unequally yoked together with unbelievers: for what fellowship hath righteousness with unrighteousness? and what communion hath light with darkness?

15- And what concord hath Christ with Be'li-al? or what part hath he that believeth with an infidel?

16- And what agreement hath the temple of God with idols? for ye are the temple of the living God; as God hath said, I will dwell in them, and walk in *them*; and I will be their God, and they shall be my people.

17- Wherefore come out from among them, and be ye separate, saith the Lord, and touch not the unclean *thing*; and I will receive you.

18- And will be a Father unto you, and ye shall be my sons and daughters, saith the Lord Almighty.

-II Corinthians 6 v 1-10, 14-18

12- For if there be first a willing mind, *it is* accepted according to that a man hath, *and* not according to that he hath not.

13- For I *mean* not that other men be eased, and ye be burdened:

14- But by an equality, *that* now at this time your abundance *may be a supply* for their want, that their abundance also may be *a supply* for your want: that there may be equality:

15- As it is written, He that *had gathered* much had nothing over, and he that *had gathered* little had no lack.

.....

21- Proving for honest things, not only in the sight of the Lord, but also in the sight of men.

-II Corinthians 8 v 12-15, 21

6- But this I *say*, He which soweth sparingly shall reap also sparingly; and he which soweth bountifully shall reap also bountifully.

7- Every man according as he purposeth in his heart, *so let him give;* not grudgingly, or of necessity: for God loveth a cheerful giver.

8- And God *is* able to make all grace abound toward you; that ye, always having all sufficiency in all *things*, may abound to every good work.

-II Corinthians 9 v 6-8

4- For though he was crucified through weakness, yet he liveth by the power of God. For we also are weak in him, but we shall live with him by the power of God toward you.

5- **Examine yourselves, whether ye be in the faith; prove your own selves. Know ye not your own selves, how that Je'sus Christ is in you,** except ye be reprobates?

6- But I trust that ye shall know that we are not reprobates.

7- Now I pray to God that ye do no evil; not that we should appear approved, but that ye should do that which is honest, though we be as reprobates.

8- For we can do nothing against the truth, but for the truth.

9- For we are glad, when we are weak, and ye are strong: and this also we wish, *even* your perfection.

10- Therefore I write these things being absent, lest being present I should use sharpness, according to the power which the Lord hath given me to edification, and not to destruction.

11- Finally, brethren, farewell. Be perfect *(spiritually mature)*, be of good comfort, be of one mind, live in peace; and the God of love and peace shall be with you.

12- Greet one another with an holy kiss *(not physically, but in the spirit)*.

-II Corinthians 13 v 4-12

The Faithway of Promise

<u>Galatians</u>

1- O foolish Galatians, who hath bewitched you, that ye should not obey the truth, before whose eyes Jesus Christ hath been evidently set forth, crucified among you?

2- This only would I learn of you, Received ye the Spirit by the works of the law, or by the hearing of faith?

3- Are ye so foolish? having begun in the Spirit, are ye now made perfect by the flesh?

4- Have ye suffered so many things in vain? if *it be* yet in vain.

5- He therefore that ministereth to you the Spirit*, and worketh miracles among you+, *doeth he it* by the works of the law, or by the hearing of faith. *(*From the written Word of God with knowledge; +The power of the Holy Spirit to change lives forever, and ever...)*

6- Even as A'bra-ham believed God, and it was accounted to him for righteousness.

7- Know ye therefore that they which are of faith *(the faith-way)*, the same are the children of A'bra-ham.

8- And the scripture, foreseeing that God would justify the heathen through faith *(the faith-way)*, preached before the gospel unto A'bra-ham, *saying,* In thee shall all nations be blessed.

9- So then they which be of faith *(the faith-way)* are blessed with faithful A'bra-ham.

10- For as many as are of the works of the law are under the curse: for it is written, Cursed *is* every one that continueth not in all things which are written in the book of the law to do them.

11- But that no man is justified by the law in the sight of God, *it is* evident: for, The just shall live by faith *(the faith-way)*.

12- And the law is not of faith *(the faith-way)*: but, The man that doeth them shall live in them.

13- Christ hath redeemed us from the curse of the law, being made a curse for us: for it is written, Cursed *is* every one that hangeth on a tree:

14- That the blessing of A'bra-ham might come on the Gen'tiles through Je'sus Christ: that we might receive the promise of the Spirit through faith *(the faith-way)*.

15- Brethren, I speak after the manner of men: Though *it be* but a man's covenant, yet *if it* be confirmed, no man disannulleth, or addeth thereto.
-Galatians 3 v 1-15

16- *This* I say then, Walk in the Spirit, and ye shall not fulfil the lust of the flesh.

17- For the flesh lusteth *(wars)* against the Spirit, and the Spirit against the flesh: and these are contrary the one to the other: so that ye cannot do the things that ye would.

18- But if ye be led of the Spirit, ye are not under the law.

19- Wherefore then *serveth* the law? It was added because of transgressions, **till the seed should come** to whom the promise was made; *and it was* ordained by angels in the hand of a mediator.

20- Now a mediator is not a *mediator* of one, but God is one.

21- Is the law then against the promises of God? God forbid: for if there had been a law given which could have given life, verily righteousness should have been by the law.

22- But the fruit of the Spirit is love, joy, peace, longsuffering, gentleness, goodness, faith,

23- Meekness, temperance: against such there is no law.

24- And they that are Christ's have crucified the flesh with the affections and lusts.

25- If we live in the Spirit, let us also walk in the Spirit.

26- Let us not be desirous of vain glory, provoking one another, envying one another.
-Galatians 5 v 16-26

5- For every man shall bear his own burden.

6- Let him that is taught in the word communicate unto him that teacheth in all good things.

7- Be not deceived; God is not mocked: for whatsoever a man soweth, that shall he also reap.

8- For he that soweth to his flesh shall of the flesh reap corruption; but **he that soweth to the Spirit shall of the Spirit reap life everlasting**.

9- And let us not be weary in well doing: for in due season we shall reap, if we faint not.

10- As we have therefore opportunity, let us do good unto all *men*, especially unto them who are of the household of faith *(the faith-way Church, the Body of Christ)*.

.....

14- But God forbid that I should glory, save in the cross of our Lord Je'sus Christ*, by whom the world is crucified unto me, and I unto the world. *(*not in the 'earthly ministry')*
15- For in Christ Je'sus neither circumcision availeth any thing, nor uncircumcision, but a new creature *(the new man born from above)*.
16- And as many as walk according to this rule, peace *be* on them, and mercy, and upon the Is'ra-el of God.
-Galatians 6 v 5-10, 14-16

<u>Ephesians</u>

10- For we are his workmanship, created in Christ Je'sus unto good works, which God hath before ordained that we should walk in them.
-Ephesians 2 v 10

1- I therefore, the prisoner of the Lord, beseech you that ye walk worthy of the vocation wherewith ye are called.
2- With all lowliness and meekness, with longsuffering, forbearing one another in love;
3- Endeavouring to keep the unity of the Spirit in the bond of peace.
4- *There is* one body, and one Spirit, even as ye are called in the hope of your calling;
5- One Lord, one faith, one baptism,
6- One God and Father of all, who *is* above all, and through all, and in you all *(the believer)*.
7- But unto every one of us is given grace according to the measure of the gift of Christ.

.....

11- And he gave some, apostles; and some prophets; and some, evangelists; and some, pastors and teachers;
12- For the perfecting of the saints, for the work of the ministry, **for the edifying of the body of Christ:**

13- Till we all come in the unity of the faith, and of the knowledge of the Son of God, unto a perfect man, unto the measure of the stature of the fullness of Christ:

14- That we *henceforth* be no more children, tossed to and fro, and carried about with every wind of doctrine, by the sleight of men, *and* cunning craftiness, whereby they lay in wait to deceive;

15- **But** speaking the truth in love, may grow up into him in all things, <u>which is the head, *even* Christ</u>:

16- From whom the whole body fitly joined together and compacted by that which every joint supplieth, according to the effectual working in the measure of every part, maketh increase of the body unto the edifying of itself in love.

.....

20- But ye have not so learned Christ;

21- If so be that ye have heard him, and have been taught by him, as the truth is in Je'sus:

22- That ye put off concerning the former conversation the old man, which is corrupt according to the deceitful lusts;

23- And be renewed in the spirit of your mind;

24- And that ye put on the new man, which after God is created in righteousness and true holiness. *(The Apostle Paul never used the words 'Born Again'. -John 3 v 3, -John 3 v 7, -I Peter 1 v 23)*

25- Wherefore putting away lying, speak every man truth with his neighbor: for we are members one of another.

26- Be ye angry, and sin not: let not the sun go down upon your wrath:

27- Neither give place to the devil.

28- Let him that stole steal no more: but rather let him labour, working with *his* hands the thing which is good, that he may have to give to him that needeth.

29- Let no corrupt communication proceed out of your mouth, but that which is good to the use of edifying, that it may minister grace unto the hearers.

30- And grieve not the holy Spirit of God, whereby **ye are sealed unto the day of redemption** *(our bodies have yet to be redeemed).*

31- Let all bitterness, and wrath, and anger, and clamour, and evil speaking, be put away from you, with all malice:

32- And be ye kind one to another, tenderhearted, forgiving one another, even as God for Christ's sake hath forgiven you.
-Ephesians 4 v 1-7, 11-16, 20-32

1- Be ye therefore followers of God, as dear children;

2- And walk in love, as Christ also hath loved us, and hath given himself for us *(Paul's Gospel)* an offering and a sacrifice to God for a sweetsmelling savour.

3- But fornication, and all uncleaness, or covetousness, let it not be once named among you, as becoming saints;

4- Neither filthiness, nor foolish talking, nor jesting, which are not convenient: but rather giving of thanks.

5- For this ye know, that no whoremonger, nor unclean person, nor covetous man, who is an idolater, hath any inheritance in the kingdom of Christ and of God.

6- Let no man deceive you with vain words: for because of these things cometh the wrath of God upon the children of disobedience.

7- Be ye not therefore partakers with them.

8- For ye were sometimes darkness, but now *are ye* light in the Lord: walk as children of light:

9- (For the fruit of the Spirit *is* in all goodness and righteousness and truth;)

10- Proving what is acceptable unto the Lord.

11- And have no fellowship with the unfruitful works of darkness, but rather reprove *them*.

12- For it is a shame even to speak of those things which are done of them in secret.

13- But all things that are reproved are made manifest by the light: for whatsoever doth make manifest is light.

14- Wherefore he saith, Awake thou that sleepest, and arise from the dead, and Christ shall give thee light.

15- See then that ye walk circumspectly, not as fools, but as wise,

16- Redeeming the time, because the days are evil.

17- Wherefore be ye not unwise, but understanding what the will of the Lord *is*.

18- And be not drunk with wine, wherein is excess; but be filled with the Spirit;

19- Speaking to yourselves in psalms and hymns and spiritual songs, singing and making melody in your heart to the Lord;

20- Giving thanks always for all things unto God and the Father in the name of our Lord Je'sus Christ;

21- Submitting yourselves one to another in the fear of God.

22- Wives, submit yourselves unto your own husbands, as unto the Lord.

23- For the husband is the head of the wife, even as Christ is the head of the church: and he is the saviour of the body

24- Therefore as the church is subject unto Christ, so let the wives *be* to their own husbands in every thing.

25- Husbands, love your wives, even as Christ also loved the church, and gave himself for it *(Paul's Gospel)*;

26- **That he might sanctify and cleanse it *(the Church, the Body of Christ)* with the washing of water by the word***, *(*-Daily read scripture)*

27- That he might present it to himself a glorious church, not having spot, or wrinkle, or any such thing; but that it should be holy and without blemish.

28- So ought men to love their wives as their own bodies. He that loveth his wife loveth himself.

29- For no man ever yet hated his own flesh; but nourisheth and cherisheth it, even as the Lord the Church:

30- For we are members of his body, of his flesh, and of his bones.

31- For this cause shall a man leave his father and mother, and shall be joined unto his wife, and they two shall be one flesh.

32- This is a great mystery: but I speak concerning Christ and the church.

33- Nevertheless let every one of you in particular so love his wife even as himself; and that the wife *see* that she reverence *her* husband.

-Ephesians 5

1- Children, obey your parents in the Lord: for this is right.

2- Honour thy father and mother; which is the first commandment with promise.

3- That it may be well with thee, and thou mayest live long on the earth.

4- And, ye fathers, provoke not your children to wrath: but bring them up in the nurture and admonition of the Lord.

5- Servants, be obedient to them that are *your* masters according to the flesh, with fear and trembling, in singleness of your heart, as unto Christ.

6- Not with eyeservice, as manpleasers; but as the servants of Christ, doing the will of God from the heart;

7- With good will doing service, as to the Lord, and not to men:

8- Knowing that whatsoever good thing any man doeth, the same shall he receive of the Lord, whether *he be* bond or free.

9- And, ye masters, do the same things unto them, forebearing threatening: knowing that your Master also is in heaven; **neither is there respect of persons with him**.

10- Finally, my brethren, be strong in the Lord, and in the power of his might.

11- Put on the whole armour of God, that ye may be able to stand against the wiles of the devil.

12- **For we wrestle not against flesh and blood, but against principalities, against powers, against the rulers of the darkness of this world, against spiritual wickedness in high *places*.**

13- Wherefore take unto you the whole armour of God, that ye may be able to withstand in the evil day, and having done all, to stand.

14- Stand therefore, having your loins girt about with truth, and having on the breastplate of righteousness

15- And your feet shod with the preparation of the gospel of peace;

16- Above all, taking the shield of faith, wherewith ye shall be able to quench all the fiery darts of the wicked.

17- And take the helmet of salvation, and the sword of the Spirit, which is the word of God:

18- Praying always with all prayer and supplication in the Spirit, and watching thereunto with all perseverance and supplication for all saints;

19- **And for me, that utterance may be given unto me, that I may open my mouth boldly, to make known the mystery of the gospel.**

20- For which I am an ambassador in bonds: **that therein I may speak boldly, as I ought to speak.**

-Ephesians 6 v 1-20

Philippians

1- If *there be* therefore any consolation in Christ, if any comfort of love, if any fellowship of the Spirit, if any bowels and mercies,

2- Fulfil ye my joy, that ye be like minded, having the same love, *being* of one accord, of one mind.

3- *Let* nothing *be done* through strife or vainglory; but in lowliness of mind let each esteem other better than themselves.

4- Look not every man on his own things, but every man also on the things of others.

5- Let this mind be in you, which was also in Christ*. *(*know scripture)*

.....

14- Do all things without murmurings and disputings:

15- That ye may be blameless and harmless, the sons of God, without rebuke, in the midst of a crooked and perverse nation, among whom ye shine as lights in the world;

-Philippians 2 v 1-5, 14, 15

1- Finally, my brethren, rejoice in the Lord. To write the same things to you, to me indeed *is* not grievous, but for you *it is* safe.

2- Beware of dogs, beware of evil workers, beware of the concision*.

*(*The Apostles Doctrine Acts 2/42?)*

3- For we are the circumcision, which worship God in the spirit, and rejoice in Christ Je'sus, and have no confidence in the flesh.

.....

13- Brethren, I count not myself to have apprehended: but *this* one thing *I do*, forgetting those things which are behind, and reaching forth unto those things which are before,

14- I press toward the mark for the prize of the high calling of God in Christ Je'sus.

.....

17- Brethren, be followers together of me, and mark them which walk so as ye have us for an ensample.

.....

20- For our conversation is in heaven; from whence also we look for the Saviour, the Lord Je'sus Christ:

-Philippians 3 v 1-3, 13, 14, 17, 20

4- Rejoice in the Lord alway: *and* again I say, Rejoice.

5- Let your moderation be known unto all men. The Lord *is* at hand.

6- Be careful for nothing; but in every thing by prayer and supplication with thanksgiving let your requests be made known unto God.

7- And the peace of God, which passeth all understanding, shall keep your hearts and minds through Christ Je'sus.

8- Finally, brethren, whatsoever things are true, whatsoever things *are* honest, whatsoever things *are* just, whatsoever things *are* pure, whatsoever things *are* lovely, whatsoever things *are* of good report; if *there be* any virtue, and if *there be* any praise, think on these things.

9- Those things, which ye have both learned, and received, and heard, and seen in me, do: and the God of peace shall be with you.

10- But I rejoiced in the Lord greatly, that now at the last your care of me hath flourished again: wherein ye were also careful, but ye lacked opportunity.

11- Not that I speak in respect of want: for I have learned, in whatsoever state I am, *therewith* to be content.

12- I know both how to be abased, and I know how to abound: every where and in all things I am instructed both to be full and to be hungry, both to abound and to suffer need.

13- I can do all things through Christ which strengtheneth me.

-Philippians 4 v 4-13

9- For this cause we also, since the day we heard *it*, do not cease to pray for you, and to desire that ye be filled with the knowledge of his will in all wisdom and spiritual understanding;

10- That ye might walk worthy of the Lord unto all pleasing, being fruitful in every good work, and increasing in the knowledge of God.

11- Strengthened with all might, according to his glorious power, unto all patience and longsuffering with joyfulness;

12- Giving thanks unto the Father, which hath made us meet to be partakers of the inheritance of the saints in light:

-Colossians 1 v 9-12

16- Let no man therefore judge you in meat, or in drink, or in respect of an holyday, or of the new moon, or of the sabbath *days*:

17- Which are a shadow of things to come; but the body is of Christ.

18- Let no man beguile you of your reward in a voluntary humility and worshipping of angels, intruding into those things which he hath not seen, vainly puffed up by his fleshly mind,

19- And not holding **the Head**, from which all the body by joints and bands having nourishment ministered, and knit together, increaseth with the increase of God.

20- Wherefore if ye be dead with Christ from the rudiments of the world, why, as though living in the world, are ye subject to ordinances,

21- (Touch not; taste not; handle not;

22- Which all are to perish with the using;) after the commandments and doctrines of men?

23- Which things have indeed a shew of wisdom in will worship, and humility, and neglecting of the body; not in any honour to the satisfying of the flesh.

-Colossians 2 v 16-23

1- If ye then be risen with Christ, seek those things which are above, where Christ sitteth on the right hand of God.

2- Set your affection on things above, not on things on the earth.

3- **For ye are dead, and your life is hid with Christ in God.**

4- **When Christ, *who is* our life, shall appear, then shall ye also appear with him in glory.**

5- Mortify therefore your members which are upon the earth; fornication, uncleanness, inordinate affection, evil concupiscence, and covetousness, which is idolatry:

6- For which things' sake the wrath of God cometh on the children of disobedience:

7- In the which ye also walked some time, when ye lived in them.

8- But now ye also put off all these; anger, wrath, malice, blasphemy, filthy communication out of your mouth.

9- Lie not one to another, seeing that ye have put off the old man with his deeds;

10- And have put on the new *man*, which is renewed in knowledge after the image of him that created him:

11- Where there is neither Greek nor Jew, circumcision nor uncircumcision, Bar-ba'ri-an, Scyth'I-an, bond *nor* free: but Christ *is* all, and in all.

12- Put on therefore, as the elect of God, holy and beloved, bowels of mercies, kindness, humbleness of mind, meekness, longsuffering;

13- **Forbearing one another, and forgiving one another, if any man have a quarrel against any: even as Christ forgave you, so also *do* ye.**

14- And above all these things *put on* charity, which is the bond of perfectness.

15- And let the peace of God rule in your hearts, to the **which also ye are called in one body;** and be ye thankful.

16- Let the word of Christ dwell in you richly in all wisdom; teaching and admonishing one another in psalms and hymns and spiritual songs, singing with grace in your hearts to the Lord.

17- **And whatsoever ye do in word or deed, *do* all in the name of the Lord Je'sus, giving thanks to God and the Father by him.**

18- Wives, submit yourselves unto your own husbands, as it is fit in the Lord.

19- Husbands, love *your* wives, and be not bitter against them.

20- Children, obey your parents in all things: for this is well pleasing unto the Lord.

21- Fathers, provoke not your children *to anger,* lest they be discouraged.

22- Servants, obey in all things *your* masters according to the flesh; not with eyeservice, as menpleasers; but in singleness of heart, fearing God:

23- **And whatsoever ye do, do it heartily, as to the Lord, and not unto men;**

24- Knowing that of the Lord ye shall receive the reward of the inheritance: for ye serve the Lord Christ.

25- But he that doeth wrong shall receive for the wrong which he hath done: and **there is no respect of persons**.

-Colossians 3

1- Masters, give unto *your* servants that which is just and equal; knowing that ye also have a Master in heaven.

2- Continue in prayer, and watch in the same with thanksgiving;

3- Withal praying also for us, that God would open unto us a door of utterance, **to speak the mystery of Christ**, for which I am also in bonds:

4- **That I may make it manifest, as I ought to speak.**

5- Walk in wisdom toward them that are without, redeeming the time.

6- Let your speech *be* alway with grace, seasoned with salt, that ye may know how ye ought to answer every man.

-Colossians 4 v 1-6

<u>I Thessalonians</u>

3- For our exhortation *was* not of deceit, nor of uncleaness, nor in guile:

4- But as we were allowed of God to be put in trust with the gospel, even so we speak; not as pleasing men, but God, which trieth our hearts.

5- For neither at any time used we flattering words, as ye know, nor a cloke of covetousness; God *is* witness:

6- Nor of men sought we glory, neither of you, nor *yet* of others, when we might have been burdensome, as the apostles of Christ.

7- But we were gentle among you, even as a nurse cherisheth her children:

.....

12- That ye walk worthy of God, who hath called you unto his kingdom and glory.

13- For this cause also thank we God without ceasing, because, when ye received the word of God which ye heard of us, **ye received *it* not *as* the word of men, but as it is in truth, the word of God, which effectually worketh also in you that believe.**

-I Thessalonians 2 v 3-7, 12, 13

1- Furthermore then we beseech you, brethren, and exhort *you* by the Lord Je'sus, that as ye have received of us how ye ought to walk and to please God, *so* ye would abound more and more.

2- For ye know what commandments we gave you by the Lord Je'sus.

3- For this is the will of God, *even* your sanctification, that ye should abstain from fornication.

4- That every one of you should know how to possess his vessel in sanctification and honour;

5- Not in the lust of concupiscence, even as the gentiles which know not God:

6- That no *man* go beyond and defraud in *any* matter: because that the Lord *is* the avenger of all such, as we also have forewarned you and testified.

7- For God hath not called us unto uncleanness, but unto holiness.

8- He therefore that despiseth, despiseth not man, but God, who hath also given us his holy Spirit.

9- But as touching brotherly love ye need not that I write unto you: for ye yourselves are taught of God to love one another.

10- And indeed ye do it toward all the brethren which are in all Mac-e-do'ni-a: but we beseech you, brethren, that ye increase more and more;

11- And that ye study to be quiet, and do your own business, and to work with your own hands, as we commanded you:

12- That ye may walk honestly toward them that are without, and *that ye* may have lack of nothing.

13- But I would not have you to be ignorant, brethren, concerning them which are asleep, that ye sorrow not, even as others have no hope.

14- For if we believe that Je'sus died and rose again *(Paul's Gospel)*, even so them also which sleep *(died)* in Je'sus will God bring with him.

15- For this we say unto you by the word of the Lord, that we which are alive *and* remain unto the coming of the Lord shall not prevent them which are asleep.

16- For the Lord himself shall descend from heaven with a shout, with the voice of the archangel, and with the trump of God: and the dead in Christ shall rise first:

17- Then we which are alive *and* remain shall be caught up together with them in the clouds, to meet the Lord in the air: and so shall we ever be with the Lord.

18- Wherefore comfort one another with these words.

-I Thessalonians 4 v 1-18

1- But of the times and the seasons, brethren, ye have no need that I write unto you.

2- For yourselves know perfectly that <u>the day of the Lord</u>* so cometh as a thief in the night. *(*the Day of Wrath, the day of the Lord is never associated with the Body of Christ. The Day of Christ is not the Day of the Lord.)*

3- For when they* shall say, peace and safety; then sudden destruction cometh upon them, as travail upon a women with child; and they* shall not escape. *(*'they' is not the Body of Christ but unbelievers.)*

4- But ye, brethren, are not in darkness, that that day should overtake you as a thief.

5- Ye are the children of light, and the children of the day: we are not of the night, nor of darkness.

6- Therefore let us not sleep, as *do* others, but let us watch and be sober

7- For they that sleep sleep in the night; and they that be drunken are drunken in the night.

8- But let us, who are of the day, be sober, putting on the breastplate of faith and love; and for an helmet, the hope of salvation.

9- For **<u>God hath not appointed us to wrath,</u>** but to obtain salvation by our Lord Je'sus Christ.

10- Who died for us *(Paul's Gospel)*, that, whether we wake or sleep, we should live together with him.

11- Wherefore comfort yourselves together, and edify one another, even as also ye do.

12- And we beseech you, brethren, to know them which labour among you, and are over you in the Lord, and admonish you;

13- And to esteem them very highly in love for their work's sake. *And* be at peace among yourselves.

14- Now we exhort you, brethren, warn them that are unruly, comfort the feebleminded, support the weak, be patient toward all *men.*

15- See that none render evil for evil unto any *man*; but ever follow that which is good, both among yourselves, and to all *men.*

16- Rejoice evermore.

17- Pray without ceasing.

18- In every thing give thanks: for this is the will of God in Christ Je'sus concerning you.

19- Quench not the Spirit.

20- Despise not prophesyings *(preaching/teaching).*

21- Prove all things; hold fast that which is good.

22- Abstain from all appearance of evil.

23- And the very God of peace sanctify you wholly; and *I pray God* your whole spirit and soul and body be preserved blameless unto the coming of our Lord Je'sus Christ.

24- Faithful *is* he that calleth you, who also will do *it.*

25- Brethren, pray for us.

26- Greet all the brethren with an holy kiss *(spiritually).*

27- I charge you by the Lord that this epistle be read unto all the holy brethren.

28- The grace of our Lord Je'sus Christ *be* with you. A'men.

-I Thessalonians 5

II Thessalonians

13- But we are bound to give thanks alway to God for you, brethren beloved of the Lord, because **God hath from the beginning chosen you to salvation*** through sanctification of the Spirit and belief of the truth.

*(*the fact your reading scripture, God chose you!)*

14- Whereunto he called you by our gospel *(Paul's ministry)*, to the obtaining of the glory of our Lord Je'sus Christ.

15- Therefore, brethren, stand fast, and hold the traditions *(manner of living)* which ye have been taught, whether by word, or our epistle.

16- Now our Lord Je'sus Christ himself, and God, even our Father, which hath loved us, and hath given *us* everlasting consolation and good hope through grace,

17- Comfort your hearts, and stablish you in every good word and work.

-II Thessalonians 2 v 13-17

6- Now we command you, brethren, in the name of our Lord Je'sus Christ, that ye withdraw yourselves from every brother that walketh disorderly, and not after the tradition which he received of us.

7- For yourselves know how ye ought to follow us: for we behaved not ourselves disorderly among you;

8- Neither did we eat any man's bread for nought; but wrought with labour and travail night and day, that we might not be chargeable to any of you.

9- Not because we have not power, but to make ourselves an ensample unto you to follow us.

10- For even when we were with you, this we commanded you, that if any would not work, neither should he eat.

11- For we hear that there are some which walk among you disorderly, working not at all, but are busybodies.

12- Now them that are such we command and exhort by our Lord Je'sus Christ, that with quietness they work, and eat their own bread.

13- But ye, brethren, be not weary in well doing.

14- And if any man obey not our word by this epistle, note that man, and have no company with him, that he may be ashamed.

15- Yet count *him* not as an enemy, but admonish *him* as a brother.

16- Now the Lord of peace himself give you peace always by all means. The Lord *be* with you all.

17- The salutation of Paul with mine own hand, which is the token in every epistle; so I write.

18- The grace of our Lord Je'sus Christ be with you all. A-man'.

-II Thessalonians 3

I Timothy

3- As **I besought thee** *(Tim'o-thy)* to abide still at Eph'e-sus, when I went into Mac-e-do'ni-a, **that thou mightest charge some that they teach no other doctrine,**

4- Neither give heed to fables and endless genealogies, which minister questions, rather than godly edifying which is in faith: *so do.*

5- Now the end of the commandment is charity out of a pure heart, and *of* a good conscience, and *of* faith unfeigned:

.....

15- This *is* a faithful saying, and worthy of all acceptation, that **Christ Je'sus came into the world to save sinners; of whom I am chief** *(first)*.

16- Howbeit for this cause I obtained mercy, **that in me first** *(chief)* **Je'sus Christ might shew forth all longsuffering, for a pattern to them which should hereafter believe on him to life everlasting**.

-I Timothy 1 v 3-5, 15, 16

1- I exhort therefore, that, first of all, supplications, prayers, intercessions, *and* giving of thanks, be made for all men;

2- For kings, and *for* all that are in authority; that we may lead a quiet and peaceable life in all godliness and honesty.

3- For this *is* good and acceptable in the sight of God our Saviour;

4- Who will have all men to be saved, and to come unto the knowledge of the truth.

5- **For** *there is* **one God, and one mediator between God and men, the man Christ Je'sus.** *(Plus the Holy Spirit = the Godhead)*

6- Who gave himself a ransom for all to be testified in due time.

7- **Whereunto I** *(Paul)* **am ordained a preacher***, and an apostle, (I speak the truth in Christ, *and* lie not;) a teacher of the Gen'tiles in faith and verity. *(*Ordained by God, not by men.)*

8- I will therefore that men pray every where, lifting up holy hands, without wrath and doubting.

9- In like manner also, that women adorn themselves in modest apparel, with shamefacedness and sobriety; not with broided hair, or gold, or pearls, or costly array;

10- But (which becometh women professing godliness) with good works.

11- Let the women learn in silence with all subjection.

12- But I suffer not a women to teach, nor to usurp authority over the man, but to be in silence. *(Early warning to the body of Christ. The Roman moral values will not work.)*

13- For Ad'am was first formed, then Eve.

14- And Ad'am was not deceived, but the women being deceived was in the transgression.

15- Notwithstanding she shall be saved in childbearing, if they continue in faith and charity and holiness with sobriety.

-I Timothy 2

1- This *is* a true saying, If a man desire the office* of a bishop, he desireth a good work. *(*-office, not the title of a man)*

2- A bishop* then must be blameless, the husband of one wife, vigilant, sober, of good behaviour, given to hospitality, apt to teach; *(*-those in office representing the Body of Christ)*

3- Not given to wine, no striker, not greedy of filthy lucre; but patient, not a brawler, not covetous;

4- One that ruleth well his own house, having his children in subjection with all gravity;

5- (For if a man know not how to rule his own house, how shall he take care of the church of God?)

6- Not a novice, lest being lifted up with pride he fall into the condemnation of the devil.

7- Moreover he must have a good report of them which are without; lest he fall into reproach and the snare of the devil.

8- Likewise *must* the deacons *be* grave, not doubletongued, not given to much wine, not greedy of filthylucre:

9- Holding the mystery of the faith in a pure conscience.

10- And let these also first be proved; then let them use the office of a deacon, being *found* blameless.

11- Even so *must their* wives *be* grave, not slanderers, sober, faithful in all things.

12- Let the deacons be the husbands of one wife, ruling their children and their own houses well.

13- For they that have used the office of a deacon well purchase to themselves a good degree, and great boldness in the faith which is in Christ Je'sus.

14- These things write I unto thee, hoping to come unto thee shortly:

15- But if I tarry long, that thou mayest know how thou oughtest to behave thyself in the house of God, which is the church of the living God, the pillar and ground of the truth.

16- And without controversy great is the mystery of godliness: God was manifest in the flesh, justified in the Spirit, seen of angels, preached unto the Gen'tiles, believed on in the world, received up into glory.

-I Timothy 3

4- For evey creature of God *is* good, and nothing to be refused, if it be received with thanksgiving:

5- For it is sanctified by the word of God and prayer.

6- If thou put the brethren in remembrance of these things, thou shalt be a good minister of Je'sus Christ, nourished up in the words of faith and of good doctrine, whereunto thou hast attained.

7- But refuse profane and old wives' fables, and exercise thyself *rather* unto godliness.

8- For bodily exercise profiteth little: but godliness is profitable unto all things, having promise of the life that now is, and of that which is to come.

9- This *is* a faithful saying and worthy of all acceptation.

10- For therefore we both labour and suffer reproach, because we trust in the living God, who is the Saviour of all men, specially of those that believe.

11- These things command and teach.

12- Let no man despise thy youth; but be thou an example of the believers, in word, in conversation, in charity, in spirit, in faith, in purity.

13- Till I come, give attendance to reading, to exhortation, to doctrine.

14- Neglect not the gift that is in thee, which was given thee by prophecy, with the laying on of the hands of the presbytery.

15- Meditate upon these things; give thyself wholly to them; that thy profiting my appear to all.

16- Take heed unto thyself, and unto the doctrine; continue in them: for in doing this thou shalt both save thyself, and them that hear thee.

-I Timothy 4 v 4-16

1- Rebuke not an elder, but intreat *him* as a father; *and* the younger men as brethren;

2- The elder women as mothers; the young as sisters, with all purity.

3- Honour widows that are widows indeed.

4- But if any widow have children or nephews, let them learn first to shew piety at home, and to requite their parents: for that is good and acceptable before God.

5- Now she that is a widow indeed, and desolate, trusteth in God, and continueth in supplication and prayers night and day.

6- But she that liveth in pleasure is dead while she liveth.

7- And these things give in charge, that they may be blameless.

8- But if any provide not for his own, and specially for those of his own house, he hath denied the faith, and is worse than an infidel.

9- Let not a widow be taken into the number under threescore years old, having been the wife of one man,

10- Well reported of for good works; if she have brought up children, if she have lodged strangers, if she have washed the saints feet, if she have relieved the afflicted, if she have diligently followed every good work.

.....

17- Let the elders that rule well be counted worthy of double honour, especially they who labour in the word and doctrine.

18- For the scripture saith, Thou shalt not muzzle the ox that treadeth out the corn. And, The labourer *is* worthy of his reward.

19- Against an elder receive not an accusation, but before two or three witnesses.

20- Them that sin rebuke before all, that others also may fear.

21- I charge *thee* before God, and the Lord Je'sus Christ, and the elect angels, that thou observe these things without preferring one before another, doing nothing by partiality.

22- Lay hands suddenly on no man, neither be partaker of other man's sins: keep thyself pure.

23- Drink no longer water, but use a little wine for thy stomach's sake and thine often infirmities.

24- Some men's sins are open beforehand, going before to judgement; and some *men* they follow after.

25- Likewise also the good works *of some* are manifested beforehand; and they that are otherwise cannot be hid.

-I Timothy 5 v 1-10, 17-25

1- Let as many servants as are under the yoke count their own masters worthy of all honour, that the name of God and *his* doctrine be not blasphemed.

2- And they that have believing masters, let them not despise *them*, because they are brethren; but rather do *them* service, because they are faithful and beloved, partakers of the benefit. These things teach and exhort.

3- If any man teach otherwise, and consent not to wholesome words, *even* the words of our Lord Je'sus Christ, and to the doctrine which is according to godliness;

4- He is proud, knowing nothing, but doting about questions and strifes of words, whereof cometh envy, strife, railings, evil surmisings,

5- Perverse disputings of men of corrupt minds, and destitute of the truth, supposing that gain is godliness: from such withdraw thyself.

6- **But godliness with contentment is great gain.**

.....

11- But thou, O man of God, flee these things; and follow after righteousness, godliness, faith, hope, love, meekness.

12- Fight the good fight of faith, lay hold on eternal life, whereunto thou art also called, and hast professed a good profession before many witnesses.

13- I give thee charge in the sight of God, who quickeneth all things, and *before* Christ Je'sus, who before Pon-ti-us Pi'late witnessed a good confession;

14- That thou keep *this* commandment* without spot, unrebukable, until the appearing of our Lord Je'sus Christ: *(*Not Law)*

15- Which in his times he shall shew, *who is* the blessed and only Potentate, the King of kings, and Lord of lords; *(The Lord Jesus Christ is and will be King of kings, and Lord of Lords, but we are fellow heirs with Christ and not subjects of a king*. *-Ephesians 3)*

16- Who only hath immortality, dwelling in the light which no man can approach unto; whom no man hath seen, nor can see: to whom *be* honour and power everlasting. A-men'

17- Charge them that are rich in this world, that they be not high minded, nor trust in uncertain riches, but in the living God, who giveth us richly all things to enjoy.

18- That they do good, that they be rich in good works, ready to distribute, willing to communicate;

19- Laying up in store for themselves a good foundation against the time to come, that they may lay hold on eternal life.

20- O Tim'o-thy, keep that which is committed to thy trust, avoid profane *and* vain babblings, and oppositions of science falsely so called:

21- Which some professing have erred concerning the faith. Grace *be* with thee. A-men'

-I Timothy 6 v 1-6, 11-21

II Timothy

7- For God hath not given us the spirit of fear; but of power, and of love, and of a sound mind.

8- Be not thou therefore ashamed of the testimony of our Lord, nor of me his prisoner: but be thou partaker of the afflictions of the gospel according to the power of God;

9- Who hath saved us, and called *us* with an holy calling, not according to our works, but according to his own purpose and grace, **which was given us in Christ Je'sus before the world began**.

10- But is now made manifest by the appearing *(resurrection)* of our Saviour Je'sus Christ, who hath abolished death, and hath brought life and immortality to light through the gospel:

11- Whereunto I am appointed a preacher, and an apostle, and teacher of the Gen'tiles.

12- For the which cause I also suffer these things: nevertheless I am not ashamed: for I know whom I have believed, and am persuaded that he is able to keep that which I have committed unto him against that day.

13- Hold fast the form of sound words, which thou hast heard of me, in faith and love which is in Christ Je'sus.

14- That good thing which was committed unto thee keep by the Ho'ly Ghost which dwelleth in us.

-II Timothy 1 v 7-14

1- Thou therefore, my son, be strong in the grace that is in Christ Je'sus.

2- And the things that thou hast heard of me among many witnesses, the same commit thou to faithful men, who shall be able to teach others also.

3- **Thou therefore endure hardness, as a good soldier of Je'sus Christ.**

4- **No man that warreth entangleth himself with the affairs of *this* life; that he may please him who hath chosen him to be a soldier.**

5- And if a man also strive for masteries, *yet* is he not crowned, except he strive lawfully.

6- The husbandmen that laboureth must be first partaker of the fruits.

7- Consider what I say; and the Lord give thee understanding in all things.

8- Remember that <u>**Je'sus Christ**</u> of the seed of Da'vid <u>**was raised from the dead according to my gospel** *(Paul's)*</u>:

9- Wherein I suffer trouble, as an evil doer, *even* unto bonds; but the word of God is not bound.

10- Therefore I endure all things for the elect's sakes, that they may also obtain the salvation which is in Christ Je'sus with eternal glory.

11- *It is* a faithful saying: For if we be dead with *him*, we shall also live with *him*:

12- If we suffer, we shall also reign with *him*: if we deny *him*, he also will deny us:

13- If we believe not, *yet* he abideth faithful: he cannot deny himself.

14- Of these things put *them* in remembrance, charging *them* before the Lord that they strive not about words to no profit, *but* to the subverting of the hearers.

15- **Study to shew thyself approved unto God, a workman that needeth not to be ashamed, rightly dividing the word of truth.**

16- But shun profane and vain babblings: for they will increase unto more ungodliness.

.....

19- Nevertheless **the foundation of God** standeth sure, having **this seal, The Lord knoweth them that are his**. And, Let every one that nameth the name of Christ depart from iniquity.

20- But in a great house there are not only vessels of gold and of silver, but also of wood and of earth; and some to honour, and some to dishonour.

21- If a man therefore purge himself of these, he shall be a vessel unto honour, sanctified, and meet for the master's use, *and* prepared unto every good work.

22- Flee also youthful lusts: but follow righteousness, faith, charity, peace, with them that call on the Lord out of a pure heart.

23- But foolish and unlearned questions avoid, knowing that they do gender strifes.

24- **And the servant of the Lord must not strive; but be gentle unto all** *men*, **apt to teach, patient,**

25- In meekness instructing those that oppose themselves; if God peradventure will give them repentance to the acknowledging of the truth; 26- And *that* they may recover themselves out of the snare of the devil, who are taken captive by him at his will.
-II Timothy 2 v 1-16, 19-26

10- But thou hast fully known my doctrine, manner of life, purpose, faith, longsuffering, charity, patience,
11- Persecutions, afflictions, which came unto me at An'ti-och, at I-co'ni-um, at Lys'tra; what persecutions I endured: but out of *them* all the Lord delivered me.
12- Yea, and all that will live godly in Christ Je'sus shall suffer persecution.
13- But evil men and seducers shall wax worse and worse, deceiving, and being deceived.
14- But continue thou in the things which thou hast learned and hast been assured of, knowing of whom thou hast learned *them*;
15- And that from a child thou hast known the holy scriptures, which are able to make thee wise unto salvation through faith which is in Christ Je'sus.
16- All scripture *is* given by inspiration of God, and *is* profitable for doctrine, for reproof, for correction, for instruction in righteousness:
17- That the man of God may be perfect, thoughly furnished unto all good works.
-II Timothy 3 v 10-17

2- Preach the word; be instant in season, out of season; reprove, rebuke, exhort with all longsuffering and doctrine.

.....

5- But watch thou in all things, endure afflictions, do the work of an evangelist, make full proof of thy ministry.
-II Timothy 4 v 2, 5

Titus

5- For this cause left I thee in Crete, that thou shouldest set in order the things that are wanting, and ordain elders in every city, as I had appointed thee:
6- If any be blameless, the husband of one wife, having faithful children not accused of riot or unruly.

7- For a bishop* must be blameless, as the steward of God; not selfwilled, not soon angry, not given to wine, no striker, not given to filthy lucre;
(-office, representing the Body of Christ)*
8- But a lover of hospitality, a lover of good men, sober, just, holy, temperate;
9- Holding fast the faithful word as he hath been taught, that he may be able by sound doctrine both to exhort and to convince the gainsayers.
10- **For there are many unruly and vain talkers and deceivers, specially they of the circumcision.**
-Titus 1 v 5-10

1- But speak thou the things which become sound doctrine:
2- That the aged men be sober, grave, temperate, sound in faith, in charity, in patience.
3- The aged women likewise, that *they be* in behaviour as becoming holiness, not false accusers, not given to much wine, teachers of good things:
4- That they may teach the young women to be sober, to love their husbands, to love their children,
5- *To be* discreet, chaste, keepers at home, good, obedient to their own husbands, that the word of God be not blasphemed.
6- Young men likewise exhort to be sober minded.
7- In all things shewing thyself a pattern of good works: in doctrine *shewing* uncorruptness, gravity, sincerity,
8- Sound speech, that cannot be condemned; that he that is of the contrary part may be ashamed, having no evil thing to say of you.
9- *Exhort* servants to be obedient unto their own masters, *and* to please *them* well in all *things*; not answering again;
10- Not purloining, but shewing all good fidelity; that they may adorn the doctrine of God our Saviour in all things.
11- For the grace of God that bringeth salvation hath appeared to all men,
12- Teaching us that, denying ungodliness and worldly lusts, we should live soberly, righteously, and godly, in this present world;
13- **Looking for that blessed hope, and the glorious appearing of <u>the great God and our Saviour Je'sus Christ</u>*;** *(*God = Jesus Christ)*
14- Who gave himself for us, that he might redeem us from all iniquity, and purify unto himself a peculiar people, zealous of good works.
15- These things speak, and exhort, and rebuke with all authority. Let no man dispise thee.
-Titus 2

1- Put them in mind to be subject to principalities and powers, to obey magistrates, to be ready to every good work,

2- To speak evil of no man, to be no brawlers, *but* gentle, shewing all meekness unto all men.

3- For we ourselves also were sometimes foolish, disobedient, deceived, serving divers lusts and pleasures, living in malice and envy, hateful, *and* hating one another.

4- But after that the kindness and love of God our Saviour toward man appeared,

5- Not by works of righteousness which we have done, but according to his mercy he saved us, by the washing of regeneration, and renewing of the Ho'ly Ghost;

6- Which he shed on us abundantly through Je'sus Christ our Saviour;

7- That being justified by his grace, we should be made <u>heirs</u> according to the hope of eternal life.

8- *This is* a faithful saying, and these things I will that thou affirm constantly, that they which have believed in God might be careful to maintain good works. These things are good and profitable unto men.

9- But avoid foolish questions, and genealogies, and contentions, and strivings about the law; for they are unprofitable and vain.

10- A man that is an heretick after the first and second admonition reject:

11- Knowing that he that is such is subverted, and sinneth, being condemned of himself.

-Titus 3 v 1-11

The Exceeding Greatness of His Power

19- And what *is* the exceeding greatness of his power to usward who believe, according to the working of his mighty power,

20- Which he wrought in Christ, when he raised him from the dead *(Paul's Gospel)*, and set *him* at his own right hand in the heavenly *places.*

21- Far above all principality, and power, and might, and dominion, and every name that is named, not only in this world, but also in that which is to come:

22- And hath put all *things* under his feet, and gave him *to be* the head over all *things* to the church,

23- Which is his body, the fulness of him that filleth all in all.

-Ephesians 1 v 19-23

The Beama Seat of Reward!

An unfortunate translation has many not seeing the truth because of the wording. In II Corinthians 5 v 10, the Greek wording of the 'Beama' seat was translated into 'the judgement seat of Christ'. Those that can't see the difference in the Body of Christ from the 'mixed mashed Gospel' have assumed that 'Judgement seat' means the 'Great White Throne' in Revelation*. *-Revelation 20 v 11-15

10- For we must all appear before the judgement seat *(beama seat)* of Christ; that every one may receive the things *done* in *his* body, according to that he hath done, whether *it be* good or bad.
-II Corinthians 5 v 10

Having read this far there is no need to further explain that the 'True Church, The Body of Christ' is not subject to Israel and the worlds coming of 'the Day of the Lord and his wrath'. The Body of Christ will be 'Caught Up', 'Gathered' and will meet the Lord in the air on that Great Resurrection Day of the Day of Christ'.

We will not be in line with the rest of the world as Jesus pronounces our eternal fate from the reading of the record of our life. We were already judged faithful, righteous and permanently sealed in Christ and hid with him in God. It is what the word of God says. You know the scriptures. You read this book.

9- For we are labourers together with God: ye are God's husbandry, *ye are* God's building.
10- According to the grace of God which is given unto me, as a wise masterbuilder, I *(Paul)* have laid the foundation, and another buildeth thereon. But let every man take heed how he buildeth thereupon.
11- For other foundation can no man lay than that is laid, which is Je'sus Christ.
12- Now if any man build upon this foundation gold, silver, precious stones, wood, hay stubble;
13- Every man's work shall be made manifest: for the day shall declare it, because it shall be revealed by fire; and the fire shall try every man's work of what sort it is.

14- If any man's work abide which he hath built thereupon, he shall receive a reward.

15- If any man's work shall be burned, he shall suffer loss: but he himself shall be saved; yet so as by fire.

16- Know ye not that ye are the temple of God, and *that* the Spirit of God dwelleth in you?

-I Corinthians 3 v 9-14

We will stand before the Lord Jesus Christ for reward at his 'Beama Seat' and will not be eternally judged at the 'Great White Throne' at the end. What did we do in our lives as ambassadors for the Resurrected Jesus Christ? To what extent did we as fellow heirs of the Kingdom of God do with Paul's Gospel? We all will be judged by Jesus Christ according to Paul's Gospel and what we did with it. We will not be judged on how close we could follow the 'earthly ministry' and 'the law' given to Israel.

In the following scriptures, simply believing Paul's Gospel of Salvation and doing very little with it for reward a person still will be saved. That's what the Word of God says. The reward will not be as much as others. In eternity there will be no sin so jealousy at this time will not be a factor. It's between you and the Lord Jesus Christ. What did you do in your life with Paul's Gospel of Salvation?

The Body of Christ is God's Heavenly people. Israel and the Jews are Gods Earthly people. Israel is promised earthly gifts while we are promised heavenly gifts. We don't know what God has in store for us other than it will be glorious, beyond description. A whole universe, worlds, galaxies forever with the Lord Jesus Christ.

The 'worldly mind' races with the possibility of what it will be like. I personally don't see why our own pets that have died could be raised again to life. I believe at this time all things are possible with Jesus Christ. What responsibilities will Jesus Christ give us? This reward will be for eternity. Run the race, reach for the prize. A few years of this life is nothing compared to eternity.

Paul writes Holy Spirit inspired:

1- What shall we say then that Abraham our father, as pertaining to the flesh, hath found?

2- For if Abraham were justified by works, he hath *whereof* to glory; but not before God.

3- For what saith the scripture? Abraham believed God, and it was counted unto him for righteousness.

4- **Now to him that worketh is the reward not reckoned of Grace but of debt.**

5- **But to him that worketh not, but believeth on him that justifieth the ungodly, his faith is counted for righteousness.**

6- Even as David also describeth the blessedness of the man, unto whom **<u>God imputeth righteousness without works</u>**.

-Romans 4 v 1-6

If any man or women were to daily do the following acts of faith (not law) such a one will receive the Holy Spirit of God. To do this for a day, a month, a year, the truth will be unavoidable! That is good news! That is Gospel! That is salvation!

1- Daily pray for the simple things with thanksgiving. Thank God first then voice your requests and concerns.

2- Thoughtfully read some scripture from the Bible. Any scripture. Read several. Accept faithfully they are the Word of God that speaks the truth 100%.

3- Pray again in the Name of the Lord Jesus Christ and ask him to open your heart and mind to the understanding of the Word of God.

Don't feel like you need to pray with full understanding and knowledge. Like a baby, we begin with milk before eating a steak. The fact that a person thoughtfully and faithfully has approached God through the Spirit has already been 'quickened'*. A connection has already been made. God already knew you were going to pray. *-Psalm 119 v 50; -Psalm 119 v 93; -Ephesians 2 v 1; -Colossians 2 v 13; -I Peter 3 v 18

Don't expect instant riches, healing and fame but do believe that your spirit that has been dormant will be 'made alive' with the 'Holy Spirit of God'. Daily do these simple acts of faith and your life will change for the better! It happens. Your daily thoughts turn toward God and not the world.

We have been sealed with the Holy Spirit of promise*. Believe it. It's what the word of God says. Now that is Good News! Gospel! This salvation is by faith and not of any works in any attempt to please God. *-Ephesians 1 v 13; -John 6 v 27; -II Corinthians 1 v 22; -Ephesians 1 v 13; -Ephesians 4 v 30

26- That he might sanctify and cleanse it *(The Church/Body of Christ)* with the **washing of water by the word,**

-Ephesians 5 v 26

The Attributes of God

Sovereign - There is no one above him. God takes no instructions from any man or anything under heaven. God can do all and anything he wants to do.

Immutable - Je'sus Christ the same yesterday, and today, and forever. God and what he has said has never changed. Sin is still sin. Though we are not under the Law, the Apostle Paul endorses 9 of the 10 Moral Commandments. We embrace the wholesome words of Jesus' earthly ministry.

Omniscience - All the sciences and medical wonders are of the full knowledge of God. There is nothing that God does not know.

Omnipresent - God is every where. From the deepest of oceans to the farthest reaches of space, God is there no matter where we go.

Infinite - There is nothing beyond God. He always was, always is, and always will be. God is eternal and forever.

Just and Righteous - Fair and makes no mistakes concerning his will. The plan of salvation was given for all people. Believe in God or believe God?

Love - God loves all people. Even sinners, but every person has to come to the place where they realize that they are nothing more than a sinful man/ women and 'hell bound' from birth. We are nothing without the love of God. We have all been 'pardoned by his grace'. When you accept and believe that God died for you individually and all the world, was buried and rose again and diligently seek the Lord through his holy scriptures, God imputes his Holy Spirit within you. We are justified when we believe Paul's Gospel of Salvation.

Grace - The 'Blessed Pardon of Grace'. Grace is the unmerited favor of God. We don't deserve it until we acknowledge the God of creation and that we seek after his truthful words and ways.

Noah's righteousness was by the 'dispensation of faith' and complete obedience to what God said. "Hey Noah, I want you to build a ship in your back yard. It may take a 100 years or so and there is no lake or sea nearby but don't worry, have faith". Dispensation is purely a 'Pauline word'. Only Paul uses the word Dispensation.

6- But without faith *it is* impossible to please *him*: for he that cometh to God must believe that he is, **and *that* he is a rewarder of them that diligently seek him**.
7- By faith No'ah, being warned of God of things not seen as yet, moved with fear, prepared an ark to the saving of his house; by the which he condemned the world, **and became heir of the righteousness which is by faith**.
-Hebrews 11 v 6, 7

Always remember and keep in mind that the Apostle Paul preached the 'Kingdom of God' as well as Jesus and his disciples. But Paul never preached the 'Gospel of the Kingdom' nor did Jesus and his disciples preach the 'Gospel of the Grace of God'. You will not find these Gospels interchanged in the scriptures of God's Holy Words. They did not preach the 'mixed mashed Gospel' like most of Christendom today. Do you? Believe in God or believe God? There is a difference.

P.S. – Finale note: not all scriptural references and tags were made. I find new things and scripture ties all the time. The KJV is the 'Living Word of God'. You can find more. I envision thousands of Bibles that have pen and pencil notes of scripture references made from this book. What a 'Blessed Day'!!! Mark your Bibles up! I pray this book has helped you and gives you 'The Solid Rock of the Resurrected Lord Jesus Christ' to stand on.

God Bless You
David Matthew